70p
4/-

INTERNATIONAL ECONOMIC ASSOCIATION

General Editors: Sir Austin Robinson (1950–80), Sir Douglas Hague (1980–6), Michael Kaser (1986–)

Béla Balassa and Herbert Giersch (*editors*)
ECONOMIC INCENTIVES

William J. Baumol (*editor*)
PUBLIC AND PRIVATE ENTERPRISE IN A MIXED ECONOMY

Ansley J. Coale (*editor*)
ECONOMIC FACTORS IN POPULATION GROWTH

Béla Csikós-Nagy and Douglas Hague (*editors*)
THE ECONOMICS OF RELATIVE PRICES

Béla Csikós-Nagy and David G. Young (*editors*)
EAST–WEST ECONOMIC RELATIONS IN THE CHANGING GLOBAL ENVIRONMENT

Marcello de Cecco and Jean-Paul Fitoussi (*editors*)
MONETARY THEORY AND ECONOMIC INSTITUTIONS

Léon H. Dupriez and Douglas Hague (*editors*)
ECONOMIC PROGRESS (Second Edition by Austin Robinson)

Martin S. Feldstein and Robert P. Inman (*editors*)
THE ECONOMICS OF PUBLIC SERVICES

Armin Gutowski, A. A. Arnaudo and Hans-Eckart Scharrer
FINANCING PROBLEMS OF DEVELOPING COUNTRIES

Karl Jungenfelt and Douglas Hague (*editors*)
STRUCTURAL ADJUSTMENT IN DEVELOPED OPEN ECONOMIES

T. S. Khachaturov and P. B. Goodwin (*editors*)
THE ECONOMICS OF LONG-DISTANCE TRANSPORTATION

Pierre Maillet, Douglas Hague and Chris Rowland (*editors*)
THE ECONOMICS OF CHOICE BETWEEN ENERGY SOURCES

Edmond Malinvaud and Jean-Paul Fitoussi (*editors*)
UNEMPLOYMENT IN WESTERN COUNTRIES

R. C. O. Matthews and G. B. Stafford (*editors*)
THE GRANTS ECONOMY AND COLLECTIVE CONSUMPTION

Franco Modigliani and Richard Hemming (*editors*)
THE DETERMINANTS OF NATIONAL SAVING AND WEALTH

Jósef Pajestka and C. H. Feinstein (*editors*)
THE RELEVANCE OF ECONOMIC THEORIES

Mark Perlman (*editor*)
THE ECONOMICS OF HEALTH AND MEDICAL CARE
THE ORGANIZATION AND RETRIEVAL OF ECONOMIC KNOWLEDGE

Austin Robinson, P. R. Brahmananda and L. K. Deshpande (*editors*)
EMPLOYMENT POLICY IN A DEVELOPING COUNTRY (2 volumes)

Paul A. Samuelson (*editor*)
INTERNATIONAL ECONOMIC RELATIONS

Christian Schmidt (*editor*)
THE ECONOMICS OF MILITARY EXPENDITURES

Joseph E. Stiglitz and G. Frank Mathewson (*editors*)
NEW DEVELOPMENTS IN THE ANALYSIS OF MARKET STRUCTURE

Richard Stone and William Peterson (*editors*)
ECONOMETRIC CONTRIBUTIONS TO PUBLIC POLICY

Nina G. M. Watts (*editor*)
ECONOMIC RELATIONS BETWEEN EAST AND WEST

ECONOMIC GROWTH AND RESOURCES

Edmond Malinvaud (*editor*)
1 THE MAJOR ISSUES

R. C. O. Matthews (*editor*)
2 TRENDS AND FACTORS

Christopher Bliss and M. Boserup (*editors*)
3 NATURAL RESOURCES

Irma Adelman (*editor*)
4 INTERNATIONAL POLICIES

Shigeto Tsuru (*editor*)
5 PROBLEMS RELATED TO JAPAN

HUMAN RESOURCES, EMPLOYMENT AND DEVELOPMENT

Shigeto Tsuru (*editor*)
1 THE ISSUES

Paul Streeten and Harry Maier (*editors*)
2 CONCEPTS, MEASUREMENT AND LONG-RUN PERSPECTIVE

Burton Weisbrod and Helen Hughes (*editors*)
3 THE PROBLEM OF DEVELOPED COUNTRIES AND THE INTERNATIONAL ECONOMY

Victor L. Urquidi and Saúl Trejo Reyes (*editors*)
4 LATIN AMERICA

Samir Amin (*editor*)
5 DEVELOPING COUNTRIES

STRUCTURAL CHANGE, ECONOMIC INTERDEPENDENCE AND WORLD DEVELOPMENT

Victor L. Urquidi (*editor*)
1 BASIC ISSUES

Silvio Borner and Alwyn Taylor (*editors*)
2 NATURAL AND FINANCIAL RESOURCES FOR DEVELOPMENT

Luigi Pasinetti and Peter Lloyd (*editors*)
3 STRUCTURAL CHANGE AND ADJUSTMENT IN THE WORLD ECONOMY

John H. Dunning and Mikito Usui (*editors*)
4 ECONOMIC INTERDEPENDENCE

The first fifty Conference volumes published by Macmillan are available as a set. Please see the foot of the copyright page for series standing order information.

Structural Change, Economic Interdependence and World Development

Proceedings of the Seventh World Congress of the
International Economic Association, Madrid, Spain

Volume 3
STRUCTURAL CHANGE AND
ADJUSTMENT IN THE WORLD
ECONOMY

Edited by
Luigi Pasinetti and Peter Lloyd

MACMILLAN
PRESS

© International Economic Association 1987

All rights reserved. No reproduction, copy or transmission of this publication may be made without written permission.

No paragraph of this publication may be reproduced, copied or transmitted save with written permission or in accordance with the provisions of the Copyright Act 1956 (as amended), or under the terms of any licence permitting limited copying issued by the Copyright Licensing Agency, 7 Ridgmount Street, London WC1E 7AE.

Any person who does any unauthorised act in relation to this publication may be liable to criminal prosecution and civil claims for damages.

First published 1987

Published by
MACMILLAN PRESS LTD
Houndmills, Basingstoke, Hampshire RG21 2XS
and London
Companies and representatives
throughout the world

Printed in Hong Kong

British Library Cataloguing in Publication Data
International Economic Association, *World Congress (7th : Madrid)*
Structural change, economic interdependence and world development : proceedings of the Seventh World Congress of the International Economic Association, Madrid, Spain.
Vol. 3 : Structural change and adjustment in the world economy
1. Economic history
I Title II. Pasinetti, Luigi L. III. Lloyd, Peter, *1936–*
330.9′048 HC59
ISBN 0–333–42846–3

Series Standing Order

If you would like to receive future titles in this series as they are published, you can make use of our standing order facility. To place a standing order please contact your bookseller or, in case of difficulty, write to us at the address below with your name and address and the name of the series. Please state with which title you wish to begin your standing order. (If you live outside the United Kingdom we may not have the rights for your area, in which case we will forward your order to the publisher concerned.)

Customer Services Department, Macmillan Distribution Ltd
Houndmills, Basingstoke, Hampshire, RG21 2XS, England.

Contents

Preface viii
Acknowledgements ix
List of Contributors x
Scientific Programme Committee xii
Principal Abbreviations and Acronyms xiv

1 **Introduction** *Luigi Pasinetti and Peter Lloyd* 1

PART I THEORETICAL ASPECTS OF CHANGE IN PRODUCTIVE STRUCTURES

2 **Economic Growth with Structural Change: An Introduction** *Luigi Pasinetti* 7
3 **Can Technology Change too Fast?** *A.P. Carter* 13
4 **Technical Change in the North: Some Implications for Southern Options** *Frances Stewart* 27
5 **Technology Transfer: Measuring the Impact of Organisational and Managerial Structures on Production Efficiency** *J.R. Marsden, V. Salas-Fumas and A. Whinston* 47
6 **Consumption and Productivity Patterns and their Implications for the Production Structure** *Jitendra G. Borpujari* 75
7 **On the Economics of Structural Change and the Evolution of Technology** *J.S. Metcalfe and M. Gibbons* 91
8 **Theoretical Aspects of Change in Productive Structures: Discussion and Conclusions** *Luigi Pasinetti* 103

PART II STRUCTURAL ADJUSTMENT IN INDUSTRIALLY ADVANCED COUNTRIES

9 **Ability to Adjust and the Problems of European Market Economies** *J. Waelbroeck* 109
10 **Trends in International Trade in Manufactured Goods and Structural Change in the Industrial Countries** *Béla Balassa* 123

11 On Using Applied General Equilibrium Models for
    Analysing Structural Change   P. B. Dixon   149
12 Micro Initiatives and Macroeconomic Adjustments in the
    Industrialised Countries   M. Didier   159
13 Structural Adjustment in Industrially Advanced
    Countries: Discussion and Conclusions
    K. Jungenfelt   177

PART III STRUCTURAL CHANGE IN A SELECTION OF
          COUNTRIES

14 Structural Effects of Increasing Australia's Imports from
    Less Developed Countries   P. G. Warr   189
15 Industrial Restructuring in a Newly Industrialising
    Country: The Case of Singapore   Chia Siow-Yue   213
16 A Multisectoral Analysis of the Structural Adjustment of
    the Brazilian Economy in the 1980s   R. L. F. Werneck   233
17 Structural Change in a Selection of Countries: Discussion
    and Conclusions   P. J. Lloyd   263

PART IV GROWTH, INFLATION AND EMPLOYMENT

18 Growth, Inflation and Employment: An Introduction
    L. R. Klein   269
19 Growth, Inflation and Employment   W. Krelle   275
20 Growth, Inflation and Unemployment in the United
    States   B. G. Hickman   293
21 Remarks on Growth, Inflation and Employment
    Shuntar Shishido   301
22 Inflation and Growth: Some Experiments on a Model for
    India   K. Krishnamurty   305
23 Growth, Inflation and Employment: Discussion and
    Conclusions   L. R. Klein   323

PART V INTERNATIONAL PRICE FLUCTUATIONS AND
       INFLATION

24 Price Inertia and Inflation: Evidence and Theoretical
    Rationale   M. I. Nadiri   329
25 The Influence of International Price Movements and
    Inflation on the Centrally Planned Economies
    S. Raczkowski   359
26 Domestic and International Sources of Brazilian Inflation
    1947–80   F. de Holanda Barbosa   381

Contents

27 International Price Fluctuations and Inflation: Discussion and Conclusions *N. Gonzalez* 395

PART VI IMPACT OF EXTERNAL MARKET FLUCTUATIONS ON CENTRALLY PLANNED AND MARKET ECONOMIES

28 World Economic Crisis, Adjustment Policies and Global Questions: An Introduction *J. Bognár* 405
29 The Impact of External Shocks on Centrally Planned Economies: Theoretical Considerations *Richard Portes* 409
30 World Markets and Socialist Economies *D. M. M. Maximova* 427
31 Adjustment to External Shocks in Socialist and Private Market Economies *B. Balassa and L. Tyson* 439
32 Impact of External Market Fluctuations on Centrally Planned and Market Economies: A Systematic Comparative Approach *W. Trzeciakowski* 465
33 Impact of External Market Fluctuations on Centrally Planned and Market Economies: Discussion and Conclusions *J. Bognár* 479

PART VII ECONOMIC ASPECTS OF ALTERNATIVE ENERGY SOURCES

34 Economic Aspects of Alternative Energy Sources: An Introduction *P. Maillet* 487
35 Main Economic Aspects of Energy Choices and Policies *P. Maillet* 491
36 The Special Source of Alternative Energy: Comparing Energy Conservation Performance of the East and West *Istvan Dobozi* 503
37 Governments in Energy Markets *M. V. Posner* 523
38 Economic Development in Third World Countries: The Role of Existing Sources of Energy and Alternative Choices *V. S. Mahajan* 537
39 Economic Aspects of Alternative Energy Sources: Discussion and Conclusions *P. Maillet* 553

Index 558

Preface

The Seventh World Congress of the International Economic Association was held in Madrid from 5–9 September 1983 on the subject of 'Structural Change, Economic Interdependence and World Development'. It covered a wide variety of topics and was designed to elucidate issues of concern in economies of all types: market orientated and centrally planned; developed and developing; and at all levels of industrialisation. There was wide participation in the Congress both on a geographical basis and from the point of view of different schools of thought and methodology. The Congress opened and closed with plenary sessions, and in between was a series of sixteen specialised sessions and a number of round table discussions. It has not been possible to publish all the papers presented, but included in the four volumes are those which give a fair representation of the views expressed. These papers are supplemented by comments from the organisers of the sessions which include some report of the discussions which took place.

The proceedings are divided into four volumes as follows:

1. *Basic Issues*, edited by Victor L. Urquidi

2. *Natural and Financial Resources for Development*, edited by Silvio Borner and Alwyn Taylor

3. *Structural Change and Adjustment in the World Economy*, edited by Luigi Pasinetti and Peter Lloyd

4. *Economic Interdependence*, edited by John H. Dunning and Mikoto Usui.

The Congress was held with the cooperation of the Consejo General de Colegios de Economistas de Espanã, the Association's member body from Spain.

Acknowledgements

The Seventh World Congress of the IEA, which took place in Madrid, was honoured by the patronage of His Majesty King Juan Carlos, and we wish to express our sincere thanks to him for his support.

The General Council of the Colleges of Economists of Spain was the principal organisation which made this Congress possible, and by the tireless efforts of its members, by its financial support, and not least by its hospitality to this international gathering, ensured its success.

Financial and practical support and hospitality came also from the Autonomous Governments of Euzkadi and Madrid, from the Municipal Government of Madrid, from the Government of Spain, and from a number of other public and private organisations which we would especially mention:

Ministerio de Economía y Hacienda
Ministerio de la Presidencia
Banco de España
Banco de Crédito Industrial
Banco de Crédito Local
Banco de Crédito Agrícola
Banco Hipoecario de España
Banco Exterior de España
Consejo Superior Bancario Comunidad Autónoma de Madrid
Instituto de Cooperación Iberoamericana
Iberia
Banco de Bilbao
Confederación Española de Cajas de Ahorror
Caja de Ahorros y Monte de Piedad de Madrid
Caja Postal de Ahorros

We wish to express our gratitude to all who participated in making this Congress a memorable and fruitful experience.

Lastly to UNESCO whose continuing support makes these meetings possible, we express our continuing appreciation.

List of Contributors

Professor Béla Balassa, Johns Hopkins University, USA and The World Bank, Washington DC, USA
Professor József Bognár, Institute for World Economics of the Hungarian Academy of Sciences, Budapest, Hungary
Dr Jitendra G. Borpujari, International Monetary Fund, Washington DC, USA
Professor Anne P. Carter, Brandeis University, Waltham, Mass. USA
Professor Chia Siow-Yue, Department of Economics and Statistics, National University of Singapore, Singapore
Professor Michel Didier, Conservatoire National des Arts et Métiers, Paris, France
Professor Peter Dixon, Institute of Applied Economic and Social Research, University of Melbourne, Australia
Professor Istvan Dobozi, Institute for World Economy, Budapest, Hungary
Professor Michael Gibbons, Department of Science and Technology Policy Studies, Manchester University, UK
Dr Norberto Gonzalez, Economic Commission for Latin America and the Caribbean, Santiago, Chile
Professor Bert G. Hickman, Stanford University, California, USA
Professor Fernando de Holanda Barbosa, Graduate School of Economics, Getulio Vargas Foundation, Rio de Janeiro, Brazil
Professor Karl Jungenfelt, Stockholm School of Economics, Sweden
Professor Lawrence R. Klein, Wharton School of Finance and Commerce, University of Pennsylvania, Philadelphia, USA.
Professor W. Krelle, Institut für Gesellschafts- und Wirtschaftswissenschaften der Universität Bonn, Bonn, FRG
Professor K. Krishnamurty, Institute of Economic Growth, Delhi School of Economics, New Delhi, India
Professor Peter Lloyd, Department of Economics, University of Melbourne, Australia
Professor V. S. Mahajan Department of Economics, Punjab University, Chandigarh, India
Professor Pierre Maillet, University of Lille I, France
Dr James R. Marsden, University of Kentucky, USA

List of Contributors

Professor M. M. Maximova, Institute of World Economy and International Relations, Academy of Sciences, USSR

Professor J. S. Metcalfe, Department of Economics, University of Manchester, UK

Professor M. Ishaq Nadiri, Department of Economics, New York University, USA and National Bureau of Economic Research

Professor Richard Portes, Birkbeck College, University of London and Centre for Economic Policy Research, London, UK

Mr Michael Posner, Pembroke College, University of Cambridge, UK

Professor Luigi Pasinetti, Universitá Cattolica del Sacro Cuore, Milan, Italy

Professor Stanislaw Raczkowski, Central School of Planning and Statistics, Warsaw, Poland

Dr Vicente Salas-Fumas, Department of Economics, University of Zaragoza, Spain

Professor Shuntaro Shishido, Institute of Socio-Economic Planning, University of Tsukuba, Sakura-Mura, Ibarahi, Japan

Dr Frances Stewart, University of Oxford, UK

Professor Witold Trzeciakowski, Institute of Economics, Polish Academy of Sciences, Warsaw, Poland

Dr Laura Tyson, International Bank for Reconstruction and Development, Washington DC, USA

Professor Jean Waelbroeck, Centre d'Economie Mathématique et d'Econometrie, University of Brussels, Belgium

Professor Peter G. Warr, Department of Economics, Research School of Pacific Studies, Australian National University, Canberra, Australia

Professor Rogerio Werneck, Department of Economics, Partifića Universidade Catòlica de Rio Janeiro, Rio de Janeiro, Brazil

Professor Andrew Whinston, Krannert Graduate School of Management, Purdue University, USA

Scientific Programme Committee

President: Victor L. Urquidi, Mexico
Co-President: Gerardo Ortega

Abdalla Ismail Sabri, Egypt
Aguilera, Manuel, Mexico
Bacha, Edmar, Brazil
Borner, Silvio, Switzerland
Bueno, Gerardo M., Mexico
Chakravarty, S., India
Csikós-Nagy, Béla, Hungary
Drakos, George E., Greece
Giersch, Herbert, West Germany
Gutowski, Armin, West Germany
Haq, Mahbub Ul, Pakistan
Helleiner, G. K., Canada
Ivanov, Ivan, USSR
Jungenfelt, Karl G., Sweden
Khachaturov, Tigran S., USSR
Kindleberger, Charles, USA
Klein, Lawrence R., USA
Kouri, Pentti J. K., Finland
León, Laureano, Cuba
Lesourne, Jacques, France
Lloyd, Peter, Australia
Maillet, Pierre, France
Malan, Pedro S., Brazil
Mennes, L. B. M., Netherlands
Modigliani, Franco, USA
Ohlin, Goran, Sweden
Onitiri, Herbert A., Nigeria
Pajestka, Jósef, Poland
Prebisch, Raúl, Argentina
Quintana, Enrique Fuentes, Spain
Rojo, Angel, Spain
Salant, Walter S., USA

Sampedror, José Luis, Spain
Sánchez-Reyes, Carlos, Spain
Seers, Dudley, UK
Silberston, Z. Aubrey, UK
Sunkel, Osvaldo, Chile
Tsuru, Shigeto, Japan
Waelbroeck, J. Belgium

Principal Abbreviations and Acronyms

AFL-CIO	American Federation of Labour, Congress for Industrial Organisation
BLS	Bureau of Labor Statistics (of the USA)
cif	cost, insurance, freight
CMEA	Council for Mutual Economic Assistance
CPE	Centrally Planned Economy
CPI	Consumer Price Index
EC	European Community
EEC	European Economic Community
EFTA	European Free Trade Association
fob	free on board
GATT	General Agreement on Tariffs and Trade
GDP	Gross Domestic Product
GNP	Gross National Product
IC	Industrialised Country
ICOR	Incremental Capital Output Ratio
IMF	International Monetary Fund
IPC	Innovation Possibility Curve
ISIC	International Standard Industrial Classification
LDC	Less Developed Country
LIBOR	London Inter-Bank Offered Rate
MDC	More Developed Country
ME	Market Economy
MKW	Mega Kilo Watts
MNC	Multinational Corporation
NIC	Newly Industrialising Country
NMP	Net Material Product
OECD	Organisation for Economic Co-operation and Development
OPEC	Organisation of Oil-Exporting Countries
R & D	Research and Development
SITC	Standard International Trade Classification
UN	United Nations
UNESCO	United Nations Educational Scientific and Cultural Organisation

1 Introduction

Luigi Pasinetti and Peter Lloyd

The general theme of this book – the third of four volumes resulting from the Seventh World Congress of the International Economic Association – is synthesised by its title: *Structural Change and Adjustment in the World Economy*.

The theme is of topical relevance today, in a heterogeneous world where adjustments of all sorts, as a consequence of internal structural change or in response to external unexpected shocks, represent a widespread and diffused feature of all economies of our time, whether they are market-oriented or centrally planned, whether they are industrially advanced or on the way to development. Indeed, any investigation that goes only slightly beyond the very short run reveals structural change and the consequent processes of adjustment to be among the most pervasive and diffused features of our economies, together with an increasing internationalisation of the problems involved. The rate of growth of world trade, since the Second World War, has been consistently about twice the rate of growth of real world output. As a consequence there is today a much greater interpenetration of the economies of the various countries, whether they are market-oriented or centrally planned, while the policies of each country, in response to structural changes, spill over into the markets of its trading partners. It thus appears more and more meaningful to talk of a world economy, and there is widespread conviction that a global view of all these problems is needed. This conviction lies deep in the background of almost all papers and discussions included in the present volume.

The papers collected here, by going right to the heart of the general theme of the IEA Seventh World Congress, cover a wide range of subjects, both on a theoretical level and on the basis of empirical investigations, with a series of comparisons of various countries and of various sectors, and with a final section explicitly devoted to the problems of energy.

The book is divided into seven parts. The title of each part roughly corresponds to the topic that was discussed either in one of the specialised sessions or in one of the round tables. An exact coincidence could not, however, be maintained: some re-arrangements had to be made, for publication purposes, in the grouping of some papers. Moreover, the reports on discussion and the conclusions that appear at the end of each part were presented by the respective authors to the concluding plenary session of the Congress.

Part I of the book is rather substantial (the longest of all) and is aimed at introducing, if not all, at least the most important theoretical aspects of structural change. It contains papers on a variety of topical subjects, all centred on structural change – from the motivation and impact of choice of technology, both in advanced and in developing countries (Frances Stewart), to the upsetting effects of competition in market-oriented economies, when technical change becomes very fast, sometimes even too fast (Anne Carter); from the obstacles to the diffusion of technical progress (Marsden, Salas-Fumas, Whinston) to the process through which technical process does in fact get diffused and constitutes an inducement to structural change (Metcalfe-Gibbons), to the interconnections and causal links between the dynamics of technology on the one side and the structural composition of consumption, and thus of production, on the other (Borpujari). An introductory essay by one of the editors of this book provides an overall theoretical framework into which the various phenomena of structural change may be inserted, both from the side of demand and from the side of production, with consequent implications for the structural dynamics of prices, levels of activities, and (most important of all) sectoral employment, or unemployment.

The papers in Part II aim to identify a number of features and similarities in the patterns of adjustment and structural change in industrially advanced countries. The major problems that are faced are those of the degree of ability of various countries to adjust (Waelbroeck, with reference to the European market economies), the trend in the trade of manufacturing goods of the advanced countries in their relations with developing countries (Balassa), the evaluation of structural change by means of a comparative state approach, within a general equilibrium model (Dixon), and the process of redistribution of employment between big business and small firms, in the USA, the UK and France (Didier). A final note by Jungenfelt examines, with reference to nine European countries in the post-war period, the so-called process of 'deindustrialisation' and the consequent structural changes in import and export shares.

Part III contains three country case studies, of Australia, Singapore and Brazil respectively. In the case of Australia, the author (Warr) investigates the effects of reduced protectionism, as it has taken place in the 1970s, on the growth of imports from both advanced and less developed countries, and the consequent impact on internal employment. In the case of Brazil the author (Werneck) uses a consistency multi-sector model to investigate the basic Brazilian problem of how to promote those bold processes of import substitution and export promotion that seem to be necessary if the present chronic deficit in the balance of payments is eventually to be reversed. The third case, Singapore, is of a more limited scale, but very interesting. The author (Chia Siow-Yue) tries to single out the major features of a striking development process which, in the course of a few decades, has entirely transformed a labour surplus economy of the underdeveloped type into a labour-scarce economy, with high skill and high capital-intensive technology. The extraordinary structural change undergone by this economy – a small city-state of two million people – appears in this case to have been strongly influenced by heavy government intervention inducing huge inflows of foreign capital.

Part IV is introduced and concluded by short notes by Lawrence Klein. It is devoted to the crucial topic of the interconnection between growth, inflation and employment. Klein and Krelle sustain their arguments with reference to the world economy, with appropriate distinctions and comparisons. A comparative analysis of what has happened in the past few decades is carried out with reference to OECD countries, developing countries and centrally planned economies. Following this, Hickman concentrates on the US economy, Shishido on Japan and Krishnamurty on India.

In Part V the focus shifts to international price movements, and to the acceleration in rates of inflation, which was such a distinguishing feature of the world economy in the 1970s. The discussion considers cases that are representative of the developed industrialised countries (Nadiri, with reference to the USA), the socialist countries of Eastern Europe (Raczkowski), and the developing countries (de Holanda Barbosa, with reference to Brazil). A welter of factors are investigated relating to commodity- or market-specific features, institutions, labour market and macroeconomic policies which are in turn related to the acceleration of inflation. All the authors investigate the role of the international transmission of price changes through international trade, both with reference to traded and untraded commodities. At the same time the investigation is extended to the lack of flexibility of prices in some markets and to the sluggishness of their adjustments, because of contracts or government regulations or restrictions on competition.

Part VI of the book is devoted to investigation, on a comparative basis, of the impact of external market fluctuations on centrally planned and on market-orientated economies. Two of the papers (by Balassa and Tyson from the USA, and by Trzeciakowski from Poland) adopt a comparative approach. The other two papers (one by a Western author, Portes, and one by an Eastern European author, Maximova) are more specifically devoted to the relations of the socialist countries with the *world* economy. Two notes by Professor Bognár, of the Hungarian Academy of Sciences, are added to open and close the discussion. It is interesting to note the strikingly different points of view adopted by the various authors, as against the common conclusion that the socialist economies, once rather isolated from the rest of the world, have lately increased considerably their international trade with the West. This has had the effect of increasing their participation in the general interdependence of the world economy. At the same time, however, this has also increased their vulnerability to outside shocks and international fluctuations.

Part VII concludes the book and is entirely devoted to the economic aspects of alternative energy sources. Professor Maillet opens with a general overview of the major economic aspects of energy choices and policies. Then, in an interesting paper by Michael Posner, the experience is scrutinised of the state energy policies of an important country (the UK) that has recently turned from being a deficit country to becoming a surplus country in the area of energy. In the two final papers, an Eastern European economist (Dobozi) compares energy conservation policies in the East and in the West, and an Indian economist (Mahajan) concentrates on the role of existing sources of energy and alternative choices in the Third World.

As the reader may realise, even from such a brief review as that presented above, the aspects dealt with and the problems investigated span a very wide spectrum indeed. It is hoped that the considerable variety of points of view presented, of approaches taken and of analyses carried out may contribute to a basic understanding of structural change – a necessary requirement for the shaping and the implementation of those economic policies that are appropriate to the economic and social development of a world economy.

Part I

Theoretical Aspects of Change in Productive Structures

2 Economic Growth with Structural Change: An Introduction

Luigi Pasinetti
UNIVERSITÀ CATTOLICA DEL SACRO CUORE, MILAN

1 FOREWORD

The dynamics of modern economic systems, since the Industrial Revolution, show that permanent changes in the absolute levels of some basic magnitudes (such as gross national product, total consumption, total investments, total employment, etc.) are generally association with changes in their *composition*, i.e. with *structural change*.

In the short run, it is not always easy to distinguish between genuine structural changes (i.e. changes in composition that are permanent and irreversible) and purely transitory and reversible changes, reflecting adjustments to temporary scarcities or to various temporary exogenous shocks. But, as time goes on, transitory changes in either direction cancel out, and long-run tendencies emerge more clearly. It thereby becomes possible to single out the interrelations between the cumulative movements of certain magnitudes and the changes that take place in their structure.

2 THREE BASIC SOURCES OF CHANGE

By taking advantage of the work I have done elsewhere on this subject (Pasinetti, 1981), I shall try to outline concisely a very general model of economic growth with structural change.

Assume an industrial economic system in which specialisation of jobs and division of labour have been taken to a very advanced stage. The economic system can produce a multitude of goods and services of great variety. As time goes on, three major sources of change can be singled out.

A first source of change is represented by the growth of population (either by natural growth or by immigration) and by changes in the ratio of active to total population.

A second source of change is represented by the application of scientific research and technical progress to the production processes, which cause in each industrial branch a change in the quantities of output per unit of 'factors' absorbed. (For expository simplicity it will be convenient here to consider all these 'factors' *as if* they were proportional to one single factor of production, to be called 'labour'). These technical changes will normally be positive, though some of them could be negative. In any case, they will normally be different from sector to sector. In quantitative terms, calling the various productive sectors, and the corresponding goods and services 1, 2, . . . m, we shall say that productivity increases at a percentage yearly rate ρ_1 (for example 20 per cent) in sector 1, at a percentage yearly rate ρ_2 in sector 2, . . . at a percentage yearly rate ρ_m in sector m. Suppose that productive sectors (and hence goods and services) have been numbered in a decreasing order, so that $\rho_1 > \rho_2 > \ldots \rho_m$. Suppose moreover, for simplicity's sake, that each sector produces one single good or service, so that a productive sector coincides with the corresponding good or service.

There is a third source of change, and this is connected with what has become known as 'Engel's law'. Technical progress generates a continuous growth of average real *per capita* incomes, and this means a corresponding growth of demand for the various goods and services.

Such growth of demand will materialise in a series of sharply differentiated increases of demand for the various goods and services and thus for the various sectors. By representing these increases in quantitative terms, we may denote by r_1 the average yearly percentage rate of growth of demand for good (or service) 1, by r_2 the average yearly percentage rate of growth of demand for good (or service) 2, and so on until r_m. There is, of course, absolutely no reason why one might expect the existence of any order in the succession $r_1, r_2, \ldots r_m$. Since real per capita incomes are rising, the rs will generally be positive, even though some of them (referring to 'inferior' goods) might be negative.

It is to be noted that all of these three sources of change are typical features of industrial systems as such, quite independently of their institutional set-ups. In other words, the dynamic movements of population, productivity and structure of demand are phenomena that are inherent in industrial development as such, whether it takes place in a market (or 'capitalist') economy or in a centrally planned (or 'socialist') economy.

3 THE STRUCTURAL DYNAMICS OF OUTPUT AND PRICES

The basic feature just mentioned is clearly very important. It leads us to ask a series of questions; and in particular to enquire into the extent to which it is possible to carry out an analysis of the dynamic movements of industrial societies in a way that is independent of their institutional set-ups, i.e. independently of whether they are organised according to socialist or capitalist principles.

It is reasonable to expect that such an analysis may not be possible for *all* aspects of economic development. Yet there is a very wide range of problems for which such an analysis is indeed possible.

To begin with, a statement of basic aims may be made in general. It seems reasonable to define as satisfactory, for capitalist and for socialist systems alike, a growth path that approximately maintains over time the full utilisation of productive capacity and the full employment of the labour force.

If this is accepted, then there are some constraints that are immediately imposed on the growth of the economic system as a whole. It can be shown that in each productive sector there is a relation that links the rate of growth of sectoral demand, the technical capital/output ratio and the amount of new investments to be undertaken. Moreover, it can be shown that there is a macro-economic relation (i.e. a relation that links together all sectors of the entire economic system) which defines the level at which total effective demand must be maintained. (See on this Pasinetti, 1981.)

When these constraints are satisfied, it is possible to sketch out a path that may be termed 'satisfactory' for the structural dynamics of the relevant magnitudes of an economic system.

In each sector i ($i = 1, 2, \ldots, m$), physical output will grow at percentage rate ($g + r_i$) per annum, where g is the annual percentage rate of growth of population and r_i is the per capita annual percentage rate of growth of demand for the ith good (or service). Since all rs are different from one another, we can thereby represent what may be called a *structural dynamics of production*.

Moreover, in each sector i ($i = 1, 2, \ldots, m$), the percentage annual rate of growth of productivity ρ_i causes a decrease of cost per unit of output. Under certain ideal conditions, that will also cause a *decrease*, at percentage rate ρ_i, of the corresponding equilibrium price, for given rewards to the factors of production. This implies a distribution of the gains of technical progress through price reductions.

There is, however, an alternative way of distributing the gains of productivity increases, which has become more common in industrial economies. This consists in maintaining the price of the output (i.e. the price of good or service i in our case) unchanged, and at the same time letting the reward for the factors of production (in our case 'labour') increase. But it is clear that, if all sectors were to behave in this way, wages and salaries would increase at different rates from sector to sector. If, as it is reasonable to expect, a certain uniformity is imposed on the increases of wages and salaries, then one obtains a whole series of differentiated rates of change of the equilibrium (i.e. efficient) prices. This means a dynamics of the *relative* prices, or, as we may well say, a *structural dynamics of prices*.

It is to be noted that exactly the same structural dynamics of prices, in an industrial system, may be associated with *different* movements of the general level of prices. To begin with, on the basis of what has been said so far, when changes in productivity are differentiated, a 'stability of prices', in the sense of a constancy through time of *all* prices, would represent an inefficient, and thus an undesirable, state of affairs. One might, however, aim at stability of prices on *average*, or, as it is generally said, with reference to the general level of prices. Let us note that such an aim implies *decreases* of prices in those sectors where productivity grows faster than average and *increases* of prices in those sectors where productivity grows slower than average. At the same time (barring changes in income distribution among different factors of production) wages and salaries may increase at an annual percentage rate equal to the average annual percentage rate of growth of productivity in the economic system as a whole. But, of course, in modern economies where the monetary unit of account is purely nominal (i.e. no longer pegged, directly or indirectly, to a physical quantity of gold), there is no objective limit to the possibilities of growth of *nominal* wages and salaries. Thus, when the growth of wages and salaries does in fact take place at a percentage rate that is higher than the average rate of growth of productivity, this will entail an increase of the general level of prices (i.e. *inflation*). In ideal conditions, with any given structural dynamics of prices, the rate of increase of the general price level (i.e. the rate of inflation) will be equal to the difference between the nominal rate of growth of wages and salaries and the average rate of growth of productivity.

4 CONSEQUENCES FOR THE STRUCTURAL DYNAMICS OF EMPLOYMENT

A further important logical step may now be taken. As time goes on, the various productive sectors are undergoing a structural dynamics of both their outputs *and* their costs (and thus prices). This evolution comes to impose very stringent consequences on the evolution of their demands for factors of production, and in particular for labour. Concentrating our analysis on labour, and supposing for a moment a stable overall population and labour force, it is quite clear that if, in sector i, labour productivity grows at percentage rate ρ_i, and at the same time demand for good i grows at percentage rate r_i, only in the unlikely event of the coincidence $\rho_i = r_i$ will the sectoral demand for labour services remain unchanged. If $r_i > \rho_i$, sector i will need expansion of its labour force, and if $r_i < \rho_i$, sector i will find itself in the position of having to lay off labour (or not taking on new workers, even if the old ones go into retirement).

This means that changes in relative sectoral demands for labour (sometimes positive, sometimes negative) will have to be faced. In other words, the structural dynamics of output and of prices will inevitably also generate a *structural dynamics of employment*.

It is precisely with reference to the structural dynamics of employment that the most serious problems are bound to emerge for industrial economic systems. Labour services cannot be separated from the people providing them. And, for each single person, it is not a matter of indifference whether he or she continues to work in the place and in the ways to which he or she is accustomed or in different geographical places or in ways and manners not necessarily suited to his or her customs, attitudes and aspirations.

5 DECLINING AND EXPANDING INDUSTRIES: A NORMAL PATTERN OF TECHNICAL CHANGE

To proceed further on these lines, one may need to introduce further hypotheses and/or further assumptions on the specific organisational and institutional features of each group of economic systems. This goes beyond the purpose of this introductory essay. It is sufficient for me to have pointed out a whole series of consequences and implications that follow directly from the mere structural dynamics of the basic non-institutional features of industrial economic systems.

Returning for a moment, as an example, to the widespread disruptive effects of technical progress, let me point out how easily this phenomenon can be inserted into the foregoing arguments. The simple model sketched out above gives it an immediate theoretical underpinning. The worrying phenomenon, that characterises any specific process of economic growth, of declining industries always coexisting with expanding industries is given a simple, clear explanation. Within the theoretical scheme sketched out above, one can see quite easily that the declining industries represent the logical counterpart of the expanding industries, within a global framework set up by continuous technical progress. When, in certain sectors, machinery is introduced which causes substantial increases of productivity, and, at the same time, the possibilities of outlets for the products do not expand at the same pace, or are saturated, then a fall of employment in *that* sector will become inevitable. This does not necessarily mean overall unemployment, but it does mean that a satisfactory level of overall employment can be kept only with an appropriate mobility of labour from sector to sector, from region to region, or with a shortening of the working week (an increase of leisure time), or with a combination of all these changes.

These structural changes cannot be expected to take place automatically, or speedily, or painlessly. From a social point of view, it is here perhaps – in these structural changes – that the industrial societies are posing to us the most difficult, exciting challenge.

REFERENCE

Painetti, L. L. (1981) *Structural Change and Economic Growth – A Theoretical Essay on the Dynamics of Nations* (Cambridge: Cambridge University Press).

3 Can Technology Change Too Fast?

A. P. Carter
BRANDEIS UNIVERSITY, WALTHAM, MASS.

1 OVERVIEW

Three incidents brought the topic of this paper to my attention. The first is the hundredth anniversary of my (deceased) father's birth in August 1883. In the 1920s, my father founded a very successful enterprise that manufactured windshield wipers and other automobile supplies. In the early 1930s, General Motors began to market its cars fully equipped. As a result, our family sustained major economic and social losses. We were only partly salvaged by the Second World War.

The second was a conversation with a Hungarian planner about Appalachia and the problems of re-employing coal-miners when the nation's energy base shifted away from coal to oil and gas. In Hungary, she assured me, coal production would be phased out very gradually, as the miners reached retirement age or left for other jobs. It was her impression that the social costs of abrupt transition would far outweigh any gain in efficiency from more rapid transition.

The third was a remark by an economist at a forum on national policy and the world economy. He raised the question of whether the effectiveness of The Japanese Ministry of International Trade and Industry (MITI) was not overrated, since Japanese steel firms are now beginning to suffer from the competition of new steel capacity coming on line in developing countries.

Each of these incidents highlights the fact that technological progress has costs as well as benefits. Only a small group of radicals and victims – Luddites and Saboteurs and a few modern environmentalists – have questioned the overall benefit of technological change to society, and I do not intend to do so here. However, there can be no doubt that the process harms some as well. If I set fire to your factory or knock it down to build a hotel in its place, I am liable;

I must recompense you for the loss of your assets. However, if I produce a competitive product that renders your productive capacity worthless, I have no liability for your loss. The insulation of competitors from such liability is a central feature of our legal-institutional framework. It makes capitalism a very powerful engine for change.

Under special assumptions that most economists know well, it has been shown that competition will assure an efficient allocation of resources. Can we rest assured that on average the competitive system does a reasonably good job in regulating the rate of innovation and diffusion of new technology? We know that some of the key assumptions on which the arguments for competitive efficiency rest are not matched by reality. This paper considers some systematic reasons why a market system will not necessarily provide optimal guidance under conditions of changing technology.

Two classes of costs are important. First, with rapid change the investment costs of adjustment will be far from negligible. If too much capacity is built or if plants are mislocated, the resources invested in them are wasted. Second, some substantial costs of change are true externalities to the system. Costs of relocation and infrastructure are generally borne by communities and individuals and not assigned as costs of producing specific goods.

Failure of the system to take some significant costs into account imparts a pro-change bias into the decision-making process. To the extent that such a bias is significant, we may conclude that technology will 'change too fast'. At this point, it is sufficient to establish, not that it necessarily does, but that it can.

Competition within a sector is discussed in Section 2. Induced investments in other sectors and the combined effects of simultaneous structural changes are considered in Sections 3 and 4. Externalities are discussed in Section 5. In the discussion that follows, the terms 'technological change', 'structural change' and 'innovation' are used interchangeably to signify a change in input combination used to produce the output of a sector or establishment. To simplify the argument it is assumed that all changes can be described in terms of inputs and outputs of fixed quality. Each technology or structure is described by fixed coefficients and no attempt is made to distinguish between substitution and structural change. Change is assumed to be capital-embodied. Conclusions should be softened to the extent that capital goods and human capital can be transferred or adapted to new uses.

2 STRUCTURAL CHANGE IN A SINGLE SECTOR

To simplify the argument, assume that all the establishments in a given sector are operating at capacity and have uniform input structures characterised by a vector of input coefficients, A_j, including a labour coefficient, 1_j.

$$A_j = \begin{bmatrix} a_{1j} \\ a_{2j} \\ . \\ . \\ . \\ a_{nj} \\ 1_j \end{bmatrix}$$

A new technology, distinguished by the prime superscript,

$$A'_j = \begin{bmatrix} a'_{1j} \\ a'_{2j} \\ . \\ . \\ . \\ a'_{nj} \\ 1'_j \end{bmatrix}$$

can be introduced at a capital cost of b'_j per unit. (A'_j cannot work with old capital.) It will pay for an existing establishment to replace old with new technology only if the savings in current input costs exceed the required investment. Capital is durable and these savings can be cumulated over its probable lifetime, T'_j. The economic lifetime of sectoral capital, T'_j, in turn, depends on future technological and economic conditions and is difficult to foresee exactly.

Assuming linear homogeneous technology and a discount rate of r, the (per unit) gain from investing in additional capacity with the new technique will be

$$\Pi_j = \sum_{t=T^0}^{T} \frac{1}{(1+r)^t} \left[pj(t) - P(t)A'_j \right] - b'_j \tag{1}$$

while the gain from replacing old capacity with new will be

$$S_j = \sum_{t=T^0}^{T'} \frac{1}{(1+r)^t} \left[P(t)\,[A_j - A'_j] \right] - b'_j \qquad (2)$$

The logic of these decision rules is simple, but in practice successful investment is an art. Future prices are not known; anticipation involves guesswork. A decision to build new capacity might be warranted if today's prices continued to prevail, but not if future shifts in technology or other conditions substantially changed them. Thus, an excess of today's price over current costs $(p_j(T^0) - P(T^0)A'_j)$ might signal the prospect of gain to investment in sector j. But any substantial new entry into the sector would tend to lower future prices relative to current ones. If this new entry and its price consequences were not correctly anticipated, the advantage of investment made at time T^0 would be different from that expected.

Two features of the economic system should be noted. First, it is clear that competitors whose economic activity brings about lower prices affect the returns on existing investments within the sector. Second, since it is impossible to anticipate future prices, nothing assures that competition will allocate investment optimally. Today's prices may suggest enormous gains from investment in a sector. Tomorrow a new discovery may belie today's expectations and render today's investment obsolete. A firm that purchases a new computer today may regret that investment in the light of next year's options.

Condition (1) governs all expansions of capacity. Thus, the owner of existing capacity might see fit to construct an addition but not to replace. The opportunity for positive profit will encourage building of new capacity. Under competitive conditions entry will drive down the price of the product, p_j. Old plants will find it worthwhile to continue to operate up to the point where their variable costs are just covered. At that point, $p_j = (P)A_j$ and criterion (2) becomes equivalent to criterion (1). Beyond that it does not pay to utilise old capacity.

If we assume that competitive equilibrium prevails at the outset, then $p_j = (P)A_j$ and hence (1) and (2) will be equivalent. Under those conditions, the signals to replace and to expand are the same. So long as profits are positive, however, expansion may be warranted while replacement is not.

Were all capacity controlled by a single decision-maker, decisions to replace and to expand could easily be distinguished. However, with decentralised decision-making an entrepreneur who puts new capacity on line may render capacity idle in other establishments without even being aware of doing so. To the extent that he adds to supply without changing demand he is likely to eliminate capacity somewhere else in the system. Thus in effect replacement in a sector may be triggered by positive values of Π_j, even though non-positive values of s_j signal that replacement of capacity in older establishments is not warranted. In the end, the distinction between 'replacement' and 'expansion' investment can only be made *ex post*. *Ex ante*, new investment may look like 'expansion'. If it crowds out old capacity, it turns out to be replacement.

If all reactions were instantaneous and foresight perfect, a price system could provide proper guidance for structural change even in a sector with many independent decision units. In practice, however, the system is likely to overshoot. Initial prices will tend to signal additions to capacity, and it will take some time for that new capacity to come on line. Prices will be driven down after, not in anticipation of, new investment. By the time the corrective price reduction comes, the system has already overreacted. New capacity replaces old 'too rapidly'.

While a decentralised market system should provide proper guidance for the introduction of new techniques 'over the long run', the system works inevitably by trial and error. In general, trials and errors involve investment; they are not cost-free. If the response to initial prices is less than optimal, opportunities to save resources are missed. If initial price conditions stimulate the creation of more capacity than is optimal, then old capacity will be scrapped prematurely.

When technology changes slowly, economic actors can be expected to learn from the trial-and-error process. Under static conditions, in any event, costs of adjustment and change may be small relative to the ongoing volume of production. With more rapid change, errors and costs of adjustment will be significant or even dominant in the overall economic picture, and experience tends to illuminate historical rather than current situations.

Costs of production with new techniques generally involve a substantial 'learning curve'. Thus new techniques can be expected to approach cost effectiveness only after an initial shakedown period. With rapid change, capacity associated with the latest techniques will drive prices down even before the learning phase for older processes is 'completed'.

Much has been made of the tendency for large firms to control, i.e. to slow, the rate of technological change. The foregoing discussion identifies some of the economic advantages of horizontal integration with rapidly changing technology. An integrated firm can exert some control over the rate of replacement in a sector and, to the extent that it controls the rate of innovation, can impose some order into the guesswork about future rates of change.

3 STRUCTURAL CHANGE IN A MULTI-SECTORAL CONTEXT

The last section dealt with the costs of rapid technological change in the context of a single sector. Structural changes in any given sector affect, in turn, the economic circumstances of the sector's suppliers and customers.

Consider a switch from steel to fibreglass in making automobile bodies. Increased demands for fibreglass should induce additional investment in the fibreglass sector while steel capacity is rendered idle. Assuming that producers of automobiles and their suppliers are not integrated, the investment cost of switching from one material to the other is external to the decision-maker in the automobile sector. He relies on the price system for information on the relative costs of the two materials. At the time when the decision is being made prices do not yet reflect idle capacity in steel nor a need for additional capacity in fibreglass. After the new fibreglass-intensive structure is introduced, excess capacity in steel and capacity shortage in fibreglass are likely to change their relative prices and hence to modify (here presumably to reduce) the originally perceived advantage of the new structure. However, the new price signals are apt to come too late, after the structural change has already been implemented. In the absence of vertical integration, there will be a pro-change bias.

To consider the general equilibrium effects of the potential innovation in sector j, consider the input vectors A_j and A'_j imbedded in the same input-output matrix. Matrix A differs from A' only with respect to column j. Similarly, assume that capital coefficient vectors B and B' are specified and that they differ only with respect to the jth column. Capital cannot be transferred among sectors or between new and old technologies in sector j. Output vectors, X and X', required to deliver a given vector of final demand, Y, with A and A' can be computed. Assume that initial capacities are equal to X. Then system-wide costs of delivering Y with old and new technology in j can be compared by computing current accout and capital requirements to produce X and X'.

Consider possible ramifications of the change in structure from A_j to A'_j on sectors other than j. These depend, of course, on the actual configuration of differences in the individual elements of A_j and A'_j. If all elements of A'_j are equal to or less than those of A_j, then economy-wide output requirements are reduced by the structural change, and the change simply renders some capacity idle in other sectors. These current account savings are reflected in sector j's cost calculation. If idle capacities lead to lower input prices, these will reinforce the advantage of the new structure but they may remain some relative advantage to the old.

Very likely the switch to A'_j will require some qualitative changes in inputs, i.e. A'_j will use some inputs not used in A_j and vice versa. Economy-wide, requirements for some products fall while others rise. In this case, while capacity will be rendered idle in some sectors, at the same time additional capacity will be required and thus new investment induced in others. The qualitative switch inputs can be represented by calling some input coefficients zero in A_j and non-zero in A'_j, and vice versa. For purposes of illustration we might set $a'_{ji} = 0$ and $a_{ji+1} = 0$ assuming all other coefficients non-zero. Hypothetically, a'_{ji} might represent steel inputs and a_{ji+1} fibreglass in the automobile example.

Among other effects, the change would be expected to increase the required output level of fibreglass and reduce that of steel. By assumption, there is initial sectoral capacity sufficient to produce X. Investment requirements in each sector will be zero if the old technology is continued in j. For sectors other than j, investment requirements, if the new technology is introduced in j, will be given by

$$\sum_{k \neq j} b_k(x'_k - x_k); x'_k > x_k \qquad (3)$$

Investment requirements are zero in sectors where $x'_k \leq x_k$. For sector j, investment is $b'_j x'_j$.

With some substitution or qualitative change in inputs used in j we normally expect that positive investment will be required, both in the innovating sector and in some sectors that deliver its inputs. In our present example we expect innovation to bring a decrease in the required output of steel ($(x'_i - x_i)$ to be negative) and an increase in the output of fibreglass ($(x'_{i+1} - x_{i+1})$ to be positive). Thus, to implement the innovation would require investement in the fibreglass industry equal to $b_{i+1}(x'_{i+1} - x_{i+1})$, while capacity in the steel industry would be rendered idle. If investment goods are not transferable among sectors, the innovation triggers new investment in the economy-wide sense.

In summary, the economy-wide effects of a structural change in sector j consist of two major components: changes in current input requirements and changes in capital requirements. Both components are likely to undergo changes in sectoral composition. Changes in input requirements will be given simply by $(x' - x)$. Some sectoral capital requirements are likely to be positive while other capital is rendered idle. System-wide, then, structural change induces net investment not only in the sector initiating the change but also in supplying sectors. Will decision-makers take proper account of all these ramifications?

If producers in sectors i, $i + 1$ and j were all united under a single decision-making unit, the cost of expansion in $i + 1$ would be included in reckoning the capital cost of innovation, and these costs would tend to offset the advantages afforded by savings in direct inputs. Thus, for an integrated operation (1) and (2) would include a term for the cost of induced investment in $i + 1$.

In the absence of vertical integration, the price system can convey information about idle capacity in other sectors, but it conveys it only with a lag. If indeed steel capacity is to be rendered idle, competition should drive steel prices down to variable costs. Lower steel prices in turn should reduce the costs of automobile producers with old structures and lower automobile prices. A reduction in the price of steel (p_i) should also make the old technique of automobile production more advantageous relative to the new. Thus, the price system can signal the existence of idle capacity in i to users of that input in j. However, as was argued in Section 2, the proper price signals will be generated only after the innovation has been made. When the decision about structural change is being initiated in sector j, prices do not constitute a firm link between the innovation decision and potential costs of investment in supplying sectors.

4 PROBLEMS OF SIMULTANEOUS STRUCTURAL CHANGE

In the modern economy, changes are implemented simultaneously in many sectors, and their indirect effects may reinforce or offset each other to some degree. If a structural change in the machinery sector induces a reduction in the demand for steel while a simultaneous structural change in construction induces an increase, effects on the steel industry will offset each other. Under conditions of rising final consumption, idle capacity may also be absorbed by general growth. In effect, the real cost of a given structural change depends not only on initial capacities but on macroeconomic conditions and on simultaneous structural changes elsewhere in the system. Perhaps the most difficult task of business judgement is to gauge possible changes elsewhere in the system and their effects. Simultaneous structural changes in other sectors are economically important, not only because of their implications for capacity utilisation, but also because they bear on the long-run advantage of any given innovation. Changes that may have economic advantage simultaneously may not be economically justifiable singly, and vice versa.

Even a well functioning market system cannot be expected to yield 'what if' information. Thus *ex ante* prices cannot provide guidance on the simultaneous advantage of two prospective changes (Carter, 1970). In Section 3 we considered multi-sectoral effects of structural change in sector j in terms of an initial economy, described by current account matrix A, and an economy with new structure in sector j, described by A'. Consider, also, a possible structural change in sector k and a matrix A'' obtained by replacing the kth column of A by the new structure for k. Let A''' represent the matrix obtained by replacing columns j and k simultaneously by the respective new structures. If X, X', X'' and X''' are the output vectors required to deliver a given final demand, Y, with the respective matrices A, A', A'' and A''', then

$$(x_j - x'''_j) = (x_j - x'_j) \frac{x'''_i}{x'_i} + (x_j - x''_j) \frac{x'''_k}{x''_k} \qquad (4)$$

(See Leontief, 1951.) The effects of the two separate changes are not additive because sectors are interdependent. Savings of labour (or any other primary resource or combination of such resources) will not be additive either. The effects on outputs and resource requirements of introducing two simultaneous structural changes are generally different from the effects of introducing them separately.

Arguments presented in earlier sections have pointed out that *ex ante* prices do not anticipate *ex post* reductions in the prices of products produced by old capacity in the face of new conditions. These arguments led to the conclusion that the *ex ante* price system imposes a pro-change bias. With this bias, technology tends to supersede the old too fast. The argument of the present section points to the inadequacy of price signals but it does not identify a consistent bias. Improvements in other sectors may either augment, diminish or leave unchanged the advantage of a proposed structural change. If techniques of producing steel and fibreglass are changing, the advantage of using one or the other in automobile production will be affected differently depending on relative economies contemplated with new technology in the two supplying sectors.

5   EXTERNALITIES AND STRUCTURAL CHANGE

The shortcomings in competitive institutions discussed in Sections 2, 3 and 4 may be seen as quasi-externalities. Prices register the effects of structural change properly only after a time lag, and they cannot anticipate the effects of unknown future changes for today's investment decisions. Since full information is never available, the system cannot guarantee 'efficient' decisions. Innovation also triggers non-trivial costs that are normally external to the innovation decision process. Structural change tends to increase demand for new labour and management skills and to render old skills obsolete. Costs of re-education will sometimes be internal to the innovating firm but most often they are not. Normally innovators are not expected to compensate members of the workforce for induced obsolescence of human capital. These costs are significant in economic as well as in non-quantifiable human terms.

One might argue that the market will function so as to reflect changing demands for labour skills and human capital through wages. However, wages are not likely to anticipate changes in demand for different types of labour. The *ex post* cost advantage of a new structure will differ from the *ex ante* value on which the original decision was based. Perhaps a skilled decision-maker might anticipate changes in the labour market as a result of structural change in a particular area, but he cannot simply rely on current wages for his judgement. Furthermore, it is doubtful whether wages ever capture the true costs of investment in human capital. Firms can only take account of those training costs that they themselves incur. Costs of nurture, schooling and training elsewhere are difficult to impute.

Costs of unemployment are definitely external in our society. Neither unemployment insurance costs nor the costs of welfare programmes will be reckoned in the innovator's decision calculus. Relocation costs represent another significant set of externalities of structural change. Of course, not all industrial relocation is induced by technological change. On the other hand, structural shifts certainly have induced substantial migration of industry and of labour. There are many costs of urban infrastructure: new housing, educational facilities, installation of utilities associated with shifts of industry from one city to another. These are assumed by various agents in the growing environment: workers, governments and to some extent private industry. Losses in asset values in declining cities are similarly diffused. For the most part the costs of regional shifts, enormous though they are, are not assigned to the changes in industrial structure that trigger them.

The evolution of a global economy, with industrial sectors of many nations in effective co-operation and competition, involves structural changes throughout the world. In addition to technological change, many important socioeconomic developments have contributed to the trend. In the global context the externalities of structural change are most striking. Developing nations make enormous investments in infrastructure to support urban manufacturing. At the same time, industrial nations sustain costs of relocation, retraining and adjustment to a 'post-industrial society'.

6 HOW IMPORTANT IS THE PRO-CHANGE BIAS?

While it is not too difficult to identify a pro-change bias in the competitive legal-institutional framework, it is hard to gauge its practical significance. The importance of the arguments in this paper depend on the significance of the costs of change in the total economic context. As a lifelong empiricist, I remain uneasy because I see no ready way to quantify the importance of these problems.

Economy-wide, there are no systematic statistics of obsolescence or economic replacement, and there is strong precedent for minimising the problem. Empirical analysis with dynamic input-output systems has not been concerned with transition costs for market economies. On the other hand, some writers suggest that these costs are not of primary importance. For example, the findings of Tsukui (1972 and Murakami *et al.*, 1970) and Brody (1970) argue against assigning significant weight to initial conditions. Both of them claim that in fact modern economies operate close to the 'turnpike paths'.

While these findings must be taken seriously, they do not provide conclusive answers to our questions. First, in both cases the computations were highly aggregative (about ten sectors) and based on necessarily crude data on capital and capacities. 'New' and 'old' technology, in both cases, are represented by input-output tables of different years, since no information on best-practice parameters was available. Perhaps most important, Tsukui assumes that new and old capital are interchangeable in any given sector. In a highly aggregative framework, this amounts to assuming away a large proportion of the costs associated with obsolescence. Finally, both Brody and Tsukui draw data from the high growth era between 1950 and 1970. If the world's economies ever operated close to turnpike paths it was then, rather than now. On the turnpike, technology will not 'change too fast' because there is no idle capacity. However, strictly speaking, on the turnpike it doesn't change at all!

Depressions, as Schumpeter pointed out, are times of 'creative destruction' (Schumpeter, 1939 and 1942). Right now, we should expect evidence of economic imbalance, excess capacity and obsolescence as we adjust to the major disruptions in the world economy since 1973. Unemployment in the United Sates exceeds 10 per cent, but there are shortages of high-tech skills. Statistics of growth of real sectoral output at 400-order detail show significant dispersion. Between 1971 and 1981, 20 per cent of sectors experienced declining output, while rates of growth for another 25 per cent exceeded 4 per cent. Individual growth rates ranged from -15.5 per cent to $+19$ per cent per annum (Data Resources, 1982). Thus the fine-grained detail shows far from proportional growth. This is a period when the problems of change stand out clearly. But the evidence of imbalance is not always so dramatic. Schumpeter himself would look forward to some years when excess capacity will be exceptional.

To be fair, general evidence on our broad question cannot be conclusive. The importance of the bias towards change remains a matter of judgement. We are all products of our economic nurture, and it is very difficult to judge economic institutions from inside the system. Can technology change too fast? Perhaps I have explained that it can. How important is the bias? I am not sure. Nor do I know how to regulate the speed of the 'engine for change' without stalling it. Centrally planned economies are noted for their conservatism with respect to structural change. Can the incentive to innovate survive in a system of stricter economic accountability?

The arguments raised in this paper are best viewed as encouragement to consider the process of structural change with more emphasis on the adjustment process itself. First, the process of structural change was characterised as a trial-and-error, rather than a truly optimising, process. Schumpeter's 'creative destruction' may well be an inevitable phase of a progressive thrust. Nevertheless, there are significant costs of change, and these costs are borne not only by decision-making entrepreneurs but by labourers and communities whose actions are only loosely tied into the market calculus. Misallocation of resources is costly not only to individual entrepreneurs but also to society at large. If mistakes can be a significant element of the system, then policies other than *laissez-faire* may be appropriate in guiding technological transition. When a system is judged less than perfect, there is less hesitation to interfere in it. Problems of transition were highlighted because transition, rather than equilibrium, is the normal state of the world. The advantages of horizontal and vertical integration in the management of change were emphasised. These advantages will continue to motivate the formation of national and multinational business organisations and to encourage government intervention in the interest of co-ordinating industrial policy. This kind of 'dynamic' advantage of integration, associated with structural change, may well be more powerful than the type of market control traditionally stressed in the theory of monopoly.

Finally, rapid and continuing change leaves very little time for 'learning'. It takes time for consumers and producers to learn to judge qualities of unfamiliar goods and services. Ever-changing options may in some sense represent rapidly expanded choice, but change also forces economic agents to rely on superficial characteristics (guesswork) or to seek costly expert advice.

If effects on other domestic producers and suppliers are external to the innovator's decisions, effects on foreign economies are even more remote. Governments that will not intervene in the economic contest among domestic producers may choose to protect domestic agents from foreign competition. The argument for free trade is significantly stronger when existing capacities are not considered than when idle capacity and consequent disruptions are apparent in the vicinity. Understandings about who may build new industrial capacity may well be essential to common-market agreements. Where the structure of the world economy threatens to change 'too fast', trade barriers can be expected to slow the process down.

Will interventionist policies stall the engine of change? In an international context we cannot afford to let that happen. Despite all the difficulties and disruptions anticipated, most thoughtful individuals agree that global problems of poverty and equity cannot be solved without substantial structural change. Acknowledging the costs of change does not preclude recognition of its essential role. By focusing explicitly on problems of timing and transition we can begin to search for a trajectory of technical transformation whose adjustment costs are manageable.

REFERENCES

Brody, A. (1970) *Proportions, Prices and Planning* (Budapest and Amsterdam: North Holland), pp. 147–59.
Carter, A. (1970) *Structural Change in the American Economy* (Cambridge, Massachusetts: Harvard University Press), pp. 177–216.
Data Resources Inc. (Spring 1982) *Interindustry Review*, pp. F83–91.
Leontief, W. (1951) 'Structural Change', Leontief, W. *et al.* *Studies in The Structure of the American Economy* (New York: Oxford University Press), pp. 17–52.
Murakami, Y., Tokoyama, K. and Tsukui, J. (1970) 'Efficient Paths of Accumulation and the Turnpike of the Japanese Economy', Carter, A. and Brody, A. (eds) *Applications of Input Output Analysis* (Amsterdam: North Holland), pp. 24–7.
Schumpeter, J. (1939) *Business Cycles* (New York: McGraw Hill), vol. 1, pp. 130–19.
Schumpeter, J. (1942) *Capitalism, Socialism and Democracy* (New York: Harper),
Tsukui, J. (1972) 'Optimal Path in a Non-Linear Dynamic Input-Output Systems – a Generalization of the Turnpike Model', Brody, A. and Carter, A. (eds) *Input–Output Techniques* (Amsterdam: North Holland), pp. 551–62.

4 Technical Change in the North: Some Implications for Southern Options

Frances Stewart
OXFORD UNIVERSITY

1 INTRODUCTION

The debate about choice of technique in developing countries has been about choice at a particular point in time.[1] Yet perhaps the most obvious fact about technology in modern economies is that it is continuously changing, both with respect to products and processes. Conclusions based on the static picture (given technology set and product) are likely to become obsolete. The nature and direction of technical change determines the set of technologies available to a developing country at a point of time, and how that set is changing: hence the nature of technical change has considerable implications for development patterns. This paper discusses aspects of this question.

Technical change has long been dominated by the advanced countries – described here as 'the North'. Evidence on significant innovations/inventions, patents issued, technology balance of payments, distribution of research and development expenditure, and scientific manpower[2] all support this conclusion. In the last decade or so, there has been a certain amount of innovative activity in the South; the development of scientific infrastructure, many minor and a few major innovations, and evidence of growing technology exports by the South (Lall, 1982). Despite this, technology change in the North still dominates, being responsible for the major directions of change, even though Southern efforts may modify the results in some respects.

Why distinguish between North and South in this way? As has often been pointed out, there is considerable heterogeneity within both groups, but especially within the South. Because of this heterogeneity it is not possible to come to conclusions which are universally applicable to all economies in the South. However, there are differences between the 'typical' Southern economy and that of the North which are of relevance to the question being considered here. These differences include the following:

1. the South has substantially lower per capita incomes;
2. the South has lower per capita savings;
3. the South generally has lower levels of education/skill per capita;
4. the South has lower levels of social and economic infrastructure per person;
5. the South has higher rates of population growth;
6. the South has smaller markets in aggregate and for most products expressed in terms of monetary demand;
7. the average size of productive unit (firm and plant) tends to be substantially smaller in the South;
8. the South has a markedly different distribution of its output between different types of goods (e.g. more agriculture, less manufacturing) and an even more marked difference in the distribution of its workforce.

Most of the differences (2)–(8) arise from, or are reflections of, the first difference – in per capita incomes: this in turn reflects differences in average labour productivity for the economy as a whole (although not necessarily for particular industries).

Because of these differences (and others not specified), the South's requirements of its technology differ in some major respects from those of the North.

Both North and South share the requirement that technologies should maximise the productivity of their resources in aggregate, which is equivalent to maximising the productivity of the total population. But technologies also affect the level and distribution of employment, the distribution of incomes, patterns of consumption, organisation and nature of work. Technologies which fulfil the output-maximising criterion may involve adverse effects on the other variables: for brevity, we shall describe these as 'distorting' effects. New technologies designed in and for the North may be assumed not to have distorting effects in the North (although many would challenge this assumption – see Norman, 1981). But even where they maximise output, they may have distorting effects in the South, given the difference in conditions (e.g. they may be associated with much underemployment). Hence new technologies from the North may:

1. Raise output in the South, without 'distorting' effects;
2. Raise output in the South, with 'distorting' effects;
3. Not raise output in the South, and not be selected;
4. Not raise output in the South, and be selected.

Obviously, the welfare effects of the new technologies will depend critically upon which category technical change (*tc*) generally falls into, as will the policy implications.

Techniques in mainstream economics, both with respect to technical choice and technical change, are usually categorised in two dimensions: these are the capital and labour requirements for the production of a given product. There are three respects in which this categorisation is inadequate. First, there are the well-known problems of measuring capital such that two techniques may turn out to be more or less capital-intensive than each other, according to the interest rate assumed. Secondly, the approach cannot deal with changes in products. Yet changes in product characteristics (minor and major) are an intrinsic aspect of technical change being the dominating motive of R & D,[3] constituting a main element in the success of new technologies, and forming a major part of increased income. Thirdly, the two dimensions selected form only one small aspect of a true description of a technology. How one describes a technology depends on the point of view of the observer. For example, an artist's description would differ from that of a transport firm whose task was to carry a machine to the factory; a worker would describe it in terms of the requirement it imposes upon the worker (e.g. monotony of operations, physical effort, etc.), while a cleaner would have a different point of view. What is the relevant point of view? In one way all these (and many others) are relevant, since all affect welfare when a technology is installed.

The major focus here is on characteristics relevent to the decision as to whether to introduce the technique, to the efficiency of the technique and to the social consequences of its introduction. (This last aspect, of course, could be interpreted to include more or less all aspects.) Major relevant characteristics, then, include the resources the technology uses, including unskilled labour and labour of various skills; the machinery involved (cost, durability, likely maintenance expenditure); the scale of production and managerial requirements; raw materials and semi-processed materials. We then have a vector, T_a, consisting of the set of characteristics of a technique a: t_i, t_{ii}, t_{iii}, ... etc. (Stewart, 1977, p. 2) which describe the technique a as a process of production. It is necessary to add a description of the product P_a, which in turn is a vector whose components, p_i, p_{ii}, p_{iii} ... describe various aspects of the product: for example, its broad function (e.g. to provide nutrition) and its specific aspects (e.g. calories, protein, process requirements). A full description of a technique, then, will include details of both product and process characteristics. For simplicity, we may include P_a as a member of T_a, so T_a consists of t_i, t_{ii}, t_{iii} ... P_a. Technical change then consists in the development of a new technology vector, say T_a', whose characteristics differ in some respects from the previous one; thus the new technique might use less energy, or be of a larger scale, or involve some major or minor improvement in product. It might also involve a change in the conventional dimensions (value of machinery, quantity of labour). But it is necessary to look at the many dimensions suggested here – first, because many technical changes may not affect the conventional dimensions at all but could still be of major significance; secondly, because many changes which do in fact fit into the usual category, changing the ratio of value of machinery to labour employed, may also be associated with other changes (in scale, material use, product characteristics) which determine the effects of the technology on patterns of development.

In practice, it is not possible to disentangle processes and products, since each process produces a (more or less) specific product, while the process itself embodies, in the form of machines, transport equipment, etc., the products of other industries. A very large proportion of changes in techniques, then, are at the same time changes in process and changes in product. Hence often if a process becomes obsolete, the product associated with it will too, while if a product is no longer demanded then the process of production associated with it is also discarded (e.g. the technology of horse-upkeep has become obsolete with the replacement of horses by mechanised horse-power). This interactive process is a major source of obsolescence, reducing the number of 'vintage' technologies which remain economic. Despite the close connection between processes and products, these are discussed separately. The next section considers technical change in processes.

2 PROCESS TECHNOLOGY

2.1 The Neoclassical Approach

As stated, most economic analysis has been concerned with a rather narrow subset of this type of change – i.e. they way in which capital/labour (K/L) requirements and capital/output requirements (K/O) change over time. The first attempt to incorporate tc into economic models did so very crudely, simply assuming that technology change occurred at some independent rate (not as an outcome of the economic system) in the form of 'increase in knowledge', with uniform effects on each of the potential techniques (Solow, 1957). Thus the whole traditional production function, embodying different combinations of capital and labour, was shifted out uniformly. Hence productivity of techniques most relevant to the South (more labour-using) was raised proportionately[4] with more capital-intensive techniques (used by the North). If this were a good description of technical change, then it would raise productivity in the South, with no adverse effects. However, the most casual of empirical evidence suggests this is an incorrect description; technical change has been uneven. Very labour-intensive technologies – the traditional technologies of the masses in the South – have been untouched by technical change, while the major new technologies have been concentrated in new industries (e.g. chemicals, and now bio-technology), generally of high capital-intensity, and often also of high skill intensity and of increasing scale of production.

There is no question, then, that the simple 'uniform' technical change neoclassical model is incorrect as a description of reality. It is also subject to severe theoretical defects. Two different types of criticism have been made; both are illuminating with respect to the nature of technical change. One accepts the basic framework of capital and labour being the main dimensions of technology but tries to locate innovatory activity in an economic setting rather than as 'manna from heaven'; it consequently sees tc as the outcome of particular economic pressures and incentives, with consequences for the rate and direction of tc.[5] The other is premised on a more radical critique of the concept of capital, thereby rejecting the use of the conventional framework, even as a starting point.

2.2 Technical Change as the Outcome of Economic Activity

Once it is accepted that the process of producing technical change, with respect to research, development and the introduction of new technologies, is an economic activity, mainly carried out by profit-making firms in order to generate (or preserve) their profits, then it can readily be shown that the actual technologies developed will be formed in the light of the economic conditions when and where they are developed. Given the big differences noted between the economic conditions in the North and South, it follows that the characteristics of the new technologies will often be unsuitable for the South. This is the broad conclusion to be derived from all the theories of technical innovation as an economic actitivity.

The simplest of these is that of Salter (1966), who argued that while in some sense the 'state of knowledge' may increase at a rate which is independent of actual economic developments, any actual technique is developed and produced in a particular context. Thus the traditional production functions cannot be a description of actual techniques in use, but, at the most generous interpretation, hypothetical techniques that might be developed, were there to be a favourable economic environment.

Techniques that are actually developed will be those which are profitable in the prevailing economic environment. As real wages rise, it can easily be shown that the low K/L ratio and, low labour productivity techniques will not generate enough output per man to pay the wage bill. Hence, over time, with rising real wages, the techniques that are developed in the North will be increasingly capital-intensive.

A major weakness of this approach is to assume the existence of a set of hypothetical production functions, representing potential techniques which may be developed according to prevailing economic conditions. While there are general scientific advances over time, which make it likely that new techniques will be more productive than old, those carrying out innovatory activity do not know what the potential set of techniques are.

In this view, the direction of tc (in terms of the K/L ratio) is indeterminate, but a greater proportion of new technologies will tend to raise the K/L ratio, the higher the real price of labour in relation to capital. The concept of an 'innovation possibility curve' (IPC) of Ahmad and others suggests that relative factor prices influence the direction of tc, with more capital-intensive (higher K/L) techniques being developed the more expensive labour is in relation to capital. Innovations in industrialised countries would tend to generate increasingly capital-intensive techniques over time.

This approach to innovation has been rightly criticised for hypothesising a curve (the IPC curve) which has no empirical foundation, and is simply a convenient theoretical device (see especially Nelson and Winters, 1982). A fundamental fact about R & D and technical development is that when decisions are made, entrepreneurs do not know what they are going to find, whereas the IPC assumes that they do. Nelson and Winters start from a much less presumptuous position, simply assuming that entrepeneurs search in a somewhat random fashion for new techniques subject to two restrictions: first, they start the search wherever they are at the moment, and the innovations tend to be clustered around that point. Secondly, they only pursue innovations which are cost-reducing. These rather modest assumptions are sufficient to lead to the conclusion that Northern innovations will tend to be biased against the needs of LDCs, as compared with own-generated innovations. A random search produces a range of research results, while the ones worth pursuing are those which reduce costs. North innovation will produce more capital-intensive results than South innovation, first because of differences in prices which lead to differences in costs associated with each technique, and secondly because of differences in starting point, with the North generally exploring new ideas in the context of a more capital-intensive environment. Over time, Northern innovation will become increasingly inappropriate for the South, with changes in factor prices and in the point of departure.

To summarise, adopting a neoclassical approach to production possibilities and innovation, there is strong theoretical support for the view that economic conditions in the North will influence the nature of tc. It seems that new technologies are likely to use more capital and less labour than would be best from the point of view of the South.

However, while the new technologies are likely to be associated with higher capital-intensity, in the sense of K/L, *there is no reason why they should be associated with higher capital requirements per unit of output.* In so far as new techniques are associated with the same, or lower, K/L than previous techniques, they will raise productivity in the South as well as the North, as compared with old techniques. In terms of the earlier classification, then, they will tend to fit into the first two categories, being output-raising. But the higher K/L may mean that they are also 'distorting', in the sense that – given limited savings – the countries can only afford to equip a minority of the labour force with them. It follows that there will be underemployment in the rest of the workforce, while inequality of income distribution is also often associated with such uneven availability of capital equipment.

Extending the discussion to include changes in skill requirements, scale and infrastructure produces similar results: new techniques will follow the supply availabilities and organisational structure of the North. Over time this means a tendency to use more skills and more sophisticated infrastructure to produce techniques designed for a larger scale of production. This does not mean that every innovation from the North will have these characteristics: science and technology can produce innovations of many kinds and some may be economic in the North, while having Southern-type characteristics. But taken together there will be broad tendency in this direction.

2.3 Capital Measurement, Technical Choice and Technical Change

The previous discussion sidestepped the issue of capital measurement. But according to Pasinetti, very different conclusions follow once it is accepted that capital is not a distinct entity, but simply labour of a different kind, i.e. indirect or embodied labour.

The basic point is that capital consists of *produced* goods; these goods are produced by labour together with machines, which were themselves produced at an earlier period. Ignoring, for the moment, the vintage machines which help make machines, capital goods consist solely of embodied or indirect labour. A rise in the wage rate, then, will affect the cost of machines (the indirect labour) as well as the labour directly employed. A rise in the real wage does not affect the cost of techniques of differing capital intensities (defined as techniques with differing ratios of indirect to direct labour) since it raises the costs of indirect labour just as much as the costs of direct labour. A change in the profit rate will affect the choice in so far as different techniques are associated with different ratios of embodied to direct labour, but 'the influence of changes in the rate of profit on the choice of technique is basically inconclusive as to the direction. In any case, whatever the direction, it is very likely in practice to be of secondary importance' (Pasinetti, 1981, p. 194).[6]

As far as choice of technique in ICs and LDCs are concerned, these propositions lead to very strong conclusions. For convenience we may assume that the profit rate is roughly the same in North and South, but the real wage is very different, being much lower in the South. According to Pasinetti (1981, p. 196):

> A different wage rate – when the rate of profit is the same and the technical possibilities are exactly the same – does not make the slightest difference to the choice of techniques!

A simple arithmetical example bears out the Pasinetti conclusion:

	'Capital' = 'indirect labour'		Direct labour		Total cost
	Quantity	Cost	Quantity	Cost	
Automated loom	10	$10w$	1	$1w$	$11w$
Hand loom	2	$2w$	10	$10w$	$12w$

In the example, the total cost of the hand loom is greater than that of the automated loom, irrespective of the wage rate. An example illustrating the reverse situation could have been chosen, but the basic conclusion would have been the same: *that the same technique turns out to be the most profitable or least cost, irrespective of the wage rate.* However, the conclusion depends on each technique being manufactured in the same country in which the technology is introduced.

Suppose initially that every technique is manufactured in the North. Then the costs of embodied labour will reflect Northern labour costs, while the costs of direct labour will reflect Southern labour costs, as follows:

	'Capital' ='indirect labour' Quantity Cost		Direct Labour Quantity Cost		Costs in North	Costs in South
			N	S		
Automated loom	10	$10Wn$	1	$1Wn$ $1Ws$	$11Wn$	$10Wn + 1Ws$
Hand loom	2	$2Wn$	10	$10Wn$ $10Ws$	$12Wn$	$2Wn + 10Ws$

In this case, Southern choice of technique will differ from Northern (in the predicted direction of lesser capital-intensity) so long as

$$(2Wn + 10Ws) < (10Wn + 1Ws) \text{ or } Ws < \frac{8}{9} Wn$$

In this example it has been assumed that the cost to the South of importing a machine can be expressed as the labour cost of producing that machine in the North. In fact the South has to expend labour resources on producing some exportable (which has its own costs) which it exports, and buys the imported machine with the proceeds. Hence a more complex procedure is required for calculating relative costs. In what follows we shall stick to the simplification of ignoring this procedure. This could well alter the results in any particular case, but would not be likely to affect the general conclusions. If one technique is produced only in the North (automated loom) and one only in the South (hand loom), the costs will be as follows:

	Capital costs N S		Direct labour N S		Total costs N	S
Automated loom	$10Wn$	$10Wn$	$1Wn$	$1Ws$	$11Wn$	$10Wn + 1Ws$
Hand loom	$2Ws$	$2Ws$	$10Wn$	$10Ws$	$2Ws + 1Wn$	$12Ws$

Hence where $Wn > 2Ws$ the North will choose the automated technique, and the South will choose the hand loom.

Only if both techniques are produced in both North and South, under the same technical conditions, will the same technique *necessarily* be best (i.e. of least cost) for both. But this is almost never the case, because of the general technological backwardness of the South relative to the North. This relative backwardness means that many Southern countries have virtually no capital goods capacity; those that do have capital goods capacity specialise in older technologies;[7] and those that attempt to produce the latest technologies tend to do so relatively inefficiently (i.e. the technical conditions are not the same). Hence we can assume that the typical case is one where the North produces the most recent technology, while older technologies are produced in the North and South, or in only one of the two. It follows that the least-cost technique in the South is not always the same as that in the North, although it may be. Where there is a difference, the lease-cost technique for the South will tend to be less capital-intensive (i.e. involve a lower ratio of indirect to direct labour) than the least-cost technique in the North. This, of course, accords with the predictions of conventional theory (although for different reasons) and of empirical findings.

Technical change will take the form of reducing the total cost (i.e. the combined quantity of indirect and direct labour). It will appear to raise capital-intensity defined as K/L, because the capital requirements (K) are normally measured as a cost (e.g. the cost of producing the machinery) and therefore rise over time with a rise in the real wage (which in turn is the consequence of technical change), while labour (L) is a physical quantity. The rise in K/L, for which there is plentiful evidence, tells us nothing, however, about what happens to capital-intensity defined as the ratio of indirect to direct labour, nor capital-intensity defined as capital requirements per unit of output. There is no reason, if the real wage-rate is the same in each sector (ignoring any influence of the profit rate) why tc should be systematically biased towards increasing or reducing the ratio of indirect to direct labour, nor why it should be capital-using or saving in terms of the K/O ratio.

As far as the South is concerned, whether or not there is such a bias is not particularly important. What is significant is that:

1. tc is labour-saving, normally in terms of indirect and direct labour requirements per unit of output; so for any given additional output fewer jobs are created;
2. the price of equipment imported from the North rises over time, with the rising real wage. This means the capital/labour ratio, or the cost of providing equipment for each worker rises; so for any given expenditure on capital fewer jobs are created;

3. there is no particular reason why the capital requirements per unit of output should rise or fall.

It follows that tc in the North may well contribute to the output-maximising object of the South, although there can be cases, as discussed above, where the output maximisation criterion suggests a different and more labour-intensive technological choice than that in the North – but it may also make it more difficult for the South to create enough extra jobs, and also to meet other objectives. The precise effects depend not only on the characteristics of the new technologies, as compared with older ones, but also where they are made – and hence the implications for relative costs and for the creation of indirect as well as direct employment opportunities. If new technologies reduce direct labour requirements while increasing indirect requirements, they may increase employment in the North, which specialises in capital goods, while decreasing it in the South, which uses these goods.

In most cases, new technologies *from* the North displace old technologies *in* the South, after a time-lag. This displacement occurs (a) because the new technology is cost-reducing and output-raising for the South; (b) because the products of the new technologies differ from those of the old, and these products displace old products because they are preferred and because they are linked to the rest of technology in use (e.g. as inputs); (c) because production of the old technology stops; (d) because of biased selection mechanisms favouring these technologies (these include capital and labour prices, exchange rate policies, the influence of multinationals on choice of technology, the influence of elites on choice of products).

If the first reason applies, the displacement will contribute to raising output in the South; with the other reasons, it may not do so. But whatever the reason, the displacement affects the pattern of development as well as output levels, because of the many characteristics of technologies noted at the beginning of this paper.

The most obvious effect is on employment. As stated, for any given capital expenditure fewer jobs are created. Since more output is normally made possible, a classic conflict between output and employment maximisation emerges.[8] In theory governments should be able to tax part of the additional output and redistribute income to the unemployed or underemployed (for example by 'creating' jobs in public works). But in practice administrative and political restraints often prevent this. The new high productivity technologies then contribute to a worsening of income distribution and an accentuation of employment problems.

In addition, as noted earlier, significant changes occur in scale, the use of materials, skill and managerial requirements, infrastructural requirements (transport, legal structure, financial services, energy) which make heavy demands on Southern economies, requiring them to devote considerable resources to meet the demands, leading to heavy reliance on imports to supplement local efforts, and notwithstanding these efforts, often involving relatively inefficient production.

Technological change from the North often creates problems for the South, not because it fails to raise output there, but because it does raise output in the South as well as the North, but the changing requirements that go along with the change are ill-suited to conditions in the South. Both types of theory considered above suggested that *tc* from the North would often, but not always, be output-raising for the South: it is precisely in these cases that the tendency towards 'distorting' impact becomes relevant.

3 PRODUCTS[9]

Any empirical investigation into *tc* at once notes the dominating feature is change in *products*. Yet theory has concentrated on change in inputs, mainly because it is difficult to deal with changing products in a conventional framework. However, the Lancaster (1966) way of dealing with products as bundles of characteristics makes it possible to treat change in products as (partly) endogenous, rather in the same way as changes in techniques. Assume any product consists of a vector of characteristcs, $P_a = P_i, P_{ii}, P_{iii}, \ldots$, where P_i, P_{ii} represent different characteristics, such as energy-giving, protein-providing, or colour. A change in product consists in a change in this vector. Let us assume, for simplicity, that the new product involves the same cost of production (however defined); a new product will be introduced if it produces more of the previous characteristics, or a different (and by some preferred) ratio of characteristics, or, perhaps, some entirely new characteristics. The new product may in practice do all of these things.

It may be assumed that an increase in quantity of characteristics always raises welfare (since we are assuming same cost); a change in the ratio of characteristics will please some (those who prefer the new ratio) and displease others.

Some significant conclusions follow: some new products improve the welfare of everyone; if tastes differ, some new products may increase the welfare of some people but not others; people only lose by new products if the availability of the old products changes (i.e. their cost increases or they are withdrawn). (The conclusions are complicated by imperfect information, the presence of advertising, and 'demonstration' effects and the interdependence of consumers' welfare.)[10]

The analysis is relevant to the North/South question because a major determinant of 'tastes' is incomes. Engels noted this in relation to the broad categories of products people spend their incomes on, and they way this changes with incomes. It is also true with respect to a narrower definition of product (e.g. the way people meet their transport needs changes from walking to cycling/riding, to buses, to private cars, to airplanes as income rises). Hence there is a tendency for a systematic difference in tastes between North and South, with the tastes for South being for goods with more 'low-income' characteristics.

New products, designed in the North, will therefore tend to be suited to high-income consumers embodying increasingly high-income type characteristics over time. While they may raise the welfare of rich consumers in the South, they will often not increase the welfare of poorer consumers, who form the majority of the population in Southern countries. Whether their welfare actually decreases absolutely will then depend on whether the old products continue to be available. In practice, they are often withdrawn, because of economies of scale, which makes it economic only to produce a limited number of products. Since the bulk of monetary demand lies with higher-income Northern consumers plus elites in the South, there will be a tendency for Northern-style products to displace low-income products. Moreover, since new processes tend to displace old ones and new processes often produce new products, new products will tend to displace old ones. However, in this situation the 'constant cost' assumption has to be relaxed, since the new technologies are often of lower cost than the old.

There is a parallel here with the development of techniques of production. There is a systematic tendency for the new products to involve more high-income and less low-income characteristics. But the tendency to lower costs as a result of technical progress means that the total available low-income characteristics may nonetheless rise. The new products will tend to be inegalitarian, in the sense that they will benefit the higher-income consumers most, while low-income consumers may not benefit at all, or may even be adversely affected.

The introduction of product change modified some of the conclusions about change in technique. It was assumed earlier that each new technique involved the 'same' product. But in practice, almost invariably, the new technologies also produce new products. In some cases the new products will be preferred in the South as well as the North, so that the superiority of new technology will be enhanced by considering product characteristics. But in others, the new product may involve 'excess' of some characteristics for low-income consumers and a deficiency of others; hence while the new technology may be output-raising in the North, it may not be in the South, since valuation of output should include valuation of the product characteristics. For example, a new technology for block-making which produces stronger and more uniform blocks may be output-raising in the North, where the new blocks save labour in sorting and testing the blocks; but not in the South, where the blocks are intended to be used for single-storey accommodation so that the additional strength is not needed.

4 CONCLUSIONS

Technical change in the North inevitably affects the South, changing, often dramatically, the technology available. Some of the changes – in both methods of production and products – undoubtedly contribute to meeting development objectives, making it possible to produce more, for a given outlay of resources. But there are other effects – intrinsically and inseparably connected – which may be undesirable. Notable among these are inegalitarian effects, resulting from the low employment potential of the new technologies and the high-income characteristics of the new products. New technologies have also often been of an excessive scale for many Third World economies; and they require increasing levels of skills, and rising levels of infrastructural facilities. In order to provide the environment and services necessary for the new technologies to operate efficiently, many economies have become excessively dependent on industrial economies, while devoting most of their investment (public and private) to serving the advanced country technologies, neglecting the tradtional sector where, often, a majority of the people find a living. The output-creating aspects of modern technology make it difficult to resist. But the 'distorting' effects make it desirable to consider policy options.

Policy Options

1. To reject modern technology. This is the Kampuchea option: it generally involves loss in output, but an increase in equality.
2. To be selective, accepting only the output-raising techniques, and products which increase the availability of low-income characteristics. This (perhaps) is exemplified by China. It is difficult politically and administratively and may also involve some loss in output. A major problem is the many links between technologies, so that it is difficult to operate part efficiently without accepting the whole. India, for example, seems to have followed an inefficient selective policy. One form of selectivity occurs automatically via the price system. A highly protected economy will tend to be less selective from this point of view than one which is open and competitive (contrast, for example, Mexico and Taiwan).
3. Generation of indigenous *tc* in both techniques and products. From one point of view, this appears the most attractive option, since it should enable the South to make use of the latest scientific and technical developments, but direct them to its own needs and thus avoid the distorting effects of Northern technology. But it can be very expensive, since the South lacks many of the resources necessary to generate *tc*. Secondly, Southern *tc* often produces technologies similar to Northern ones, because of the organisation of R & D and the structure of incentives. Since the very poor lack purchasing power and access to credit, there is little incentive to produce technologies which they need (either machines or products).
4. Adaptation of Northern technologies to Southern condition. This less ambitious than (3) above. There is more possibility of some success, but it implies that the Southern economies would continue to accept the broad sweep of Northern *tc*, providing minor modifications. It seems, empirically, that there has been more success in modifying methods of production than in modifying product characteristics.
5. Individual Southern economies also have the option, increasingly being exercised, or getting their technology from other Southern economies. Collectively, because of the larger markets and

greater resources, the South is likely to make more headway in creating alternative technologies, but many Southern economies are too closely linked with the North to wish to do so.

The discussion in this paper suggests that it is not possible to come to any *general* conclusion about whether *tc* in the North benefits or disadvantages the South. While this might not seem a strong conclusion, it contradicts both those who have argued that modern technology is always the best, and those who argue the opposite, that it is always disadvantageous.[11] Each technology has to be judged on its own merits, paying especial attention to the source and terms of acquisition of capital goods and the nature of product characteristics. Innovation in and for the South potentially offers *tc* with more desirable characteristics, but it has a cost in terms of resource use and levels of output, at least in the short run.

NOTES

1. See, for example, Sen (1968), Dobb (1956–7), Kahn (1951), Galenson and Leibenstein (1955).
2. See, for example, Annerstadt (1979).
3. According to a McGraw-Hill survey, 83 per cent of R & D among manufacturing firms was devoted to product innovations. See Link in Sahal (ed.), p.48.
4. The precise meaning of 'proportionately' in this context depends on the precise assumptions made about the process of technical change. It is not necessary to specify these here.
5. See Binswanger *et al.* (1978) for a survey of work adopting this approach and some applications to developing countries.
6. This conclusion follows where the stream of costs and benefits of a project are even. However, with very simple assumptions about the timing (where, for example, the two projects consist of different ratios of labour at time t to labour at time $t-1$, and the output is identical and occurs at time t) it seems that a higher rate of interest would increase the cost of the capital-intensive techniques, that is the one with the higher ratio of labour at time $t-1$. However, the paper follows the Pasinetti conclusion.
7. In general there is a much greater time-lag between transfer of technology from the North to developing countries and transfer to other developed countries. See Mansfield in Sahal (ed.), p.16. It seems probable that the lag is greater in capital goods production.
8. This is discussed at length in Stewart and Streeten (1971).
9. See James and Stewart (1981), which elaborates on some of the discussion here.

10. Some of these are discussed in more detail in James and Stewart (1981).
11. Each view has strong advocates. Emmanuel (1982) is a recent adherent of the 'latest is best' school. Some of those promoting intermediate technology come near to arguing the opposite – see Schumacher (1973).

REFERENCES

Ahmad, S. (1966) 'On the Theory of Induced Invention', *Economic Journal*, vol.76, no. 302.
Amsalem, M. (1983) *Technology Choice in Developing Countries: the Impact of Differences in Factor Costs* (Cambridge, Mass.: MIT Press).
Annerstadt, J. (1979) 'On the Present Distribution of R & D Resources', occasional paper, 79/1, Vienna Institute for Development.
Binswanger, H. P., Ruttan, V. W. *et al.* (1978) *Induced Innovation* (Baltimore: John Hopkins University Press).
Dobb, M. (1956–7), 'Second Thoughts on Capital-intensity of investment', *Review of Economic Studies*, vol. XXIV, no. 63.
Eckaus, R. S. (1955) 'The Factor Proportions Problem in Underdeveloped Areas', *American Economic Review*, vol. XLV, no. 4.
Emmanuel, A. (1982) *Appropriate or Underdeveloped Technology*, (Chichester: John Wiley).
Galenson, S. and Leibenstein, H. (1955) 'Investment Criteria, Productivity and Economic Development', *Quarterly Journal of Economics*, vol. LXIX, no. 3.
James, J. and Stewart, F. (1981) 'New Products: a Discussion of the Welfare Effects of the Introduction of New Products in Developing Countries', *Oxford Economic Papers*, vol. 33. no. 1.
Kahn, A. E. (1951) 'Investment Criteria in Development Programs', *Quarterly Journal of Economics*, vol. LXV, no. 1.
Lall, S. (1982) *Developing Countries as Exporters of Technology* (London: Macmillan).
Lancaster, K. (1966) 'Change and Innovation in the Technology of Consumption', *American Economic Review*, vol. LVI, no. 2.
Nelson, R. R. and Winters, S. (1974) 'Neo-classical versus Evolutionary Theories of Economic Growth: Critique and Prospects', *Economic Journal*, vol. 336, no. 4.
Nelson, R. R. and Winters, S. (1982) *An Evolutionary Theory of Economic Change* (Cambridge Mass: Harvard University Press).
Norman, C. (1981) *The God that Limps* (London:Norton).
Pasinetti, L. (1981) *Structural Change and Economic Growth* (Cambridge: Cambridge University Press).
Ranis, G. (1973) 'Industrial Sector Labor Absorption', *Economic Development and Cultural Change*, vol. 21, no. 3.
Sahal, D. (ed.) (1982) *The Transfer and Utilisation of Technical Knowledge* (Lexington: Heath).

Salter, W. E. G. (1966) *Productivity and Technical Change* (Cambridge: Cambridge University Press).
Schumacher, E. F. (1973) *Small is Beautiful* (London: Blond and Briggs).
Sen, A. K. (1968) *Choice of Techniques* (Oxford: Blackwell).
Solow, R. (1957) 'Technical Change and the Aggregate Production Function', *Review of Economic and Statistics*, vol. XXXIX, no. 3.
Stewart, F. (1977) *Technology and Underdevelopment* (London: Macmillan).
Stewart, F. and Streeten, P. (1971) 'Conflicts between Output and Employment Objectives in Developing Countries', *Oxford Economic Papers*, vol. 23, no. 3.

5 Technology Transfer: Measuring the Impact of Organisational and Managerial Structures on Production Efficiency

J. R. Marsden[1],
KRANNERT GRADUATE SCHOOL OF MANAGEMENT
V. Salas-Fumas
UNIVERSITY OF ZARAGOZA and
A. Whinston
UNIVERSITY OF KENTUCKY

1 INTRODUCTION

Inter-country transfer of technology offers the lure of the productivity advances so fundamentally necessary for continued economic growth. Increasingly, however, notable failures in such transfers have raised questions about the adaptability of technology to new environments. The introduction of unfamiliar processes, working conditions and management structures has involved the nagging repercussions of production problems and lingering societal upheaval that work against the realisation of the anticipated gains. Although there are ample examples of technology transfer, some resulting in resounding success and others in equally resounding failure, there remains a void in terms of the formulation of a workable analytic process for indentifying and measuring the 'transferability' (across the spectrum from likely failure to likely success) of particular technologies between specific countries or regions within a given country. Further, for industries such as high technology industries, easily measurable inputs do not take on the same importance as they do for primary, heavy resource-using industries. Instead such industries rely more heavily on unmeasurable factors including organisational structure and incentive formation. Indeed, changes in this direction have accompanied the natural progression of time. In the 1800s the availability of natural resources, particularly land, was the key to successful economic development, to successful technology transfer. By the early 1900s the focus had shifted to labour and raw materials, the inputs then needed to fuel industrial expansion and facilitate technology transfer. Today, we must deal more and more with technologies that depend on highly skilled, relatively unique individual contributors rather than on easily measurable and substitutable resources. In software development, in robotics, in modern manufacturing, the successful introduction of new technologies requires the application of appropriate organisational and incentive structures. The evolution of production technologies has led us to a situation where successful introduction of new or transferred technologies must focus on dealing with and modifying behaviour through organisational effort rather than on dealing with or modifying physical resources or controlling an adverse natural environment. One may well wonder about the precise role that differing organisational and incentive structures played in determining the dichotomy presently observed in robotics where, though the technology was primarily developed in the United States, the major applications are occurring in Japan.

In the present paper our objectives are two-fold:
1. to develop procedures for distinguishing between or 'disentangling' engineering and managerial capability; and
2. to structure a framework for the measurement and control of technological transfer across countries.

By utilising an engineering process model approach, we are able to analyse the efficiency of a firm's input choice set for producing a specified output level. With benchmark theoretical frontier values estimated using repeated process model solutions and with world and country frontier benchmarks estimated using worldwide or country-specific data, we can decompose a specific firm's inefficiency into measures of allocative inefficiency and various forms of X-inefficiency (see Farrell, 1957, and Leibenstein, 1978). In our terminology, *engineering technology* is the key to technological progress, while *managerial technology* is the key to technical efficiency in the Farrell sense. The core problem with which our framework deals is the possible sensitivity of production processes to country- or region-specific management techniques and organisational structure, either of which may be directly or indirectly representative of local underlying political or cultural structure. As the latter two may not be empirically quantifiable, the present analysis focuses on developing information about response patterns from various structures rather than on quantifications of the structures themselves.[2]

Our analytical framework uses Leibenstein's X-efficiency concept, which, we argue, can actually be made measurable by utilising detailed mathematical models of production processes, or *process models*, such as those developed and in use in industries such as petroleum refining, electricity generation, and steel fabrication.

Further by utilising an updated process model incorporating new technologies, the basic analysis used in the static context can be extended to a dynamic context.

We begin the sections that follow with a consideration of production efficiency, including X-efficiency, and the issues relevant to the development of the problem presented here. We follow this in Section 3 with a discussion centring on the relations between efficiency, transfer costs and technology transfer, emphasising the relationship between previous work in the efficiency area and the present approach. The fourth section details the generalised process model framework, indicating its usefulness in developing the all-important frontier values required for empirical measurement. This crucial fourth section outlines our suggested integrated approach and includes a consideration of the role of four data forms – historic, process model, experimental, and panel – in actually estimating the suggested measures. The final section of the paper presents a brief summary and suggestions for implementation.

2 EFFICIENCY AND TECHNICAL PROGRESS

The concept of efficiency analysed in this paper is closely related to Farrell's technological efficiency. In his well-known paper, Farrell (1957) addressed the concept of economic efficiency, pointing to two ways in which the actual resource allocation of a firm may depart from the cost-minimising solution: (a) the firm is not determining the input levels that make the value of marginal products per dollar spent equal across inputs (assignative or allocative inefficiency), or (b) the firm is not utilising the best technique available for output production (technical inefficiency).[3] The two measures suggested by Farrell were expanded by Leibenstein (1966), who suggested the additional possibility that the firm knows the best practice or technology but does not have the incentives or competitive pressure to employ it. Thus the actual choices of resource allocation that are observed are determined by organisational forces in conjunction with the knowledge of available technology. Such organisational laxity results in what Leibenstein terms 'X-inefficiency', which in his use includes both ineffectiveness of decisions concerning how to use inputs and the resulting actual performance based on those decisions.

In empirical work, Farrell's technical efficiency has been closely related to the frontier production function defining the outer boundary of possible input-output combinations for a set of observations. At a given moment of time, the level of Farrell's technical inefficiency may be viewed as related to the distance from the frontier estimate. Over time the distance from the frontier may change due to alterations in the technical efficiency of the firm, a situation easily detected if the frontier remains unchanged. However, location of the frontier is itself subject to change because of technical progress. Comparing actual resource allocations at two points in time, it is important to know the underlying forces that have determined their displacement and the relative importance of such determinants. As pointed out by Nishimizu and Page (1982), there has been little attention to the problem of 'knowing how far one is off the technological frontier at any point in time, and how quickly one can reach the frontier' (p. 921).

Both statics and time dynamics of efficiency are of central interest and importance in understanding the problem of technology transfer. We introduce Figure 5.1 to help elucidate these problems. Point X_{ij} in the figure indicates the actual resource allocation of inputs '1' and '2' utilised to obtain the specified level of output, say Y, for firm i in country j. X_{ij} represents firm i's input combination choice from the relevant alternative input sets the firm faces (i.e. firm i's perceived Y isoquant). Similarly, point F corresponds to the cost-minimising (global frontier) resource allocation for the same output level and for a given set on input prices which are here assumed to be world prices. Our concern is thus to understand the reasons that would explain why the resource allocation selected differs from the global optimum and to measure the sources contributing to such inefficiency.

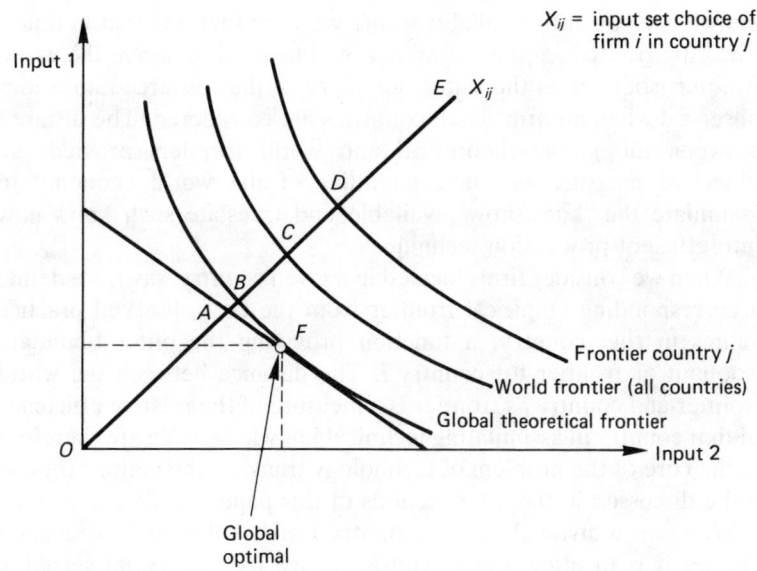

Figure 5.1 Global efficiency: cross-country comparisons

The global theoretical frontier, represented in Figure 5.1 by the isoquant lying closest to the origin, differs from the conventional frontier notion since it has no reference to actual observed data. Rather, the reference is to a set of solutions that would result from parameterising the optimisation problem of cost minimisation, given a specified output level and the scientific, technical and engineering knowledge currently available in the world at that moment in time.[4] The empirical concept of frontier would be used to derive the world frontier isoquant as the outer boundary of the resource allocations observed when all firms in all countries are considered. The distance between the global theoretical and world frontiers provides an objective measure of the capabilities of the world economy to assimilate the 'know-how' available and translate such know-how into efficient production techniques.

When we consider firms located in a given country, say j, we define a corresponding empirical frontier from the best observed practice values in that country, a function providing the outer boundary isoquant or frontier for country j. The distance between the world frontier and country j's frontier is a measure of the relative efficiency of that country in assimilating technical knowledge. We are therefore at the core of the problem of technology transfer, the major problem to be discussed in the later sections of this paper.

When an individual firm in country j makes the final production choice, it is in effect putting into practice its managerial selection from the available technology set. Referring again to Figure 5.1, the distance between firm i's perceived isoquant and the frontier isoquant of country j provides a general respresentation of firm-specific inefficiency without regard to input prices. In particular, the distance along the ray from the origin from X_{ij} (firm i's chosen input combination set) to the frontier isoquant of country j measures the degree of technical inefficiency in the conventional and most technical sense. For a given set of input prices, this measure can be viewed in terms of relative costs, i.e. the difference between firm i's total cost at its chosen operating point, X_{ij}, and the lower cost for obtaining the same output level (Y) if firm i's input mix were utilised with the frontier technology available in country j. This representation focuses on the input mix that firm i actually chooses and compares the level (X_{ij}) of the input mix firm i utilises to produce Y with the lower level (indicated by point D) of the same input mix proportion that the frontier firm in country j could use to reach the same output level, Y. The measurement is along a ray from the origin (or fixed proportions input usage) passing through the actual usage choice of firm i; thus it has no necessary direct correspondence to cost-minimising solutions for either firm i or for the frontier firm in country j.

In addition to the above measures related to technical efficiency, we can also utilise Figure 5.1 to 'visualise' Farrell's assignative inefficiency as the distance from the global theoretical frontier to the isocost line along the actual input proportions ray.

Summarising the above discussion, we can decompose the static measurement for our hypothetical firm i operating in country j of relative global efficiency as follows:

$$\underset{\substack{\text{global} \\ \text{efficiency}}}{\frac{OA}{OE}} = \underset{\substack{\text{allocative} \\ \text{(assignment)} \\ \text{efficiency}}}{\frac{QA}{OB}} \times \underset{\substack{\text{world} \\ \text{technical} \\ \text{efficiency}}}{\frac{OB}{OC}} \times \underset{\substack{\text{country-} \\ \text{specific} \\ \text{technical} \\ \text{efficiency}}}{\frac{OC}{OD}} \times \underset{\substack{\text{firm-specific} \\ \text{technical} \\ \text{efficiency}}}{\frac{OD}{OE}}$$

Such a static decomposition of efficiency measures aids our understanding of distribution of competitive advantage among different countries at a given point in time, but it also possible to translate the approach into a dynamic context focusing on the nature of technological progress over time. For this purpose, consider Figure 5.2, a restrictive representation, where isoquants T_1 and T_2 indicate the theoretical frontier isoquant for the same output level at two different points in time. We assume that existing relative prices are the same for both points in time and that input proportions lie along the same ray from the origin. $X_1(E)$ shows that the resource allocation of period one and $X_2(D)$ that of period two.[5] The figure suggests two distinct phenomena that may have contributed, in very different ways, to the improvement in efficiency measured by the relative reductions in inputs used to achieve the specified output level. We may write the conventional measure of productivity gain in quotient form as follows:

$$\frac{OE}{OD} = \frac{OA}{OD} \bigg/ \frac{OA}{OE}$$

– that is, as the ratio of technical efficiency of period two of the technical efficiency of period one. Alternatively, the technical efficiency of period two may be written as the product of the technical efficiency of period one and the productivity gain between the two periods, i.e.:

$$\frac{OA}{OD} = \frac{OA}{OE} \times \frac{OE}{OD}$$

On the other hand, productivity gains are in part attributable to the technological progress that is implied by the displacement of the frontier isoquant. To measure this we utilise point C in Figure 5.2 which is located along the given ray at a distance from E just equal to the distance from A to B along the ray; that is, the distance CE

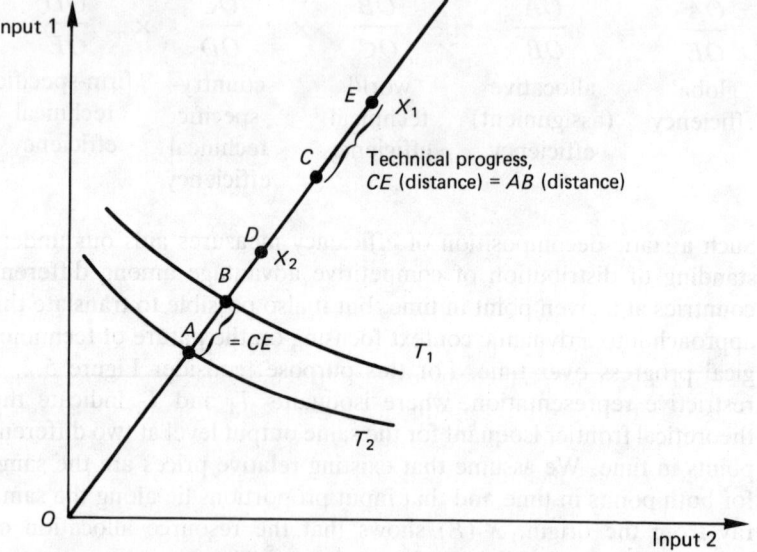

Figure 5.2 Determinants of technical efficiency over time

corresponds to the gains achievable from technical progress occurring between the two points in time. The distance in fact can be viewed as the input set reductions attributable to technological progress embodied in the frontier displacement. In our illustration, X_2, point D, is located below point C and therefore we can conclude that technical efficiency in period two is an improvement over the technical efficiency in period one, the distance from D to C measuring the improvement. If point D lay at point C, no improvement over time in the firm's technological efficiency would be in evidence, while D lying above C would evidence a slippage over time in the firm's technical efficiency. Productivity gains (or losses) can thus be rewritten as:

$$\frac{OE}{OD} = \frac{OE}{OC} \times \frac{OC}{OD}$$

or, substituting into the previous expression:

$$\frac{OA}{OD} = \frac{OA}{OE} \times \frac{OE}{OC} \times \frac{OC}{OD}$$

technical   technical   technical   gain in
efficiency of   efficiency of   progress   technical
period two   period one   efficiency

The above provides several implications. Nishimizu and Page (1982) call its importance into notice in studies of productivity measurement and explanations of productivity gains over time:

> Conventional measures of total factor productivity change cannot distinguish between technological progress and changes in technical efficiency, yet the two are analytically distinct and may have quite different policy implications. Technological progress, generally defined, is the consequence of innovation or adoption of new technology by best practice firms. Total factor productivity change, however, is the sum of the rate of technological progress and changes in technical efficiency . . . Policy actions intended to improve the rate of total factor productivity growth might be badly misdirected if focused on accelerating the rate of innovation, for example in circumstances where the cause of lagging total factor productivity change is a low rate of mastery or diffusion of best practice technology. (p. 924)

In the context of Figure 5.1 and our interest in the problems of technology transfer, the above results suggest an important distinction in the determinants of efficiency gains over time across national economies. Technical progress in a strict sense can be attributed only to displacements towards the origin of the theoretical frontier. When the world frontier, estimated over actual observations, moves closer to the origin, this reflects institutional improvements in the ability to transmit and utilise the best practice technologies available. Correspondingly, if the relative improvements in such capabilities by firms operating in country j were greater than in other countries, country j's frontier would move closer to the world frontier. Such suggested shifts would result from improved management decision-making within firms.

Because of the wide differences in the nature of the various potential efficiency gains, the development and use of new techniques and processes must be accompanied by policy actions at multiple levels if efficiency gains are to be maximised over time. Before positing our integrated analytic approach to these problems, completeness requires consideration of two important topics: (a) the impact of institutional structure and organisational behaviour on the success of technology transfer, and (b) the various theoretical concepts and empirical measurements of efficiency suggested by earlier authors.

3 TRANSACTION COSTS, EFFICIENCY, AND THE TRANSFER OF TECHNOLOGY

3.1 Conceptual Framework

Any difference in the theoretical global frontier and the actual world frontier can be attributed to institutional difficulties encountered in the process of diffusion and the use of available technology. Moreover, any relative disadvantage of a particular country in the acquisition of existing knowledge will likely increase the difficulty of that country in participating in the creation and utilisation of future technological advances.

Among the several ways of analysing the structure and process of technology is one we shall term the transaction costs approach. The heart of the approach is the concept that the appropriate organisational mode for effective exchange activities is endogenously determined by efficiency criteria. The two competing mechanisms for governing transactions are *complete contracts* (markets) and *incomplete contracts* (firms or other hierarchical structures). The two mechanisms are mutually exclusive institutional forms for accomplishing technology transfer, and under efficiency conditions each would specialise in transactions for which it has a comparative advantage *vis-à-vis* the other.[6]

But regardless of the mechanism used in attempting technology transfer, there are major difficulties in the process. Previous authors (Buckley and Casson, 1976, and Williamson, 1981) have focused on three major areas of difficulty which we now consider in turn: (1) small numbers, (2) disclosure, and (3) transfer-team organisation and control.

The production of knowledge through R & D and its implementation in new processes or products are lengthy projects requiring detailed long-term appraisal and careful short term synchronisation. Future markets may play the role of achieving such synchronisation, but they are not always present. When prospective purchasers, having control of local markets through ownership of distributive outlets, try to buy the knowledge produced, a bilateral monopoly relation arises, since the proprietor of knowledge is effectively a monopolist. The bargaining costs under such conditions of exchange involving small numbers form very well-known problems.

Disclosure, on the other hand, is related to the asymmetric information which appears at the moment of writing a possible transfer contract. The buyer is much less informed than the seller, who may be tempted to pursue opportunistic behaviour towards the buyer. Even in more evenly structured contests, differences in language and/or technology base may complicate the exchange. Finally, cultural difference may compound the difficulties, increasing suspicion and furthering lack of trust. Williamson recalled Arrow's (1971) fundamental information paradox under which falls any attempt to reduce the initial information asymmetry by disclosure: 'The value of information for the purchaser is not known until he has the information, but then he has in effect acquired it without costs'.

When benefits of technology transfer are sufficiently large, exchange may be accomplished by devising a complex trade in which technology and associated know-how are transferred as a package. Since the know-how is concentrated in the human input already familiar with the technology, such a trade scheme entails the creation of a 'consulting team' by the seller to accompany the physical technology transfer, the object being to overcome start-up difficulties and to familiarise the employees of the receiving firm, through teaching and demonstration, with the idiosyncrasies of operating the technology. There are, however, intrinsic difficulties in writing a contract to regulate the role of such a consulting team due to the contingencies arising in performance. One possibility is the utilisation of an independent consulting team located in the importing country, an alternative which might help alleviate communication problems but which may not be feasible due to limited familiarity with the technology to be transferred.

Such difficulties in transfers across markets have fostered increased emphasis on an alternative institutional mode of governing cross-country exchanges – the multinational corporation (MNC). Modern theory explains the development of this particular corporation form as a response to the costs of market exchange of technology and know-how. The MNC internalises the transactions and substitutes for the market by a hierarchial structure of incomplete contracts and authority lines. With this organisation, the lack of future markets is compensated for by internal planning and co-ordination. Similarly, bilateral exchange by independent parties is now executed between two units largely dependent on the same authority who can resolve disputes by fiat. The information value paradox can also be resolved using such a structure. The seller of the technology has a strong incentive to assume the buyer risk and internalise the knowledge by integrating forward into the buyer's industry. Further, under the potential costs of policing licences when a licence system is used, together with the risks that restricted practices are violated, firms will be encouraged to exploit the knowledge themselves or to acquire by takeover the potential licencees. Finally, the organisations of the firms are likely to allow more effective team organisation.

Although the multinational corporation appears as an efficient institution to carry out the diffusion of technology and know-how across countries, it has also been criticised as likely to restrict competition and result in a variety of inefficiencies. The dual view of multinational corporations has perhaps been most strongly pointed out by Hymer (1970):

> Multinational corporations enlarge the domain of centrally planned world production and decrease the domain of decentralized market directed specialization and exchange. Bigness is then paid for in part by fewness and a decline in competition since the size of the market is limited by the size of the firms . . . Direct foreign investment thus has a dual nature. It is an instrument which allows business firms to transfer capital, technology and organizational skill from one country to another. It is also an instrument for restraining competition between firms of different nations. (p. 443)

The efficiency argument, or transaction costs elimination, and the competitive restriction argument, or potential oligopolistic and monopolistic practices, are in fact arguments which imply possible trade-off between allocative and technical efficiency gains in the process of technology creation and diffusion. If the growth and structure of the multinational corporation implies a reduction of free trade and free factor movements, it is in fact a source of assignative or allocative inefficiency. On the other hand, to the extent of the validity of the transaction costs argument, the growth of the MNC firm evidences important potential gains in technical efficiency, since the MNC is exchanging knowledge more efficiently than the competitive market. Potential gains and losses must be analysed to form conclusions about efficiency implications of the MNC.

Until now, the MNC has been viewed as something of a 'black box'. To achieve more a precise evaluation of its potential role in the creation and diffusion of technology, it is important to understand its internal functioning and that of its subsidiaries. Although generally the alternative organisational structures and managerial styles available to an MNC will form a very large set, recent studies have dealt with two main idealised forms of organisation: bureaucratic forms and Z forms. The bureaucratic organisation form is characteristic of American and European-based MNCs, while the Z form, with its implicit, informal control mechanisms (control based on organisational, cultural and social norms) leans heavily on the Japanese managerial style and organisation.[7]

Jaeger (1982) has conducted a study contrasting control modes and the implications for MNCs. At least three of his conclusions are worthy of note for our purposes:

1. Type Z firms, employing cultural control, appear to be importing their own company culture into the host (or technology receiving) country, and tend to import more valuable management skills into the country;
2. Firms with bureaucratic control are potentially freer to carry out their activities in accordance with local practices than their Z counterparts. Thus, in theory, the firms can better adapt the technology to local culture, including changing government regulations impacting their operations;
3. The situation for type Z culture control subsidiaries is more problematic with respect to company–government relations. If the company culture is in serious conflict with local laws or customs, it may be difficult for the firm to modify its behaviour in order to comply. On the other hand, where the corporate culture is in harmony with local laws, type Z subsidiaries can be expected to be easily in compliance with the letter and spirit of the local laws since there is no need to activate decision-making procedures to alter activities.

The internal organisation of the MNC may influence the way in which interaction between the firm and the host country may proceed. But there may also be influences from the actual response that the receiving economic community gives to the technological change accompanying the arriving firm. This is the point raised by Leibenstein (1978) under the application of X-efficiency theory to the problem of technical change. According to Leibenstein, where switches in techniques are involved, one may distinguish two types of X-inefficiency: transitional X-inefficiency, and a shift in the comparative degree of X-inefficiency. The first is a temporary phenomenon by nature explained in two ways: (a) individuals committed to traditional work habits resist work arrangements appropriate for the new technique, and (b) expectations of decreased employment opportunities due to the new technology lead to individuals resisting its introduction. Leibenstein suggests that changes in the degree of X-inefficiency may occur for any of a number of reasons: the degree of co-ordination and factory discipline required may be greater for the new technique than for the old; the existing technique may be carried out fairly efficiently but in a highly rigid manner, a rigidity that is detrimental to the synchronisation of activities required to utilise the new technique successfully; the new technique may require a scale of operations different from the old one, but the skill mix in the population may be more amenable to the smaller scale than to the larger. The list goes on, and we do not attempt to enumerate fully all the possibilities. It is important to note that the exchange of technology and know-how across countries is subject to potential assignative (allocative), technical and X-inefficiencies which may arise at different levels and which may be industry-specific, country-specific, or international in nature. Further, the exact degree and nature of the various forms of inefficiency will depend upon the organisational forms involved and their associated incentive and reward mechanisms.

Up to this point we have used a conceptual framework to outline the efficiency problem and have suggested the important role which organisational form and structure have to play in determining the precise character and level of inefficiency. We now move to specifics, beginning with a discussion of methodologies for use in actually measuring the potential sources of inefficiencies in order to establish trade-offs and to provide the accurate information necessary for appropriate policy determination. After summarising the suggestions for earlier authors using the present context and notation, we present an integrated alternative employing the theoretical and empirical frontier isoquants discussed earlier.

3.2 Measuring Efficiency

Recently, the problem of measuring efficiency has received significant attention in the literature. At the same time the theoretical basis underlying Farrell's original work has been completed with extended frontier models which allow for important generalisations. Here we briefly summarise some of these extensions, focusing on the problem of separating technical and allocative efficiency in a static context, and technical progress from technical efficiency in a dynamic one. In the next section we consider the further problem of measuring the inefficiency due to differences between actual frontiers and theoretical frontiers, i.e. the various existing limitations on the use of available technologies.

The problem of separating technical and allocative efficiency has been addressed in a paper by Kopp and Diewert (1982) as a straightforward generalisation of Farrell's original work. The basic idea of the paper, following a previous contribution by Kopp (1981), is to substitute for the frontier unit isocost (which assumes linear homogeneity), a frontier cost function which is dual to a non-homothetic production frontier. Farrell's original measures are then specified in terms of cost ratios. Though not set in a cross-country framework, we can illustrate these concepts by reference to Figure 5.1, ignoring the world and country references and slightly altering the notation to indicate the use of a vector approach. For example, we use $X^{A'}$ to refer to the two-tuple [i.e. (X_1^A, X_2^A)] of input levels associated with point A in Figure 5.1. Similarly, X^E input levels associated with point E (X_{ij}), the actual level chosen by the particular firm under study. Given point X^E, representing the actual resource allocation to obtain a given output level, y, and the point X^F, which would be the cost-minimising solution to obtain the output y, the production efficiency of the firm would be measured by the ratio of the production costs corresponding to the two, i.e. by $p'X^F/p'X^E$, where p is the vector of input prices. If X^B is the point of intersection of the frontier and the ray from the origin that goes through point X^E, and X^A the intersection of the same ray with the isocost line which is tangent to the frontier isoquant at point X^F, we can write:

$$\underbrace{\frac{p'X^F}{p'X^E}}_{\text{productive efficiency}} = \frac{p'X^A}{p'X^E} = \underbrace{\frac{p'X^A}{p'X^B}}_{\substack{\text{assignative} \\ \text{(allocative)} \\ \text{efficiency}}} \times \underbrace{\frac{p'X^B}{p'X^E}}_{\substack{\text{technical} \\ \text{efficiency}}}$$

The method proposed by Kopp and Diewert is intended to measure X^A and X^B which will allow obtaining the efficiency measures. Defining $C(y,p)$ as the dual cost function of output and input prices, we have the well-known result:

$$X^F = \nabla_p C(y^*, p^*)$$

where $\nabla_p C(y^*, p^*) = \delta C(y^*, p^*)/\delta p_1^*, \ldots, \delta C(y^*, p^*)/\delta p_n^*]$ and $y^* > 0$ is the output that the inefficient point X^E produces.

To solve for X^A, they solve for the intersection of the line segment joining the origin to X^E with the cost plane or

$$\{X: p'^* X = p^{*\prime} X^F\} = \{X: p'^* X^F\} = \{X: p'^* X = C(y^*, p^*)\}, \text{ i.e.}$$

$$X^A = \lambda^A X^E, \text{ where } \lambda^A = C(y^*, p'^* X^E).$$

There remains the problem of finding X^B. Since it is a frontier point, there must exist a set of prices p^B such that:

$$X^B = \nabla_p C(y^*, p^B). \tag{1}$$

At the same time X^B lies on the ray through X^E, i.e.:

$$X^B = \lambda^B X^E \tag{2}$$

where λ^B is an unknown scalar. The preceding two equation sets are regarded as a system of $2N$ equations in $2N + 1$ unknowns indicated by X^B, p^B and λ^B. The additional equation required to permit a solution is provided by a normalisation rule of input prices, for example, $p_N^B = 1$. Dividing through the left- and right-hand side of equation set (1) by X_1^B and $\lambda^B X_1^E$ respectively, the following equation set is obtained:

$$X_2^B/X_1^B = X_2^E/X_1^E, \ldots, X_N^B/X_1^B = X_N^E/X_1^E \tag{3}$$

Equations (1) and (3) together with $p_N^B = 1$ provide $2N - 1$ equations in the $2N - 1$ unknowns $X_1^B, \ldots X_N^B, \ldots p_{N-1}^B$. The solutions of this equation set can then be used to decompose the measures of efficiency.

In the process model approach outlined in detail below, the minimum cost solution (X^F) under existing world prices can be calculated directly. Further, by shifting input price levels and solving the process model cost minimisation problem for each such input price set iteration, the frontier isoquant can be mapped out, including the required solution X^B, where the input mix corresponds to the actual input mix of firm X_{ij}.

In a dynamic context, technical progress appears combined with gains in technical efficiency, jointly determining productivity changes over time. The methodology necessary to separate the two components in such a setting has been provided by Nishimizu and Page (1982). Their basic approach can be modified to relate it to the dual cost frontier, as follows.

Define the cost function giving the cost of producing output of (s, t) by firm s in period t,

$$C(y(s, t), s, t) = p'X^E(s, t) \tag{4}$$

where p' is the vector if input prices and X^E is the vector of inputs actually employed by the firm.

For the same output level and given the actual input vector of a particular firm, equation (4) will hold only as an inequality when the observed firm is not employing its inputs with the 'best practice' productivity level. Denoting by $\hat{s}$, $\hat{t}$ and $\hat{X}$ (or X^A) the best practice, productivity and input levels, equation (4), for a firm not operating at such level, will be:

$$p'X^E = C(y(s, t), s, t) > C(y(s, t), \hat{s}, \hat{t}) = p'X(s, t) \tag{5}$$

The potential level of total factor productivity relative to the actually observed level for such a firm is defined as the maximum possible factor of reduction in total cost that can be obtained with the observed inputs employed at potential productivity levels; that is:

$$e(s, t) \, (p'X^E(s, t)) = C(y(s, t), \hat{s}, \hat{t}) \tag{6}$$

From equation (4) the role of total factor productivity observed for a firm is given by:

$$\dot{C}(y(s, t), s, t) = p'\dot{X}^E(s, t) - C_y(s, t)\dot{y}(s, t) \tag{7}$$

where $C_y(s, t)$ is the vector of cost elasticities for each component of output y and the superscript denotes logarithmic time derivatives. But from equation (6), equation (7) can be rewritten as

$$\dot{C}(y, s, t) = \dot{C}(y, \hat{s}, t) - \dot{e}(s, t) + (C_y(\hat{s}, t) - C_y(s, t))\dot{y}(s, t) \quad (8)$$

In equation (8) the rate of technological change of the 'best practice' cost frontier $\dot{C}(y, \hat{s}, t)$ in a sense represents the 'true' rate of technological progress. Over any given set of firms, the cost frontier provides information on the subject of firms which define the technological state of the art. Its movements over time, however, must not be confused with changes in the relative efficiency with which known technologies are employed. These effects are captured by $\dot{e}(s, t)$ in equation (8). As defined, $\dot{e}(s, t)$ represents the rate at which any observed firm is moving towards or away from the best practice cost frontier. The term $\dot{e}$ is defined as the role of technical efficiency change in the sense discussed in the previous section above. Finally, at any given level of output, an interior (non-frontier since it is not using the best practice technique) firm's effort to reach its potential cost may entail changes in cost elasticities represented by the last component in (8). Therefore equation (8) provides the decomposition of the conventional measure of total factor productivity change into three components: technological progress, technical efficiency change and cost elasticity differences between the frontier and the interior. The methods proposed by Kopp–Diewert and Nishimizu–Page make possible the actual computation of the alternative efficiency measures from observed data. Thus they provide the basis for application of the methods to evaluate the efficiency of the process of technology diffusion discussed in the opening sections of this paper. However, there still remains the crucial problem of evaluating or estimating the distance from the frontier estimated from actual data and the theoretical frontier estimated from the solution of an optimisation problem. But this void can be filled and the analytic structure made complete by the use of process models. While this final process model step can be utilised in the various frameworks suggested by earlier authors, it also can serve as the basis for a generalised procedure incorporating the informational content of a variety of data forms. The following section begins with a presentation of the use of process models in generating the theoretical frontier isoquants referred to above. This is followed by a proposed generalisation presenting an integrated alternative enabling comparative measurement of efficiency even in situations where production alternatives or technological choices have not been previously employed.

4 PROCESS MODELS AND THE ESTIMATION OF PRODUCTION FRONTIERS

4.1 Process Model

As suggested earlier, the global frontier notion has reference to solutions to an optimisation problem. In our particular use here, the solution set is that obtained from parameterising the optimisation problem of cost minimisation gives a specified output level and the scientific, technical and engineering knowledge currently available, though not necessarily in actual operation. A natural candidate for use in determining the solution set is a production process model, a detailed mathematical representation characterising the physical relationships inherent in the process represented. It incorporates not only the mapping relationships of the process, but also the relevant mass balance constraints and physical restrictions on process relationships. Such a model is not simply a representation of actually existing production. Rather, it incorporates engineering knowledge and technological alternatives perhaps not available, or not chosen, when existing procedures were implemented. Thus, an accurate process model includes within its scope the information necessary to solve for the frontier relationships of the production transformation modelled. In fairly simple summary form, the mathematical statement of the problem of solving for the output frontier for a specified input set combination may be structured as:

$$\max_{x_1, x_2, \ldots x_n} Y$$
$$\text{s. t.} \quad T(X_0, y) = O, \; X_0 = (x_{10}, x_{20}, \ldots, x_{n0})$$

where Y is the chosen output measure; X_0 is a vector of specified levels for the inputs $x_1, \ldots, x_n$; and $T(X_0, Y)$ is the set of physical, chemical and engineering laws within which the input-output transformation process is technologically feasible. Each solution value for such a maximisation problem (one corresponding to each chosen set of inputs) would be represented as a single point lying on a global frontier isoquant corresponding to the output level determined by the problem solution.

In order to trace out or approximate a given isoquant, it is convenient to approach the problem in the dual cost realm. In doing so, the approach will conform to the context in which Figure 5.1 was presented earlier. Considering the cost-minimising means to attain a specified output level, the firm faces a problem which can be structured as:

$$\min_{x_1, \ldots, x_n} \sum_{i=1}^{n} p_i x_i$$

$$s.\ t. \quad T(X, Y) = 0 \quad X = (x_1, \ldots, x_n)$$
$$Y \geq \bar{Y}$$
$$X_i \geq 0$$

where the x_is represent the input levels, Y the output measure, the p_is the specified input levels, and $T(X, Y)$ the relevant physical, chemical and engineering laws (including the input-output relationship(s)) of the process technology represented. Using this approach, mapping out the theoretical global frontier isoquant for a specific output quantity, say $\bar{Y}_i$ (i.e., a theoretical global frontier isoquant such as shown in Figure 5.1) is equivalent to solving the cost minimisation problem for repeated shifts in the input price levels, each solution corresponding to a tangency point between the isoquant and the appropriate price line with slope determined by the relative prices specified for the particular cost minimisation problem.[8] It is important to note that such theoretical frontier isoquants differ from the actual frontier isoquants since the solution values used in their construction are determined under the implicit assumption of total efficiency.

To summarise, repeated solutions of a process model for differing input price combinations enables us to trace out or approximate the theoretical frontier isoquants. Thus we have the ability to complete the first step in our task of measuring the transferability of technology – the frontier benchmark from which to measure process sensitivity to management structure, decision-making capacity, or other specific attributes accompanying production location. In order to complete the necessary analytic structure, we may utilise the procedures suggested by the various authors cited above or we may generalise the process model approach to enable the incorporation of the information necessary to develop world and country frontier isoquants related to technology and practices actually utilised.

Having discussed the former above, we focus here on the latter. Our task is to restructure the suggested process model to incorporate sensitivities of the production process to organisational and social patterns. To facilitate such a generalisation it is helpful first to consider the variety of data forms that are available and the role each will play in our analysis.

4.2 Historical, Experimental and Panel Data and their Use

Historical or naturally occurring data have by their nature limited informational content, for they refer only to alternatives that have been tried and not to those which could have been tried. Further, such data may not be in the form amenable to the required analytic use (for example, they might be too aggregated or perhaps too incomplete). There are, however, other data forms which serve to augment the historical data and provide desired additional information for our task: *panel data* obtained through contact with industry decision-makers, and *experimental data* obtained through experiments specifically structured to identify behavioural responses (or sensitivities) to various control variable alterations. Proper structuring of the data developed from these latter two sources can enable the attainment of the necessary informational input for incorporating behavioural relationships into our analysis. If, for example, the country or area under consideration has dominant characteristics in its management structure (see, for example, Ouchi's (1980) discussion of markets, bureaucracies and clans) or if the firm involved has distinct organisational characteristics such as suggested earlier for MNCs (bureaucratic or type Z), the exact nature of such structures may be explored in the development of the panel data set and then utilised as informational input into the structuring of the experiments used to derive the experimental data set.

To illustrate the use of the four distinct data forms, we proceed in two steps, beginning with a verbal sketch and following this with a more formal summary presentation.

Consider a hypothetical country A pondering subsidising the importation of technology in a given industry. We may view the additional data forms as adding to the information derived from the process model (i.e. to the informational content of the theoretical frontier isoquant). The additional experimental data input would be derived by structuring the 'rules of the game' to mirror various incentive patterns and organisational structures rewarding subjects based upon their performance while acting within such constraints.

The role of panel data, developed through contact with various industry representatives including those who are to participate in country A or those familiar with conditions in the country, would be in structuring the experimental setting and in relating experimental outcomes to performance possibilities in country A. In our formulation, historical data play a dual role: first, as an input into the estimation of points on the isoquants (actual, not theoretical frontier) relating to quantities that have actually been produced using the technology; and secondly, and perhaps more importantly, as a means to check the accuracy (and thus applicability) of the derived data over the range of input price combinations historically occurring (i.e. over the range to which the actual frontier functions of the previous section are limited). Once the generated experimental and panel data have been reviewed for accuracy over the range of the historically observed values, they become information for inclusion in an expanded process model formulation for use in generation of the country- or region-specific isoquants.

The main attraction of utilising an expanded process model approach now becomes apparent, for it facilitates the consideration of alternative production methods to those historically observed. The technique takes detailed notice of behavioural information garnered from panel and experimental data in determining likely outcomes rather than just extrapolating from observed values. It provides the vehicle for incorporating organisational structures and constraints (such as outlined earlier for MNCs) in the estimation procedure. Each of these is especially important for the optimal selection of technology transfers and for decomposing and measuring the various types of inefficiencies potentially present in a specific production process to be operated at a given location. The comparison techniques mirror these suggested by earlier authors, but the computation of the world and country-specific frontier isoquants diverge sharply.

Because of the flexibility of the generalised process model approach, the technique facilitates efficiency comparisons of a wide variety of alternatives under varying organisational structures. Further, the very key determination of the global theoretical frontier enables the determination of whether or not specific technologies suffer from large diffusion inefficiencies (i.e., whether the world frontier deviates greatly from the global theoretical frontier).

More formally we sketch the use of a generalised process model representation with the following restated cost minimisation problem:

$$\min_{x_1 \ldots x_n} \sum_{i=1}^{n} p_i x_i$$

$$\text{s. t. } T^j(X, Y) = 0 \quad R^k(X, Y) = 0 \quad W(X, Y) = 0$$
$$x = (x_1, \ldots x_n), \quad Y \geq \bar{Y}$$
$$x_i \geq 0$$

where $T^j(X, Y)$ provides the chemical, physical and engineering laws including the input-output relationships for process j; $R^k(X, Y)$ details the specific restrictions or constraints, or limitations on operation of the technology within country k; $W(X,Y)$ specifies the world or general constraints, if any, on the process; and X and Y are the input level vector and output measure respectively. (Perhaps a simpler representation would combine the T, R and W constraint sets and denote the applicable constraints for technology j in country k by $T^{jkw}(X, Y)$, but we shall utilise the separate representations to emphasise that they are developed quite differently, one relying on engineering developments and testing, the other two relying on the derived economic information concerning general behavioural responses and those peculiar to the structures representing country k).

Utilising the generalised process model formulation, determining the varying isoquants for a specified output level Y, amounts to the repeated solution of differing process models (varying according to the complexity of the constraint set) for different input price combinations. For the global theoretical frontier isoquant neither $R^k(X, Y)$ would appear. Generating the relevant world frontier and country k-specific frontier isoquants would require the repeated solution of process model formulations which included, respectively, the $W(X, Y)$ and $R^k(X, Y)$ constraints.

The flowchart in Figure 5.3 presents an overview of our integrated approach. As suggested throughout this paper, the proposed analysis, which can be lengthy and perhaps quite complicated, is aimed at tackling the difficult and important questions inherent in multimillion dollar technology transfers. Successful application requires more than an accurate engineering representation of the technologies under consideration. Accurate behavioural and organisational constraint representation must be determined through the experimental and panel data developed and checked over the historical range against the naturally occurring data. The approach is general in its theoretical applicability but demanding in its informational require-

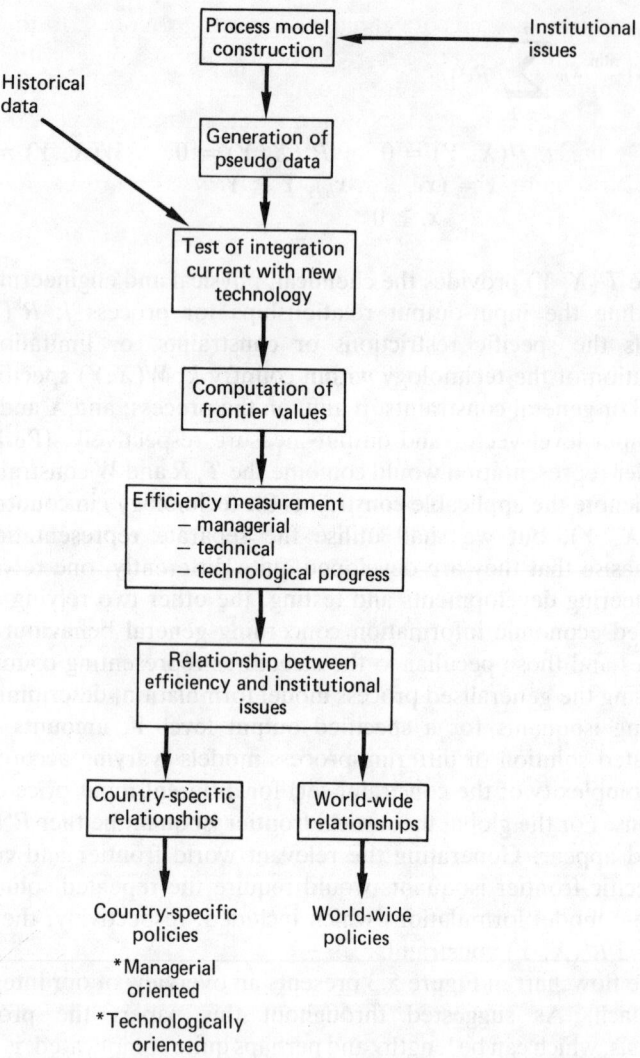

Figure 5.3 An integrated approach

ments. In the form presented, estimation of even the global theoretical frontier is limited to areas where accurate process models exist. Although this almost certainly rules out specific industries, it still permits analysis of many high-technology and capital-intensive industries such as electrical power generation, oil refining, and manufacturing using advanced techniques involving robotics. In the latter industries, the engineering process model information is at the heart of determining if and how to introduce various possible new technologies. Utilising complex robotics in manufacturing process requires engineering knowledge to be able to simulate the processes – in other words, it requires the use of what we refer to as a process model.

5 SUMMARY AND CONCLUSIONS

The methodology we have outlined above focuses on measuring efficiency and utilising the various measures developed as crucial inputs into the decision process for analysing various technology transfer alternatives. We began by noting that there is an optimal technology in the world-wide context for which we used a process model frontier representation. The distance from the theoretical frontier to the world frontier provides a measure of how efficient world-wide institutions are in making the technology available. Distances from the world frontier to country frontier point to country-specific efficiency problems, while deviations of the individual firm values point to firm-specific problems. Within this framework we indicated the need and suggested the methodology for disentangling in an operational way managerial inefficiencies from engineering inefficiencies. Following an integration of earlier work into the present context, we outlined an integrated approach utilising a generalised process model for completing the desired analysis. As pointed out above, the implementation of the analysis is by no means an easy task. To achieve accurate answers to the important questions successfully will require the participation of world-wide organisations in building the process models and in developing the necessary information on institutional and socially related restrictions. The tasks are indeed enormous, but the approach holds the possibility of developing real answers to real-world problems.

Even a cursory look at the problem exposes the severity of the difficulties to be overcome and the enormity of the task. Yet such obstacles must be kept in perspective and weighed against the potential benefits from successful completion of the procedures. Erring in the introduction of new technologies can involve the loss of millions of dollars and serve as a severe setback to economic development. Both can be avoided by properly investigating the potential and assessing the likelihood of success for such transfer. It is with such views in mind that we suggest the above outlined approach and urge the initiation of the steps necessary to bring it to fruition.

NOTES

1. This research was in part made possible by a Summer Research Grant from the College of Business and Economics of the University of Kentucky. The grant was made possible by a donation of funds to the College by Ashland Oil Inc.
2. The authors are currently working on implementing an experimental structure to measure the response pattern under varying organisational structures and incentive patterns.
3. The theoretical support of the original Farrell measures have been reformulated and generalised by Kopp (1981), who also gives a complete set of related references.
4. Here, for pedagogical ease, we focus on the dual cost-minimising problem. Though the procedures we later outline are amenable to either output-maximisation or cost-minimisation formulation, we find it easier to use the latter.
5. We consider the simplified case of no relative price change in the two periods so that the firm does not changethe input mix proportions. The more general case would not alter the main ideas suggested in our argument.
6. A more detailed explanation of the relevance of transaction costs in economic analysis can be found in Williamson (1981), together with a list of main references on the topic.
7. See Ouchi (1981).
8. Similarly, the theoretical frontier for a particular region or country could be developed in exactly the same manner and would differ from the theoretical global frontier only through the effects of legal, environmental or locational restrictions which can be added to the general process model formulation in the form of additional constraints in the set represented by $T(X,y)$. If such additional constraints are present (and indeed effective in the solution) then the country- or area- specific theoretical frontier isoquant would lie above the global frontier isoquant corresponding to the same output level.

REFERENCES

Arrow, K. (1971) *Essays in the Theory of Risk Bearing* (New York:Markham; and Amsterdam: North Holland 1970).

Bever, R., Marsden, J. R., Salas-Fumas, V. and Whinston, A. (1982) 'Aggregate Summary Functions: Heterogeneity and the Use of Random Coefficient Models', *Advances in Applied Micro-Economics*, vol. III.
Verifying the Usefulness of Engineering Process Models Applied to Forecasting, Electric Power Research Institute, Final Report, Project 867–1 (EPRI EA–2441), June.

Buckley, P. and Casson, M. (1976) *The Future of the Multinational Enterprise* (New York: Helmes and Meier).
Farrell, M. (1957) 'The Measurement of Productive Efficiency', *Journal of the Royal Statistical Society*, 120, Series A (General), pp. 253-81.
Griffin, J. M. (1977) 'Long-Run Production Modelling with Pseudo Data: Electric Power Generation', *Bell Journal of Economics*, vol. 8, no. 1, Spring, pp. 112-27.
(1972) 'The Process of Analysis Alternative to Statistical Cost Functions: an Application to Petroleum Refining', *American Economic Review*, vol. 62, March, pp. 46-56.
Hymer, S. (1970) 'The Efficiency (Contradictions) of Multinational Corporations', *American Economic Review*, 60, May, pp. 441-8.
Jaeger, A. (1982) 'Contrasting Control Modes in the Multinational Corporation: Theory, Practice and Implications', *International Studies of Management and Organization*.
Kopp, R.J. and Smith, V.K. (1979) 'The Perceived Role of Materials in Neoclassical Models of Production Technology', Resources for the Future, Discussion Paper, January.
Kopp, R. (1981) 'The Measurement of Productive Efficiency: A Reconsideration', *Quarterly Journal of Economics*, 96, August, pp. 477-503.
Kopp, R. and Diewert, E. (1982) 'The Decomposition of Frontier Cost Functions Deviations into Measure of Technical and Allocative Efficiency', *Journal of Econometrics*, 19, pp. 319-31.
Leibenstein, H. (1968) 'Allocative Efficiency vs. X-Efficiency', *American Economic Review*, 56, June, pp. 392-415.
Leibenstein, H. (1978) *General X-Efficiency Theory and Economic Development* (London: Oxford University Press).
Marsden, J.R., Pingry, D.E. and Whinston, A.B. (1974a) 'Engineering Foundations of the Production Function', *Journal of Economic Theory*, 9, pp. 124-40.
(1974b) 'The Process Analysis Alternative to Statistical Cost Functions: Comment', *American Economic Review*, 64, pp. 773-6.
Nishimizu, M. and Page, T. Jr. (1982) 'Total Factor Productivity Growth, Technological Progress and Technical Efficiency Change: Dimensions of Productivity Change in Yugoslavia, 1965-78', *The Economic Journal*, 92, December, pp. 920-36.
Ouchi, W. G. (1980) 'Markets, Bureaucracies and Clans', *Administrative Science Quarterly*, vol. 25, March, pp. 129-41.
Ouchi, W. G. (1981) *Theory Z: How American Business Can Meet the Japanese Challenge* (Reading, Mass.: Adison-Wesley Publishing Company).
Plott, C. R. and Smith, V. L. (1976) 'Experimental Economics: Induced Value Theory' *American Economic Review*, 66, pp. 274-79.
Plott, C.R. and Smith, V.L. (1978) 'An Experimental Analysis of Two Exchange Institutions', *Review of Economic Studies*, 45, pp. 133-53.
Smith, V.L. (1982) 'Microeconomic Systems As An Experimental Science', *American Economic Review*, vol. 72, no. 5, December, pp. 923-55.
Williamson, O.E. (1981) 'The Modern Corporation: Origins, Evolution, Attributes', *Journal of Economic Literature*, 19, December, pp. 1537-70.

6 Consumption and Productivity Patterns and their Implications for the Production Structure

Jitendra G. Borpujari
INTERNATIONAL MONETARY FUND,
WASHINGTON, DC

> Man is the only creature who refuses to be what he is.
> (Albert Camus)

1 PURPOSE

This paper[1] traces the intellectual lineage, empirical relevance and practical implications of a 'New Approach' which places consumer spending at the centre of macroeconomic policies for maintaining full employment in an economy that is technologically progressive and experiencing a continual rise in per capita incomes.

2 THE BECHER PRINCIPLE AND THE SAVINGS SCHOOL

Economic analysis of consumption patterns – which dates back to perhaps no earlier than the seventeenth century writings of Johann Becher (1635–82) – can be grouped broadly, depending on whether the stress is on consumption or on saving as an economy's prime mover.

Becher emphasised that differences in income distributions bring about various consumption patterns which lead to growth rates that differ from one commodity to another (Schumpeter, 1954). He anticipated a number of Keynesian measures and was generally an advocate of economic expansion through increased mass consumption. Boisguillebert (1646–1714) had the same notion, except that he considered landlords rather than the masses to be the main sources of consumer spending. But the first to present a systematic theory were the physiocrats who saw the dynamics of production structures as dependent on a specific evolution of the effective demand for raw products, and viewed savings that are not offset by spending elsewhere as wholly undesirable. This stand was developed into a more general theory of consumption by Lauderdale and Spence (Fetter, 1945). The argument's income distributional aspects were developed by Sismondi (1773–1842) and the Russian Narodniks (Lustig, 1979).

Mainstream economics since Adam Smith has, however, mostly forgotten the earlier warnings against uncompensated parsimony and extreme income inequalities. With the desire to consume treated as inherently expansionary and limited only by the dearth of the means for satisfying consumption, the emphasis of economists has in general shifted sharply to a concentration on savings of which an economy is assumed incapable of having too much. In classical economics, the disappearance of consumption studies was virtually complete except for the under-consumptionists (Shoul, 1957). Subsequently, the very quest for the determinants of production became unimportant with the emergence of the marginalists, who focused on the dramatically narrower problem of optimally allocating scarce resources among competing ends.

The Savings School – and the attendant 'Treasury View of 1929' (J. Robinson, 1978) – received a setback with Keynes's demonstration that the *ex post* equality of savings and investments can be at any level of income and employment, thus effectively vindicating the policy prescriptions of Becher. But Keynes concentrated on the short run, kept his consumption analysis at the aggregate level, and was concerned not with the determination of production's commmodity-mix but with labour market equilibrium which may be consistent with a number of different production structures. By contrast, Kalecki (1976) concentrated on production patterns and showed how an economy's viability and expansion are contingent upon the development of an appropriate commodity-mix of output for domestic consumption and exports (Borpujari, 1980, 1981). He pointed out that increases in income – whatever their origin – translate into particular commodity mixes of consumer demand which have to be met with *pari passu* increases in product supplies if economic growth is to be achieved without exacerbating domestic inflationary pressures or adding to difficulties in managing the balance of payments. As such, Kalecki took consumption analysis beyond the aggregative level and integrated it into his production theory by effectively invoking the empirical findings of Ernst Engel which were curiously neglected by most other theorists. However, Kalecki also developed these issues out of a concern for immediate problems of policy rather than identifying the fundamentals of how production structures expand in the long run.

3 A NEW APPROACH

The Becher Principle has received a far-reaching restatement in a new approach which shows that consumer demand is the ultimate arbiter of what the commodity composition of value added will be in a developing economy (Pasinetti, 1981). With this approach, one continues the customary search of economists for conditions of equilibrium, but equilibirum itself is defined simply as the state of full employment (and full capacity utilisation). The maintenance of such an equilibrium over time is accepted to be the central aim of macroeconomic policy, since all other states of the economy are obviously undesirable as they involve either unemployment (and/or excess capacity) or inflation (and/or balance of payments difficulties). The new approach analyses how consumer demand channels the *increments* of income arising from technological progress into various commodities; but the focus is on consumer demand at rising levels of income, and not on optimum allocation at a given level of income.

The argument is presented in terms of reproducible commodities. A fundamental human urge to reduce the drudgery of labour, as well as the sheer exigency of survival in a competitive setting that calls for a continual reduction in labour costs and innovation of new goods, are taken as the primary sources of technological progress. Symmetrically, a fundamental human urge to consume is accepted to be the exogenous determinant of consumer demand.[2] This historical fact that technological progress has occurred at various rates for individual commodities, but always to reduce monotonically the direct and indirect labour needed to produce a unit of ouput, is taken to be the definitive feature of the productivity pattern. By contrast, the per capita demand coefficients, although displaying generally an offsetting upward movement, have no comparable monotonicity but follow Engel's Law instead. In other words, the per capita demand for various commodities increases, but only up to a point of satiety and always following a lexicographic pattern that makes the entry of a commodity into one's consumption basket dependent on one's prior consumption of another commodity. Moreover, there is no single commodity for which per capita demand rises indefinitely with increases in income.

The asymmetries in man's natural processes of learning as producer and as consumer result in a chronic tendency towards disequilibrium and unemployment in an economy where per capita income is rising. The pattern of productivity increases determines the evolution of relative costs/prices and the level of per capita income. Consumer preferences, on the other hand, determine how the income increments are allocated among the various commodities depending on the position of each good in the Engel hierarchy. But only by fluke will the structural evolution of productivity and of consumer demand take place in an exactly offsetting manner so as to maintain full employment equilibrium over time. In other words, Engel's Law signals that the consumers transmit and the growth patterns of productivity under which the suppliers operate are inherently incongruent, so that the dialogue between consumers and producers takes the form of a succession of overproduction and underproduction with no built-in tendency towards equilibrium. As such, for full employment to be maintained, there is a need in all technologically progressive economies for macroeconomic surveillance and policies so as to ensure that trends in consumer spending counteract, and no exacerbate, the unemployment-generating impact of productivity growth.

The greater knowledge of consumption structures thus turns out to be crucial, especially as consumption behaviour is more amenable to policy manipulation than technological progress in the short run. In an open economy, consumers will have to decide not only what they will buy with their incremental income, but also where they will buy from. This second question is likely to be resolved primarily by the rate of rise of relative prices. However, whereas a rise in productivity usually increases an economy's per capita income, for there to be also a rise in the country's exports, the productivity rise has to be high relative to that of other countries.[3] To look at it the other way round, a country that experiences a rise in exports of a particular commodity, relative to the exports of the same commodity from other countries, can be expected generally to have enjoyed a relatively high rate of productivity growth in that commodity.[4]

All earlier studies of consumption and savings treated the former as a prior claim on income. By contrast, the new approach considers the savings needed for investments that are necessary to maintain full employment to be a prior claim on income so that consumption becomes logically a 'surplus', the maximisation of which is the economists' *summum bonum*. Moreover, consumption is studied disaggregatively and the focus is on the long run. Also, the Savings School's faith that whatever is not consumed will be always invested is replaced by making the macroeconomic equality of savings and investments a condition of equilibrium. Above all, the new approach discards the more usual treatment of consumer behaviour as a phenomenon that can be defined at one level of income for all commodities and then extended to all other levels of income. Instead, consumer preferences are studied as 'more a *local* phenomenon, operating through a kind of limited "search" in the immediate neighbourhood of experienced consumption' (Harris, 1982). The study of productivity structures as determinants of the composition of international trade, on the other hand, is focused on relative trends in commodity-specific productivity changes rather than on the relative levels of comparative productivity at a point in time.

The various conclusions under the new approach are derived solely as logical requirements for maintaining full employment in a technologically progressive economy. Inasmuch as full employment is indisputably a desirable policy objective, the conclusions therefore require verification only as to the empirical relevance of the underlying premises. What follows below are indications that the evidence is overwhelmingly supportive of the new approach.

4 CONSUMPTION PATTERNS

The cross-sectional data in Table 6.1 show how consumption patterns change sharply from a concentration of about 57 per cent of total consumer spending upon essentials at the lowest level of income to an allocation of over 80 per cent of the consumption budget to commodities other than food by the richest consumers. The share of bread and cereals – obviously the most elementary consumables – declines across the income spectrum from about 20 per cent to under 2 per cent, while all other foods display a milder fall or fluctuate narrowly over a wide range of incomes. The share of clothing and footwear rises as incomes increase from the lowest levels, but then falls as

Table 8.1 Consumption structures for country groups by per capita income levels in 1975* (in per cents of total)

	Less than 0.15	Country groups				
		0.15–0.30	0.30–0.45	0.45–0.60	0.60–0.90	0.90–1.00
Food, beverages and tobacco	56.6	43.7	37.0	35.5	22.8	16.0
Bread and cereals	19.5	10.5	6.2	3.2	2.6	1.8
Meat and fish	8.2	8.6	9.0	10.0	6.1	3.7
Milk, cheese and eggs	4.7	3.8	4.6	4.1	2.3	1.5
Oils, fats, fruits and vegetables	12.7	10.3	7.3	7.7	4.0	3.6
Other	11.5	10.5	9.9	10.5	7.7	5.3
Clothing, footwear	7.5	8.3	9.4	10.1	7.9	6.5
Rent, fuel and home supplies	13.3	15.6	18.6	18.0	23.9	24.1
Medical care	3.9	4.4	6.8	7.2	8.6	12.6
Transport, communications	5.6	9.2	8.3	8.6	11.2	13.3
Recreation, education	8.0	9.3	10.4	11.4	14.2	15.1
Miscellaneous services	5.1	9.5	9.5	9.2	11.5	12.4
Total	100.0	100.0	100.0	100.0	100.0	100.0
Shares in combined population						
in millions	795.0	187.4	140.2	135.9	318.5	213.6
in per cent	44.4	10.5	7.8	7.6	17.8	11.9

*A total of 34 countries with Malawi as the poorest and the USA as the richest and classified by relative per capita real gross domestic product (USA = 1.00).

Source: based on Kravis, Heston and Summers (1982, p.188).

incomes grow further. All other types of consumer spending generally rise in relative importance at speeds that vary from one income level to another, with recreation, education and various other services making the most remarkable gains at higher income levels. These resutls relate, of course, to averages and remain valid although some consumers in the 'richest countries' may be considerably worse off than a minority in the poorest countries. Moreover, the richer countries in fact spend more in absolute terms on almost all commodities; spending a relatively small proportion of a considerably higher income is sufficient to satisfy the essential physiological needs, allowing higher proportions of income to be spend on such items as education and medical care.

The cross-sectional data of Table 6.1 can be seen also as the experience of a single economy at various levels of income, as is borne out by Kuznets (1962). Further, one can equally view the world's economies as a pecking order of consumption structures in which one economy moves from its own erstwhile consumption structure into that of the adjacent country higher up in the per capita income totem pole. Such a structured view of consumer learning applies, of course, as much to regions within a country as to the countries internationally. Also, one thus gathers a hierarchic view of any commodity set as comprising an elementary group that loses in relative share over time, a secondary group that gains correspondingly, and a tertiary group that queues up to catch consumer attention as per capita income rises. As such, far from making consumption choices at a point of time for all income levels as in the usual text-book paradigm, the consumer decides continually in accordance with the pecking order of consumption structures and the ranking of available as well as yet-to-be commodities. Furthermore, whereas the usual text books dwell at length upon the heterogeneity of consumer preferences from one individual to another, the data point towards a striking homogeneity of consumption patterns among millions of individuals who fall within a particular income band. For instance, whatever one's sophistries in utility analysis, Table 6.1 suggests that bread and cereals accounted for nearly eleven times as much of consumer spending by an average individual from among the poorest 44 per cent as by one from among the richest 12 per cent of the combined population of some 1.8 billion in the thirty-four countries considered for 1975. By contrast, the relative importance of medical care triples as one moves from the poorest to the richest. Thus, the pecking order of consumption structures can provide a simple, comprehensive and analytical classification of economies by consumption patterns.[5]

The irrelevance of aggregative or pseudo-structural consumption studies for an understanding of economies at various income levels can be made apparent also by applying a standard demand-theoretic model to a wide range of commodities. The equation reported in Table 6.2 is chosen from among a number of alternative forms which yielded broadly the same conclusions about consumption structures in a developing economy. The data relating to thirty-four countries at various income levels and for 158 commodities are used to examine commodity-specific per capita consumptions relative to the US levels as a loglinear function of comparably defined indices for per capita income and relative prices. To save space, the presentation is limited to sixteen commodities that are intuitively grouped as 'essential', 'necessaries', and 'luxuries' in Table 6.2.

As is obvious from Table 6.2, the explanatory power of the model varies sharply from one income class to another across the country groups. Also, irrespective of income classes, little or nothing can be explained thus of consumer behaviour for elementary consumer goods and services of which some amounts are consumed irrespective of the levels of relative prices and incomes. The income effect turns out to be statistically significant for a number of commodities for which the model provides little by way of overall explanation. The higher a commodity is in the commodity hierarchy, generally the better seems to be the explanatory power of the standard demand-theoretic model, with both the income and the price variables contributing significantly to explaining differences in consumption patterns.

Notwithstanding the preliminary nature of the statistical evidence presented above, there can be no disagreement on the basic point that any integrated theory of economic growth must treat consumption as a structure that expands non-proportionately from one commodity to another across various levels of income. Indeed, the conclusion is so obvious that the effort to provide a demonstration is justifiable only in view of the surprisingly persistent and pervasive consideration in economics of consumption as an aggregate or a pseudo-structure.

Table 6.2 Estimated equations for per capita consumption patterns by levels of income (all variables entered in log form: t statistics in parentheses)ᵃ

Commodities	Coefficient of determination (R^2)			Constant			Income elasticity			Price elasticity		
	Poorer countries	Richer countries	All countries	Poorer countries	Richer countries	All countries	Poorer countries	Richer countries	All countries	Poorer countries	Richer countries	All countries
Essentials												
Cereals	0.33	0.08	0.32	5.58 (4.66)	7.24 (2.05)	7.35 (8.69)	−0.14 (−0.33)	−0.91 (−1.07)	−0.91 (−3.84)	−1.47 (−2.57)	−0.43 (−0.32)	−0.90 (−1.83)
Clothing materials	0.31	0.02	0.04	2.74 (2.00)	5.19 (1.71)	4.53 (5.17)	1.02 (2.36)	−0.11 (−0.15)	0.20 (0.95)	−0.56 (−0.73)	0.33 (0.44)	−0.22 (−0.40)
Bus transport	0.12	0.31	0.04	4.91 (3.65)	12.54 (3.48)	6.16 (5.74)	0.66 (1.88)	−1.56 (−1.88)	0.02 (0.10)	−0.08 (−0.73)	−0.47 (−0.32)	−0.38 (−1.83)
Household utensils	0.00	0.53	0.08	3.93 (3.65)	−1.67 (−0.71)	−2.68 (−0.50)	−0.85 (−1.88)	1.54 (−2.74)	1.63 (1.20)	−1.55 (−2.57)	−0.86 (−0.32)	−0.45 (−1.83)
Necessities												
Milk products	0.63	0.45	0.72	0.00 (0.00)	−0.66 (−0.34)	0.44 (0.47)	1.24 (2.58)	1.22 (2.66)	1.00 (4.37)	−1.41 (−1.74)	−0.41 (−0.72)	−1.14 (−2.19)
Bread	0.70	0.69	0.73	−2.43 (−2.00)	3.86 (3.10)	−0.51 (−0.79)	1.94 (4.49)	0.10 (0.33)	1.19 (6.43)	−1.50 (−3.17)	−1.58 (−5.12)	−1.57 (−4.65)
Drugs	0.77	0.49	0.86	−1.81 (−2.78)	0.26 (0.20)	−1.30 (−3.75)	1.45 (6.26)	0.87 (2.88)	1.25 (12.81)	−1.09 (−2.55)	−0.86 (−2.15)	−1.03 (−3.50)
Rents	0.85	0.73	0.92	−1.25 (−2.40)	−2.71 (−2.53)	−1.83 (−6.46)	1.10 (5.84)	1.57 (6.13)	1.33 (16.23)	−0.77 (−1.09)	−0.40 (−1.41)	−0.66 (−4.73)
Men's clothing	0.66	0.04	0.73	−2.61 (−2.17)	2.01 (1.59)	−1.35 (−2.19)	1.69 (4.39)	0.20 (0.43)	1.26 (7.82)	0.04 (−0.22)	−0.38 (−1.14)	−0.44 (−0.12)
Luxuries												
Radios, TVs, phonographs	0.24	0.89	0.34	−2.26 (−0.23)	−6.41 (−3.06)	−4.63 (−0.83)	2.80 (1.12)	2.45 (5.08)	2.23 (1.77)	−5.59 (−1.28)	−0.64 (−2.03)	−2.28 (−1.15)
Books, papers and magazines	0.62	0.62	0.84	−1.52 (−1.99)	−1.53 (−0.69)	−1.90 (−3.83)	1.28 (4.74)	1.39 (2.60)	1.48 (10.74)	−0.44 (−0.88)	−1.41 (−3.03)	−0.95 (−2.89)
Educational facilities	0.66	0.58	0.79	−2.89 (−2.34)	−4.79 (−1.90)	3.17 (−4.85)	1.54 (3.82)	2.29 (3.67)	1.69 (9.85)	−0.64 (−1.21)	−2.95 (−3.25)	−0.86 (−2.12)
Medical supplies	0.42	0.33	0.43	1.41 (0.89)	−2.88 (−0.63)	0.67 (0.86)	0.47 (1.16)	1.64 (1.40)	0.71 (3.52)	−1.92 (−1.80)	−2.18 (−2.61)	−1.76 (−3.37)

Table 6.2 Estimated equations for per capita consumption patterns by levels of income (all variables entered in log form; t statistics in parenthesis)[a]*

Commodities	Coefficient of determination (R^2)			Constant			Income elasticity			Price elasticity		
	Poorer countries	Richer countries	All countries	Poorer countries	Richer countries	All countries	Poorer countries	Richer countries	All countries	Poorer countries	Richer countries	All countries
Therapeutic equipment	0.96	0.63	0.94	−1.66 (−1.02)	−10.58 (−3.39)	−1.19 (−1.18)	1.37 (2.42)	3.27 (4.38)	1.14 (4.05)	0.97 (17.05)	−1.20 (−2.18)	0.97 (18.13)
Household textiles	0.45	0.64	0.78	−1.60 (−1.15)	−0.92 (−0.82)	−2.57 (−3.60)	1.19 (2.78)	1.14 (4.51)	1.54 (9.29)	−0.92 (−0.98)	−0.25 (−0.49)	−0.69 (−1.12)
Cleaning appliances	0.64	0.86	0.72	−28.28 (−2.17)	−6.39 (−3.35)	−20.00 (−3.64)	8.66 (1.98)	2.47 (5.77)	5.63 (3.74)	0.54 (2.31)	−0.58 (−2.24)	0.62 (4.28)

*Per capita consumption in 1975 of the various commodities and services, relative to the US levels of per capita consumption, for 34 countries arranged in the rising order of per capita income, with Malawi as the poorest and the USA as the richest country; the income and the relative price variables are defined comparably. The 'poorer' refer to the first seventeen, and the 'richer' to the last seventeen, in the ranking of economies by per capita income. The equation fitted is: $LN(QJK) = a + b^* LN(QGK) - c^* LN(PJK/PCK)$, where QJK are the per capita consumptions (USA = 100) in real terms of $J (J = 1,2,...,158)$ commodities in $K (K = 1,2,...,34)$ countries; QGK are the real gross domestic products per capita (USA = 100) for K countries; PJK are the purchasing power parities per US$ for J commodities in K countries; and PCK are the purchasing power parities per US$ for total consumption in K countries.

Source: based on data in Kravis, Heston and Summers (1982).

5 PRODUCTIVITY PATTERNS AND EXPORT PERFORMANCE

The usual advice that an economy should specialise in the exportation of a commodity in which it has a comparative advantage is incomplete and sometimes even meaningless in a dynamic setting because of differences among economies in the rates of growth of productivity for any given commodity. The advice has to be to specialise in the exportation of commodities in which an economy has achieved, and is likely to maintain, rates of productivity growth higher than in the competing economies. Notably, an advantage that did not exist before can be created through appropriate policies. Furthermore, productivity growth and market expansion are themselves interlinked, as evidenced by the celebrated Verdoorn Law, so that a simplistic policy based on static comparative advantage can be entirely inappropriate.

Since labour accounts for the largest single input cost in any production and also because other input costs usually are relatively stable, the rates of price changes are likely to reflect mostly the rates of changes in labour productivities. The data provide ample justification for these claims. For instance, as is well known, exports from Japan have increased dramatically in recent decades, raising that country's share in the world market from less than 6 per cent to about 15 per cent in the period 1963–79 (Green, 1982). At the same time, a recent cross-national comparison of innovation patterns has indicated a decline in the US share of major newly marketed products and processes from 76 per cent during 1953–9 to 56 per cent in 1967–73 (Chakrabarti, Feinman and Fuentivilla, 1982). That study also illustrated Japan's unique commitment to improve productivity; the proportion of Japanese innovations that were for the innovating firms' own use was twice the corresponding ratio for the major competitors of Japan in the period 1953–73.

An identification of the likely areas of demand growth abroad, the higher achievable growth rates of productivity for a country that starts from a relatively low level of output per hour, and the ability to pass on a substantial part of the productivity increases to price reductions appear to be the major factors underlying Japan's superior export performance. Space forbids reproduction here of the numerous charts presented at the Madrid Congress – based on data from Japan Productivity Center (1982) and US Bureau of Labor Statistics (1982) – indicating how productivity growth has varied between different periods of time, from one industry to another within the same country, and for the same industry in different countries with Japan as the reference country. It appears that conscious policy oriented Japan's production structure to components of foreign consumer spending which were identified as not only substantial but, most importantly, also as likely to grow rapidly over time.

As the front-runner in productivity performance, Japan was naturally able to attract consumers in all accessible markets. The close correspondence between export performance and productivity growth can be indicated for a number of industries by expressing Japanese exports to the United States as a function of US productivities relative to Japan. While the results that were presented at the Madrid Congress are only indicative, the productivity variable turns out to be statistically significant for almost all industries, and the R^2 value is also high in most cases. Data are amply available for further analyses of the variability of productivities across countries, industries and time, as well as for the close dependence of export performance on trends in relative productivities. For instance, it would appear that while static and dynamic comparative advantages may coincide in specific cases, the former alone is neither a necessary nor a sufficient basis for specialisation in international trade. Also, the conclusion seems irresistible that, if Japan's ascendancy as an exporter is to be preserved, then Japanese industry must above all continually change the commodity-mix of export production so as to move out of goods for which demand is growing relatively slowly or approaching satiety, and go instead into the production of items that are likely to dominate the spending patterns of those whose incomes are expected to grow.

6 A FEW PRACTICAL IMPLICATIONS

The acceptance of consumption and productivity as asymmetrically expanding patterns and the adoption of full employment equilibrium as the desirable aim of public policy are the only premises from which the conclusions of the new approach are drawn. Given these assumptions, the conclusions follow logically, so that the only remaining question is whether anyone willing to accept such an analytical framework indeed has a new basis for formulating practical public policies. That public policy alone can bring about and maintain full employment in such a setting is obvious, since, left to itself, a technologically progressive economy has a manifest tendency to generate unemployment as time goes on and per capita income rises.

Full employment equilibrium will require the maintenance of effective demand at a level sufficient to generate a quantity of production required to keep the available labour force fully employed at a given state of technology. There is thus a need to monitor the incidence of technological progress in various sectors and to anticiipate the consumer demand that the resulting increase in income would entail. Even in the absence of precise and large-scale computations, one can have a general idea of where productivity is rising and what the nature of the next cluster of commodities in demand will be so that the movements in productivity and consumption have at least opposing effects on employment levels.

Technological unemployment, the unwelcome side of productivity increases, will call for a manpower policy that would ease the transition through changes in retirement provisions, working hours, training schemes, and other such measures local to the industries affected. But, in the main, the pressure on employment will have to be offset by ensuring that the unemployed can go into the production of those commodities for which demand will expand as a result of the income rise incidental to the growth of productivity. This will call for a co-ordination of monetary, fiscal and development policies to facilitate a matching of production increments with the likely commodity-mix of marginal demand.

In the short run, demand structures are clearly more amenable to public policy manipulations than productivity patterns. Research into consumer preferences could identify the particular clusters of goods that are likely to absorb the incremental income. Such demand is, in fact, routinely generated in market economies through appropriate advertisements and other consumption-creating efforts. Economies lower down in the pecking order of consumption structures will, of course, simply imitate the patterns of consumption already realised in countries higher up in the Engel hierarchy. Moreover, even in the absence of domestic productivity increases, scope for increasing production may exist through exports following income increases in the rest of the world.

By the same token, attempts to exceed the full employment level of effective demand through measures such as deficit financing will create inflationary pressures (and/or balance of payments financing difficulties) that will have to be corrected through an appropriate restraint on demand and/or increases in the full employment output through productivity increases or increased immigration. Inflationary financing is self-defeating and results in serious inequities, especially in economies that are technologically less progressive. Attempts to export the inflationary pressures through balance of payments deficits result in a growing debt burden which has to be adjusted subsequently, often with serious setbacks for economic growth.

The new approach fully recognises the problem of mobilising savings for capital formation which continues to be of central importance. Policies have to be implemented so as to ensure that the necessary volume of savings is generated and invested either indirectly through an appropriate mix of monetary and fiscal policies or directly through public sector operations. The crucial macroeconomic condition that will have to be satisfied is the elimination of uncompensated parsimony by ensuring that every act of saving in one part of the economy is offset by dissavings or investments elsewhere.

Countries that are technologically stagnant in the sense of unchanging labour productivities and lack of commodity innovations have to look into the factors underlying such stagnation, leading possibly to such institutional changes as land reforms, which may be a precondition for releasing a populations's natural urge to increase labour productivity and to innovate new commodities. Besides, productivity can be increased in such countries by acquiring techniques and commodities that are already in use abroad. Moreover, as already indicated, increases in incomes in the rest of the world may take the place of domestic productivity increase as a stimulus to local production. The particular commodity cluster for which demand will increase in this manner will depend on the location of the income gains. For instance, the commodity mix of demand resulting from income increases in India is likely to be very different from that originating in income gains in the USA.

While the harvest of novel hypotheses is rich and diverse, what the new approach basically calls for is a close attention to the full employment output capacity, and to the commodity composition of incremental consumer demand, at the particular income level at which a developing economy finds itself at a point in time. Further, specialisation for exports has to be directed to commodities in which the country has not only achieved but is likely to maintain a comparative cost advantage. Notably, the problem of achieving and maintaining full employment equilibrium in a technologically progressive economy where per capita income is rising turns out to be essentially the same irrespective of who owns the means of production, so that the policy prescriptions apply as much to a fully socialised economy as to an economy that is partly or wholly under private enterprise. In addition, the arbitrary and often misleading distinction now drawn between 'less developed' and 'developed' countries is replaced under the new approach by a continuous ranking of economies by their respective productivity patterns and a pecking order of consumption structures that ranges from the most elementary to the highly sophisticated extremity at the very edge of man's knowledge about what can be economically produced and consumed.

NOTES

1. The paper has benefited from comments by especially Manmohan Kumar (Cambridge), Jitendralal Borkakoti (Middlesex Polytechnic), and Azizali F. Mohammed and Patrick L. Clawson (both of the International Monetary Fund). Aroona S. Borpujari (University of District of Columbia) improved the statistical analysis. Opinions expressed in the paper are the author's own and not necessarily those of the International Monetary Fund; presentation of the paper in Madrid was made possible by a grant from the organisers of the Madrid Congress.
2. These assumptions, unlike the usual rationality postulate, have support in other disciplines (Marcuse, 1969).
3. There are also terms of trade effects that are quite independent of income growth resulting from technological progress.
4. Whether such gains in export shares are advantageous to the exporting country as a whole is a different matter that has to be addressed separately (Pasinetti, 1981, pp. 268–71). also, the gains in export shares can be an exchange rate-cum-subsidy phenomenon.
5. Such a classification could provide a basis for giving up the habit acquired in the decades since the Second World War of treating the problems of the poorer countries as special issues belonging to a hodge-podge called 'development Economics'.

REFERENCES

Bleaney, M. (1976) *Underconsumption Theories* (New York: International).
Borpujari, J.G. (1980) 'Toward a Basic Needs Approach to Economic Development with Financial Stability', *Departmental Memorandum Series* (Washington: International Monetary Fund) 28 February.

Borpujari, J.G. (1981) 'Savings Generation and Financial Programming in a Basic Need Constrained Developing Economy', *Departmental Memorandum Series* (Washington: International Monetary Fund), 14 December; paper presented at a Round Table Meeting of the International Economic Association on 'Financing Problems of Developing Countries', Buenos Aires, Argentina, October 26–30, 1981.

Chakrabarti, A. K., Feinman, S. and Fuentivilla, W. (1982) 'A Cross-National Comparison of Patterns of Industrial Innovations', *The Columbia Journal of World Business*, vol. XVII, no. 3, Fall.

Fetter, F. A. (1945) 'Lauderdale's Oversaving Theory', *The American Economic Review*, vol. XXXV, no. 3, June.

Green, R. T. (1982) 'Changing National Concentrations of High Technology Exports, 1974–79', *The Columbia Journal of World Business*, vol. XVII, no. 3, Fall.

Harris, D. J. (1982) 'Structural Change and Economic Growth: a Review Article', *Contributions to Political Economy*, vol. I, March.

Japan Productivity Center (1982) *Research on International Comparisons of Labor Productivity* (Tokyo: National research Institute).

Kalecki, M. (1976) *Essays on Developing Economies* (Sussex: Harvester).

Kravis, I. B., Heston, A., and Summers, R. (1982) *World Product and Income, International Comparisons of Real Gross Product*, Phase III (Baltimore: Johns Hopkins University Press).

Kuznets, S. (1962) 'Quantitative Aspects of the Economic Growth of Nations: the Share and Structure of Consumption', *Economic Development and Cultural Change*, vol. X, no. 2, January.

Lustig, N. C. (1979) *Distribution of Income, Structure of Consumption and Economic Growth: the Case of Mexico*, unpublished PhD dissertation, University of California, Berkeley.

Marcuse, H. (1969) *Eros and Civilisation* (London: Sphere).

Pasinetti, L. L. (1981) *Structural Change and Economic Growth: a Theoretical Essay on the Dynamics of the Wealth of Nations* (Cambridge: Cambridge University Press).

Robinson, J. (1978) 'The Second Crisis of Economic Theory', Richard T. Ely Lecture, 1971, reproduced in Robinson, J. (1978) *Contributions to Modern Economics* (Oxford: Basil Blackwell).

Schumpeter, J. A. (1954) *History of Economic Analysis* (New York: Oxford University Press).

Shoul, B. (1957) 'Karl Marx and Say's Law', *Quarterly Journal of Economics*, vol. LXXI, no. 4, November.

Spengler, J. J. (1945) 'The Physiocrats and Say's Law of Markets', *The Journal of Political Economy*, vol. LIII, nos. 3–4, September and December.

US Bureau of Labor Statistics (1982) 'International Comparisons of Productivity and Labor Costs in the Steel Industry: United States, Japan, France, Germany, United Kingdom: 1964–80', Department of Labor, Office of Productivity and Technology, September 1981 and January 1982 (unpublished data).

7 On the Economics of Structural Change and the Evolution of Technology

J. S. Metcalfe and M. Gibbons
UNIVERSITY OF MANCHESTER

1 FRAMEWORK AND ASSUMPTIONS

The problem with which we are concerned in this paper is the relationship between technological change and structural change. The historical record shows new technology to be of central importance in the history of modern industrial nations, and yet this same phenomenon has proved resilient to attempts to incorporate it within formal economic theory. Our purpose is to develop a framework for the integration of technical change into the economic analysis of structural growth and development. In particular we wish to understand the forces which determine the growth rate of an industry and how these forces change over time in a systematic way.

Our starting point is to recognise the all-pervasive nature of the forgotten stylised fact, namely that economic growth is never a smooth balanced process. It inevitably involves the changing relative importance of different nation states, of broad economic sectors within nations (agriculture, manufacturing, services) and of specific activities within these broad sectors. We argue that the phenomenon of structural change is central to an understanding of the economic effects of new technology and, conversely, that the process of evolution of technology can properly be understood only in the context of structural change. A macroeconomic perspective is simply inconsistent with an adequate analysis of technological change.[1]

In a progressive economy, scientific advances continually create a basis for new economic activity, and our framework is designed to model the growth of new technology systems – groups of interrelated innovations – from the moment the innovations occur, through the process of growth and technical development, until the technologies have matured and the activities settled into their economic niches.[2] Our framework owes much to the writing of Schumpeter, Kuznets and Burns, and more recently to the work of Hicks, Leon and Pasinetti.[3]

The assumptions with which we work are as follows. The economy is initially in equilibrium and a scientific advance occurs which permits the development of a series of new technologies for producing different products. To keep the exposition manageable, only two new industries will be considered. The new industries need not be established simultaneously, but our analysis of development begins with the moment both are competing for markets and productive inputs. As we show below, the time-lag between the two innovations has a significant effect on the growth paths.

To each new industry we assign a process technology and a product technology. The product technology defines the single product in terms of a bundle of given and time-invariant characteristics. This product is a non-durable commodity. The process technology defines a single, constant returns-to-scale productive process specifying the various inputs required to produce a unit output. In this first pass at the problem produced means of production are available to the new industries as unlimited quantities at given prices.

To analyse the process of development we proceed in two stages. A long period niche is defined for the new industries and then the dynamics of adjustment to this position are introduced.

2 THE LONG-PERIOD POSITION

The introduction of the two new industries creates a discontinuity, a structural break in the pattern of equilibrium economic relations existing in the economy. A new long-period position is created which may be quite different in terms of output and price structures from the previous equilibrium. In this section we will focus on the long-period positions of the two new industries, ignoring the spillover effects of the rest of the economy. Indeed, the two new industries define a simple general equilibrium system which stands in a partial equilibrium relation with the rest of the economy. The generalisation of this argument would not appear to raise any issues of principle additional to those discussed below.

To determine the long-period niche for the new industries we must specify the production, input supply, and market demand relationships for each industry. The process technology of both industries is such that inputs of machines, materials and labour are required to support production. We shall treat labour and materials as a single aggregate input bundle and assume that the supply price, w, is an increasing function of the quantity of that input which is employed. Further disaggregation of the inputs will not influence the substance of our argument. If l_i is the quantity of input per unit of output and x_i is the scale of output in industry, i, then we can write

$$w = w_0 + w_1(l_1 x_1 + l_2 x_2) \tag{1}$$

relating the supply price to the output of both new industries one and two.[4]

Let v_i be the given value capital:output ratio in each industry, p_i the price of its output, and r_i and d_i the percentage rates of profit and depreciation respectively; then we can write the price equations

$$p_1 = (r_1 + d_1)v_1 + w l_1$$
$$p_2 = (r_2 + d_2)v_2 + w l_2 \tag{2}$$

Taking account of (1) these can be written as the long-period supply price schedules

$$p_1 = h_{01} + j_{11} x_1 + j_{12} x_2$$
$$p_2 = h_{02} + j_{21} x_1 + j_{22} x_2 \tag{3}$$

Along these schedules price is equal to unit cost with capital charges evaluated at the normal rate of profit for the industry.[5] One implication of (3) is that the equilibrium cost structures depend on the output of both industries.

On the demand side we also proceed by means of linear approximations and assume that the outputs of the new industries are gross substitutes with each other. Let n_i be the long-periods demand level; then

$$n_1 = a_{01} - b_{11} p_1 + b_{12} p_2$$
$$n_2 = a_{02} + b_{21} p_1 - b_{21} p_2 \tag{4}$$

Combining (4) and (3) we can write the following equilibrium excess demand relations for the new industries.[6]

$$E_1 = n_1 - x_1 = d_{01} + d_{11}x_1 + d_{12}x_2$$
$$E_2 = n_2 - x_2 = d_{02} + d_{21}x_1 + d_{22}x_2$$
(5)

Setting both excess demands equal to zero enables (5) to be solved for the long-period output levels x_1 and x_2, and for expositional purposes we shall assume that both magnitudes are positive.[7] We shall see subsequently that the dynamics of the industrial growth paths are related to the static stability properties of the excess demand system (5). The stability of this system requires that both d_{ii} coefficients be negative and that the determinant $|D|$ be positive. In the following we shall assume that these conditions are satisfied and, moreover, that all the d coefficients are negative, apart from d_{01} and d_{02}, which are positive. Thus an increase in the output of x_1 reduces both the excess demand for x_1 and the excess demand for x_2. The postulate of negative cross-industry effects places the two new industries in a competitive relationship.

3 THE ADJUSTMENT PROCESS

It is central to a Schumpeterian development process that the long-period position is not achieved immediately the initial innovations are made. Technical change is a process of economic adjustment. The innovations act as an impulse to industrial growth, but the working out of this impulse necessarily takes time. We shall argue that two dynamic mechanisms determine the time profile with which the given new technologies are absorbed into the economic system – a process of learning by the users of the innovations, and a process of capital accumulation in anticipation of the profits to be earned exploiting the new technology system. Consider first the dynamics of demand growth. Here the essential point is that potential consumers have to learn new preference patterns before they purchase the new commodity.[8] As Hoffmann put it, an industry may experience a rapid rate of growth, not because of Engel Law effects but,

> because of it is a 'young' industry busy creating a market for itself in the place of other products; in contrast to an 'old' industry when

the public has had a long time to decide on how much to use. (Hoffman, 1949, p. 171)[9]

The dynamic forces behind this learning phenomenon relate to ignorance and lack of information on relevant characteristics of the new technology. Many studies of innovation diffusion have been based upon learning processes which dispel ignorance and create bandwagon effects, a form of social learning by doing.[10] The point of relevance here is that these diffusion studies are examples in miniature of our process of industrial growth. A familiar pattern for the diffusion process is captured by the logistic curve in which the level of demand, x, evolves according to the following differential equation:

$$\frac{dx}{dt} = \beta x[n - x] \qquad (6)$$

From an initial value $x(0)$, demand grows towards a long-period equilibrium level n, at a pace dictated by the adoption coefficient, β. This later coefficient is dependent on the dynamics of information transmission between potential and actual purchases of the innovation. Notice that the rate of growth of demand is subject to continuous retardation: the smaller is the gap $(n - x)$, the lower is the growth rate of demand. It will be clear that the mechanism specified in (6) is incomplete, for the equilibrium demand level will depend on the relative prices of the new commodities, and these are likely to change during the diffusion process. Instead of one diffusion curve we have many curves each appropriate to a particular pattern of prices. Any observed diffusion curve is likely to be an envelope curve which, depending on the pattern of price variations, will not generally be logistic. To take account of this possibility we must provide an explanation of how prices change during the course of industrial growth. This brings us directly to the second dynamic element, the growth of productive capacity to produce each new commodity.

Our starting point is the proposition that the growth of productive capacity depends on the rate of profit on investments in each new industry. For expositional purposes we assume that investment in capacity expansion occurs as long as the expected rate of profit stands above the appropriate long-period normal level, $\bar{r}$, and we equate the expected profit rate with the current profit rate, r. To finance investment there are two sources of funds: profits generated internally by the existing firms in the industry, and external funds, including the possibility of new entrants. As a first approximation, we assume that the flow of funds is generated by a stable fraction, f, of industry profits reinvested in capacity expansion, and a fixed ratio, e, between external and internal capital funds. These assumptions take us close to a classical savings postulate, for the proportionate rate of growth of productive capacity in each industry, g_i, is related to the corresponding rate of profits by

$$g_i = f_i(1 + e_i)r_i = \pi_i r_i \tag{7}$$

For the purpose of the present exercise we shall treat the 'saving' ratios π_i as constant.[11] If we now substitute the growth profit relations (7) into the price equations (2) we immediately define a relation between the price of each new commodity and the rate of growth of capacity to produce it. The greater is g_i, the greater has to be the margin between price and long-period unit cost in order to provide the appropriate flow of investible funds. Thus in place of (3) we write

$$p_1 = k_1 g_1 + h_{01} + j_{11} x_1 + j_{12} x_2$$
$$p_2 = k_2 g_2 + h_{02} + j_{21} x_1 + j_{22} x_2 \tag{8}$$

where $k_i = v_i/\pi_i$, the profit which must be earned in order to finance a unit increase in capacity. In the long-period position, the growth rates of capacity are zero and equation (8) becomes equation (3), but during the transition the relation between prices and growth rates must be taken into account explicitly. Imagine now the following experiment, in which we consider each industry in isolation. Holding the price of the new commodity constant, its path of demand will follow a logistic curve (6) towards the appropriate upper asymptote, n_i. Similarly, from (8) the capacity output level will also follow a logistic curve towards an upper asymptote. However, except by fluke, the two asymptotes will differ, as will the levels of capacity and demand at each point on the adjustment paths. For such an arbitrary price, the dynamics of demand and capacity growth are incompatible. Clearly some rule about prices is needed to eliminate this inconsistency; a rule which also recognises the element of interdependence between the cost and demand structures of the two industries.

Our provisional solution to the pricing problem will be to let the price of each new commodity adjust to maintain equality between the level of demand and productive capacity at each point on the industrial growth path. Such a path is a path of secular trend, and we shall refer to it as the balanced path for the industry. It is, of course, an ideal, a reference position and no more. Nevertheless it represents precisely that situation in which profit-conscious entrepreneurs would wish to find themselves with neither a surplus nor a shortage of capacity. Of course, mistakes and false hopes will drive the actual growth path from the secular trend, but our working hypothesis is that such deviations are short-lived and self-correcting.

4 THE BALANCED PATH

In a closed economy, it follows that the level and growth rate of capacity must exactly equal the level and growth rate of demand at all points on the balanced path. From (8), (4), (6) and (7) we then obtain

$$g_1 = \beta_1[a_{01} - b_{11}(k_1 g_1 + h_{01} + j_{11} x_1 + j_{12} x_2) + b_{12}(k_2 g_2 + h_{02} + j_{21} x_1 + j_{22} x_2) - x_1]$$

and (9)

$$g_2 = \beta_2[a_{01} + b_{21}(k_1 g_1 + h_{02} + j_{11} x_1 + j_{12} x_2) - b_{22}(k_2 g_2 + h_{02} + j_{21} x_1 + j_{22} x_2) - x_2]$$

Choosing time units such that $\beta_2 = 1$, we may then rearrange these equations as

$$\begin{bmatrix} 1 + \mu_{11}, \mu_{12} \\ \mu_{21}, 1 + \mu_{22} \end{bmatrix} \begin{bmatrix} g_1 \\ g_2 \end{bmatrix} = \begin{bmatrix} d_{01} + d_{11} x_1 + d_{12} x_2 \\ d_{02} + d_{21} x_1 + d_{22} x_2 \end{bmatrix} \quad (10)$$

where the terms on the right-hand side are the static excess demand functions discussed previously. The terms in the left-hand matrix are dynamic adjustment coefficients.[12] Equations (10) may now be solved to yield a pair of simultaneous, non-linear differential equations in the secular output levels x_1 and x_2. Thus

$$\frac{dx_1}{dt} = \frac{-x_1}{\Delta} \{e_{11}(\bar{x}_1 - x_1) + e_{12}(\bar{x}_2 - x_2)\}$$

$$\frac{dx_2}{dt} = \frac{-x_2}{\Delta} \{e_{21}(\bar{x}_1 - x_1) + e_{22}(\bar{x}_2 - x_2)\} \quad (11)$$

where $(1 + \mu_{11})(1 + \mu_{22}) - \mu_{12}\mu_{21}$, and the e coefficient are combinations of the d and μ coefficients.[13] Given our assumptions about the d coefficients, it follows that the e coefficients are negative. At each point in time the 'tilt' of an industry's secular trend is a product of its current level of output and the current adjustment gaps of *both* industries. With cross effects zero, each secular trend would be a logistic curve, but in the presence of the cross effects we have departures from logistic growth. How significant these are depend upon the cross adjustment gaps and the cross coefficients, e_{ij}.

Given the initial conditions, the dynamics of industrial growth are determined by (11), and it is of interest to investigate the following properties of the system. Is the long-period position a centre of gravity for the new technology system? Do the growth paths of output exhibit retardation? What is the time-path of the rate of profits, and how do prices and costs evolve during the adjustment process? These are complicated issues, since the expansion of each industry influences the growth of the other. As levels of output grow, prices change, so shifting the long-period equilibrium demand and cost structures. Before we proceed it is useful to note the formal analogy between equations (11) and simple models of population dynamics between interacting species. Instead of competition between life forms for a biological niche, we have competition between technologies for a long-period position.[14] By analogy with these ecological models it can be shown that the dynamic system (11) has two general types of solution. Either one industry entirely dominates the other in the final equilibrium, or both industries may co-exist, with positive equilibrium output levels. This latter case may be further subdivided into one for which the final equilibrium is stable ($|E| = e_{11}e_{22} - e_{12}e_{21} > 0$) and the contrasting unstable position ($|E| < 0$). A knowledge of the initial conditions then permits the investigator to determine the simultaneous paths of industrial growth, noting that if one of the industries should reach a period of decline its dynamics of contraction will differ sharply from the dynamics of expansion.

5 SUMMARY AND EXTENSIONS

The principal theme of the previous section has been the determination of the growth rates of output following the establishment of a new industry – a situation of Schumpeterian development.

It is important to ask whether our conclusions are robust and how useful they might be as a guide to historical experience in particular cases. The following discussion is intended as a brief guide to some of the issues which should be considered.

A first modification might be to allow the cross growth effects, e_{ij}, to be positive so that in dynamic terms the industries are complements. The structure of the argument is unaffected, but the interesting possibility now emerges of acceleration of growth rates in the early stages of the growth process. Retardation clearly depends on a particular pattern of competitive inter-industry relationships.

A second set of possibilities is provided by a more detailed specification of the input structure, introducing many primary inputs and many produced inputs – not all in perfectly elastic supply. An even fuller treatment would require that the capacity growth process in the industries supplying produced means of production be incorporated into the argument. This would introduce several complex issues, but it is unlikely that our general conclusions would change. One simple way of illustrating this is to make the output of industry one an input in two and *vice versa*. The network of input-output relations introduces elements of technological complementarity in demand, and means that each price depends directly on the other – irrespective of output levels or growth rates. The structure of the argument is enriched, but system (11) still applies with appropriate redefinition of the coefficients.[15] Hence all the qualitative properties of our simpler system hold in a world of complicated input-output relations.

A more important set of modifications relates to changes in underlying conditions during the adjustment process. Exogenous changes related to technological developments in other sectors, Engel Law effects, or other shifts in preference raise no new issues of principle. Of course, they redefine long-period positions and impose structural breaks on the growth paths, but the effects of such changes can be readily understood within our framework. Only space precludes further discussion of them at this point.

Of far greater significance are endogenous changes in the various coefficients as the industries grow. In general one might expect the β_i

and π_i coefficients to vary over time and for the technical coefficients to evolve in particular directions. Changes in the β_i and π_i coefficients will influence paths of adjustment but not the long-period positions. Changes in technology – process or product improvements – have deeper effects, and the need here is to link the patterns of industrial growth with the inducement and learning mechanisms which shape the post-innovation improvement of each technology. This important development is beyond the limited scope of this paper.

6 CONCLUDING REMARKS

This paper has attempted a provisional statement of a Schumpeterian model of economic development. It will be clear that much remains to be done, but we venture to hope that we have provided a basis for interpreting some important connections between structural change and technical progress. Certainly we consider that our framewrok is consistent with a vast body of historical research into technical change, if not with a macroeconomic approach. We find that the patterns of industrial growth identified by Kuznets, Burns and others are natural consequences of our analysis, which is flexible enough to accommodate both industrial growth and industrial decline. We hope we have identified a valuable focus for future investigation, namely the linking together of mechanisms diffusing new technology with the mechanisms inducing particular patterns of technical change.

NOTES

1. On the problem of macro 'balanced' growth theory see Pasinetti (1981), chs 4 and 10, where the critique is also extended to macroeconomic theories of cyclical behaviour. The sectoral approach to technical progress and growth is, of course, the stock of trade of economic historians. Landes (1969) remains the best reference, but see also Rostow (1960) and Coleman (1956).
2. The concept of a new technology system is introduced in Freeman *et al.* (1982), ch.4, with related discussion of the synthetic materials and microelectronics industries. Related concepts are Rostow's leading sector complexes (1960) and Rosenberg's clusters of basic innovations (1979).
3. Schumpeter (1934) and (1939), Kuznets (1930) and (1954), Burns (1934), Hicks (1977), Leon (1967) and Pasinetti (1981).
4. In general terms (1) can be treated as a suitable linear approximation to any non-linear inverse supply function. Throughout we shall simplify through linear approximations.

5. $\dot{h}_{01} = (\bar{r} + d_1)v_1 + w_0 l_1$; $\dot{h}_{02} = (\bar{r}_2 + d_2)v_2 + w_0 l_2$;
   $j_{11} = w_1 l_1^2$; $j_2 = w_1 l_2^2$, $j_{12} = w_1 l_1 l_2 = j_{21}$
   Note the symmetry of cross effects and that $j_{11}j_{22} - j_{12}j_{21} = 0$.

6. $d_{01} = a_{01} - b_{11}h_{01} + b_{12}h_{02}$; $d_{02} = a_{02} + b_{21}h_{01} - b_{22}h_{02}$;
   $d_{11} + b_{12}j_{21} - b_{11}j_{11} - 1$; $d_{22} = b_{21}j_{12} - b_{22}j_{22} - 1$;
   $d_{12} = b_{12}j_{22} - b_{11}j_{12}$; $d_{21} = b_{21}j_{11} - b_{22}j_{21}$.

7. let $/D/ = d_{11}d - d_{21}d_{12}$. Then $\bar{x}_1/D/^{-1}[d_{02}d_{12} - d_{01}d_{22}]$
   and $\bar{x}_2 = /D/^{-1}[d_{01}d_{21} - d_{02}d_{11}]$. The condition that $^{-1}/\bar{x}$, $< 0, \bar{x}_2 < 0$.
   requires that the following inequalities be satisfied
   $d_{22}/d_{12} > d_{02}/d_{01} > d_{21}/d_{11}$.

8. See Pasinetti, 1981, pp. 75–6.

9. See also Burns (1934), pp. 127–8.

10. The diffusion literature is immense. Davies (1979) provides an excellent survey, and a critical review of diffusion models is contained in Metcalfe (1981). Papers of Ozga (1961), Lekvall and Wahlbin (1973) and Hernes (1976) discuss simple deterministic diffusion processes.

11. With $\pi_i = 1$ we have Pasinetti's case of natural growth. See Pasinetti, ch.7.

12. They are defined as followes:
    $1 + \mu_{11} = (1 + \beta_1 k_1 b_{11})/\beta_1$; $\mu_{22} = 1 + k_2 b_{22}$; $\mu_{12} = k_2 b_{12}$;   and
    $\mu_{21} = k_1 b_{21}$.

13. Thus, $e_{01} = (1 + \mu_{22})d_{01} + \mu_{12}d_{01} = (1 + \mu_{11})d_{02} + \mu_{21}d_{01}$
    $e_{11} = (1 + \mu_{22})_{11} + \mu_{12}d_{21}$, $e_{22} = (1 + \mu_{11})d_{22} + \mu_{21}d_{12}$
    $e_{12} = (1 - \mu_{22})d_{1\,2} + \mu_{12}d_{22}$, $e_{21} = (1 + \mu_{11})d_{21} + \mu_{21}d_{11}$

14. On the ecological analogy, consult Slobodkin (1961) and Roughgardan (1979), ch.21.

15. Stability requires that the Hawkins–Simon condition for the pair of industries be satisfied, together with $/E/>0$.

REFERENCES

Burns, A. F. (1934) *Production Trends in the United States Since 1870* (New York: NBER).

Coleman, D. C. (1956) 'Industrial Growth and Industrial Revolutions', *Economica*, vol. 23, pp. 1–22.

Coleman, J. S. (1964) *Introduction to Mathematical Sociology* (Glencoe: Free Press).

Davies, S. (1979) *The Diffusion of Process Innovation* (Cambridge: Cambridge University Press).

Freeman, C., Clark, J. and Soete, L. (1982) *Unemployment and Technical Innovation* (London: Frances Pinter).

Hernes, G. (1976) 'Diffusion and Growth: the Non-Homogeneous Case', *Swedish Journal of Economics*, vol. 78, pp. 427–36.

Hicks, J. (1977) *Economic Perspectives* (London: Oxford University Press).

Hoffman, W. G. (1949) 'The Growth of Industrial Production in Great Britain: a Quantitative Study', *Economic History Review*, vol. 4, pp. 162–80.

Kuznets, S. (1930) *Secular Movements in Production and Prices* (Boston: Houghton Miflin).

Kuznets, S. (1954) *Economic Change* (London: Heinemann).

Landes, D. S. (1969 *The Unbound Prometheus* (Cambridge: Cambridge University Press).

Lekvall, P. and Wahlbin, C. (1973) 'A Study of Some Assumptions Underlying Innovative Diffusion Functions', *Swedish Journal of Economics*, vol. 75, pp. 362–77.

Leon, P. (1967) *Structural Change and Growth in Capitalism* (Baltimore: Johns Hopkins).

Metcalfe, J. S. (1981) 'Impulse and Diffusion in the Study of Technological Change, *Futures*, vol. 13, pp. 347–59.

Ozga, S. A. (1961) 'Imperfect Markets Through Lack of Knowledge', *Quarterly Journal of Economics*, vol. 75, pp. 39–52.

Pasinetti, L. (1981) *Structural Change and Economic Growth* (Cambridge: Cambridge University Press).

Roughgardan, J. (1979) *Theory of Population Genetics and Evolutionary Ecology: an Introduction* (New York: Macmillan).

Rosenberg, N. (1979) 'Technological Interdependence in the American Economy', *Technology and Culture*, vol. 20, pp. 25–50.

Rostow, W. (1960) *The Process of Economic Growth* (London: Oxford University Press).

Schumpeter, J. A. (1934) *The Theory of Economic Development* (New York: Oxford University Press).

Schumpeter, J. A. (1939) *Business Cycles Vols I and II* (New York: McGraw-Hill).

Slobodkin, L. B. (1961) *Growth and Regulation in Animal Populations* (New York: Dover).

8 Theoretical Aspects of Change in Productive Structures: Discussion and Conclusions

Luigi Pasinetti
UNIVERSITÀ CATTOLICA DEL SACRO CUORE, MILAN

The session that discussed the topic 'Theoretical Aspects of Change in Productive Structures' was the only session of the 7th World Congress of the IEA that was *specifically* devoted to theoretical problems. Three authors were invited to present papers: Professor Anne Carter of Brandeis University, Dr Frances Stewart of the University of Oxford, and Dr Jitendra Borpujari of the IMF, Washington. Seven other contributed papers were accepted. Altogether ten papers were presented. A further (invited) paper, by Professors Marsden, Sala-Fumas and Whinston, has been added here, for reasons of relatedness of contents, although the paper was actually presented in another session of the Congress. Space has only permitted the publication of the invited papers, slightly shortened, and of an abridged version of one contributed paper (by Professors Metcalfe and Gibbons of Manchester University).

Anne Carter and Frances Stewart, as the reader will be aware, have dealt with two of what might be considered classical problems arising from changes in technology: the disruption aspect of technical change (what Schumpeter called the 'creative destruction' of technical progress in capitalist economies) and the problem of choice of technique, respectively. A Schumpeterian view of technical change has also been proposed in the paper by Metcalfe and Gibbons, with a model aimed at showing the links between the diffusion of technical progress and the inducement of structural change. On the other hand, Marsden *et al.* have dealt with the related, but in a sense opposite, phenomenon of the obstacles to the diffusion of technical change. Transfers of technology from one country to another, and even from one firm to another, are sometimes very quick but at other times surprisingly painful. We must take note of the successes, but we must also reckon with the failures. The authors focus their attention on the problem of measuring what they call 'transferability' of technology, and they distinguish between engineering aspects and managerial aspects. Finally, in his paper, Jitendra Borpujari, has taken a more ambitious, overall, approach to structural change in a growing economy, by inserting a series of recent empirical data into a comprehensive multi-sector model of growth and structural change.

The six contributed papers which are not published here have dealt with a number of other theoretical problems which I shall try here to relate to those dealt with by the authors of the invited papers.

Professors Okólski and Winiecki (from Warsaw) have reviewed investment and trade policies in socialist countries, especially with reference to Poland, bringing to light the interesting feature that in socialist countries the proportion of national income devoted to investment is, in a consistent way, considerably higher than in capitalist countries.

Professors Amendola and Gaffard (Strasbourg University) have proposed a sequential approach to the analysis of the process of innovation. Their idea is that technical change may be viewed as a process in which the outcomes of each period constrain the decisions that can be taken in the following periods. Anne Carter's idea recurs here that any innovation cannot be looked at in isolation from what happened earlier in time.

Two very highly theoretical papers were also discussed. Professor Lombardini (in co-authorship with Dr Donati and Dr Villa of the University of Torino, Italy) presented an elaborate model of economic growth. The model, though using simplifying assumptions, illuminates many relevant aspects of growth, both in equilibrium and in disequilibrium situations. And Frank Englemann (University of Tübingen) presented a theoretical paper in which he explores the problem of uniqueness or multiplicity of a uniform rate of profit in a multi-sector model in which different sectors grow at different rates.

Finally, two other papers were discussed that have adopted the same approach proposed in Borpujari's paper. Dieter Kattermann (University of Bremen), while using traditional tools of analysis (offer curves), has used the hierarchical order that can be depicted in the expansion of demand for the various commodities to obtain new results concerning theories and policies of international trade. And Professor Nardozzi (Univeristy of Florence) has put forward some proposals aimed at the introduction of specific institutional features relating to money and banking into multi-sectoral growth models.

The discussion has been wide-ranging, lively, and on the whole satisfactory.

It is not possible, within the space limits of this report, even to summarise the abundance of comments, remarks and interchange of views expressed by the numerous speakers. But at least two sets of problems should be mentioned, as they arose again and again both in the papers and in the discussion.

The first set of problems concerns the two opposite faces of technical progress. On the one hand, technical progress brings about the benefits of productivity increase; on the other hand it causes disruption by rendering part of the existing capital equipment obsolete and by displacing workers. There were many contributions on this subject. The speakers talked of 'creative destruction', of Darwinian processes, of market competition, etc. Some speakers tended to claim that the institutions of capitalist economies are biased in the direction of too much or too fast technical change; but this view appeared controversial. Other speakers, from socialist countries, forcibly made the point that there are too few incentives to technical change in socialist economies.

The other set of problems that was discussed very widely concern the *policy* implications that emerge when one looks at structural change from within a theoretical framework in which per capita demand, by expanding in a non-proportional way according to what is known as Engel's Law, does not necessarily offset the deflationary effects generated by increasing productivity. It was recognised that in such a framework, characterised by structural change, there is no automatic tendency towards full employment. It follows that economic policies will have to be drawn up which facilitate the absorption of the technologically unemployed into the production of those commodities and services for which demand expands, as a result of the income increases that accompany the growth of productivity, or as a result of export promotion. Internationally, export specialisation will have to be directed at products in which an economy has not only achieved, but is likely to maintain, an advantage in comparative rates of change of productivity. These implications apply as much to centrally planned economies as to those that are more market-oriented.

There also was a general recognition that a considerable volume of empirical work will have to be accomplished in this area in order to refine and adapt the theoretical models to those features of our economic system that emerge as the most characteristic and persistent.

The authors of the papers and all the participants in the discussion hope that their work (part of which is published here, while other parts are finding publication elsewhere) will be of some use not only to theoretical economists, but also to those in charge of economic policies.

Part II

Structural Adjustment in Industrially Advanced Countries

Part II

Structural Adjustment in Industrially Advanced Countries

9 Ability to Adjust and the Problems of European Market Economies

J. Waelbroeck
UNIVERSITY OF BRUSSELS

1 THE PROBLEM OF ECONOMIC THEORY

This paper discusses the ability of the modern welfare states, particularly in Europe, to adjust to economic shocks. Loss of flexibility is widely perceived to be at the root of the present recession, from which Europe is finding it so difficult to extricate itself. The problem is often presented as though there were single-pronged policies which could increase flexibility without jeopardising other objectives which European states have prized highly. To a certain extent this is true. But it is a delusion to reason as though there were no conflict between objectives, and no need to decide what is the best trade-off between goals which cannot be fully achieved simultaneously.

From a theoretical point of view, I will rely on the convenient but somewhat intuitive approach according to which economies are at any point of time in disequilibrium, tending only to the equilibrium state which implies that resources are used efficiently.[1] Equilibrium is but a target. It is assumed that the movement of equilibrium is stable,[2] but it may be so slow as to be imperceptible. The organisation of particular markets may block the corresponding adjustment mechanism. It is claimed that a number of markets in Europe are malfunctioning from this point of view.

What is wrong? To start the discussion on this, I will examine the institutional evolution of three markets which play key roles in the functioning of modern economies: the labour market, the market for entrepreneurs, and what economists have begun to speak of as the 'market for government assistance'.

2 LABOUR MARKET ADJUSTMENT: THE DEMISE OF THE PHILLIPS CURVE

The discovery of the Phillips curve caused quite a stir at the time. Explaining wage changes filled a major gap in Keynesian theory, which assumed that wages were fixed. The specification of the curve happened to fit neatly the idea on which there was a great deal of research at the time that prices adjust to excess demand on the markets for the corresponding goods. Here was, properly estimated, a *tâtonnement* process of continuous adjustment.

The curve, which Phillips showed to have determined wages in Britain for decades, appears to have vanished upon discovery, like rare species such as the dodo, which disappeared soon after being discovered by the early explorers. It seems to have survived on the continent for some years. I found one easily in Belgium. But extinction came quickly there also. Econometricians are tenacious individuals, and there are still occasional reports that something like the Phillips curve has been estimated, as Himalayan explorers still announce that they have sighted tracks of the yeti. These reports meet disbelief. Economists do still usually agree that there is a vague relation between wages and unemployment, but the idea that this can be quantified meets wide scepticism in Europe.

What was remarkable about Phillips' discovery was not that the labour market adjusted, but that it adjusted slowly enough to make the process observable. It is only recently that economics has begun to be interested in the underlying unique features of the labour market. This work starts from the observation that labour has never been a commodity like others – not as some would have it, because workers are persons and not things, a difference which has no theoretical interest, but because of the stability of the typical employer–employee relation. Hall (1980), for example has shown that even in the United States, workers work for most of their lives for a single employer. This among other facts is recognised by implicit contract theory, which stresses that even apart from any formal contract or collective agreement, workers and their employers consider themselves bound by *de facto* understandings about the rights and obligations of both parties. Given the *de facto* stability of the employment relation, there is obviously scope for divergences between the wage and marginal product of workers, either between individuals, or over time. Disabled workers will be kept on; workers will not be laid off in periods of slack demand. The employers know that there are other workers who produce more than what they cost, or that there will be times when marginal product exceeds the wage. This kind of reasoning exists in other markets in which buyer-seller relations are stable, and this has given rise to the so-called 'administered prices'. The labour market is an extreme instance of this type of relationship.

Workers have thus always been insulated to some degree from the pressure of market forces. This is not because of any social consciousness of enterprises, but because of the structure of the market. This insulation has probably always been greater in Europe than in the United States, because employer–employee relationships have historically been more stable in the old continent than in the new. There is, however, a natural limit to such natural insulation: the employer's solvency – his ability to borrow his way through a recession, and his willingness to bear risk, since income stability for workers means profit instability for him.

This discussion implies that the price of labour has never been the amount of money paid to a worker at a particular time and place, as equilibrium theory tends to assume, but a (in part vague) commitment to pay definite amounts under various possible future circumstances. *Ex ante*, this implies a given statistical distribution of future earnings. Both the mean and the variance of this distribution are of importance to the two parties, and negotiations will *inter alia* involve trade-offs between the two: 'I can offer you a higher wage, but you must accept that you can be laid off under particular circumstances'.

Of course, the state has come to be very much involved in these relations. It has intervened in three ways to support the pressure of workers for greater income stability. It intervenes in determining the structure of collective agreements. Dismissing workers may be possible only after lengthy negotiations with the authorities in Sweden firms were even given employment targets in the mid-1970s; in Portugal it was made unconstitutional to dismiss workers. Law also prescribes the payment of large redundancy benefits, which in Belgium can amount to two years' wages for a worker and five for a salaried employee. Minimum wage legislation is effective in blocking wage cuts in important industries such as textiles and clothing.

It was remarked that the security which a firm can offer its workers is limited by its solvency; the state therefore also supplements the security offered by enterprises by giving money from its own budget. The main form of such payment is, of course, unemployment insurance. But early pension schemes are also used to help laid off workers who are too old to find other jobs. Some countries have schemes to pay severance benefits if bankruptcy of the employer prevents him from making the redundancy payments prescribed by law.

Employment is more than just money for the workers: it is friends, an occupation, status, and probably other things. The ultimate unemployment insurance is therefore to keep bankrupt firms alive through subsidies – to remove the solvency constraint on producers by a host of direct and indirect aid schemes: subsidies, support through public contracts, and even nationalisation. Often one has led to the other, in a process which has become familiar and predictable.

Through the years, workers have come to be vastly better insulated against business cycle risks than in previous times. This is a great social progress. But by impairing the adjustment mechanism on the labour market, it forces governments to increase unemployment much more than used to be necessary if they wish to reduce the increase of wages. Possibly they should be looking for other ways of curbing excessive wage increases. But so far, none has been found that works for more than a couple of years.

The other consequence of the institutional evolution of the labour market is an apparent shift in the balance of bargaining power between workers and employers. This means that, other things being equal, wages will tend to rise more than they would have ten or twenty years ago.

The insulation of workers from market pressures is, of course, a basic cause of this change in the shopfloor balance of forces. Two more factors should also be mentioned. Workers have everywhere become subject to fairly high marginal tax rates today, and this limits the cost of striking as a fraction of a year's income. They also draw social security transfers and sometimes benefits from subsidised housing, which maintains income during a strike.

High marginal tax rates exert an upward pressure on wages by reducing the incentive to move to a higher paid job. This makes it harder for employers who need to increase output rapidly to attract extra labour, and forces them to raise wages. Worker mobility has probably also been reduced by the increase in the number of working wives; but this factor is probably rather minor in most West European countries, which are so densely populated that it is usually possible for both man and wife to find a suitable job in any area. The Scandinavian countries may be an exception.

Job stability for individual workers and income redistribution via numerous devices have had a high priority in Europe and rightly so. The measures taken to promote these goals have, however, reduced the flexibility of the labour market, and made it very difficult to maintain price stability. The Phillips curve has disappeared as an econometrically observable phenomenon, but the rather weak connection that remains between wages and unemployment has turned out to be the only anti-inflation weapon that works. Because price stability is also highly prized by voters, governments have resorted increasingly to deflation to stop inflation, whatever the employment cost – and won elections after that.

In this indirect way, the policies meant to guarantee job and income stability to individual workers, or to the workers of particular factories, have made the achievement of full employment very difficult – surely a strange paradox. The general discussion will perhaps debate whether this line of argument is justified, and if so, how the countries of Europe can move in the direction of full employment policies which are not self-destructive.

3 THE MARKET FOR ENTREPRENEURS

I will now discuss a market which economists do not normally encompass in the list which they usually envisage: the market for entrepreneurs.

No such market exists in the usual general equilibrium microeconomic theory. In neoclassical analysis, factors of production combine by a kind of spontaneous combustion, a peculiar chemical process which associates elements in proportions dictated by market prices. 'Producers' are mere mailboxes, where profits accumulate before being redistributed to the owners of the firms.

Many years ago, Schumpeter brought analysis closer to reality by stressing that there are individuals who are indispensable catalysts in this process: the entrepreneurs who combine factors of production in new ways, or discover ways of producing goods that were not thought of before. Entrepreneurs are obviously a very important factor of production; therefore there must be a market for them. How can the market be described? Has it been distored by economic policies? Is it somehow in disequilibrium, yet failing to adjust? This is the problem addressed in this section.

It is often asserted that the countries of Europe lack entrepreneurs. In a way, that is a strange assertion. I do not think that there is any country that does not have in abundance men with the qualities required of an entrepreneur.[3]

What is 'the price' of entrepreneurs? in Discussing the labour market, it was mentioned that there is not 'a' price of labour, but a conditional understanding about the evolution of what is expected to be a long-term relation. The price of entrepreneurs is even stranger: it is what society leaves them after subtracting from the value of sales the cost of the inputs used. Entrepreneurship is both a risky and a long-term commitment, so that the price is the expected present value of a stream of earnings. And surely, as for workers, the variance of that stream of earnings is as relevant to its recipients as the mathematical expectation.

Of course, the market for entrepreneurs adjusts. Commitment to a new venture is a decision that implies consideration of all alternatives, such as keeping a safe job in an existing enterprise or government or exploiting a safe niche of the market economy, investing in bonds to take advantage of high real rates of interest and the ease of tax cheating. It is often pointed out, usually as an argument for protectionism, that there are innumerable products which any country does not produce, for no obvious reason from the point of view of apparent comparative advantage, that the necessary labour and capital are there. The proper catalyst is not protection, but a man with the skills and knowledge needed to initiate profitable production; often the man probably exists, but does not come forward because starting a new venture seems too risky and not profitable enough. As the Italian black economy shows, entrepreneurs come forth when profits are adequate.

Adjustment of the market for entrepreneurs is probably slow. It takes time for new firms to develop and for their success to encourage more risk-taking, and for weeding out through competition those who are less effective as managers than they thought. The process may take as long as ten years: but it does not take generations.

The contention of this paper is that the market for entrepreneurs is distorted by various economic policies, but that it is not in disequilibrium. There are enough potential entrepreneurs in every country of Europe to generate the dynamism needed to re-establish adequate growth, but the profits that they can hope to get are not enough to encourage them to come forward; they are not unemployed, simply employed in other ways which happen to be more attractive. There are many ways in which a talented man can use his gifts.

Business has become more risky as the earnings of workers have become safeguarded more effectively through legislation: that relation is as direct as that between an object and its reverse image in a mirror. That nowadays loss-making firms can often obtain subsidies does not reduce risks. Almost always, what the subsidies do is to prolong a process of slow death: a clean bankruptcy would often have been more advantageous to the owner.

Everywhere in Europe also, the stability of institutions is not assured as it was in happier times. European governments are obviously at a loss about the right way to cope with today's economic difficulties; voters are unhappy with their performance, voting one party in with a big majority and voting it out four year later equally convincingly; strange recipes are advocated, which could conceivably be implemented as a result of another electoral upset. 'Exceptional taxes' have become customary, and are often meant to convince trade unions to accept wage moderation by showing them that the rich are being hit too. Deep institutional change is perhaps at hand: that possibility cannot be rejected as long as the continent's politico-economic system is so clearly malfunctioning.

While the variance of expected entrepreneurial gains is very large, the mean is probably low. There are, of course, no statistical series to measure how much potential entrepreneurs can hope to get. But the trend of profits has been negative for many years – the slide began before the recession. The shift became apparent at the time of the wave of strikes in the late 1960s and early 197s, which suggests that it reflects the rising bargaining strength of workers discussed earlier. Rightly or wrongly, there is widespread expectation that any reduction in the unemployment rate would generate widespread demands for higher wages. Even if the expectation is wrong, the fact that it is so prevalent reduces the present value of future earnings of entrepreneurs: 'the price' which influences their supply.

Marginal tax rates on high incomes are far higher by and large than in the 1960s. A last negative factor is the bias of governments in favour of large firms, with their policital strength, their willingness to keep them going with subsidies at any cost, whatever the impact on smaller, more efficient producers. It would be easy to draw up pages of examples; the present debate over the rationalisation of steel policy is as good as illustration as any, with the Federal Republic of

Germany letting the entrepreneurial Korff conern go under and subsidising inefficient Saarstahl, Italy fighting hard to be allowed to close efficient small mills to preserve inefficient plants near Naples and Genoa, the United Kingdom reserving its enormous subsidies to British Steel and letting small private mills sink or swim. A similar picture could be constructed for the computer industry, with a list of the huge amounts wasted in subsidies to large enterprises with very limited results, and very limited help to the industry's small entrepreneurial firms.

4 THE MARKET FOR GOVERNMENT ASSISTANCE

Next to that for labour, the biggest market in Europe has come to be what economists are beginning to call the market for government assistance. The totals are formidable indeed. Industrial subsidies typically amount to 5 to 7 per cent of industrial value added: they have gone up to 15 per cent of that aggregate in Sweden in some years. These figures are incomplete: covert subsidies should be added, extended via tax rebates, social security tax forgiveness, and other devices. A second type of government assistance is extended via tariff and non-tariff barriers, the latter being by far the larger. The tariff equivalent of import controls under the Multifibre Arrangement amounts to 50 to 100 per cent for many goods; informal cartelisation arrangements in the EC keep automobile prices and those of consumer electronics products as much as 50 to 60 per cent higher than the prices paid in other EC countries. Agricultural protection exceeds 100 per cent for many products. Steel and automobile prices are kept above the world level by voluntary export restraint arrangements with suppliers. The margin of protection on public procurement is, according to observers, as high as 50 to 60 per cent in many cases. No one has to my knowledge added up the numbers for Europe (such a calculation by Magee exists for the United States). But it is clear that the totals would be formidable indeed.

Economics has long treated the decisions to grant protection as though they were exogenous, the only problem being to assess their effect on the economy. This is clearly unsatisfactory, given their large impact on the distribution of incomes. Our discipline has taught us that if there is money to be earned, economic agents will struggle to get it, spending money for that purpose until the marginal cost equals the marginal revenue earned. European government assistance is a richer source of wealth than the Klondyke gold miners ever dreamed of: why should it be less an object of greed than gold mines? Obviously, economic analysis of market imperfections is incomplete unless it considers the costs and benefits of the lobbying activities undertaken to influence policy decisions.

The market for government assistance is a market of an unusual kind. It is well to describe its peculiarities.

Assistance is supplied by politicians (some authors also consider the role of bureaucrats), who balance the losses and gains in votes from yielding to the demands for protection of the various lobbies. The latter represent producers mainly (see below), and balance the marginal income gains secured through the assistance procured with the marginal cost of the required lobbying. The third group of agents are, of course, the voters, whose decisions ultimately decide the outcome of the process.

The 'price' on the market for government assistance is high indeed; for the producers, the amounts involved are huge; for the politician what is at stake is political power. Yet nothing useful is produced: in fact the 'product' is a bad, not a good. Bhagwati (1982) stresses this by speaking of directly unproductive activities, suggesting that the acronym DUP, to be pronounced 'dupe', characterises well what is taking place. The driving force is the greed for rents (Krueger, 1974), but society suffers a double loss. A first component of the loss is the resources used up in lobbying for assistance – which represent much more than the visible cost of the overt lobbies. Like tax cheating and the black economy, political lobbying has to be discreet to be effective. The protection secured is a source of misallocation of resources, which is far from negligible given the amount of assistance granted, often as large as most of the value added of a sector or its total wage bill. The cost of this resource misallocation should be added to that of the lobbying.

In brief, DUP activities are costly efforts to make the market function badly. The analogy drawn above with the Klondyke gold rush is perhaps appropriate. The miners got rich, but all that the world got was inflation.

That such a thing can happen is itself a surprise for the economist, which requires an explanation. If the political process worked perfectly, it could generate only Pareto optimal patterns of production and consumption. Any inefficient pattern would be transformed by common agreement into an efficient one, to the benefit of all concerned. It was Downs (1957) who pointed out many years ago that this is unlikely to take place if, as so often happens, the cost of what a few gain is distributed over a very large number of persons, for each of whom the loss is so small that it is not worthwhile to do something about it. Only the first cares enough to make the effort to understand the implications of the measures taken, and they will tailor them both to maximise their gains and to make them so obscure that others will be unable to understand their implications easily. The losers will be passive.

What about adjustment in the market for government assistance? As stressed by Usher (1981), there is a basic problem of instability involved in any democratic redistribution of incomes. An optimal coalition should be just large enough – half the voters plus one ideally – and take everything from the minority. But it is not viable, as the voters left out can always form another winning majority by offering to just one member of the first coalition just enough to convince him to join them. Reality is not so stark as this reasoning implies, but observation does suggest that a heavy involvement in redistribution of incomes through assistance and other schemes is a cause of instability of democratic systems: and the more voters understand what is happening and act accordingly, the more unstable they become. It is, for example, assumed too easily that the 'poor' can form a majority automatically, because they are many and the rich are few; but electors above the median can band with the median voter to win an election – and something like that has happened of late in a number of countries.

In practice, however, this instability is limited by the fact that coalitions cannot form arbitrarily. There has to be a nucleus, which for lobbies is often a professional association created for other purposes. Olson (1965) has stressed that the gains sought by interest groups have the character of public goods: all butter producers in the European Community benefit from the high price granted by the Common Agricultural Policy, whether they contributed to lobbying efforts or not. Effective coalitions have to rely on loyalties that take time to develop (for example, it took time for the textile and clothing interests to learn to work together in the UK and for the synthetic fibre producers to decide to put their full backing behind downstream users of fibres (Cable and Rebelo, 1980)).

The world of interest groups is more lumpy therefore than envisgated in Usher's reasoning sketched above, but the latter is not irrelevant. The AFL-CIO can decide not to support a democratic candidate to punish statements which he has made, or a farmers' group might decide not to put its weight behind a candidate of the right in France; jugglings of traditional alliances do occur. Lumpiness also implies that the market for assistance is not a perfect market, but one in which power meets power. Tumlir and Wolf (1983) stressed, for example, that in the recent steel negotiations between the USA and the European Community, the Reagan administration had as much trouble negotiating with steel interests as with the Community.

The other implication of Olson's remark (it is the implication which he stresses) is that it takes a long time for interest groups to form and to become effective: 'adjustment on the market for government assistance' is slow. Likewise, the interests groups once formed, cannot easily be undone. The loyalties formed tend to be strong and lasting. The interest groups become so enmeshed in the country's political life that no political surgery could sever the links. Like a drug, assistance is addictive; fat men don't like to run and become fatter, and assisted industries become inefficient as uncompetitive producers are not weeded out by competition, generating a ratchet mechanism in which assistance granted cannot be removed, and a further escalation of protection becomes unavoidable. The European Community's steel policy is a beautiful example of this, which merits study by all those interested in the topic.

5 CONCLUSION

A friend from an Asian country has made a habit of joking about the contrast between the 'old men' which the countries of Europe have become, compared with the 'young men' which the countries of his group represent. Certainly, the last decade does suggest that our countries suffer from the ills of old age, which seem to have struck even those of Southern Europe which reached an industrialised status rather later than the rest. The United States appears to have retained a vitality which our countries have lost.

In this paper I have set out, in a way that will hopefully provoke discussion, the idea that the cause of this loss of vitality is a breakdown of the adjustment process of key markets. In brief

— The labour market adjusts only weakly to market forces; there has been a shift in the balance of forces which has increased dramatically the 'natural unemployment rate' compatible with price stability.

— Various policy measures have unwittingly driven the price of entrepreneurs too low, and its variance too high. A shortage has developed, akin to the housing shortages in countries which have implemented rent controls.

— The growth of DUP activities has led not only to considerable waste, but to a deterioration of the ability of all markets to adjust, as government assistance has become a generally used substitute for adjustment. To some extent, this has been accompanied by a perversion of the democratic system, the functioning of which has come to be dominated more and more by the struggles of interest groups in favour of their members.

NOTES

1. This way of looking at things, which inspired for example the work on *non-tâtonnement* theory and the more recent research of fix-price equilibria is currently out of fashion among economists across the Atlantic, who prefer to think that at each point in time, agents act optimally, subject to existing contracts and the information available to them. Since contracts and the information gathered are themselves subject to utility and profit-maximising calculations, this way of looking at things is not best suited as the basis of a paper that is concerned with the reasons why some countries adjust better than others.
2. Theoretically, *tâtonnement* and *non-tâtonnement* process can be unstable, as Scarf (1960) and others have shown. I cannot see that this work has led to useful insights about the functioning of the real world, and will therefore assume stability.
3. I am aware that there is a risk of overdramatisation in the emphasis in this section on the role of the individual entrepreneur, to the extent of making him a unique and rather peculiar commodity. There is entrepreneurial activity in big business and in government. But it is true that much that is important and dynamic in market economies is created by men who spot an opportunity, and plunge in to take it in the hope of making a lot of money. Hopefully, the approach in this paper will help to focus thinking on the entrepreneurial function in general and how it may be promoted, instead of on piecemeal approaches that stress particular measures such as the creation of institutions to finance venture capitalists, and which are decided in ignorance of the fact that other aspects of economic policy have a negative impact which by far outweighs these measures.

REFERENCES

Azariadis, C. (1975), 'Implicit Contracts and Underemployment Equilibria' *Journal of Political Economy*, 83, December, pp. 1183–202.

Baldwin, R. E. (1982) 'The Political Economy of Protection', in Bhagwati, J. (ed.) *Import Competition and Adjustment*, (Chicago: University of Chicago Press).

Bhagwati, J. (1982) 'Directly-unproductive Profit-seeking (DUP) Activities', *Journal of Political Economy*, 90, no. 5, pp. 998–1002.

Cable, V. and Rebelo, I. (1980) 'Britain's Pattern of Specialization in Manufactured Goods with Developing Countries and Trade Protection', *World Bank Staff Working Paper*, no. 425.

Donges, J. B. and Spinanger, D. (1983) 'Intervention in Labour Markets–an Overview', Working Paper 175, *Kiel Institute for World Economy*.

Downs, A. (1957) *An Economic Theory of Democracy* (New York: Harper & Row).

Giersch, H. (1981) 'Aspects of Growth, Structural Change, and Unemployment–a Schumpeterian Perspective' in Giersch, H. (ed.) *Macroeconomic Policies for Growth and Stability: a Schumpeterian Perspective* (Tübingen: J. C. B. Mohr).

Hall, R. E. (1980) 'The Importance of Lifetime Employment in the US Economy', *National Bureau of Economic Research* Working Paper 560.

Hicks, J. R. (1974) *The Crisis of Keynesian Economics*, Chapter 3 (New York: Basic Books).

Krueger, A. (1974) 'The Political Economy of Rent Seeking', *American Economic Review*, 64, June, pp. 291–303.

Olson, M. (1965) *The Logic of Collective Action* (Cambridge: Cambridge University Press).

Olson, M. (1982) *The Rise and Decline of Nations–Economic Growth, Stagflation, and Social Rigidities* (New Haven: Yale University Press).

Sachs, J. D. (1979) 'Wages, Profits, and Macroeconomic Adjustment: a Comparative Study', *Brookings Papers on Economic Activity* no. 2.

Scarf, H. (1960) 'Some Examples of Global Instability of Competitive Equilibrium', *International Economic Review*, 1/3 Sept.

Tumlir, J. and Wolf, M. (1983) 'The Way Back to Sustained Growth', *The World Economy*, vol. 6 no. 2, June, pp. 106–22.

Usher, D. (1981) *The Economic Prerequisites to Democracy* (Oxford: Blackwell).

10 Trends in International Trade in Manufactured Goods and Structural Change in the Industrial Countries

Béla Balassa[1]
with the assistance of Kenneth Meyers
JOHNS HOPKINS UNIVERSITY

This paper will examine recent trends in manufactured goods between the industrial and the developing countries and will indicate the implications of these trends for structural change in the industrial countries. It will update and extend earlier papers by the author, which dealt with the experience of the years 1973–8 (Balassa, 1979a, 1980a and 1981b). The present paper will cover the period 1973–81, with consideration given to changes during the sub-periods 1973–8 and 1978–81, each of which began with an oil shock, followed by a world recession.

Section 1 of the paper will provide information on changes over time in the current dollar value of trade in manufactured goods between the industrial and the developing countries. It will further analyse the trends in the volume of trade in manufactured goods, and its relationship with economic activity, in the two groups of countries. Finally, the relative importance of trade with the developing countries for the manufacturing sector of the industrial nations, and changes thereof, will be indicated.

The commodity composition of trade in manufactured goods between the industrial and the developing countries will be the subject of Section 2 of the paper. It will examine the changing importance of trade with the developing countries for the manufacturing sector of the industrial nations in a seven-commodity group breakdown. The discussion will also cover the employment effects of trade in manufactured goods as well as its conformity to the comparative advantage of the two groups of countries. The paper will conclude with policy recommendations that aim at promoting international trade and structural change.

For the purposes of the statistical analysis, industrial countries have been defined to include the United States, Canada, the European Common Market (EC),[2] the European Free Trade Association (EFTA)[3] and Japan; among developing countries, distinction has been made between OPEC[4] and non-OPEC countries. The two groupings exclude Southern Europe other than Greece and Portugal; Australia, New Zealand, and South Africa; and the centrally planned economies.

1 TRADE IN MANUFACTURED GOODS BETWEEN THE INDUSTRIAL AND THE DEVELOPING COUNTRIES

1.1 Changes in Export and Import Flows, 1973–81

The period beginning with the first oil shock saw considerable increases in the surplus of the industrial countries in their trade in manufactured goods[5] with the developing countries. In terms of current dollars, the surplus grew from $36 billion in 1973 to $114 billion in 1978 and, again, to $172 billion in 1981 (Table 10.1).

In 1981, over one-half of the surplus in this trade was with the OPEC countries. In that year, OPEC provided markets for two-fifths of the manufactured exports of the industrial nations to the developing countries, but supplied a negligible proportion of their imports of these commodities. The export share of the OPEC countries rose from one-fourth in 1973 to two-fifths in 1978 and stabilised afterwards.

In 1973, the industrial nations covered 43 per cent of their oil imports from OPEC by the exports of manufactured goods. This ratio rose to 62 per cent in 1978, but declined to 48 per cent in 1981. The increased coverage of oil imports by manufactured exports between 1973 and 1978 reflects the rise in the spending of oil revenues by OPEC, while the subsequent decline indicates delays in using increases in these revenues following the 1979–80 oil price rise.

The extent of coverage of oil imports by the exports of manufactured goods, and changes in this coverage over time, vary to a considerable extent among the industrial countries. Between 1973 and 1981, the ratio increased from 41 to 61 per cent in the European

Table 10.1 Trade between the industrial countries and the developing countries in manufactured goods (US$ billion)

Trading partner	United States			Canada			EC			EFTA			Japan			Industrial countries		
	Export	Import	Balance	Export	Import	Balance	Export	Import	Balance	Export	Import	Balance	Export	Import	Balance	Export	Import	Balance
Oil-exporting developing countries																		
1973	2.43	0.06	2.37	0.17	0.00	0.17	7.00	0.42	6.58	0.69	0.05	0.64	2.57	0.02	2.55	12.86	0.55	12.31
1974	4.28	0.10	4.18	0.31	0.00	0.31	11.63	0.42	11.21	1.19	0.07	1.12	5.16	0.03	5.13	22.59	0.62	21.95
1975	8.00	0.09	7.91	0.57	0.00	0.57	20.00	0.46	19.54	1.97	0.05	1.92	8.12	0.01	8.11	38.66	0.61	38.05
1976	9.90	0.09	9.81	0.75	0.01	0.75	23.10	0.53	22.57	2.80	0.06	2.74	8.93	0.02	8.91	45.49	0.71	44.78
1977	10.50	0.10	10.40	0.84	0.00	0.84	29.43	0.67	28.76	3.21	0.08	3.13	11.51	0.04	11.47	55.49	0.89	54.60
1978	11.97	0.14	11.83	1.04	0.00	1.04	34.56	1.11	33.45	3.72	0.09	3.63	13.57	0.05	13.52	64.09	1.39	62.70
1979	11.41	0.21	11.20	0.99	0.01	0.98	33.32	1.63	31.69	3.81	0.11	3.70	12.80	0.09	12.71	62.33	2.05	60.28
1980	13.38	0.23	13.15	1.14	0.01	1.13	42.12	1.80	40.32	4.91	0.15	4.76	17.72	0.11	17.61	79.27	2.30	76.97
1981	16.38	0.34	16.04	1.51	0.01	1.50	48.40	1.31	47.09	5.47	0.16	5.31	22.14	0.11	22.03	93.90	1.93	91.97
Oil-importing developing countries																		
1973	10.35	7.33	3.02	0.57	0.53	0.04	16.01	4.68	11.33	2.56	0.75	1.81	9.96	2.22	7.74	39.45	15.51	23.94
1974	16.10	9.73	6.39	0.87	0.76	0.11	23.03	5.83	17.20	3.54	1.01	2.53	14.90	2.52	12.38	58.44	19.85	38.59
1975	17.75	8.89	8.86	1.05	0.76	0.30	25.82	6.85	18.97	3.74	1.18	2.56	14.25	2.00	12.25	62.62	19.65	42.54
1976	18.25	12.95	5.30	1.05	1.21	-0.15	25.35	8.92	16.43	3.82	1.38	2.44	16.05	2.89	13.16	64.53	27.35	37.18
1977	18.84	15.61	3.23	1.08	1.16	-0.08	29.98	10.87	19.11	4.57	1.81	2.76	20.14	2.97	17.17	74.61	32.42	42.19
1978	23.54	20.93	2.61	1.24	1.27	-0.03	37.28	14.10	23.18	5.89	1.93	3.96	25.64	4.27	21.37	93.59	42.50	51.09
1979	32.33	25.75	6.47	1.67	1.72	-0.05	46.56	19.33	27.23	7.31	2.41	4.90	29.40	6.01	23.39	117.16	55.22	61.94
1980	42.36	29.38	12.98	2.38	1.77	0.61	53.11	23.52	29.59	8.14	3.21	4.93	35.23	5.73	29.50	141.22	63.61	77.61
1981	45.25	34.87	10.38	2.39	2.29	0.10	52.41	20.65	31.76	8.28	3.03	5.25	39.11	6.36	32.75	147.44	67.20	80.24
Developing countries together																		
1973	12.78	7.39	5.39	0.74	0.53	0.21	23.01	5.10	17.91	3.25	0.80	2.45	12.53	2.24	10.29	52.31	16.06	36.25
1974	20.38	9.83	10.55	1.18	0.76	0.42	34.66	6.25	28.41	4.73	1.08	3.65	20.06	2.55	17.51	81.03	20.47	60.54
1975	25.75	8.98	16.77	1.63	0.76	0.87	45.82	7.31	38.51	5.71	1.23	4.48	22.37	2.01	20.36	101.28	20.29	60.99
1976	28.15	13.04	15.11	1.82	1.22	0.60	48.45	9.45	39.00	6.62	1.44	5.18	24.98	2.91	22.07	110.02	28.06	81.96
1977	29.34	15.71	13.63	1.92	1.16	0.76	59.41	11.54	47.87	7.78	1.89	5.89	31.65	3.01	28.64	130.10	33.31	96.79
1978	35.51	21.07	14.44	2.28	1.27	1.01	71.84	15.21	56.63	9.61	2.02	7.59	39.21	4.32	34.89	157.68	43.89	113.79
1979	43.63	25.96	17.67	2.66	1.73	0.93	79.88	20.96	58.92	11.12	2.52	8.60	42.40	6.10	36.10	179.49	57.27	122.22
1980	55.74	29.61	26.13	3.52	1.78	1.74	95.23	25.32	69.91	13.05	3.36	9.69	52.95	5.84	47.11	220.49	65.91	154.58
1981	61.63	35.21	26.42	3.90	2.30	1.60	100.81	21.96	76.85	13.75	3.19	10.56	61.25	6.47	54.78	241.34	69.13	172.21

Source: GATT, *International Trade*, Geneva, various issues.

Note: Exports are expressed in fob prices, imports in cif prices, except for Canada and the United States where imports are also in fob prices.

Common Market and from 19 to 33 per cent in Canada; it remained practically unchanged in the European Free Trade Association (68 and 69 per cent) and in Japan (43 and 42 per cent); and it declined from 52 to 33 per cent in the United States.[6]

The results for the European Common Market were not, however, due to rapid increases of manufactured exports to OPEC; together with the United States, the EC was at the lower end of the range as far as the growth of these exports is concerned. But while the current dollar value of oil imports from OPEC rose more than tenfold in the United States, oil imports into the EC increased less than five times. In turn, EFTA and Japan expanded their manufactured exports *pari passu*, with an approximately eightfold rise in their oil imports from OPEC, and export increases of a similar magnitude were more than sufficient to compensate for the fivefold increase of oil imports into Canada.

In the trade of the industrial countries with the non-OPEC developing countries, changes in the ratio of their manufactured imports to the exports of these commodities are of interest. It can be seen in Table 10.1 that, for the industrial countries taken together, this ratio rose from 39 per cent in 1973 to 45 per cent in 1978. Nevertheless, given the small ratio in the initial year, the surplus of the industrial countries in manufactured trade with the non-OPEC developing countries grew from $24 billion in 1973 to $51 billion in 1978. The surplus increased further, to $80 billion in 1981, when the import-export ratio reached 46 per cent.

Import-export ratios in trade in manufactured goods with the developing countries increased in all industrial countries and country groups, the exception being Japan. While Japan was only slightly above the industrial country average in terms of the growth of manufactured exports to the non-OPEC developing countries, the increase in its imports of manufactured goods from these countries hardly exceeded one-half of the industrial country average. In turn, US manufactured exports to the non-OPEC developing countries grew more rapidly than those of Japan, but imports into the United States rose at double the Japanese rate. As a result, the US import-export ratio in manufactured trade with the non-OPEC developing countries increased from 71 per cent in 1973 to 77 per cent in 1981; by contrast, the ratio for Japan fell from 22 to 16 per cent.

In the same period, the ratio of the imports of manufactured goods to the exports of these commodities in trade with the non-OPEC developing countries rose from 29 to 39 per cent in the European

Common Market and from 29 to 37 per cent in the European Free Trade Association, reflecting below-average increases in their exports and roughly average changes in their imports. Finally, Canada had an approximate balance in its trade in manufactured goods with the non-OPEC developing countries throughout the period under consideration.

1.2 Trends in the Volume of Manufactured Trade and in the Gross Domestic Product

In Table 10.1, trade in manufactured goods between the industrial and the developing countries was reported in terms of current dollars. Table 10.2 provides data on this trade in terms of constant prices. It further provides information on the rate of increase of the gross domestic product in the industrial countries and on their 'apparent' income elasticities of import demand, defined as the ratio of the rate of growth of imports to that of the gross domestic product.[7]

The apparent income elasticity of demand for manufactured imports originating in the developing countries averaged 3.6 in the industrial countries during the 1963–73 period; the volume of imports into these countries rose at an average annual rate of 16.5 per cent, while their combined GDP grew at 4.6 per cent a year. The apparent income elasticity increased to 4.1 in 1973–8 as the rate of growth of imports was 10.2 per cent and that of GDP 2.5 per cent; it increased further to 4.2 per cent in 1978–81, when import growth was 8.4 per cent and GDP growth 2.0 per cent; and it averaged 4.1 for the entire 1973–81 period.

Considerable differences are observed, however, among the industrial countries and country groups. While Japan leads in both periods in terms of GDP growth, it had the lowest import growth rate in 1973–8 and the second lowest (next to the EC) in 1978–81. Correspondingly, Japan had by far the lowest income elasticity of import demand for manufactured goods originating from the developing countries. In fact, between 1973 and 1981, Japan's imports of manufactured goods from these countries increased hardly more than its gross domestic product.

The EC and EFTA had the highest income elasticities of import demand in 1973–8, but relatively low elasticities in 1978–81. In turn, the elasticity rose to a considerable extent in the United States between 1973–8 and 1978–81, approaching the EC average for the entire period. Increases also occurred in Canada, but the average for

Table 10.2 Change in the volume of trad in manufactured goods between industrial and developing countries and in the Gross Domestic Product of the industrial countries

	Exports to			Imports from all LDC	GDP per cent	Apparent income elasticity*
	OPEC	non-OPEC	all LDC			
		average annual rate of growth				
1963–73						
Industrial countries	–	–	8.2	16.5	4.6	3.6
1973–78						
United States	23.7	6.3	10.6	11.1	2.5	4.4
Canada	33.7	8.8	16.5	6.8	3.4	2.0
EC	23.3	6.2	12.5	12.1	2.1	5.8
EFTA	23.8	5.4	10.7	8.4	1.5	5.6
Japan	26.4	9.9	14.2	3.0	3.6	0.8
Industrial countries	24.2	7.2	12.5	10.2	2.5	4.1
1978–81						
United States	–1.3	10.6	6.9	10.5	1.6	6.6
Canada	2.5	13.9	8.2	13.6	2.0	6.8
EC	7.8	7.9	7.9	5.3	1.4	3.8
EFTA	8.5	6.8	7.5	8.6	2.6	3.3
Japan	10.3	7.9	8.8	6.6	4.1	1.6
Industrial countries	6.9	9.5	8.3	8.4	2.0	4.2
1973–81						
United States	13.7	7.9	9.2	10.8	2.2	4.9
Canada	21.0	10.7	13.3	9.3	2.9	3.2
EEC	17.2	6.8	10.8	9.5	1.8	5.3
EFTA	17.8	5.9	9.5	8.5	1.9	4.5
Japan	20.1	9.1	12.1	4.3	3.8	1.1
Industrial countries	17.4	7.1	11.7	9.5	2.3	4.1

*The apparent income elasticity has been defined as the ratio of the average annual rate of growth of imports to that of the gross domestic product.
Sources: 1963–73 and 1973–78: B. Balassa (1981b).
1978–81: Value of trade – GATT, *International Trade*, 1980/81 and 1981/82. unit values – Industrial countries: United Nations, *Monthly Bulletin of Statistics*; Developing countries: estimated from the export unit value indices of the principal developing country exporters of manufactured goods, accounting for 72 per cent of the total. Gross domestic product – World Bank economic and social data base.

the entire period was reduced by the low 1973–8 income elasticity of import demand.

Apparent income elasticities have also been calculated in regard to the developing countries' imports of manufactured goods from the industrial countries. In 1973–8, increases in GDP averaged 8.2 per cent in the OPEC countries, while the volume of imports grew at an average annual rate of 24.2 per cent, resulting in an income elasticity of 3.0. The corresponding figures for the non-OPEC developing countries were 4.1 and 7.2 per cent, with an income elasticity of 1.8.[8]

In 1978–81, however, the gross domestic product of the OPEC countries declined, reflecting in part the political events in Iran and in part the unfavourable economic developments that occurred in several large oil-exporting countries. During this period, the volume of imports of manufactured goods increased at an average annual rate of 6.9 per cent. In turn, imports grew by 9.5 per cent, and GDP increased 4.3 per cent a year in the non-OPEC developing countries, resulting in an apparent income elasticity of demand of 2.2.

A longer time perspective may be taken in regard to the combined manufactured imports of all developing countries from the industrial nations. In the 1963–73 period, the apparent income elasticity of demand for these imports was 1.3, with the gross domestic product and the volume of imports growing at average annual rates of 6.2 and 8.2 per cent respectively[9]. The elasticity rose to 2.4 in 1973–8 and increased again to 3.5 in 1978–81; GDP increased at an average rate of 5.3 per cent and the imports of manufactured goods from the industrial countries 12.5 per cent in the first sub-period, and at average rates of 2.4 and 8.3 per cent in the second.

A comparison of export and import volume growth rates is of further interest. In their trade in manufactured goods with the developing countries, the volume of the industrial countries' exports and imports rose at average annual rates of 8.2 and 16.5 per cent respectively, between 1963 and 1973. Average increases were 12.5 and 10.2 per cent a year in 1973–8, when manufactured exports to OPEC grew particularly rapidly.

The rate of increase of the industrial countries' exports of manufactured goods to the developing countries declined, however, in 1978–81, as the acceleration of the growth of exports to the non-OPEC developing countries did not compensate for the deceleration of short expansion to OPEC. The average volume growth rate of 8.3 per cent for the manufactured exports of the industrial nations to the developing countries approximately equalled their import growth rate of 8.4 per cent.

The conclusions are modified if value rather than volume data are compared. Thus, the current dollar value of manufactured exports from the industrial to the developing countries rose by 53 per cent between 1978 and 1981, while the imports of these commodities from the developing countries increased by 53 per cent.

The results reflect an improvement in the terms of trade of the developing countries in manufactured goods. The improvement occurred in 1981, when European countries did not raise their export prices in terms of domestic currency to offset fully the appreciation of the dollar, whereas developing country exporters, which generally link their currencies to the US dollar, continued to increase their prices in dollar terms.

1.3 Changes in the Relative Importance of Trade in Manufactured Goods between the Industrial and the Developing Countries

In the 1973 period, the developing countries assumed increased importance as markets for the manufactured exports of the industrial nations. Thus, it can be seen from Table 10.3 that their share in the extraregional exports of manufactured goods of the industrial countries rose from 37 per cent in 1973 to 47 per cent in 1978 and to 49 per cent in 1981.[10] And while data on average shares would seem to indicate a deceleration over time, incremental shares remained practically constant – 54 per cent in 1973–8 and 53 per cent in 1978–81.

The developing countries also assumed increased importance as sources of supply for manufactured goods imported by industrial countries; their share in the industrial countries' extra-regional imports of these commodities increased from 20 per cent in 1973 to 24 per cent in 1978 and to 25 per cent in 1981. Again, incremental shares showed little change; they were 29 per cent in 1973–8 and 27 per cent in 1978–81.

In 1973, the developing countries accounted for the largest share of extra-regional manufactured exports in the United States (42 per cent), with EFTA (31 per cent) at the lower end of the range. In turn, in 1981, these countries had the highest share in the extra-regional exports of the EC (54 per cent), followed by the United States (51 per cent), with Japan falling to last place (42 per cent). The results reflect differences in incremental export shares that were especially high in the EC (63 per cent) and much below average in Japan (44 per cent) during the period.

However, the United States retained first place as far as the relative importance of developing countries in the extra-regional imports of manufactured goods is concerned. The US import shares were 23 per cent in 1973 and 30 per cent in 1981, with an incremental share of 33 per cent. In turn, EFTA remained in last place, the relevant figures being 14, 19 and 21 per cent. Finally, the share of the developing countries in Japanese imports of manufactured goods rose between 1973 and 1978, but declined slightly afterwards as incremental import shares in 1978–81 did not exceed the average share at the beginning of the period (23 per cent).

International trade in manufactured goods increased more rapidly than manufacturing output in the industrial countries throughout the period under consideration. Correspondingly, the share of exports to the developing countries in the production of manufactured goods in the industrial countries increased even more than their share in the extra-regional exports of these countries. The relevant proportions were 2.9 per cent in 1973, 5.2 per cent in 1978, and 6.4 per cent in 1981. The deceleration in the rise of average shares notwithstanding, incremental shares rose from 8.5 per cent in 1973–8 and 11.3 per cent in 1978–81, averaging 9.5 per cent for the entire period (Table 10.3).

Similar trends are observed in regard to the share of imports from the developing countries in the consumption of manufactured goods in the industrial countries. These shares increased from 0.9 per cent in 1973 to 1.5 per cent in 1978 and to 2.0 per cent in 1981, with incremental shares being 2.4 per cent and 3.8 per cent in 1973–8 and 1978–81 respectively.

Exports to the developing countries had a higher than average share in the production, and lower than average share in the consumption, of manufactured goods in Japan. Developing countries made little headway in entering the Japanese market, with their share in the consumption of manufactured goods rising only from 0.7 per cent in 1973 to 1.0 per cent in 1981. During this period, their incremental share in consumption was 1.2 per cent in Japan, compared to a range of 3.1 to 3.5 per cent in the other industrial countries and country groups, excepting Canada.

As a result of these changes, in 1981 the developing countries had the highest share in the consumption of manufactured goods in the United States and EFTA (2.3 per cent), followed by the EC (2.0 per

Table 10.3 The relative importance for the industrial nations of trade in manufactured goods* with the developing countries**

	1973				1978				1981			
	$\frac{X_{LDC}}{X}$	$\frac{X_{LDC}}{P}$	$\frac{M_{LDC}}{M}$	$\frac{M_{LDC}}{C}$	$\frac{X_{LDC}}{X}$	$\frac{X_{LDC}}{P}$	$\frac{M_{LDC}}{M}$	$\frac{M_{LDC}}{C}$	$\frac{X_{LDC}}{X}$	$\frac{X_{LDC}}{P}$	$\frac{M_{LDC}}{M}$	$\frac{M_{LDC}}{C}$
United States	41.6	1.8	22.9	1.1	51.1	3.0	27.4	1.8	50.6	4.1	30.2	2.3
Canada	35.9	1.2	12.5	0.8	50.7	2.4	17.4	1.3	47.7	3.0	20.4	1.6
EC	37.3	3.7	18.1	0.9	49.8	6.8	23.3	1.6	54.4	8.3	24.4	2.0
EFTA	31.0	5.2	14.4	1.2	39.7	8.9	17.8	1.9	43.7	10.0	19.2	2.3
Japan	36.0	3.7	22.6	0.7	42.6	6.3	24.4	0.8	42.1	7.9	23.9	1.0
Industrial countries	37.4	2.9	19.7	0.9	47.4	5.2	24.4	1.5	49.0	6.4	25.5	2.0

	1973–8				1978–81				1973–81			
	$\frac{\Delta X_{LDC}}{\Delta X}$	ΔP	$\frac{\Delta M_{LDC}}{\Delta M}$	ΔC	$\frac{\Delta X_{LDC}}{\Delta X}$	ΔP	$\frac{\Delta M_{LDC}}{\Delta M}$	ΔC	$\frac{\Delta X_{LDC}}{\Delta X}$	ΔP	$\frac{\Delta M_{LDC}}{\Delta M}$	ΔC
United States	58.7	4.9	30.7	2.9	49.9	7.5	34.8	4.2	53.6	6.0	33.0	3.5
Canada	63.1	4.5	23.9	2.0	44.0	4.7	26.6	2.6	51.6	4.6	25.2	2.3
EC	59.1	11.5	27.2	2.6	70.8	17.2	21.7	4.3	62.9	13.1	26.8	3.1
EFTA	46.2	13.8	23.7	2.9	57.3	13.9	19.3	3.7	50.0	13.9	21.3	3.3
Japan	46.4	9.2	26.8	0.9	41.4	15.1	22.8	2.2	44.1	11.1	24.6	1.2
Industrial countries	54.4	8.5	28.6	2.4	52.5	11.3	27.2	3.8	53.6	9.5	27.7	2.9

*The definition of manufactured goods used here corresponds to that employed in trade statistics (SITC classes 5 to 8 less 68). For 1981 production figures had to be estimated on the basis of incomplete information.
**Explanation of symbols = X = exports, M = imports, P = production, C = consumption ($P+M-X$), LDC = developing countries.

cent) and Canada (1.6 per cent). In the same year, the developing countries provided markets for 10.0 per cent of manufacturing output in EFTA, 8.3 per cent in the EC, 7.9 per cent in Japan, 4.1 per cent in the United States, and 3.0 per cent in Canada.

1.4 Policy Implications of the Results

Changes in the manufactured imports of the OPEC countries are largely explained by the effects that the 1973–4 and 1979–80 oil price increases had on their foreign exchange revenue and by the speed at which increases in these revenues were translated into higher imports. Following the quadrupling of oil prices, the merchandise trade surplus of the OPEC countries increased from $21 billion in 1973 to $84 billion in 1974. It declined to $43 billion by 1978 as manufactured imports were catching up with the higher revenues. The OPEC surplus rose again to $113 billion in 1979 and to $168 billion in 1980, when oil prices increased two and a half times; it declines only to $120 billion in 1981, indicating the time-lag involved in adjusting to higher revenues.

Nevertheless, differences are observed within OPEC as the capital-surplus countries continued to accumulate reserves, while some other OPEC countries borrowed abroad in order to finance their ambitious development programmes. The non-OPEC developing countries also stepped up their foreign borrowing during the period under consideration, so as to finance their rising merchandise trade deficit, which grew from $15 billion in 1973 to $37 billion in 1978 and to $78 billion in 1981.

Foreign borrowing represented one of several possible policy responses of the non-OPEC developing countries to the external shocks they experienced in the form of the oil price increases of 1973–4 and 1979–80 and the ensuing world recessions. Other policy responses included export promotion, import substitution, and deflationary policies.

The observed increases in the apparent income elasticity of the import demand – defined as negative import substitution – more than offset the import effects of the decline in rates of economic growth in the non-OPEC developing countries, so that the rise of their imports accelerated. Also, while these countries increased their export market shares in manufactured goods, the net result was a rise in foreign borrowing as a proportion of imports.

Foreign borrowing made it possible for the non-OPEC developing countries to finance their growing deficit in manufactured trade with the industrial countries, notwithstanding their higher oil bill. This increase in turn benefited the industrial countries in a situation of underutilised capacity. Assuming that the increment in net exports, over and above what would have occurred if the 1973 ratio of net exports to production had remained unchanged, added to manufacturing output in the industrial countries, incremental output between 1973 and 1981 was 4.6 per cent larger than it would have been otherwise.[11]

The trade-induced rise in incremental output appears to have been the largest in the EC (7.2 per cent), followed by Japan (6.9 per cent), EFTA (6.6 per cent), with Canada (1.9 per cent) and the United States (1.6 per cent) at the other end of the scale. At the same time, these figures represent an underestimate, inasmuch as they do not allow for multiplier effects, and an overestimate, inasmuch as they do not take account of alternative uses of the capital outflow from the industrial countries in their own economies.

In turn, the observed rise in the industrial countries' income elasticity of demand for the imports of manufactured goods originating in the developing countries, and the increased developing country share in their consumption of these commodities, do not provide an indication of increased protectionism in the industrial countries.[12] Japan provides an exception, however, as it had by far the lowest income elasticity of demand for manufactured imports from the developing countries, and these countries had by far the lowest share in its domestic consumption of manufactured goods.

These results cannot be explained on the grounds that factor endowments are more similar between the developing countries and Japan than between the developing countries and other industrial countries. Although such might have been the case during the 1960s, the situation changed to a considerable extent afterwards. At the same time, with relatively high economic growth rates, Japan's factor endowment changed rapidly, and this should have led to rapid increases in imports from the developing countries if these imports had not been subject to restrictions.

This is not to say that the expansion of the developing countries' manufactured exports could be explained by demand considerations alone. In this regard, a statement made by the author concerning the 1973–8 period continues to apply:

While access to industrial country markets has provided opportunities for export expansion, the exports of manufactured goods from the developing countries had responded to the policies followed by these countries. A number of developing countries adopted an export-oriented strategy during the 1960s and have continued with this strategy after 1973. Available evidence suggests that countries following an export-oriented strategy were better able to surmount the adverse effects of the quadrupling of oil prices and the 1974–75 world recession than countries with an import-substitution orientation. (Balassa, 1981b, p. 267)

Developing countries following an export-oriented strategy also relied less on foreign borrowing than import substitution-oriented countries (Balassa, 1981a). In turn, with lower indebtedness, they escaped the difficulties that the latter group of countries experienced as world interest rates rose. Excessive foreign borrowing under import substitution orientation, then, helped the expansion of manufacturing output in the industrial countries in a situation of under-utilised capacity, but subsequently created difficulties for the borrowing countries themselves.

2 EFFECTS OF TRADE ON PRODUCTION, EMPLOYMENT, AND RESOURCE ALLOCATION

2.1 Recent Trends in the Trade of Individual Commodity Groups

We have seen that the developing countries assumed increased importance as markets for the industrial nations between 1973 and 1981. The same picture emerges in regard to individual commodity groups, for which comparable production and trade data are available for the entire period. They include iron and steel, chemicals and other semi-manufactures, engineering products, textiles, clothing, and other consumer goods. For all these commodity groups, the share of the developing countries in the extra-regional exports and in the production of the industrial countries rose between 1973 and 1978 and, again, between 1978 and 1981 (Table 10.4).

In 1973, the developing countries' share in the extra-regional exports of the industrial countries varied from 26 per cent in the other consumer goods category and 29 per cent in clothing to 42 per cent in chemicals and 43 per cent in textiles. The difference narrowed to a

Table 10.4 The relative importance for the industrial nations of trade in industrial commodity groups with the developing countries*

	1973				1978				1981			
	$\frac{X_{LDC}}{X}$	$\frac{X_{LDC}}{P}$	$\frac{M_{LDC}}{M}$	$\frac{M_{LDC}}{C}$	$\frac{X_{LDC}}{X}$	$\frac{X_{LDC}}{P}$	$\frac{M_{LDC}}{M}$	$\frac{M_{LDC}}{C}$	$\frac{X_{LDC}}{X}$	$\frac{X_{LDC}}{P}$	$\frac{M_{LDC}}{M}$	$\frac{M_{LDC}}{C}$
Iron and steel	41.0	3.5	10.7	0.4	44.8	5.0	11.6	0.5	49.7	6.5	16.1	1.0
Chemicals	42.2	3.4	11.2	0.4	45.5	4.6	12.1	0.6	47.5	4.9	13.7	0.7
Other semi-manufactures	36.7	1.1	34.0	1.0	50.7	2.5	38.1	1.6	53.0	3.0	34.8	1.5
Engineering products	36.6	3.7	9.9	0.5	48.2	7.0	15.1	1.0	48.9	8.7	16.2	1.5
Textiles	43.0	2.8	39.8	1.3	49.3	3.6	45.8	2.7	52.6	5.0	45.2	3.0
Clothing	28.7	0.9	63.3	6.0	40.8	1.7	69.1	10.9	46.5	2.6	73.8	14.4
Other consumer goods	26.2	1.2	27.7	1.4	41.2	2.3	37.0	2.4	46.2	3.3	44.4	3.3
Total manufacturing	37.4	2.9	19.7	0.9	47.4	5.2	24.4	1.5	49.0	6.4	25.5	2.0

	1973–8				1978–81				1973–81			
	$\frac{\Delta X_{LDC}}{\Delta P}$	$\frac{\Delta X_{LDC}}{\Delta MC}$	$\frac{\Delta M_{LDC}}{\Delta C}$	$\frac{\Delta M_{LDC}}{\Delta X}$	$\frac{\Delta X_{LDC}}{\Delta P}$	$\frac{\Delta X_{LDC}}{\Delta C}$	$\frac{\Delta M_{LDC}}{\Delta C}$	$\frac{\Delta M_{LDC}}{\Delta P}$	$\frac{\Delta X_{LDC}}{\Delta X}$	$\frac{\Delta X_{LDC}}{\Delta P}$	$\frac{\Delta M_{LDC}}{\Delta M}$	$\frac{\Delta M_{LDC}}{\Delta X}$
Iron and steel	47.6	7.3	11.5	0.7	64.8	17.5	25.4	4.8	54.3	10.0	18.9	1.8
Chemicals	47.8	5.9	12.7	0.7	51.9	5.8	15.8	1.0	49.7	5.8	14.3	0.9
Other semi-manufactures	61.5	6.5	42.3	3.4	58.0	5.2	22.0	1.1	60.0	5.9	35.3	2.3
Engineering products	55.7	11.2	19.0	1.6	50.4	15.9	18.0	3.8	53.4	12.8	18.5	2.3
Textiles	59.5	5.6	49.1	6.1	61.7	17.2	45.0	6.3	60.7	8.7	48.0	6.1
Clothing	50.0	3.2	73.3	19.6	56.3	12.2	84.5	41.5	53.1	5.2	77.8	25.5
Other consumer goods	53.2	3.6	43.4	3.5	54.9	7.8	63.6	7.5	54.1	4.9	51.9	4.7
Total manufacturing	54.4	8.5	28.6	2.4	52.5	11.3	27.2	3.8	53.6	9.5	27.7	2.9

*The classification system used corresponds to that applied in GATT, *International Trade*. For an explanation of symbols see Table 3.
Sources: see table 3

considerable extent between 1973 and 1981. Other consumer goods and clothing (46 per cent) remained at the lower end of the range; semi-manufactures joined textiles (53 per cent) at the upper end; and the developing countries came to account for 49 per cent of the industrial countries' extra of engineering products.

The share of exports to developing country markets in production in the industrial countries also increased in every commodity group. At the lower end of the range, this share rose from 0.9 to 2.6 per cent in the case of clothing, from 1.1 to 3.0 per cent for other semi-manufactures, and from 1.2 to 3.3 per cent for the other consumer goods category; at the upper end, the relevant shares were 3.4 and 4.9 per cent for chemicals, 3.5 and 6.5 per cent for iron and steel, and 3.7 and 8.7 per cent for engineering products. In the latter category, increases in exports to the developing countries provided 12.8 per cent of incremental output in the industrial countries between 1973 and 1981. Incremental shares varied from 4.9 per cent (other consumer goods) to 10.0 per cent (steel) in the other commodity groups.

The developing countries also increased their share in the extra-regional imports of the industrial countries in every commodity group between 1973 and 1981. While this share remained relatively low in engineering products (9.9 per cent in 1973 and 16.2 per cent in 1981), iron and steel (10.7 and 16.1 per cent) and chemicals (11.2 and 13.7 per cent), it increased from 39.8 to 45.2 per cent in textiles, from 63.3 to 73.8 per cent in clothing, and from 27.7 to 44.4 per cent in the other consumer goods category.

Imports from the developing countries, expressed as a percentage of consumption in the industrial countries, also rose in all commodity groups. Varying between 0.4 and 0.5 per cent in 1973, these imports reached 1.0 per cent of consumption in the case of iron and steel, 0.7 per cent for chemicals, and 1.5 per cent for engineering products in 1981. At the other end of the scale, the share of imports rose from 6.0 per cent to 14.4 per cent in the case of clothing, followed by textiles (1.3 and 3.0 per cent) and other consumer goods (1.4 and 3.3 per cent).

Clothing also leads in terms of incremental consumption shares (25.5 per cent between 1973 and 1981), followed by textiles (6.1 per cent) and other consumer goods (4.7 per cent). These results occurred, notwithstanding the continued operation of the Multifibre Arrangement and the restrictions imposed on some of the other consumer goods originating in the developing countries. Moreover, incremental shares doubled between 1973–8 and 1978–81 in the case of clothing and other consumer goods, exceeding the increases shown for total manufacturing, while they remained constant for textiles.

The next question concerns the extent to which changes in net exports in trade with the developing countries affected manufacturing output in the industrial countries. Under the assumption made earlier, the average 4.6 per cent increase in output between 1973 and 1981, associated with increases in the ratio of net exports to production, covers considerable differences among commodity groups. The resulting rise in incremental output appears to be the largest for engineering products (7.3 per cent) and iron and steel (5.1 per cent), followed by chemicals (2.9 per cent), other semi-manufactures (2.5 per cent), and textiles (1.1 per cent). In turn, no changes occurred in other consumer goods, while trade in clothing with the developing countries appears to have reduced incremental output by 15.2 per cent.

2.2 Employment Effects

Trade in manufactures also affects employment in the industrial nations. Table 10.5 shows that, during the period under consideration, average labour input coefficients were two-fifths higher in the industrial countries' imports than in their exports of manufactured goods in trade with the developing countries. The ratios exhibited considerable stability over time; differences among industrial countries and country groups were relatively small. The exception is Canada, where labour input coefficients were lower for exports, and higher for imports, than the industrial country average.

The results reflect inter-industry differences in labour input coefficient, calculated from the 1975 US Census of Manufacturing in a eleven-commodity group breakdown by subdividing the engineering product group into five categories (machinery for specialised industry, office and telecommunications equipment, road motor vehicles, other machinery and transport equipment and household appliances). Labour input coefficients, expressed in man-years per million dollars of output, are lower than the manufacturing average for engineering products (18.6), with a range from 6.9 for motor vehicles to 21.0 for household appliances; other semi-manufactures (18.0); iron and steel (15.9); and chemicals (13.2). By contrast, labour input coefficients exceed the manufacturing average in the case of clothing (40.6), other consumer goods (28.9), and textiles (26.7).[13]

Table 10.5 Employment and capital/labour coefficients in the trade of the industrial countries with the developing countries in manufactured goods

	E/O		PK/e		Stocks HK/E		Stocks TK/E		Flows PK/E		Flows HK/E		Flows TK/E	
	X	M	X	M	X	M	X	M	X	M	X	M	X	M
USA														
1973	18.4	25.5	12.8	9.8	28.1	25.0	40.9	34.8	9.0	6.7	9.4	8.0	18.4	14.7
1978	18.2	25.8	12.5	9.3	28.1	25.4	40.6	34.7	9.1	6.7	9.4	8.1	18.5	14.8
1981	18.5	25.3	12.5	9.3	28.1	25.9	40.6	35.2	9.0	6.8	9.4	8.2	18.4	15.0
Canada														
1973	17.0	28.0	14.0	8.8	27.9	22.0	41.9	30.8	9.0	5.8	9.4	7.3	18.4	13.1
1978	15.5	27.4	13.8	8.6	27.5	22.7	41.3	31.3	9.7	6.3	9.8	7.4	19.5	13.7
1981	15.4	26.7	13.0	9.0	26.7	24.0	39.7	33.0	9.4	6.4	9.4	7.7	18.8	14.1
EC														
1973	18.0	25.6	13.7	11.4	27.3	21.8	41.0	33.2	9.2	6.6	9.3	7.5	18.5	14.1
1978	18.4	25.7	12.8	10.5	27.5	22.8	40.4	33.3	8.6	6.6	9.3	7.7	17.9	14.3
1981	18.1	25.9	12.9	9.8	27.2	23.3	40.1	33.1	8.7	6.7	9.2	7.7	17.9	14.4
EFTA														
1973	18.7	23.9	13.2	11.1	28.5	19.6	41.7	30.7	9.0	7.1	9.2	6.9	18.2	14.0
1978	18.8	26.6	13.1	9.9	28.4	22.1	41.5	32.0	8.7	6.8	9.2	7.4	17.9	14.2
1981	18.7	26.4	13.0	9.9	28.0	22.5	41.0	32.4	8.8	6.9	9.2	7.5	18.0	14.4
Japan														
1973	18.5	25.4	14.9	11.7	27.5	21.2	42.4	32.9	8.0	6.4	9.3	7.4	17.3	13.8
1978	17.8	25.6	13.8	11.7	28.3	23.0	42.1	34.7	8.3	7.2	9.5	7.8	17.8	15.0
1981	17.7	23.9	13.7	12.4	28.4	23.8	42.1	36.2	8.4	7.4	9.5	8.0	17.9	15.4
Industrial countries														
1973	18.2	25.6	13.7	10.6	27.6	23.2	41.3	33.8	8.8	6.6	9.3	7.7	18.1	14.3
1978	18.2	25.8	13.1	9.9	27.9	24.0	41.0	33.9	8.7	6.7	9.4	7.8	18.1	14.5
1981	18.2	25.5	13.1	9.8	28.0	24.7	41.1	34.5	8.8	6.8	9.4	8.0	18.2	14.8

Notes: X = exports, M = imports, E = employment, O = production, PK = physical capital, HK = human capital, TK = total capital. For explanation of 'stocks' and 'flows', see text.

Sources: Balassa (1979a) and (1979b).

The observed differences in average labour input coefficients for the industrial countries' manufactured exports and imports in trade with the developing countries were more than offset by their surplus in this trade, resulting in a net gain in employment.[14] The estimated gain was 701,000 jobs in 1973, 1,439,000 jobs in 1978, and 1,474,000 jobs in 1981 (Table 10.6); the slowdown after 1978 is explained by the decline in export-import ratios in trade with the developing countries.

Among the industrial countries and country groups, employment gains decreased after 1978 in the EC and EFTA, they underwent little change in Canada, while continued increases were shown in Japan and, in particular, in the United States. Nevertheless, in 1981, net employment gains were by far the largest in the European Common Market (710,000) and Japan (523,000), followed by the United States (142,000) and the European Free Trade Association (98,000), with Canada showing an approximate balance. The relatively low US net employment gain, compared to its trade balance in manufactures with the developing countries, is explained by its low export-import ratio. The same considerations account for the lack of a net employment gain in Canada.

Among individual commodity groups, iron and steel, chemicals, other semi-manufactures, all categories of engineering products, and textiles exhibited net employment gains in the industrial countries. These gains increased between 1973 and 1978 and showed litle change afterwards, the exception being the 'other semi-manufactures' category, which experienced large increases in net employment gains as the trade surplus of the industrial countries increased to a considerable extent.

In 1981, net losses in employment were shown in only one commodity group, clothing, with practically no net effect for the other consumer goods category. In the case of clothing, net employment losses for the industrial countries, due to their trade with the developing countries, were estimated at 163,000 in 1973, 279,000 in 1978, and 283,000 in 1981.

To put these figures into perspective, they should be compared with actual employment statistics. The results show that, in 1981, net employment losses due to trade with the developing countries did not reach 3 per cent of employment in the textiles, clothing, and leather products sector of the indusrial countries.[15] The ratio was the highest for the United States, but it did not exceed 6 per cent in this case either.

Table 10.6 Employment effects of trade in manufactured goods with the developing countries (thousands of jobs)

	United States			Canada			EC			EFTA			Japan			Industrial countries		
	1973	1978	1981	1973	1978	1981	1973	1978	1981	1973	1978	1981	1973	1978	1981	1973	1978	1981
Iron and steel	7	3	3	1	1	1	33	57	54	2	3	3	54	75	74	97	139	135
Chemicals	32	56	68	1	2	2	63	92	91	8	12	12	19	28	23	123	190	196
Other semi-manufacturers	−8	−9	0	2	3	4	9	27	35	6	18	15	−2	13	20	7	52	74
Engineering products	118	239	286	8	14	15	302	622	553	48	86	79	149	351	368	625	1312	1301
of which:																		
Machinery for specialised industries	47	129	155	2	3	4	131	258	222	15	28	28	45	99	105	240	517	514
Office and telecommunications equipment	4	−6	−14	2	1	0	19	32	27	6	8	7	12	27	31	43	62	51
Road motor vehicles	10	19	19	1	4	4	25	42	47	1	3	3	11	32	38	48	100	112
Other machinery and equipment	70	119	147	4	8	9	121	283	255	16	35	32	56	145	127	267	590	570
Household appliances	−13	−22	−21	−1	−2	−2	6	7	2	10	12	9	25	48	67	27	43	54
Textiles	−9	−3	1	−3	−2	−2	4	1	7	0	2	3	36	37	45	28	35	54
Clothing	−72	−134	−138	−8	−12	−12	−53	−92	−94	−9	−16	−17	−21	−25	−22	−163	−279	−283
Other consumer goods	−37	−71	−78	−3	−5	−7	20	56	64	1	1	3	3	9	15	−16	−10	−3
Total manufacturing	31	81	143	−2	−1	1	378	763	710	56	106	98	238	488	523	701	1439	1474

Sources: Table 10.5 and GATT, *International Trade*, 1980–1 and 1981–2.

Alternatively, one may compare changes in trade-induced employment losses with changes in employment. Between 1973 and 1980, employment in the textiles, clothing and leather products sector of the industrial countries declined by 1.7 million, compared to an increase of 0.1 million in net employment losses due to trade with the developing countries. In none of the industrial countries and country groups did the increase in the trade-induced loss in employment reach 15 per cent of the decline in employment in this sector.

2.3 Comparative Advantage in Trade in Manufactured Goods

We have considered the effects of trade in manufactured goods between the industrial and the developing countries on employment in the former group of countries. Next, the factor intensity of this trade will be examined, with separate consideration given to physical and human capital.

Physical capital-labour and human capital-labour ratios have been derived from US data with calculations made in 'stock' and 'flow' terms. The former have been defined as the value of fixed capital per worker (physical capital) and the discounted value of the difference between the average wage and the unskilled wage (human capital), and the latter as non-wage value added per worker (physical capital) and the average wage (human capital).

Table 10.5 provides information on average capital-labour ratios for the exports and imports of manufactured goods in trade between the industrial and the developing countries. As is apparent from the table, capital-labour ratios are substantially higher for the exports than for the imports of the industrial countries. In 1973, the ratio for exports exceeded that for imports by 29 per cent for physical and by 19 per cent for human capital, utilising the stock measure, and by 33 per cent for physical and 21 per cent for human capital, utilising the flow measure.

Between 1973 and 1981, the aggregate ratios (physical and human capital combined) changed little for exports, and increased slightly for imports. The results were practically the same under the stock and the flow measures, with a 3 to 4 percentage points reduction in the difference in capital-labour ratios between exports and imports.

It appears, then, that trade in manufactured goods between the industrial and the developing countries conformed to their comparative advantage. While textiles may appear to be an aberrant case, it should be recognised that the industrial countries and, in particular, the United States export high-quality textiles and import low-quality textile products from the developing countries (Balassa, 1983).

By and large, similar results are obtained for the trade of individual countries and country groups with the developing countries; exceptions are Canada, whose exports tend to be relatively more capital-intensive compared to its imports from the developing countries, and EFTA, where the opposite is the case. In Canada, the high export share of the capital-intensive, natural resource-based other intermediate products category contributed to this result, while the EFTA countries are the most liberal among industrial countries in admitting labour-intensive manufactures from the developing countries.

The results changed little between 1973 and 1981. An exception is engineering products, where the developing countries increased their exports to a considerable extent. This change also conformed to the comparative advantage of the two groups of countries, with the developing countries gaining in the exports of labour-intensive radios and television sets as well as in exporting labour-intensive parts, components and accessories in the framework of the international division of the production process.

2.4 Policy Implications of the Results

The data show that the industrial countries tend to exchange manufactured goods intensive in physical and in human capital for products intensive in unskilled labour. Such an exchange apparently occurs through inter-industry as well as through intra-industry specialisation.

The large differences observed in capital-labour ratios among commodity groups are indicative of the mutual gains that the industrial and the developing countries can obtain through specialisation according to comparative advantage. This result is strengthened if account is taken of differences in capital-labour ratios within individual commodity groups. It receives further support if consideration is given to the high research intensity of the manufactured exports of the industrial countries.

Apart from traditional gains owing to differences in factor proportions, the industrial countries derive benefits from trade in manufactured goods with the developing countries through the exploitation of economies of scale. This source of gain has assumed increased importance as the share of the developing countries in the domestic production of manufactured goods in the industrial countries has risen. Apart from economies of scale in production, gains are obtained through economies of scale in research inasmuch as a larger scale volume permits reducing unit expenditure on research and development.

Further gains can be obtained through intra-industry trade in the form of horizontal or product specialisation, such as the exchange of capital-intensive for labour-intensive textiles, and vertical specialisation in the framework of the international division of the production process, involving the importance of labour-intensive parts, components and accessories from the developing countries. Horizontal specialisation permits the reduction of costs by concentrating on fewer commodities, while vertical specialisation reduces costs through the purchase of lower-priced inputs. Finally, increased competition from developing countries provides inducements for technological improvements, as has been the case in the textile industry.

The developing countries, too, enjoy gains from improved resource allocation, the exploitation of economies of scale, and competition through inter-industry and intra-industry trade in manufactured goods with the industrial countries. They enjoy the further benefit of procuring sophisticated machinery and equipment in a world of rapidly changing technology.

International specialisation in manufactured goods also affects employment. While at the actual level of trade the industrial countries have a net employment gain, a balanced expansion of exports and imports would have negative employment effects for them. This is because labour input coefficients are, on average, two-fifths higher for the imports than for the exports of the industrial countries in their trade in manufactured goods with the developing countries.

Nevertheless, projections made earlier by the author indicate that the net employment effects of the expansion of trade in manufactured goods are likely to be negligible. This estimate was made for the 1976–86 period on the assumption that the exports of manufactured goods from the industrial to the developing countries would rise at an average annual rate of 5.7 per cent, and their imports at a rate of 12.6 per cent (Balassa, 1979a).

According to the same article, the expansion of trade in manufactured goods would involve the upgrading of the labour force, with increases in the number of professional, technical and highly skilled workers, and a decline in unskilled and semi-skilled workers in the industrial countries. The upgrading of the labour-force, in turn, would contribute to the increases in the productivity and higher rates of economic growth.

3 CONCLUSIONS

This paper has examined the increased importance of the developing countries as markets for the manufactured goods produced in the industrial nations. In particular, in the 1973–81 period, developing countries accounted for one-half of the increment in the extra-regional exports of manufactured goods by the industrial countries and provides markets for one-tenth of the increment in their manufacturing output. These shares were higher than the average for engineering products, where economies of scale are of especial importance.

In turn, the industrial countries increased their imports of manufactured goods from the developing countries at four times the rate of growth of their GDP. In the 1973–81 period, the developing countries provided over one-fourth of the increment in the extra-regional imports, and three per cent of the increment in manufacturing consumption of the industrial countries. Their share was the highest in clothing, accounting for over three-quarters of the increase in extra-regional imports and for one-quarter of the rise in consumption.

It further appears that increases in the industrial countries' net exports of manufactured goods in trade with the developing countries had multiplier effects on their economies in a situation of underutilised capacity. In turn, the rapid rise of their manufactured exports to the industrial countries had favourable effects on the growth process of the developing countries.

The two groups of countries derive further benefits from improved resource allocation, economies of scale, and increased competiton through inter-industry and intra-industry trade in manufactured goods. In the industrial countries, this trade contributes to structural change, involving the exchange of capital for labour, the upgrading of the labour force, and the expansion of research-intensive activities.

It follows that trade liberalisation is in the mutual interests of the industrial and the developing countries. In particular, the reduction of trade barriers in the industrial countries becomes an agent for structural change, which is, in turn, a condition for increases in productivity and higher rates of economic growth.

The lowering of trade barriers would also permit increased trade among the developing countries which is presently limited by these barriers. Inter-regional trade may occur between countries at the same level of development as well as between the newly-industrialising and the less developing countries. Also, if appropriate policies are followed, the less developing countries can replace the newly industrialising countries in exporting simple, unskilled labour-intensive products, while the latter group of countries can upgrade and diversify their exports.

NOTES

1. Professor Balassa alone is responsible for the opinions expressed in the paper, which should not be interpreted to reflect the views of the World Bank.
2. Belgium-Luxembourg, Denmark, Germany, France, Greece, Ireland, Italy, the Netherlands and the United Kingdom. Data for 1981–3 include Greece; this causes little distortion in the results as Greece accounts for less than 1 per cent of EC trade in manufactured goods.
3. Austria, Finland, Iceland, Norway, Portugal, Sweden and Switzerland.
4. Algeria, Ecuador, Gabon, Indonesia, Iran, Iraq, Kuwait, Libyan Arab Jamahiriya, Nigeria, Qatar, Saudi Arabia, United Arab Emirates and Venezuela.
5. Manufactured goods have been defined as commodity classes 5 to 8 in the UN Standard International Trade Classification, less non-ferrous metals (68). The same definition is used throughout the paper.
6. Data on oil imports are provided in GATT, *International Trade*, Geneva, various issues.
7. The expression 'apparent' income elasticity is used to refer to the fact that this measure neglects the effects of changes in relative prices on the volume of imports. Nor does the measure consider the interactions of changes in demand and supply.
8. Estimates based on United Nations, *Monthly Bulletin of Statistics*, various issues, and World Bank economic and social data base.
9. Estimated by regression analysis from data published in United Nations, *Monthly Bulletin of Statistics* and *Yearbook of National Accounts Statistics*.
10. Extra-regional trade has been defined to exclude trade in manufactured goods between the United States and Canada, one-third of which is exempt from duty under the US-Canadian Automotive Agreement, while a substantial part of the remainder represents intra-company transactions, as well as trade within the European free trade area that encompasses the EC and EFTA. All data are in current prices.
11. The calculations have been made by relating the difference between the incremental ratio of net exports to output in the 1973–81 period and the

average ratio in 1973 to the increment in output between 1973 and 1981. Needless to say, the results are subject to qualifications due to the use of current price data.
12. For supporting evidence, see Balassa (1980b).
13. The calculations reflect the assumption that the same coefficients apply to the other industrial countries and that they are invariant within a particular category, irrespective of whether the products are exported or replace imports. Employment gains and losses have been calculated by adjusting the coefficients for changes in industrial prices.
14. The calculation assumes constant labour input coefficients and disregards the loss in employment associated with the outflow of capital.
15. Employment data pertain to 1980 and originate in OECD, *Labour Force Statistics, 1961–1980*. While data on the employment effects of trade are not available for leather products, this represents a relatively small fraction of the total.

REFERENCES

Balassa, B. (1979a) 'The Changing International Division of Labour', *Banca Nazionale del Lavoro Quarterly Review*, no. 130, pp. 243–85.
— (1979b) 'A "Stages" Approach to Comparative Advantage', in Adelman, I. (ed.) *Economic Growth and Resources*, vol. 4, *National and International Issues* (London, Macmillan), pp. 121–56.
— (1980a) 'Prospects for Trade in Manufactured Goods between Industrial and Developing Countries, 1978–90', *Journal of Policy Modelling*, vol. 2, no. 3, pp. 437–53.
— (1980b) 'The Tokyo Round and the Developing Countries', *Journal of World Trade Law*, vol. 14, no. 2, pp. 243–85.
— (1981a) 'Adjustment to External Shocks in Developing Countries', in Csikós-Nagy, B. and Hague, D. (eds) *The Economics of Relative Prices*, International Economic Association (London: Macmillan).
— (1981b) 'Trade in Manufactured Goods: Pattern of Change', *World Development*, vol. 9, pp. 263–75.
— (1983) 'Industrial Prospects and Policies in Developed Countries' in Machlup, F., Fels, G. and Muller-Groeling, H. (eds) *Reflections on a Troubled World Economy*, Essays in Honor of Herbert Giersch (London: Trade Policy Research Centre), pp. 257–78.

11 On Using Applied General Equilibrium Models for Analysing Structural Change

P. B. Dixon
INSTITUTE OF APPLIED ECONOMIC AND SOCIAL RESEARCH, UNIVERSITY OF MELBOURNE

1 INTRODUCTION

Structural change refers to changes in the industrial composition of the GDP, the regional allocation of economic activity and the occupational composition of the demand for labour. Structural changes are caused by, among other things, changes in tariffs, capital accumulation, technical change, changes in consumer tastes and changes in world commodity prices. Structural changes are of little concern during periods of overall growth when all sectors of the economy are achieving positive growth rates and intersectoral shifts of existing resources are not required. However, in a period of low overall growth, structural change may require committed resources to be transferred to alternative uses. These transfers may involve becoming idle for lengthy periods, imposing costs on the possessors of particular labour skills and on the owners of specific types of capital. In these circumstances, we often find strong resistance to structural change from trade unions and capitalists in threatened industries. It is in the interests of these groups to overstate the effects of structural change on their members. The result is often panicky moves towards protectionism and other undesirable policies.

It is important, therefore, that economists provide convincing measures of the extent of the structural changes that are likely to follow various policy initiatives and other exogenous shocks which affect national economic activity. For example, it is important that economists quantify the structural effects of reductions in protection so as (a) to provide a counter-balance to the exaggerated claims of adversely affected groups and (b) to alert other groups to the losses that are being imposed upon them from the continuation and escalation of high rates of protection.

Over the next few years, I expect general equilibrium modelling to become an increasingly popular approach for attempting to quantify the extent of the structural change that would follow from various shocks. General equilibrium computations can provide detailed comparisons between alternative equilibrium states of the economy. If we are interested in the effects of a 25 per cent tariff cut, say, then we can use a general equilibrium model to compare two equlibrium states, one with the tariff cut implemented and one without.

For these comparative static exercises to be useful in policy debates, they must
(a) be highly disaggregated and
(b) give some indication of the rate of structural change as well as its extent.

I will briefly discuss each of these points, devoting most of my paper to point (b), because this is closest to the particular aspect of applied general equilibrium modelling that I wish to discuss, namely internal adjustment mechanisms.

2 DISAGGREGATION

One cannot give a convincing description of structural effects using a model with only a few industrial sectors, one type of labour and no regional detail. One needs, for example, to be able to talk about the displacement of textile workers in Tasmania. Fortunately, it is now possible to build highly disaggregated models and to use them quite routinely. For instance, in Australia at the IMPACT Project we have made innumerable simulations with the ORANI model.[1] ORANI, which incorporates advanced specifications of numerous substitution possibilities, is normally run with 113 industrial sectors, 230 commodities, 71 types of labour and 7 regions. The paper that I distributed at the conference contained examples of disaggregated ORANI simulations.[2] After a period of experimentation during the 1970s with some unnecessarily mathematically sophisticated and computationally inefficient techniques, it has been found that very large general equilibrium models can be solved quite easily using older, simpler approaches. For the ORANI model we adopt a straightforward extension of the method used in Johansen's pioneering work of the

1950s (see Johansen, 1960). ORANI solutions cost only a few dollars. It seems that computational problems should no longer be an inhibiting factor on the level of detail included in general equilibrium models.

A much more important factor in determining the feasible level of disaggregation is the availability of data. Most advanced countries and many developing countries now have input-output tables distinguishing at least 100 sectors. Where these tables are supplemented by information on the regional location of industries and the occupational composition of industrial labour forces, worthwhile general equilibrium analysis of policy-relevant structural issues becomes possible. Ideally, we should also have time-series data to facilitate the estimation of important price-response elasticities (e.g. elasticities of substitution between primary factors and between imported and domestic goods). However, even where inadequate data are available for elasticity estimation, we can still build useful, disaggregated general equilibrium models. Much of what we find out from general equilibrium computations reflects not the elasticities but the information on the composition of inputs to industries and the patterns of industrial sales contained in input-output matrices and supplementary tables.

Although I believe that it is now possible for most advanced countries to have general equilibrium models which can provide valuable insights on structural issues, I should emphasise that even the currently most sophisticated general equilibrium models are not a complete analytical tool-kit. For example, assume that we have a model that can give us a reasonable story on how many Tasmanian textile workers are likely to be displaced by a 25 per cent tariff cut. In assessing the costs and benefits of the tariff-cutting policy, we will want to know about the mobility characteristics of Tasmanian textile workers. Is it costly for them to change occupation and/or location? What period of unemployment is likely? Are there adequate social welfare support schemes in place? While some work has been done on these topics (see Bale, 1976, 1977; Cheh, 1974 and Baldwin et al., 1980) much remains to be done. In the paper I distributed at the conference, we did not attempt to attach a cost to particular occupational and regional shifts. Instead, we tried to indicate the shifts associated with a simulated shock (a 25 per cent tariff cut) are quantatitively significant in relation to occupational mobility observed in recent history.

Let me now turn to the second point, the rate of structural change.

3 RATE OF STRUCTURAL CHANGE

A major problem with general equilibrium models is timing. If we increase tariffs by 25 per cent, we might find that automobile production will be 7 per cent higher than it otherwise would have been. But when does this happen? Can we expect the rate of output to be 7 per cent higher one month after the tariff increase, or do we have to wait five years? While general equilibrium models tell us the effect of a shock on the equilibrium situation, they do not tell us how long it will be before that effect becomes apparent. Consequently they do not tell us about the rate of structural change that will accompany various shocks.

In applications of the ORANI model, we have made a distinction between short- and long-run simulations. In short-run simulations, capital capacity in each industry is treated as an exogenous variable. It is assumed that although the shock under consideration may affect investment plans, insufficient time elapses for there to be a resulting impact on industrial capacities. Most users of the ORANI model have assumed that the short-run is between one and a half and two years.

At the IMPACT Project we have been particularly concerned with trying to measure the length of the ORANI short run, which we have usually assumed to be one and a half to two years. Recent work by Cooper, McLaren and Powell[3] has provided an empirical justification for this assumption. What I intend to do in the rest of my paper is to give a brief overview of their work.

4 MEASURING THE ORANI SHORT RUN

For many years, builders of macro models have paid close attention to issues of timing. The estimation of the length of lags has been a primary concern. The approach adopted by Cooper, McLaren and Powell to the estimation of the ORANI short run is to borrow the estimated dynamics built into one of the macro models of Australia developed at the Reserve Bank. I will refer to the particular macro model which was chosen as MACRO. MACRO is a slightly modified version of the model described in Jonson and Trevor (1981).

MACRO produces explicitly timed responses to exogenous shocks. Given a path for the vector of MACRO's exogenous variables, we can generate a path for the vector of MACRO's endogenous variables. The percentage effects of a sustained shock can be calculated for each point of time by comparing two MACRO solutions whose path of exogenous inputs differ by a constant (time-invariant) vector. For example, if we were interested in the effects of a sustained or permanent 25 per cent increase in the average level of tariffs, we would compare two MACRO solutions whose paths of exogenous inputs were identical apart from the average tariff level, which would be 25 per cent higher at each point of time on one path than on the other.

The interpretation of MACRO results, $y_M(\tau)$, for the effects of a sustained shock is similar to that of ORANI results, y_O. Both y_M and y_O are vectors of changes in the values of endogenous variables caused by maintained shifts in the exogenous variables. Furthermore, some of MACRO's endogenous variables (aggregate output, the price level, aggregate employment and aggregate imports) are also endogenous variables in short-run ORANI simulations. Similarly, some of MACRO's exogenous variables (real government expenditure and the average level of tariffs) are exogenous in ORANI. Therefore, both models can be used to estimate the effects of, say, a sustained 10 per cent increase in real government expenditure on real output, the price level, aggregate employment and aggregate imports. However, whereas MACRO will produce a time-path for the deviations from control for the double endogenous variables, ORANI will produce a single set of values. The Cooper, McLaren and Powell approach to estimating the length of the ORANI short run is to pick the time $t^* \in [0,\infty)$, where the MACRO results for the doubly endogenous variables come closest to the single set of ORANI results.

From a technical point of view, the Cooper, McLaren and Powell problem of choosing t^* would be simple if ORANI's exogenous variables included none of MACRO's endogenous variables and vice versa. However, in short-run ORANI simulations, the exchange rate, real wages, real household expenditure, real investment and the aggregate capital stock are normally included in the ORANI exogenous set. These five variables are endogenous in MACRO.[4] Consequently, when we simulate a 10 per cent increase in government expenditure in ORANI we are holding constant a different set of variables from those being held constant when we increase government expenditure by 10 per cent in MACRO. Before we use MACRO to estimate ORANI's short run, we must design comparable ORANI and MACRO experiments.

For the purpose of exposition only, let us assume that MACRO's exogenous variables include none of ORANI's endogenous variables. This allows us to think recursively. First we shock MACRO by a 10 per cent increase in government spending. Then we shock ORANI not only with a 10 per cent increase in government spending but also with appropriate changes in the five ORANI-exogenous variables which are endogenised in MACRO. But what are the appropriate changes? If we want to check the compatibility of ORANI results with two year MACRO results (say), by how much should we shock the ORANI exchange rate? If a 10 per cent increase in government spending in MACRO increase the exchange rate by 5 per cent after two years, should we shock the ORANI exchange rate by five? The answer will usually be no. A 5 per cent shock would be appropriate only if MACRO told us that the increase in the exchange rate was instantaneous. Our problem is that ORANI (as with all other applied general equilibrium models) is set up to accept only sustained, time-invariant shocks (deviations from control). Yet MACRO is giving us a time-varying response path for the exchange rate which must be fed into ORANI. It appears that before we can run comparable experiments in ORANI and MACRO, we must teach ORANI to accept time-varying shocks. This will involve the addition of some dynamic features to ORANI.

Cooper, McLaren and Powell have assumed that ORANI has the dynamic form:

$$D\, Y_O(t) = A_O\, Y_O(t) + B_O\, Z_O(t),\ t \in [0,\infty) \qquad (1)$$

where A_O and B_O are matrices of parameters and $Y_O(t)$ and $Z_O(t)$ are the vectors of logarithms of ORANI's endogenous and exogenous variables. Those of you who work with differential equations will recognise that (1) implies that

$$y_O(t) = C_O(t)\, z_O \qquad (2)$$

where

$$C_O(t) = A_O^{-1}\, (e^{A_O t} - I)\, B_O \qquad (3)$$

and $y_O(t)$ is the vector of deviations from control for the endogenous variables caused by a time-invariant or sustained deviation, z_O, from control for the exogenous variables. From short-run, comparative static computations we can evaluate $C_O(t^*)$, where t^* is the unknown ORANI short-run. $C_O(t^*)$ is the matrix showing the short-run elasticities of the ORANI endogenous variables with respect to the ORANI exogenous variables. This suggests that a starting point for estimating A_O, B_O and t^* is the system

$$C_O(t^*) = A_O^{-1} (e^{A_O t^*} - I) B_O \tag{4}$$

The system (4) contains mn equations, where m is the number of rows in $C_O(t^*)$ and n is the number of columns. The unknown parameters to be estimated are t^* and the m^2 components of A_O and the mn components of B_O. It is obvious that for estimating t^*, A_O and B_O, (4) by itself is not sufficient.

Cooper, McLaren and Powell reduce the estimation problem by assuming that A_O is diagonal. Sometimes they assume that it is a scalar matrix (i.e. of the form $ßI$ where $ß$ is a scalar). In their most recent paper, Powell, Cooper and McLaren (1983), they allow the diagonal components of A_O to have six different values, so that the number of unknowns in system (4) exceeds the number of equations by seven. To eliminate these remaining seven degrees of freedom they proceed as follows.

First, they adopt as a standard shock a sustained 10 per cent increase in government expenditure. They record for this shock the deviations from control, $y_M(t)$, $t \in [0,\infty)$, of the MACRO endogenous variables. Next, they assume values for A_O, B_O and t^* which are consistent with (4). Using these assumed values in (1), they compute the vector of ORANI deviations from control, $y_O(t)$, $t \in [0,\infty)$, caused by a sustained 10 per cent increase in government expenditure combined with the changes implied by MACRO for the five ORANI-exogenous variables (the exchange rate, real wages, real household expenditure, real investment and the aggregate capital stock). The $y_M(t)$ and $y_O(t)$ vectors calculated in this way are comparable. Cooper, McLaren and Powell have eliminated the incompatibility between stand-alone ORANI and MACRO experiments that arises from the different assumptions that are built into the two models as to what is being held constant. Finally, they vary their choice of A_O, B_O and t^* so as to minimise the incompatibility between the ORANI results for the doubly endogenous variables (aggregate output, the price level, aggregate employment and aggregate imports) and the MACRO results for these variables.

While much work remains to be done, the results to date have been very promising. Cooper, McLaren and Powell have estimated the ORANI short run as 7.94 quarters; that is, they have shown that inconsistencies between the ORANI and MACRO results for the four double endogenous variables under the standard shock are minimised when $t^* = 7.94$ quarters. With $t^* = 7.94$, A_O and B_O can be chosen so that only minute differences remain between the results for ORANI's and MACRO's doubly endogenous variables, even with A_O restricted to being a diagonal matrix.

5 CONCLUSIONS

It is now feasible for many countries to have highly disaggregated general equilibrium models. Such models can be valuable tools for indicating the extent of structural changes that are likely to be associated with policy changes and other shocks. Most advanced countries have adequate data bases to support the construction of large models, and computational problems no longer seem to be a difficult obstacle.

Probably the greatest weakness of the general equilibrium approach is its lack of dynamics. While comparative static general equilibrium calculations give us an estimate of the extent of structural change, they give us very little idea about the rate of structural change. An attempt is being made in Australia to give the ORANI model some dynamics by borrowing the estimated dynamics from a conventional macro model. One attractive feature of this work is that it allows a continuation of the specialisation that currently exists in the model-building profession. On the one hand we have macro-econometricians who are experts in the estimation of dynamic relations using time-series techniques applied to macroeconomic data. On the other hand, we have applied general equilibrium modellers who are experts in the use of input-output tables and other micro information. The work of Cooper, McLaren and Powell brings together a dynamic macroeconometric model with a static general equilibrium model without requiring modifications in the construction of either model.

NOTES

1. IMPACT is an economic and demographic research project conducted by agencies of the Commonwealth Government of Australia in

association with the Faculty of Economics and Commerce at the University of Melbourne and the School of Economics of La Trobe University. The Project is directed by Alan A. Powell. Since 1975 the Project has created an inter-industry model, ORANI, and a demographic model, BACHUROO. It also uses a version, MACRO, of the Reserve Bank's macroeconometric model. One of the long-term objectives of the IMPACT Project is to interface the three models, ORANI, MACRO and BACHUROO (see Powell, 1977).
2. See Dixon, Parmenter and Powell (1983). For a complete description of ORANI, see Dixon, Parmenter, Sutton and Vincent (1982).
3. See Cooper (1983), Cooper and McLaren, (1980, 1982, 1983) and Powell, Cooper and McLaren (1983).
4. Similarly, among MACRO's exogenous variables which are endogenous in ORANI are the price of wool, the volume of exports and the price of exports. Here, however, we will ignore this complication and assume that ORANI endogenises none of MACRO's exogenous variables.

REFERENCES

Baldwin, R. E., Mutti, J. H. and Richardson, J. D. (1980) 'Welfare Effects on the United States of a Significant Multilateral Tariff Reduction', *Journal of International Economics*, vol. 10, p.p. 405–23.
Bale, M. D. (1976) 'Estimates of Trade-Displacement Costs for US Workers', *Journal of International Economics*, vol. 6, pp. 245–50.
Bale, M. D. (1977) 'United States Concessions in the Kennedy Round and Short-Run Labour Adjustment Costs: Further Evidence', *Journal of International Economics*, vol. 7, pp. 145–8.
Cheh, J. H. (1974) 'United States Concession in the Kennedy Round and Short-Run Labour Adjustment Costs', *Journal of International Economics*, vol. 4, pp. 323–40.
Cooper, R. J. (1983) 'A Tariff Experiment on the Interfaced ORANI-MACRO System', IMPACT Project *Preliminary Working Paper* no. IP-18, University of Melbourne, p.29.
Cooper, R. J. and McLaren, K. R. (1980) 'The ORANI-MACRO Interface', IMPACT Project *Preliminary Working Paper* No. IP-10, University of Melbourne, p. 83.
Cooper, R. J. and McLaren, K. R. (1982) 'An Approach to the Macroeconomic Closure of General Equilibrium Models', IMPACT Project *Preliminary Working Paper* No. IP-15, University of Melbourne, p. 28.
Cooper, R. J. and McLaren, K. R. (1983) 'The ORANI-MACRO Interface: an Illustrative Exposition', *Economic Record*, 59, June, pp. 166–79.
Cooper, R. J. and McLaren, K. R. (1980) 'The ORANI-MACRO Interface', IMPACT Project *Preliminary Working Paper* No. IP-10, University of Melbourne, pp. 83.
Dixon, P. B., Parmenter, B. R. and Powell, A. A. (1983) 'Trade Liberalization and Labour Market Disruption', Discussion paper no. 990, Harvard Institute for Economic Research, Harvard University, July p. 26.

Dixon, P. B., Parmenter, B. R, Sutton, J. and Vincent, D. P. (1982) *ORANI: A Multisectoral Model of the Australian Economy* (Amsterdam: North Holland).

Johansen, L. (1960) *A Multi−Sectoral Study of Economic Growth* (Amsterdam: North Holland) (second edition, 1974).

Jonson, P. D. and Trevor, R. G. (1981) 'Monetary Rules: a Preliminary Analysis', *Economic Record*, 57, June, pp. 150–67.

Powell, A. A. (1977) *The IMPACT Project: An Overview–First Progress Report of the IMPACT Project*, Vol. 1, Canberra: Australian Government Publishing Service.

Powell, A. A., Cooper, R. J. and McLaren, K. R. (1983) 'Macroeconomic Closure in Applied General Equilibrium Modeling: Experience from ORANI and Agenda for Further Research', paper presented to the Numerical Micro Models Conference, Australian National University, August 1983. Available from IMPACT Project, University of Melbourne.

12 Micro Initiatives and Macroeconomic Adjustments in the Industrialised Countries

M. Didier
ECOLE POLYTECHNIQUE, FRANCE

Since the turn of the twentieth century, the functioning of the capitalist economies has been radically changing. The structures of the production sector were upset as the agricultural population dwindled, as the large companies and the wages system developed, and mass production and industrial and urban concentration burgeoned. The competitive capitalism of the early years of the century gave way to monopolistic capitalism, the apex of which may be associated with the thirty years of rapid growth after the Second World War. In some ways, the crisis of the 1970s, manifested notably in the sudden and persistent rise in unemployment, can be interpreted as a jamming of the monopolistic system.

Among those adjustments which are affecting the structures of production, the reversal of the tendency towards industrial concentration deserves particular attention. The development of 'micro initiatives' and small companies, and the decline of the larger structures, previously considered the primary source of productivity, are both new on the economic scene. For the first time in many years, jobs are being generated from the other side of the fence; large companies are phasing out jobs and small companies are creating them. In response to the economic crisis, the structural pendulum would appear to be swinging in such a way as to modify the parameters of macroeconomic adjustments. This paper will attempt to find the origins of the swing, and to assess its extent.

In the first section, we will briefly review the manner in which macroeconomic regulation is affected by the economic crisis. The structural adjustments affecting the concentration of employment for the last decade will then be examined, on the basis of the statistical data available. The last two sections will explore the causes of these adjustments and their consequences.

1 FROM GROWTH MECHANISMS TO DEPRESSION MECHANISMS

The macroeconomic equilibrium which has prevailed in most of the Western economies since the Second World War has been dubbed 'monopolistic'. It was established during the Depression in the 1930s. In Galbraith's view, the need for protection against economic insecurity largely explains transformations which began or solidified during the era.

These transformations primarily concern institutional structures. Pressure from the rapidly developing unions led governments to intervene, and to set up funds for welfare and emergency situations, to insure workers against unemployment, to offer retirement pensions to elderly workers, to guarantee medical care and in some cases protection against falls in prices. Legislative and regulatory measures were sustained by a growing awareness of the responsibility of government for macroeconomic control.

These institutional and intellectual patterns were to be reinforced during, and indeed would dominate, the entire post-war period through the 1960s. But they would have had little effect without modifications in the behaviour and structures of the system of production. Galbraith (1958) observes that 'the elimination of economic insecurity was pioneered by the business firm in respect of its own operations. The greatest source of insecurity . . . lay in competition and free and unpredictable movement of competitive market prices.'

Companies thus set about to eliminate risk, and since size makes possible a diversified line, and greatly diversifies the opportunities of the firm in raising money, the tendency towards industrial concentration which had begun before the dawn of the twentieth century was reinforced.

1.1 Concentration and Productivity

The long-term trend towards industrial concentration is still the object of a good deal of debate. In the 1950s, Jewkes (1952) noted that 'no spectacular change has taken place in the size of industrial establishment over the past thirty to forty years'. Shortly afterwards, Florence (1954) argued that 'the average size of the factories slowly increased just about everywhere'. Nearer to our present concerns Pryor (1972), returned to this question and explored it more deeply. He noted accentuated trends toward concentration in the Federal Republic of Germany, and more moderate ones in France and the USA, based on the percentage of persons working in companies of over 1,000 employees. The percentage is sharply increasing in all three countries at the present time.

In France, Didier and Malinvaud (1969) and Didier (1982) have examined the evolution of concentration in industrial establishments since the beginning of the century. They stress the slow disappearance of those employing fewer than ten workers. In 1906, 58 per cent of industrial jobs were offered by companies employing 9 or less workers; the figure was 39 per cent in 1936, and by 1981 it was 18 per cent.

Another characteristic of post-war growth has been the leap in industrial productivity. In the classic pattern of mass production (see Rothwell and Zegveld, 1982), new goods are produced by relatively small, inefficient production units. When demand and the size of the market increase, techniques improve as a result of learning by doing. Productivity increases, production units become larger, the market matures and is progressively transformed into a replacement market with production heavily concentrated in a few firms. During the phase in which the market is extending, gains in productivity recede, investment is principally directed towards increasing capacities, and jobs are created. As the market matures, the effects on capacity are less clear; investment is directed towards rationalisation, and employment is stabilised. In the last phase, investment for rationalisation takes precedence over capacity investment, and employment wanes.

1.2 Management of Manpower

Boyer and Mistral (1982) emphasised the role of the organisation of work in the mechanism of manpower regulation. They state that postwar regulation was marked by

— persistent high productivity linked with the intensive exploitation of techniques of mass production, the systematic use of scientific methods of organising work and the technical and financial concentration of the factors in industrial production;

— considerable development in the institutional factors in relations with employees – new forms of wage bargaining, closer indexation of salaries with prices and anticipated production, and a spectacular leap of indirect remuneration (which is derived from regulation and not from the market, and now amounts to between half and two-thirds of the direct salaries in Western Europe).

The evolution of Western economies since the beginning of the 1960s shows that this form of regulation comports serious contradictions which call for a transformation.

Studies of the present economic crisis highlight the extent and diversity of breakdowns which are concerned precisely with the mechanisms of regulation. To Dubois (1980) they appear to stem neither from exhaustion of the dynamics of supply nor from an upset in the behaviour of demand, but must be looked for 'in the mechanisms of regulating supply and demand, production and employment (a substitution of capital for labour, regulations of working hours, etc. . .), and pricing and revenue (wage and profit structures)'. Monopolistic mechanisms of regulation now appear to have effects which are incompatible, and their incoherence postpones the possibility of returning to a balanced system of regulation. Several authors have demonstrated the risk of incompatibility between new conditions of growth and the mechanisms of forming direct and indirect remuneration systems and profit structures. Certain structural adjustments may be initiating an evolution towards new forms of mechanisms.

2 STRUCTURAL CHANGE: BIG BUSINESS REDUCING EMPLOYMENT, SMALL BUSINESS CREATING IT

Among the structural adjustments involved in the crisis, the reversal in concentration in employment most clearly indicates a break with time-honoured tradition. Small units of production are no longer dying out; they are proliferating and generating jobs, while the big companies suffer severe cutbacks in their personnel. A number of converging views have recently been published in the literature.

In the United States, Birch (1979) has examined variations in employment in 5.6 million industrial and service establishments between 1969 and 1976. The procedures he utilised make it possible to distinguish several causes of the final net variation – the appearance and disappearance of new units of production, and the creation of employment by existing companies. The main inferences drawn for the USA are as follows:

1. About 8 per cent of the yearly reduction in employment in the USA occurs through closing down or reductions in the workforce.
2. In the creation of gross employment, 50 per cent is the result of the expansion of existing companies, 50 per cent evolves from the creation of new enterprises.
3. Small companies employing fewer than 20 persons (in 1969) were responsible for 66 per cent of the net variation in employment in the USA between 1969 and 1976.

Economists found this last conclusion very surprising. Out of a little over 6.5 million jobs created in the USA between 1969 and 1976 throughout all sectors, 4.5 million were in small production units (of 0 to 20 employees in 1969), and fewer than 900,000, that is around a fifth, were in companies employing 500 or more workers, which had until then been presumed to be the moving force in development.

Part of the explanation lies in the relative imbalance among the sectors. More jobs were created in the trades (2,600,000) and services (2,300,000), than in industry (where in fact 150,000 jobs were lost). The tertiary sector is traditionally composed of small production units, yet the vitality of the small companies is manifest in every sector of activity.

In the United Kingdom, we do not have as complete a study. Fothergill and Gudgin (1979) examined the movements in the industrial employment of the East Midlands between 1968 and 1975. Their conclusions were similar to those drawn from the United States.

Storey (1982) estimated the share of jobs created by new enterprises at less than 15 per cent in the UK, as opposed to 50 per cent in the USA).

In France, several recent studies confirm the dynamism of small companies in creating employment. Didier (1982) studied about 13.5 million wage-earners in industry and trade – that is, virtually all of them except those in agriculture, public enterprises, and, of course, the administration. Valid statistics are available for France through UNEDIC (the National Union for Employment and Industry and Trade) throughout the period 1968–80, and these give breakdowns of workers by size of establishment. In 1967 the affiliation of UNEDIC was considerably widened, and has remained fairly constant since, so that valid comparisons can be made over a period of several years before and after the first oil crisis.

During the years of expansion before the crisis, the number of wage-earners grew by between 300,000 and 400,000 yearly; a very large part of this increase took place in large enterprises, with somewhat less in the medium-sized companies. The crisis years saw a change in the proportion of workers in each category. Between 1974 and 1980 the total number of employed workers remained stable, but within the total, 550,000 workers were gained by small companies (of less than 20 employees), and about the same number were lost by the large ones (with over 200 employees).

Analysis of the sectors shows that the phenomenon of growth in the small units of production and diminution in the large ones is very widespread. It is seen in all activities, including the tertiary sector.

Delattre's (1982) study includes important data pertaining to industrial companies. This study drawn from fiscal statistics formulated over the period 1974–9, concerns companies rather than employees. During this time industry lost about 400,000 jobs, of which 300,000 were from enterprises employing over 500 workers, 100,000 from those employing between 100 and 499. In the smaller units employment remained stable.

As Birch has demonstrated in the USA, this evolution was the result of two distinct movements, one from differences in the employment in those large and small enterprises that endured throughout the period, the other in the appearance and disappearance of enterprises. Since the crisis, more firms have been created than have disappeared, but it is difficult to isolate the direct effect of this balance on employment. To distinguish the two causes of variation in employment, Delattre took a constant sample of 5,000 companies, 2,800 of which were in industry. All endured throughout the period 1974–9; none were restructured during that time. The results show that the increase in employment in the small and medium-sized companies cannot be explained solely by demographic movements. Over five years, the manpower of large companies in the sample (more than 500 salaried workers in 1974) diminished by 6 per cent; it remained stable in the medium-sized units (100–500 workers in 1974), and increased in the small units (20–100 workers in 1974; units with less than 20 workers were not included in the sample). The result applied generally over all sectors of industry. Without exception, small enterprises created jobs while in sixteen out of nineteen sectors large enterprises showed losses. It should be noted that the two inquiries, which include companies of fewer than 20 employees (Birch, 1979, and Didier, 1982) show that it is this category that created most of the employment.

To conclude, the dynamism of the small units – particularly the very smallest – in creating employment appears to be general and obvious in virtually all sectors of activity. It occurs both through the development of existing companies and through the net positive creation of new production units. The change in the overall structure is taking place at a rapid rate, and is eliciting substantial changes in the organisation of the production sector; it would appear to be advisable to explore its causes before going on to estimate its extent and effects on macroeconomic regulation.

3 MICROECONOMIC MANAGEMENT AND STRUCTURAL ADJUSTMENTS: THE CAUSES OF THE TRANSFORMATION

It was observed during the Depression of the 1930s that small companies showed better resistance than large ones. Their share in industrial employment grew at that time. But the mechanisms now in play appear to be different, and the adjustments of today must be explained at the levels of demand, production technology and organisation, profit structures, and, lastly, manpower management.

3.1 The Market and Demand

The study undertaken by Delattre (1982) confirms the gain of a greater share of the markets on the part of the small companies through an examination of their value-added volume between 1974 and 1979. Over this period the annual growth of small industrial enterprises (fewer than 100 employees in 1974) was 2.6 per cent, that of the large enterprises (over 500 employees in 1974) was 1 per cent. Similar ratios were found in almost all other sectors.

It is possible that the development of the newly industrialised countries will be less encouraging to large enterprises than to small ones. Large enterprises tend to produce rather 'banalised', technologically tested products, which can be mass-produced. The newly industrialised countries, in which salaries are low, are formidable competitors in the sale of such goods.

Yet the conclusions of research on global exportation, which view the small companies as handicapped on the world market, are not borne out by the experience of recent years, at least not in France. The most comprehensive study of the bulk of French industrial enterprises for the year 1977 (Roncin, 1982), which determines whether or not and to what extent the companies export (i.e. the proportion of export sales in total sales), observed that the propensity to export increased with size; 25 per cent of the companies employing 2 and 9 persons exported, as compared to 96 per cent of those employing more than 1,000. However, among the companies which export, a positive and significant link is noted between size and tendency to export in only 12 out of 47 sectors.

3.2 Technology and Innovation

A good deal of work has been devoted to comparing the innovative capacities of small and large companies. Theoretical considerations usually stress the disadvantage of small size in the innovation process, and conclude that large enterprises are in a better position to innovate. They cite the lack of highly qualified personnel, the lack of access to information on scientific and technical discoveries, financial limitations, and management problems in small companies. In fact, financial resources directed towards R & D usually vary with the size of the enterprise in some sectors of activity, but Freeman (1971) showed that in some sectors the correlation between size of company and expenditure for research was inverse. Moreover, expenditure for research does not necessarily correspond to rate or quality of invention.

One of the most comprehensive data bases on the relationship between company size and innovation is that of the research unit at the University of Sussex. Information on some 2,100 important innovations achieved in British enterprises between 1945 and 1980, classified by size of the enterprise and the size of the unit which developed the innovation (laboratory, separate department, etc.) is collected there. Rothwell and Zegveld (1982) have published results for 35 industrial sectors; a few of the figures for industry in general are reproduced in Table 12.1.

The dynamism of the small companies (of less than 200 employees), and a coincident diminution of the largest (500 and over) is clearly seen in the 1970s, and the tendency is even more evident in the innovative units. Their share in the 2,154 innovations recorded in the data bank goes from 18 per cent to 31 per cent from one decade to the next. It should be noted that some 'small' units are part of 'large'

Table 12.1 Number of innovations by size of company and by size of research unit

	Distribution by company size			Distribution by size of innovating unit (laboratory, separate department, etc.)		
	1-199	200-499	500 and over	1-199	200-499	500 and over
	(in % of total innovations)					
From 1960 to 1969	12	6	82	18	14	68
From 1970 to 1980	17	8	75	31	14	55

Sources: Townsend, Henwood and Thomas, SPRU innovation data bank (1981), as quoted by Rothwell and Zegveld (1982).

enterprises; but the tendency is just as clear if one considers only small independent companies.

3.3 The Internal Organisation of the Production Sector

Many small companies undertake subcontracting activities for larger ones. According to a 1980 study of small and medium-sized enterprises in France (CEPME, 1981), 38 per cent of the companies employing between 10 and 49 workers stated that they worked as subcontractors. Only 26 per cent of the companies employing 200 to 499 workers took subcontracted work. Lydall (1958) divided small English industrial enterprises into 'subcontractors' (of which 58 per cent of his sample were in the group employing 10–19 persons, and 25 per cent were in the group employing 200–499) and 'independents'. He found that the subcontractors, rather than competing with the large companies, complemented them. Small enterprises are active subcontractors in all countries.

In a time of crisis, one might presume that the tendency to subcontract would be less accentuated, and that the large companies would have their subcontracted work done by their own employees. On the contrary, the share of work assigned to outside contractors has increased. Some activities appear to have been exteriorised. The early use of outside enterprises for such activities as cleaning and maintenance has subsequently been extended to a wide range of service activities, and this exteriorisation has worked to the benefit of small enterprises, partially explaining the rapid growth of the sector servicing companies.

3.4 Profit Structures

Analysis of the ledgers and operating budgets of small enterprises and comparison with those of large ones highlights the structural differences in their financial management. These differences were the object of a detailed study (Vassille, 1982) of the non-financial French companies employing more than 20 persons in 1979 (in industry, construction, trades and services). The study covers more than 72,000 companies; the very smallest are not included. Vassille's salient conclusions are as follows.

1. Average profitability (profits on capital) is higher in small companies. The mean net profit rate of the companies employing

20–99 salaried workers is 7.5 per cent; that of companies employing 100–499 is 5.1 per cent; and that of companies employing over 500 is 2.7 per cent. In industry the differences are particularly wide – 9.1 per cent among the small companies, 7.2 per cent in the medium-sized, 2.5 per cent in the large.
2. Profits are more consistent in enterprises belonging to a financial group than in independent ones; 20 per cent of the medium-sized companies belong to large groups, as compared to 4 per cent of the small ones. It seems that the former run fewer risks and suffer less profit variability.
3. Although the smallest companies seem the most fragile, as indicated by their greater profit variability and their more frequent need of short-term credit, they are also the most profitable. Moreover, statistics show that the differences in profitability increased during the crisis, and that large companies suffered greater profit losses than did small ones.

In summary, small companies weathered the general fall in activity better than large companies; indeed, they often improved their positions during the period of crisis.

3.5 Management of Manpower Costs

The smaller the company, the less capitalistic it is, and the more manpower it uses. Labour productivity rates are generally lower in small companies than in large ones. Yet in terms of profitability, the results do not indicate overall inefficiency. What we would like to show here is that in terms of managing manpower costs, small companies were better able to adapt to crisis conditions than large ones, and this adaptability was one of the primary explanations for their better performance.

Several studies have shown that average wage and salary levels (or personnel expenditure, including social charges) are generally higher in large companies than in small ones (see Brocard and Gandois, 1978, for example). The quarterly wage index shows that the difference between wages in large and small enterprises has widened in France since the beginning of the crisis. The constant sample of Delattre (1982) confirmed this observation. The increase in the average wage was still relatively more rapid in the large companies in 1975 and in 1976 (more than two years after the first oil crisis), although it had already slowed in the small ones by 1975. In that year, the gap between the growth rates of average wages reached six points. Between 1974 and 1979 the share of wages in value-added increased by 3.7 points in companies employing 20 to 99 workers, and by 6.5 points in companies employing 500 and over. The greater flexibility of small companies in manpower management is one of the key factors in the structural adjustments now likely to alter macroeconomic regulation. We shall return to this observation in Section 4.

4 TOWARDS NEW FORMS OF MACROECONOMIC ADJUSTMENTS

Investigation of the causes of the present ongoing structural adjustments invites research into their extent and their effects on macroeconomic adjustments. Is there a return towards competitive capitalism in the emerging small firms and the retreating large ones, after a seeming stalemate in monopolistic capitalism? This explanation may be partly valid, but it certainly does not suffice without a much more precise description of the modes of the adjustment.

As mentioned above, there are indications that small companies are more often complementary to large ones than competitive with them. But on the other hand it is clear that the rigidity of large companies in managing manpower makes it much easier for adaptable units to withstand macroeconomic hardships in times of crisis.

4.1 Complementarity of Small and Large Units

It happens sometimes that small and large companies find themselves competing in the same market, but certainly not all the time. Small and large companies usually complement each other in market and financial terms.

On the product level, firms and their subcontractors are obviously complementary; independent producers compete, but product differentiation is extensive enough to fragment the market considerably, and thus reduce competition. An inquiry carried out by CEPME (1981) on 1,900 companies employing fewer than 500 persons is particularly revealing. Two-thirds of the companies questioned estimated that their markets were at least national (that is, national and worldwide); half of them described their markets as worldwide. Among the companies employing fewer than 50 workers, 62 per cent considered their markets at least national, and 24 per cent worldwide.

Of this group of companies, which is generally considered small, 67 per cent considered themselves among the average or largest producers in their markets.

Complementarity is also evident in the new organisational trends in the production sector. The shift of activity towards services is often linked with the exteriorisation of activities by the large companies. This is true notably of software, public relations, marketing, and technical counselling.

Lastly, companies within groups are financially complementary. In France it was possible to measure these relations precisely (Thollon and Pommerol, 1982). Enterprises which belong to groups constitute 20 per cent of the medium-sized companies (100–499 employees) and 4 per cent of the small ones (20–199 workers). In some respects, these companies appear to be somewhere between the independent companies of the same size and the large enterprises to which they belong. Their profitability is thus rather weaker, all things being equal, than that of the independent companies (see Vassille, 1982). On the other hand, employment growth is greater in the small or medium-sized companies belonging to groups than in comparable independent companies, which would seem to indicate that groups favour the development of their smallest units.

4.2 New Forms of Manpower Management

As observed earlier, small enterprises reacted more rapidly to deteriorating economic conditions than did large companies, by sharply reducing wages. In the face of management standards which have become particularly rigid, it was the capacities of the small units to adapt that made them more resistant in terms of profit and employment. Wages are generally lower in small companies than in large ones, but their greater ability to adapt is explained better by the skill structure and the nature of the manpower employed by small enterprises, which is younger, more often female, and tends toward greater seniority in the company (see Eymard–Duvernay, 1981). It is also less skilled, particularly in medium-sized companies. In short, it is less stable, less structured, less often unionised, and, in the smallest companies, more dispersed.

Pay bands are narrower in large companies. In the face of the evolution in rates of pay which they assume, the principal variables of adjustment available to large companies are staff size (which can be sharply reduced in spite of the legal and financial obstacles to firing) and profits (which can be much narrower than in small companies). Growing recourse to temporary personnel is one of the alternatives opted for by the large units to obviate rigidity in pay. An inquiry by the French Ministry of Labour showed that 45 per cent of French companies with over 500 salaried workers used temporary workers, as opposed to about 5 per cent of those employing 10–49 (see Rerat, 1979, and Revoil, 1979). This form of employment remains marginal, however.

One might say briefly that adjustments in personnel costs are made by adjusting wage levels in the small business sector, and by adjusting the number of employees in the big business sector. The profit situation has deteriorated less in small companies, but they have had to 'pay' through higher and growing failure rates.

4.3 Company Creation and Destruction – New Adjustment Variables

Several studies have stressed the fact that a resurgence in new companies occurred during the 1970s, particularly in France and the United Kingdom. Fairly consistent and complete data on the total number of companies are available for France (Didier, 1982), based on annual accounting. After a period of frequent company failures, a resurgence in company creation began in 1973, and it is likely that variations in the total number of companies occurred principally among the smallest.

Two other sets of statistics confirm this new tendency – the registers of the trades and that of the commerce tribunals. The first concerns enterprises of artisans, meaning generally companies which do not employ more than 10 workers, which produce goods, perform transformations or repairs, or offer services, and of which the trade guilds keep lists. On the one hand, there were increases simultaneously in the creation and the disappearance of companies from the beginning of the crisis, indicating greater mobility in the craft sector; on the other hand, perceptibly more companies were created than died, and the difference is too great to be explained solely by statistical error.

The second source concerns the number of actions registered by the courts to create or dissolve companies. Creations have gone from 20,000 to 40,000 a year; dissolutions have increased as well, but to a considerably lesser degree.

In conclusion, it seems certain that a significant resurgence in the creation of companies has taken place over the past few years, but it is accompanied by an increase in the number of failures.

Storey (1982) traces the number of companies registered in the United Kingdom between 1945 and 1979. He shows considerable fluctuations in this number, and a tendency toward a heavy increase in the annual formations since the beginning of the 1970s. The number of failures has also increased. Some studies have shown that around a third of the new companies do not survive the first year.

On the macroeconomic level, there has been an increase in the rate of turnover of companies. When an enterprise fails, in favour of a new enterprise or of those which survive it, it is logical to assume that production will cost less. If the market of the failed enterprise gravitates to existing enterprises, they will profit by savings accruing from better productivity. If the market is taken over by a new enterprise, the workers may be persuaded to accept lower salaries in order to remain employed. This situation often applies when floundering companies are taken over. Macroeconomic models of demand structures do not usually take account of these phenomena which normally occur in the restoration phase of a crisis. However, they show how important supply factors are in economic regulation.

4.4 An Ideological and Institutional Context to Favour Small Business

In the 1960s it was fashionable to decorate economic speeches with arguments in favour of large-scale production. Slowdown in productivity and growth was generally attributed to the 'outmoded technologies' of the smallest companies. Economic policy strained to regroup and to concentrate companies. Since then, new arguments and theories have appeared, developed notably by Schumacher (1973), which cast doubt on the universal validity of growth and concentration, and these have not been without influence on workers' aspirations. 'People can only be themselves in small, suitably sized groups', wrote Schumacher (1973). 'We must thus learn to think in terms of articulated structures capable of dealing with many small units'. Autonomy, and perhaps a certain degree of conviviality, to which one can aspire in small groups, have been sought by workers and by some company heads as well.

It is, for example, significant that company growth is no longer a management objective. According to the inquiry among small companies cited above (CEPME, 1981), 77 per cent of the directors questioned thought in 1978 that above all, they needed to 'try not to go over a certain size, so as not to lose their originality as a small enterprise'. This proportion, which already appeared to be very high, had increased to 81 per cent by 1980.

Governments have adapted their behaviour to these ideas, and are trying to encourage small units. A strong movement has developed in support of local micro initiatives through assistance in creating jobs in new activities not covered in the public sphere or in the traditional private sector. a report by the French Minister of Employment (Gaudin, 1982) shows that these new forms of undertaking are not negligible, but they are still marginal. Thus policy for encouraging employment is principally focused on the small enterprise in the free market sector. Policies of this kind are operating in most of the market economies offering fiscal incentives, direct financial assistance, low-interest loans and practical help. It is not yet possible to evaluate the impact of such a policy, and there is no assessment of the spontaneous movement that might have occurred without help. But it is certain that the regulatory measures taken cannot fail to contribute to the dynamism of small companies.

Emphasis over several decades on macroeconomic theory may have obscured the role of microeconomic structural adjustments in overall regulation. It seems that important transformations are taking place in Western economies, and they are linked to the need for finding new ways of reconciling microeconomic management with macroeconomic coherence.

REFERENCES

Birch, D. (1979) *The Job Generation Process*, Cambridge Program on Neighbourhood and Regional Change (Cambridge, Mass.: MIT Press).
Boyer, R. (1982) 'Les transformations due rapport salarial dans la crise: une interprétation de ses aspects sociaux et économiques', Mémo (Paris: CEPREMAP).
Boyer, R. and Mistral, J. (1982) *Accumulation, inflation, crises* (Paris: Presses Universitaires de France) (2nd edition).
Boyer, R. and Mistral, J. (1983) 'La crise actuelle; d'une analyse historique à une vue prospective', memo, (CEPREMAP).
Brocard, R. and Gandois, J. M. (1978) 'Grandes entreprises et PME', *Economie et Statisique*, no. 96, January.
Cepme (1981) 'Les petites et moyennes industries en 1981. Credit d'équipment des PME June 1981', (Paris: CEPME).

Delattre, M. (1982) 'Les PME face aux grandes entreprises', *Economie et Statistique*, no. 148, October.
Didier, M. (1982) 'Crise et concentration du secteur productif', *Economie et Statistique*, no. 144, May.
Didier, M. et Malinvaud, E. (1969) 'La concentration de l'industrie française s'est-elle accentuée depuis 1900?', *Economie et Statistique*, no. 2, June.
Dubois, P. (1980) 'La rupture de 1974', *Economie et Statistique*, no. 124, August.
Eymard–Duvernay, F. (1981) 'Les secteurs de l'industrie et leurs ouvriers', *Economie et Statistique*, no. 138.
Florence, P. S. (1954) 'The Size of the Factory: a Reply', *Economic Journal*, vol. 64, September.
Fothergill, S. and Gudgin, G. (1979) 'The job generation process in Britain', Centre for Environmental Studies, research series no. 32, November.
Freeman, C. (1971) *The Role of Small Firms in Innovations in the UK Since 1945*, research report no. 6, Committee of Inquiry on Small Firms (London: HMSO).
Galbraith, J. K. (1958) *The Affluent Society* (London:Hamish Hamilton).
Gaudin, J. (1982) *Initiatives locales et création d'emplois,* Report by the Minister for Employment Paris, La documentation francaise.
Jewkes, J. (1952) 'The Size of the Factory', *Economic Journal*, vol. 62, June, pp. 237–51.
Lydall, H. F. (1958) 'Aspects of Competition in the Manufacturing Industry', *Bulletin of the Oxford Institute of Economics and Statistics*, vol. 20, no. 4, November, pp 319–37.
Pryor, F. L. (1972) 'Size of Establishments in Manufacturing', *Economic Journal*, vol. 82, June, pp. 547–68.
Rerat, F. (1979) 'Roles de l'intérim dans l'industrie', *Economie et Statistique*, no. 112, June.
Revoil, J. P. (1979) 'La croissance lente marque l'emploi', *Economie et Statistique*, no. 112, June.
Roncin, A. (1982) 'L'engagement des PMI dans l'exportation', *Economie et Statistique*, no. 148, October.
Rothwell, R. et Zegveld, W. (1982) *Innovation and the Small and Medium Sized Firm* (London: Frances Pinter).
Schumacher, E. F. (1973) *Small is Beautiful* (London: Blond and Briggs).
Storey, D. J. (1982) *Entrepreneurship and the New Firm* (London: Croom Helm).
Thollon and Pommerol (1982) 'Les groupes publics et privés'. *Economie et Statistique*, no. 147, September.
Vassille, L. (1982) 'Les PME: fragilité financière, forte rentabilité', *Economie et Statistique*, no. 148, October.

13 Structural Adjustment in Industrially Advanced Countries: Discussion and Conclusions

K. Jungenfelt
STOCKHOLM SCHOOL OF ECONOMICS,
STOCKHOLM

1 THE 'DEINDUSTRIALISATION PHENOMENON'

The concept of 'structural change' has been used in connection with a wide range of economic development problems. It is therefore necessary to limit the scope of the topics to be treated at the beginning. In the following, structural change will be used to describe only long-run development problems for those parts of the advanced economies that are usually termed manufacturing industries.

The recent interest in this field has coined the expression 'deindustrialisation' to describe the process whereby manufacturing industries have tended to become a less dynamic factor in the growth process. It is only too well known that the earlier experience was the opposite one: production and employment grew faster in manufacturing than in the rest of the economy. The explanation for this is to be found in the rapid increase of productivity in nearly all industries and a certain combination of price and income elasticities for consumers' demand. Industrialisation accordingly accompanied rapid growth. It may well be natural that an observed *de*-industrialisation creates fear for less rapid growth in the future.

What, then, is the evidence for a reversal of this kind among the advanced economies? The development of some West European countries may serve as an illustration.[1] From Table 13.1 it can easily be seen that in the 1970s stagnation is pronounced in all countries. On average, real output growth fell to one-third of its value during the 1960s, and the earlier increase in employment was turned into a decrease of the same order of magnitude. This deceleration or stagnation did not start at the same time in all countries. In some, it was present already in 1970; in others, it began after 1974. For growth of productivity, measured by output per man-year, it did not matter whether the stagnation was late or early. All countries experienced a drop, with an average of approximately one-third of the level in the 1960s. These rough measures may well be interpreted as a tendency for the considered economies to have begun a process of deindustrialsation during the 1970s.

Table 13.1 Growth of real output, employment and productivity in nine countries, 1960s and 1970s (per cent per annum), manufacturing

Country	Real output* 1958–60 to 1968–70	1970–78	Employment** 1958–60 to 1968–70	1970–78	Productivity 1960 to 1968–70	1970–78
Belgium	6.5	3.4	0.3	−2.0	6.1	5.5
Finland	6.9	3.1	2.0	0.6	4.8	2.5
France	6.3	4.4	0.8	−0.3	5.5	4.8
Germany, Federal Republic of	6.3	2.0	0.4	−1.6	5.8	3.7
Italy	8.3	2.9	1.7	0.3	6.5	2.6
Netherlands	6.8	2.9	0.8	−2.6	6.0	5.7
Norway	5.3	1.5	1.1	0.1	1.1	1.4
Sweden	6.9	0.7	0.3	−0.9	6.6	1.6
United Kingdom	3.3	0.7	0.1	−1.4	3.2	2.1

*Value added at factor cost, 1963 prices for the 1960s and 1970 prices for the 1970s.
**Includes the self-employed.

Source: Economic Commission of the United Nations, *Economic Survey of Europe in 1980* (New York: United Nations), p.186.

2 THE PACE AND DIRECTION OF STRUCTURAL CHANGE IN PRODUCTION

It is perhaps trivial to point out that growth is uneven between the different sectors of manufacturing. When growth in general is as strong as in the 1960s these differences are established on the positive side: for example in the 18-sector study of West European manufacturing referred to here, all sectors had positive growth rates for output. For the 1970s, this is no longer true. Some appear on the negative side. One might then expect that structural change becomes more pronounced as growth is retarded. But the evidence here is not clearcut. Two indices of the pace of structural change presented by the cited study are given in Table 13.2.

Table 13.2 Two indices of structural change for total manufacturing in nine West European countries.

'Structural' variable	Index of structural change*	
	1958–60 to 1968–70	1970 to 1978
Value added at constant prices	7.4**	6.9
Employment	5.8	4.4

*The index is calculated as the sum of the *positive* differences between a sector's percentage share of the relevant variable in total manufacturing at the end and at the beginning of the period. The sum is taken over all sectors.
**Includes Yugoslavia.
Source: ECE (1980), p.189.

The index takes on a large value for the 1960s, so structural change measured in this way was inevitably more pronounced earlier. But with slower growth during the 1970s, one would have expected the pace of structural change to be reduced more than is actually registered by the fall index. Furthermore, a calculation of these indices on a yearly basis shows little variation during 1970–8. This is somewhat surprising if one considers the pronounced drop in the overall growth rate for manufacturing during the latter half of the period. It seems safest to conclude that the pace of structural change remained remarkably stable from the 1960s into the 1970s in spite of the deceleration in growth. The development of individual sectors underlying this structural change is too rich to be considered here. A few points of more general interest will be taken up, however. The first relates to the consistency of change in two different dimensions. One is consistency between the two time periods considered, the other is consistency between countries. It turns out that for sectors with extreme development patterns there is a pronounced consistency in both dimensions. Table 13.3 below shows where to find the clear winners and losers during the 1970s. It turns out that there are very few examples of reversals, i.e. a change from rising to falling or vice versa, from the 1960s.

Table 13.3 Rising, stable and falling shares of total manufacturing in nine West European countries, 1968–78.

Sector	Output at constant prices			Employment		
	Rising	Stable	Falling	Rising	Stable	Falling
Chemicals	7	2	0	8	1	0
Electrical machinery	7	2	0	8	1	0
Non-electrical machinery	5	4	0	5	4	0
Manufacturing n.c.s.	4	2	3	3	3	3
Transport equipment	3	3	3	8	1	0
Wood and furniture	3	4	2	3	1	5
Food and drink	2	5	2	2	4	3
Petroleum products	1	5	3	2	3	4
Non-metallic minerals	0	5	4	0	1	8
Basic metals	2	3	4	5	0	4
Metal products	2	2	5	7	2	0
Tobacco products	1	2	6	1	3	5
Printing and publishing	2	1	6	4	5	0
Rubber products	1	1	7	1	4	4
Paper	0	2	7	1	4	4
Leather	0	2	7	0	1	8
Clothing and footwear	1	1	7	0	2	7
Textiles	0	1	8	0	0	9

Source: ECE (1980), p.205.

A second point is related to the labour intensity among fast-, average- and slow-growth sectors. If sectors are grouped according to their growth performance with respect to output, the following table (Table 13.4) can be constructed:
It is seen here that the fast-growing sectors have a lower share of employment than of output. For slow-growing sectors the opposite is true, while average-growing sectors have approximately the same

Table 13.4 Labour intensity and rate of growth of sector

Sectors	Percentage share of			
	Output		Employment	
	1970	1978	1970	1978
Fast-growing	20.7	25.3	17.3	19.1
Average-growing	36.3	37.3	36.4	38.0
Slow-growing	43.0	37.4	45.7	42.9

Source: ECE (1980), p.194.

shares. It is thus possible to classify the dynamic sectors as being *less* labour-intensive than the average. The stagnating sectors are in the same sense *more* labour-intensive. Moreover, these difficulties tended to be accentuated over the period as labour productivity rose more in the fast growth sectors.

It is also of interest to see that about half the number of all sectors are approximately average-growing. The overall index of structural change presented above is to its largest extent (80 per cent) determined (positively) by six sectors. On the negative side four sectors contribute 75 per cent of the total change.

The aspects of structure and structural change reported so far are all common to the different countries covered by the report. It should not be forgotten, however, that the sector structure differs pronouncedly between themselves. Due to their natural resource endowments, the Nordic countries are strongly specialised in forest industries, Italy and Belgium seem to have the most striking specialisation in labour-intensive products among the countries concerned. There is no general tendency for specialisation to converge or diverge during the period.

3 INTERNATIONAL TRADE AND STRUCTURE OF PRODUCTION

The development during the 1970s shows an increasing dependence of manufacturing upon international specialisation. In the aggregates, this can be demonstrated by the rise in imports as well as exports relative to gross output in nearly all countries (Table 13.5).

Table 13.5 The shares of imports and exports in gross output of total manufacturing output in 1970 and 1978 (current prices), eight countries, percentages

Country	Imports 1970	Imports 1978	Exports 1970	Exports 1978
Finland	27.8	25.0	28.9	36.2
France	15.1	18.8	16.5	22.4
Germany, Federal Republic of	11.9	15.3	18.0	23.2
Italy	17.7	19.7	22.0	30.5
Netherlands*	42.2	47.5**	37.9	47.1**
Norway	42.5	40.1	30.1	31.4
Sweden	28.5	31.5	29.5	38.1
United Kingdom	13.1	20.0	15.3	20.8

*Excluding petroleum and cost products.
**1977

Source: ECE (1980), p.218.

Indices of structural change for imports and exports show that the change in import structure was considerably larger. One interpretation is that exports of the concerned countries reacted relatively slowly to changing world trade conditions. However, the different countries vary considerably in this respect.

The most striking feature for the development of individual sector shares in that the trend is at least non-decreasing in nearly all cases. i.e. eighteen sectors in eight countries. The heavy import penetration in labour-intensive products is well established in all markets. But the very same sectors also exhibit strong upward trends in export ratios. For most countries there exists a striking similarity in export and import ratios. This evidence demonstrates the importance of intra-industry trade among developed nations. It also suggests that heavy import penetration is beneficial to efficiency, which in turn creates strong competitiveness in export markets. For the Nordic countries, however, the specialisation of exports is heavily dominated by their natural resource endowments.

4 SUMMARY AND CONCLUSIONS

The slowing down of overall growth in manufacturing industries in the West European advanced economies in the 1970s did not affect structural change to any large extent. The pace of change remained stable from the 1960s. Also the directions of change represent a continuation of earlier established trends: a shift *from* production of low-skilled, labour-intensive products to specialisation in high-technology and capital-intensive production. The development of international trade is mainly responsible for increasing specialisation, even though trade has tended to stagnate during the period.

This empirical evidence offers little or no support for the view that structural change problems in industrialised countries have their origin in disturbing *import competition* from developing countries. Professor Balassa's paper elaborates on these issues in much more detail. There it is seen that imports from developing countries have been growing in importance as a source to satisfy demand for manufactured goods in industrialised economies. But at the same time, the markets in developing countries are absorbing an increasing share of exports from the industrialised world. This, of course, is an empirical demonstration of the classical mechanism that trade can be mutually beneficial to participants. In this way, structural change is in itself a means to achieve welfare improvements and should accordingly not be counteracted by policy.

One is then left with factors that are *internal* to the industrial countries to explain the structural change problems. Here, we have first of all the possibility of a shift in the parameter combination. Where, as earlier, growth tended to favour the industrial sector, we may now be in a situation where it favours the service sectors. This should happen, for example, if productivity increases have become more labour-saving than earlier, a case which may well be advanced with reference to the info-revolution. Then capital-intensive indusry sectors gain little or nothing and accordingly make a loss in internal competitiveness. Growth will shift to labour-intensive service sectors and 'de-industrialisation' will be the typical outcome of this process. Again, this type of structural change is welfare-improving, even though it does not replicate the historically established pattern.

The expansion of the public sector can be seen as part of this mechanism. Demand for goods that are publicly provided has been unusually expansive in the last decade. But here we have also a second explanation which is related to structural change in a somewhat different way. By its very nature, structural change will create unemployment – at least temporarily. In reality, structural phenomena of this type can never be distinguished from short-run problems, and employment policies are bound to affect both. Where the industrialised countries have committed themselves to ambitious goals concerning cyclical unemployment, they have automatically affected the structural change process. It may even be that these effects have been particularly strong because of the means that have been used. Public employment that becomes more or less permanent must have a crowding-out effect on the private sector in the labour market, even in those cases where it is used as a policy to reduce unemployment.

Professor Waelbroeck's paper also discusses the implications of egalitarian welfare policies for an economy's ability to adjust itself in response to pressures for structural change. Taxation and other income distribution policy measures have strongly reduced the incentives for entrepreneurs to create new development in new sectors of the economy. In this way, the structural change process has been left with only the negative side of development. This, in turn, has created demand for policies to ensure that *existing* employment opportunities survive. For this reason, the governments in many industrialised countries have become engaged in large subsidies and/or public production programmes in those sectors that are presently declining due to lack of competitive strength. Policies of this type do not only have the crowding-out effect discussed above. They also preserve an inefficient production structure and retard economic growth.

The conflicting goals of economic policy meet a very severe dilemma at this point. Social gains from income and employment stability are easy to visualise and even represent by empirical estimates of production and employment otherwise foregone. The gains from structural change are visible only in the long run, and accordingly they tend to become drowned by subsequent short-term changes. This also makes it difficult to identify what groups are benefiting from structural change. Professor Dixon presents in his paper a methodology to overcome the difficulties in assessing returns to specific policy proposals related to structural adjustment. In the computable general equilibrium framework he is using, one can calculate not only the immediate effects of policy change, e.g. a tariff reduction, but also the indirect effects and it is here that this methodology scores. There is no doubt that calculations of this type make important contributions to our understanding of structural change, and they can also serve as a firm basis for the evaluation of alternatives on specific policy issues.

By focusing on the firm as the unit of production, Michel Didier's study of the pattern of growth in the private sector of the national economies shows that most growth of output and employment occurs in firms that are smaller than average in size. This is particularly true in France and the UK, but the phenomenon appears to be universal. This dynamism of small firms is associated with a higher rate of innovation. Smaller units have more flexible personnel policies, including salary relativities among their staff. Smallness is not therefore to be discouraged, and the entry of new small firms is to be encouraged.

NOTE

1. All data presented are from a careful study of structural change in Western Europe by the Secretariat of the European Economic Commission. The report is presented as chapter 4 of the *Economic Survey of Europe in 1980*. In this chapter, this study is referred to as ECE (1980).

Part III

Structural Change in a Selection of Countries

14 Structural Effects of Increasing Australia's Imports from Less Developed Countries

P. G. Warr
AUSTRALIAN NATIONAL UNIVERSITY

1 INTRODUCTION[1]

By OECD standards, Australia is a highly protectionist country.[2] The relationship between this protection and the export prospects of the less developed countries (LDCs) has been the subject of extensive popular and professional debate in Australia, from two quite different directions. First, there has been growing recognition that Australia's heavy protection of its manufacturing sector adversely affects the export prospects of the LDCs.[3] This recognition has in part reflected a sympathetic response to demands from representatives of the LDCs for greater access to the markets of the more developed countries (MDCs) for LDC exports, and has in part been a by-product of the growing political importance to Australia of the developing countries of East and South East Asia. Reductions in Australian protection have thus been advocated partly for this reason.

Second, and from a quite different direction, there has been a popular fear that a flood of imports from cheap-labour countries may result from continued improvements in the export competitiveness of the LDCs, particularly in manufacturing, or from reduced protection within Australia. It is believed that this would cause increased unemployment within Australia and would affect the structure of the Australian economy in ways that are not desired. Fears of this kind are not unique to Australia, and there is nothing new about them. They derive emotional support from Australia's historical fear of the densely populated countries of Asia, and indeed continued public tolerance of the heavy protection of Australia's manufacturing sector testifies in part to their historical persuasiveness. It also testifies to the political attractiveness of protectionist arguments which assume the desirability of maintaining a substantial manufacturing sector within the Australian economy.

This paper attempts to examine these two aspects of the debate together. First, Section 2 discusses the effects that Australian protection has on its imports from LDCs. Both the overall effects of Australia's system of protection and the effects of the protection of particular industries are examined. Next, Section 3 looks at the structural effects of reduced protection. Although the undesired structural effects of reduced protection are usually not well defined, reductions in the share of the manufacturing sector in national output and employment appear to be of central concern. The analysis focuses on the effects of reduced protection of those commodities where such reductions would be of most benefit to the LDCs.[4]

2 AUSTRALIA'S IMPORTS FROM LDCS AND THE EFFECTS OF REDUCED PROTECTION

Australia's imports from LDCs in recent years as a proportion of its total imports are summarised in Table 14.1.[5] This proportion rose from around 15 per cent in the early 1960s to around 20 per cent in the late 1970s. The LDCs' share of world exports of all commodities was consistently somewhat greater than this. For example, this share was 19 per cent in 1968 and 26 per cent in 1977.[6] In the case of manufactured commodities, this situation is reversed, with Australia's imports from LDCs rising over the period 1968–6 to 1977–8 from 7 to 13 per cent of its total imports of these commodities, whereas the LDCs' share of world exports of manfactures rose from 5 to 8 per cent over this period.

Australia's trade policies affect its imports from the LDCs in two ways. *Direct discrimination* between trading partners operates through Australia's system of trade preferences. The countries receiving these preferences include both MDCs and LDCs. Since the United Kingdom joined the EEC in 1973, the balance of these preferences has shifted in favour of the LDCs, but their commodity coverage remains very limited. *Indirect discrimination* is much more important. It occurs as a result of Australia's uneven system of industrial protection. Obviously, this protection is intended to assist particular Australian industries. Its differential effects on Australia's

Table 14.1 Australia'a imports from LDCs (three-year averages, per cent of total imports)

Source of imports	1963–4 to 1965–6	1966–7 to 1968–9	1969–70 to 1971–2	1972–3 to 1974–5	1975–6 to 1977–8	1978–9 to 1980–1
ASEAN	3.9	3.1	2.4	2.9	4.3	5.4
NICs	1.2	1.8	2.9	5.5	7.4	7.9
Other LDC – low income	5.3	5.0	3.6	3.4	2.9	3.2
Other LDC – middle income	4.8	3.8	4.1	5.6	5.4	4.1
LDC total	14.9	13.4	12.4	16.1	18.1	19.7
MDC total	85.1	86.6	87.6	83.9	81.9	80.3

Source: Industries Assistance Commission

trading partners are an unintended but nevertheless significant side-effect.

In an earlier paper (Warr and Lloyd, 1983) it was shown that the effect of Australia's trade preferences on its imports from the LDCs is far less important than even quite small changes in overall rates of protection. As a means of increasing Australia's imports from the LDCs, changes in overall rates of protection are of much greater importance than changes to Australia's system of trade preferences would probably be. Consequently, this paper focuses on the effects of Australia's protection (indirect discrimination) on its imports from the LDCs.

Obviously, the high but variable rates of protection seen in Australia have differential effects on its various trading partners. One way to show this would be to construct weighted averages of the nominal rates of protection applying to various commodities, with the commodity weights used for each trading partner reflecting the share of the commodity concerned in Australia's total imports from that country. The well-known difficulty with this procedure is that actual import shares reflect existing rates of protection. Commodities subject to high rates of protection consequently receive too low a weight. Nevertheless, while free trade import shares would be preferable for this purpose, they are unobserved. Actual import shares have therefore been used in the construction of Table 14.2. It is not clear that any systematic bias between trading partners would be likely to result from this procedure. These calculations suggest that Australian protection was slightly heavier against commodities exported by MDCs than those exported by LDCs throughout the period 1968–6 to 1980–1 but that the difference between them diminished over time.[7]

The impact of a country's protection on its imports from particular trading partners depends not only on the rates of protection it applies to the commodities exported by those trading partners, but also on the degree to which its imports of those commodities respond to changes in rates of protection. This depends on domestic supply and demand conditions. Countries exporting commodities which have highly elastic import demand within Australia could be more adversely affected by Australian protection than others which export commodities subject to higher rates of protection but for which Australia's import demand is less elastic. Differences among countries in this respect are missed by the sort of analysis presented in Table 14.2, but these differences are clearly central to an assessment

Table 14.2 Australia's implicit protection against LDC exports (nominal rate of protection, per cent)

	1968–9	1971–2	1974–5	1977–8	1980–1
ASEAN	10.8	18.6	6.7	8.8	8.6
NICs	30.1	28.6	21.5	24.4	22.9
Other LDC – low income	24.1	19.4	13.1	17.8	4.7
Other LDC – middle income	16.1	15.6	6.1	7.5	10.8
LDC total	20.3	24.0	13.1	17.2	16.2
MDC total	26.5	27.7	17.7	19.2	18.6
All countries	25.6	26.6	16.9	18.8	18.1

Source: Calculated from data provided by Industries Assistance Commission.

of the degree to which imports from particular groups of countries would respond to reduced Australian protection.

This issue is studied in this paper with the aid of a multi-sectoral general equilibrium model of the Australian economy. This 109-sector model, known as the ORANI model, is discussed in detail in Dixon et al. (1977 and 1982).[8] It belongs to the general class of Johansen multi-sectoral models and is linear in the percentage response of endogenous variables to given percentage shocks in exogenous variables. For a given specification of endogenous and exogenous variables, the model thus computes a matrix of elasticities giving the response of the former to variations in the latter. The ORANI model has now been widely applied in policy-related economic research within Australia and its structure is particularly well suited to the analysis of the general equilibrium effects of changes in protection.

Two variants of the ORANI model are used. These are referred to as the 1968–9 and 1977–8 variants, and are respectively based on the 1968–9 and 1974–5 Australian input-output tables, 1968–9 and 1977–8 import shares, and 1968–9 and 1977–8 data on tariff equivalent rates of protection by input-output commodity. In other respects, such as in the econometric estimates of domestic consumer demand elasticities, export demand elasticities and other parameters which underly the model, the two variants are the same. In both variants, real aggregate absorption (consumer spending plus investment plus government spending, all in real terms) is held constant, and in both variants real wages are held fixed and labour markets are therefore slack. All imported commodities are assumed to be available in infinitely elastic supply.

In this exercise, the ORANI model is used in conjunction with the Australian trade data to estimate the effects of reduced Australian protection on its imports from various trading partners. The assumption is made that for each commodity the proportion of Australia's imports coming from any one country is unaffected by changes in levels of protection. Changes in protection will thus affect individual countries' exports to Australia in different proportions, provided the proportional response of Australia's imports to a change in protection differs from one commodity to the other.

The simulated effects that reduced protection has on imports from LDCs are summarised in two ways. First, the dollar value of the increased imports from particular groups of countries that would result from a 30 per cent reduction in all rates of protection is estimated.[9] Second, the discriminatory impact of a uniform reduction in protection is captured by computing for each group of countries an *index of discrimination*.[10] This consists of a ratio of that group of countries' marginal share to its average share. The marginal share is that group of countries' share of the increased volume of imports which enter Australia in response to the uniform reduction in protection. The average share is simply Australia's total imports from that country or group of countries as a share of Australia's total imports.

The index of discrimination can be represented most clearly in terms of elasticities. For country group k, the index is given by

$$I_k = \eta_{kt}/\eta_{.t} \tag{1}$$

where η_{kt} denotes Australia's elasticity of demand for imports from country k with respect to the rate of protection, t (in general, changes in t can represent across-the-board changes in protection or, in other applications, changes in individual rates), and $\eta_{.t}$ denotes the elasticity of demand for imports from all countries with respect to the rate of protection.

Alternatively, writing M_{ik} for imports of commodity i from country k, and dM_{ik} for the change in that variable resulting from a given change in protection,

$$I_k = \frac{\sum_{i=1}^{n} dM_{ik} / \sum_{k=1}^{m} \sum_{i=1}^{n} dM_{ik}}{\sum_{i=1}^{n} M_{ik} / \sum_{k=1}^{m} \sum_{i=1}^{n} M_{ik}} \qquad (2)$$

where n and m denote the number of commodities and the number of countries supplying imports, respectively. This expression is estimated by means of the maintained assumption that $dM_{ik}/dM_{i.} = M_{ik}/M_{i} \equiv \alpha_{ik}$, where $M_i \equiv \sum_{k=1}^{m} M_{ik}$ denotes total imports of commodity i. That is, $dM_{ik} = \alpha_{ik} dM_{i.}$, and the estimated value of I_k is thus

$$I_k = \frac{\sum_{i=1}^{n} \alpha_{ik} dM_{i.} / \sum_{i=1}^{n} dM_{i.}}{\sum_{i=1}^{n} \alpha_{ik} M_{i.} / \sum_{i=1}^{n} M_{i.}}$$

Clearly, a country or group of countries for which the index of discrimination exceeds unity is one whose share of Australia's imports would *rise* if Australia's protection was reduced, while a country for which the index is less than unity one whose share of Australia's imports would fall. The higher the index of discrimination, the more heavily Australia's protection discrimates against imports from that country *vis-à-vis* others. Obviously, the weighted average of all indices of discrimination across trading partners is unity.[11] Therefore, a country whose index is greater (less) than unity is one against which Australia's protection discriminates more (less) heavily than against the average of all other countries.

The results of this exercise are summarised in Tables 14.3 and 14.4. Table 14.3 relates to uniform across-the-board reductions in protection. Table 14.4 presents the effects on imports of *all* commodities of reductions in the protection of individual manufactured commodities, holding all other rates constant. The results of this exercise are presented for each of two years, 1968–9 and 1977–8. The 1968–9 and

Table 14.3 Australia's imports from LDCs and effects of a general cut in protection

	Actual share of total imports (%)		Increased imports from 30% cut in protection				Index of discrimination	
			Value ($m)		Per cent total imports			
	1968–9	1977–8	1968–9	1977–8	1968–9	1977–8	1968–9	1977–8
ASEAN	3.2	5.3	0.147	6.027	0.1	1.1	0.050	0.477
NICs	2.0	7.8	3.216	34.839	4.8	3.9	1.753	1.699
Other LDC – lower income	5.1	4.4	2.500	10.818	1.5	2.5	0.526	1.060
Other LDC – middle income	3.0	4.4	1.023	5.670	1.0	1.1	0.361	0.465
LDC total	12.9	20.3	6.822	56.181	1.6	2.6	0.567	1.138
MDC total	87.1	79.7	85.332	197.865	2.9	2.2	1.065	0.967

Table 14.4 Australia's imports of specific manufactured commodities and effects of reduced protection

	Commodity (Input-Output Number)	LDC share of imports (%)		Nominal rate of protection (%)		Increase in total imports from a 30% general cut in protection				Index of discrimination For LDCs	
						Value ($'000)		% of total change in LDC imports			
		1968–9	1977–8	1968–9	1977–8	1968–9	1977–8	1968–9	1977–8	1968–9	1977–8
1	Knitted goods (24.01)	0	62	44	53.4	108	30,756	1.6	54.7	2.71	18.983
2	Plywood (25.02)	4	80	29	22.8	261	1,167	3.8	2.1	5.39	6.256
3	Fibreboard (26.02)	81	84	46	20.4	261	456	3.8	0.8	8.76	5.448
4	Joining and wood products (25.03)	41	71	24	14.3	69	939	1.0	1.7	6.20	5.212
5	Clothing (24.02)	2	69	58	69.5	954	11,085	14.0	19.7	5.65	4.622
6	Footwear (24.03)	0	65	51	57.4	528	10,305	7.7	18.3	2.68	4.355
7	Cotton, silk, etc. (23.03)	42	54	33	39.6	753	5,787	11.0	10.3	6.25	4.072
8	Margarine, oils, fats (21.04)	57	44	15	8.9	96	651	1.4	1.2	5.07	3.383
9	Man-made fibres (23.02)	3	4	25	33.8	−297	−1,002	4.4	−1.8	−7.96	−1.278
10	Motor vehicles, parts (32.01)	0	4	35	55.8	−306	−4,278	4.5	−7.6	−0.15	−0.242

1977–8 results use the 1968–9 and 1977–8 variants of the ORA[NI] model in conjunction with the Australian trade data correspondin[g to] 1968–9 and 1977–8, respectively. These years are chosen beca[use] readily available variants of the ORANI model exist for these ye[ars] and because the period 1968–9 to 1977–8 captures important chan[ges] in Australian protection policy. In particular, both the text[ile,] clothing and footwear commodity group and the transport equipm[ent] commodity group, which includes motor vehicles, became m[ore] heavily protected over this period, while protection was lowered [in] other areas.

The results in Table 14.3 indicate that a 30 per cent reduction in rates of protection would have caused imports from the LDCs a[s a] whole to rise by 1.6 per cent in 1968–9 and 2.6 per cent in 1977[.] These seem surprisingly low, considering the amount of concern [the] issue has generated in Australia. On the other hand, a sim[ilar] qualitative conclusion holds for imports from the MDCs.[12] [The] results for the index of discrimination are more revealing. The in[dex] of discrimination against LDC imports rose significantly over [the] period from well below unity to just above unity. Over this peri[od] the incidence of Australia's system of protection shifted hea[vily] against the interests of the LDCs relative to the more advan[ced] countries.[13] Within the LDCs, this same qualitative statement app[lies] to the ASEAN countries and to other low-income LDCs, particul[arly] China and India.[14] The index of discrimination rose slightly [for] middle-income LDCs and fell marginally for the newly industriali[sed] countries, but from a high level.

There are two possible explanations for this change in the incide[nce] of Australian protection. First, it could be due to changes in [the] structure of the Australian system of protection, discriminatin[g in] recent years more heavily than before against commodities wh[ich] happen to be exported by the LDCs. Second, it could be due [to] changes in the comparative advantage of the LDCs, whose exp[orts] now consist to a greater extent than before of commodities wh[ich] have always been subject to high rates of protection in Australia. [Of] course, these explanations are not mutually exclusive. Their rela[tive] importance has been examined by means of the following exp[eri]ment. First, the 1968–9 variant of the simulation model was combi[ned] with the 1977–8 trade data. The index of discrimination for the LD[Cs] was then 0.916. Reversing this, and combining the 1977–8 varian[t of] the model with the 1968–9 trade data, this index becomes 0.638[.]

Clearly, the second of the two possible explanations is the more important. It is primarily changes in the types of commodities Australia imports from the LDCs (as captured in the trade data), rather than changes in the structure of Australian protection (as captured in the simulation model), which accounts for the fact that Australian protection has come to discriminate more heavily against imports from the LDCs as a group. Of course, this shift in the composition of Australia's imports from the LDCs towards commodities which are highly responsive to reduced protection, reflects a shift in the comparative advantage of the LDCs towards commodities against which Australia maintains high rates of protection.

It is useful to examine the effects of reduced protection at a more disaggregated level. Of the 109 commodities specified in the Australian input-output tables, eighty are traded goods and twenty-nine are non-traded. Of the traded goods, positive rates of nominal protection have been estimated for sixty-two items, most of which are manufactured commodities. The ORANI model is capable of estimating the effects of reduced protection on each of the individual items separately, holding the others constant, as well as the effects of reducing all, or groups of items, simultaneously. The results presented relate to the general equilibrium effect that reductions in the rates of protection of *individual* commodities have on Australia's total imports of *all* commodities from the LDCs. The effect on imports from the LDCs of reducing protection on individual commodities varies widely. Even the signs of these effects vary. Reduced protection of many items actually causes total imports from the LDCs to decline. This is true for fifteen of the sixty-two tariff items in 1977–8 and for seventeen items in 1968–9.

This variation in the response of imports from LDCs to reduced protection at an individual commodity level is illustrated in Table 14.4. The effects of reduced protection on each of the sixty-two tariff items have been estimated and, of these, ten commodities have been selected for inclusion in the table and for the analysis in the following section. These items were selected on the basis of the index of discrimination for the LDCs.[15] The first eight commodities are ones for which reductions in their rates of protection cause increased imports from the LDCs, while the other two commodities are selected to illustrate the opposite possibility. The first eight commodities had the highest indices of discrimination against the LDCs in 1977–8 and are arranged in order of their indices of discrimination in that year. Reduced protection of these eight items together represents 107 per cent of the value of an equal percentage reduction in the rates of protection of all manufactured commodities in 1977–8 and 91 per cent in 1968–9. The increase over the decade in the LDCs' share of Australia's imports of these commodities is especially notable.

The other two commodities included in the table – (9) man-made fibres and (10) motor vehicles and parts – are selected to illustrate the fact that reduced MDC protection of some commodities will actually reduce imports from the LDCs. To understand this, it is necessary to note first that only a very small proportion of Australia's imports of these two items comes from the LDCs.

Consider man-made fibres first. Two mechanisms are operating. First, man-made fibres are a substitute for cotton and silk-based textiles, the latter imported heavily from LDCs. Reduced protection of man-made fibres thus stimulates their use as an intermediate good and demand for imports of natural fibre-based textiles declines. Because of the Leontief input-output assumptions used in the simulation model, this effect is muted within the analysis, and operates only through adjustments in industry outputs. The more important mechanism is that reduced protection of man-made fibres improves the competitiveness of the domestic clothing industry, causing imports of finished clothing items from the LDCs to decline as well.

The mechanism of adjustment is less direct in the case of motor vehicles. Reduced protection of automobiles stimulates production generally in the remainder of the manufacturing sector. The primary reason for this derives from the fixed real wage assumption. The price of motor vehicles is a major component of the consumer price index (CPI). Reduced motor vehicle protection lowers this price component of the CPI, and the money wage corresponding to a fixed real wage thus falls in terms of the domestic prices of other manufactured goods. A lesser reason is that transport equipment is itself an input into the production of many other manufactured commodities. For both these reasons, reduced protection of motor vehicles improves the competitiveness of other import-competing manufacturing industries and thus causes imports of these commodities to decline, harming the LDCs.

It would seem that the share of LDCs in the change in total imports (of all commodities) which results from a reduction in the rate of protection of a particular commodity (the LDCs' marginal share for that tariff item) would be positively related to the share of LDCs in Australia's actual imports of that commodity. But how well does information on the latter serve as a predictor of the former? The answer is, not especially well. The correlation coefficient between these two variables across all tariff items has been computed, and results of 0.50 for 1968–9 and 0.65 for 1977–8 were obtained. These correlation coefficients are both significantly greater than zero at the 5 per cent significance level, but the difference between them and unity suggests that other factors are also important. In particular, differences between commodities in the responsiveness of imports to reductions in their own rates of protection (own price elasticity of import demand) and differences in the cross-elasticity of import demand clearly play an important role).

3 STRUCTURAL EFFECTS

The effects that reduced protection has on employment and on the structure of the Australian economy will now be considered. It is important to recall that in the version of the ORANI model being used, labour markets are slack and real wages are held fixed. Attention will be focused on the effects of Australian output and employment of reduced protection of the ten commodities included in Table 14.4, and these effects will be compared with the effects of reduced protection on imports from LDCs. The aim is to show the trade-off between the (politically undesired) structural effects of reduced protection and the (allegedly desired) effect on imports from LDCs.

3.1 Output Effects

We summarise the output effects of reduced protection of the ten selected industries by concentrating on the sectoral distribution of the change in the value of output at producer prices. First, we look at the change in the value of output in the industry in which protection is being reduced, followed by the change in the value of output in the manufacturing sector as a whole. The rest of the economy is then divided into two sectors, referred to as the 'primary sector', comprising the agricultural and mining industries, and the 'non-traded sector', comprising the service industries, utilities and construction. To show the trade-offs involved, the dollar value of the output effects at producer prices are presented in Table 14.5 relative to the dollar value of the change in imports from LDCs at cif prices.

Table 14.5 Output effects per unit change in LDC imports from reduced protection (output change in dollars per dollar of increased LDC imports)

Commodity	Protected industry 1968–9	1977–8	Manufacturing sector 1968–9	1977–8	Primary sector 1968–9	1977–8	Non-traded sector 1968–9	1977–8
1 Knitted goods	−16.8	−1.3	−16.7	−0.5	3.0	0.2	0.9	0.1
2 Plywood	−3.9	−2.6	−2.8	−1.1	0.6	0	−1.0	−0.3
3 Fibreboard	−2.8	−1.6	−3.5	−0.9	0.6	0.3	0	0
4 Joining and wood products	−10.1	−2.2	−6.8	−1.4	1.7	0.2	−1.5	−0.4
5 Clothing	−8.2	−4.3	−7.7	−2.8	1.2	0.7	−0.1	−0.2
6 Footwear	−14.7	−5.8	−16.5	−5.4	1.4	0.5	−2.5	−0.5
7 Cotton, silk, etc.	−17.4	−6.1	−4.1	0.3	3.1	1.0	3.7	1.2
8 Margarine, oils, fats	−6.3	−3.6	4.3	2.1	1.7	0.5	1.2	0.3
9 Man-made fibres	178.5	125.7	157.2	−97.3	−1.4	−9.8	0	0.5
10 Motor vehicles, parts	28.8	31.3	2.8	−14.7	−5.2	−5.4	−5.4	−6.1
Commodities 1–8	−11.1	−3.4	−7.5	−1.6	1.7	0.4	0.3	0
Across the board	—	—	−14.7	−8.5	5.0	2.1	1.9	1.7

For example, in the case of commodity 1 in Table 14.5, knitted goods, the amount by which reduced protection causes imports from LDCs to rise in relation to its structural effects rose dramatically over the period 1968–9 to 1977–8. In the latter year, reduced protection of this industry causes output to decline by 1.3 dollars per dollar of increased imports from LDCs, but output rises in other industries. Surprisingly, most of this rise in output occurs within the manufacturing sector itself. Output of other manufacturing industries rises by 80 cents per dollar of additional LDC imports, giving a net decline of manufacturing output of 50 cents. Output in the primary sector and in the non-traded sector rises by 20 cents and 10 cents per dollar of additional LDC imports, respectively. Aggregate output declines by 15 cents per dollar of additional LDC imports. It must be stressed that these output effects are calculated at domestic producer prices and that these prices are distorted by trade interventions such as tariffs and import quotas, by excise taxes, and by wage controls. Consequently, the sign of aggregate output effects does not necessarily have any direct welfare significance.

This general pattern is seen in each of the first eight commodities presented in Table 14.5. The trade-off between the structural effects of reduced protection and the effect on imports from LDCs appears to have improved substantially over the decade in the case of each of these commodities. Focusing on the results for 1977–8, output declines in the industry in which protection is reduced, but rises in the rest of the economy, taken together. In all cases, the major part of this rise in output in the rest of the economy occurs elsewhere in the manufacturing sector itself, and not in the primary or non-trade sectors, as might have been expected.[16] This is an interesting result and occurs primarily because of the fixed real wage assumption, as outline dearlier. Reduced protection of one manufactured commodity lowers wage costs in other manufacturing industries, via its effects on the consumer price index. In the case of two commodities (7 and 8), aggregate output in the manufacturing sector actually rises.[17]

An equiproportional reduction in the protection of these eight commodities together accounts in 1977–8 for more additional imports from the LDCs than an across-the-board reduction of the same proportion; but it causes only 21 per cent of the decline in total output in the manufacturing sector that results from an across-the-board cut of the same proportion. Moreover, if protection of motor vehicles is increased slightly (by 8 per cent) the effect on manufacturing output of a 30 per cent reduction in the protection of the other eight commodities is cancelled out. But, for the reasons explained earlier, both of these changes cause imports from the LDCs to rise. The combination of these two adjustments to protection leaves manufacturing output unchanged, but imports from the LDCs increase by 112 per cent of the increase resulting from a 30 per cent across-the-board cut in all rates of protection.[18] Needless to say, this is not the sort of policy that would be recommended if the objective were to improve economic welfare within Australia; but if the aim of policy was to increase imports from the LDCs without reducing the size of the manufacturing sector, this combination of adjustments could achieve it.

3.2 Employment Effects

Popular discussion of protection, in Australia and elsewhere, focuses on the effect that changes in protection may have on employment in the protected industries themselves. Economists have pointed out, with growing political success, that the protection of one industry reduces output and employment in others. The effect that reduced protection has on aggregate employment will thus be very different from its effect on employment in the protected industry. The Australian trade union movement has been especially resistant to this line of argument. One interpretation of this resistance is that protection is believed to discriminate in favour of employment of particular categories of labour – those represented by the trade unions – and that these workers would be especially disadvantaged by reduced protection. This section of the paper attempts to capture these elements of the debate by estimating the effects of reduced protection on employment in the protected industry, on aggregate employment, on the sectoral distribution of employment, and finally on 'blue-collar' employment.[19]

Table 14.6 summarises the estimated employment effects of reduced protection of these ten commodities, as well as the effects of an across-the-board cut. Employment effects are expressed as the change in the number of workers per million dollars of additional imports from LDCs resulting from a cut in protection. The comparison of employment effects for 1977–8 and 1968–9 is similar to the comparison of output effects for those years discussed above, so the discussion will be confined to the results for 1977–8. Column (1) indicates the effect of reduced protection of the industry concerned

Table 14.6 Employment effects per unit change in LDC imports from reduced protection, 1977–8 (number of workers per million dollars of LDC imports)

Commodity	(1) Protected industry	(2) Manufacturing sector	(3) Primary sector	(4) Non-traded sector	(5) Aggregate	(6) Blue-collar
1 Knitted goods	−38	−18	26	5	13	−3
2 Plywood	−77	−37	19	−15	−33	−41
3 Fibreboard	−46	−30	123	−2	91	−3
4 Joining and wood products	−88	−78	31	−16	−63	−51
5 Clothing	−182	−149	77	−3	−75	−69
6 Footwear	−212	−207	56	−18	−169	−146
7 Cotton, silk, etc.	−114	51	109	57	217	96
8 Margarine, oils, fats	−35	95	54	23	172	111
9 Man-made fibres	615	−580	−621	−423	−1,624	713
10 Motor vehicles, parts	2,467	1,883	−1,146	−58	379	1,364
Commodities 1–8	−100	−67	49	8	−10	−30
Across the board	—	−204	245	37	78	−29

on employment in that industry, relative to the increase in LDC imports. Column (5) shows the change in aggregate employment and columns (2) and (4) show the sectoral distribution of this aggregate employment effect. Finally, column (6) shows the effect on blue-collar employment.

The sectoral distribution of employment effects is qualitatively similar to the output effects discussed above. The effects on aggregate employment of reduced protection of the first eight commodities are small and vary considerably. These net aggregate employment effects are estimated by summing across the estimated sectoral employment effects, the signs of which vary. It should be emphasised that the small residual which is obtained magnifies errors in the estimated sectoral components. The resulting estimates of aggregate employment effects are consequently the least reliable of the results presented in the table. But a comparison of the estimated aggregate employment effects with the estimated blue-collar employment effects does lend moderate support to the notion that the employment effects of reduced protection are biased against the interests of blue-collar workers. In the four cases where aggregate employment falls, most or all of this decline is experienced by blue-collar workers, and blue-collar employment declines in two cases where aggregate employment rises.

Comparing the effects of reduced protection on commodities 1 to 8 with the effects of an across-the-board reduction, the former is more cost-effective (loss of employment per unit of LDC imports) in terms of manufacturing employment, less so in terms of aggregate employment (which rises in response to an across-the-board cut) and about equally as effective in relation to blue-collar employment. Comparison of the last two rows of columns (5) and (6) suggests that the net employment effects of reduced protection of commodities 1 to 8 are indeed biased against the interests of blue-collar workers *vis-à-vis* other workers, but less so than is the case with an across-the-board cut.

4 SUMMARY AND CONCLUSIONS

This paper studies the trade-off between two effects of reduced Australian protection. These are, on the one hand, the desired effect of increasing imports from less developed countries (LDCs), and, on the other, the politically undesired structural effects of reduced protection. These undesired structural effects primarily involve reductions in the share of the manufacturing sector in national output and employment. The paper focuses on the decade 1968–9 to 1977–8 and the analysis utilises the ORANI general equilibrium model of the Australian economy in conjunction with the Australian trade data.

It is argued that the effects of Australian protection came to descriminate much more heavily against the LDCs, relative to Australia's other trading partners, over this decade. Nevertheless, reductions in rates of protection at the individual commodity level have widely varying effects on Australia's total imports from LDCs. Reductions in some rates would increase imports from LDCs quite considerably, while reductions in others would actually cause total imports from the LDCs to decline. Negative effects of this type seem paradoxical, but they arise from the fact that reduced protection of one commodity can cause imports of other commodities to decline. Obviously, a general equilibrium analysis is essential if effects of this sort are to be detected. A partial equilibrium analysis will necessarily miss the fact that the LDCs have an interest (in the short run, at least) in *increased* developed country protection of some commodities.

Of the sixty-two input-output commodities subject to protection, a given proportional reduction in the rates of protection of only eight particular commodities would have a greater effect on imports from the LDCs than that same proportional reduction applied to all sixty-two rates. Reduced protection of these eight commodities would in addition have much smaller structural effects than an equal across-the-board reduction. Moreover, virtually any undesired structural effect of reduced protection of these eight items could be counteracted by increased protection of one or more of the commodities for which increased protection would benefit the LDCs. These adjustments to protection would not necessarily improve economic welfare within Australia, but if the objective of policy was to increase Australia's imports from the LDCs without causing undesired structural effects, then adjustments of this kind could achieve it.

NOTES

1. This paper has benefited greatly from the author's discussions with P. J. Lloyd. The analytic approach used in Section 2 draws in part on our joint paper (Warr and Lloyd, 1983). The paper also benefited from the comments of Max Corden and from the research assistance of Prue Phillips and Chris Cheah. The research makes extensive use of the

ORANI general equilibrium model of the Australian economy developed as a component of the IMPACT Project and described in Dixon et al. (1982). Assistance with the ORANI simulations was provided by Robert Butterworth and Brian Parmenter. Tony Lawson assisted with provision of data and the interpretation of some ORANI results.

2. Average nominal rates of protection on dutiable items were estimated by Cline et al. (1978, p.10). In 1973, these were United States 9 per cent, Canada 14 per cent, Japan 11 per cent and EEC 9 per cent. For Australia (not included in Cline's data), the comparable rate in 1973–4 was 18 per cent. The data on economy-wide rates of protection for Japan and the EEC miss the increase in the rate of agricultural protection occurring in the late 1970s, and also the increased use generally of non-tariff barriers. When attention is confined to manufactured goods the corresponding rates were: United States 9.5 per cent, Canada 14.2 per cent, Japan 12.5 per cent, EEC 9 per cent and Australia 23 per cent.

3. See, for example, the report of the influential, government-appointed Harries Committee (Committee on Australia's Relations with the Third World, 1979). This report strongly advocates (p.131) that rather than 'to seek to use our trade policies to isolate ourselves from the consequences of Third World industrialisation', Australia should 'set out deliberately and energetically to facilitate the transition to a more outward-looking Australian industrial structure'.

4. Other studies along these general lines include Krueger (1971), 1978a, 1978b), Cline et al. (1978) and Birnberg (1979). Krueger (1971) draws on the US input-output tables to argue that US import quotas on LDC exports do not succeed in raising employment in the USA. Krueger (1978a and 1978b) draws on time series data for the USA to argue that increased LDC exports of manufactured goods to the USA have little discernible effect on employment or output in the American industries affected. Cline et al. (1978) and Birnberg (1979) utilise econometrically estimated aggregate price elasticities of demand for imports from various countries to project the import effects of reduced protection. Several significant and interesting conclusions emerge from this. The present study takes this a step further by conducting the analysis within a full general equilibrium model of the domestic economy. The qualitative conclusions that emerge for Australia generally support those obtained for other OECD countries by Cline and Birnberg.

5. The LDCs are defined, as in World Bank (1981), to be those countries with 1979 GNP per capital below US $4,400. The ASEAN (Association of South East Asian Nations) countries comprise Indonesia, the Philippines, Singapore, Thailand and Malaysia. The NICs (newly industrialising countries) comprise Taiwan, South Korea, Hong Kong and Singapore. These two groups of LDCs are isolated because of their political importance to Australia. Note that Singapore belongs to both ASEAN and the NICs. The other LDCs are divided into 'low' and 'middle' income groups, as in World Bank (1981), which makes the separation at a 1979 GNP per capita of US $375.

6. See Industries Assistance Commission (1981). For a more detailed discussion of trends in Australia's imports from the LDCs see Garnaut and Anderson (1982).
7. The nominal rates of protection by input–output category on which these calculations are based represent the *tariff equivalent* of all major forms of protection including tariffs, excise taxes and import quotas.
8. Further details of the characteristics of the simulation model used are presented in Warr (1983). Copies are available from the author.
9. As before, 'rate of protection' means the *tariff equivalent* of all forms of protection which are present. A 30 per cent reduction means, for example, that the rate of protection applying to a commodity receiving a 40 per cent rate of protection is reduced by 12 points, to 28 per cent. It does not mean a 30 per cent reduction in the domestic price. In the above case, the domestic price falls from an index of 140 to 128, a reduction of 8.6 per cent.
10. I am particularly indebted to P. J. Lloyd for suggesting this term.
11. The relevant weights are average shares. Writing m_k and a_k for country group ks marginal and average shares, respectively,

$$I_k = m_k/a_k \text{ and so } \sum_{k=1}^{m} a_k I_k = \sum_{k=1}^{m} m_k = 1$$

12. The simulated effect of reduced protection on most endogenous variables is smaller than might have been expected. The reason is that the price elasticity of demand for imports which the parameters of the model imply is relatively low. A 30 per cent reduction in all rates of protection leads to a 1.79 per cent rise in aggregate imports. Assuming an average rate of protection of 18 per cent, this implies a 4.57 per cent reduction in the domestic price, implying a price elasticity of demand for aggregate imports of around −0.4. This lies within, but towards the lower end of, the range of estimates for other OECD countries provided by Cline et al. (1978).
13. It has been possible to extend the trade data series to include the years 1978–9 and 1979–80. The index of discrimination against LDCs for these years was calculated at 1.013 and 1.004, respectively. Problems caused by the revised commodity classification introduced in these years make these calculations less reliable than those for the earlier years.
14. The indices of discrimination for China and India rose over the period from 1.41 to 2.41 and 0.80 to 1.95, respectively.
15. These indices of discrimination represent the change in imports of *all* commodities from LDCs in response to a cut in the rate of protection applying to a specific commodity relative to the corresponding change in total imports from all countries (LDCs' marginal share) divided by the LDCs' share of imports of *all* commodities (LDCs' average share).
16. Output rises in the primary sector in all cases but falls in the non-traded sector in four cases. This occurs because the production of these

commodities is intensive in the use of electricity and domestic transport facilities.
17. In interpreting the results for commodities 9 and 10 it should be kept in mind that reduced protection of these commodities causes LDC imports to fall, and this reverses the sign of the employment effects presented.
18. It should be stressed that this result is based on a static analysis and that dynamic considerations may point in a very different direction. As the comparative advantage of the most advanced LDCs shifts towards more capital–and skill-intensive goods, a system of MDS protection which favours the most labour-intensive goods would inhibit this transition. For example, Korea is already becoming a significant exporter of motor vehicles, and MDS protection which favoured imports of textiles, clothing and footwear at the expense of motor vehicles may not be in Korea's long-term interests.
19. This breakdown is possible because the ORANI model distinguishes nine types of labour. Four of these are 'blue-collar' categories, three are 'white-collar' and the other two are 'rural workers' and 'armed services'. Blue-collar workers account for 46 per cent of the workforce. The simulations hold the real wage of *each* of these categories of labour constant, so the average real wage of all employed workers will change slightly in response to a change in the composition of the workforce.

REFERENCES

Birnberg, T. B. (1979) 'Trade Reform Options: Economic Effects on Developing and Developed Countries', in Cline, W. R. (ed.) *Policy Alternatives for a New International Economic Order* (New York: Praeger), pp. 217–83.

Cline, W. R., Kawanabe, N., Kronsjo, T. O. M. and Williams, T. (1978) *Trade Negotiations in the Tokyo Round: a Quantitative Assessment* (Washington, DC: Brookings Institution).

Committee on Australia's Relations with the Third World (Harries Committee) (1979) *Australia and the Third World* (Canberra: Australian Government Printing Service).

Dixon, P. B., Parmenter, B. R., Ryland, G. J. and Sutton, J. (1977) *ORANI, A General Equilibrium Model of the Australian Economy: Current Specification and Illustration of Use for Policy Analysis* (Canberra: Australian Government Publishing Service).

Dixon, P. B., Powell, A. A. and Parmenter, B. R. (1979) *Structural Adaptation in an Ailing Macroeconomy* (Melbourne: Melbourne University Press).

Dixon, P. B., Parmenter, B. R., Sutton, J. and Vincent, D. P. (1982) *ORANI: a Multisectoral Model of the Australian Economy* (Amsterdam: North Holland).

Garnaut, R. and Anderson, K. (1982) *Australian Protection and Trade with Developing Countries* (forthcoming volume in a series to be published for the World Bank).

Industries Assistance Commission (1981) *Trends in Australia's Trade in Manufactures, Approaches to General Reductions in Protection*, Information Paper No. (Canberra: Australian Government Printing Service).

Krueger, A. O. (1971) 'Quotas on American Imports Reduce Employment in American Industry', *Public Policy*, vol. 19, pp. 653–9.

Krueger, A. O. (1978a) 'Effects of Exports from New Industrial Countries on US Industries', in Kasper, W. and Parry, T. C. (eds) *Growth, Trade and Structural Change in an Open Australian Economy* (Kensington, NSW: Centre for Applied Economic Research, University of New South Wales).

Krueger, A. O. (1978b) 'Impact of LDC Exports on Employment in American Industry' mimeo (London: Trade Policy Research Centre).

Salant, W. S. (1978) 'The effects of Increases in Imports on Domestic Employment: a Clarification of Concepts', Special Report No. 18 (Washington, DC: National Commission for Manpower Policy).

Warr, P. G. (1983) 'Structural Effects of Increasing Australia's Imports from Developing Countries', Discussion Paper No. 72, May, Centre for Economic Policy Research, Australian National University.

Warr, P. G. and Lloyd, P. J. (1983) 'Do Australian Trade Policies Discriminate Against Less Developed Countries?' *Economic Record*, vol. 59, December, pp. 351–64.

World Bank (1981) *World Development Report 1981* (Washington, DC: World Bank).

Yeats, A. J. *Trade Barriers Facing Developing Countries* (New York: St. Martin's).

15 Industrial Restructuring in a Newly Industrialising Country: The Case of Singapore

Chia Siow-Yue
NATIONAL UNIVERSITY OF SINGAPORE

1 INTRODUCTION

Singapore is a small city-state of 618 square kilometres and 2.5 million people. It has overcome land and natural resource constraints by exploiting its geographical location in South East Asia and developing its human resources. As a newly industrialising country with a per capita GNP of S$13,783 (US$6,563) in 1983, it is on the threshold of becoming a developed economy.

Since 1960, per capita GNP growth has averaged 7.0 per cent a year. This has been made possible by a GDP growth rate of 9.0 per cent in 1960–83, and a rapid decline in population growth. Economic growth was increasingly broad-based, led at various times by manufacturing, trade, transport and communications, and financial and business services. It was accompanied by rapid employment absorption, price stability, trickle down effects, and internal and external balance. Employment grew at over 4 per cent a year, and massive unemployment gave way to labour shortage and dependence on foreign workers. The increase in GDP deflator averaged 3.5 per cent a year. Wage levels stagnated in the 1960s but rose rapidly after the mid-1970s, leading to highly visible improvements in living standards and declining incidence of poverty. Buoyant government revenues led to budget surpluses and a reduction in personal income tax rates. The persistent balance of payments, as service exports and capital inflows offset the chronic merchandise trade deficit, resulted in the large build-up of foreign reserves and an appreciating Singapore dollar.

A major source of economic growth are the high rates of investment and saving. The fixed investment/GNP ratio rose to 48.2 per cent and the gross national savings/GNP ratio to 40.1 per cent by 1983. Other growth factors include an outward-looking development strategy that emphasises exports of manufactures and services and inflows of foreign investment and expertise, sound economic management, and an accommodating external environment. The first restructuring programme was implemented in 1960 and the second in 1979. The recent upward progression is hindered by the slow restructuring process in the advanced industrial countries and pressured by the emergence of labour-abundant less developed countries as exporters of labour-intensive manufactures.

2 CHANGING PRODUCTION AND EXPORT STRUCTURES

Singapore's development pattern has been shaped by its *entrepôt* heritage, city-state status, geographical location, and restructuring policies. A natural harbour, strategic geographical location, and British colonial policy which fostered political stability, free trade and private enterprise, provided the initial advantages that established Singapore as the *entrepôt* of South East Asia. The growth of transportation and commercial and financial institutions and services consolidated Singapore's *entrepôt* role for over a century. Eventual challenge emerged from neighbouring countries via the growth of competing ports, direct shipping and trading, the domestic processing of raw materials, and import-substituting industrialisation. By the late 1950s *entrepôt* trade had stagnated.

Following self-government in 1959, industrialisation was actively promoted. The development of tourism and financial, transport and communications services followed in the 1970s, while after 1979 the emphasis shifted towards higher technology and higher value-added industries and services. The structural transformation from an *entrepôt* to a manufacturing service economy is depicted in Table 15.1. The small agricultural sector declined to only 1.0 per cent of GDP by 1983. The share of manufacturing peaked at 23.9 per cent in 1980–1, then dipped with the recession. Structural change also took place within sectors and industries. In the services sector, the share of

Table 15.1 Singapore: percentage distribution and growth rate of GDP by industrial origin, 1960–83

Sector	Per cent distribution				Average annual growth rate (%)			
	1960	1970	1980	1983	1960–70	1970–80	1980–3	1960–83
Agriculture & fishing	4.1	2.5	1.3	1.0	3.9	2.2	−2.6	2.3
Quarrying	0.4	0.4	0.4	0.6	9.9	8.6	26.3	11.3
Manufacturing	13.2	19.7	23.9	20.0	13.7	11.2	1.9	11.0
Utilities	2.5	2.8	2.9	2.9	10.5	9.4	7.0	9.6
Construction	3.7	6.7	5.0	8.2	15.8	6.0	27.2	12.8
Trade	33.6	30.1	25.8	23.9	8.0	7.4	5.3	7.4
Transport & communications	14.0	11.6	19.2	20.8	7.1	14.7	10.9	10.9
Financial & business services	11.7	14.0	17.8	21.9	11.2	11.7	15.8	12.0
Other services	18.5	14.2	11.0	11.0	6.4	6.3	7.9	6.5
Less: imputed bank service charge	1.7	2.1	7.3	10.1	11.6	23.7	20.3	17.8
GDP at 1968 factor cost:								
Per cent	100.0	100.0	100.0	100.0	9.2	9.1	8.0	9.0
S$million	2,122.3	5,107.0	12,160.5	15,339.7				

entrepôt activities declined, while those of transport and communications and financial services grew under the strategy of developing Singapore as centres of transport, telecommunications and finance. Within the manufacturing sector, the pattern of industries changed to reflect market orientation, factor endowment, and stage of industrial development. Initially the small domestic market severely limited both the extent and range of industrial production; with the switch to export manufacturing, scale economies became possible and domestic human resources were augmented by inflows of managerial, technical and marketing expertise. By 1978 export demand accounted for 65 per cent of manufacturing output. Table 15.2 shows the changing distribution of industry value added between 1960 and 1982. The early industries were those that enjoyed natural protection, processed raw materials as an extension of the *entrepôt* trade, or provided engineering services ancillary to the British naval base. Food manufacturing, beverages and printing and publishing together accounted for 42.8 per cent of total value added in the manufacturing sector in 1960, but their share had declined to only 9.1 per cent by 1982. Petroleum refining emerged as the industry with the largest value added, followed by electronics, transport equipment and non-electrical machinery. The electronics industry led in employment with 24.6 per cent of the manufacturing total, followed by textiles and garments and transport equipment.

Singapore is heavily dependent on foreign trade. In 1983, exports amounted to 189 per cent of GNP. The city-state is thus extremely sensitive to developments in world trade and the trade policies of its trading partners. Attempts at product and market diversifications have reduced to a limited extent the trade-transmitted instabilities. The *entrepôt* share of exports declined from over 90 per cent in the early 1960s to one-third in recent years. As shown in Table 15.3, the major non-*entrepôt* exports are petroleum products (including oil bunkers), machinery and transport equipment (mainly electronic components, television and radio sets, electric motors and resistors, office machines, and boats and oil rigs), and textiles and garments. There has been a gradual shift away from exports of processed materials and labour-intensive manufactures towards exports of higher skill and technology products. Geographical location, good infrastructure, efficient low-cost labour, and active investment promotion were the dominant factors in the development of Singapore's leading export industries and services. Direct foreign investment is dominant in all the major export industries and services. In fact, of

Table 15.2 Singapore: percentage distribution of value added by industry, manufacturing sector, 1960–82

ISIC industry group		1960	1970	1982
311+2	Food manufacturing	11.7	7.0	3.5
313	Beverages	13.9	2.3	1.5
314	Tobacco products	5.4	2.3	1.0
321	Textiles	3.4	2.2	1.1
322	Wearing apparel		2.2	3.5
323	Leather products		0.2	0.1
324	Footwear		0.6	0.2
331	Wood & wood products	7.1	5.5	1.5
332	Furniture & fixtures	1.0	1.0	1.1
341	Paper & paper products	1.3	1.1	1.3
342	Printing & publishing	17.2	4.7	4.1
351	Industrial chemicals & gases	6.8	1.5	1.5
352	Paints, pharmaceuticals & other chemical products		3.1	3.9
353+4	Petroleum refineries & products		19.2	17.3
355	Processing of jelutong & gums	2.3	0.1	–
356	Rubber products		1.7	0.4
361–9	Non-metallic mineral products	3.8	3.0	3.3
371	Iron & steel	1.3	1.6	1.5
372	Non-ferrous metals		0.5	0.3
381	Fabricated metal products	7.6	6.6	7.0
382	Machinery, except electrical/electrtonic	4.6	2.6	10.8
383	Electrical machinery, apparatus, appliances & supplies	5.5	11.7	4.1
383	Electronic products & components			15.8
385	Transport equipment (incl. oil rigs)	5.8	14.6	10.8
386	Instrumentation equipment, photographic & optical goods	1.3	0.3	1.3
357	Plastic products		1.1	1.9
390	Other miscellaneous industries		2.6	1.2

Note: The data include only those establishments with 10 or more workers in the manufacturing sector, excluding quarrying and rubber processings.

Source: Singapore, Department of Statistics, *Report on the Census of Industrial Production*, various years.

total exports by the manufacturing sector in 1982, wholly foreign-owned establishments accounted for 64.9 per cent and joint ventures for 25.9 per cent.[1]

Table 15.3 Singapore: percentage distribution of non-*entrepôt* exports by SITC groupings, 1960–83

SITC groupings	1960	1970	1975	1980	1983
Food	22.3	5.8	3.7	2.3	1.6
Beverages & tobacco	9.6	0.6	0.3	0.4	0.4
Crude materials	4.1	1.6	0.6	0.6	0.6
Mineral fuels	–	43.2	42.9	45.0	41.7
Animal & vegetable oils	9.4	2.7	0.7	1.5	1.4
Chemicals, of which	12.3	2.4	2.8	2.2	3.0
Medicinal products	1.1	0.5	1.8	1.0	0.8
Plastic materials	–	0.2	0.3	0.4	0.4
Manufactured goods by materials, of which	23.3	9.3	6.4	5.1	3.7
Veneer & plywood	0.6	2.3	1.8	1.3	0.7
Textile yarn & fabrics	3.5	1.3	1.4	1.0	0.5
Machinery & transport, of which	7.6	10.8	22.4	25.4	29.9
Office machines	–	1.9	2.3	1.0	2.8
Electric motors & resistors	–	0.3	0.3	1.3	3.5
Television & radio	–	1.1	3.7	7.3	6.0
Electronic components	–	–	6.7	8.5	8.1
Ships, boats & oil rigs	–	0.5	3.7	2.3	3.4
Miscellaneous manufac. articles, of which	11.3	7.9	8.9	7.3	7.2
Clothing	2.4	3.6	3.1	2.9	2.6
Scientific instruments	–	0.2	2.7	1.2	0.7
Miscellaneous transactions, of which	–	15.8	11.3	10.1	10.5
Oil bunkers	–	15.3	11.1	10.0	10.4
Total : per cent	100.0	100.0	100.0	100.0	100.0
S$million	217.1	1,832.2	7,540.4	25,805.2	29,206.4

Source: Singapore, Ministry of Trade and Industry *Economic Survey of Singapore*, various years.

Petroleum refining is a highly capital-intensive industry. It depends on imported crude to supply the large bunkering demand of Singapore's port and markets in the Asia-Pacific. Strategic location and a favourable investment climate have established Singapore as a major refining centre. But its comparative advantage is being eroded by the global trend towards locating refineries in proximity to oil-fields rather than to markets.[2] The transport equipment industry is dominated by shipyards and oil-rig firms. Comparative advantage was established by the heritage of the British naval base and Singapore's strategic location in relation to major shipping lanes and oil exploration activities. For the electronics industry, the product cycle, ready availability of low-cost labour and infrastructure, and generous investment incentives have been important factors in attracting multinational corporations. The labour-intensive textiles and garments export industry was promoted during the years of labour surplus. Service exports account for about one-third of total exports. Geographical location is a major factor in the comparative advantage in finance, transport and communications, and tourism.

3 INDUSTRIAL RESTRUCTURING: RATIONALE AND STRATEGY

In analysing the structural transformation of a economy, it is necessary to distinguish between secular structural change which accompanies economic growth and which is due to changing demand, factor endowment and technology, and industrial restructuring which involves government intervention. Government intervention can seek either to enhance the effectiveness of competitive market forces or substitute for them. The former generally entails policy measures to improve trade, domestic competition, and capital and labour markets, while the latter involves adjustment assistance and rationalisation policies that focus on specific sectors and industries facing technological and/or import challenges. A necessary condition for effective industrial restructuring is that it must rationalise investment and production in line with underlying shifts in technology, cost structures and market demands, and channel investment resources to those industries and activities in which the economy has a longer-term comparative advantage, and phase out inefficient industries and firms. The basic issue is how much government intervention is warranted and whether bureaucrats are better than private enterprise in picking 'winners' among sectors and industries. Rapid changes in technology and markets can severely limit the ability of any government to anticipate fully future viable industries.

The Singapore government has been active in industrial restructuring for a quarter of a century. In 1960 the restructuring programme focused on industrialisation to replace *entrepôt* trade as the leading sector. The manufacturing sector was underdeveloped relative to the economy's per capita income level.[3] The small domestic market, lack of import restrictions, lack of natural resources and industrial know-how, and the high wage levels set by the *entrepôt* sector, hindered the emergence of resource-based, technology-based and even labour-intensive industries. Industrial policy emphasised private enterprise, with government fostering a favourable investment climate. It was also outward-looking, emphasising direct foreign investment and exports. Direct foreign investments were actively promoted to provide industrial entrepreneurship, technology and markets. Export manufacturing ensured efficient and sufficient industrialisation through scale economies and international competition, although there was an initial short phase of import substitution.[4] With high unemployment, investment promotion was directed at labour-intensive industries. The main investment incentives were tax holidays, provision of industrial estates and facilities, enforcement of industrial peace and discipline, and provision of an educated and skilled labour force. Restructuring was undertaken in an environment of expanding world trade and investment. The end result was an upsurge in direct foreign investments, manufacturing production, employment and exports. This was followed by policies to develop service exports in tourism, transport and communications and financial services. Labour-intensive industries and services led to rapid employment growth and eventual labour shortages and wage pressures.

Domestic full employment and external market conditions necessitated a new development by the early 1970s. Unlike the restructuring programme pursued by South Korea, land and natural resource scarcity precluded any extensive promotion of basic heavy and chemical industries.[5] Like Taiwan, however, Singapore opted for skill-intensive industries dependent on human resources; in addition, Singapore focused on high value-added service exports. Further efforts were thus directed at manpower development, with foreign investment continuing to fill the resource gaps. However, this time restructuring coincided with a world economy beset by monetary and oil crises and recession. As foreign investments and manufactured exports declined in 1974–5, restructuring was postponed.

With economic recovery, restructuring was resumed in 1979 in view of growing domestic and external constraints. Domestically, sustained economic growth has created stresses and strains in the economic structure, which called for rationalisation. Primarily, labour-intensive development slowed down productivity growth, and coupled with slowdown in the growth of the domestic labour force, led to growing labour shortage. The shift in comparative advantage in

Singapore has been much more rapid than for larger and slower growing economies with less dramatic demographic transitions.[6] The necessity to restructure had, in fact, been postponed for some time as comparative advantage in labour-intensive manufacturing was maintained by the Lewis-type of labour inflow from neighbouring countries, so that labour supply continued to expand rapidly and the market wage rate stagnated. Externally, NICs like Singapore face the growing threat of OECD protectionist pressures directed largely at labour-intensive manufactures, as well as competitive pressures from low-wage LDCs embarking on export manufacturing.

A dynamic economy with minimal market distortions and flexible institutional responses may be expected to undergo structural change as a normal process of growth and development. For Singapore, however, the labour market distortions and demand and technology changes were such that structural change could not be left to market forces alone. Restructuring was necessary to rationalise factor use and to channel resources towards activities with long-term comparative advantage, namely higher value-added goods and services embodying more advanced technology, and larger physical and human capital inputs. Unlike larger NICs where the structural balance is between agriculture and manufacturing, Singapore has to strike a balance between manufacturing and services. In manufacturing, priority Schumpeterian and high value-added industries include chemical process and machinery industries, precision and aerospace engineering, shipbuilding and ship machinery, electrical and electronic products, parts and components manufacture, and industrial servicing of sophisticated machinery and aircrafts. In services, the emphasis is on finance, transport and communications, computer services, and medical, engineering and consultancy services. In view of the global uncertainties, 1979 was still a risky period to resume restructuring. However, a young and mobile workforce and a cooperative trade union movement help lessen the stresses and strains. Moreover, the widespread presence of foreign investors and labour also facilitate the redeployment of enterprise and labour.

The promotion of new and the upgrading of existing industries and services has to be accompanied by wide-ranging policies and measures pertaining to productivity growth, research and development, manpower training, labour-management relations and institutional changes. Of these, the most important are those affecting the labour market, by allowing wages to find their market levels, reducing the inflow of foreign works, and accelerating manpower development.

High unemployment, an inflow of labour and the curbing of trade union powers contributed to wage stagnation in the 1960s. With the emergence of full employment and the need for a stable market to maintain investor confidence, the tripartite National Wages Council (NWC) was formed in 1972 to ensure 'orderly wage increases' through annual non-mandatory wage guidelines. In the period 1972–8, earnings of production and manual workers grew at an annual average rate of 9.5 per cent nominally and 2.5 per cent in real terms. In retrospect, the NWC guidelines were conservative and, together with the inflow of foreign workers, contributed to growing labour market distortions. A corrective wage policy was instituted, with NWC wage recommendations averaging 14–20 per cent a year in 1979–82. Increases in average earnings or production and manual workers averaged 14.0 per cent a year, or 7 per cent in real terms, Escalating labour costs from higher wages and contributions to the Central Provident Fund and the Skills Development Fund[7] and weak export demand dampened employment growth and spurred mechanisation and computerisation. Wage increases have moderated, and the government has adopted a low profile in NWC deliberations so that collective bargaining may reflect supply and demand forces more sensitively.

Immigration control imposed soon after political independence in 1965 was relaxed a decade later to supplement domestic skills and ease labour shortages. By 1980, non-citizens accounted for 120,000 or 11 per cent of the workforce.[8] The majority were poorly educated, and only 9.9 per cent had tertiary qualifications. Only 17.8 per cent were employed in administrative, managerial, professional and technical positions. The dependence on foreign workers was highest in construction and manufacturing, with nearly half of them in manufacturing alone; the dependence was very high in textiles and garments, wood processing, and to a lesser extent electronics. The presence of foreign labour reflects both the general scarcity of high-level manpower in Singapore as well as the 'white-collar' preference of Singaporeans with lesser skills. Labour importation reduced the economic rent and dampened the general wage level but allowed Singaporean workers to exercise their job preferences. The two categories of foreign labour exerted opposite impacts on comparative advantage and economic upgrading as one increased the stock of human capital while the other enlarged the pool of cheap labour. While the policy of inducting 'foreign brains' is being continued to ensure a successful restructuring towards the information age, the inflow of unskilled and semi-skilled labour is being increasingly restricted and will be eventually stopped.

The upgrading of domestic human resources embraces not only education and training but also the inculcation of industrial discipline and appropriate work attitudes. Budgetary resources for education and training have increased rapidly, and emphasis has been given to technical, engineering, managerial and computer education. Training institutions and programmes by public agencies (the Vocational and Industrial Training Board and the Economic Development Board), joint government–industry training programmes, and private training schemes financed by the Skills Development Fund have proliferated in the past decade. To enable the existing poorly educated workforce to meet the challenge of technological obsolescence, a continuing education programme has been mounted in recent years.[9] Efforts to improve industrial relations and industrial discipline date from 1960, with measures to control the excesses of trade unions. Since the late 1970s the policy emphasis has been on inculcating appropriate work attitudes, productivity consciousness, and better labour–management relations through a national productivity movement, the introduction of Japanese-style quality control circles and human resources development courses, and a symbiotic relationship between the trade union movement and the political leadership.

Apart from labour market interventions, restructuring policy makes liberal use of fiscal incentives. A free trade philosophy and the small domestic market circumscribed the role of protection.[10] Tax holidays, however, raise the question of their efficacy in attracting investments, while direct and overt export subsidies attract countervailing duties and other retaliatory measures. While investments in resource development and processing and in import substitution are largely location-specific, those in export manufacturing are generally footloose and thus can be highly sensitive to the availability of tax and other investment incentives.[11] The pioneer tax holiday was introduced in 1959, but has been applied with growing selectivity to promote export manufacturing and restructuring. Awards in recent years have been directed at more technologically advanced industries and products such as computers, computer peripherals and precision instruments. By the end of 1982, there were 432 pioneer manufacturing establishments with total gross fixed assets of S$8.4 billion, employment of 106,000, and output of S$19.9 billion. After 1967 tax concessions were used to encourage exports, foreign borrowings for machinery and equipment purchases and technology inflows. In 1979 several new tax incentives were introduced to stimulate restructuring. The investment allowance aims at promoting automation, upgrading, expansion and diversification in industry. Tax incentives were also introduced to expand and upgrade warehousing and servicing operations for engineering products and international consultancy services, and to encourage the development of Singapore as a financial centre. Preferential loans to industry for technological upgrading are provided under the Capital Assistance Scheme (CAS) and the Small Industries Finance Scheme (SIFS).

Promotion of new technology industries goes hand in hand with research and development (R & D) activities. An official survey in 1978 highlighted the dismal state of R & D activities in Singapore.[12] Technological capability for a small city-state is obviously limited; nonetheless, R & D in selected sectors is feasible and desirable and can be enhanced by support from multinational corporations. Increased government support for industrial R & D in recent years includes the slanting of existing tax incentives toward projects with an R & D component, double tax deductions on R & D expenditures, and financial assistance under the Product Development Assistance Scheme (PDAS) and the Research and Development Assistance Scheme (RDAS). An increasing number of industrial enterprises are undertaking some form of R & D, and there has been some success in promoting R & D in biotechnology, robotics and microcomputers, but it remains an uphill task to induce multinational corporations to establish R & D facilities.

Table 15.4 shows the net investment commitments in manufacturing for 1972-83. The data for 1979-83 reflect the twin effects of global recession and industrial restructuring policies. Overall investment commitments of recent years were concentrated in electrical goods and electronics, petroleum refining, non-electrical machinery, chemicals, transport equipment, fabricated metal products and food manufacturing, and include new skill- and technology-intensive products and processes. There were only limited investment commitments in the traditional labour-intensive industries such as textiles and garments. Re-investments have been larger than investments in new projects; this is somewhat worrisome since the latter provides a faster method of technological upgrading and establishing new product mix. Although there have been re-investments for diversification and upgrading into new and higher value-added products, a major part of it is directed at expansion, mechanisation and automation.

Table 15.4 Singapore: percentage distribution by industry of net investment commitments in manufacturing, 1972–82

ISIC Industry group	1972–5	1976–9	1980–3
Food & beverages	0.7	3.7	6.9
Textiles	3.5	1.4	1.0
Wearing apparel	0.6	0.4	0.4
Wood products	2.9	2.3	0.9
Paper products & printing	0.7	0.5	4.7
Industrial chemicals	3.7	1.2	3.1
Plastic products	1.6	2.8	2.7
Other chemical products	1.9	1.9	5.2
Petroleum	12.4	25.9	16.2
Non-metallic mineral products	3.3	0.3	4.4
Basic metals	2.8	0.8	1.6
Fabricated metal products	2.4	3.8	6.6
Machinery except electrical	22.9	13.3	9.8
Electrical machinery & appliances	13.3	32.9	22.8
Transport equipment	19.3	2.3	8.6
Precision equipment	1.8	3.2	2.8
Other products	6.2	3.3	0.9
Servicing/engineering	–	–	1.4
Total:			
Per cent	100.0	100.0	100.0
S$million:	1,088.6	2,455.7	6,824.5
Foreign	796.0	2,212.2	4,834.4
Local	292.6	243.5	1,990.1

Source: Singapore, Ministry of Trade and Industry, *Economic Survey of Singapore*, various years.

4 SECTORAL DEVELOPMENTS IN TEXTILES, GARMENTS AND ELECTRONICS

The textiles and garments and electronics industries in Singapore share the common characteristics of being labour-intensive and paying low wages, and thus they are most seriously affected by the labour shortage and rising wage levels in Singapore. They are also highly export-oriented and dependent on markets in the advanced countries, and are adversely affected by OECD protectionism and by competition from less developed countries. However, the two industries differ substantially in their growth and restructuring prospects. The Singapore electronics industry is highly integrated into a global industry experiencing rapid technological change and demand growth. The textiles and garments industry is not internationally integrated, depends on relatively standardised technology, and has limited prospects of demand growth.

The export segment of the textiles and garments industry was established in the early 1960s by investors from Hong Kong and Taiwan who were spurred by push factors from their homelands and pull factors in Singapore.[13] The garments segment is larger than the textiles segment. In 1982 the industry had 95 textile and 406 garment establishments employing ten or more workers. Of these, only 34 were wholly foreign-owned and 105 were joint ventures. The industry employed 35,000 workers, or 12.7 per cent of the manufacturing workforce; however, a very high proportion of the female operatives were foreign workers. Gross output amounted to S$1.3 billion and value added amounted to S$0.4 billion, or 3.4 per cent and 4.6 per cent of the manufacturing total respectively. The export/total sales ratio was 63.1 per cent, and export sales of S$799 million were largely from the foreign-owned firms and accounted for 3.7 per cent of manufacturing exports.

The industry is highly labour-intensive, has low labour productivity and pays low wages. In 1982 the wage/value added ratio was 57 per cent for textiles and 62 per cent for garments, ranking the second and fourth highest among thirty-one three-digit industries. Value added per worker for textiles was the fifth lowest in the manufacturing sector and was less than half the manufacturing average; for garments, it was the lowest in rank and only one-third of the manufacturing average. The average annual remuneration of operatives for textiles was only S$7,590 or 16 per cent below the manufacturing average, and for garments was only S$6,325 or 30 per cent below the manufacturing average. Employment in the industry peaked in 1979 and declined steadily thereafter, while production value and exports declined sharply in 1982–3 under the impact of the global recession and restricted quotas under the Multi-Fibre Arrangement.

In retrospect, the textiles and garments industry should not have been vigorously promoted through tax and other incentives in the early 1960s as it had no long-term comparative advantage; it is an example of a 'loser' being picked. It has limited prospects of expansion, and the appropriate structural adjustment policy would be to encourage disinvestment of firms that have become non-competitive and unable to upgrade, as it is not possible to protect the export industry and unwise to subsidise it, particularly as the major investors and a large proportion of the workers are foreign. There are no specific financial assistance schemes for this ailing industry facing both demand and supply problems. Nonetheless, the general tax incentives have encouraged some upgrading efforts through automation and mechanisation to improve operational efficiency, and an up-market movement into high-quality textiles and fashion garments to improve value added. A Textile and Garment Industry Training Centre has been established to provide better-skilled operatives, but it faces the problem of labour shortage, which will be even more acute with the phasing out of foreign workers. The government has been assisting the garments sector to move up-market through the trade promotion and marketing efforts of the Trade Development Board

The electronics industry was first established in Singapore in the mid-1960s and expanded rapidly in response to external and domestic factors. Externally, the 1960s witnessed the internationalisation of the industry, as both product cycle and market developments led major OECD multinational corporations to relocate labour-intensive processes in low-wages countries, while retaining in the home countries the more capital- and technology-intensive processes and the R & D. Domestically, efforts to encourage export-oriented labour-intensive industries intensified in the latter half of the 1960s, supported by the rapid infrastructure build-up and generous investment incentives.

Electronics has been the fastest growing industry in the manufacturing sector, but it is characterised by the boom and bust cycles that mirror the global industry. During the period 1968–74, the influx of multinational corporations led to rapidly expanding production, exports and employment. Production cutbacks and retrenchments occurred in 1975 and in 1981–2. In 1982, there were 186 establishments producing electronic products and components, with 106 wholly foreign-owned, 41 joint ventures and only 39 wholly locally-owned. Foreign investments were largely from the USA, Japan and Western Europe. Employment in the industry is dominated by young females, and after peaking in 1980 with 72,000 workers, declined to 61,000 in 1982 to account for 22.1 per cent of total manufacturing employment.

In 1982 production and exports were S$5.3 billion and S$4.6 billion respectively. The industry is highly export-oriented, with an export/total sales ratio of 86.1 per cent.

In recent years the industry has been upgrading its operations towards more skill- and technology-intensive products and processes. However, although labour productivity has improved substantially in the last decade, in 1982 it remained at 28 per cent below the average for the manufacturing sector. Similarly, although the average remuneration of workers in the industry increased rapidly in the same period, it remained at 17 per cent below the manufacturing average. Recent developments, however, will result in significant technological upgrading and improvements in labour productivity. Labour shortages and rising wages are driving both multinational corporations and local firms to relocate labour-intensive operations in neighbouring countries. Processes remaining in Singapore are increasingly automated and mechanised under the various incentive schemes, and newer products of higher value and embodying more advanced technology have been introduced in response to the accumulation of skills and experience and to world technology and market developments. In the semiconductor sector, a major development is the establishment of local wafer fabrication. Industrial electronics including computers is being actively promoted. The bulk of new fixed investments are by manufacturers installing automated equipment and by new companies producing higher technology and higher value-added computer equipment and electronic components. The new computer projects are attracted by Singapore's ready accommodation to the quick start-up in operations required. Exports are increasingly of higher value-added products such as computer systems and subassemblies and computer peripherals, integrated circuits, industrial-grade printed circuit boards, stereo-radio cassette recorders and colour television sets. In 1983 the share of electronic components in the industry's exports declined to 50.5 per cent, while the share of consumer electronics rose to 30.7 per cent and that of industrial electronics to 18.8 per cent.

5 CONCLUSION

In the course of two decades Singapore has progressed from a labour-surplus to a labour-scarce economy. As as a result, comparative advantage in labour-intensive production has eroded and new advantages are emerging for skill- and capital-intensive activities. The structural transformation is being achieved through active government intervention. Several factors have contributed to a less traumatic process in Singapore as compared with developments in the mature industrial economies. First, restructuring is occurring in an environment of labour shortage; in the 1979–83 period, foreign labour accounted for 10–14 per cent of the labour force. Retrenched domestic labour can be readily redeployed without serious hardship, and the inflow of foreign labour can be reversed. Second, the domestic workforce is relatively youthful, with half below 30 years old; work ethics remain strong in a newly industrialising country, so that labour is readily amenable to further skills upgrading and occupational and industrial redeployment. In the small city-state geographical mobility is also ensured. Third, the large presence of foreign investment makes the redeployment of investment and entrepreneurial/managerial resources easier. Disinvestment in Singapore is followed by the relocation of firms and processes in neighbouring countries offering cost advantages. New injections of investment from abroad speed up technological upgrading.

As is evident from the above, the success of the current restructuring exercise depends very much on the ability to continue to attract the necessary volume and quality of direct foreign investment. Skill-intensive and higher-technology industries are not attracted by abundant low-wage labour. Instead, the government has to ensure political stability, an innovative environment, a critical mass of scientists and technologists, abundant skilled labour, and a wide range of fiscal incentives.

In view of the inherent uncertainties of a heavy dependence on direct foreign investment, more effort needs to be directed at the development and upgrading of domestic resources and to reduce the 'export processing' character of the economy. It is noteworthy that in the other Asian NICs – Hong Kong, South Korea, and Taiwan – there is a much greater reliance on domestic human resources. In particular, Singaporean entrepreneurial talent has been somewhat bypassed in the rapid industrialisation of the last two decades. There is an abundance of entrepreneurship in the non-industrial sector, and greater attention needs to be paid to finding ways of transforming them into modern-day industrial entrepreneurs. Management and production skills are trainable, and considerable resources are already being channelled in this direction. Technology is a thorny issue. There has been very little official concern over technology transfer from abroad. Both institutional and fiscal measures can be directed at facilitating the transfer of technology, including the more vigorous promotion of joint ventures between domestic and foreign entrepreneurs and at promoting indigenous technological capability. In all these areas of government intervention it is essential to maintain a fine balance, so that promotional efforts are not negated by the stifling of private enterprise and innovation as a result of excessive regulation and control.

NOTES

1. See Department of Statistics (1982).
2. Fears of a drastic cutback in refining did not materialise as neighbouring countries continued to send their crude for processing. However, with the completion of new refineries in the region, the industry faces increased competition. In anticipation of this development, the petroleum refineries have undertaken substantial investments to improve operating efficiency through computer control systems, energy conservation and storage facilities. They have also diversified into secondary processing capability to extend refining flexibility, strengthen market position and increase value added.
3. In 1960 the per capita GNP was S$1,330 or US$429, but manufacturing's share of current factor cost was only 11.9 per cent. At that time, many of the Latin American Economies, East and South East Asian economies with lower per capita incomes had relatively larger manufacturing sectors. In the city-state of Hong Kong manufacturing already accounted for 26 per cent of GDP. See World Bank (1984), Table 3.
4. The domestic market was too small for viable industrialisation. Nonetheless, prospects of merger with Malaysia and an ensuing common market, as well as difficulties in initiating export manufacturing, led to an initial short and mild phase of import substitution during 1961–5. Political separation from Malaysia and the abortion of the common market scheme in 1965, and the 1967 British decision to withdraw its Singapore military base, necessitated a policy switch to export manufacturing to provide employment, income and foreign exchange, and further dependence on direct foreign investment to achieve the objective.
5. The promotion of a petrochemical complex represented the main exception, as it was regarded as the logical extension of the petroleum refining industry. However, the S$2 billion petrochemical complex was beset by difficulties, and it finally came onstream in February 1984 with the completion of upstream facilities and three downstream plants.
6. The population growth rate declined from over 4 per cent in the

mid-1950s to only 1.2 after the late 1970s. Its impact on labour force growth had to be ameliorated by policy measures encouraging greater female labour force participation.

7. Employer contributions to the government-managed Central Provident Fund for employees originated in the mid-1950s. The rates of contribution from both employer and employee were progressively raised, but escalated after the late 1970s. By 1984, an employer has to contribute to the Fund at the rate of 23 per cent of the employee's wage, thus considerably adding on to labour cost. In addition, the Skills Development Fund was instituted in 1979, since when the employer contributes 4 per cent of payroll to the Fund, which is used to subsidise approved training schemes run by employers.

8. From the 1980 population census: see Department of Statistics (1981).

9. The 1980 population census showed that 22.3 per cent of the labour force had no qualifications whatsoever, while another 50.3 per cent had only primary school qualifications, making a total of 72.6 per cent of the labour force with inadequate educational levels. The continuing education programme (BEST) aims to provide literacy and numeracy so that these works can be more readily absorbed into training programmes.

10. For a study of the extent of protection, see Tan and Ow (1982).

11. An early study by Helen Hughes had determined that tax incentives were not significant in the locational decisions of foreign firms in Singapore. However, the study was conducted in 1966, a time when export processing investments were still unimportant. See Hughes (1969).

12. There were only 90 establishments engaged in R & D activities, 63 in the private sector and 27 in the public sector, employing a full-time equivalent of 461 scientists and engineers, with total R &n D expenditures of only S$37.2 million or 0.2 per cent of GDP. The private sector R & D establishments comprised 36 foreign and 27 local firms with 2 consultancy firms, 2 scientific laboratories, and 59 R & D outfits in manufacturing firms, and with total R & D expenditures of S$24.9 million for the year. Most of the private sector R & D personnel and expenditures were from five larage multinational corporations. See Ministry of Science and Technology (1980).

13. The decision to invest in Singapore was associated with quota restrictions imposed on Hong Kong and Taiwan textile exports to major markets in developed countries and the absence of similar restrictions on Singapore. The pull factors were geographical proximity, cultural affinity and a favourable investment climate.

REFERENCES

Department of Statistics (1981) *Census of Population 1980, Singapore, Release No. 4: Economic Characteristics* (Singapore: Government Printers).

Department of Statistics (1982) *Report on the Census of Industrial Production* (Singapore: Government Printers).

Economic Development Board, *Annual Report* (Singapore), various issues.

Hughes, H. and You, P. S. (eds) (1969) *Foreign Investment and Industrialisation in Singapore* (Canberra: Australian National University Press).

Ministry of Trade and Industry, *Economic Survey of Singapore* (Singapore), various issues.

Ministry of Science and Technology (1980) *Survey of Research and Development Activities in Singapore 1979* (Singapore).

Tan, A. H. H. and Ow, C. H. (1982) 'Singapore', in Balassa, B. *et al. Development Strategies in Semi−industrial Economies* (Washington DC: World Bank).

World Bank (1984) *World Development Report* (Washington DC: World Bank).

16 A Multisectoral Analysis of the Structural Adjustment of the Brazilian Economy in the 1980s

R. L. F. Werneck
PONTIFIĆA UNIVERSIDADE
CATÓLICA RIO DE JANEIRO

1 INTRODUCTION

A retrospective look at the ways in which economic policy in Brazil has been tackling the mounting foreign sector difficulties in the country over the last few years would hardly allow any clear-cut identification of the strategy which has been followed, particularly as far as short- and medium-run policies are concerned. What has been observed is a succession of experiments which is far from a plan of action. However, there is a clearer thread to detect in long-run policy – notwithstanding occasional contradictions. The essence of the policy designed to overcome the external disequilibrium in the long run seems to be a deep change in the sectoral growth pattern of the economy to generate the structural adjustment consistent with the adoption of bold programmes of import substitution and export expansion, which will eventually give rise to substantial improvements in the trade balance.

This is clearly an optimistic strategy, particularly in expectations of export performance, over a period for which most forecasts of world trade growth are extremely pessimistic. Nonetheless, if it is accepted, merely as a working hypothesis, that this strategy is reasonably realistic, then one has to worry about other kinds of questions. More specifically, what is the nature, the magnitude and speed of the structural changes required to allow such a strategy to be successful? What does this mean precisely in terms of changes in the growth pattern of the economy? What is the nature of the necessary reallocation of investments? In particular, how should state investments be reallocated?

These are key questions about the consistency of the long-run strategy adopted to overcome the external disequilibrium of the Brazilian economy. So far, however, the adoption of such a strategy has been based on analyses which – though intuitively attractive – leave more room for merely impressionistic considerations than would seem fit. It is necessary, therefore, to try to examine in a more consistent and systematic way how such strategy really unfolds.

This paper is a contribution to that complex task. In the next section we present a multisectoral consistency model that will allow an exploration – using simulations – of the logical consequences of the adoption of strategies designed to overcome the external disequilibrium of the Brazilian economy in the 1980s, on the basis of bold programmes of import substitution and export expansion. The objective is to be able to visualise the extent and nature of the required changes in the productive structure and the growth pattern, as well as to outline the investment programme involved. The hypotheses about key exogenous variables are discussed in Section 3. The results of the simulations relating to the growth pattern and the productive structure are presented in Section 4. Those relating to the investment pattern are given in Sections 5 and 6. The main conclusions are assessed in Section 7.

2 THE MODEL

The model is a consistency model in the sense that it does not deal with questions of feasibility,[1] but with what has been called 'requirements analysis'.[2] The economy is disaggregated into thirty sectors, following what might be seen as a two-digit industry classification altered to allow singling out sectors which, according to *a priori* considerations, were expected to play particularly important roles in the process under analysis.

As to the logical structure of the model, a distinguishing feature is that all endogenous variables relate to the same year, namely the terminal year of the planning period. That means that one may deal with changes which might take place during a period of time, but not with the phasing of change within that period.[3]

The base and terminal year are 1978 and 1990 respectively.[4] Key exogenous variables are the sectoral import substitution and export expansion targets, as well as the aggregate output growth rate. Once their values are established, the model is supposed to generate the required sectoral growth rates, the related investment programme and the implicit changes, also on a sectoral basis, in the productive structure.

Table 16.1 provides a list of the model's variables and parameters. Variables with a zero subscript refer to values at the base year of the planning period. Those which refer to values at the terminal year are written without any numerical subscript. The model's formulation is given by the set of equations presented in Table 16.2.

Table 16.1 List of the model's variables and parameters

EXOGENOUS VARIABLES

T = Length of the planning period
Y_o = Gross domestic output at the base year
g = Target average annual growth rate of GDP
x_{io} = Output of the ith sector at the base year
β_{io} = Ratio of imports to domestic production for the ith sector at the base year
β_i = Ratio of imports to domestic production for the ith sector at the terminal year
v_i = Expected average annual growth rate for the ith sector's export
V_{io} = Export demand for the ith sector's output at the base year
C_{io} = Consumers' demand for the ith sector's output at the base year
Con_o = Aggregate consumers' demand at the base year
g_N = Population growth rate
I_o^H = Gross residential investment at the base year

ENDOGENOUS VARIABLES

Y = Gross domestic output at the terminal year
X_i = Output of the ith sector at the terminal year
C_i = Consumers' demand for the ith sector's output at the terminal year

G_i = Government's consumption demand for the ith sector's output at the terminal year
I_i = Investment demand for the ith sector's output at the terminal year
M_i = Imports competitive to the ith sector's output at the terminal year
g_i = Average annual growth rate of the ith sector's output
Imp = Total imports at the terminal year
V_i = Export demand for the ith sector's output at the terminal year
Exp = Total exports at the terminal year
Inv = Aggregate investment at the terminal year
I^D = Non-residential net investment at the terminal year
I^R = Non-residential replacement investment at the terminal year
I^H = Gross residential investment at the terminal year
J_i = Net investment in the ith sector at the terminal year
r_i = Stock-flow conversion factor of the ith sector
R_i = Accumulated net requirement of investment in the ith sector
Gov = Aggregate government consumption demand at the terminal year
Con = Aggregate consumers' demand at the terminal year
g_i = Share of the ith sector in total value added at the terminal year
k = Aggregate incremental capital-output ratio (output measured as gross production)
k' = Aggregate incremental capital-output ratio (output measured as value added)
Z_i = Share of the ith destination sector in the total net accumulated investment requirements
z_i = Share of the ith destination sector in the terminal year investment
R_i^E = Accumulated net requirement of state investment in the ith sector
J_i^E = Net state investment in the ith sector at the terminal year
I^E = Aggregate net state investment at the terminal year
Z_i^E = Share of the ith destination sector in total net accumulated state investment requirements

z_i^E = Share of the ith destination sector in the terminal year net state investments
U = State's share in the total net accumulated investment requirements
u = State's share in non-residential net investment

PARAMETERS

a_{ij} = Input-output coefficient
k_i = Incremental capital-output ratio of the ith sector
δ = Depreciation coefficient (as percentage of GDP)
ζ_i = Proportion of the net investment in the ith sector that is made in constructions
$\bar{\zeta}$ = Proportion of the replacement made in constructions
θ'_i = Distribution coefficient of the demand for investment in equipments
b = Ratio of aggregate government's consumption to GDP
γ_i = Government's consumption demand distribution coefficient
ϵ_i = Engel's elasticity of the consumers' demand for the ith sector's output
ϵ_H = Engels's elasticity of the residential investment demand
α_i^E = State's share of the ith sector

Equation (1) is a straightforward determination of the GDP at the terminal year, given an exogenous target for the average annual growth rate during the course of the planning period. In equation (2) sectoral gross output levels are determined in the usual way. Stock variations are supposed to be nil, I_i comprising only gross fixed investment demand for what is produced in the ith sector. Sectoral growth rates are given by equation (3).

Imports and exports at the terminal year are determined in equations (4) to (7) through import substitution targets ($\beta_{io} - \beta_i$) and annual average growth rates of exports from the various sectors (v_i), which are established exogenously. Given the nature of the issues to be analysed, this seems to be a proper way to deal with exports and imports in the model. It may be noticed that all imports are treated as competitive. The scale and degree of complexity already attained by the Brazilian economy make that a reasonable hypothesis to be assumed in a multisectoral model with the level of aggregation that is adopted here.[5]

Table 16.2D The model's formulation

Gross domestic output

$$Y = (1 + g)^T Y_o \qquad (1)$$

Output by sector

$$X_i = \sum_{j=1}^{30} a_{ij} X_j + C_i + G_i + I_i + V_i - M_i \qquad i = i, 2, \ldots, 30 \quad (2)$$

Growth rate by sector

$$g_i = \frac{X_i}{X_{io}} \frac{1}{T} - 1 \qquad i = 1, 2, \ldots, 30 \quad (3)$$

Imports (competitive) by sector

$$M_i = \beta_{io} X_i - (\beta_{io} - \beta_i) X_i = \beta_i X_i \qquad i = 1, 2, \ldots, 30 \quad (4)$$

Total imports

$$Imp = \sum_{i=1}^{30} M_i \qquad (5)$$

Exports by sector

$$V_i = (1 + v_i)^T V_{io} \qquad i = 1, 2, \ldots, 30 \quad (6)$$

Total exports

$$Exp = \sum_{i=1}^{30} V_i \qquad (7)$$

Aggregate investment

$$Inv = I^D + I^R + I^H \tag{8}$$

Non-residential net investment

$$I^D = \sum_{i=1}^{30} J_i \tag{9}$$

Net investment by sector of destination

$$J_i = r_i R_i \qquad i = 1,2,\ldots,30 \tag{10}$$

Accumulated net investment requirement by sector of destination

$$R_i = k_i (X_i - X_{io}) \tag{11}$$

Stock-flow conversion factor by sector

$$r_i = \frac{g_i}{1 - e^{-g_i T}} \qquad i = 1,2,\ldots,30 \tag{12}$$

Non-residential replacement investment

$$I^R = \delta Y \tag{13}$$

Investment by sector of origin

$$I_{25} = \sum_{j=1}^{30} \zeta_j J_j + \overline{\zeta} I^R + I^H \tag{14}$$

$$I_i = \theta_i' [\sum_{j=1}^{30} (1 - \zeta_j) J_j + (1 - \overline{\zeta}) I^R] \quad i = 1,2,\ldots,24,26,\ldots,30 \tag{15}$$

Aggregate government's consumption demand

$$Gov = by \tag{16}$$

Government's consumption demand by sector

$$G_i = \gamma_i Gov \qquad\qquad i = 1,2,\ldots,30 \quad (17)$$

Aggregate consumers' demand

$$Con = Y - Gov - Inv - Exp + Imp \quad (18)$$

Consumers' demand by sector

$$C_i = \epsilon_i \frac{C_{io}}{Con_o} Con + (1 + g_N)^T C_{io}(1 - \epsilon_i) \qquad i = 1,2,\ldots,30 \quad (19)$$

Residential gross investment

$$I^H = \epsilon_H \frac{I_o^H}{Con_o} Con_o + (1 + g_N)^T I_o^H (1 - \epsilon_H) \quad (20)$$

Composition of the total value added by sector

$$q_i = \frac{\lambda_i X_i}{\sum_{i=1}^{30} \lambda_i X_i} \qquad\qquad i + 1,2,\ldots,30 \quad (21)$$

Aggregate incremental capital-output ratios

$$k = \frac{\sum_{i=1}^{30} k_i (X_i - X_{io})}{\sum_{i=1}^{30} (X_i - X_{io})} \quad (22)$$

$$k' = \frac{\sum\limits_{i=1}^{30} k_i (X_i - X_{io})}{\sum\limits_{i=1}^{30} \lambda_i (X_i - X_{io})} \qquad (23)$$

Composition of the total net accumulated investment requirements by sector of destination

$$Z_i = \frac{R_i}{\sum\limits_{i=1}^{30} R_i} \qquad i = 1,2,\ldots,30 \quad (24)$$

Composition of the net investment by sector of destination

$$z_i = \frac{I_i}{I^D} \qquad i = 1,2,\ldots,30 \quad (25)$$

Accumulated net requirement of state investment by sector of destination

$$R_i^E = \alpha_i^E R_i \qquad i = 1,2,\ldots,30 \quad (26)$$

State net investment by sector of destination

$$J_i^E = \alpha_i^E J_i \qquad i = 1,2,\ldots,30 \quad (27)$$

Aggregate state net investment

$$I^E = \sum_{i=1}^{30} J_i^E \qquad (28)$$

Composition of the total net accumulated state investment requirement by sector of destination

$$Z_i^E = \frac{R_i^E}{\sum_{i=1}^{30} R_i^E} \qquad i = 1,2,\ldots,30 \quad (29)$$

Composition of the net state investment by sector of destination

$$Z_i^E = \frac{J_i^E}{J^E} \qquad i = 1,2,\ldots,30 \quad (30)$$

State's share in the total net acumulated investment requirements

$$U = \frac{\sum_{i=1}^{30} R_i^E}{\sum_{i=1}^{30} R_i} \quad (31)$$

State's share in the non-residential net investment

$$u = \frac{I^E}{I^D} \quad (32)$$

In equation (8) aggregate investment at the terminal year is divided into non-residential net investment (I^D), non-residential replacement investment (I^R) and gross residential investment (I^H). The first of these components is given by equation (9), as the summation of net investments by sector of destination. Those in turn are determined in equation (10), which establishes that the net investment in a given sector at the terminal year is a fraction (r_i) of the investment requirement, accumulated over T years, in the sector. Such requirement is obtained in equation (11), where k_i is the ith sector's capital-output ratio.

The fraction r_i – known in the literature as the stock-flow conversion factor – may be obtained for the various sectors through equation (12). It is assumed that net investment in each sector grows over the period at an exponential rate equal to the respective sector's output growth rate. That being the case, net investment made at year T as a proportion of total net investment, accumulated over T years, is given by equation (12). A similar equation may be found in Manne, (1966), who, however, adopts the same factor value for all sectors, based on what is expected to be the average sectoral growth rate. In the specification adopted in (12), not only do we have different stock-flow conversion factors for each sector, but we also have an endogenous determination of such factors.[6]

Non-residential replacement investment in year T is given by equation (13). In fact, the greatest advantage of such specification is that it is fully consistent with the method by which depreciation is estimated in the Brazilian national accounts – a fixed proportion of the aggregate output.[7]

Equations (14) and (15) determine investment by sector of origin at the terminal year. There is a basic differentiation between investment in construction and in equipment.[8] The demand for construction is given by equation (14). To the residential investment (I^H) is added the part of non-residential replacement investment that takes place in the form of construction (ζI^R), as well as the summation of construction net investments made in the various sectors. Notice that it is assumed that the investment in construction is a fixed proportion – for each sector, though variable across sectors – of the next investment made. It is also assumed that a fixed proportion (ζ) of replacement investment takes the form of expenditure in construction.[9]

Equation (15) determines the demand for equipment, supplied by the other capital goods-producing sectors. Total demand for equipment – resulting from the aggregation of the net investment in equipment in the various sectors and the replacement investment made in equipment – is broken down among the various capital goods-producing sectors through distribution coefficients Θ.[10]

Government's consumption demand for the goods and services produced by each sector at year T is obtained from equations (16) to (17). Government's aggregate consumption is estimated as a fixed proportion of GDP in (16) and broken down among the various sectors according to coefficients γ_i in (17).

Aggregate consumers' demand is determined by equation (18) in a residual fashion. It is implicitly assumed that the economy is always able to adapt its consumption level in order to attain the required savings ratio. That equation is consistent with several different hypotheses about the adjusting process. Equation (19) simply shows linearisations of a logarithmic specification of Engel curves, which allow breaking down aggregate consumers' demand at year T among the various sectors. The same specification is used in (20) to determine gross residential investment.[11] The output's composition at year T is obtained from equation (21), which determines each sector's share in total value added. Comparisons with the sectoral distribution of value added at the base year may allow visualisation of the direction of the main structural changes implied by a given growth pattern.

The implications in terms of the aggregate incremental capital-output ratio are determined by equations (22) and (23). The first estimates the ratio on the basis of gross output, the second on the basis of value added.

The composition – by sector of destination – of the total net investment requirements accumulated over T years is given by equation (24). Equation (25) gives the composition of the total net investment at year T. The following equations relate to state investment. The net state investment requirements, accumulated over T years, by sector of destination, are determined in (26); the net state investment in year T, by sector of destination, in (27). Notice that in both (26) and (27) it is assumed that the state's share in each sector remains constant over the period under analysis. That must be understood much more as a working hypothesis than as a forecast. In fact, the sensitivity of the results of the simulations to changes in that particular hypothesis is reasonably easy to perceive.

In (28) net state investment in year T is obtained through the aggregation of the state investment in the various sectors. Similarly, (24) and (25), (29) and (30) allow a breakdown of the state investment by sector of destination. The state's share in the accumulated investment is given by (31); and the investment in year T by (32).

The model is block-recursive. The solution is obtained by first solving the system formed by equations (1) to (20) and then that which comprises equations (21) to (32).[12]

3 HYPOTHESES AND KEY EXOGENOUS VARIABLES

We are basically concerned with exploring the sensitivity of the growth and investment patterns, as well as of the productive structure at the terminal year, to different hypotheses about export expansion and import substitution during the period under analysis.

In the first place we had to find a way of adopting different assumptions about the sectoral exports growth rate (v_i) that would allow a reasonably simple sensitivity analysis. The starting point was the sectoral exports growth rates ($\bar{v}_i$), observed for the period 1970–8. The substitution of these rates in (6) and the use of (7) lead to

$$Exp = \sum_{i=1}^{30} (1 + \bar{v}_i)^T V_{io} = (1 + \bar{v})^T Exp_o \qquad (33)$$

where Exp_o is the level of total exports in 1978, the base year of the model, and $\bar{v}$ the implicit growth rate of total exports.

Naturally, given the excellent performance of exports during the period – made feasible by peculiar and extremely favourable conditions in terms of world trade expansion – $\bar{v}$ represents an excessively optimistic hypothesis concerning total export growth during the period 1978–90. The question is how to adopt a less optimistic hypothesis concerning export expansion and, at the same time, take into account the distinct dynamism shown by exports from different sectors during the period 1970–8.

Let v – instead of $\bar{v}$ – be a reasonable hypothesis for the total export growth rate. On the basis of the rates $\bar{v}_i$, how could we also adopt a more reasonable hypothesis relating to the sectoral export growth rates (v_i) that are consistent with the rate v?

From (33) the accumulated growth of total exports, in the case where the adopted rate was $\bar{v}$ – consistent with sectoral rates $\bar{v}_i$ – would be given by

$$\Delta Exp\,(\bar{v}) = [(1 + \bar{v})^T - 1]\,Exp_o = \sum_{i=1}^{30} [1 + \bar{v}_i)^T - 1]V_{io}. \qquad (34)$$

Similarly, with a rate v – consistent with sectoral rates v_i – we would have

$$\Delta Exp(v) = [(1+v)^T - 1] Exp_o = \sum_{i=1}^{30} [(1+v_i)^T - 1] V_{io}. \quad (35)$$

From (34) and (35) we get

$$\frac{\sum_{i=1}^{30} [(1+v_i)^T - 1] V_{io}}{\sum_{i=1}^{30} [(1+\bar{v}_i)^T - 1] V_{io}} = \frac{(1+v)^T - 1}{(1+\bar{v})^T - 1}$$

which may lead to

$$v_i = \left\{ \frac{(1+v)^T - 1}{(1+\bar{v})^T - 1} [(1+\bar{v}_i)^T - 1] + 1 \right\}^{1/T} - 1$$

$$i = 1, 2, \ldots, 30 \quad (36)$$

which establish sectoral exports growth rates, obtained on the basis of the rates $\bar{v}_i$ and consistent with the assumption of total exports growing at a rate v. In other words, equation (36) allows a normalisation of the sectoral rates $\bar{v}_i$, according to the aggregate rate v.[13]

In the simulations discussed below, four different hypotheses about total export expansion during the period 1978–90 were adopted, making v equal to 2.5, 5.0, 7.5 and 10 per cent. Using equation (36), each one of these values led to consistent assumptions about the sectoral exports growth rates (v_i).

In the adoption of hypotheses about the intensity of the import substitution process, attention was concentrated in three basic intermediary goods-producing sectors and in the mineral fuels extraction sector [3].[14] It was assumed that the import coefficients β_i of the sectors iron and steel [5] and paper pulp [12] would be reduced to zero at the end of the period under analysis. The corresponding estimated values of these coefficients for 1978 were 0.066 and 0.121 respectively. For the non-ferrous metals [7] sector, it was assumed that the import coefficient would be reduced from 0.915 in 1978 to 0.25 in 1990. All values were estimated on the basis of existing sectoral expansion plans.[15] Finally, for the mineral fuels extraction sector [3], the value of the import coefficient – which was found to be equal to 6.505 in 1978 – was initially assumed to reach 1.5 in 1990. Since such a coefficient is defined as the ratio of imports to domestic production, that amounts to an assumption that imports would account for 60 per cent of the total supply of mineral fuels at the end of the period. Later, a sensitivity analysis of the results of that particular hypothesis was made. For the remaining sector it was simply assumed that the import coefficients would not change during the period, which means no import substitution in those sectors. Again, that should rather be seen as a working hypothesis than as a forecast.

As to the assumptions about the GDP growth rate, we considered values between 3 and 8 per cent yearly.

4 THE GROWTH PATTERN AND PRODUCTIVE STRUCTURE

Table 16.3 presents the average annual growth rates, g_i, for the various sectors, where it is assumed that the average yearly aggregate growth rates g from 1978 to 1990 will be equal to 3 per cent. As indicated in the table, the results are presented for different hypotheses on the export expansion rate, v ranging between 2.5 and 10 per cent.

It is easy to single out sectors with a performance that is extremely sensitive to the assumption about export expansion. The growth rate of non-fuels mining [2], for example, becomes three times larger when the most optimistic assumption about v is adopted, instead of the most pessimistic one. Also extremely sensitive are the rates g_i corresponding to machinery [8] and electric and electronic goods [9]. With a somewhat lower sensitivity – though still significant – are the cases of non-ferrous metals [7], transportation goods [10], paper pulp [12], paper and cardboard [13], refinery and heavy petrochemicals [17], other chemicals [18], rail transportation [27] and waterborne transportation [28].[16]

The sensitivity of the growth rates g_i of non-ferrous metals [7] and paper pulp [12] are not higher still because – as mentioned above and indicated in Table 16.3 – the simulations assume quite intense import substitution processes in both sectors, which reduces the relative importance of the dynamic effect stemming from export expansion. It may be seen that even for $v = 2.5$ per cent the growth rates of both

Table 16.3 Average annual growth rates by sector (g_i)

		3%			
Assumptions		$\beta_3=1.5$, $\beta_5=0$, $\beta_7=0.25$, $\beta_{12}=0$			
	β_i	$\beta_i=\beta_{io}$, $i=1,2,4,6,8,9,10,11,13,\ldots,30$			
	v	2.5%	5.0%	7.5%	10.0%

Sectors:
1. Agriculture & livestock	3.00	3.00	2.99	2.98
2. Non-fuels mining	1.45	2.38	3.48	4.73
3. Mineral fuels extraction	13.11	13.58	14.17	14.87
4. Non-metallic minerals	.32	.35	.39	.45
5. Iron & steel	1.89	2.54	3.34	4.27
6. Foundry & metal processing	1.26	1.67	2.17	2.79
7. Non-ferrous metals	6.86	7.62	8.54	9.62
8. Machinery	0.79	1.86	3.10	4.49
9. Electric & electronic goods	1.35	2.30	3.42	4.70
10. Transportation goods	1.54	1.98	2.53	3.20
11. Wood & furniture	2.62	2.51	2.36	2.17
12. Paper pulp	5.05	6.77	8.62	10.60
13. Paper & cardboard	3.61	4.32	5.18	6.17
14. Rubber, leather & plastic	2.45	2.67	2.95	3.31
15. Fertilizers, alkalis & others	2.78	3.05	3.39	3.81
16. Alcohol & vegetable oils	5.76	6.02	6.36	6.77
17. Refinery & heavy petrochemicals	2.63	3.06	3.59	4.24
18. Other chemicals	2.38	2.79	3.30	3.92
19. Perfumery & pharmaceutical	3.83	3.72	3.58	3.39
20. Textile, clothing & footwear	3.41	3.57	3.76	4.01
21. Food, beverages & tobacco	3.03	3.00	2.97	2.93
22. Printing, publishing & others	3.48	3.47	3.46	3.45
23. Electricity	3.05	3.13	3.23	3.36
24. Water & sewerage	3.22	3.13	3.02	2.87
25. Construction	−.52	−.59	−.68	−.79
26. Commerce, storage, road & air transportation	3.10	3.05	2.97	2.88
27. Rail transportation	2.19	2.65	3.22	3.90
28. Waterborne transportation	1.48	1.89	2.40	3.02
29. Communications	4.72	4.48	4.17	3.75
30. Other services	3.89	3.77	3.61	3.40

sectors are well above the average sectoral growth rate. This same discrepancy may be observed, in a much more significant way, in the case of mineral fuels extraction [3].[17]

It should also be noted that the growth rates of the non-tradeable goods-producing sectors are, in general, lower the higher the assumed export expansion rate. This is to be expected, since the economy's growth rate is being kept constant. Besides construction [25] may be listed other services [30], communications [29], commerce, storage, etc. [26] and water & sewerage [24].[18] Electricity constitutes an important exception.

A growth pattern characterised by the leadership of exporting and import-substituting sectors seems to emerge from the simulations. One should include among the import substituting sectors the special case of alcohol & vegetable oils [16]. The outstanding performance of this sector stems, however, not from a reduction in the sectoral import coefficient, but from a change in the consumption pattern, implied in the adopted value for the sector's Engel's elasticity.[19]

What has to be analysed now is the impact of this new growth pattern on the productive structure of the economy. This may be done using data in Table 16.4, which presents – for the same set of hypotheses that generated the results of Table 16.3 – the importance of the various sectors in terms of value-added generation at the terminal year g_i. To make comparisons easier, values referring to the base year are also presented.

Especially outstanding is the increase, between 1978 and 1990, in the share of sectors for which import substitution was assumed: mineral fuels extraction [3],[20] non-ferrous metals [7] and paper pulp [12]. The exception is iron & steel [5], which presents a fall in its share when the most pessimistic assumption about export expansion is adopted. This is a consequence of that sector's low import coefficient at the base year. Even a reduction of this coefficient to zero does not lead to a very significant effect upon the sector's growth. However, it should be noted that its share is highly sensitive to the assumption about export expansion.

Quite a high sensitivity may also be observed for other sectors, particularly non-fuel mining [2], machinery [8], electric & electronic goods [9] and transportation goods [10]. Nonetheless, those sectors would only show higher shares at the terminal year, under extremely optimistic assumptions about export expansion. The sensitivity of non-ferrous metals [7] and paper pulp [12] to v is also very clear, even though the increase in their shares follows to a large extent from the

Table 16.4 Sectoral shares in total value added

	1978		1990			
		g		3%		
Assumptions		β_i	$\beta_3=1.5$, $\beta_5=0$, $\beta_7=0.25$, $\beta_{12}=0$ $\beta_i=\beta_{io}$, $i=1,2,4,6,8,9,10,11,13,\ldots,30$			
		v	2.5%	5.0%	7.5%	10.0%

Sectors:					
1. Agriculture & livestock	10.97	11.26	11.16	11.03	10.87
2. Non-fuels mining	.50	.43	.47	.53	.61
3. Mineral fuels extraction	.17	.54	.56	.59	.63
4. Non-metallic minerals	2.04	1.52	1.52	1.51	1.50
5. Iron & steel	1.75	1.57	1.69	1.83	2.01
6. Foundry & metal processing	2.38	1.98	2.06	2.17	2.30
7. Non-ferrous metals	.25	.39	.42	.46	.51
8. Machinery	2.88	2.27	2.56	2.92	3.39
9. Electric & electronic goods	1.78	1.50	1.66	1.88	2.14
10. Transportation goods	3.79	3.27	3.42	3.61	3.85
11. Wood & furniture	1.82	1.78	1.74	1.70	1.63
12. Paper pulp	.06	.07	.09	.11	.14
13. Paper & cardboard	.86	.95	1.02	1.11	1.23
14. Rubber, leather & plastic	1.26	1.20	1.23	1.25	1.29
15. Fertilizers, alkalis & others	.57	.57	.58	.60	.62
16. Alcohol & vegetable oils	.32	.45	.46	.47	.49
17. Refinery & heavy petrochemicals	1.43	1.40	1.46	1.53	1.63
18. Other chemicals	.82	.78	.81	.85	.91
19. Perfumery & pharmaceutical	1.88	2.12	2.08	2.02	1.95
20. Textile, clothing & footwear	2.52	2.71	2.74	2.77	2.81
21. Food, beverages & tobacco	5.99	6.16	6.09	6.00	5.89
22. Printing, publishing & others	3.06	3.31	3.28	3.24	3.19
23. Electricity	2.27	2.34	2.34	2.34	2.35
24. Water & sewerage	.22	.23	.22	.22	.21
25. Construction	7.70	5.20	5.12	5.01	4.88
26. Commerce, storage, road & air transportation	26.34	27.35	26.95	26.44	25.79
27. Rail transportation	.16	.15	.15	.16	.17
28. Waterborne transportation	.86	.73	.76	.80	.85
29. Communications	1.50	1.87	1.80	1.72	1.62
30. Other services	13.86	15.77	15.42	14.97	14.41
Total	100.00	100.00	100.00	100.00	100.00

import substitution hypotheses, as was seen above. The rise in the importance of alcohol and vegetable oils [16] as a consequence of changes in the pattern of fuels consumption should also be noted.

As expected, the share of non-tradeable goods-producing sectors is, in general, lower the higher the v value, although shares below the base year level may be observed only under an extremely optimistic assumption about export expansion. The exception is the significant reduction in the importance of the construction industry [25] which stems, however, from the assumption of a relatively low aggregate growth rate, as was explained above. This same assumption is responsible for the reduction in the shares of the remaining capital goods-producing sectors, which may be observed for low v values.[21]

This suggests an analysis of the sensitivity of the sectoral growth rates g_i and value added shares at the terminal year g_i to different hypotheses about the aggregate growth rate g. As a general statement, one may say that the impact of import substitution and export expansion upon the growth pattern and productive structure tends to be substantial when it is assumed that the economy will grow at a relatively slow rate. But the impact tends to become less significant when more optimistic assumptions about the expansion of the aggregate output over the period under analysis are considered. As the difficulties facing the Brazilian economy do not leave much room for optimism on that matter, it is reasonable to assume that scenarios that take into account slower growth rates represent more faithful outlines of what the expansion pattern and consequent changes in the productive structure will be over the next few years.

5 THE BROAD INVESTMENT SITUATION

Table 16.5 presents the composition of the next accumulated investment requirements by sector of destination, when a 3 per cent annual aggregate growth rate is assumed, and the basic import substitution hypothesis previously adopted is maintained. The results are presented for different values assigned to the export expansion rate, v. The percentage of the net investment requirement that has the ith sector as destination is given by Z_i. Analogously the percentage of the state investment requirement that has the ith sector as destination.

Naturally, those sectors with a performance that proved to be sensitive to the hypothesis about v in the previous section, show a

Table 16.5 Composition of the net accumulated investment requirements by sector of destination

	g		3%					
Assumptions	β_i		$\beta_3=1.5, \beta_5=0, \beta_7=0.25, \beta_{12}=0$ $\beta_i=\beta_{io}, i=1,2,4,6,8,\ldots,11,13,\ldots,30$					
	v	2.5%		5.0%		7.5%		10.%
Sectors:		Z_i	Z_i^E	Z_i	Z_i^E	Z_i	Z_i^E	Z_i	Z_i^E
1. Agriculture & livestock		11.53	0	11.24	0	10.87	0	10.43	0
2. Non-fuels mining		.26	.57	.44	.94	.67	1.38	.94	1.87
3. Mineral fuels extraction		7.69	28.93	8.00	29.46	8.39	30.07	8.86	30.77
4. Non-metallic minerals		.18	0	.19	0	.21	0	.23	0
5. Iron & steel		1.52	3.53	2.07	4.70	2.76	6.09	3.59	7.68
6. Foundry & metal processing		.82	.04	1.08	.05	1.40	.07	1.80	.08
7. Non-ferrous metals		.85	.84	.96	.93	1.11	1.04	1.28	1.16
8. Machinery		.27	.04	.66	.09	1.14	0	1.72	.22
9. Electric & electronic goods		.28	0	.49	0	.75	0	1.06	0
10. Transportation goods		.91	.15	1.18	.18	1.5	.23	1.90	.28
11. Wood & furniture		.68	0	.63	0	.57	0	.5	0
12. Paper pulp		.13	.12	.18	.17	.25	.23	.34	.3
13. Paper & cardboard		1.04	0	1.26	0	1.54	0	1.87	0
14. Rubber, leather & plastic		.5	0	.54	0	.59	0	.64	0
15. Fertilizers, alkalis & others		.4	.37	.44	.40	.48	.42	.53	.46
16. Alcohol & vegetable oils		.93	.05	.96	.05	1.01	.05	1.06	.06
17. Refinery & heavy petrochemicals		1.10	3.35	1.28	3.82	1.51	4.36	1.78	4.98
18. Other chemicals		.5	.07	.58	.08	.68	.09	.81	.1
19. Perfumery & pharmaceutical		1.0	.06	.95	.06	.88	.05	.79	.04
20. Textile, clothing & footwear		3.83	.33	3.95	.34	4.09	.34	4.25	.34
21. Food, beverages & tobacco		5.86	.31	5.67	.29	5.43	.27	5.15	.25
22. Printing, publishing & others		1.25	.21	1.22	.20	1.18	.19	1.13	.18
23. Electricity		4.14	15.47	4.16	15.21	4.19	14.91	4.22	14.57
24. Water & sewerage		.42	1.60	.4	1.48	.37	1.34	.34	1.18
25. Construction		0	0	0	0	0	0	0	0
26. Commerce, storage, road & air transportation		23.63	11.82	22.59	11.05	21.31	10.15	19.76	9.12
27. Rail transportation		.51	1.93	.62	2.29	.75	2.71	.91	3.19
28. Waterborne transportation		1.10	2.25	1.38	2.81	1.75	3.47	2.20	4.22
29. Communications		3.51	12.49	3.21	11.19	2.85	9.66	2.40	7.90
30. Other services		25.20	15.47	23.68	14.21	21.79	12.73	19.50	11.04
Total		100.00	100.00	100.00	100.00	100.00	100.00	100.00	100.00

share in investment that is equally sensitive to that same hypothesis. Thus, as increasingly optimistic assumptions about export expansion are adopted, the Z_i and Z_i^E values are altered, outlining a reallocation of investments that, in general, are characterised by a fall in the share of non-tradeable goods-producing sectors and an increase in the share of the exporting sectors. Taking state investment, it may be seen that a rise in the v value generates significant increases in the participation of sectors such as non-fuels mining [2], iron & steel [5], non-ferrous metals [7], paper pulp [12] and rail transportation [27],[22] and a sharp fall in the participation of sectors which typically produce non-tradeable goods, as it the case of communications [29]. When one takes total investment requirements, the gains in participation of for example, machinery [8], electric and electronic goods [9] and transportation goods [10] may be noticed, and also the losses of commerce, etc. [26] and other services [30].

Two points need to be made about some non-tradeable goods-producing sectors. The first concerns the stability of the participation of electricity [23] which follows from the relative sensitivity of the aggregate demand of electricity to the composition of the aggregate output. The second concerns the zero participation of construction [25]. With a negative growth rate, that sector's investment requirements should also be negative according to equation (11). However, in the model's solution, we adopted the convention that in such cases the requirements would be considered equal to zero, which amounts to using (11) only when $X_i \geq X_{io}$.

Reflecting the analysis in the previous section, import-substituting and exporting sectors tend to show less important shares in the investment programme when more optimistic hypotheses about the aggregate growth rate are assumed. In other words, the impact of import substitution and export expansion fades as higher expansion rates for the economy are assumed.

The investment pattern proved to be rather sensitive to the hypotheses about the import-substitution process. In particular, it was easy to detect a clear growing prominence of the share of mineral fuels extraction [3], as bolder hypotheses about import substitution in the sector were adopted. In fact, the value of β_3 proved to be a basic determinant of the composition of state investments. Naturally, this sensitivity to the import-substitution targets is partially weakened when scenarios that contemplate more optimistic hypotheses about the aggregate growth rate are simulated.

With further regard to the investment pattern, it is worth making some comments on the results of the simulations for some of the aggregate variables. For low growth rates g, the aggregate capital-output ratios, either in terms of gross output, k, or in terms of value added, k, show some sensitivity to the hypothesis about export expansion, both tending to diminish with an increase in v. On the other hand, this same increase gives rise, in general, to an increment, though not very significant, in the state's share in total investment requirement (U). The sensitivity of these three variables to v tends to diminish when higher g values are assumed. As to import substitution, the adoption of the basic set of assumptions – described in Section 3 – causes k, k' and U to be higher than they would be had we assumed no import substitution in all sectors.

6 INVESTMENT REALLOCATION

With the results presented above one may visualise in some detail the outlines of the investment reallocation process involved in the probable structural adjustment of the Brazilian economy in the 1980s. However, given the need to make a reasonably simple sensitivity analysis, there was an unavoidable bunching of a large number of exogenous variables – as was done with the sectoral export growth rates – as well as a limit to the scope of the hypotheses about import substitution. That, undoubtedly, may impose upon the results a certain degree of arbitrariness. What will be done now is to remedy that deficiency in part by presenting a more detailed sensitivity analysis of the investment reallocation process. Such analysis in fact allows the estimation of sectoral parameters that may be used as guidelines in that process.

The starting point is a particular solution for the model corresponding to reasonable assumptions about the values of the key exogenous variables. For that purpose g was set equal to 4 per cent, v to 5 per cent and the same basic set of import-substitution hypotheses – described in Section 3 and widely used above – was adopted. Once that solution was obtained, we tried to check the sensitivity of the net accumulated investment requirements, by sector of destination, to relatively small increments in a given sector's demand in the terminal year. That increment may in fact be interpreted either as a rise in the sector's exports or as the substitution of imports that are competitive with that sector's output. Thus, we could obtain estimations of the direct and indirect net investment requirements associated with the production corresponding to this increment in demand, distributed by sectors of destination of the investment. This exercise was repeated for various sectors, always using the same value for the demand increment – Cr$ 100 million at 1970 prices – in such a way as to obtain results that are comparable across sectors.

Hence it was possible to generate a set of parameters that permit the estimation of the impact on the investment pattern of any rise in exports or of import substitution in any sector of the economy. It also permits the identification of important linkages between investments that are made in different sectors, as well as between private and state investments. It permits further comparison of investment efforts required by the same increment in exports – or import substitution – in different sectors.[23]

A space constraint allows us to present here only a sample of the results obtained, relating to an important exporting sector (Table 16.6) and a sector for which an intense import substitution process has been assumed (Table 16.7).[24] Comprehension of those results may be made easier by some brief comments. According to Table 16.7, a Cr$ 100 million cruzeiros rise in exports – or import substitution – in non-ferrous metals [7] requires an investment effort amounting to Cr$ 280.93, of which only 62.57 per cent relates to investment outlays in the sector itself. The total requirement of state investment amounts to Cr$ 101.25, of which 45.14 per cent is in the sector itself, 27.87 per cent in electricity [25], 6.71 per cent in rail transportation [27] and 5.79 per cent in non-fuels mining [2]. On the other hand, comparison of tables 16.6 and 16.7 allows the conclusion that although the direct and indirect investment required by a given increment in sectoral exports (or import substitution) is roughly comparable in both sectors, the requirements referring to non-fuels mining [2] involve a much larger participation of state investment.

7 CONCLUSIONS

There is evidence that the impact of import substitution and export expansion on the performance of most sectors of the Brazilian economy during the 1970s was rather limited, to the point of not affecting in a significant way the growth pattern observed during that period.[25]

Table 16.6 Direct and indirect investment requirements, by sector of destination, of an increment in exports, or in import substitution, amounting to Cr$ 100 millions in the non-fuels mining sector

Sectors of destination of the investment	Total additional investment		Additional state investment	
	Cr$ millions	%	Cr$ millions	%
1. Agriculture & livestock	.98	.36	0	0
2. Non-fuels mining	220.28	82.23	126.22	81.46
3. Mineral fuels extraction	6.85	2.55	6.80	4.39
4. Non-metallic minerals	1.06	.39	0	0
5. Iron & steel	1.64	.61	1.00	.65
6. Foundry & metal processing	1.53	.57	.02	.01
7. Non-ferrous metals	.40	.15	.10	.06
8. Machinery	2.91	1.08	.10	.07
9. Electric & electronic goods	.30	.11	0	0
10. Transportation goods	.22	.08	0	0
11. Wood & furniture	.05	.02	0	0
12. Paper pulp	.17	0	0	0
13. Paper & cardboard	.14	.05	0	0
14. Rubber, leather & plastic	.20	.07	0	0
15. Fertilizers, alkalis & others	.95	.35	.23	.15
16. Alcohol & vegetable oils	.06	.02	0	0
17. Refinery & heavy petrochemicals	2.90	1.08	2.32	1.50
18. Other chemicals	.93	.35	.03	.02
19. Perfumery & pharmaceutical	.02	0	0	0
20. Textile, clothing & footwear	.07	.02	0	0
21. Food, beverages & tobacco	.04	.01	0	0
22. Printing, publishing & others	.08	.03	0	0
23. Electricity	12.48	4.65	12.32	7.95
24. Water & sewerage	0	0	0	0
25. Construction	.36	.13	.03	.02
26. Commerce, storage, road & air transportation	8.00	2.98	1.05	.68
27. Rail transportation	4.06	1.51	4.06	2.62
28. Waterborne transportation	.87	.32	.48	.31
29. Communications	.01	0	.01	0
30. Other services	.18	.07	.03	.02
Total:	267.87	100.00	154.93	100.00

Table 16.7 Direct and indirect investment requirements, by sector of destination, of an increment in exports, or in import substitution, amounting to Cr$ 100 millions in the non-ferrous metals sector

Sectors of destination of the investment	Total additional investment		Additional state investment	
	Cr$ millions	%	Cr$ millions	%
1. Agriculture & livestock	.86	.30	0	0
2. Non-fuels mining	10.24	3.64	5.87	5.79
3. Mineral fuels extraction	5.27	1.87	5.24	5.17
4. Non-metallic minerals	.61	.21	0	0
5. Iron & steel	3.64	1.29	2.23	2.20
6. Foundry & metal processing	6.36	2.26	.08	.08
7. Non-ferrous metals	175.80	62.57	45.70	45.14
8. Machinery	1.26	.44	.04	.04
9. Electric & electronic goods	.34	.12	0	0
10. Transportation goods	.41	.14	.01	.01
11. Wood & furniture	.08	.03	0	0
12. Paper pulp	.05	.02	.01	.01
13. Paper & cardboard	.73	.26	0	0
14. Rubber, leather & plastic	.32	.11	0	0
15. Fertilizers, alkalis & others	2.24	.79	.54	.54
16. Alcohol & vegetable oils	.11	.03	0	0
17. Refinery & heavy petrochemicals	2.12	.75	1.70	1.68
18. Other chemicals	1.42	.50	.05	.05
19. Perfumery & pharmaceutical	.05	.02	0	0
20. Textile, clothing & footwear	.19	.06	0	0
21. Food, beverages & tobacco	.14	.05	0	0
22. Printing, publishing & others	.27	.09	.01	.01
23. Electricity	28.58	10.17	28.21	27.87
24. Water & sewerage	0	0	0	0
25. Construction	.61	.22	.05	.05
26. Commerce, storage, road & air transportation	30.81	10.96	4.06	4.01
27. Rail transportation	6.79	2.41	6.79	6.71
28. Waterborne transportation	.71	.25	.39	.38
29. Communications	.0	0	0	0
30. Other services	.68	.24	.11	.11
Total:	280.93	100.00	101.25	100.00

However, the analysis developed in the previous section suggests that during the 1980s such impact may become quite substantial. That analysis allowed a visualisation of the probable consequences of a strategy designed to overcome the structural external disequilibrium of the Brazilian economy, on the basis of bold programmes of import substitution and export expansion during the period.

The results of the simulations, using the model presented in Section 2, in fact indicate that unless very optimistic assumptions about the aggregate growth rate are made, import substitution and export expansion may prove to be fundamental determinants of the economy's growth and investment patterns. During the 1970s those effects were much less significant due to the dynamism that the economy was able to maintain. Under slower growth conditions, such as those that will probably have to be faced during the 1980s, such effects may become very important.

Broadly, the simulations reveal the outlines of a probable, and natural, increment in the importance of tradeable goods-producing sectors, particularly those engaged in import-substitution programmes or more directly in export activities. As has been seen, this may require considerable changes in the investment pattern, especially in the composition of state investment, that is bound to be determined to a large extent by the intensity of the oil import-substitution effort that will effectively be made until the end of this decade.

NOTES

1. See (Clark, 1975) for a good discussion of the difference between consistency and feasibility models.
2. See, for example, Bergsman and Manne (1966).
3. In this sense the model is similar to those developed by, for example, Bruno (1966), Manne (1966), Lopes (1972) and Werneck (1980).
4. We did not choose a more recent base year for several reasons. In the first place, the model assumes that each sector's growth, as well as the investment requirements, are determined by demand expansion. That may be a realistic hypothesis only if such expansion is related to an initial situation for which it is fair to suppose full employment or, at least, low idle capacity. That being the case, more recent years would be less appropriate than 1978. Second, the implementation of the present long-run strategy, involving bold import substitution and export expansion programmes, becomes significantly more aggressive after 1979, with the mounting foreign sector difficulties. If we take into account the natural lags involved in investment maturation, the

estimation of investment requirements using a more recent base year could lead to an exaggeration of the required capital outlays, since there would be no allowance for the investment effort already made. Finally, the most recent year for which we could get reasonably reliable data for the model was precisely 1978.
5. This is a common way to deal with competitive imports in multisectoral models. See Srinivasan (1975).
6. Notice that we are using the stock-flow method to determine investment by sector of destination. This method has often been used for the determination of investment by sector of origin, on the basis of the accumulated requirements of various kinds of capital goods. On the use of the stock-flow conversion factor see also Manne and Rudra (1965), Chenery and Bruno (1962), Manne (1963), Clark (1975) and Taylor (1975).
7. See Fundação Gefúlio Vargas (1972).
8. This is the basic differentiation used in Johansen (1960 and 1974), which allows 'to take care of the more important differences in capital structure, without adding too greatly to the complexity of the model' (Johansen, 1960, p.42).
9. Similar assumptions are adopted in Johansen (1960 and 1974).
10. As opposed to Johansen, who assumes a single equipment-producing sector, we are working with several capital goods-producing sectors, besides construction.
11. A similar specification for the determination of residential investment may be found in Bruno (1966). Notice that both the model and the input–output data do not consider residential investment as consumers' demand, which does *not* mean that we cannot use a specification as in (20).
12. For details of the solution and the utilised data see Werneck (1982).
13. It should be noted that this amounts to estimating the increment in a given sector's exports using the observed elasticity of that sector's exports with respect to total exports.
14. The name of every sector mentioned will be followed by its number in our classification in square brackets.
15. See Secretaria de Planejamento da Presidencia da Republica (1982) and Conselho de Desenvolvimento Industrial (1981).
16. The observed sensivity for rail transportation [27] is explained by the way the input-output matrix deals with the gross rail transportation margin associated with exports, which is treated as exports from sector[27].
17. The fact that the construction sector [25] shows negative growth rates–though close to zero–is easily explained. This is basically a capital goods-producing sector, and the low investment ratio, required to make the economy grow at only 3 per cent annually, causes the sectoral output at the terminal year to be lower than it was at the base year, when the investment ratio was much higher. The same kind of effect

appears in other capital goods-producing sectors, such as machinery [8], electric and electronic goods [9] and transportation goods [10] although it does not lead to negative growth rates either because they do not produce only capital goods or because the capital goods produced are tradeable goods, which allows those sectors' growth rates to be sensitive to the hypothesis about export expansion.

18. It must be remembered that, due to the way the input-output matrix deals with the exports' commercialisation and transportation margins, the production of rail transportation [27] and part of sector [26], commerce, storage, etc, may in fact be classified as tradeable.
19. Since the mid-1970s Brazil has been engaged in an important and original programme designed to disseminate the use of alcohol in passengers' cars as a substitute for gasoline. So far that programme has been surprisingly successful. The adopted value for the sector's Engel's elasticity assumes the fulfilment of the programme's targets.
20. It should be pointed out that, as all data are estimated at 1970 prices–to be consistent with the input-output matrix–the share of the mineral fuels extraction sector [3] is well below what it would be, had the data been estimated at prices referring to 1978, for example.
21. Similar reductions may be observed for sectors strongly linked to the capital goods-producing sectors, including construction [25]. That is the case of non-metallic minerals [4] and foundry and metal processing [6].
22. As was pointed out before, the rail transportation margin associated to exports is considered as exports from sector 27, which explains the high sensitivity of Z^E27 to v.
23. In fact, it would be preferable to work with the same foreign exchange generation value in each sector measured in dollars instead of cruzeiros. Unhappily, that was not possible.
24. Results referring to other sectors are presented in Werneck (1982).
25. This evidence is presented in Werneck (1983).

REFERENCES

Adelman, I. and Thorbeck, E. (eds) (1966) *The Theory and Design of Economic Development* (Baltimore: Johns Hopkins Press).

Bergsman, J. and Manne, A. S. (1966) 'An Almost Consistent Intertemporal Model for India's Fourth and Fifth Plan', in Adelman, I. and Thorbecke, E. (eds) (1966).

Blitzer, C., Clark, P. B. and Taylor, L. (eds) (1975) *Economy Wide Models and Development Planning* (Oxford: Oxford University Press).

Bruno, M. (1966) 'A Programming Model for Israel', in Adelman, I. and Thorbecke, E. (eds) (1966).

Chenery, H. B. and Bruno, M. (1962) 'Development Alternatives in an Open Economy', *Economic Journal*, vol 72.

Clark, P. B. (1975) 'Inter-Sectoral Consistency and Macroeconomic Planning', in Blitzer, C. *et al.* (eds) (1975).

Conselho de Desenvolvimento Industrial (1981) *Relatório Anual-1980* (Brasilia: CDI-MIC).

Fundação Gefúlio Vargas (1972) *Contas Nacionais do Brasil: Conceitos e Metodolgia* (Rio de Janeiro: FGV/IBRE).
Johansen, L. (1960) *A multi–Sectoral Study of Economic Growth* (Amsterdam: North Holland).
Johansen, L. (1974) *A Multi–Sectoral Study of Economic Growth*, second enlarged edition (Amsterdam: North Holland).
Lopes, F. L. P. (1972) 'Desigualdade e Crescimento: Um Modelo de Programaçáo com Aplicaçáo ao Brasil', *Pesquisa e Planejamento Económico*, vol 2, no. 2, December.
Manne, A. S. (1963) 'Key Sectors of the Mexican Economy: 1960–70', in Manne, A. S. and Markowitz, H. M. (eds) (1963).
Manne, A. S. (1966) 'Key Sectors of the Mexican Economy, 1962–70', in Adelman, I. and Thorbecke, E. (eds) (1966).
Manne, A. S. and Markowitz, H. M. (eds) (1963) *Studies in Process Analysis: Economy–Wide Production Capabilities* (New York: John Wiley).
Manne, A. S. and Rudra, A. (1965) 'A Consistency Model for India's Fourth Plan', *Sankhya*, serie B, vol. 27.
Secretaria de Planejamento de Presidéncia de República (1982) 'Consolidaçáo Plurianual de Programas de Governo (Uma Antevisão da Demanda de Recursos)', IPLAN/IPEA, mimeo.
Srinivasan, T. N. (1975) 'The Foreign Trade Sector in Planning Models', in Blitzer, C. *et al.* (eds) (1975).
Taylor, L. (1975) 'Theoretical Foundations and Technical Implications', in Blitzer, C. *et al.* (eds) (1975).
Werneck, R. L. F. (1980) 'Rapid Growth, Distributional Equity and the Size of the Public Sector: Trade–offs Facing the Brazilian Economic Policy in the 1980s', doctoral dissertation, Harvard University, mimeo.
Werneck, R. L. F. (1982) 'Disequilibrio Externo e Reorientaçáo do Crescimento e dos Investimentos: Uma Analise Multisetorial das Perspectivas da Economia Brasileira', Relatorio de Pesquisa, Departamento de Economia, PUC–RJ, Rio de Janeiro, mimeo.
Werneck, R. L. F. (1983) 'Expansao de Exportações, Substituição de Importações e Crescimento Setorial: A Experiéncia dos Anos 70', Texto para discussão no. 43, Departamento de Economia, PUC–RJ, Rio de Janeiro, mimeo.

17 Structural Change in a Selection of Countries: Discussion and Conclusions

P. J. Lloyd
UNIVERSITY OF MELBOURNE

Structural changes in a selection of countries were discussed in terms of the 'branch level'. The term 'branch level' refers to the level of sectors of an economy and the changes in their component industries. Structural changes at the level of industries are of interest to economists, it was felt, primarily because many of the resources employed are specific to the industries that employ them – that is, the capital and labour embody features or skills which cannot be transferred to other industries. The concern has been mainly with industries that are contracting and whose contraction reduces the incomes of the workers who possess industry-specific skills and the owners of the capital assets.

While the analyses presented were microeconomic at the level of the industry, there was a widespread view that it was also necessary to use the tools of general equilibrium analysis for the whole economy. This is because the expansion or contraction of one group has significant effects on others; for example, events or policies which raise the prices of the outputs of an industry group producing intermediate outputs will raise the costs of production of downstream industries and reduce their competitiveness or, as another example, the expansion of booming industries which utilise new discoveries of natural resources will reduce the profitability of other industries, chiefly by an appreciation of the exchange rate if they are export industries. The general equilibrium effects were emphasised particularly in the papers by Dr Rogerio Werneck of Brazil and Dr Peter Warr of Australia, but they were implicit in all papers.

As there was a variety of experiences reported for several countries (Brazil, Singapore, Australia, the Netherlands, Poland and Sweden, not all of which are published here) generalisations are somewhat difficult. Moreover, the shock of these economies which brought about changes in the structure of industries have varied greatly from economy to economy, and this was reflected in the aspects which the individual authors chose to examine.

In the case of Brazil, examined by Dr Rogerio Werneck, the fundamental problem is a chronic balance of payments desequilibrium and growing international indebtedness. This has prompted policies of import substitution and export expansion at the same time, which are intended to switch resources to the tradeable goods sector so as to restore equilibrium in the balance of payments. This strategy raises questions concerning the reallocation of resources that is consistent with the target rates of growth of exports and of the ratio of imports to domestic production (and hence in the rates of imports to domestic consumption). The period considered was 1978 to 1990. A sensitivity analysis revealed that some sectors such as machinery, electric and electronic goods and non-fuels mining are extremely sensitive to the assumptions concerning the target rates of import substitution and export growth. As a generalisation, the impact of the import substitution export expansion policies on sectoral growth rates is reduced when the rate of growth for the whole economy is assumed to be greater, apparently because the effects of the assumed average rate of growth of all industries swamps those of the switches of resources required to effect the import substitution and export growth. Thus acceleration of growth is the more important source of structural change. One query for this method of analysis is why the government should plan these industrial growth rates instead of allowing the exchange rate to determine the changes in relative prices which will effect the desired improvement in the balance of payments.

The Singapore experience has been quite different. Over the 22-year period 1960 to 1982 per capita GNP grew at an average rate of 7.0 per cent, and at the same time the unemployment rate fell from 10 per cent initially to less than 3 per cent; this real economic growth was spread widely over all income groups. Dr Chia attributed the success story in part to the role of foreign investment. Under a regime which offered various financial incentives to the production and exports of MNCs, direct foreign investment has financed more than 50 per cent of gross capital formation, which is currently at the exceptionally high level of 48 per cent of GNP. Foreign investment also supplied entrepreneurial and skilled labour resources which were in scarce supply. Policies of free trade and a disciplined labour force, which permitted real wages to grow at only 2.5 per cent in real terms, a rate well below the growth of labour productivity, also distinguish the performance of this economy from most developing and developed countries. These experiences may provide important lessons for less rapidly growing economies. Another feature that deserves attention is that, in an environment of sustained rapid growth, it was necessary for the Singapore government to switch policies several times: first away from a brief period of import substitution to one of free trade led by foreign investment, and later to one of deliberately raising real wages more rapidly and encouraging a switch to higher technology and less labour-intensive industries which have better growth prospects on world markets. Some questions remain as to the role of high rates of interest in encouraging investment and the role of family business enterprise as the means of promoting entrepreneurship in service and financial activities.

The Australian experience presented by Dr Warr is quite different again. As in many other developed countries, debate and public policy have concentrated on the appropriate levels of production for sensitive industries such as textiles, clothing and footwear and automotive assembly. Dr Warr questioned the popular belief, espoused by the Brandt Report and others, that the policies of tariff escalation and high barriers to labour-intensive imports really do discriminate against imports from less developed countries *vis-à-vis* imports from more developed (high-income) countries. He concluded, on the basis of a general equilibrium model which takes account of inter-industry import requirements and differences among industries in the demand and supply elasticities, that Australian policies have not in fact discriminated significantly against the LDCs. Moreover, reductions in the present rates of protection for individual industries have widely varying effects on Australia's imports from LDCs. Remarkably, in about one-fourth of the protected industries reductions in rates of protection would *reduce* total imports from LDCs. This is due to inter-industry effects. It was suggested that these results should be examined for different levels of constant real wages in the model. It was also conjectured that these results, which have important policy implications for the LDCs, may hold for other industrial countries. It was suggested that the long-run effects might differ from the short-run effects due to changes in comparative advantage over time.

As another case study (not published here) the paper by Drs van Gemert and de Groof examined the nature and causes of the 'Dutch disease' in the Netherlands by comparing Dutch experience with that of other OECD countries. The deviations in the changes in the distribution of employment by industry in the Netherlands from the 'normal' pattern of other OECD countries were dominated by a relatively strong reallocation of labour from manufacturing to non-market government activities and other services. They concluded that this feature of the Dutch economy was indeed due to the effects of the booming natural gas sector of the economy. Some questions were asked whether the role of the expenditure of revenues from taxation of natural gas was as important in determining the structural changes as the authors had maintained.

Despite the recognition of differences among this sample of countries and among other countries, some themes emerged. One was the importance of up-to-date information on market trends and the structure of the economy if governments are to make decisions which reduce the burdens of structural change. All agreed that governments had an important role to play, though there was no agreement, as the papers showed, on what objectives policy should be directed towards and what instruments should be assigned to the objectives. The Polish example emphasised the necessity to ensure that benefits of change be distributed to all income groups rather than being concentrated on elite groups, often as a result of government policies themselves. There was some optimism deriving from the realisation that structural change creates opportunities for higher aggregate consumption possibilities and, therefore, higher real incomes of most households. But it is not possible or desirable if these changes are to occur to protect the real incomes of all factor owners. Government policies should be directed towards ensuring that these potential benefits are realised. It became apparent that the nature of the major structural problems identified and the nature of the debate about the policies to resolve these problems differed markedly in those countries which had experienced slow growth. Hence the those countries which had experienced slow growth. Hence the policies to facilitate structural change at the industry level must be, to a considerable extent, country-specific. This suggests, in turn, that it may be possible for the developed countries at least to move from protectionist policies as a response to structural change to more constructive policies if and when the world economy moves out of the current recession.

Part IV

Growth, Inflation and Employment

18 Growth, Inflation and Employment: An Introduction

L. R. Klein
WHARTON SCHOOL OF FINANCE AND
COMMERCE, UNIVERSITY OF PENNSYLVANIA,
PHILADELPHIA

1 THE HISTORICAL BACKGROUND

If we date an era of economic expansion as the period after the Second World War and extending up to the present time, we may note that this era did get off to a fine start in terms of macroeconomic indicators of growth, inflation and employment. As is shown in Table 18.1, the 1950s and 1960s were basically decades of good growth (in excess of 4 per cent for the world as a whole) with low or moderate inflation of about 3 to 4 per cent. Unemployment was not high. In the industrial world (OECD countries) unemployment also averaged no more than about 3 to 4 per cent.

Table 18.1 The world series (percentage change)

	1950–60	1960–70	1970–80
GDP, world total	4.9	5.3	4.3
OECD	4.1	5.3	3.5
Developing	4.9	5.6	5.7
Centrally planned	6.0	5.0	5.5
World trade volume	7.2	8.3	5.6
Inflation, OECD	2.9	4.6	8.2

Source: Wharton Econometrics.

The succeeding decade was one of high inflation, near 10 per cent, and higher unemployment, about 4 to 6 per cent. Overall growth slowed very little, but non-OPEC developing countries held steady at about 5.6 per cent and OECD countries slowed to a rate of 3.5 per cent.

The world entered the war of 1939 from a situation of lengthy depression (one decade) and high unemployment. The fear that we would quickly return to that state after the stimulus of war production was taken away proved to be groundless, and the expansion of the post-war period unprecedented. Economic conditions improved all over the world, and people enjoyed the fruits of progress to an unusual degree.

In these early years of the 1980s there is a fear of returning to the high inflation with high unemployment of the 1970s. Will these fears prove to be groundless, too?

2 THREE KEY QUESTIONS

In the economic environment that presently exists, there is a tendency for inflation to abate and growth to revive, but unemployment persists. As the world emerges from the recession of 1980–3, there are obvious questions to be asked about the issues that are being discussed by this panel.

1. *How* did the world economy reach its present state? An understanding of the factors responsible for this development may help us in understanding how to extricate the world economy from its present predicament.
2. *Why* is the prospect considered by many to be one of continuing inflation at high levels of unemployment, with a growth slow-down?
3. *What* are some of the economic policies that may lead to an improvement in economic prospects for the 1980s?

There are many questions to be asked, but these are quite comprehensive, and if we can provide some answers to them, we will probably have done as much good for the world as economists can ever expect to achieve.

1. *How*? As far as the United States are concerned, the start of our inflation is best dated from 1965, when we engaged in reckless war finance – carrying out a major military expedition without raising taxes to cover the costs and trying at the same time to support

expanding social legislation at home. A falling dollar and rising commodity prices sealed our inflationary fate. Other industrial countries expanded social programmes, neglected to foster productivity growth, and also paid high prices for international raw materials.

Industrial nations as a whole, with a few oil-exporting exceptions, were hit severely and simultaneously with very high terms of trade for fuel. As workers tried to compensate for the high prices with high wage demands, an inflationary spiral was set in motion. It was not unusual to find widespread wage gains of 25–30 per cent following price rises of similar magnitude.

Amidst the turbulence of floating exchange rates, high fuel and food prices and strong wage demands, there was a complicating factor of a worldwide productivity slowdown resulting from energy substitutions, environmental protection, absorption of the baby-boom generation into the labour force, and a second wave of oil price rises a few years later.

It is little wonder that we had stagflation in the 1970s, with simultaneous high unemployment and large price rises. Japan, through a restrictive wage policy and aggressive export promotion, managed to escape much of the effects of stagflation, especially in the latter part of the decade. Switzerland, Germany and other countries used their buffer of guest workers to alleviate the problem of unemployment for a while, but they had slow growth to accompany their lower rates of inflation.

2. *Why?* Economists often tend to extrapolate present conditions far into the future. They see continuing stagflation. Any attempt to break out into expansionary programmes to bring down unemployment would be accompanied by rising inflation, and this would cancel the programme. We have been having, instead, restrictive programmes (except for defence) that created even higher levels of unemployment – levels that would have been considered astronomical at the beginning of the 1970s – which worked via the Phillips curve to hold down wage growth and therefore lessen inflation. External shocks determined stagflation – a positive relation between unemployment and inflation – while internal policies of recent years determined the shape of the trade-off, meaning a negative relation between unemployment and inflation.

The world recession of 1980–3, engineered by the restrictive policies of the United Kingdom, United States, Germany and other countries, provides a weak start for the statistics of performance of the economy in this decade. Many economists are simply extrapolating these unfavourable tendencies. At the moment, they are more vocal and have an upper hand in the debate, but my considered view is that a significant expansion, larger than most people contemplate, can possibly be achieved in the remainder of this decade in spite of the legacy of the 1970s and the extremely poor start during the first three years of the present decade.

3. *What*? What instruments of economic policy can be activated in order to bring about the preferred pattern of performance for the 1980s? This is a worldwide economic slump and must be dealt with on a broad international level. The key is policy co-ordination (across countries). If one country tries to go it alone, there are likely to be setbacks rather than the lasting expansion that we are searching for. We have already experienced some of these temporary solutions which soon turned adverse again. And when some countries tried to fight the general trend of policy, their situations deteriorated rapidly.

In world modelling exercises, it has been found that co-ordinated interest rate reductions, in the present context through easier monetary policies, together with fiscal expansions where budgetary conditions permit, public spending, the liberalisation of trade, and special stimuli for capital formation, in order to restore productivity growth, form a good recovery package that promises to be of lasting value.

Table 18.2 Effects of co-ordinated monetary-fiscal policies supplemented by investment tax credits (deviations of poicy simulation from baseline)

	1984	1985	1986	1987	1988
World GDP (%)	0.50	1.31	2.06	2.62	2.41
OECD GDP (%)	0.70	1.90	3.00	3.82	3.44
Inflation rate (%)	−0.42	−0.67	−0.14	0.27	0.65
Trade balance ($bn)	3.45	0.84	−2.11	−5.08	−7.25
Unemployment (%)	−0.23	−0.50	−0.94	−1.37	−1.37
LDC GDP (%)	0.39	0.61	0.86	1.16	1.44
Trade balance ($bn)	−5.39	−4.57	−2.73	−0.78	0.34
CPE GDP (%)	0.02	0.06	0.11	0.16	0.22
Trade balance ($bn)	1.36	2.28	2.66	3.18	3.34

Source: Project LINK.

Many things could happen to worsen the outlook – military outbreaks, further restrictions on the world supply of crude oil, severe drought, more serious cases of debt failure (or near failure), or other disturbances. The most unruly and close at hand is the overpowering force of the debt burden of several developing countries. During the past year, the debt problem has been contained, not solved. As long as it can be contained, recovery can continue. In the worst of cases, a financial panic could be generated. In the best of cases, each problem could be dealt with, one at a time, and problems could be worked out.

3 STRUCTURAL POLICIES

The considerations so far have been concerned only with broad macro policy for attaining the goals of good growth, inflation and unemployment. It is time now to turn to other policies, known as structural policies.

Structural or specific policies cover many areas, but some promising cases are those that address the following issues:
(a) demographic imbalances;
(b) environmental protection;
(c) industrial policy.

Demographic Imbalances

It is quite natural to find that a consequence of the dislocations of the Second World War was a surge in births after the war, first in the United States, then in Europe. The baby-boom children came into the American labour force during the 1970s. This caused increments in youth unemployment and probably contributed to the productivity slowdown. In addition, many women entered the labour force during this period.

European countries are now dealing with these labour force issues, and moderate economic growth permitted under restrictive policies cannot hold down unemployment. We therefore need, on both sides of the Atlantic, specific manpower policies designed to deal directly with youth unemployment. These policies would consist of job training, special labour exchanges for youth, low minimum wages for youth, and other specific measures.

Environmental Protection

Unrestricted growth has made many aspects of urban life quite unpleasant. In addition, the pollution of the air, streams and land surface are problems all over the world. Growth must be monitored and directed so as to improve the quality of life, without choking off the expansion. This requires great skill and precision in policy formation. Macro policies are not going to be able to deal with the issues from this source.

Industrial Policy

Industrial policy means many things to different people. Broadly speaking it deals with such specific policies as public support of research and development, support for higher education, identification for support in strategic growth industries, the promotion of trade, and support for techniques of productivity improvement. To a large extent, the investment tax credit policies imbedded in the results of Table 18.2 aim to enhance capital formation and thereby productivity gains. The whole range of industrial policies is much more comprehensive and takes us far beyond general fiscal and monetary measures.

This statement is not intended to provide a blueprint for achieving good growth, inflation and employment rates. It is meant to point out the issues and to indicate some promising policy lines to be followed. It is meant to introduce the problems and issues that the distinguished panelists will take up in more detail.

19 Growth, Inflation and Employment

W. Krelle
BONN UNIVERSITY

1 INTRODUCTION: THE MAIN PROBLEMS

This paper approaches the problems of growth, inflation and employment from the point of view of economic theory. First, the *long-term aspects* are considered:

1. Is it possible to continue the process of economic growth that we have experienced in the last thirty years such that the less developed countries can reach the standard of life of the industrialised ones? This problem has to be analysed considering the limitations of natural resources and the continued growth of the world's population.
2. Since the world economy consists of different national economies which are connected by trade and capital flows, we have to ask whether the international trade and monetary system is appropriate to serve the needs of the world economy as a whole. In other words, does the system of international trade serve the needs of all nations or is it a system of exploitation, as Professor Bogomolov suggested at this conference?

Second, the following *short-term problems*, which are more or less common to all nations, are taken up:

1. The Keynesian type of employment policy does not seem to work any more. An expansion of the money supply pushes up the rate of inflation rather than pulls down the rate of unemployment. How can that be explained, and is there a way of reviving the Keynesian type of employment policy without the inflationary effects?
2. Usually, growth is connected with structural change. But most countries, industrialised as well as developing ones, have difficul-

ties in accomplishing the necessary change. This restrains or even stops the process of growth. What can be done about this?

Third, some *special problems* will be dealt with:

1. The high interest rate in the United States.
2. The high debts of several important developing countries.
3. The high fluctuations of exchange rates and their divergence from the purchasing power parity.
4. Some internal problems of industrialised countries (high transfer payments, budget deficits, structural inflexibility, resistance to investment) and of developing countries (over-ambitious developing plans, underestimation of the time necessary to establish the necessary infrastructure, and the social and psychological preconditions for change).

The mathematical models which form the basis of the paper cannot be produced here due to lack of space. They form the appendix to the original paper and are available on request.

2 LONG-TERM PROBLEMS OF THE WORLD ECONOMY

2.1 Can the Growth Process be Continued in spite of the Limitations of Natural Resources and in spite of Environmental Difficulties?

The present situation of the world economy is unsatisfactory, to say the least. There are some countries, namely the industrialised ones, with a high standard of life and with problems of affluence, and there are other countries which remain far behind and where the population is struggling for survival. This may be tolerable if it is a transitory phenomenon. Some 200 years ago the industrialised countries were in the same condition as the less developed countries are now. May we hope that the latter will keep up or even pass the industrialised countries after a while? The World Bank sees the situation this way. The statistical figures seem to indicate that at least the upper group of the developing countries may reach self-sustaining growth paths with a higher rate of growth than the industrialised countries. But are there sufficient natural resources for all nations, or do the industrialised countries eat up the natural wealth of the earth and deprive the developing countries of their fair share of total wealth? In this section we deal with this problem from the point of view of the world as a whole. The distributional aspects will be dealt with later.

Problems such as these can only be answered using a model. Consider a world in which three products are produced or extracted according to neoclassical production functions: a reproducible good which may be used for consumption or for investment, an exhaustible resource which is extracted from finite deposits, and technical progress which is produced in laboratories. There are four factors of production: labour which is not produced, reproducible capital, land (where the supply is fixed), and the exhaustible resource. Assume Harrod-neutral technical progress. The production functions are supposed to be homogeneous of degree one in the arguments: labour, capital, land and the natural resource. We assume a constant savings ratio, cost minimising firms and perfect competition. The model may now be solved. Figure 19.1 shows some results for Cobb–Douglas production functions, if the savings ratio varies. Labour supply is supposed to be constant; the research ratio (= proportion of research cost in GDP) is assumed to be 0.0105, the rate of depletion of the natural resource is assumed to be 0.05. Figure 19.2 shows the same for various research ratios (the savings ratio is kept constant at 0.0532). These are all equilibrium values.

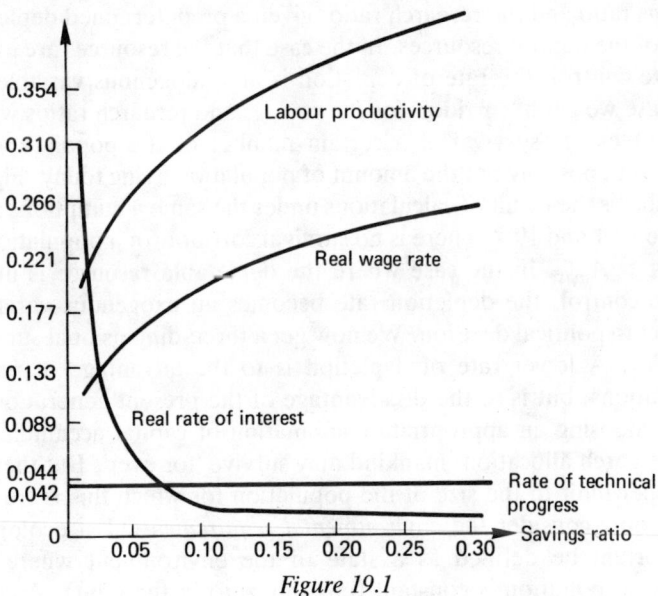

Figure 19.1

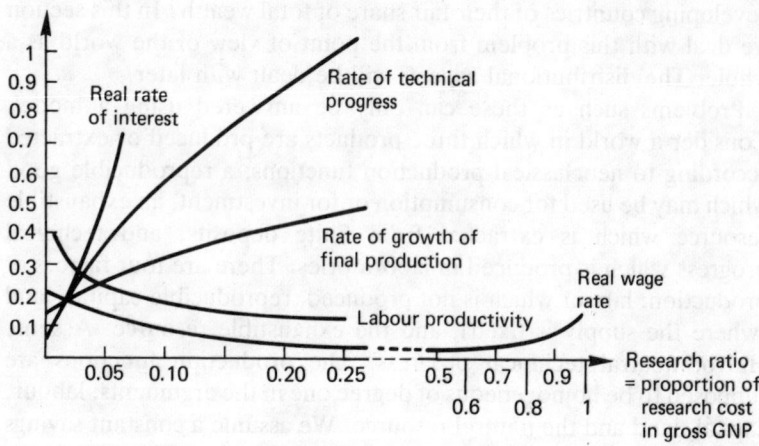

Figure 19.2

In order to guarantee the survival of mankind, the real consumption per head on the equilibrium path must be larger than the subsistence level at a given time, and simultaneously the rate of growth of the real wage rate must not be negative. These two conditions guarantee that the amount of population which exists at a given time can survive for ever. They limit the feasible ranges of the savings ratio and the research ratio, given a predetermined depletion ratio of the natural resources. In the case that the resources are under private control, the rate of depletion is an endogenous variable. In this case we get a 'corridor' for the savings and research ratios which guarantees the survival of a certain number of the population for ever — but possibly not the amount of population living today. Figure 19.3 shows the result of calculations under the same assumptions as in Figure 19.1 and 19.2. There is no survival corridor for a population of size $A > A_{max}$. In the case where the depletable resource is under public control, the depletion rate becomes an exogenous variable, subject to political decision. We now get a three-dimensional survival corridor. A lower rate of depletion is to the advantage of future generations, but is to the disadvantage of the present generation.

By choosing an appropriate combination of capital accumulation and research allocation, mankind may survive 'for ever'. But there is an upper limit to the size of the population for which this is true.

We now consider the *environmental requirements*. Let ecological equilibrium be defined as a state of the environment where the degree of pollution is constant (possibly zero in the limit). Assume

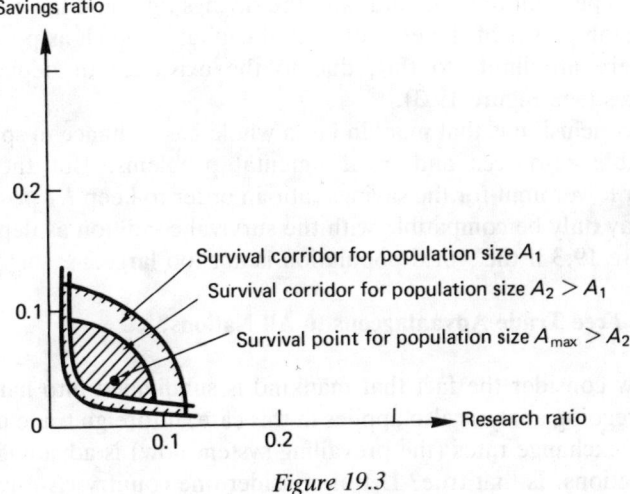

Figure 19.3

that there is a certain self-cleaning power of nature. A part (or the whole) of capital accumulation may be diverted to investment in environmental protection. We assume an exogenous rate of growth of the labour force and Harrod-neutral technical progress such that the economy is capable of growing at an equilibrium path and this growth is stable. Ecological equilibrium prevails if capital to protect the environment is accumulated at a rate which keeps the rate of pollution constant. It follows from the model that economic as well as ecological equilibrium coexist, if the capital which protects the environment (K_R) and the productive capital (K_P) keep the ratio:

$$\frac{K_R}{K_P} = \frac{1}{\dfrac{rs}{vw_Y} - 1} \tag{1}$$

where: r = amount of pollution which can be removed by one unit of capital devoted to environmental protection
s = savings ratio
v = amount of pollution per unit of GDP
$w_Y = \dot{Y}/Y$ = real rate of growth of GDP.

Only if the denominator of the expression above is positive, is the survival of mankind guaranteed as far as environmental protection is concerned. This means that we have to try to reduce the amount of pollution per unit of GDP and raise the savings ratio and the amount of cleaning power of the environmental capital as much as possible. But there are limits to this, due to the existence of depletable resources (see Figure 19.3).

The conclusion is that mankind as a whole has a chance in spite of depletable resources and environmental problems. But there is another lower limit for the savings ratio in order to keep K_R positive. This may only be compatible with the survival condition as depicted in Figure 19.3 if the world population is not too large.

2.2 Is Free Trade Advantageous to All Nations?

We now consider the fact that mankind is subdivided into nations. The foregoing analysis also applies in this case, if foreign trade under flexible exchange rates (the prevailing system now) is advantageous to all nations. Is that true? Let us consider one country *vis-à-vis* the world market. The country should be relatively small, such that it is not able to affect the market conditions substantially. Let the country produce two commodities: a consumption and an investment good. Let there be a constant savings ratio, an exogenous growth of labour supply, a constant rate of Harrod-neutral technical progress and neoclassical production functions for both sectors. If the country opens up its borders for foreign trade it has to adapt to the price ratio p_w of the investment good to the consumption good on the world market. The capital-labour ratio in both sectors depends on this ratio (see Figure 19.4; this figure and the following ones are constructed according to a numerical example using Cobb–Douglas production functions). Thus the same applies for the wage-profit ratio, the allocation of capital and labour to the two sectors, and the level of production of the two commodities.

Figure 19.5 shows the equilibrium levels of production of the two commodities per head as a function of the price ratio p_w of the two goods on the world market. The equilibrium growth rate is equal to both sectors (because of Harrod-neutral technical progress connected with labour in general, independent of its allocations) and independent of the price ratio on the world market. It depends only on the rate of technical progress. There is a price ratio $\hat{p}$ which is equal to the price ratio under autarchy. No trade takes place if the world market prices keep this ratio. If this ratio is not maintained there will be trade flows and a reallocation of resources. Is it advantageous for the country? That depends on the measure we use. Surely, the usual

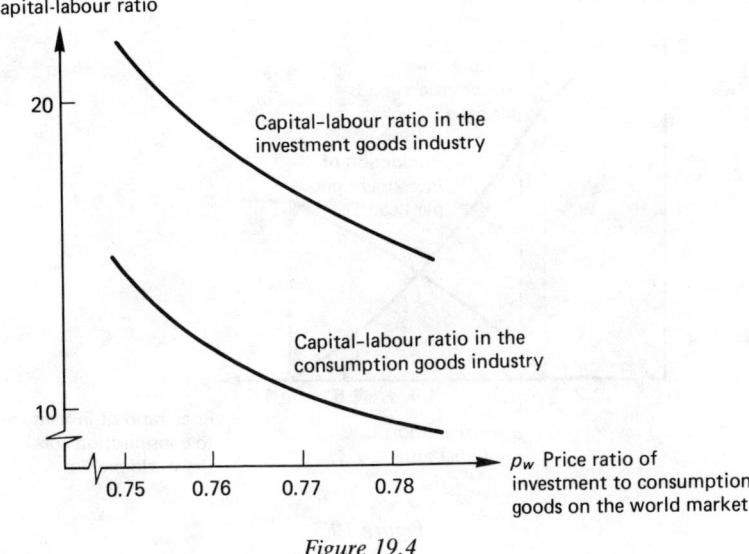

Figure 19.4

textbook version of Figure 19.6, which is supposed to prove that foreign trade is advantageous, is inappropriate for our dynamic approach. The short-term transformation curve is drawn under the assumptions that total capital and labour are fixed and may only be allocated differently to the sectors. The gradient angle of the tangent to the production point p equals the reciprocal of the price ratio p_w on the world market. If one assumes social indifference curves of the usual type, it is clear that a tangent point B on the exchange line is always better for the country than a tangent point A on the short-term transformation curve, which indicates the situation under autarchy.

But is this also true for the benefit of foreign trade in the long run? The long-run transformation curve (defined as the set of productions per head which will be produced under different world market prices on the equilibrium growth path at a given time) cuts the short-term curve at the production point P. Thus the proof breaks down. We have to look for other welfare measures.

We may choose the amount of commodities available within the country, evaluated in units of consumption goods. In this case there might be a small disadvantage from trade for a certain range of world market prices comprable to that which we shall analyse below. If we take as a measure the potential amount of consumption goods which

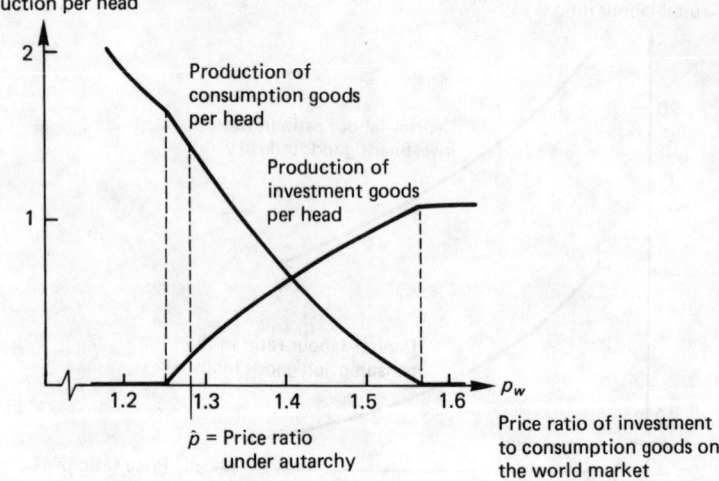

Figure 19.5

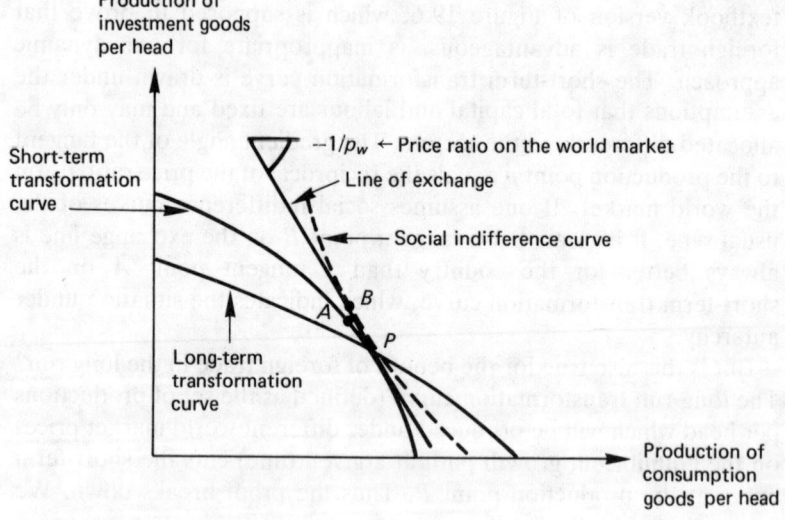

Figure 19.6

the country could get from the world market after it has procured the same amount of investment goods as would be available under autarchy, foreign trade would always be advantageous. A more natural measure would be the actual amount of consumption goods available in the country. A detailed analysis shows that three cases may arise (see Figure 19.7). In case A, foreign trade is always advantageous. This case arises if the savings ratio is optimal in the sense that equilibrium consumption under autarchy reaches its maximum and if the savings ratio keeps a certain relation to the production elasticities of labour and to the growth rate (this is an uninteresting special case). Thus we may say: if the economy is already in an optimal state, it could only improve by foreign trade. If it is not (cases B and C), there are small 'grooves' of price ratios on the world market in the neighbourhood of the autarchy price ratio where foreign trade is detrimental. But if the domestic and the world market prices differ enough, foreign trade always becomes advantageous also in the long run. Thus we may conclude this section on long-term problems of the world economy by stating:

1. The process of economic development may be continued even under depletable resource and by environment protection if the savings ratio and the research ratio lie within certain limits (especially if they are bound away from zero), if the population stays below a certain limit, and if a sufficient part of investment is used for environmental protection.
2. Free world trade is (in general, disregarding small exceptional cases) to the advantage of all nations.

The following statements are given without proof. They may be found in the extended version of this paper.

3. World GDP will be maximised if there is (in addition to a free flow of commodities) also a free flow of capital such that capital flows to the countries where the marginal product of capital is highest.
4. In the case the real growth rates of all countries will be asymptotically equal. But since rates of growth of population, technical progress, production functions and savings ratios will be different, the real wage rates and the standard of life will differ from country to country. There will be an uneven distribution of income and wealth on the world scale. But the countries which are leading on the scale of standard of life and technology may change and surely will change. In the past, China, India, Mesopotamia, Egypt, Greece, Rome, the Arabian countries,

Growth, Inflation and Employment

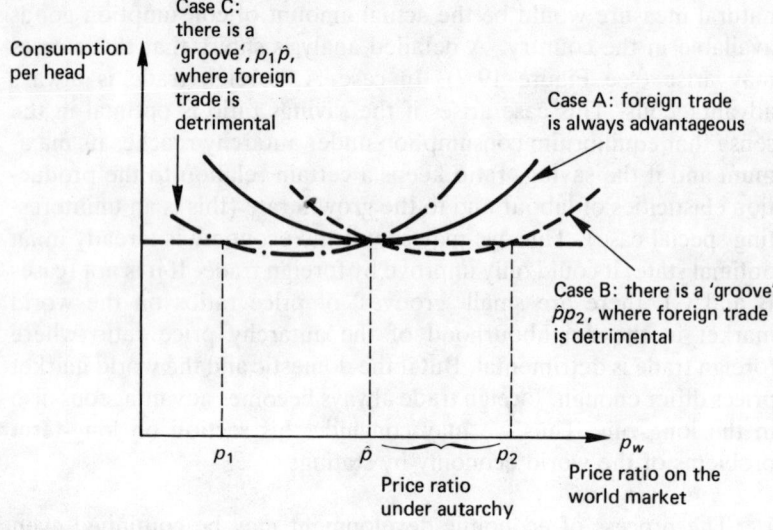

Figure 19.7

Europe and the United States have been in the forefront of development and enjoyed the highest standard of life. Now the East Asians under the guidance of Japan seem to be to the front. Perhaps Mexico and Brazil will follow after a while. Thus each nation may have its chance.

3 SHORT-TERM PROBLEMS OF THE WORLD ECONOMY

We turn now to urgent short-term problems which almost all nations have to face: the simultaneity of inflation and unemployment (or, to put it otherwise, the inefficiency of the usual Keynesian-type employment policy) and the difficulties to accomplish the structural change which is a precondition for economic growth.

3.1 Inflation and Unemployment. Why May an Employment Policy of the Keynesian Type Fail?

Stagflation, high government deficits and high international indebtedness of many countries have been prominent features in the economic picture of the last five years. One reason seems to be that many governments tried Keynesian-type employment measures in order to raise employment. But this did not work in the long-run. Why? In the first eighteen chapters of the 'General Theory', Keynes assumed fixed wage rates and fixed prices. In the nineteenth chapter (which is neglected by most readers) Keynes introduces flexible wages and comes to the end conclusion that there are several conflicting tendencies. The best advice would be to keep the nominal wage rate constant in case of unemployment. Actually, prices and wages are not constant today if there is unemployment; on the contrary, most nations experience high wage and price inflation in spite of unemployment. This is what has to be explained, not the consequences of fixed prices and wages. Unfortunately, too much effort has been devoted to explaining unemployment by fixed prices and wages in connection with rationing. Interesting as this may be in itself, it cannot explain what we have experienced, namely inflation and unemployment simultaneously. What is wrong with the Keynesian advice of curing unemployment by extending the money supply and running government deficits? We shall explain it on the base of the following model.

Let us use the familiar LM–IS approach which results from the Keynesian system, but introduce a price and a wage function into it. The real demand for money is a function of real income (which also may be a measure for real wealth) and of the interest rate and the rate of inflation. Real final demand for commodities (i.e. the sum of consumption, investment and government demand) is a function of the change of the real money supply (the additional money is used for additional demand), of the real final demand of the period before and of the interest rate.

The wage rate is determined by labour productivity, by the price level of the period before and by the unemployment rate of the period before. The price level is a function of real unit labour cost and of the amount of money per unit of GDP in the period before. Thus we consider the cost-push effect of higher wages and the demand-pull effect of a larger money supply simultaneously. The mathematical model may be found in the extended version of this paper. By substituting the wage and price functions into the money demand and commodity demand functions and solving for GDP, we get the usual LM- and IS-curves (see Figure 19.8). These curves also depend on the variables of the period before. The results of the model are as follows.

Assume that there is unemployment and the authorities decide to expand the money supply. The model shows the usual Keynesian-type

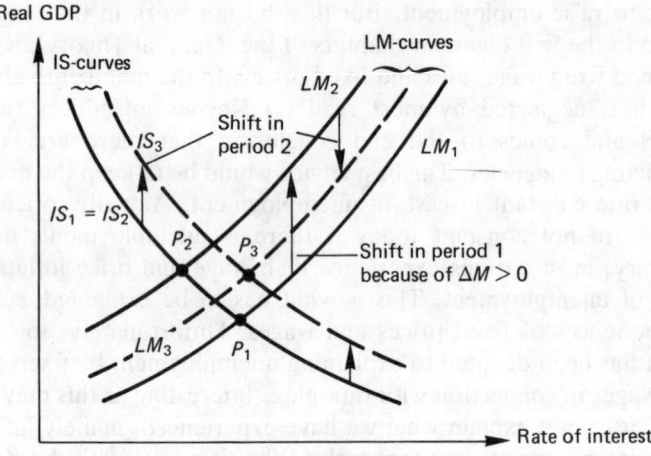

Figure 19.8

results: the LM-curve shifts upward (from LM_1 to LM_2), the IS-curve stays as it is ($IS_1 = IS_2$). Thus real GDP goes up and the interest rate declines (the system moves from P_1 to P_2). Of course, the rate of unemployment will go down. But there is a setback in the next period. Let us assume that the money supply stays as it is in the next period, because the authorities hope that the expansion of money may induce a real multiplier process which pulls the economy out of the recession. But in the next period the LM-curve will shift downward (e.g. from LM_2 to LM_3). Even if the IS-curve moves upward (from IS_2 to IS_3), GDP may decline and the rate of interest will rise again (see Figure 19.8 – the system moves from P_2 to P_3). But the IS-curve may as well stay unaffected if expectations do not change. Thus a new monetary push seems to be needed, and the game will repeat itself with the consequence that the price level and the government deficit will rise, but the effect on employment will be small or even negative, the real interest rate stays in the same range, and the rate of inflation rises.

If the real rate of interest stays unchanged, real demand and therefore real production grows by a rate which is independent of the money supply and the rate of inflation. In the long run, the rate of inflation is simply the difference of the rate of monetary expansion and the rate of real growth of GDP. Thus a change in investment and consumption behaviour and in pricing and wage-setting behaviour is needed in order to increase the rate of growth of real demand and therefore raise employment. Monetary expansion has only transitory effects. These may be helpful if they change consumption and especially investment behaviour by changing the expectations, but if this behaviour remains the same, the additional employment induced by higher money supply is only transitory.

3.2 Structural Change, Growth and Unemployment

Industrial countries as well as developing countries have difficulties in accomplishing the structural change that is necessary to regain a rate of growth which would abolish unemployment. In many industrialised countries people are living in a sort of welfare state where they think that everything is possible and efforts and sacrifices are no longer necessary to guarantee the preservation of the current state and to secure future growth. This leads to a sort of conservativism, where everybody considers his or her current working place as a sort of private property. But in an interdependent world of competition and technical progress this is impossible. Since there are no linear Engel curves (and no linear production functions), growth is connected with structural change: the demand structure changes with rising GDP. In a democracy there is strong pressure from the trade unions (as representatives of the common worker) and from other institutions on the parties and on the government to keep the structure as it is. Thus firms are subsidised which otherwise could not stay in business in order to preserve jobs. For the same reason, there is strong pressure for protectionism and against technical progress. This undermines the very base of the current wealth and yields unemployment and stagnation in the future.

The developing countries also have problems in accomplishing the necessary structural change, but for different reasons. The resistance stems partly from the fear of losing their cultural or national identity. People want to keep their social and political structure, which usually is inappropriate for an industrialised status and must be changed if these countries want to participate in the general process of economic growth. There is no fast solution to these sociological, political and cultural problems. We now turn to some special problems.

4 SPECIAL PROBLEMS

4.1 The US Budget Deficit and High Interest Rates

There is no question that a capitalist economy cannot work with interest rates on government bonds which are substantially higher than profit rates in the producing sector of the economy. But the political and economic interests of governments may bring about just this. The present US administration wants (among other things) to re-arm the United States in order to turn the tide of rising military and political influence of the Soviet Union. Moreover, it wants to boost private economic activity by keeping down the tax rate. Thus, the US government runs high budget deficits which in turn yield high rates of interest. This attracts foreign capital and raises the exchange rate of the dollar above purchasing power parity. The inflow of foreign capital helps to finance the US budget deficit. Of course, the other side of the coin is the high US current account deficit. This is a wrong position from the point of view of the world as a whole. Rich countries should have a capital *outflow* and should finance the development of the poor countries, not the other way round. It is understandable that from the point of view of the US administration the capital inflow is an attractive feature. But the disturbing influences on the world economy should be taken into account.

4.2 The High Indebtedness of Important Developing Countries

This is a consequence of over-ambitious development plans, but also of the high level of interest rates. It is especially after rates of inflation fall substantially that the burden of debt from these high interest rates becomes heavier. But all major partners in world trade must be trustworthy debtors. This is a necessary condition for the functioning of the whole world market system. It is most important that capital should flow again from the industrialised countries to the developing countries. This is in the interests of the developing countries as well as of the industrialised countries, but it is not possible if interest payments cannot be guaranteed. Since the marginal product of capital, on average and as a rule, cannot reach the heights of current interest rates in financial markets, these interest rates have to be reduced. According to UN estimates, for some countries interest and amortisation payments amount to almost two thirds of their total earnings of foreign currency. But reducing interest rates creates difficulties for the credit banks, since they would have to revalue their assets according to the lower interest rates. Perhaps central banks or governments should step in to help the banks accomplish this interest rate conversion.

4.3 High Fluctuations in Exchange Rates

When the regime of flexible exchange rates was introduced in 1973, those economists who advocated this change expected a stable movement of exchange rates more or less in line with purchasing power parities. Unfortunately, this did not come true. There have not only been daily and weekly fluctuations, but also the yearly exchange rate averages moved substantially and without any connection with the relative purchasing power of the currencies involved. Take, for instance, the yearly average of the DM exchange rate *vis-à-vis* the US $. This exchange rate was 2.00 in 1978; 1.83 in 1979; 1.86 in 1980; 2.26 in 1981; 2.43 in 1982. Of course, these movements have nothing to do with purchasing power parity. Thus substantial risk is involved in foreign trade which – due to lack of efficient forward markets of different terms – cannot be shifted totally to speculators or others who are willing to take the risk. Perhaps markets for currency options may develop after a while. But they will not take over the total risk. As the situation is now, the large fluctuations in exchange rates reduce the international division of labour. Unemployment and job insecurity follow. It is time to reconsider the international monetary system with the aim of reducing fluctuations and keeping exchange rates more in line with purchasing power parity. This could be done by agreement on the upper and lower bounds of exchange rates and on the intervention rules of the central banks, similar to the arrangements in the European Currency System. This also may help to reduce inflation and to stimulate employment.

4.4 Some Internal Problems of Industrialised Countries

There is a whole range of factors responsible for high rates of inflation and for unemployment in industrialised countries. Structural inflexibility has already been mentioned above. There is a resistance against investment, partly for ideological reasons, partly because of conservationist considerations. This has induced a whole net of regulations which make it very difficult for a firm to invest, especially if it wants to start a new business in a new location. Transfer payments have risen substantially. Thus the burden of taxes and social insurance payments has become heavier and heavier. This diverts funds from productive to unproductive use and gives high incentives to black market labour. The black market in labour aggravates the financial problems of the social security system, since those who work in this market profit from the social insurance system but do not pay contributions. The trade unions are under pressure from their members to press for higher wages in spite of the high rate of unemployment. The members of the trade unions are the employed workers, not the unemployed (who as a rule leave the union). Thus the characteristic attitude of the trade unions is to maximise the income of their members by raising the wage rate as high as they are able and leave the problem of unemployment to governments. This, of course, is no contribution to solving the unemployment problem.

It is difficult to change these attitudes, or the institutions which represent them, in a short time. But nevertheless, this must be done.

4.5 Some Internal Problems of Developing Countries

Most developing countries (not all) have tried to follow development plans which were much too ambitious. The time necessary to accomplish the social and political changes which are preconditions for industrialisation has been substantially underestimated. It is now clear that development does not simply mean buying machinery or whole factories from industrialised countries and putting them to work. This also takes much more time than usually estimated. Development also means education, change in behaviour, and change in the social and political structure, and all this needs much more time. In most developing countries there is a dual economy: large backward agricultural areas and some large cities where the process of industrialisation is starting. These attract labour from the rural locations. Large unemployment figures and slums in the cities follow from this. Monetary expansion can only induce inflation without helping to solve problems which lie on the real side of the economy, especially in the field of education. Land reform, emphasis on rural development, birth control and similar measures may help to raise the standard of life and to abolish illiteracy. When this has been accomplished, the process of industrialisation will have a much greater chance of success.

The fastest way to industrialisation seems to be to let a country participate in world trade. This is especially true for smaller countries. South Korea, Taiwan, Hong Kong, Singapore and other countries have succeeded in this way. Development aid and private capital flows may substantially facilitate this process.

5 SOME CONCLUSIONS

The world economy is now passing through a difficult phase. There are urgent short-term problems which mostly emerge from the general decline of the average growth rate. There is no reason why the process of growth cannot be resumed in spite of exhaustible resources and necessary investment in (short-run) 'unproductive' areas of environmental protection. Mankind need not come to an end. But the behaviour of individuals and institutions has to be changed in order to achieve better results. Some modest suggestions have been made above to this end.

20 Growth, Inflation and Unemployment in the United States

B. G. Hickman
STANFORD UNIVERSITY,
CALIFORNIA

In this paper I will focus on the stagflation in the United States during the 1970s and the prospects for the 1980s. For the most part, my remarks summarise the principal findings from several studies which I have conducted jointly with Robert M. Coen concerning the macroeconomic impact of the energy shocks of the 1970s and the extent to which the tax incentives embodied in the Economic Recovery Tax Act (ERTA) of 1981 may be expected to stimulate US growth in the 1980s.

1 THE STAGFLATION

The average annual growth rate of real GNP was 3.6 per cent during the period 1955–73. It dropped to 2.8 per cent in 1973–9 and to −0.1 per cent in 1979–82. Meanwhile, the annual inflation rate rose from 3.1 to 7.3 to 7.9 per cent and unemployment averaged 5.2, 6.8, and 8.1 per cent during the three intervals.

Although unemployment rose during the stagflation, the growth deceleration was due as much or more to supply-side factors as to demand constraints. Moreover, the onset of slower growth began prior to the energy shock of 1973–4. Actual output rose almost as fast during 1968–73 as before–3.4 per cent a year instead of 3.6–but the growth rate of potential output decelerated from 3.6 in 1955–68 to 2.9 per cent in 1968–73. In keeping with the deceleration of potential in the face of a relatively unchanged actual growth rate, the unemployment percentage dropped a little during 1968–73, and the inflation rate doubled to 5.0 per cent. In contrast, both rising unemployment and higher inflation accompanied the further deceleration of growth as stagflation set in during the remainder of the decade (Table 20.1).

Table 20.1 Selected economic indicators, actual (1955–82) and projected (1982–9)

Variable	1955–68	1968–73	1973–9	1979–82	1982–4	1984–9
		Growth rate (per cent)				
Potential GNP	3.6	2.9	2.5	2.2	2.4	2.6
Real GNP	3.6	3.4	2.8	−0.1	4.2	2.7
GNP deflator	2.4	5.0	7.3	7.9	4.1	5.5
		Average (per cent)				
Unemployment	5.3	5.0	6.8	8.1	9.3	7.8

Sources: 1955–82, *Economic Report of the President*, February 1983. 1982–9, Coen and Hickman (1983a).

What factors were responsible for the retardation of potential output during the 1970s? According to the Hickman–Coen (HC) model, the slowdown of productivity growth during 1968–73 is directly attributable to a reduced rate of capital deepening and a deceleration of technical progress (Coen and Hickman, 1980b). The further retardation of productivity growth after 1973 is largely a result of the same factors, with additional reductions occurring in both the deepening rate and technical progress. To some extent these productivity slowdowns were offset by faster growth in man-hours, but the growth rate of potential output declined nonetheless.

Higher energy prices account for much of the deceleration of capital deepening, and hence of the growth of potential labour productivity, after 1973. That is, the increase in energy prices raised the price of capital goods, and hence the rental price of capital, relative to the cost of labour, and thereby reduced the desired capital-labour ratio. If this were the only channel by which an adverse energy shock could affect productivity, the level of the potential growth path would be permanently reduced by a permanent increase in the real price of energy, but the growth rate would fall only during the transition to the lower growth path.

Empirical evidence on these issues is obtained in the HC model from joint maximum likelihood estimation of the production function and the derived demand functions for capital and labour. In rather exhaustive tests, we have found that the hypothesis that the quadrupling of the OPEC oil price in 1973–4 caused a downshift of the production function, representing a once-and-for-all loss of total factor productivity, could be decisively rejected (Coen and Hickman, 1980a). Successive reductions do appear to have occurred in the rate of technical progress, from 1.9 per cent in 1955–68 to 1.4 in 1968–73 and 0.7 in 19739, although the t-ratios on the coefficients for the trend breaks after 1968 and 1973 are rather weakly significant at 1.8 and 1.6 respectively.

These results unfortunately leave important issues unresolved. The apparent deceleration of technical progress well before the first energy shock suggests that other, unexplained factors were at work to reduce productivity growth during the 1970s. If the apparent further deceleration of technical progress after 1973 was independent of the energy shock, then the effects of the latter were captured entirely in the capital-deepening process. The assumption of independence is plausible, since it is hard to understand how a step increase in the real price of energy could permanently affect the rate of growth of productivity, and since there is no evidence of a production function downshift from the shock. Nevertheless, one cannot rule out the possibility that at least part of the estimated deceleration of technical progress after the shock was energy-induced.

The stagflationary character of the 1970s was strongly influenced from the supply side by the Soviet grain purchases of 1972 and the oil shock of 1973–4. The resulting leftward shift of the aggregate supply function raised the price level even as it was depressing output, and the initial rise of consumer prices increased inflationary expectations and fostered catch-up wage attempts. The real money supply declined sharply as monetary policy was tightened to inhibit a wage-price spiral, putting added downward pressure on demand and output.

The performance of the economy during 1979–82 was adversely affected by the second energy shock and especially by the subsequent tightening of monetary policy to contain inflationary pressures. Potential growth decelerated slightly during the period, but actual growth was negative and unemployment increased sharply, averaging

8.1 per cent for the period and reaching 9.7 per cent in 1982. After rising to a peak of 9.4 per cent in 1981, the inflation rate dropped to 6.0 in 1982, owing to slack conditions in the labour and product markets.

2 FUTURE PROSPECTS

United States economic activity reached a cyclical trough in November 1982, and the recovery was well underway by the end of 1983. Unless curtailed by a restrictive monetary or fiscal policy, the upswing will cumulate for a time, but the pace must eventually slow as excess capacity is reduced. A conditional forecast for the 1980s is shown in Table 20.2.

The forecast was the baseline solution for a study of the effects of the 1981–2 tax legislation on the growth prospects of the economy. As such, it is an attempt to preserve the spirit of contemporary policy for the remainder of the decade. It therefore assumes continuing monetary restraint to curb inflation and eschews stimulative fiscal policies. The growth rate of the money stock (M1) is held to 7.0 per cent throughout the period. 1983 tax provisions are incorporated in the forecast, including the automatic indexation of tax brackets, exemptions, and the standard deduction to inflation beginning in 1985. The baseline solution also includes the prospective increases in social security contribution rates for 1985 and 1986 which were in place before the additional increases legislated this March.

The general pattern of the forecast is for a moderate recovery of real GNP at an average rate of about 4.2 per cent between 1982 and 1984, followed by a deceleration to 2.4 per cent in 1985 and 1986 and a pick-up to 2.8 per cent thereafter. Unemployment is forecast to peak at 9.9 per cent in 1983, and then to decline slowly to 8.0 per cent in 1986 and 7.2 per cent in 1989. Inflation averages 4.1 per cent between 1982 and 1984 and rises moderately to 5.5 per cent from 1984 to 1989. The pace of expansion could be expected to moderate after two years of recovery in any event, but the slowdown during 1985–6 is partly attributable also to the social security tax increases scheduled for those years. The basic growth constraint is from the supply side, however, with the growth rates of actual and potential output projected to be virtually identical during 1984–9 (Table 20.1).

Table 20.2 Selected economic indicators

Variable	1982	1983	1984	1985	1986	1987	1988	1989
GNP ($billion in 1972 prices)	1475.5	1529.0	1606.3	1645.1	1686.7	1734.6	1787.0	1837.1
% change	−1.8	3.6	5.1	2.4	2.5	2.8	3.0	2.8
GNP deflator	207.2	216.1	225.1	237.3	251.1	265.3	280.2	296.5
% change	6.0	4.2	4.2	5.5	5.8	5.7	5.6	5.8
Unemployment %	9.7	9.9	8.7	8.5	8.0	7.9	7.6	7.2

Source: Coen and Hickman (1983a).

The forecasted potential GNP growth rate is 2.6 per cent in 1984–9, or about the same as in 1973–9. About 0.4 of the 2.6 represents the rate of increase of real income originating in government employment and housing rent, neither of which is included in the gross private non-residential product, or the concept of output entering the production function. Potential output in the private non-residential sector increases by about 2.2 per cent a year, with half the increase due to rising man-hours and the remainder to higher man-hour productivity. The rate of increase of potential employment is slightly higher–1.2 instead of 1.1 per cent–than for man-hours, since average hours of work are forecasted to decrease by about 0.1 per cent per year. With regard to man-hour productivity, 0.7 of the projected annual gain of 1.1 percentage points is attributable to technical progress and 0.4 to capital deepening.

This is a gloomy outlook. Instead of increasing at nearly 3 per cent a year, as in 1955–68, or 1.5 per cent, as in 1968–73, the prospective potential annual productivity gain is placed at about 1 per cent, as in 1973–9. The greatest source of uncertainty in the projection is the assumed rate of technical progress. For example, if the decrease in the rate of technical progress of 0.7 percentage points estimated to have occurred after 1973 were presumed to be transitory instead of permanent, the projected rate of productivity growth would be increased by the same amount, or from 1.1 to 1.8 per cent. Discounting only part of the estimated post-1973 deceleration could easily raise the projected growth rate of potential GNP from 2.6 to 3 per cent in 1984–9.

With regard to energy, the baseline forecast incorporates the 1983 reduction in the OPEC price and assumes an average increase of oil prices of 7 per cent a year from 1984 to 1989. Should a large and unexpected increase in energy prices occur in the future, it could adversely affect output in both the short and long runs. According to the HC model, a once-and-for-all increase of 50 per cent in the OPEC oil price would reduce the level of potential GNP by about 0.5 per cent after four years, although the maximum cyclical reduction in actual GNP, reached within two years, would be four times as large (Coen and Hickman, 1983b). Thus the effect of such a shock on the potential growth rate over a period of four years would be on the order of only 0.1 percentage points.

Could monetary or fiscal policies significantly increase the level or growth rate of potential output? A once-and-for-all increase in the nominal money supply increases actual GNP in the short run but leaves potential GNP largely unaffected, owing to the property of long-run neutrality of money in the HC model (Coen and Hickman, 1983b).

As for fiscal policy, our simulations showed that reductions in personal tax rates could stimulate a cyclical expansion but would not lead to a significant increase in potential GNP, because neither labour force growth nor business fixed investment was much affected (Coen and Hickman, 1983a). More could be accomplished by direct tax subsidies to business fixed investment. The liberalisation of depreciation guidelines under the tax legislation of 1981–2 is estimated to have raised the level of the potential path by over 1 per cent in the 1980s by encouraging capital deepening. Most of the once-and-for-all adjustment to the higher desired capital-labour ratio will be accomplished by 1986, however. The growth rate is increased temporarily during the transition to the higher path, but it reverts thereafter to the long-term value determined by the underlying rates of population increase and technical progress. The favourable effects from the liberalised depreciation guidelines of 1981–2 are already embodied in the baseline forecast quoted in Table 20.2, of course, so that additional new investment incentives would be needed for yet another boost to the potential path.

It is noteworthy that unemployment declines slowly in the forecast and still exceeds 7 per cent in 1989, even though the 'natural' or 'full employment' unemployment rate is estimated to be about 6.5 per cent in the later 1980s. Why doesn't the real wage rate fall rapidly to restore full employment? Real wage rigidity is a common property of econometric models of the US economy, and the present case is no exception. Real wages are sticky because prices typically are set as a mark-up over unit cost and are insensitive to demand pressures. Thus even though labour demand responds positively to real wage reductions in the HC model, the neoclassical adjustment mechanism works slowly. Unemployment does reduce nominal wages, but prices decline along with labour costs and the real wage is largely unaffected. Unemployment could be reduced more rapidly by stimulative monetary or fiscal actions, but at the expense of a higher inflation rate than in the baseline forecast.

3 SUMMARY

The United States entered a period of stagflation during the 1970s, combining markedly slower growth with unprecedentedly high rates of inflation and unemployment. Although unemployment rose, the growth deceleration was due as much or more to supply-side factors as to demand restrictions. The energy shocks of 1973–4 and 1979–80 contributed to the slowdown, but other factors appear to have led to a prior deceleration of technical progress beginning in the late 1960s, and a further deceleration may have occurred after 1973. The outlook is reasonably bright for a substantial cyclical recovery in 1983–4, but the economy may revert to the slow growth rates of the 1970s thereafter, albeit with a lower level of inflation. The major uncertainty is over the underlying rate of technical progress. An unexpected energy shock could further depress the level of potential output but it would have to be quite large to have much effect on even the transitional growth rate. Personal tax reductions appear to have little effect on potential output, but direct investment incentives can raise the growth rate temporarily as the economy adjusts to a higher growth path through capital deepening.

REFERENCES

Coen, R. M. and Hickman, B. G. (1980a) *Testing Factor Demands for Monetary Influences and Technical Change in the Postwar Economy*, Research Memorandum no. 241, Center for Research in Economic Growth, Stanford University, May.

Coen, R. M. and Hickman, B. G. (1980b) *The Natural Growth Path of Potential Output*, WP–80–132, International Institute of Applied Systems Analysis, Laxenburg, Austria, August.

Coen, R. M. and Hickman, B. G. (1983a) *Tax Policy, Federal Deficits, and US Growth in the 1980s*, Discussion Paper no. 6, Center for Economic Policy Research, Stanford University, April.

Coen, R. M. and Hickman, B. G. (1983b) *Energy Shocks and macroeconomic Activity: Simulation Results from the Hickman–Coen Model*, paper prepared for Working Group 7 of the Energy Modelling Forum, Stanford University, June.

Hickman, B. G. and Coen, R. M. (1976) *Annual Growth Model of the US Economy* (Amsterdam: North Holland).

21 Remarks on Growth, Inflation and Employment

Shuntaro Shishido
UNIVERSITY OF TSUKUBA, SAKURA

The unsatisfactory economic performance of the industrial world since 1974 is mostly due to OPEC's oil price increases, but also to the lack of consensus among policy-makers and economists. Now that inflationary expectations among the industrial countries seem to have almost disappeared, except for some primary commodity markets due to unusual weather, it is high time for economists to analyse the causes of the past stagflation and the present slow recovery of the world economy in a much more analytical way, instead of through ideological arguments over monetarism versus non-monetarism, etc. Many policy proposals based on ideological models with weaker empirical ground seem to have failed to revitalise the industrial world. There have been, for instance, proposals for a policy mix with high real interest rates and low corporate tax rates to promote private savings and to expand business investment, and lower personal rates to stimulate output and employment, etc. Now we need a more pragmatic policy approach based on scientific efforts with rich empirical content. Recent volatile movements in exchange rates and heavy fiscal debts, however, might lay the basis for more active policy responses to the present economic diseases, whether macroeconomic or structural. In my opinion, economic theories and empirical findings have steadily accumulated in recent years, such as in the field of exchange rates, asset preference, price-wage behaviour, tax incentives, industrial technical progress, multi-country relationships, etc. and there are growing possibilities for policy-makers to utilise more sophisticated econometric tools to deal with present and future economic issues. (See Table 21.1 on a global simulation.)

Table 21.1 Impacts on real GNP (in per cent) resulting from an increase in the US discount rate (Tsukuba–FAIS world model)*

	1983	1984	1985	1986
Japan	−0.046	−0.310	−0.737	−0.999
USA	−0.121	−0.627	−1.271	−1.410
Canada	0.027	−0.034	−0.523	−1.254
Great Britain	−0.002	−0.096	−0.207	−0.270
France	−0.002	−0.056	−0.230	−0.556
Germany	−0.014	−0.118	−0.334	−0.529
Italy	0.005	−0.033	−0.206	−0.419
Austria	−0.008	−0.074	−0.148	−0.121
Other developing countries	−0.007	−0.140	−0.487	−0.881
Developing countries	−0.053	−0.327	−0.755	−0.988
OPEC	−0.003	−0.034	−0.111	−0.210
Non-oil developing countries	−0.006	−0.042	−0.102	−0.134
World**	−0.039	−0.244	−0.564	−0.740

*See Shishido (1983).
**World excludes centrally planned economies. The figures are shown in terms of per cent deviation from Base-line simulation. Exchange rates are endogenised for developed countries. The US discount rate increases are 0.5, 1.0, 1.0, 0.5 per cent respectively.

Source: National Institute of Research Advancement, *Symposium on World Economy: World Economic Outlook and International Economic Cooperation*, Technical Supplement on Alternative Scenarios with Tsukuba–FAIS World Econometric Model, FAIS, Project LINK and Japan Economic Journal (1983, Tokyo).

Secondly, recent inflationary forces have tended to be related to social factors which are sensitive to inflationary expectations based on uncertainties over the future and lack of information. National and international efforts to clear those uncertainties seem to be urgently needed, such as formulating an industrial outlook on output, employment and prices by sector in collaboration with government, business and trade unions. International collaboration through the OECD, etc. is also vital to clear the future uncertainties and to reduce business risk in investment. Confidence should be restored as a result of these efforts by the public sector.

Thirdly, growth should be revitalised among industrial countries through collaboration on industrial policies including science and technologies. Military and mercantile barriers on technical know-how need to be kept to a minimum by opening and exchanging information, especially the results of R & D in frontier technologies for peaceful purposes. It remains true that acceleration in technical progress is the only way to foster growth and price stability, as long as macroeconomic policy works properly.

REFERENCE

Shishido, S. (1983) 'Long-Term Forecasts and Policy Implications: Simulations with a World Econometric Model (T-FAIS IV)', in Hickman, B. G. (ed.) *Global International Economic Models* (Amsterdam: North Holland), pp. 53–66.

22 Inflation and Growth: Some Experiments on a Model for India

K. Krishnamurty
INSTITUTE OF ECONOMIC GROWTH
UNIVERSITY ENCLAVE, INDIA

This paper is based on the study *Inflation and Growth: A Model for India, 1961–80* by the present author, assisted by Messrs. Saibaba and Kazmi (Krishnamurty, 1984).

I shall make some introductory observations about the focus of the study and the nature of inflation and growth in a developing economy like India. This will be followed by a presentation of the salient features of the Indian economy during the sample period, an outline of the model and the broad nature of the results, and, finally, the outcome of simulation experiments.

1 INTRODUCTORY OBSERVATIONS

The focus of this study is to examine inflation-inducing and growth-generating forces, and their interaction in a developing country with predominant agriculture and abundant labour supply. With this in view, an econometric model for India is constructed for the period 1961–80 with emphasis on the supply side, money and prices. The role of government in promoting economic growth through its investment activities on the one hand, and the impact of its fiscal operations on money supply on the other, is stressed.

Important inflation-generating impulses in developing countries with dominant agriculture are weather failures that lead to supply shortfalls, fiscal and monetary policies that result in monetary expansion, and external factors which push up domestic costs and prices and lead to balance of payments problems. An important external factor is the fuel oil price escalations that started in the early 1970s. These inflation-inducing impulses are not necessarily independent of each other; each may activate the other.

Monetary expansion is an important source of inflation in developing countries. Budgetary deficits are a major cause of monetary expansion. They arise on account of current and investment expenditures. The government plays a dominant role in promoting economic growth by its direct investments. Revenues lag behind expenditures for various reasons, and monetary policy is often secondary to fiscal policy.

The impact of budgetary deficits arising from investment activity is more involved than that associated with harvest failures, external factors or increased current expenditures. The immediate impact of such deficits on prices may be different from the ultimate impact: it depends on the nature of public investments, and the direct and indirect effects of these investments on output generation and on private investments.

Many developing countries suffer from resource constraint. Investment needs and priorities for promoting growth exceed savings, thereby necessitating government intervention. In the process, pressures build up within the system and prices rise at least in the short run because of attempts to pierce resource constraint in the face of lags and rigidities that exist in the system.

The special features of the model constructed by us are (a) the introduction of the role of public investment, particularly in infrastructure; (b) an elaborate treatment of supply for the agriculture–food and non-food–industry, infrastructure and tertiary sectors; (c) the indentification of the links between public and private investments for each of the sectors to trace the complementarity and crowding out effects of public investment; (d) the incorporation of the response of public revenues and expenditures to inflation, and the consequent generation of deficits, high-powered money and money supply and their interaction; (e) price determination for each of the sectors incorporating supply, demand, cost, monetary factors and the impact of import prices; (f) the introduction of a price-wage nexus for the non-agricultural sectors; and (g) the determination of private savings, distinguishing differential propensities between agricultural and non-agricultural sectors on the one hand, and between wage and non-wage incomes in the non-agricultural sector on the other. A limitation of the model, notwithstanding import quantities and prices influencing the system, is the absence of an explanation for imports, exports and the balance of payments. This imposes certain limitations on the analysis of inflation and growth.

In the simulation experiments, the impact of weather, import prices and quantities, money supply and public investment on inflation and growth, among other things, is explored.

2 THE INDIAN ECONOMY: SALIENT FEATURES

Let us look at some salient features of the Indian economy during the period 1961–80.

India experienced moderate inflation in comparison with many developing countries. The inflation rate during the period 1961–80 averaged 8 per cent per annum. However, there were considerable year-to-year fluctuations, ranging from negative values to as high as 20 per cent and more per annum. These fluctuations were closely associated with fluctuations in the growth of real GDP and variations in the money supply. Agriculture being dominant, fluctuations in output growth were influenced by agricultural performance. Agriculture is still prone to the vagaries of the weather as only one-third of the acreage is irrigated, even in recent years.

The inflation rate was higher in the 1970s (9 per cent) than in the 1960s (7 per cent). In the 1960s, however, the rate of increase in food prices was the highest among various commodity groups, but it declined in the 1970s. For all the other commodity groups, and particularly the fuel group it increased. Also, import prices rose faster. Among imports, the price of fuels and raw materials recorded higher increases.

Real GDP rose at an average rate of 3.5 per cent per annum during 1961–80. The rate of increase was somewhat higher in the 1970s–3.6 per cent in contrast to 3.2 per cent in the 1960s. This better performance was associated with a higher rate of growth achieved in agriculture as a result of the Green Revolution ushered in in the mid-1960s.

Money supply increased much faster than output. It rose at 11 per cent per annum in the 1970s in contrast to 9.5 per cent in the preceding decade. Reserve Bank credit to the government was the dominant component of high–powered money (over 50 per cent) and an important source of expansion in the money supply. However, in the second half of the 1970s, increases in foreign exchange reserves assumed importance. Foreign exchange reserves rose and stood at an all-time high as a result of the dramatic increase in the remittances from Indian nationals abroad.

Domestic savings rose to one-quarter of GDP and thereby reduced dependence of foreign inflows. The household sector alone contributed three-fourths of domestic savings.

Performance of public sector savings was tardy. Public sector revenues, which were less than 15 per cent of GDP in the early 1960s, rose to 20 per cent in the late 1970s. But because of a faster increase in current expenditures, its savings as a proportion of GDP remained below 5 per cent. The public sector resource gap (capital expenditures less its savings) related to GDP stood at around 7 per cent. Nearly 50 per cent of the resource gap was financed by domestic borrowings. Reserve Bank credit to the government as a per cent of the resource gap increased at the cost of external borrowings. In the closing years of the 1970s, Reserve Bank credit financed two-fifths of the public sector resource gap.

Aggregate real investment increased at 5 per cent per annum during 1961–80. Public sector investment was about two-fifths of the total investment in the economy and it rose at a higher rate in the 1970s than in the 1960s. Infrastructure was dominant in public investment, with about two-fifths' share, followed by industry, the tertiary sector, and agriculture.

India had an adverse balance of trade for most of these years, but its severity varied. The trade gap averaged over one billion rupees in the second half of the 1970s due to the price increase of fuel oil. However, favourable foreign exchange reserves resulting from the remittances of Indian nationals abroad helped to ease the situation.

The single most important drain on foreign exchange reserves in the second half of the 1970s was the rising fuel bill. Its share of the total import bill rose from less than one-tenth to over one-third. The share of capital goods declined, partly reflecting growth in the domestic capital goods industry due to import substitution policies and the existence of excess capacity.

3 THE MODEL

The model, consisting of seventy-seven equations, is estimated by the ordinary least squares (OLS) for the period 1962–80. Not all equations in the model are behaviourial or technological. Apart from identities, there are several estimating or linking equations which are statistical in nature. All equations are linear.

The real side of the economy is divided into four sectors: (1) agricultural–(food and non-food); (2) industry (mining and manufacturing combined); (3) public sector infrastructure defined in the traditional way as comprising electricity, transport and communications, and finally (4) the tertiary sector, defined to include all other activities. Productivity per unit of land in agriculture and productivity per unit of capital in other sectors are explained.

The agricultural sub-model contains eighteen equations, industry twelve, public sector infrastructure ten, tertiary nine, savings and other macro aggregates six, public sector revenues, expenditures and deficits fifteen, and finally, money, general price level and consumer prices seven.

We now present the basic feature of the model by sector.

3.1 Agriculture

The key production relationships are productivity in agriculture and the decomposition of total output into food and non-food. Productivity per unit of land is well explained by the capital-land ratio, rainfall and a dummy variable to account for the effect of new technology. In terms of elasticities, capital-land ratio has an edge over rainfall. Capital includes public irrigation works, and therefore water is the key factor in agricultural development, given land. Expansion of output by land extension was almost exhausted in the 1950s.

Determination of the share of foodgrain in output is implicitly based on the well-established empirical finding that relative price within agriculture influences the allocation of fixed (land) and variable factors between alternative crops. The relative price of food in relation to the general price of agriculture is a significant determinant of food share.

Private real investment responds well to terms of trade and agricultural income. Public investment has a strong complementarity effect on private investment. Every rupee of public investment activates more than a rupee of private investment.

Prices are explained by supply-demand imbalance. Demand is related not only to real income but also to excess supply of money, i.e. it is related to money demand for output. Supply of money in excess of aggregate output growth exerts pressure on commodity markets.

Food and non-food prices are adequately explained by per capita availability, per capita real income, and money per unit of real GDP. Also, imports and import prices have an impact on prices. Food and non-food agricultural prices together account for nearly one-third of the weight in the wholesale price index for 'all commodities'.

The implicit GDP deflator is related to the wholesale price of agricultural products. The investment goods price for agriculture is linked to the price of industrial goods and the price of imported capital. The former has a stronger impact.

To summarise, the agricultural sub-model underlines the importance of public investment for agricultural development. Public investment provides infrastructure for agriculture and thereby assured irrigation. Short-run variations in output are weather-determined. Supply, demand and monetary factors influence price behaviour. Prices, given other factors, move almost at the same rate as money supply. Imports and import prices do matter.

3.2 Industry

Output in industry is determined by labour, capital, agricultural raw materials and imported raw materials inclusive of fuels. Capital stock is augmented by both public and private investments. Private investment decisions are influenced by the non-wage income of industry, aggregate public investment reflecting its acceleration facet, and total resources in the economy less public investment and private investment in agriculture reflecting the crowding-out facet. While demand for labour is determined by the real wage rate defined in terms of product price and output, nominal wage is governed by the cost of living. Together they constitute the wage bill. Industrial prices are cost-determined. The mark-up factor is seen as varying with excess demand pressures in the economy represented by the money-real GDP ratio. The investment goods price is related to its own price and the price of imported capital goods. The implicit price deflator for GDP is linked to industrial prices.

The results confirm the two facets of public investment–one as a promoter of output and private investment, the other as a dampener on private investment, at least in the short run. Capital productivity, which mirrors capital utilisation, is influenced by infrastructural facilities and the availability of raw materials, both domestic-agriculture-based and imported. Private investment is very positively associated with factor income distribution within the sector. Employment is governed by the scale of output. The wage rate seems to have no effect on it. Nominal wages adjust to the cost of living gradually. Industrial prices are cost-determined but excess demand pressures – monetary expansion in excess of aggregate output growth – exert stronger influence than cost factors, namely wages and the price of raw materials. Agriculture has an impact on the industrial performance.

3.3 Public Sector Infrastructure

This is the first time, perhaps, that specific and detailed treatment has been accorded to this vital sector in macro behaviouristic econometric models for India. The structure is similar to industry, particularly with regard to output, employment and wage equations.

Capital and labour influence output, but capital is more important than labour in the public sector infrastructure. Capital grows with public investment. Capital productivity is affected by fuel imports. Public sector pricing adjusts with a lag to the general price situation and concurrently with the import price of fuels. Employment is output-determined. Wages adjust slowly to the cost of living. The price of imported capital goods has a stronger influence on the capital goods price in the infrastructure compared to other sectors.

3.4 Tertiary Sector

Output in the tertiary sector is demand–determined, given capital and other variables. Private investment adjusts to the needs of other sectors, given resources (domestic savings and foreign capital inflow). GDP identity in nominal terms determines the tertiary sector implicit price deflator, given other elements.

Real GDP is determined by demand (the output of all other sectors), the output of the public sector infrastructure, public and private capital, and imports of fuels; labour does not find a place. The specification assumes constant labour output and capital-output ratios. The wage bill is well accounted for by real GDP, consumer prices and its own lagged value. The investment goods price is influenced by industrial prices and the prices of imported capital goods.

3.5 Savings and Other Macro Aggregates

In this group the only behaviourial equation is the private savings function. Private disposable income is related to real GDP through an estimating relationship. The rest of the equations are standard identities.

The marginal propensity to save out of private disposable incomes is one-third. This implies a multiplier of the order of three. As expected, the two income distribution variables, namely GDP in agriculture to GDP, and wage income to GDP, have a negative impact on savings. The negative influence of agricultural income is stronger than wage income. The rate of inflation shows some positive effect on savings.

Real private disposable income has a stable relationship with real GDP. It has unit elasticity.

3.6 Public Sector: Revenues, Expenditures and Deficits

The public sector consists of general government (government proper plus departmental undertakings) and non-departmental undertakings of the government as defined in the *National Accounts Statistics*. We distinguish between the two wherever necessary.

The treatment of public sector resources and expenditures is aggregative. It merely distinguishes between revenues and borrowings on the resource side, and between current expenditures, investment expenditures and net capital transfers of the government on the expenditure side. The aim of this exercise is only to establish interdependence between budget deficits and prices. The purpose is well served by the level of disaggregation adopted. It is not intended to explain specific revenues and expenditures.

The analysis rests on the basic hypotheses that revenues are targeted in nominal terms in relation to nominal GDP, expenditures are targeted in real terms in relation to real GDP, and both adjust to the target gradually. Consequently, the deficit becomes a function of price and its rate of change, among other factors.

The resource gap of the public sector, i.e. total expenditures inclusive of current and capital expenditures less current revenues, is filled by the public sector borrowing abroad and domestically, and government's borrowing from the Reserve Bank. Domestic borrowing is explained by the resource gap less external borrowing, which is treated as exogenous. At the margin, on average, an increase in the gap results in nearly 90 per cent of it being financed by domestic borrowing other than from the Reserve Bank.

The results reveal that expenditures adjust towards the target level at a faster rate than revenue and, within expenditures, current expenditures adjust more speedily than investment expenditures. This makes the public sector resource gap a positive function of price level and rate of inflation. At the margin, the resource gap is filled more by domestic borrowings than by Reserve Bank credit to the government. The empirical results establish interdependence among budget deficits, money supply and prices.

3.7 Money, the General Price Level and Consumer Prices

The stock of high-powered money consists of stock of Reserve Bank net credit to government plus government currency liabilities to the public (its change represents the high-powered deficit of the government), Reserve Bank credit to the commercial sector, its foreign exchange assets, and non-monetary liabilities.

The dominant component of changes in high-powered money was Reserve Bank credit to the government. Changes in foreign exchange reserves were important in certain periods. Credit to the commercial sector was much less important than credit to government.

Money and high-powered money are stocks at the end of the year and therefore, to allow time for the money supply to adjust to changes in high-powered money, the money supply is treated as a function of high-powered money and lagged money supply. The long run marginal money multiplier is 1.7.

The general price level is measured by two indicators, namely the wholesale price index and the GDP implicit price deflator. The components of the wholesale price index were explained earlier. The ratio of money supply to real GDP was found to be a dominant factor in the explanation of sectoral prices. These prices aggregate to the wholesale price index of 'all commodities' with the weights assigned to them in the official index. The GDP price deflator is explained in terms of quantity theory in the partial adjustment framework. The money to real GDP ratio bears a strong relationship with the price level. The long-term elasticity of implicit price deflator with respect to money-real GDP ratio is one. Thus, prices move at the same rate as the money supply in the long run, given output. This result, by and large, is borne out by sectoral price analysis.

Consumer prices adjust slowly to the general price level represented by the wholesale price index. The long-term elasticity of consumer prices with respect to the wholesale price index is less than unity.

In brief, the Reserve Bank credit to the government is the most important component of high-powered money. High powered money determines money supply *à la* money multiplier. Money supply has a strong influence on prices. Sectoral and general prices move, by and large, at about the same rate as the money supply, given other factors.

3.8 An Overview

The empirical results have brought out the basic links in the economy. Public sector investment, which acts as an engine of growth, augments output in all sectors. It has a complementarity effect on private investment in agriculture, and both complementarity and crowding out effects in industry. Public sector infrastructure improves productivity in industry and tertiary sectors.

While relative prices within agriculture influence the composition of the sectoral output, terms of trade between agriculture and the rest of the economy affect private investment decisions in agriculture. Terms of trade between agriculture and the rest of the economy influence private savings. Shifts in terms of trade in favour of agriculture promote private investment in agriculture but have adverse effects on private savings.

Agricultural performance in the short run is weather-influenced and in the long run public investment-determined. Agriculture affects industry through raw material supplies and prices.

Employment in non-agricultural sectors is determined by scale of output. Nominal wages react slowly to consumer prices, which in turn move tardily with the general price level. Therefore, factor income distribution shifts in favour of non-wage incomes in periods of price rise. Such shifts favourably affect private investment in industry and private savings.

Import and import prices affect activity in the economy, the former favourably and the latter adversely. Import prices have a sizeable impact on domestic prices. Supply factors do matter, but the single most important factor influencing prices is monetary expansion, which is out of alignment with output growth. Import prices assumed significance, particularly after 1974.

Monetary expansion is fuelled by budget deficits. Public expenditures, specifically investment expenditures, not only add to growth potential but also increase inflationary potential, as revenues expand slower than expenditures. Budget deficits widen with inflation, and therefore money supply and prices are interdependent. The strength of this interdependence rests on the pattern of financing of the resource gap of the public sector. The larger is the Reserve Bank financing of the resource gap, the stronger is the interdependence between money and prices. Inflation could be self-perpetuating in character.

4. SIMULATION EXPERIMENTS

The estimated model is put on trial. Apart from historical validation of the model, the following experiments were conducted to assess the impact of:

1. Weather (rainfall)–assuming it was normal in years when it was below normal;
2. import prices – had they remained constant at 1974 level: and import quantities – had they been larger than the actual ones;
3. money supply – if it had grown according to some rule: (a) at a constant rate from year to year or (b) at the same rate from year to year as real GDP but with a mark-up over and above the estimated level;
4. an increase in public investment on private investment – complementarity and crowding out effects;
5. an increase in public investment on prices and output; and, finally,
6. stepping up public investment for the period 1967–80.

These experiments, which are counter-factual, only suggest the direction of change and broad dimensions of change under the conditions specified in each experiment.

All simulations are dynamic and non-stochastic. The results of controlled experiments are compared with the corresponding reference solutions.

4.1 Historical Validation

Judged by mean square percentage error, the model performs well. Quite a large number of endogenous variables (72 out of 75) have errors of less than 5 or 10 per cent for the period 1962–80. The model traces the second period (1971–80) more closely than the first (1962–70).

The error for outputs is less than 2 per cent; for prices, employment, public sector real investment, money supply and related aggregates, it is less than 5 per cent. Private investment is traced better in agriculture than in industry and the tertiary sector. Similarly, public sector expenditures were better replicated than its revenues.

4.2 Weather

Rainfall was below normal in six years in the period 1962–70, in contrast to four in 1971–80. Had normal weather prevailed and everything else remained unchanged, as can be expected, output levels would have been higher and prices lower. A larger effect is found in the first period (1962–70) than in the second (1971–80) as the former had more sub–normal years. In the first period, real GDP in agriculture would have been larger by 2 per cent, food production by 4 per cent, aggregate real GDP by 2 per cent, and food and 'all commodity' price indices would have been lower by 6 and 3 per cent respectively. Private investment, public investment and private savings would also have been higher. All these favourable effects would have resulted in a 5 per cent increase in the rate of growth of real GDP and an equivalent reduction in the rate of inflation.

4.3 Import Prices and Quantities

Import prices rocketed from 1974 onwards. Fuel prices more than doubled and the import price for 'all commodities' rose more than 50 per cent in 1974 as compared to the previous year. This was the first major increase in prices. Between 1973 and 1980, fuel prices recorded a tenfold increase, raw material prices doubled, and capital goods prices experienced a threefold increase.

An attempt is made to assess the impact of an increase in import prices on inflation and economic activity. The model is simulated by allowing an initial rise in prices in 1974 and maintaining it at that level

(1974) for the subsequent years, i.e. 1975 to 1980. All other exogenous variables including import quantities assume their historical values.

The major impact is on the wholesale prices of 'fuel, power, light and lubricants', followed by capital goods. The wholesale price index for all commodities would have been lower by 11 per cent and the price of capital goods by about 20 per cent, had import prices remained at the 1974 level.

The rate of inflation would have been 10 per cent less during the period 1975–80 if import prices had remained constant at the 1974 level with unchanged imports. The rate of growth of private investment in industry and the tertiary sector would have been higher. However, the impact on output is negligible.

An alternative set of simulations was run by maintaining import prices at the 1974 level, but raising for each year during 1975–80 the import quantities of raw materials and intermediates, fuels and non-food agricultural products from the observed level, by 5 to 25 per cent, with increments of 5 percentage points. The impact of an increase in imports is on the output of the tertiary sector, public sector infrastructure and industry, in that order. But prices are not very sensitive to import quantities.

The growth rate of output increases with an increase in imports, given import prices at the 1974 level. Elasticity of the real GDP growth rate with respect to import quantities (raw materials and intermediates, fuels and non-food agricultural imports) is somewhat less than half (0.4). An increase in the real GDP growth rate exerts some pressure on food price, but the general price level (wholesale price index) is not sensitive to changes in imports of raw materials, fuels or non-food agricultural products.

4.4 Money Supply

In this exercise, the effects of a change in the growth of the money supply on prices and on other important variables are evaluated. Thus, the money supply becomes exogenous, and all equations pertaining to money supply generation are delinked from the model. It is made to change according to two rules: (a) changes from year to year at a constant rate, and (b) changes from year to year at the same rate as real GDP but with a mark-up over and above the estimated level of the money supply as given by the rule.

Public investment in real terms is treated as exogenous. This and other exogenous variables are made to follow their respective historical paths. In reference simulations, however, the money supply assumes observed values.

These exercises assume that resources for public investment, which is maintained at historical levels, are somehow found from within, as the foreign inflow of capital is fixed at historical levels, in such a way that it ensures that the money supply grows as specified.

Restraint on money supply growth contains the rate of inflation. Reduction in the growth rate of the money supply brings down the rate of inflation dramatically.

Concentrating on the recent decade, a reduction in the growth of the money supply from the observed 11 per cent per annum to 8 per cent would result in about a one-quarter reduction in the rate of inflation (wholesale prices and consumer price indices), while a step-down in the money supply growth rate from 11 to 5 per cent would have halved the rate of inflation. The rate of reduction in the implicit price deflator is much more.

The results do not indicate sensitivity of aggregate real GDP growth to changes in money supply growth, but the industry sector does show reaction. The insensitivity of real GDP is contrived, as the model does not consider credit as an input in the production process. It would be affected adversely, at least to some extent, in so far as reduction in the growth of the money supply reduces production credit.

The industry sector reacts favourably to an increase in the inflation rate as the mark-up factor over costs increases with excess demand pressures and, consequently, non-wage incomes increase as wages lag behind prices and factor income distribution shifts in favour of non-wage incomes. Simulation results confirm this scenario. The opposite prevails when the inflation rate is reduced. Reduction in inflation affects somewhat adversely private savings, private investment in industry, and output growth in industry. This contrasts with the impact of the reduced rate of inflation on industry which results from cost reductions resulting from import prices.

The results are similar in terms of broad trends when the growth of the money supply follows rule (b). It is interesting to note that the observed rate of growth of the money supply of 11 per cent per annum during 1962–80 and 1971–80 is associated with a mark-up factor of 7.5 per cent.

Although the broad directions and dimensions of change in the rate of inflation over a long period and of several important variables are similar, whether money supply changes from year to year at a constant rate, or at a rate consistent with real GDP growth plus a mark-up factor, year-to-year variations in the rate of price change would be different. The latter rule is procyclical with respect to real GDP, and therefore changes in the money supply consistent with output growth would restrain price increases in years of low growth of output, while constant rate of growth of the money supply will accentuate price increases in such years.

4.5 Complementarity and Crowding Out Effects

The model is simulated to assess complementarity and the crowding out effects of public investment on private investment and on output, assuming average conditions prevailing during the period 1975–80. All exogenous variables are maintained at their respective mean levels for all years. Weather is assumed to be normal for all years. Public real investment is stepped up for one year and for all times by 5 per cent from the average of the period 1975–80 (44 billion rupees).

Consider the case of an increase in public investment for one year only. In agriculture, complementarity prevails as no crowding out effect is postulated in the specification itself. However, in industry and the tertiary sector the crowding out effect dominates the complementarity effect in the year of increase of public investment. Private investment recovers subsequently. There is a turnaround in private investment in industry and in aggregate private investment in the second year. While the loss of private investment in industry is recovered by the eighth year, aggregate private investment is recouped by the eleventh year. However, aggregate real GDP suffers no loss except for a tiny tenth of 1 per cent in the first year. The gain in public sector output and its favourable impact on productivity in other sectors more than compensates for the loss in private output.

Stepping up public investment for all times is more realistic. Even in this case, there is no loss of aggregate real GDP, except for a very small one in the first year (one-tenth of one per cent). Private investment in industry is crowded out for six years and aggregate private investment for eleven years. The loss is recouped in the twelfth year for industry and in the twenty-first year for aggregate private investment.

In short, although public investment crowds out private investment in some sectors and for some years, aggregate real GDP does not suffer losses. Public sector output supplants private output.

4.6 Public Investment, Prices and Output

Public sector real investment is raised, maintaining the historical pattern of financing the public sector resource gap, as captured in the relevant equations, and with unchanged foreign capital inflow. Public sector real investment is increased for six years from the average levels of 1975–80, with all the other exogenous variables assuming their respective mean values of the period for each year. Weather is assumed to be normal. This exercise imitates average conditions prevailing during 1975–80, and assumes that excess capacity exists in industry to meet additional demand for capital goods arising from increased public investment as imports are left unchanged.

The medium term is viewed as the period during which public investment is raised (six years) and the long term as the period in which dynamic effects are, by and large, worked out after bringing it back in the seventh year to the initial level. The dynamic solution is allowed to run for twenty-one years after the year of step-down.

Real GDP, the price level (implicit GDP deflator), nominal GDP and the money supply are higher than the reference solution. However, the long-term price impact on nominal GDP is less than that in the medium term. The decomposition exercise reveals that the increase in nominal GDP is shared in the medium term by a price increase which is little over half (52–4 per cent) and output a little over four-tenths (about 42 per cent), while in the long run the contribution of output picks up (about 48 per cent) and price effects dwindle (about 50 per cent). This is a type of trade-off between inflation and growth.

4.7 Stepping up Public Investment, 1967–80

Several authors have emphasised that post-1966 years represent a departure from the trends established in the first three five-year plans (1951–65). The below-average performance of the economy since 1966 has been ascribed, among other reasons, to a slowing down of public sector investment, and specifically in public sector infrastructure. It did slow down even in absolute terms during the years 1966–70.

With this background in mind, public investment is increased in this simulation exercise from the observed levels for each of the years 1967 to 1980 by a constant rate. All exogenous variables including the foreign inflow of capital and imports, are maintained on their respective historical paths. This assumes that the additional demand for capital goods generated by an increase in public investment will be met by activating idle capacity. The financing pattern of the public sector resource gap is assumed to follow the historical pattern set out in the relevant equations. In the reference solution, all exogenous variables, including public investment, assume historical values.

An increase in public investment tones up activity all around. It increases the growth rate of output in all sectors, private real investment in agriculture and in industry, and private savings. However, the rate of inflation also rises as a result of an increase in the growth of the money supply, but the increase in the rate of inflation is less than the increase in output growth.

An increase in public sector real investment benefits growth of output in the tertiary sector most, followed by public sector infrastructure, agriculture and industry. An increase of one-quarter in the level of public investment would have raised the growth rate of real GDP by 14 per cent, i.e. from 3.5 per cent per annum to 4.0 per cent. The elasticity of the growth rate of real GDP with respect to the level of real public investment is about one-half, while it is over one-half (0.6) for both public sector infrastructure and the tertiary sector, and less than one half (0.4) for both agriculture and industry.

Private investment in industry derives a stronger fillip in contrast to other sectors. An increase of one-quarter in public investment pushes up the growth of private investment in industry more than twofold, while in agriculture it raises the growth rate of investment only by one-fifth.

The growth of the money supply increases with an increase in public investment, since a part of the resource gap resulting from it is financed by central bank credit and, consequently, the rate of inflation also increases. A one-quarter increase in public investment results in a little more than a one-tenth increase in the growth rate of the money supply and little less than a one-tenth increase in the rate of inflation. Elasticity of the rate of inflation with respect to the level of real public investment (about 0.4) is less than that of real GDP (0.5).

In a nutshell, assuming the same historical pattern of financing the public sector resource gap and given foreign capital inflow, a rise in public investment increases output growth more than the rate of inflation. This is the trade-off between inflation and growth.

5 CONCLUDING REMARKS

To sum up: sustained good weather improves growth performance and lowers inflation. Imported inflation is a significant contributor to domestic inflation in the post-1974 years. An increase in the availability of raw materials and intermediates and fuels improves growth performance. Restraint on monetary expansion is the single most important factor in containing inflation. An increase in public sector real investment is the key to growth. Although it crowds out private investment in some sectors and for some years, the immediate and ultimate impact favours growth of output. An increase in public investment tones up activity all around. It increases growth more than inflation, if inflationary financing is moderate.

The message of the model is clear and policy implications are obvious. An increase in public sector investment is a must for growth but needs to be accomplished without excessive dependence on inflationary financing. Monetary expansion is the single most contributory factor to inflationary trends in the Indian economy. Monetary policy has limits. The control of budget deficits without the curtailment of productive expenditures and monetary expansion, among other measures, is the key to growth with price stability. This has been stressed time and again by economists and policy-makers in India.

REFERENCE

Krishnamurty, K. (1984) 'Inflation and Growth: a Model for India', *Indian Economic Review* Jan–June 1984; reprinted in Krishnamurty, K. and Pandit, V. (1985) *Macroeconometric Modelling of the Indian Economy: Studies in Inflation and Growth* (Delhi: Hindustan Publishing Corp.)

23 Growth, Inflation and Employment: Discussion and Conclusions

L. R. Klein
WHARTON SCHOOL OF FINANCE AND COMMERCE,
UNIVERSITY OF PENNSYLVANIA,
PHILADELPHIA

The papers presented under the topic 'Growth, Inflation and Employment' covered the advanced industrial and the developing world economies, in both instances by reference to specific cases. The industrial country presentations by Professor Hickman, Krelle and Shishido dealt respectively with the United States, Germany and Japan. These are the three most important OECD countries in terms of GDP contributions. They are all large, dynamic and generally important from an economic point of view. They are, in fact, key countries or 'swing' economies in the industrial world.

The contribution from the developing countries comes from Professor Krishnamurty and is based on the case of India. The developing world is highly diverse, but India plays a key role. It is the second largest country in the world. If China is placed among the centrally planned group of countries and not strictly classified as a Third World country, although that may not be entirely appropriate, then India emerges as the largest country in the developing world. It is, no matter how one classifies countries, one of the most important developing countries, although it may not be 'typical'. In a sense, no single developing country is typical, because there is so much diversity among such countries. India has been so much studied and observed closely from a social scientific viewpoint that it commands a great deal of attention, even though it may not be fully typical.

All authors are concerned about inflation – about the need to bring it under control now and to keep it under control while achieving future growth. None is, however, very optimistic about growth prospects. There is clear recognition, in all the papers, of the fact that concern about inflation has a moderating influence on future expansion. Growth without inflation means moderate growth. No one is looking for a large-scale boom during the 1980s. It is not ruled out, for the economy can (and has) responded in excess of present expectations, but the prevalent projection and recommendation is for *moderate* growth in the intermediate future, until, say, the end of the decade.

Professor Krishnamurty is mainly concerned about deficits, which are built into the Indian fiscal system. Revenues are targeted in nominal terms, while expenditures are targeted in real terms. Revenues adjust more slowly to the target values; thus, deficits develop and these lead to increases in money supply, which, in turn, generate inflation. His arguments are thus much in line with those being put forward in leading industrial countries with large budget deficits. A separate factor contributing to fast growth of the money supply has also been the strong inflow of funds in the form of worker remittances from Indian nationals working abroad, especially in the Middle East. This source of international flow of funds may be slackening a little now, but it is of great importance for many developing countries throughout the Third World.

The industrial country papers are concerned with productivity problems and generally look for help through capital formation. In a sense, Professor Krishnamurty's paper follows the same lines of argument because he places great emphasis on the need to stimulate public sector capital formation, and that would be associated indirectly with productivity growth. He believes that it is productive infrastructure investment that is needed in India. Professor Hickman, however, attaches a great deal of significance to the changes in terms of trade for energy as a reason for the productivity slowdown in the United States. Changed relative prices for energy explain only a part of the productivity slowdown in his econometric model simulations and do not account for the persistently low rate of progress. It accounts mainly for a lowering of the level of potential output. The greatest source of uncertainty in his relatively pessimistic projection of continuing stagflation is the assumed rate of technical progress. Steady real wages, monetary restraint, and the lack of power of tax reductions all contribute to his outlook for moderate growth in this decade.

As for contemporary problems that need some resolution in the interests of good growth once again, most of the papers recognise full well the oppressive effects of high interest rates, large deficits, and high dollar exchange valuation, all in the United States, as being responsible for world ills, as well as domestic American ills. Policies for steady, non-inflationary growth with improving employment opportunities would have to be directed towards bringing down US interest rates and dollar exchange values.

Among the papers, there is hesitation to look towards 'industrial policy' as a way out of the bind of stagflation in all cases except that of Japan. Professor Shishido, not surprisingly, argues convincingly for bold and direct policy action through the promotion of R&D and the flow of scientific-technological information. Industrial policy has served Japan well in past and should continue to do so in the future.

Professor Krelle reminds us that Keynesian policies of the purest sort do not seem to be doing as much good as we once thought they did, but they are not dismissed to the extent that some of the new generation theorists would like. He is mainly concerned that increased money supply and inflation will accompany positive employment policies. Other obstacles to recovery with strong growth are, in his view, the indebtedness of developing countries and large fluctuations in exchange rates. He also believes that industrial countries have unduly raised the burden of domestic transfer payments, allowed the underground economy to flourish, and developed rigid wage structures.

Professor Krishnamurty states unequivocally that monetary control is the single most important item in controlling inflation, but he does recognise clearly that weather, for crop yield, is all-important for India. A good crop does much to hold inflation in check. Professor Hickman notes that high oil prices have led to general price rises in the past and lurk under cover as a potential threat in the future.

All in all, a note of cautious optimism emerges from these papers. All the authors stress careful quantitative research. They are all model builders and use that methodology to *understand* the stagflation problems, while at the same time thinking about policies that could work their way through the model structures towards better results.

The world economy is fully recognised to be in trouble, but is capable of emerging on a better growth path with sustainable low inflation. No one, however, expects to get back to full employment as we once knew it: several percentage points lower, all over the world.

Part V

International Price Fluctuations and Inflation

24 Price Inertia and Inflation: Evidence and Theoretical Rationale

M. I. Nadiri
NEW YORK UNIVERSITY AND NBER

1 INTRODUCTION

The phenomenon of price insensitivity to changes in demand in the advanced Western economies has been a subject of considerable discussion among macroeconomists and policy-makers. In recent years prices have not only been rigid downward but have even risen in the face of slack demand. Short-run inflexibility of prices is critical for the success of fiscal and monetary stablisation policies and the ability of economic systems to accommodate external shocks. The question is, what are the causes of price inflexibility and is this consistent with private maximisation principles? How do the dynamic interactions among various stages and types of economic activity lead to price stickiness of the aggregate price level?

The debate on aggregate price adjustment has been joined by two schools of thought: the neo Keynesian approach, which assumes that markets do not clear because of institutional and informational arrangements, and the 'new classical' equilibrium approach to business cycles, which postulates market clearance and instantaneous prices adjustment in response to changes in nominal demand. The empirical evidence, as shown by Gordon (1982a) and others is that prices are neither perfectly fixed nor perfectly flexible; they vary over time and across industries, markets and countries. Neither of the two approaches seems as yet to provide a consistent explanation of this empirical finding. This has led to a search for developing the micro foundations for price rigidity from an optimisation viewpoint and models which explicitly take account of the structure of markets and input-output relationships in the economy. As yet there is no general consensus model available to explain the observed degree of pervasiveness of price inflexibility.

In this paper our purpose is to sketch some illustrative empirical findings on price adjustment at the aggregate and industry levels in some of the Western industrialised economies and to discuss some of the microeconomic models of price adjustment that have been proposed. The second objective of the paper is to examine the relationship of market structure and pricing behaviour and assemble some of the evidence on differential price behaviour in competitive and oligopolistic markets. The third issue considered is how these differential price behaviours may lead to the price adjustment observed at the aggregate economy level. The paper is concluded with a few final remarks and policy suggestions.

2 THE EXTENT AND DEGREE OF PRICE INFLEXIBILITY

The empirical evidence on the question of price vs output flexibility has been quite extensive. The evidence comes partly from macro econometric studies, surveys of transactions in different markets, and studies of disaggregated price series. We shall briefly discuss each of these types of evidence before examining some of the theoretical rationale provided for the phenomenon of price inertia in the context of profit-maximising models.

2.1 Evidence from Macro Price Models

Gordon (1982a) has been chief among those in the USA who have addressed empirically the question of price inertia in aggregate price level. His results indicate that nominal GNP has been divided consistently over the last 90 years of US history, with about two-thirds taking the form of output changes and the remaining one-third the form of price changes; the structure of price expectations changed some time before the Second World War from a regressive to an extrapolative form possibly due to the recognition of the stabilising role of government policies and the emergence of overlapping wage contracts in the USA. However, when the experience of the US economy is compared to that of Japan and the UK, Gordon finds that wages and prices are more flexible in the latter countries. The degree of price inflexibility therefore varies among countries and over time. Nonetheless, the evidence of price inertia, particularly in the post-war US economy, suggests a sluggish response of prices to restrictive demand policies and the resulting high unemployment, thus constituting a dilemma for policy-makers.

Evidence of price inflexibility in the post-war US economy and in the European economies has also been reported by other studies. Eckstein and Fromm (1968), using US annual data, found that both prices and outputs react within three to six months to changes in costs and demand. Hay (1970) found for two US industries that a temporary increase in demand caused a small increase in price but a large increase in output. Using aggregate data for the USA, de Minel (1974) reached similar conclusions. The evidence provided for the nineteen OECD countries by Grubb, Jackman and Layard (1982) suggests different degrees of price and wage inertia in these countries over the post-war period. Coutts, Godley and Nordhaus (1978), using British data for several industries, reached the conclusion that prices are mainly determined by costs and affected little by changes in demand. Studies using time series data for Germany found that firms keep their prices at their planned level and adjust their outputs when demand changes (Kawasaki, McMillan and Zimmerman, 1983). The econometric results obtained by Nadiri and Gupta (1977) and Eckstein and Wyss (1977) for different US manufacturing industries provide evidence of price inertia at the industry level. These results indicate that effects of demand changes on prices are small in most of the industries considered, and there is evidence of considerable inertia in price adjustments. The degree of demand effect and price adjustment, however, varies among industries.

The studies differ in their coverage, level of aggregation and span of time. However, they all seem to point to the slow adjustment of prices and more rapid adjustment of outputs when the demand level changes in the short run. But a potential shortcoming of all these studies is that they are based not on transaction but list prices. Stigler and Kindahl (1970) have argued that the relevant series is prices at which buyers and sellers transact a sale. They have indicated, based on their study, that transaction prices are highly variable and the price stickiness reported above may be an illusion. However, Weiss (1977) has argued persuasively that changes in Stigler-Kindahl price series and BLS data (which is often used in the studies mentioned above) reflect each other and therefore that the Stigler-Kindahl conclusion is not valid. Further new econometric studies using transaction prices indicate that firms, in their immediate response to disequilibrium, are more likely to react with an output change than a price change.

2.2 Survey of Market Transactions

Another source of evidence of whether prices are inflexible is provided in an interesting study by Carlton (1979). Tables 24.1 and 24.2 provide evidence on the pattern of transaction prices in a sample of businesses during a relatively non-inflationary period, 1957–66. Table 24.1 lists by product the average duration of price inflexibility in months and the standard deviation of duration. The results suggest several important points. For many transactions between individual buyers and sellers, price, once set, tends to remain unchanged for a substantial period of time. This suggests that quantity adjustment and not prices may be the mechanism used to allocate some goods when supply or demand changes. Since the standard deviation of length of price rigidity is quite high, we can infer that a wide variety of contracts have differing price flexibility; that is, some contracts have very

Table 24.1 Price rigidity by product

Product	Number of contracts observed*	Average duration of price rigidity (months)	Standard deviation of duration (months)
Steel	348	13.0	18.3
Non-ferrous metals	209	4.3	6.1
Petroleum	245	5.9	5.3
Rubber tyres	123	8.1	12.0
Paper	128	8.7	14.0
Chemicals	658	12.8	10.7
Cement	40	13.2	14.7
Glass	22	10.2	12.1
Truck motors	59	5.4	6.3
Plywood	46	4.7	7.7

*'Number of contracts' means the number of price series between individual buyers and sellers for a good of specified characteristics

Source: Table 6.1 in Carlton (1982).

flexible prices while others have very inflexible prices within the same broad commodity group. Finally, there are very large differences across industries in degree of price inflexibility.

The results in Table 24.2 show the frequency of price rigidity by the duration of contract, i.e. annual and monthly. It seems that the contracting structure for each product is not only different, but that there are many annual contracts whose prices change well before one year has elapsed, while there are many monthly contracts whose prices often do not change for one year. Thus the contract terms seem to be very flexible and adaptable to changes in market conditions. Perhaps ongoing relations between buyer and seller account for this behaviour. Also, the monthly contract prices vary more frequently than those for the annual contracts, which implies that there are contracts whose prices remain unchanged at the same time that demand and supply forces are changing other contract prices for the same commodity group.

From these results the conjecture may be drawn that some markets resemble liquid markets with flexible prices performing the allocative role, and other markets resemble illiquid markets with fixed prices where quantity changes perform the allocative role. Non-ferrous metals, petroleum and plywood are likely to have sub-markets that are highly liquid, while steel, paper and chemicals seem likely to have sub-markets that are highly illiquid. For some goods highly liquid and illiquid sub-markets may exist side by side. These observations suggest there are different degrees of price inflexibility in different markets and for different products which are likely to change over time and among different industries.

An econometric study using monthly transaction prices and output changes of individual firms in various German industries substantiates the results noted above and confirms the hypothesis of differentiated behaviour in different markets. Kawasaki *et al.* (1982) develop a dynamic disequilibrium model taking account of inventories and unfilled orders in determining the adjustment path of prices and output in response to changes in demand. Their results show that both prices and output flexibility vary markedly across industries, reflecting some of the differences among industries noted above. They show, too, that prices are in the short-run inflexible in industries such as stone and clay machinery, electrical equipment, iron, tin and other products, glass and products and clothing. By contrast, non-ferrous metals, textiles, and plastic and products exhibit short-run price flexibility. The results also indicate that each firm

Table 24.2 Frequency of duration of price rigidity for annual and monthly contracts based on spells of price rigidity*

Product	Contract type	Number of contracts**	0–3 months	3 months 1 year	1–2 years	2–4 years	Over 4 years
Steel	Annual	11	0.11	0.41	0.24	0.22	0.03
	Monthly	111	0.48	0.27	0.15	0.07	0.04
Non-ferrous metals	Annual	8	0.16	0.69	0.12	0.03	0.00
	Monthly	87	0.78	0.20	0.02	0.01	0.00
Petroleum	Annual	66	0.20	0.69	0.07	0.04	0.00
	Monthly	16	0.83	0.15	0.07	0.00	0.00
Rubber tyres	Annual	32	0.19	0.72	0.07	0.01	0.01
	Monthly	24	0.44	0.42	0.07	0.01	0.06
Paper	Annual	22	0.04	0.69	0.18	0.08	0.01
	Monthly	36	0.46	0.36	0.12	0.04	0.02
Chemicals	Annual	286	0.11	0.58	0.17	0.09	0.06
	Monthly	134	0.53	0.27	0.09	0.06	0.04
Cement	Annual	8	0.04	0.78	0.13	0.04	0.00
	Monthly	4	0.64	0.29	0.02	0.04	0.02
Glass	Annual	8	0.00	0.87	0.10	0.03	0.00
	Monthly	9	0.51	0.22	0.18	0.09	0.00
Truck motors	Annual	8	0.05	0.86	0.09	0.00	00.0
	Monthly	34	0.69	0.26	0.04	0.01	0.00
Plywood	Annual	0					
	Monthly	2	0.99	0.02	0.00	0.00	0.00

*The numbers in the rows of the table may not add to one because of rounding.

**'number of contracts' means the number of price series between individual buyers and sellers far a good of specified characteristics. Note that this is not the same as the number of spells of price rigidity in all contracts.
Source: Table 6.2 in Carlton (1982).

changes its output whenever there is an inventory or unfilled order disequilibrium but changes its price only when disequilibrium persists long enough to reflect permanent changes in demand or costs. However, there is no evidence of asymmetry in their price behaviour; that is, prices are no less flexible downwards than upwards. When firms face a high level of inventories, they are just as likely to cut their prices as they are to raise their prices when inventories are too low.

2.3 Evidence from Disaggregated Prices Studies

The most thorough study of the behaviour of prices during periods of recession has been published by Cagan (1975). Using approximately 1,100 BLS wholesale price series for 1947–70, he demonstrated that in each succeeding recession since the Second World War there was a tendency for a smaller average decline in prices. The pattern is especially clear when the rate of price change in a recession is regarded as a decline from the rate of price increase in the immediately preceding expansion. The important question is whether the distribution of recession rates of price change differs between classes of industries with different levels of concentration ratio. Cagan's results are unequivocal for all recessions except the 1969–70 period. The average decrease in the rate of price change has been greater for less concentrated industries. In the 1969–70 recession the average price of the high concentration group increased less than the mean price of the intermediate group, but both average rates increased, whereas the average rate for the least concentrated group declined relative to the preceding expansion.

There are two principal points to be noted in connection with Cagan's study:
1. The responsiveness of all prices to recessions declined during the post-Second World War period.
2. The prices in less concentrated industries were more responsive than the prices in more concentrated industries.

The evidence seems to favour the view that all prices have become less responsive to a decline in aggregate demand. Wachtel and Adelsheim's (1977) results imply that, even if cost changes are taken into account, the conclusion reached by Cagan on the growing downward inflexibility of prices in successive recessions is reaffirmed.

An examination of the empirical evidence of other disaggregated studies suggests several important conclusions:

1. Factor costs, such as wage rates and material prices, are the dominant determinants of industry price changes. The importance of factor costs is overwhelmingly supported by cross-sectional and time-series studies. This finding is consistent with studies of aggregate price behaviour.
2. Prices are generally much less sensitive to demand changes than to cost changes.
3. Pricing behaviour is related to the level of industry concentration. Although costs are important determinants of prices in all industries, the influence of demand varies considerably among industries. Short-run demand changes have an effect on price changes in the competitive industries. In contrast, the long-run trend of aggregate demand influences prices in more concentrated industries. This implies that a short-run decline in demand can be expected to have a minimal effect on many industry prices. This finding of disaggregate studies may explain why the demand variable has often been found insignificant in aggregate price equations.
4. Prices are often perversely affected by a decline in demand; that is, a type of compensatory pricing behaviour seems to have occurred in some industries.
5. An important conclusion is that the structure of the economy changed in the 1960s towards domination of costs on prices. This is manifested in the upward shift in the distribution of price changes; there is less downward flexibility of prices in recessions. In the most recent recessions wholesale prices have not generally fallen.

From the evidence presented here it seems that prices have been subject to sluggish adjustment in the post-war period. However, the degree and pervasiveness of price adjustment vary considerably over time, markets, industries and countries. The response to a change in demand in the short run, however, is mainly to adjust output and to a much smaller extent prices. The questions that arise are: Why is there such asymmetry in the response of prices and quantities in a majority of industries? Has the market structure, such as the degree of concentration, some relationship with price inflexibility? And how do the various degrees of price inflexibility in different markets, for whatever reason, lead to aggregate price level inflexibility? These are some of the questions we shall attempt to address below.

3 THE THEORETICAL RATIONALE FOR PRICE INFLEXIBILITY

There is a variety of theoretical rationales to explain why firms are reluctant to change their prices in face of a short-term change in demand. If firms are interested in long-term profits they may equate their long-term marginal revenue to long-term marginal cost and then prices may become invariant to changes in the short run. If firms are producing multiple output they will face the problem of jointly setting prices for all of their product. The cost associated with price adjustments may induce the firms to have a stable price policy even if the demand for the individual product fluctuates. Firms may be interested in goals other than profit maximisation, such as increasing market share, a stable profit margin or target rate of return on investment. In such cases firms may want to change their prices infrequently. It is not possible here to present all the theoretical arguments and evidence for why prices are inflexible. We shall discuss some of the main theoretical models put forward to rationalise why price inertia may arise from an optimising behaviour.

3.1 Industrial Structure and Price Behaviour

One of the most important structural features of the Western industrial economies is the difference between individual industries in the extent to which particular markets are dominated by one or a few large sellers. The traditional view has relied on the difference in the discretionary power over the price as the main explanation of the differences in the pricing behaviour between oligopolistic and competitive industries. Thus prices in competitive markets are supposed to arise out of interaction between market demand and supply, whereas prices in oligopolistic industries are set by some implicit collusive agreement between the few oligopolistic firms dominating the industry.

The notion of differential price behaviour in concentrated and unconcentrated industries was first raised by Means (1962). He advanced the 'administered price' thesis, which holds that administrative control over prices in markets where there are relatively small numbers of firms results in less price flexibility than is found in more competitive markets; prices in concentrated industries tend to fall less than competitive prices during periods of recession and to rise less than the market-determined prices during expansionary periods.

Studies attempting to verify or reject Means's hypothesis have been basically empirical, with little theoretical explanation of the process underlying the differential pricing behaviour of the concentrated and unconcentrated industries. The usual criticism of the traditional view has centred on the lack of an explicit price determination mechanism in both types of industries. In the absence of a Walrasian auctioneer, it is not clear how prices in the competitive markets are in fact 'made' as a result of the interaction of supply and demand. On the other hand, theories of oligopolistic pricing have been generally *ad hoc* and lack rigorous theoretical foundations (Frydman and Nadiri, 1977). However, recent studies have clarified to some extent the basic issues involved and have led to a more sophisticated understanding of the possible relationship between industrial structure and pricing behaviour.

Phelps and Winter (1970) have developed an atomistic competition made of price behaviour. In a significant departure from traditional analysis, the authors assume that each atomistic firm is in a position of a transient monopolist and is a price setter. Due to imperfect and costly information as to the currently set prices, the result will be not one price in the competitive market, but a distribution of prices. Thus, each firm will not lose its customers instantaneously when it raises its price above the average of competitors' prices and will also not attract a substantial number of customers at the instant in which it lowers its prices below the average of market prices. The firm will fix its price according to standard theory of price settings under monopoly conditions, with the significant difference that it will have to take explicitly into account the cost of setting the price which is different from the mean industry price. The Phelps–Winter model replaces the fiction of the Walrasian auctioneer with an explicit account of price setting under conditions of atomistic competition. The recent advance in the theory of disequilibrium pricing suggested by F. Fisher (1981) and others, also substantiates the rationale of inertia or the relative inflexibility of prices in the competitive industries.

From the point of view of our discussion, the importance of the Phelps–Winter model lies in the apparent blurring of the distinction between oligopolistic and competitive pricing behaviour. The differential pricing behaviour is dependent on the degree of response of rivals. It is important to note the information aspects of price setting that underlie price information in *all* markets (Frydman and Nadiri, 1977). This, however, does not lead to the conclusion that prices in oligopolistic and competitive industries are set in the same way. The crucial difference lies in the likelihood of collusion among firms in a given industry. Stigler (1964) has argued that when the number of sellers is lower, the ability to detect price cutters is much stronger and a collusive agreement easier to maintain. This argument provides an essential link between the likelihood of collusion among firms and the degree of industry concentration. Recently Phlips (1980) has derived a price rule which links price behaviour to the parameters representing market structure, degree of co-operation among firms and the possibility of entry. It is shown that price rigidities can result from an intertemporal optimising behaviour. The optimal path of the firm's price rule is obtained from an intertemporal price discrimination model where firms accumulate inventories and the possibility of entry exists. The industry price equation takes the following form:

$$P = \left(\frac{\delta}{m+\delta}\right)\alpha + \left(\frac{m}{m+\delta}\right)\bar{k} - \left(\frac{\delta m}{m+\delta}\right)\Psi \frac{\partial h}{\partial P}\frac{\partial P}{\partial Q}$$

where δ reflects the degree of co-operation among firms in the industry, m is the number of firms, α is the slope of the linear industry demand schedule, k is the average normalised marginal cost, while

$$\Psi \frac{\partial h}{\partial P}\frac{\partial P}{\partial Q}$$

is the average cost (or loss of profit) due to entry. It is likely that the degree of co-operation δ will depend on the degree of concentration, m. Also, barrier to entry represented by

$$\Psi \frac{\partial h}{\partial P}\frac{\partial P}{\partial Q}$$

should have a positive effect on industry price, and the better the co-operation among firms (for given m) then the larger is δ and the stronger is the negative impact of the threat of entry on price. Other implications of this model are as follows: in more concentrated industries cost increases are less fully transmitted into prices than in less concentrated industries; changes in demand are transmitted more fully into prices in concentrated industries than in more competitive industries; for a given industry structure an increase in industry demand will have a smaller impact on prices than an increase in average marginal normalised costs. These are testable hypotheses, and Phlips' empirical results for a select group of industries in Belgium, the Netherlands and France confirm them. Particularly costs turn out to be the dominant factors affecting prices in different categories of industries and the barrier to entry has a highly significant positive effect on prices.

An important question is to substantiate whether there is a link between the likelihood of collusion among firms and the degree of industry concentration. We noted Stigler's (1964) argument in favour of this proposition. However, to establish its validity, it is important to show whether collusion among firms leads to higher long-term profits. Some evidence is provided by the studies of the relationship between concentration and profits. Weiss (1974) concludes on the basis of an extensive survey of empirical evidence that, 'The bulk of the studies show a significant positive effect of concentration of profits or margins'. Since implicit co-operation is usually found in concentrated industries, these findings imply that collusion seems to be profitable for co-operating firms.

But how does the process work? Ross and Wachter (1975) provide an explanation for an observation that firms in oligopolistic industries act so as to maintain fixed pricing strategies (although not necessarily or generally fixed prices), which they alter at regular points of time. The interval of time in which the pricing strategy is unchanged is called the planning period. Thus their model is not an explanation of price determination under oligopoly, but it provides an analysis of timing of price changes in concentrated industries. They assume that the firms are denied a possibility of outright collusion and that particular equilibrium industry structure has developed. The implication of this equilibrium is that none of the firms or any coalition of firms, bound by the implicit collusive agreement, views it to be in their interest to alter the equilibrium structure. As the demand and supply conditions of the industry change, then in deciding on whether or not to adjust to the new developments, the firm is forced to balance the loss of profits due to an inappropriate price structure against the potential profit loss if an attempt to alter prices should lead to a breakdown in the level of oligopoly co-operation.

The significance of Ross–Wachter's model lies in its applicability to a wide variety of market structures. The firms in the competitive industries will respond continuously to changes in market conditions, since the atomistic firms find it impossible to collude and therefore will not face the trade-off between benefits of collusion and losses due to inappropriate price structure. On the other hand, the firms in oligopolistic industries will move in discrete time intervals. The conclusion regarding competitive firms should be modified, however, to take account of the factors elaborated in the Phelps–Winter model, i.e. informational structure of the market would cause firms in the competitive markets to respond, also in discrete time intervals.

3.2 Inventory and Price Stickiness

A firm's profit-maximising inventory strategy may also cause the firm to react differently to a change in demand depending on whether the firm perceives the change to be transitory or permanent. The assumption about the demand fluctuation is essential in models which link inventory decisions and price inflexibility. Since demand fluctuates randomly around a given mean, the firms respond to these fluctuations by changing their level of inventories because they cannot instantaneously adjust their prices or outputs. The inventory change is followed in the next period by a change in the rate of production to restore their equilibrium inventory stocks while leaving their prices unchanged. Kawasaki *et al.* (1983) construct a model of dynamic profit maximisation under uncertainty and imperfect competition to derive an analogue of a repeated Cournot equilibrium framework. Using such an analytical framework they demonstrate that firms change their output in response to *any* demand change but change their prices in response to only permanent demand changes. Blinder (1982) reaches similar conclusions, though using a different analytical framework: both prices and output respond less to a transitory demand stock than to a permanent demand change and prices will become sticky when inventories can be stored without much cost and when the demand shocks are transitory. In both of these models the existence of inventories reduced the flexibility of prices in all states of demand and in both directions. In fact, the empirical results reported by Kawasaki *et al.* (1982), as was noted earlier, suggest no evidence of an asymmetrical response of prices, i.e. prices are less flexible downwards than upwards.

Note that these models provide an explanation of the relative price inflexibility and not sluggish absolute prices. However, changes in relative prices can affect the rate of inflation (see Fischer, 1982). The models described here can be modified to relate firms' price decisions to their expectations about aggregate price expectations or demand fluctuation. If the mean of the firms' demand functions stated above shifts, a new equilibrium emerges, with each firm having a new target inventory stock and perhaps a new price. This can arise if firms form expectations about future changes in aggregate demand or general price levels and use them as indicators of how the mean of the individual demand functions will shift. This will lead to the possibility of linking the sluggishness of relative prices and absolute prices, as shown by Rotemberg (1982) and Gordon (1981).

3.3 Adjustment in Changing Prices

The degree of price inflexibility in econometric price equations is measured by the coefficient of the lagged price variable. The estimates of this coefficient imply that firms incur costs for not being able to change their price readily. The partial adjustments of prices in these equations are mainly *ad hoc*, in the same way as the adjustment lags were postulated in econometric investment functions prior to the advent of the cost of adjustment models. If the firms know the costs involved in adjusting their prices in face of a changed demand condition, it is logical for them to take these costs into account in their optimisation behaviour. The adjustment costs for changing prices are due to the administrative cost of changing the price lists and similar matters, and, more importantly, due to the potential unfavourable reaction of consumers to frequent price changes. Rotemberg (1982) has developed an interesting equilibrium model of monopolistic price adjustment with the cost of price adjustment explicitly taken into account. The model is like the Lucas (1972) equilibrium model of business cycle and incorporates the Phelps–Winter type of monopolistic pricing behaviour. Firms optimise their objective function taking the prices set by other firms as given; they make the best full use of the current information – that is, they form their expectations rationally. The firms produce differentiated products; they observe their demand and cost functions before setting their prices; they know the prices of their suppliers, the price level and the level of aggregate nominal money balances. The cost to changing prices is assumed to be a function of the square of the price change, and the monopolists set their prices optimally, given that it is costly to change them. Rotemberg shows that, in the presence of adjustment costs, changing prices today will affect tomorrow's profit, and the pricing rule for the firm will be the usual partial adjustment equation used in most empirical studies, namely:

$$P_{it} = \gamma P_{it-1} + (1 - \gamma) P^*_{it}$$

where P^*_{it} is the expectation formed by firm i of its optimal price; p_i depends on the cost of changing prices, say c; and ρ the discount rate. When c increases price increases, i.e. it will take longer for current prices to adjust towards their long-run value. The effect of changes in ρ on speed of adjustment is ambiguous; a decrease in ρ makes it relatively cheaper to change prices in the future, but it also penalises the monopolists relatively more for current deviations of actual prices from their long-run values.

If each firm picks its own P^*_{it} optimally, given the prices charged by other firms, and expects its decision not to influence the path of aggregate variables, such as the stock of money or the aggregate price level, then Rotemberg shows that the industry equilibrium can be established and an aggregate price equation analogous to the one stated above can be derived, namely:

$$P_t = \lambda P_{t-1} + (1 - \lambda) P^*_t$$

where P^*_t is the price level 'desired' at t, and λ is the partial adjustment coefficient of aggregate price level. This type of equation is often used to estimate the aggregate price level (Gordon, 1981; Nadiri and Gupta, 1977). The virtue of Rotemberg's model is that it derives the partial adjustment price equations for both individual and aggregate prices from an optimisation model; links the parameters of the aggregate and individual price equations; and develops a cost of adjustment model of prices based on rational expectations in which producers are aware of their true trading opportunities and of information in aggregate statistics concerning the present.

3.4 Uncertainty and Price Inflexibility

Production is essentially a dynamic phenomenon, i.e. it takes time and therefore is subject to uncertainty. Firms may take different steps to reduce uncertainty. In a world of dynamic uncertainty firms will perform intertemporal arbitrage. The market variation is met only in part by market adjustment in sales and the remainder is met by the firms' internal adjustment in inventory and to a lesser degree in production. In a world of static certainty, when the market is purely competitive through price and the entry and exit of firms, the market adjusts to variation in demand and supply. When the firm faces an uncertain market environment and a multi-period decision horizon, price flexibility may not be a necessary condition for the efficient allocation of resources (Wu, 1979). A stable price will have certain benefits both to the sellers and buyers: it will cut the search costs of buyers from the firm and eliminate the necessity for buyers to accumulate a precautionary inventory to guard against price uncertainty. These factors may encourage buyers to buy more at a given price or pay more for a given quantity of goods in exchange for a reduction in price uncertainty. This could mean a higher demand put to sellers. On the other hand, any price cut could be construed in most industries as an attempt to obtain a larger market share which will be resisted by rivals and may lead to lower revenue for the seller.

Another way to mitigate the haphazard results of uncertainty in a world where production takes time is the use of a contract (Davidson, 1977). The wage contract, implicit or explicit, is the most pervasive agreement in the economy. If it were constantly revised and recontracted, the transaction cost would be so high that it would likely inhibit production in a decentralised market economy. To a lesser degree the same argument applies to other types of costs and products. When contracts are taken into consideration, then the past and future of economic activities becomes part of the economic process and provides the element of inertia, i.e. the overlapping labour contract as a source of inflexibility of prices. This is because if money wages are determined outside the theoretical market system over the forthcoming three-year interval, then prices will adjust to money wages rather the converse.

The inflexibility of wages arises from a number of factors. The most widely accepted is based on the behaviour of unions, where collective bargaining introduces lags in wage response of some industries. In the absence of unions firms may want to pay premium wages in order to have a queue of available skilled labour, and therefore the firms will not change wages immediately as labour conditions change (Wachter, 1976). Also, firms may desire an ongoing relationship with their labour force, especially if the jobs are idiosyncratic in nature and require specific skills and training. The wages for these type of jobs will be determined by the internal wage structure, and the short-run market forces will be ignored in this situation.

3.5 Heterogeneity of Markets and Price Inertia

A number of models have been proposed which emphasise the diversity and heterogeneity of different markets as the source of inertia of the aggregate price level. The basic notion is that the economy is composed of a variety of markets with different characteristics and different rules of behaviour. Sticky prices may be a rational outcome in certain markets in the economy which in turn may impart the price inertia at the aggregate level. Arthur Okun, W. Nordhaus and R. J. Gordon have discussed various aspects of how models of heterogeneous markets may lead to price inertia at the aggregate level.

The Okun (1981) model is based on a 'contract-theoretic' framework and states that in order to economise on transaction costs with one another, economic agents will trade repeatedly with each other. Wages and price behaviour are explained in a search-theoretic framework. In markets with heterogeneous products prices tend to be inflexible because information about prices is difficult to obtain and there is a continuing relationship between the buyer and seller. The transaction costs are very high and price stability is in the interest of both parties. In these types of markets, called 'customer markets', both customers and producers have an interest in stable prices. The customers would like to avoid an excessive search cost and are willing to pay a premium to do business with customary suppliers. Firms have an incentive in stable prices to encourage customers to return, using yesterday's prices as a guide. But if permanent changes in demand and costs have accrued and both the customers and firms have this knowledge, prices could change without inducing customers to do comparison shopping. Price stability is considered as a service in Okun's model, which is a complete reversal of Means's model of administered prices noted earlier. The auction, or what we called liquid markets, clears instantaneously and there is no incentive to induce long-term contractual arrangements, infrequent price changes and quantity rationing. In markets with homogeneous products information flows rapidly and the market mechanism is impersonal.

Nordhaus (1976) elaborates further on this line of thinking. The economy can be divided into 'auction' and 'administered' markets. In the auction markets competitive supply and demand forces prevail and prices are flexible. In the administered markets either buyers or sellers have significant market power, and one use of that power has been to restrain price movements. Prices and wages are set in these markets on some principle of 'normal pricing', that is, cyclical fluctuations are largely removed in setting prices and wages. The effect of demand on aggregate price will be fairly weak and there will be what Nordhaus calls the 'momentum effect'. Demand changes affect prices through three channels: through the mark-up in the administered market prices equation, through unemployment in the wage equation, and from 'auction' markets. The combination of these forces, due to non-linearities, are likely to be weak at low levels of demand but high when the economy operates at capacity. The 'momentum effect' of current and past wages and prices in the administered markets of the economy dominates their short-term movements. The effect of demand policies will be small in the initial stage but would be spread out over a long period. The third effect comes from the auction prices which may be due to such factors as oil price increases, increases in commodity prices, changes in weather, speculation, etc. If these changes are significant, then, as Bruno and Sachs (1982) have shown, input price shocks can affect aggregate prices significantly.

An elaborate model of price behaviour is outlined by Gordon (1981). No adjustment costs are formally included in the analysis but the emphasis is put on the diversity of circumstances facing firms in different markets and the cost of communication and co-ordination through a complex input-output network of relationships among firms. Firms may face diverse sets of circumstances in various markets. They may have distinct technologies, produce heterogeneous products, discover information about changes in their own demand and costs and the aggregate demand and cost changes with different degrees of certainty. The learning capacity of firms usually differs (Frydman, 1981), i.e. there may be long lags in the formation of expectations (Maccini, 1981). What emerges in Gordon's model is the crucial role of the local vs aggregate components of demand and costs, that is, on the one hand, the ratio of the variance of local to the sum of variances of local and aggregate components of demand shift and, on the other hand, the ratio of the local to the sum of the local and aggregate components of costs. These ratios are likely to be zero in periods of war and hyperinflation, when there is extreme pressure for prices to change; the variance of the aggregate components of demand and costs will dominate in such periods and individual prices will respond immediately to changes in aggregate demand and costs.

A further extension of the idea that the network of input–output or stages of production matter in pricing behaviour of firms has been developed recently by Blanchard (1983). Some of the simplifying assumptions are that production is instantaneous, all goods are perishable, input supply is an increasing function of its real price, output demand depends positively on real money balances, and money is neutral and affects only the level of all prices. Firms choose their relative prices every two periods and their prices depend on current and expected input prices for the next two periods. Assuming rational expectations and uncertainty, Blanchard shows that if the firm's price decisions are not completely synchronised, the price level will depend on three elements: the actual and expected past input prices, the actual value and past expectations of current input prices, and both past and current expectations of input prices. As the number of stages of production increases, so does the dependence of the price level on input prices further back in the past and expected in the future. The price level will react less and adjust more slowly to changes in money if real input prices are insensitive to market conditions. An increase in money affects the structure of prices: prices early in the chain of production move more and adjust faster; prices further in the chain move less and adjust more slowly. When a nominal disturbance requires a change in the price level, a likely consequence is a change in the complex structure of prices of final goods, intermediate goods and inputs. These adjustments will not be taken continuously nor in the same manner in different markets or industries. Thus the desynchronisation of individual price decisions can generate price level inertia observed at the aggregate economy or industry level.

There is some empirical evidence to suggest that the response of prices at stages of process to a change in demand differ substantially. The model of stage of process developed by Popkin in (1977) links the movements of crude, intermediate and finished goods components of the Wholesale Price Index with each other and with the Consumer Price Index. The results of the twenty-one sector price model, when viewed as a whole, suggest that it is in the primary and semi-finished goods industries, rather than in the finished goods-producing and distributing sectors, that changes in demand affect the relationship between the output and input prices. The initial response in the finished goods industries is to reduce output and not prices. Cutbacks in orders for materials and supplies placed by these industries are often larger than they would be if prices had been flexible. The fluctuations in output are much larger at the earlier stage than at the later stage of production. Also, the ratio of price of output to the weighted price of inputs behaves not procyclically in the finished goods sectors, while for the primary and semi-finished products it moves procyclically. In response to a cut-back in orders from the finished product manufacturers, the prices in the primary product manufacturing industries weaken. Such weakness then feeds forward to final demand prices, with a lag, affecting prices in all finished manufacturing and service sectors. Thus the amplitude of output and price responses to changes in final demand vary considerably among different stages of production, and there is a dynamic relationship in the response pattern through the input-output structure of the economy.

4 ASYMMETRICAL PRICE INCREASE

We have noted that no only have most prices become less responsive to a decline in aggregate demand, but they may also rise in a recession. What can explain this perverse behaviour? There are several reasons why this phenomenon can occur.

Under the conditions of monopoly the traditional theoretical explanation for rigidity of prices in the presence of contraction in demand is based on the difference between short- and long-run price elasticity of demand. Since the short-run elasticity of demand is less than the long-run elasticity, and in many cases must be less than one, a monopolist considering a price cut to deal with a temporary recession would face a possibly negative marginal revenue, compared to the marginal revenue it would face in making general price policy. The natural conclusion seems to be that optimal price policy in a recession would often be to hold prices stable or to change them only in response to changes in long-run expectations.

This reasoning has some relevance to the explanation of the price inflexibility of oligopolistic prices during recessions. Spence, (1976) has suggested the concept of market share equilibrium and shown that there exists a set of market shares such that no firm can increase its profits if all others react by maintaining their market share. In this framework market shares serve as basis of strategic interaction among firms in oligopolistic industry. Suppose now that the fall in industry demand affects all firms proportionately so they continue to be in market share equilibrium. It is clear that if industry demand becomes inelastic, the firm would not find it profitable to lower its prices given that other firms will react to maintain their market shares. Lowering of the price by one individual firm may be considered by other firms as 'competitive' price cutting and lead to the breakdown of implicit collusive agreements and the loss of benefits associated with such agreements. Moreover, considerable uncertainty will exist as to the true value of the industry's price elasticity of demand. Therefore, it is very likely that known benefits of implicit collusion will outweigh highly uncertain benefits of contemplated price reduction. On the other hand, if costs rise during the recession because of the 'momentum effect' built into past contracts, the firm will be likely to pass on these costs without any danger of retaliation from its competitors. Cost increases are likely to be experienced by all the firms in the oligopolistic industry where firms are likely to follow a normal pricing decision rule with respect to the prices of inputs and outputs.

Another rationale for asymmetric pricing behaviour is suggested by Kuran (1983). He argues that the prices of monopolistic firms with non-increasing price elasticity of demand and non-increasing marginal costs can be relatively more rigid downwards than upwards. Such firms raise their prices to a greater extent when they expect inflation than they lower them when they expect an equivalent reduction in demand. In response to an increase in price level uncertainty, these firms will increase their prices. These results follow from the notion that the monopolist's loss is greater from charging a price below the monopoly price than the loss from charging above it by a proportionately equivalent amount. A price cut may trigger a reaction from competitors, while an increase in prices may not.

To show that relative price variability can be linked to variation in the rate of inflation requires that prices respond asymmetrically to disturbances. If prices behave asymmetrically in either direction, the association between relative prices and the rate of inflation can be established, but it cannot be established if prices are equally sticky in recessionary and expansionary phases of the business cycle. Fischer's (1982) results indicate that there is a strong link between unanticipated inflation and relative price variability for both the US and Germany. There are weaker links between the variation of relative prices and the rate of inflation. Unanticipated inflation was found to affect relative price variability much more than a deflation, suggesting support for the asymmetric price response hypothesis.

But why should many firms in the competitive industry raise prices when demand falls? The only conceivable circumstance is the perception of the decrease in the short-run elasticity of demand coupled with increases in the marginal costs of firms in the competitive industry. In such a case, if properly perceived by individual firms, the proper profit-maximising response is to increase, not decrease, prices. Since the firm contemplating the price change will be highly uncertain as to the price elasticity of demand for its product, but will be able to observe the increases in its costs, it might decide to increase its price. If all firms perceive the situation in this way the fall in demand will be mostly reflected in the output changes.

The overall conclusion from the above reasoning is that when contraction of demand is accompanied by increases in direct costs, the rational response of both competitive and oligopolistic firms might be to raise prices. This phenomenon will be considerably strengthened if the firms in both oligopolistic and competitive industries expect the contraction in demand to be temporary, while cost increases are perceived to be permanent. It is also clear that due to the element of implicit collusion in oligopolistic industries, the increase in prices should be more widely observed in more concentrated industries.

An interesting explanation of this perverse behaviour of prices is provided by Cagan (1979). If the anticipated trend of prices is upward and price changes over the cycle are the cyclical deviations from the trend, then prices will rise in the recession, though less than the trend. The long trend in prices can be subject to rational expectations. This anticipation factor will be incorporated in the contract prices of inputs, or some input supplies will be withheld from the market. Thus the anticipated rise in the price trend can limit the decline of prices in the recession and may cause prices to rise if the anticipated trend is rising fast enough. But the anticipated price trend will be revised by rational agents depending on the severity and duration of current and past business cycles.

5 INTERNATIONAL COMPETITION AND PRICING BEHAVIOUR

In the previous sections we have examined pricing behaviour across industries in the domestic economy. A number of the industries considered produce goods that are sold in foreign markets. In many industries foreign firms have a significant share of the domestic markets. Moreover, many industries use inputs that are traded internationally. Therefore, the developments in the world markets, trade patterns and currency fluctuations have a potentially important role in understanding pricing adjustment in domestic industries. Unfortunately, no systematic theoretical and empirical analysis of price formation seems to exist for industries producing exportable or import-competing goods. Therefore the discussion in this section will necessarily be limited to a few observations on the possible significance of these issues.

We noted earlier that barriers to entry could play an important role in the pricing behaviour of firms. Competition in the world market could have the same effect as the entry of a competitor in the domestic economy. For example, Wachtel and Adelsheim (1977) have argued that in the US automobile industry, foreign competition provides an extraordinary intense competitive check on what had traditionally been a mature oligopoly with routinised pricing behaviour. Due to this competition, price increases for domestically produced cars have been restrained and price mark-ups in the automobile industry have declined in recent years.

Even though similar calculations have not been performed for other industries, the potentially significant effect of imports can be inferred by noting that between 1960 and 1970 imports increased in high-concentration industries by the following percentages: machinery and transportation equipment, 662 per cent; rubber tyres and tubes, 876 per cent; iron and steel mill products, 352 per cent. These developments suggest caution in the use of concentration ratios as a basis for studying price behaviour across industries. In the presence of a substantial volume of imports, the concentration ratios might significantly overstate the degree of market power or the possibility of implicit price co-ordination in domestic industries (Frydman and Nadiri, 1977).

As we noted earlier, material costs are generally very significant in explaining industry price behaviour. Since many raw materials are traded internationally, it is clear that domestic prices will be strongly affected by the conditions in the world commodity markets. Also, the effect of changes in the exchange rate, in addition to having an effect on import prices, will have an effect on the domestic prices of import-competing goods.

Some empirical results are available on the role played by changes in import prices and particularly the recent increase in material prices. Nordhaus and Shoven (1977) have broken down the rate of inflation of 58 sectors in the US economy during 1972–4 into its components. They have considered the effect of acceleration in agricultural prices, the rise in mining and domestic fuel prices, import price increases, and increases in labour costs. Several results stand out. First, the contribution of these components varies considerably in different sectors: in some, import prices dominate; in a few, the rise in agricultural prices stands out; while in some others the labour cost increase seems to be the major component of the sectoral inflation rates. Second, about 85 per cent of the inflation was explained by the passing on of increases in commodity prices and wages, suggesting the dominance of costs in price behaviour. Third, there were shifts in the composition of the inflation over the two-year period 1972–4. In the early parts of the period wage increases constituted the major contributory factor to inflation, while the prices of agricultural products accounted for two-thirds of the inflation from November 1972 to August 1973; imports contributed about 16 per cent to inflation in this period. In the last part of the 1973–4 period imports dominated the picture. Thirty-six per cent of total inflation was due to a rise in import prices, and the price rise of domestic crude oil and natural gas contributed significantly to inflation in this period.

Grubb et al. (1982) explore the causes of stagflation in nineteen OECD countries and estimate the contribution of the slowdown in productivity growth, the unfavourable trends in relative import prices and the higher level of unemployment. They show that, in the average OECD country, relative import prices made inflation in 1980 5 per cent higher than it would have been if import prices had continued their pre-1973 trend. Lower productivity growth had an equal effect in raising inflation. These two effects were offset by the consequences of higher unemployment measured as a deviation from its trend. Bruno and Sachs (1982) have also argued that input price shocks can lead to a decline in growth of output and productivity, real wages and capital accumulation. When real wages are sticky these effects are greatly magnified, leading to greater unemployment and a decline in output. With real wage inertia, profitability is reduced significantly by the rise in input prices, and investment tends to become sharply reduced. Their empirical analysis suggests that recent sharp increases in material prices have been a major contributor to the increase in the rate of inflation in most of the OECD countries. Since materials are a major component of the imports in these countries, the exogenous increase in prices of materials and oil since

1973 was one of the major factors in the stagflation of Western economies.

6 CONCLUDING REMARKS

In this paper we have looked at some empirical evidence on price inflexibility and presented some of the theoretical bases for why price stability, in the face of a decrease in short-run demand, may be an outcome of rational maximisation behaviour. The response of firms to uncertainty, the cost of adjusting prices, the contents of long-term contracts (explicit or implicit) in the goods and input markets, and the extent and variability of excess demand may differ among firms and industries. The structure of the industry, the degree of heterogeneity of the products in a market, the network of input-output relationships among industries, the nature of international competition, and the process of formation of expectations of shocks from monetary and fiscal policies and input price increases, may all interact and create the ever-changing environment of firms. There is a continual interplay of institutional forces, market arrangements and cultural factors and customs that govern the behaviour of firms, together with government policies and macroeconomic forces, which will result in price rigidities in the short run. These rigidities will evolve over time and will vary across different markets, industries or countries. In the long run the institutions and market arrangements will also change when they are no longer useful.

In the presence of price rigidities, the conventional monetary and fiscal restraint can achieve price stability at a cost of high unemployment. This would result from the momentum of built-in lags in costs and from people forming their expectations by extrapolating past rates of inflation. The cost of restraining inflation could be fairly substantial, as recently documented by Gordon (1982b). On the other hand, there is convincing evidence that monetary and fiscal restraints have been very successful in reversing the inflationary spiral in the hyperinflation experienced by a number of countries in the early 1920s (Sargent, 1982). The cause of such hyperinflation may have been due to the excess increase of money and people's expectations that the government would accomodate the inflationary developments. To end the hyperinflation governments were forced to adopt the dramatic new strategy of a co-ordinated set of policies. An abrupt change in government policies and an effective enforcement of the new legislation were the prerequisites for ending the hyperinflation. Although there are no specific estimates of the costs of such anti-inflationary policies, it seems they did not lead to any widespread unemployment, as is implied in the models discussed in this paper.

In hyperinflationary situations the transaction costs of holding money are so high that all contracts expressed in money terms become excessively burdensome and the length of contracts dramatically shrinks; the distortive effects of high inflation on incentives could lead to disorientation of the business and consumers, the distribution of income and wealth gets distorted, and finally the self-generating nature of inflationary expectations become very much understood by the public and the government. In such situations the government will receive a mandate to follow dramatic anti-inflationary policies to break the inflationary expectations and put the economy on a stable course. However, at low rates of inflation a consensus often does not exist for decisive action. In democratic societies, governments will not have the ability to sustain anti-inflationary policies for too long and with sufficient force to achieve growth with stable prices. The central point to stress is that the ability of governments to combat inflationary expectations is endogenous in the system. There is a non-linear relationship between the costs of inflation, the ability of the government to pursue effective and anti-inflationary policies, and the public's acceptance of the necessary adjustments.

What kind of policy options are open in an economy with moderate rates of inflation which exhibits, in the short run, price inflexibility for the reasons described in this paper? This is a very difficult question and would require considerable analysis and space beyond the scope of this paper. A few such options can be mentioned here, but only briefly. If the price inflexibility is partly due to imperfect and costly information or its uneven distribution and utilisation, then such a market failure can be corrected with timely and relevant information provided by policy-makers and by the emergence of firms that could make the needed information available. If the problem is partly due to overlapping wage contracts and institutional rigidities in other markets, or if it is due to the unsynchronised nature of the pricing decision, then the possibility of success in the short run is not encouraging. Only a consistent policy targeted at the disaggregated industry levels and sustained for a number of years might dampen the effects of these structural forces.

If the price inflexibility is partly in response to uncertainty and an inability to determine precisely the changes in aggregate demand, then governmental policies should attempt to minimise potential disturbances by avoiding erratic and sizeable shifts in its monetary and fiscal policies. The government could promote policies to lessen the degree of concentration in domestic markets and encourage international competition to dampen the potential effects of monopoly power on prices. But it must also reach international agreements to stabilise prices of inputs such as raw materials, which can exert a significant effect on the level of prices when the domestic prices are inflexible. Promoting increases in productivity and technical change may be one of the important ways to lower the rate of inflation and reduce price inflexibility. Further, the price structure of government services and the effect of governmental regulations on price behaviour must be examined carefully, for they may impart significant inflexibility to the price structure.

REFERENCES

Blanchard, O. J. (983) 'Price Desynchronisation and Price Level Inertia', National Bureau of Economic Research Working Paper Number 900.

Blinder, A. (1982) 'Inventories and Sticky Prices: More on the Microfoundations of Macroecomomics', *American Economic Review*, vol. 72, no. 3, pp. 33448.

Bruno, M. and Sachs, J. (1982) 'Input Price Shocks and the Slowdown in Economic Growth: the Case of UK Manufacturing', *Review of Economic Studies*, vol. 49, no. 5, pp. 679–705.

Cagan, P. (1975) 'Changes in the Recession Behaviour of Wholesale Prices in the 1920's and Post-World War II', Occasional Paper of the National Bureau of Economic Research.

Cagan, P. (1979) *Persistent Inflation: Historical and Policy Essays*, (New York: Columbia University Press), pp. 227–52.

Carlton, D. (1979) 'Contracts, Price Rigidity, and Market Equilibrium', *Journal of Political Economy*, vol. 87, no. 5, Part I, pp. 1,034–62.

Carlton, D. (1982) 'The Disruptive Effect of Inflation on the Organisation of Markets' in Hall, R. E. (ed.) *Inflation: Causes and Effects* (Chicago: Chicago University Press for NBER) pp. 139–52.

Coutts, K., Godley, W. and Nordhaus, W. (1978) *Industrial Pricing in the United Kingdom* (Cambridge, NY: Columbia University Press).

Davidson, P. (1977) 'Post-Keynes Monetary Theory and Inflation', in S. Weintraub (ed.) *Modern Economic Thought* (Philadelphia: University of Pennsylvannia Press), pp. 275–93.

Eckstein, O. and Fromm, G. (1968) 'The Price Equation', *American Economic Review*, vol. 58, pp. 1159–83.

Eckstein, O. and Wyss, P. (1971) 'Industry Price Equations', in Eckstein (ed.) *The Econometrics of Price Determination* (Washington: Publication Services, Division of Administrative Services, Board of Governors & Federal Revenue System), pp. 133–56.

Fischer, S. (1982) 'Relative Price Variability and Inflation in US and Germany', *European Economy Review*, vol. 18, no. 2, May-June, pp. 171–96.

Fisher, F. M. (1981) 'Stability, Disequilibrium Awareness and the Perception of New Opportunities, *Econometrica*, pp. 279–317.

Frydman, R. and Nadiri, M. I. (1977) 'Price Behavior, Industrial Structure, and Inflationary Bias in the U.S. Economy', mimeo.

Frydman, R. (1981) 'Sluggish Price Adjustments and the Effectiveness of Monetary Policy Under Rational Expectations: a Comment', *Journal of Money, Credit, Banking*, vol. 13, no. 1, pp. 94–102.

Gordon, R. J. (1980) 'A Consistent Characterisation of a Near Century of Price Behavior', *American Economic Review*, vol. 70, no. 2, pp. 243–9.

Gordon, R. J. (1981) 'Output Fluctuations and Gradual Price Adjustment', *Journal of Economic Literature*, vol. 19, no. 2, pp. 493–530.

Gordon, R. J. (1982a) 'Wages and Prices Are Not Always Sticky: a Century of Evidence of US, UK and Japan', National Bureau of Economic Research working paper No. 847.

Gordon, R. J. (1982b) 'Why Stopping Inflation May be Costly: Evidence from Fourteen Historical Episodes', in R. E. Hall (ed.) *Inflation: Causes and Effects* (Chicago and London: University of Chicago Press), pp. 11–40.

Grubb, D., Jackman, R. and Layard, R. (1982) Causes of the Current Stagflation', *Review of Economic Studies*, vol. 49, no. 5, pp. 707–30.

Hay, G. (1970) 'Production, Price and Inventory Theory', *American Economic Review*, vol. 60, no. 4, pp. 531–45.

Kawasaki, S., McMillan, J. and Zimmermann, K. F. (1982) 'Disequilibrium Economics', *American Economic Review*, vol. 72, no. 5, pp. 992–1004.

Kawasaki, S. (1983)'Inventories and Price Inflexibility', *Econometrica*, vol. 51, no. 3, pp. 599–610.

Kuran, T. (1983) 'Asymmetric Price Rigidity and Inflationary Bias', *American Economic Review*, vol. 73, no. 3, pp. 373–82.

Lucas, R. E. (1972) 'Expectations and Neutrality of Money', *Journal of Economic Theory*, vol. 4, no. 2, pp. 103–24.

Maccini, L. (1981) 'Adjustment Lags, Economically Rational Expectations, and Price Behavior', *Review of Economic Statistics*, vol. 63, no. 2, pp. 213–22.

Means, G. C. (1962) 'The Administered Price Thesis Reconfirmed', *American Economic Review*, vol. 52, no. 3, pp. 292–306.

Minel, G. de (1974) 'Aggregate Price Dynamics', *Review of Economics and Statistics*, 56, pp. 129–40.

Nadiri, M. I. and Gupta, V. (1977) 'Price and Wage Behavior in the US Aggregate Economy and in Manufacturing Industries', in J. Popkin (ed.) *Analysis of Inflation: 1965–1974* (Cambridge, Mass.: Ballinger for the National Bureau of Economic Research), pp. 195–234.

Nordhaus, W. (1976) 'The Flexibility of Wages and Prices', *American Economic Review*, vol. 66, no. 2, pp. 59–64.

Nordhaus, W. and Shoven, J. (1977) 'A Technique for Analyzing and Decomposing Inflation', in J. Popkin (ed.) *Analysis of Inflation: 1965–1974*, (Cambridge, Mass.: Ballinger), pp. 333–55.

Okun, A. M. (1975) 'Inflation: Its Mechanics and Welfare Costs', *Brooking Papers on Economic Activity*, no. 2, pp. 351–401.

Okun, A. M. (1981) *Prices and Quantities: a Macroeconomic Analysis* (Washington DC: The Brookings Institution).

Phelps, E. S. and S. G. Winter, Jr (1970) 'Optimal Price Policy Under Atomistic Competition', in Phelps (ed.) *Microeconomic Foundations of Employment and Inflation Theory* (New York: Norton).

Phlips, L. (1980) 'Intertemporal Price Discrimination and Sticky Prices', *Quarterly Journal of Economics*, vol. 94, no. 3, pp. 525–542.

Popkin, J. (1977) 'An Integrated Model of Final and Intermediate Demand by Stage of Process: a Progress Report, *American Economic Review*, vol. 67, no. 1, pp. 141–7.

Ross, S. A. and Wachter, M. L. (1975) 'Pricing and Timing Decision in Oligopoly Industries', *Quarterly Journal of Economics*, vol. 89, no. 1, pp. 115–37.

Rotemberg, J. J. (1982) 'Monopolistic Price Adjustment and Aggregate Output', *Review of Economic Studies*, vol. 49, no. 4, pp. 517–31.

Sargent, T. (1982) 'The Ends of Four Big Inflations', in Hall, R. H. (ed.) *Inflation: Causes and Effects*, (Chicago and London: National Bureau of Economic Research, University of Chicago Press), pp. 41–98.

Spence, M. (1976) 'Market Shares and Tacit Co-ordination', Discussion Paper number 464, Institute of Economic Research, Harvard University.

Stigler, G. J. (1964) 'A Theory of Oligopoly', *Journal of Political Economy*, no. 72, pp. 44–61.

Stigler, G. J. and Kindahl, J. K. (1970) *The Behavior of Industrial Prices* (New York: National Bureau of Economic Research).

Wachtel, H. M. and Adelsheim, P. D. (1977) 'How Recession Feeds Inflation: Price Markups in a Concentrated Economy', *Challenge*.

Wachter, M. L. (1976) 'Some Problems in Wage Stabilization', *American Economic Review*, vol. 66, no. 2, pp. 65–71.

Weiss, L. W. (1974) 'The Concentration-Profits Relationship and Antitrust', in Goldschmid, H. J., Mann, M. H. and Weston, J. F. (eds), *Industrial Concentration: The New Learning* (Boston, Mass.: Little, Brown).

Weiss, L. W. (1977) 'Stigler–Kindahl and Means on Administered Prices', *American Economic Review*, vol. 67, no. 4, pp. 610–19.

Wu, S. T. (1979) 'An Essay on Monopoly Power and Stable Price Policy', *American Economic Review*, vol. 69, no. 2, pp. 60–72.

25 The Influence of International Price Movements and Inflation on the Centrally Planned Economies

S. Raczkowski
POLAND

Among the countries with planned economies the most important are the seven European socialist countries belonging to the Council for Mutual Economic Assistance: the USSR, Bulgaria, Czechoslovakia, the German Democratic Republic, Poland, Rumania and Hungary. In our report we shall use for them the terms 'socialist countries' and 'member countries of the CMEA'. We shall not concern ourselves with other centrally planned economies, particularly with the Asiatic ones, the Republic of Cuba or Yugoslavia, whose economic systems differ from that of the CMEA member countries.

The institutional framework of economic relations between the CMEA countries and the foreign non-CMEA countries shows many familiar common characteristics, but at the same time some individual differences. The latter arise from the different evolution of the planning and management systems in those countries. Since the late 1960s, this evolution followed the course of moderating the role of central administrative directives and of limiting the scope of centrally allocated material resources. At the same time, it strengthened the degree of decentralisation of decision-making and influenced the economy by parametric instruments of regulation, such as prices, rates of exchange, rates of interest, taxes, subsidies, etc. In some socialist countries, such as Hungary and Poland, this evolution went much further than in the others.

In investigating the influence of international price movements and of foreign inflation on the economies of socialist countries we shall first describe the extent of the foreign trade of the socialist countries and its role in their economy. We shall further consider the influence of inflationary changes in foreign prices on those countries' terms of trade, on their domestic wholesale and retail prices, and on their balances of payments. This will allow us to estimate the extent and nature of this influence during the 1970s, particularly from 1975 to 1981.

1 THE SIZE AND ROLE OF FOREIGN TRADE

The foreign trade of the seven socialist countries has already attained considerable proportions, but recently it has been developing at a slower pace than the international trend. Between 1975 and 1981, the share of those countries in world imports dropped from 9.8 to 7.8 per cent in current prices, and in world exports from 8.9 to 8.1 per cent. The size of the foreign trade of individual countries is represented, in current prices, against their population in Table 25.1.

Table 25.1 Trade and population of seven CMEA countries

Country	Population (millions)	Imports (millions of US $)		Exports (millions of US $)	
		1975	1981	1975	1981
Bulgaria	8.9	5,408	10,509	4,691	10,725
Czechoslovakia	15.3	9,077	14,727	8,356	13,699
GDR	16.7	11,290	18,933	10,088	19,909
Poland	35.9	12,545	15,476	10,289	13,294
Rumania	22.4	5,342	12,990	5,341	12,597
Hungary	10.7	7,176	9,128	6,091	8,712
Sub-total	110.5	50,838	81,760	44,856	78,891
USSR	267.7	36,971	74,000	33,316	78,360
Total	378.2	87,909	155,760	78,172	157,251

Source: *Rocznik Statystyczny*, 1982 (Warsaw), p. 551.

Table 25.1 shows that joint imports as well as joint exports of the six East European countries were always larger than those of the USSR, but their predominance in this respect was less in 1981, partially on account of the sudden decrease of Polish foreign trade in this year. Both Polish imports and exports diminished at that time.

The role of foreign trade in the economy of the lesser socialist countries is, of course, much more important than that in the USSR. The latter, as a world power, is less dependent on imports. Considering the very specific system of domestic prices and foreign exchange rates in those countries, it is difficult to quantify this role and compare it with the data for Western countries. Approximately, it may be estimated that the ratio of the value of imports to that of the total GNP amounts to 5–6 per cent for the USSR and to 20–30 per cent for other socialist countries. The influence of changing foreign prices, exerted by way of foreign trade, on the lesser socialist economies is, accordingly, stronger.

2 TERMS OF TRADE

Changes in prices in international markets undoubtedly influence the terms of trade of the socialist countries. The scope of this influence depends on four main factors:

1. The system of price formation in the mutual trade of socialist countries and in their trade with market economies.
2. The share of their mutual trade in their joint foreign trade.
3. The commodity structure of their imports and exports.
4. The fluctuations of foreign exchange rates used in settling their foreign trade transactions.

The prices applied in the foreign trade of socialist countries are always quoted in foreign currencies and based on world market prices. But in the mutual trade of the CMEA countries they are calculated differently.

In the trade with market economies current world market prices are applied. They are expressed in convertible currencies. Consequently, upward and downward tendencies of prices on the world market exert an immediate and direct influence on the terms of trade of the socialist countries.

In the mutual trade of the CMEA countries a modified system of world prices is applied. During the IX Session of the CMEA in 1958, it was decided that the prices used in this trade would be those of the world market, but averaged over the last five years and changed every fifth year. This system aimed at eliminating short-term price fluctuations on the world market, often resulting from speculation. The prices thus modified would, better than the current ones, reflect the international value of goods. With this system of pricing, the prices in the mutual trade of the CMEA countries were stabilised over long periods of time, and the influence of world price changes on their terms of trade was considerably delayed.

As a consequence of the price stabilisation in the mutual trade of socialist countries, their prices of imported and exported goods differed from those applied at the same time in their trade with the market economies. In the 1960s, when world prices changed little, those differences were insignificant and did not exceed a few per cent. But in the 1970s, the prices of primary commodities as well as of manufactured goods rose considerably, particularly after the fourfold increase in the crude oil price in 1973. It is worth noting that, as late as 1974 and 1975, the socialist countries still applied average prices from the period 1966–70, that is considerably lower than the current prices on the world market, particularly in the case of oil. To prevent the continuation of this disparity, it was decided that from 1976 on, the prices in mutual trade would be changed yearly, but still on the basis of the last five-year average.

Thus the changes in world prices are still exerting a delayed influence on the terms of trade between socialist countries, not in the form of considerable and rapid changes every fifth year, but of gradual yearly modifications. That is why the prices in the mutual trade of socialist countries each year differ less from the current world prices than they did before 1976. Thus, while the 1979–80 doubling of the oil price had its influence on the socialist market as early as 1981 and 1982, its full effect will be felt only in 1985.

While the changes in world prices exert an immediate influence on the terms of trade of the socialist countries in their trade with market economies, and a delayed one in the mutual trade, the general terms of trade of those countries depend to a considerable degree on the relative share of their trade with those two geographic regions. This share varies with the individual countries, as is shown in Table 25.2 for 1980 and 1981.

Table 25.2 Share of socialist and other countries in trade of seven CMEA countries (per cent)

Country	Imports		Exports	
	Socialist countries	Remaining countries	Socialist countries	Remaining countries
Bulgaria	75.6	24.4	69.1	30.9
Czechoslovakia	72.8	27.2	71.1	28.9
GDR*	63.3	36.7	68.7	31.3
Poland	65.0	35.0	50.9	41.1
Rumania*	37.8	62.2	43.5	56.5
Hungary	52.0	48.0	58.1	41.9
USSR*	53.2	46.8	54.2	45.8

*1980.
Source: *Rocznik Statystyczny 1982* (Warsaw), pp. 553–4.

The greater is the share of the country's trade with market economies, the more rapid is the influence of foreign price changes on its general terms of trade. We can conclude from Table 25.2 that world price changes have their quickest effect on general terms of trade in Rumania. Their effect is also prompt in the case of the USSR and Hungary. It is somewhat delayed in the case of Poland and the GDR and very greatly so in the case of Bulgaria and Czechoslovakia.

The prices of individual goods in the foreign trade of socialist countries change differently on the world market. Some rise quicker than others, and they can even change in opposite directions during the same year. That is why the commodity structure of foreign trade is so important to the terms of trade of those countries.

Generally speaking, this commodity structure of the European socialist countries does not greatly differ from that of the European market economies, which are net importers of oil. With the exception of the USSR, the most important part of those countries' commodity structure consists of industrial goods, particularly machines and equipment, oil and other primary commodities.

Annual percentage changes in the prices of those main categories of goods between 1963 and 1981 were as shown in Table 25.3. As we see, the range of yearly fluctuations in prices was much greater after 1973 than in the preceding decade. By 1981, all prices were much higher than ten years earlier.

Table 25.3 Annual change in price (US $) of categories of goods in seven CMEA countries

Year	Industrial goods	Oil	Remaining primary commodities
Average 1963–72	3.0	3.0	2.5
1973	17.7	40.0	53.2
1974	21.8	225.8	28.0
1975	12.3	5.1	−18.2
1976	–	6.1	13.3
1977	9.0	9.3	20.7
1978	14.7	0.1	− 4.7
1979	14.5	48.7	16.5
1980	11.0	61.9	9.7
1981	− 5.0	10.1	−14.8

Source: International Monetary Fund (1982).

The price of oil rose thirteen times, the largest increases occurring in 1973–4 and 1979–80. According to GATT, the index of prices of industrial goods exported by industrialised countries rose yearly, until it reached 232 in 1980 (1973 = 100). For non-electric machines the index was 201 and for electric ones 155. Only in 1981 did this index drop a little, to 220, 194 and 147 respectively.

The index of prices for primary commodities other than oil, exported by industrialised and developing countries, is shown in Table 25.4.

In the case of primary commodities, the index also dropped in 1981, but some decreases were observed in 1975 and 1978.

Within the above-mentioned categories of goods, the prices of individual products imported or exported by the socialist countries were subject to various changes and that is why, without detailed data, it is impossible to evaluate the influence of the foreign trade commodity structure of individual CMEA countries on their terms of trade. But it can be stated with conviction that the influence of the enormous increase in oil price was undoubtedly negative in all those countries except the USSR, which is a big oil exporter.

Exchange rate fluctuations of convertible currencies used in settling foreign trade transactions also affected the terms of trade of socialist countries. Those fluctuations were considerable during the 1970s, particularly since the introduction of floating rates for the US

Table 25.4 Price indices for primary products in industrialised and developing countries (1973 = 100)

	Industrialised countries		Developing countries	
	1980	*1981*	*1980*	*1981*
Total primary commodities, excluding oil	176	168	200	173
Food	167	154	203	171
Agricultural raw materials	161	151	198	172
Minerals and non-ferous metals	223	227	188	183

Source: *International Trade 1981/82* (Geneva: GATT), p.26.

dollar and other important capitalistic currencies in 1973. Those fluctuations, depending on their direction, contributed to the improvement or to the deterioration of terms of trade. The fluctuations in the US dollar naturally exerted the biggest influence, since the socialist countries conclude many contracts and make payments in their trade with market economies in this currency. In Poland, about one-half of foreign trade is transacted in dollars.

However, the fluctuations in the dollar rate and in other convertible currencies also influence the terms of trade in the mutual trade of socialist countries, because the prices expressed in those currencies are converted each year into transferable rubles, according to changing rates on the world market.

It is, unfortunately, impossible to evaluate with any precision the joint influence of the above factors on the terms of trade of individual socialist countries, because only two of them, Hungary and Poland, publish the data concerning their terms of trade. But bearing in mind the example of those two countries, it is possible to approximate this influence on the terms of trade of those lesser East European countries which have a similar commodity and geographic structure in their trade. The changes in the terms of trade of the USSR can be estimated only in a very general way.

Hungary publishes its terms of trade separately for ruble transactions and those in other currencies. This corresponds, in principle, to the distribution of its trade between the socialist countries and the market economies. For the period 1973–80, the data are shown in Table 25.5.

Characteristically, in the years 1973 and 1974, when prices of oil and other primary commodities increased considerably on the world market and prices in the mutual trade of socialist countries remained unchanged, Hungary's terms of trade in its ruble transactions were positive, while those with market economies were negative. But since 1975, terms of trade in ruble transactions have been constantly negative, while transactions in other currencies were negative every second year and positive in the remaining years. In ruble transactions this deterioration was undoubtedly due to constant yearly increases in prices of oil and other primary commodities imported from USSR.

Table 25.5 Terms of trade of Hungary in rubles and other currencies (percentage of previous year)

Year	Rubles	Other currencies
1973	100.3	97.5
1974	100.4	85.2
1975	91.2	93.0
1976	97.9	106.5
1977	97.0	96.2
1978	97.7	100.8
1979	90.2	98.8
1980	98.9	101.6

Source: *Statisztikai Evkönyzv 1980* (Budapest), p.321

A similar phenomenon occurred in the case of Poland. In the period 1976–81, Poland's terms of trade in transactions with the socialist countries, those with the market economies and the general terms of trade were as shown in Table 25.6.

Since 1977, Poland's terms of trade with the socialist countries have always been worse than with the market economies. This fact influenced its general terms of trade negatively. In 1981, the index of import prices was 143.1 (1975 = 100) and that of export prices was 132.1. This was undoubtedly due to the gradual increase in prices of

Table 25.6 Terms of trade of Poland by country groups (percentage of previous years)

Year	Socialist countries	Remaining countries	General terms of trade
1976	101.8	99.6	102.0
1977	97.7	98.6	97.7
1978	98.3	102.2	100.0
1979	97.4	99.0	97.5
1980	97.7	100.2	98.4
1981	96.2	98.6	97.2

Source: *Rocznik Statystyczny 1982* (Warsaw), p.307. Selected data on Polish foreign trade, Foreign Trade Institute, Warsaw, 1981 and 1983.

oil, natural gas and other primary commodities imported from the USSR, consistent with the principles of price formation in the mutual trade of the CMEA countries.

With the examples of Hungary and Poland in mind, we can assume that during the 1970s, in other socialist countries importing primary commodities from the CMEA area, a considerable deterioration in terms of trade also took place. At the same time, the terms of trade of the USSR considerably improved.

According to the estimates of the UN Economic Commission for Europe, during the period 1975–80 the general terms of trade of the six European socialist countries importing oil deteriorated by 8 per cent and in 1981 by a further 4 per cent. On the other hand, the terms of trade of the USSR improved, particularly in its trade with market economies. Over the years 1975–80, its terms of trade with those countries improved by 44 per cent and in 1981 by a further 13 per cent. Owing to a delayed increase in the prices of oil and other primary commodities, the USSR's terms of trade with socialist countries improved over the same period only by 9 per cent and in 1981 by a further 6 per cent. The UN Economic Commission for Europe (1981) rightly draws attention to the fact that 'The large difference between the two measures (though not its precise numerical value) can be taken as an indication of the high economic opportunity cost to the Soviet Union of the lagged adjustment of intra-CMEA trade prices to the world market price structure'.

3 INFLUENCE OF FOREIGN PRICE CHANGES ON DOMESTIC WHOLESALE PRICES

In the socialist countries, wholesale prices of home-produced goods are formed, generally speaking, on the basis of production costs, with the producer's profit taken into account. But the systems of price formation are not the same in individual countries and they vary over time. Often they do not reflect real costs. Foreign price changes can influence, to some extent, domestic wholesale prices of important goods, and, through them, production costs and, finally, domestic prices.

During the 1970s, in all industrialised market economies a constant inflationary increase in domestic prices occurred. This was mainly due to internal factors, but was also partly connected with the rise in the price of oil and other primary commodities on world markets. While the weighted average of annual increases in the GNP deflators of the seven largest industrial countries was 4 per cent during the period 1962–72, it rose to 7.3, 12.2 and 10.8 per cent respectively in the years 1973, 1974 and 1975. In 1976–8 it amounted to 7–8 per cent and in 1979–80 it rose once more to 10.2 and 11 per cent. In 1981 it dropped to 9 per cent (IMF, 1978, p. 4, and 1982, p. 55).

This considerable increase in domestic prices in the market economies was bound to affect, through foreign trade, production costs and, through them, prices in the socialist countries. It influenced, first of all, wholesale prices. The scope of this influence depended on the system of domestic price formation for imported and exported goods and on exchange-rate policy. It was also related to the degree of dependence of the economy on imports.

In the socialist countries, two kinds of domestic wholesale prices of imported and exported goods are applied: stable prices and variable ones.

Stable prices are fixed by the state authorities for long periods of time, usually for more than a year. They apply to basic primary commodities and food products. In the planned economy, the policy of stable prices aims at stabilising the production costs and the living standard of the population. In the formation of those prices the existing price relations on world markets are taken into account, but, once fixed, domestic prices are applied regardless of later changes in world prices. As a result, importers and exporters can find themselves faced with considerable differences between domestic wholesale prices of goods and their prices in foreign exchange, converted into domestic currency at the official rate of exchange. Such price differences would bring unjustified profits or undeserved losses to importing or exporting enterprises. To obviate this difficulty, a special system of compensations on a state-wide scale was established. The state monopoly of foreign trade provides for a special compensatory account in the state budget. The enterprises pay into this account extra profits arising from price differences or obtain from it compensation for similarly incurred losses. In most socialist countries the application of this system depends on the range of application of stable prices.

As a result of this practice of compensatory accounts, every socialist country can maintain an autonomous system of stable domestic prices for imported and exported goods. In this system, domestic price relations differ from world price relations.

The weakness of this system, however, is that the price differences and their balance (negative or positive) in the state budget are in no way connected with the profits or losses of the enterprises using imported goods or producing exported merchandise. Those price differences do not affect their financial results and do not encourage the enterprises to follow a more rational import and export policy, better adapted to the situations and trends on international markets.

Variable domestic wholesale prices of imported and exported goods are formed by converting into domestic currency foreign prices paid by domestic buyers, increased by margins covering the costs and profits of foreign trade enterprises and—if necessary—by tariffs. The producers of exported goods obtain the equivalent of foreign exchange prices, expressed in domestic currency, minus the margins and commissions of intermediaries. In this way, world price changes affect directly and immediately domestic wholesale prices and, by the same token, the level of profits of domestic enterprises.

Until the late 1960s, all socialist countries applied stable domestic prices of imported and exported goods almost exclusively. Only in the case of certain machines and equipment were variable prices used. In the course of time, along with changes in the planning and management systems in the sense of taking better advantage of parametric instruments of regulation, the scope of application of variable prices was extended. But in all socialist countries stable prices for basic primary commodities and food are applied. In the USSR, the scope of application of stable prices is the largest, both in imports and exports. Variable prices are used only for imports of those machines and equipment that have no analogue in domestic products. In its imports and exports Bulgaria applies stable domestic prices, corrected yearly with regard to changes in world prices. In the remaining countries variable prices are used more and more often, particularly in exports. The widest scope of their application is observed in Hungary. In consideration of balance-of-payments needs, variable prices can be modified by means of various financial instruments, such as tariffs and taxes imposed on importers or the refund of indirect taxes to producers of exported goods.

Stable domestic wholesale prices cannot be maintained unchanged for too long. First, because, for economic reasons, permanent changes in world price relations between certain producers have to be taken into account. A permanent relative decrease in prices, such as for oil, other fuels and some primary commodities in the 1970s, should be reflected in the system of domestic wholesale prices. Whenever the price of an imported primary commodity increases permanently, domestic enterprises should use it economically, try to employ its substitutes, change their technologies of production, and undertake other similar measures. With the domestic price unchanged, they are in no way interested in changing their old methods.

Secondly, the change in stable domestic prices becomes unavoidable after a time, since owing to interior factors, the costs of producing primary commodities increase. For instance, the costs of coal production in Poland rise continuously, since Poland excavates deposits that are more and more deeply situated, and the outlays on labour protection and environmental preservation are increasing rapidly.

As a consequence of those changes, the level and mutual relations of stable domestic wholesale prices deviate after a time from real costs of their purchase abroad or their production at home. This fact necessitates adequate changes in the prices of domestic primary commodities and intermediate goods. The need for such changes is felt particularly by the smaller socialist countries, importing considerable amounts of primary commodities. If a country, such as the USSR, is self-sufficient with regard to primary commodities, it can maintain its prices at a stable level for a long time, modifying them *pari passu* with changes in domestic costs and conditions of production. But if a drastic change occurs, such as in the price of oil, even such a country is bound to increase domestic prices in order to avoid the indiscriminate use of a valuable commodity which could be allocated to profitable exports.

Budgetary considerations constitute another reason for changes in stable domestic prices. The increase in world prices while the domestic ones remain unchanged causes larger and larger sums in domestic currency to pass through the special compensatory account in the state budget. If the prices of imported and exported goods change at the same rate, the balance on this account can remain unchanged. But in the case of deteriorating terms of trade, this balance can become negative. The resulting deficits may necessitate cuts in certain budgetary expenses or rises in taxes. All this could have an adverse influence on the development of the national economy. A proper solution to this problem lies in an adequate modification of domestic prices.

It is thus evident that in due course appropriate changes in stable wholesale prices become inevitable in every socialist country. They take the form of general wholesale price reforms. These reforms take into account trends in world prices and are prepared well in advance, to become effective on a given date.[1]

A reform of this kind may embrace simultaneous changes in all prices or it can be realised in stages. The Czechoslovakian reform of 1977, the Hungarian one of 1980 and the Polish one of 1982 are examples of simultaneous changes in all prices. In the GDR a reform in stages took place, in which the wholesale prices of some groups of goods were changed each year, for instance oil in 1976 and 1981.

During a price reform not all wholesale prices are changed in the same direction or in the same proportion. Price increases of some goods may be neutralised by price decreases of other articles, so that the general level of prices does not change much. Such was the case of the Czechoslovakian reform of 1977. The prices of main imported primary commodities were increased considerably, but at the same time the prices of many manufactured products were diminished, thanks to reducing the rate of profits contained in the previous prices or economising on production costs. In the USSR reform of 1982, the prices of oil, natural gas, coal and various primary commodities and intermediate goods were increased, while prices in many branches of manufacturing industry were reduced.

In price reforms, various elements are taken into account. In the reforms at the turn of the 1970s, changes in prices were usually aimed at inducing enterprises to economise on fuel and energy and to cut down on their use of imported primary commodities and intermediate goods. They were also meant to bring domestic price relations closer to those of world prices. Moreover, domestic prices were so fixed as to eliminate the subsidies from the state budget.

Generally speaking, price reforms in all socialist countries resulted in an increase in domestic wholesale prices, particularly those of oil and other fuels. In further consequence, they also brought about an increase in transport tariffs and the prices of finished goods, manufactured from imported raw materials.

In view of the fact that stable prices are widely applied in a socialist economy, increases in domestic prices always took place with a certain delay in relation to those in world prices. On the other hand, the inflationary growth of world prices brings about an immediate increase in domestic wholesale prices, but of course only within the limited range of application of variable prices.

In the case of both stable and variable prices, an important factor to be taken into consideration is the exchange rate applied for converting foreign prices into domestic currency. In some countries the conversion is based on the official, published rate, while in others it is based on the same rate, multiplied by an appropriate coefficient, often not published. This coefficient was introduced with the object of bringing the real value of domestic currency closer to the value of foreign currency, within the existing system of domestic prices and costs. Whenever the level of domestic or foreign prices is changed, the rate of exchange or its coefficient is also changed.

The most important aim of the exchange rate policy is the fixing of rates applied in foreign trade at a level that would, on the one hand, ensure the profitability of a vast majority of exports, and, on the other, maintain the equilibrium of the balance of payments. This rate should not be such as to ensure the profitability of exports even when goods are produced at the highest cost. With such a rate and with stable prices, too big sums would pass through the special compensatory account in the state budget. The rate should not be average, either, because then the exports of too many goods would become unprofitable. In practice, the sub-marginal rate is most advisable.

The above considerations indicate that in the past decade price increases on world primary commodity markets and the inflationary rise in prices in the industrialised countries undoubtedly caused a certain increase in domestic wholesale prices in the socialist countries. It is very difficult, however, to evaluate the extent of this influence, first, because in the socialist countries indices of wholesale prices are not published and, secondly, because the growth of domestic wholesale prices can result from some internal causes, only part of it being due to external influence. In the course of economic development, an internal inflationary pressure, due to various factors, can appear. In periods of accelerated rate of growth, bottlenecks can arise in various branches of the economy. Their elimination involves additional costs and, in consequence, an increase in the wholesale prices of the goods concerned. Moreover, in those periods, capital investment and output of the means of production grow rapidly, unaccompanied by an adequate growth of production of consumption goods. This can call for increases in prices of the latter.

In some periods, an excessive increase in nominal wages may occur, without an adequate increase of labour productivity. This growth in wages may be due to social pressure, as for instance in Poland in 1981, when wages rose by 27 per cent, while the volume of production and labour productivity dropped. The resulting increase in costs was responsible for a substantial rise in wholesale prices in the following years.

An increase in wholesale prices can also result from a tolerant attitude of state authorities towards excessive production costs in the state enterprises and – in consequence – higher prices of their products. It can take the form of supporting unprofitable enterprises, subsidising them from the state budget, or reducing their taxes.[2]

As already mentioned, the socialist countries do not publish the index of their wholesale prices. Nevertheless, the increase in those prices can be evaluated to some extent on the basis of published data relating to national income in current and stable prices. It is possible to calculate the implicit deflator of the net material product over several years. The deflator will be only implicit, since the product includes not only goods passing through the market but also natural elements of consumption. In this calculation, the parallelism of changes in retail and wholesale prices is taken for granted – an obviously realistic assumption in the case of socialist countries. In the period 1976–80, the implicit deflator for Poland, obtained by dividing the net material product in current prices by the same product in constant prices is shown in Table 25.7.

As can be seen, over the 1976–80 period, the implicit deflator, used here as a measure of increase in wholesale prices, grew every year. A faster rate of its growth in 1976 and 1978 can be attributed to a reform of wholesale prices that took place in those years. The acceleration of the deflator's rate of growth in 1980 and its sudden violent growth in 1981 results undoubtedly from the then manifest internal inflationary

Table 25.7 Implied deflator of the net material product in Poland, 1976–80

Year	Previous year = 100	1975 = 100
1976	109.9	109.9
1977	104.8	115.2
1978	107.7	124.0
1979	105.2	130.5
1980	108.2	141.2
1981	122.9	173.5

Source: Calculated from data in *Rocznik Statystyczny* for the years 1976–81.

pressure. During those six years the level of wholesale prices, measured by the implicit deflator, grew by 73.5 per cent in Poland. As much as 32.3 per cent of this increase took place in 1981.

Just how strong was the influence of the foreign price increase on the growth of domestic wholesale prices in Poland (measured with the aid of the implicit deflator) during those years? In 1975–81, prices paid for imports grew by 43.1 per cent, while domestic wholesale prices increased by 73.5 per cent. In 1981 alone, import prices increased by 9.9 per cent and wholesale prices by 22.9 per cent. This shows clearly that the rise in wholesale prices, particularly in 1981, was influenced above all by internal factors. But how strong was the influence of foreign price increases? It should be noted that their increase only affected imported goods, and total Polish imports in 1980 amounted only to 20 per cent of material costs. It cannot be assumed that out of the general increase of 73.5 per cent in wholesale prices, only one-fifth or about 9 per cent can be attributed to the increase in import prices. We should take into account the fact that along with the rise in prices of imported primary commodities and intermediate goods, the prices of manufactured goods, transport tariffs, etc., also grew. It is difficult to gauge this growth. Assuming that it amounted to another fifth, it would follow that about 18 per cent of the total growth of 73.5 per cent of wholesale prices in Poland in the period 1976–81 could be attributed to external causes. The rest, that is almost three-quarters, resulted from internal causes. The above figures are, of necessity, only approximate. In individual socialist countries they may be different, the more so as in none of them did the internal inflationary pressure reach such proportions as in Poland.

4 CHANGES IN DOMESTIC RETAIL PRICES

In the socialist countries, the retail prices of basic consumption goods and services vital to the large masses of the population are fixed by the proper authorities and kept unchanged for long periods of time as official stable prices. For instance, in the USSR, the retail prices of natural gas and electricity used in housekeeping, telephone charges and public transport fares remained unchanged for 30 years. In Poland, prices of butter were kept unchanged for 20 years, those of bread for 17 years, and of meat for 14 years. But prices of the remaining, less essential consumption goods were changed once in a while by the appropriate authorities, organisations and economic units, in accordance with centrally fixed rules of price calculation. Those prices can be maxima. Some of them may be left to the free play of supply and demand. In recent years, the range of application of the latter kind of prices grew considerably, particularly in Poland and Hungary.

Indices of retail prices are published in socialist countries, and for the years 1970, 1975 and 1980 are shown in Table 25.8.

Table 25.8 Indices of retail prices in seven CMEA countries (1970 = 100)

Country	1975	1980
Bulgaria	101	123
Czechoslovakia	101	111
GDR	98	99
Poland	113	157
Rumania	103	108
Hungary	116	159
USSR	100	103

Source: Rocznik Statystyczny, 1982 (Warsaw), p.555.

Table 25.8 shows that in the late 1970s the rise in retail prices accelerated in all these countries, particularly in Poland and Hungary. It should be noted that price indices in these two countries cover a much wider assortment of goods and services than in the remaining ones. For instance, in Poland the retail price index contains 1,800 items, while in some other countries its range is narrower, being limited to basic goods and services only. In the latter case, changes in the prices of less important goods may not be fully reflected in the retail price index.

The USSR and some other countries have observed, as far as possible, the rule of maintaining the general level of retail prices unchanged. If the rise in the prices of certain selected goods became inevitable, other prices were lowered at the same time.

The increase in prices on world markets and in the industrialised countries, our partners in foreign trade, does not affect the retail prices in the socialist countries directly. It can affect them only indirectly, through an increase in the wholesale prices of goods indispensable for the production of consumption goods. Only in exceptional cases may the variations in wholesale prices of imported consumption goods, such as citrus fruit, be directly reflected in their retail prices. Usually, the influence on retail prices of the rise in production costs of consumption goods is neutralised with the help of appropriate financial instruments. For instance, the rate of turnover tax on some consumption goods or the rate of profit in wholesale prices may be lowered. Or subsidies from the state budget can be granted or increased. In the first instance, however, budget receipts will be diminished, and in the second budget outlays increased. The government may follow such policy for a long time if it is determined to maintain the living standard of the population. But it involves a great strain on the budget.

If, however, the level and the relations of world prices are being changed permanently, domestic retail price relations of consumption goods, established under essentially different external conditions, cannot be kept unchanged. In the socialist countries, the changes in domestic prices were made in the late 1970s. Apart from allowing for the consequences of world price increases, the changes in retail prices may also aim at restoring the market equilibrium and at eliminating budgetary subsidies to the prices of some goods.

In practice, in all countries changes in retail prices involved general price reforms, although once in a while changes in individual prices, for instance, those of alcoholic beverages and cigarettes, also occurred. In Bulgaria and Rumania the reforms of 1979 were aimed at ensuring greater consistency in retail prices in relation to production costs. In Rumania increases in wholesale prices are transferred to retail prices gradually, over five years. In the USSR and the GDR, price reforms stabilise the prices of basic consumption goods for long periods of time, while considerably increasing those of luxury goods. In Hungary, a flexible policy of retail prices (official and maximum) is followed and their changes are relatively frequent.

The most radical reform of retail prices was recently carried out in Poland. On 1 February, 1982, retail prices of basic food articles and of fuel and energy were increased. Food prices were raised by about 241 per cent on average, and those of fuel and energy by 171 per cent. This reform improved the relationship between various retail prices and reduced food price subsidies. In 1981, those subsidies amounted to about 150 per cent of the value of subsidised food articles. After the reform they dropped to 30 per cent. The increase in the retail prices of food, fuel and energy in the socialised trade was fully compensated by appropriate wage increases. But rises in the remaining retail prices were not compensated, and this resulted in a drop in real wages.

5 INFLUENCE ON THE BALANCE OF PAYMENTS

The rise in prices on world markets and in the industrialised countries affected the balance of payments of the socialist countries in several ways.

First of all, in the late 1970s, the foreign currency expenditures of a majority of smaller countries rose more rapidly than receipts, owing to the deterioration in the terms of trade. The resulting deficit had to be covered partly by drawing on foreign currency reserves and partly by utilising foreign credits. During those years, the foreign debt of socialist countries increased. But it is very difficult to estimate how much of this increase in foreign debt was due to the deterioration in the terms of trade and how much to raising new foreign loans for imports of investment goods needed for the development and modernisation of their economy. But certainly the part played by the deterioration in terms of trade should not be underestimated. The necessity of repaying this debt will be a burden to the economy of the socialist countries for years to come.

Inflation in the industrialised countries had, however, a more direct influence on the balance of payments of the CMEA countries. It resulted in a considerable increase in the rate of interest on financial markets where socialist countries negotiated their loans. The amount of their credits grew rapidly during the 1970s. Estimates of the Wharton Econometric Forecasting Associates are shown in Table 25.9.

Table 25.9 Estimated debt of seven CMEA countries (billion US $)

	1970	1975	1981
Six Eastern European countries	6.0	21.2	59.6
USSR	1.0	7.8	15.5
Total	7.0	29.0	75.1

Source: *Institutional Investor*, January 1982, p.80.

It can be seen from Table 25.9 that the total amount of debt increased tenfold during this period. The cost of interest payments grew correspondingly. In the years 1978–81, the rate of interest increased rapidly in the most important creditor countries and on the Euromarket. We can assume that the average rate of interest (including the margin over LIBOR) paid toward the end of this period by the socialist countries, was not lower than 12–14 per cent, and in some cases might have been even higher. In 1981, with the level of indebtedness of those countries reaching 75.1 billion dollars, the joint burden to their balance of payments amounted to at least 9 billion dollars annually. The drop of the rate of interest by 1 per cent would mean a reduction of yearly payments by about 750 million dollars and its increase by 1 per cent an additional burden of the same amount. The lowering of the interest rate on the world market in 1982 and 1983 diminished the nominal burden of annual payments for the debtor socialist countries. But the real rate of interest should also be taken into account. Depending on the relation between the nominal rate of interest and the rate of inflation in individual creditor countries in the late 1970s, the real rate of interest was generally lower than the nominal rate, and in some years, for instance in

1978–9 in the USA, it was even negative. But from 1980 on, the real rate grew considerably and, consequently, the repayment of interest rate requires, and will require, a larger volume of exports than before.

6 FINAL REMARKS

The increase in prices of goods on world markets and the high rate of inflation in the industrialised market economies in the 1970s influenced the planned economy countries in several different ways:

First of all, the terms of trade of the six East European countries importing oil and many other primary commodities deteriorated. Owing to a specific system of price formation in the CMEA countries, this effect was lessened and delayed. Only in the USSR did terms of trade improve, but also with a certain delay.

Second, the influence of increasing world prices on domestic wholesale prices in socialist countries depended on the relative size of their imports, particularly from the market economies, and on the scope of application of variable prices in their foreign trade. If the stable prices were widely applied, this influence was delayed and took the form of general price reforms. But domestic wholesale prices could also grow under the influence of internal factors, among others changing conditions of production.

Third, in the socialist countries retail prices were maintained at a stable level for long periods of time. The influence of the increase in world prices was indirect and delayed. It made itself felt only after a subsequent price reform that took into account the increase in production costs of import-based consumption goods.

Fourth, in the centrally planned economies the influence of world price increases on domestic wholesale and retail prices was neutralised by means of appropriate financial instruments. The state budget played the part of 'shock absorber': it made it possible for the economic units to implement their plans regardless of changes in world prices. But after a time domestic prices had to be adjusted to permanently changed relations of world prices in order to prevent the uneconomical use of resources and to avoid state-budget deficits.

Fifth, the balances of payments of the six socialist countries deteriorated because their terms of trade worsened. Only in the case of the USSR did the terms of trade improve. All the remaining countries felt an increased strain on their balance of payments, due to a higher rate of interest on their credits. This burden became particularly heavy when not only the nominal but also the real rate of interest increased.

All these phenomena are evidence of the high degree of economic interrelations between socialist countries and the market economies. That is why the socialist countries are not indifferent to price movements on world markets nor to the inflation in the industrialised market economies.

NOTES

1. The principles of wholesale price formation and the wholesale price reforms realised in the period 1959–78 in the USSR and the six East European countries are described in Lavigne (1979, pp. 279–95).
2. Kornai (1980, p. 561) draws attention to this 'Paternalistic' attitude of state authorities towards state enterprises.

REFERENCES

International Monetary Fund (1978) *Annual Report* (Washington, DC: International Monetary Fund).

International Monetary Fund (1982) *Annual Report* (Washington, DC: International Monetary Fund).

Kornai, J. (1980) *Economics of Shortage* (Amsterdam: North-Holland).

Lavigne, M. (1979) *Les Economies Socialistes*, 3rd edition (Paris: Armand Colin).

United Nations Commission for Europe (1981) *Economic Survey of Europe in 1981* (New York: United Nations).

26 Domestic and International Sources of Brazilian Inflation: 1947–80

F. de Holanda Barbosa
GRADUATE SCHOOL OF ECONOMICS
GETÚLIO VARGAS FOUNDATION,
BRAZIL

1 INTRODUCTION

Inflation is a phenomenon so imbedded in the Brazilian economy that perhaps like Carnival and football it has become a trademark of our society.

The Brazilian experience with regard to inflation during the post-war period is so rich that it cuts across different political regimes and governments. It has lived together with democracy and authoritarianism and witnessed the suicide, resignation and deposition of Presidents. It has been managed by Ministers who identified it as a powerful enemy that had to be attacked with all kinds of weapons and by others who did not even bother with its presence. It has witnessed the transformation of a predominantly rural society into an urban-industrial economy, was held accountable by some economists as one of the causes of the concentration in the distribution of income that occurred during part of the period, and used by others to redistribute income towards low wage-earners. A large spectrum of sources have been selected to explain its vitality, some of them as charming and exotic as the prices of xuxu vegetables, the price of a regular hair cut, and the whims of Arab sheiks. A good number of medicines have been developed in order to curb its effects; and even so it goes on benefiting some people and harming others.

Before monetarism became very popular in the northern hemisphere, the term was used in Latin America to name a group of economists who identified monetary policy as the main source of the high rates of inflation that were observed in those less developed countries. By the same token, before supply shocks became very popular among economists in the United States and Western Europe, after the OPEC cartel, a group of Latin America economists, called structuralists, identified changes in relative prices as the major source of inflation in less developed countries which tried to change the path of economic growth by means of economic policy.[1]

The aim of this chapter is to identify the domestic and international sources that lie behind the Brazilian inflation during the period 1947–80. The approach we use here is based on an aggregate supply and demand model, which combines some traits of the monetarist and structuralist schools to build up a final form equation for the rate of inflation that identifies monetary and fiscal policies, as well as supply shocks due to external and internal factors, as the main sources of inflation.[2]

This paper is structured as follows. Section 2 presents a very simple structural model which offers a rationale for the final form equation for the inflation rate that we use in the empirical part of the paper. Section 3 presents the empirical evidence for the period 1947–80, and Section 4 gives a summary of our major conclusions.

2 STRUCTURE AND FINAL FORM OF THE MODEL

The structure of the model that we present in this section illustrates the fact that the final form equation we use in the empirical part of this paper for the inflation rate is based and indeed can be deduced from a very simple model in which some basic features of economic policy such as monetary and fiscal policy instruments are included, as well as some supply shock variables.

We start by assuming that real cash balances m_t are related to real income y_t and nominal interest rate i_t according to:

$$\log m_t = \alpha_o + \alpha_1 \log y_t - \alpha_2 i_t \tag{1}$$

The nominal interest rate depends upon the expected rate of inflation p^e_{t+1} and the size of public deficit as a proportion of output:

$$i_t = p^e_{t+1} + \delta \log \frac{F_t}{Y_t} \tag{2}$$

where F_t is equal to the difference between government expenditures and tax revenues; $F_t = G_t - T_t$, and nominal output Y_t is equal to the price index P_t times real income y_t. Equation (2) embodies the hypothesis that the government deficit is always positive, otherwise the logarithm would not be defined in the set of real numbers. We would like to remark that such an assumption is not such a strong one when we consider countries which have a historical record of great and sustained public deficits.

The rate of inflation is by definition equal to the difference between the rate of growth of money supply μ_t and the rate of increase in real cash balance demanded:

$$p_t = \mu - Dm_t \tag{3}$$

where $Dm_t = \log m_t/m_{t-1}$.

By combining equations (1), (2) and (3), and taking into account that $y_t = P_t y_t$, we get:

$$p_t = \frac{\mu_t}{1+\alpha_2\delta} - \frac{\alpha_1+\alpha_2\delta}{1+\alpha_2\delta} DY_t + \frac{\alpha_2}{1+\alpha_2\delta} \Delta p^e_{t+1} + \frac{\alpha_2\delta}{1+\alpha_2\delta} DF_t \tag{4}$$

where $DF_t = \log F_t/F_{t-1}$ is the public deficit of growth. This equation can be seen as an aggregate demand equation that results from a set of IS and LM curves. The rate of inflation is negatively related to the rate of growth of real income, and positively related to the rate of increase in money supply, to the acceleration in the expected rate of inflation and to the rate of growth of public deficit.

With regard to the process of expectation formation we suppose that the past is extrapolated to the future as:

$$p^e_{t+1} = p_t \tag{5}$$

This assumption is made to keep things simple and is not intended as an accurate description of reality. Other more elaborate schemes of expectation formation could be introduced into the model at the cost of increasing the algebra but without any gains in terms of content of the final form equation for the rate of inflation that would be generated by the model.

From the supply side, we start by assuming that the rate of inflation is a weighted average of the rate of increase in industrial and agricultural prices:[3]

$$p_t = (1 - \Phi) p_{it} + \Phi p_{at} = p_{it} + \Phi (p_{at} - p_{it}) \qquad (6)$$

The rate of change in the terms of trade between agriculture and industry depends basically upon the behaviour of agricultural production. We assume that

$$p_{at} - p_{it} = \Theta A_t \qquad (7)$$

where A_t is equal to the difference between the actual rate of growth of agricultural production Dy_{at} and the trend rate of growth of this sector, that is $A_t = Dy_{at} - D\bar{y}_{at}$.

With regard to industrial prices, we use the hypothesis that the market structure of the industrial sector is an oligopolistic one in which prices are determined by a mark-up over unit costs. Therefore, the rate of increase in industrial prices is equal to a weighted average of the rate of growth of wages s_t, corrected for increases in labour productivity q_t and the rate of growth of imported raw materials prices Π_t

$$p_{it} = \gamma (s_t - q_t) + (1 - \gamma) \Pi_t \qquad (8)$$

The rate of increase in imported raw material prices depends upon the rate of growth of international prices of those goods Π_{mt} and the precentage variation e_t of the exchange rate according to:

$$\pi_t = e_t + \pi_{mt} \qquad (9)$$

The exchange rate policy is such that it intends to maintain the same purchasing power parity in relation to a basket that includes other goods, such as capital goods, besides raw materials. Thus,

$$e_t = p_t - \pi_t \qquad (10)$$

where π_t is a measure of the international inflation rate.

The rate of increase in wages is related to the past inflation rate, to the prevailing conditions in the labour market, and also to the desired rate of growth of real wages, according to: [5]

$$s_t = p_{t-1} - \beta h_t + \bar{s}_t \tag{11}$$

where the output gap h_t is defined by $h_t = \log \bar{y}_t/y_t$, and $\bar{y}_t$ is the level of potential output.

When we substitute equations (7)–(11) in equation (6) we obtain the following result:

$$p_t = p_{t-1} - \beta h_t + \frac{1-\gamma}{\gamma} O_t - \frac{\phi\theta}{\gamma} A_t + \bar{s}_t - q_t \tag{12}$$

where $O_t = \pi_{mt} - \pi_t$ measures supply shocks due to changes in the prices of imported raw materials.[6]

This equation can be interpreted as an aggregate supply equation, and it shows that the rate of inflation depends upon the past rate of inflation, the level of idle capacity in the economy, supply shocks due to changes in prices of imported raw materials, agricultural shocks, and increases in real wages greater than the rate of growth of labour productivity.

The rate of growth of real output and changes in output gap are related by the following identity:

$$Dy_t \equiv D\bar{y}_t - h_t + h_{t-1} \tag{13}$$

By combining this expression with (5) and (4), the aggregate demand and supply equations can be written in the following system:

$$\begin{bmatrix} 1 & \beta \\ 1 - \dfrac{\alpha_1 + \alpha_2\delta}{1 + \alpha_2\delta - \alpha_2} \end{bmatrix} \begin{bmatrix} p_t \\ h_t \end{bmatrix} = \begin{bmatrix} 1 & 0 \\ -\dfrac{\alpha_2}{1 + \alpha_2\delta - \alpha_2} & -\dfrac{\alpha_1 + \alpha_2\delta}{1 + \alpha_2\delta - \alpha_2} \end{bmatrix} \begin{bmatrix} p_{t-1} \\ h_{t-1} \end{bmatrix} +$$

$$+ \begin{bmatrix} \dfrac{1-\gamma}{\gamma} O_t - \dfrac{\theta \phi}{\gamma} A_t + \bar{s}_t - q_t \\ \dfrac{\mu_t}{1 + \alpha_2\delta - \alpha_2} + \dfrac{\alpha_2\delta}{1 + \alpha_2\delta - \alpha_2} DF_t - \dfrac{\alpha_1 + \alpha_2\delta}{1 + \alpha_2\delta - \alpha_2} Dy_t \end{bmatrix} \quad (14)$$

The solution for this system of difference equations, without taking into account transient terms, will be given by:[7]

$$p_t = p + \omega_1(L)\mu_t + \omega_2(L)DF_t + \omega_3(L)O_t + \omega_4(L)A_t \quad (15)$$
$$h_t = \omega^*_1(L)\mu_t + \omega^*_2(L)DF_t + \omega^*_3(L)O_t + \omega^*_4(L)A_t \quad (16)$$

where we assume a constant rate of growth of potential output and a rate of growth of real wages equal to the increase in labour productivity. The letter p stands for the inflation rate when both u_t and DF_t are equal to zero and there are no supply shocks. The polynomials $\omega_i(L)$ and $\omega^*_i(L)$, $i = 1,2,3,4$, in the lag operator $L(LZ_t = Z_{t-1})$ depend upon the structural parameters of the model according to the following expressions:

$$\omega_1(L) = \dfrac{\beta}{\Delta}; \qquad \omega_2(L) = \dfrac{\beta \alpha_2 \delta}{\Delta}$$

$$\omega_3(L) = \dfrac{(\alpha_1 + \alpha_2\delta)(1 - \gamma)}{\Delta\gamma}; \qquad \omega_4(L) \dfrac{(\alpha_1 + \alpha_2\delta)\theta\phi}{\Delta\gamma}$$

$$\omega_1^*(L) = \dfrac{-(1-L)}{\Delta}; \qquad \omega_2^*(L) = \dfrac{-\alpha_2\gamma(1-L)}{\Delta}$$

$$\omega_3^*(L) = \dfrac{1 + \alpha_2\delta - \alpha_2(1-L)(1-\gamma)}{\Delta\gamma};$$

$$\omega_4^*(L) = \dfrac{-1 + \alpha_2\delta\alpha(1-L)\theta\phi}{\Delta\gamma}$$

$$\Delta = (1-L)^2(\alpha_1 + \alpha_2\delta) + \beta[1 + \alpha_2\delta - \alpha_2(1-L)]$$

When $L = 1$, Δ is equal to:

$$\Delta(1) = \beta (1 + \alpha_2 \delta)$$

Thus it is not difficult to prove that the polynomials $\omega_i(L)$ and $\omega^*_i(L)$ satisfy the following restrictions:[8]

$$\omega_1(1) + \omega_2(1) = 1$$

$$\omega^*_1(1) = 0$$

$$\omega^*_2(1) = 0$$

These results can be interpreted in a very simple way. First of all, let us take a look at the meaning of the two last restrictions that belong to the output gap final form equation. When supply shocks are not present, equation (15) can be written in the following way:

$$h_t = \sum_{i=0}^{\infty} \omega^*_{1i} \mu_{t-1} + \sum_{i=0}^{\infty} \omega^*_{2i} DF_{t-i} \qquad (17)$$

If the rates of growth of money supply and public deficit were constants and equal to μ and DF respectively, the output gap would be given by:

$$h_t = \left(\sum_{i=0}^{\infty} \omega^*_{1i} \right) \mu + \left(\sum_{i=0}^{\infty} \omega^*_{2i} \right) DF$$

Since the sum of each set of weights is equal to zero, then it follows that in the long run both monetary and fiscal policies do not affect the level of economic activity.

With regard to the inflation rate, its final form equation shows that it depends on the historical evolution of the monetary and fiscal policies, as well as on the time path, from the past to the present, of the supply shocks. That is:

$$p_t = p + \sum_{i=0}^{\infty} \omega_{1i} \mu_{t-1} + \sum_{i=0}^{\infty} \omega_{2i} DF_{t-i} +$$

$$\sum_{i=0}^{\infty} \omega_{3i} O_{t-i} + \sum_{i=0}^{\infty} \omega_{4i} A_{t-i} \qquad (18)$$

In the long run, in a situation defined when there are no supply shocks, inflation is fully expected and the proportion of the public deficit in relation to nominal output is constant, the rate of growth of money supply will be equal to the rate of growth of the public deficit subtracted from the rate of growth of income velocity that comes from the increase in potential output. Under these conditions we arrive at the monetarist proposition that in the long run inflation is a purely monetary phenomenon, due to the fact that the sum of the weights ω_1s and ω_2s is equal to one.

Therefore for constant rates of growth of money supply and potential output we conclude that, in the long run, the rate of inflation is equal to the difference between the rate of increase in money supply and the product of money demand income elasticity times the rate of growth of potential output: $p_t = \mu - \alpha_1 D\bar{y}$.

3 EMPIRICAL EVIDENCE FOR THE PERIOD 1947–80

The final form equation for the inflation rate depends upon the historical record of fiscal and monetary policies. It also includes two variables that measure supply shocks due to increases in agricultural and imported raw material prices. Equation (18) was estimated by ordinary least squares by using annual data for the period 1947–80. We measure the rate of inflation by four different indices: the General Price Index (GPI), the Wholesale Price Index (WPI), the Cost of Living Index of Rio de Janeiro City (CLIRJ) and the Implicit Output Deflator (IOD).[9]

The money supply rate of growth is indeed an endogenous variable because it is not directly controlled by monetary policy. Thus, we prefer to use the rate of growth of monetary base.

Due to some peculiar aspects of Brazilian monetary institutions, it is a very difficult job to quantify the true federal government deficit.

This is so because the National Monetary Council has the legal power to create expenditures without having to include it in the fiscal budget, and the monetary budget is not required to be approved by the Congress. We use as a proxy for the rate of growth of the public deficit the rate of growth of government expenditures as measured by the national accounting system. At this point we would like to make two remarks. First, these expenditures include all levels, i.e. federal, state and municipal governments. Second, we are aware of the possibility that the use of this proxy may bias some coefficient estimates.

The variable that captures external shocks is measured by the acceleration in the rate of growth of oil products' domestic prices.

With regard to the agricultural supply shock variable, this is measured by the difference between the actual rate of growth of agricultural production and its trend rate of growth.

The number of lags for each variable in equation (18) is basically an empirical problem. The best results we arrived at included only one lag for the monetary and fiscal variables, and no lags for the supply shocks variables. Table 26.1 presents the results obtained for the following equation:

$$p_t = -p + \omega_{10} B_t + \omega_{11} B_{t-1} + \omega_{20} DG_t +$$

$$\omega_{21} DG_{t-1} + \omega_{30} O_t + \omega_{40} A_t + \varepsilon_t \qquad (19)$$

where ε is the stochastic disturbance, and B and G stand respectively for the rate of growth of monetary base and government expenditure.

The Durbin–Watson statistics do not show serially correlated residuals, the determination coefficients R^2 are high and the signs of the estimated coefficients are as expected. However, some standard errors are high probably because of multicollinearity in the data.

The sum of the monetary base coefficients is greater than the sum of government expenditure coefficients, except for the IOD equation. However, the thrust of fiscal policy is greater in the first period for the GPI, WPI and IOD equations.

As suggested by the model we presented in the previous section, the sum of the weights for the two variables B and DG is very close to one. Indeed, in all cases we cannot reject the hypothesis that the sum of those weights is equal to one. Thus we may conclude tentatively, based on the empirical evidence, that when there are no supply shocks, inflation is in the long run a monetary phenomenon.

Table 26.1

Regression: $p_t = -p + \omega_{10} B_t + \omega_{11} B_{t-1} + \omega_{20} DG_t + \omega_{21} DG_{t-1} + \omega_{30} O_t + \omega_{40} A_t$

Dependent variable	$-p$	ω_{10}	ω_{11}	ω_{20}	ω_{21}	ω_{30}	ω_{40}	$\Sigma\omega_{1i} + \Sigma\omega_{2i}$	$D-W$	R^2
GPI	−8,417 (4,804)	0,381 (0,166)	0,219 (0,189)	0,706 (0,208)	−0,235 (0,206)	0,042 (0,049)	−0,842 (0,349)	1,071 (0,111)	2,08	0,86
WPI	−5,999 (5,446)	0,347 (0,188)	0,433 (0,214)	0,740 (0,236)	−0,487 (0,234)	0,033 (0,055)	−0,885 (0,396)	1,033 (0,124)	1,97	0,83
CLIRJ	−6,501 (4,579)	0,508 (0,158)	0,238 (0,180)	0,427 (0,198)	−0,137 (0,196)	0,018 (0,047)	−0,572 (0,333)	1,036 (0,104)	2,34	0,84
IOD	−10,976 (2,894)	0,227 (0,100)	0,192 (0,114)	0,608 (0,125)	0,072 (0,124)	0,036 (0,030)	−0,388 (0,210)	1,099 (0,066)	2,05	0,94

The estimated coefficients for the oil supply shock variable are small, and they have high standard errors. Therefore, we cannot accept the hypothesis that the oil shock played an important role in the Brazilian inflation during the period we studied.

With regard to agricultural shocks, the empirical evidence points out that, as structuralists usually emphasise, fluctuations in agricultural production do affect the inflation rate since the estimated coefficients of this variable are statistically significant. However, the potency of agricultural shocks is small when compared with the long-run potency of fiscal and monetary variables.

4 CONCLUDING REMARKS

The sources of Brazilian inflation during the post-war period were mainly domestically created and its connection with international events cannot be grounded on empirical evidence. This statement is based on the fact that monetary and fiscal policies plus agricultural shocks were the most important variables in explaining the Brazilian inflationary experience.

When one looks at periods of high inflation rates the contribution of agricultural shocks is minor. When one wants to disentangle the effects of the monetary and fiscal policy variables in the short run, this becomes a very difficult task due to the high degree of multicollinearity between the two variables.

The allegation of a substantial contribution of the oil shock to the acceleration in the inflation rate observed after 1973 is not warranted. This finding contradicts the hypothesis that attributes an important role to the behaviour of the OPEC cartel in explaining that event.

The most important result, based on the empirical evidence presented here, is that in the long run inflation is a monetary phenomenon. It follows that the most challenging task for Brazilian society in the near future is to shape a monetary-fiscal constitution that precludes financing much of the budget deficit through the inflation tax.

NOTES

1. The controversy between monetarists and structuralists developed during the 1950s and still goes on today. For an earlier account of this debate see, for example, Prebisch (1961), Campos (1961), Seers (1962), Olivera

(1964) and the more recent survey article by Kirkpatrick and Nixson (1976). For a test of these two alternative models for Brazil see Barbosa (1983). It is interesting to note that Latin American monetarists could, in the taxonomy of schools of thought (Davidson, 1982), be described either as Monetarist-Neoclassical or as Neoclassical Synthesis Keynesians. A structuralist would be more inclined, according to the same classification, to be affiliated with the Keynesian, Neo-Keynesian or the Socialist Radical School of thought.
2. The theoretical framework we apply here is one that follows the main stream as represented by Dornbusch and Fischer (1981). The econometric approach is based on the final form equation introduced by Theil and Boot (1962).
3. We use here the assumption that consumer goods are not imported. This is a stylised fact of the Brazilian economy with some minor qualifications.
4. It is assumed that the productivity of imported inputs is constant through time.
5. In specifying the wage rate equation we use the past rate of inflation instead of the expected rate in order to take into account Brazilian wage policy, which establishes a minimum rate of change for the wage based on past inflation. Of course, firms can offer a different adjustment by using promotion to give more than the law requires or by increasing the turnover rate when the market wage is below the one that would be set by the official rate.
6. It is not difficult to show that o_t measures not only changes in imported raw material international prices but also changes in the exchange rate which do not obey the parity rule.
7. We assume that the model structural parameters are such that the model is a stable one.
8. There is also the following restriction among the coefficients of the two equations: $\omega_4(1)/\omega^*_4(1) = \omega_3(1)/\omega^*_3(1)$.
9. The General Price Index (GPI) has a long tradition in Brazilian price statistics and is a weighted average of the Wholesale Price Index, Cost of Living Index of Rio de Janeiro City and the Civil Construction Cost Index, with the following weights: 0.6, 0.3 and 0.1.

REFERENCES

Barbosa, F. de H. (1983) *A Inflação Brasileira no Pós-Guerra: Monetarismo x Estruturalismo* (Rio de Janeiro: PNPE).

Campos, R. de O. (1961) 'Two Views on Inflation in Latin America', in A. O. Hirschman (ed.) *Latin American Issues: Essays and Comments* (New York: Twentieth Century Fund).

Davidson, P. (1982) *International Money and the Real World* (London: Macmillan).

Dornbusch, R. and Fischer, S. (1981) *Macroeconomics*, 2nd edition (New York: McGraw-Hill).

Kirkpatrick, C. H. and Nixson, F. I. (1976) 'The Origins of Inflation in Less Developed Countries: a Selective Review', in M. Parkin and G. Zis (eds)

Inflation in Open Economies (Manchester: Manchester University Press).

Olivera, J. H. G. (1964) 'On Structural Inflation and Latin American Structuralism', *Oxford Economic Papers*, vol. 16, pp. 321–32.

Prebisch, R. (1961) 'Economic Development or Monetary Stability: the False Dilemma', *Economic Bulletin for Latin America*.

Seers, D. (1962) 'A Theory of Inflation and Growth in Underdeveloped Economies Based on the Experience of Latin America', *Oxford Economic Papers*, vol. 14, pp. 173–95.

Theil, H. and Boot, J. C. (1962) 'The Final Form of Econometric Equation Systems', *Review of the International Statistical Institute*, vol. 30, pp. 136–52.

27 International Price Fluctuations and Inflation: Discussion and Conclusions

N. Gonzalez
ECONOMIC COMMISSION FOR LATIN AMERICA AND THE CARIBBEAN

After the end of the Second World War, the international economy enjoyed a long period of dynamic growth and stable prices. Only a few countries, especially those in Latin America, experienced continued inflationary pressures. In these countries a lively discussion took place between monetarist and structuralist schools of thought. Both schools had different interpretations of the causes of inflation, and hence both recommended different policy combinations to correct it.

During the 1970s, inflation became an acute and widespread world problem. International trade and capital flows were important vehicles for this propagation. Inflationary price increases affected not only developing countries but also developed market and socialist economies.

The reactions of countries to inflation were heterogeneous. Different countries assigned different priorities to fighting inflation *vis-à-vis* maintaining a specified rate of economic growth and employment.

Approaches to anti-inflationary policies also adopted different combinations of income and demand policies; in some cases orthodox monetarist policies were adopted.

Stagflation, practically unknown before this time in most countries, became a widespread phenomenon. Difficulties in mastering inflation contributed to casting doubts on the effectiveness of Keynesian and monetarist economic policies.

A specific Specialised Session of the Congress was devoted to an examination of some of these problems. The central focus was an analysis of international price movements and their impact on the internal inflation and relative prices of each country. The main subjects covered during the meeting fell under three main groups: (a) factors that generate international price rises, (b) the relative importance of international factors of inflation compared to domestic ones, for different countries, and (c) the possibility of applying policies to neutralise inflationary pressures coming from abroad.

The subject of inflation was discussed distinguishing three cases: developed market economies, socialist countries of Eastern Europe, and developing countries. These three types of economies have different institutional structures (economic policies and price determination differ from one case to another); they show wide differences in the structure of their production activities and in their international economic relations; and they also have different ways of reacting to inflationary impulses coming from abroad. Analysis of these three cases led to some interesting suggestions concerning similarities and differences between them, although no attempt was made to compare them systematically.

Three of the papers presented to the Congress are published in this book, namely those by Professor Nadiri (developed market economies), Professor Raczkowski (socialist economies), and Professor de Holanda Barbosa (developing countries).

The list of papers that were also presented but are not published here is as follows:

Quadrio Curzio, A., 'Turning Points of Post-War behaviour of Primary Commodity Prices
Gionnaros, D. and Kolluri, B. 'Deficit Spending, Money and Infla-
Primary Commodity Prices'
Tandon, R. 'Prebisch Hypothesis and Terms of Trade'
Wilczynski, W., 'Remarks on the Impact of External Price Fluctuations and Inflation on Home Economy'.

The main aspects covered in the session are outlined below.

1 FACTORS THAT GENERATE INTERNATIONAL PRICE RISES

During the last fifteen years the international prices of commodities have experienced wide fluctuations, with booms during the early and late 1970s and declines in the early 1980s. The following factors which generate fluctuations were stressed:

1. The disorder in the international monetary system and inflationary expectations created additional demand for raw materials as a hedge against inflation.
2. The OPEC agreements sharply raised the price of oil, after a long period of depressed prices.
3. The rate of technical progress, linked to the production of capital goods, has been uneven. When technical progress in agriculture or mining slowed down, it increased pressures on natural resources and primary commodities, generating scarcities which produced inflationary pressures.
4. The accumulation of strategic stockpiles increased in certain periods.

International prices of manufactures also increased for several reasons:

1. Internal inflationary pressures of developed market economies resulting from social pressures leading to cost-push and to structural factors (such as the loss of competitiveness of traditional manufacturing sectors). These inflationary pressures increased the export prices of these countries.
2. Fluctuations in the main world currencies due to the floating exchange rate system.
3. The increase in international liquidity as a consequence of abundant financial surpluses of oil-exporting countries recycled by private international banks.

2 RELATIVE IMPORTANCE OF INTERNATIONAL CAUSES OF INFLATION COMPARED TO DOMESTIC ONES

Although the focus of the meeting was on the relationship between domestic inflation and external trade, the discussions emphasised the fact that the phenomenon of inflation is complex. Neither monetary and fiscal causes, nor external factors, nor autonomous increases in domestic prices of productive factors or specific goods, can in isolation explain the process of inflation, notwithstanding the fact that in each case some of these causes have greater weight than others. Anti-inflationary policies must thus consider all the different aspects involved.

The intensity of the effects of external price increases in comparison with domestic demand-inflationary factors (such as the increase in money supply and the fiscal deficit) appears to have been high in certain periods of the last ten years in developed capitalist countries, even when both were important. The paper by Professor Nadiri concludes that material (intermediate goods) costs are generally very signficant in explaining industry price behaviour. Since many raw materials are traded internationally, domestic prices are strongly affected by conditions in the world market. Sharp increases in material prices have made an important contribution to the rate of inflation in many OECD countries.

However, the relative importance of external price increases should not be overemphasised. Some participants stressed the fact that, before the first increase in oil prices, inflationary pressures of internal origin were already present in developed market economies. Also, the devaluation of a national currency might affect import prices as well as domestic prices of import-competing goods.

In developing countries with a tradition of heavy inflation, the situation seems to have been different. According to some of the experiences analysed during the meeting, the importance of international prices was not very high in comparison with such domestic factors as demand imbalances and sectoral price variations.

In several Latin American countries inflation is a very old problem. The discussion emphasised the fact that during the post-Second World War period, monetary and fiscal policies were essential variables in explaining inflationary experience. The inflationary effects of variations in sectoral prices were also important: fluctuations in agricultural prices resulting from variations in production are a good example. This factor is stressed by the structuralist economists who are quite influential in Latin America. The impact of external supply factors such as the oil shock was, at least in the case of Brazil, of little significance in comparison with the two above-mentioned factors.

According to the conclusions of Professor Barbosa's paper, monetary and fiscal policies plus agricultural shocks were the most important variables in explaining the Brazilian inflationary experience. During periods of high inflation, the contribution of agricultural shocks is minor. The contribution of the oil shock to the acceleration in the inflation rate observed after 1973 does not seem to have been very important.

However, the fact that internal causes of inflation predominate in comparison with external (as has often been true for high-inflation countries) cannot be extended to all developing countries. Many of them had enjoyed long periods of price stability until the early 1970s. After that, increases in international prices of tradables, both manufactures and raw materials, started internal inflationary spirals.

In the socialist countries both factors, external and domestic, were important. According to Professor Raczkowski's paper, in the past decade price increases on world primary commodity markets and the inflationary rise in prices in the industrialised market-economy countries caused increases in domestic wholesale and retail prices in socialist countries.

At the same time, there were internal inflationary pressures. In periods of accelerated growth rates, bottlenecks arise in various branches of the economy and rapid growth in capital investment and the production of capital goods (production means) is not accompanied by an adequate growth in the production of consumption goods; this can call for increases in prices of the latter. Increases in nominal wages without an adequate growth in labour productivity, due to social pressures, were also responsible for rises in internal prices. Similar effects can result from high production costs of state enterprises subsidised from the state budget.

The impact of external price variations on the domestic inflation of each country depends on several factors. A few of them were mentioned during the discussion:

1. The relative importance of international trade with respect to gross product; more open economies are likely to receive a stronger impact.
2. The external trade structure and the specific links between internal production and international trade at the sectoral level. If a few raw materials represent a high proportion of exports, then the fluctuations in international prices that are so characteristic of primary commodities are likely to affect internal prices strongly.
3. If a high proportion of imports consists of essential consumption

or intermediate goods, then the impact of international price fluctuations is likely to be great.
4. Policies which attempt to delay or attenuate the internal impact of external factors; reference to these policies will be made later on.

3 POSSIBILITIES OF APPLYING POLICIES TO NEUTRALISE INFLATIONARY PROCESSES COMING FROM ABROAD

The meeting discussed some important institutional aspects that are relevant for the internal propagation of external inflation and for the effectiveness of certain anti-inflationary policies. In the case of developed capitalist countries, emphasis was placed on the lack of flexibility of prices to meet short-term decreases in demand. Inflexibilities vary from one sector to another. As causes of these rigidities, mention was made of:
1. The existence of long-term contracts for goods and factors of production.
2. The fact that enterprises not only consider short-term but also long-term elements when setting prices. If they are interested in long-term profits, they may equate their long-term marginal revenue to long-term marginal costs and then prices may become less responsive to changes in the short run; they may pursue an increasing market share or a stable profit margin.
3. Uncertainty, as a price cut may be seen as an attempt to obtain a larger market share which will be resisted by rivals and may lead to lower revenue; price stability diminishes the necessity for buyers to accumulate precautionary inventories.
4. The lack of synchronisation of prices changes in different sectors.
5. Imperfect competition. Due to these inflexibilities, in the face of short-term reductions in demand, entrepreneurs adjust the quantities produced rather than the prices. This raises a policy dilemma between inflation and employment, as will be seen later on.

With respect to the socialist countries, an examination was made of the effects of state regulations on the prices of goods traded among them, and on domestic wholesale prices.

In the intra-zonal trade of the CMEA countries, prices applied are those of the world market, but averaged over the last five years. This system aims at eliminating the influence of short-term price fluctuations on the world markets, often resulting from speculation.

The other type of regulation concerns internal wholesale prices of some goods (basic primary commodities and food products). These are fixed in some relation to world prices, but are kept stable for long periods despite modifications in international prices. Consequently, there can be considerable differences between the domestic wholesale prices of goods, and their prices in foreign exchange converted into domestic currency at the official rate of exchange. To avoid profits or losses to exporting or importing enterprises that could result from this, subsidies and taxes are applied.

Both types of regulation slow down the domestic price adjustment of these countries in the face of international price variations.

If the international price fluctuations are short-term, frequently caused by speculation, this system can have favourable effects: it allows domestic prices, which are more stable, better to reflect the international value of goods.

Conversely, if international price variations are permanent and strong, as in the case of oil, the regulation of domestic prices may have undesirable consequences. Such regulation may delay the adjustment of the economy to the new situation because it does not encourage enterprises and consumers to conserve commodities whose prices have increased; nor to employ substitutes; nor to change technologies of production and other similar measures. All this can affect efficiency and competitiveness. It can also be burdensome for the state budget which must compensate the difference between internal and external prices.

This point is also applicable to the developing and developed market economies, although to a different extent. In some of them, the regulation of oil prices meant that domestic price adjustment did not follow international prices immediately, with consequent effects on consumption, the productive apparatus, the budget deficit and the balance of payments.

With regard to policies for combating the impact of international price variations on domestic inflation, the following points were mentioned.

In the domestic sphere, three types of measures were identified:
1. Those designed to delay the impact of external price variations

on domestic prices, such as those mentioned above in connection with socialist and other countries.
2. Monetary and fiscal measures.
3. Income measures.

The most appropriate mix of these three types of measures varies from one country to another.

Conventional monetary and fiscal policies may prove not to be very effective by themselves, in developed capitalist countries and in developing countries with moderate inflation, for combating the inflationary effects of external shocks. This is so, among other reasons, because of the rigidity of prices in the face of reductions in demand, as was mentioned above. These policies may entail high costs in terms of unemployment. On the other hand, they may be inevitable in developing countries with acute and chronic inflation.

It was stated that income policies should generally accompany monetary and fiscal policies.

Mention was made of the limitations of economic policies for combating inflation in countries where these policies are, to a certain extent, endogenous with respect to the economic and social system, i.e. where governments cannot act completely autonomously to combat the increase in prices.

Part VI

Impact of External Market Fluctuations on Centrally Planned and Market Economies

28 World Economic Crisis, Adjustment Policies and Global Questions: An Introduction

J. Bognár
INSTITUTE FOR WORLD ECONOMICS OF THE
HUNGARIAN ACADEMY OF SCIENCES

The various sessions of this World Congress of the International Economic Association analyse the reactions developed both by planned economies and market economies to the world economic crisis. Obviously, the analysis of these reactions provides a wide basis for comparison of national economies operating in different socio-economic systems. Social economic systems have a decisive influence on the conduct and adjustment abilities of various national economies. The reverse is also true: the implementation of economically necessary interventions exerts an influence on the forms and structures of socio-political systems.

If negative external factors (external shocks) occur, the economic policy-making authorities are forced to make decisions on whether the economy chooses to adjust or tries to minimise or 'prevent' unfavourable effects.

A reasonable decision depends on the character, intensity and durability of negative external factors, and also on the availability of resources.

It is obvious that the more intensive and lasting the negative world effects, the more they reduce the quantity of available resources, since these have to be drawn away from their earlier utilisation. This brings about a series of chain reactions in the 'internal' sphere of the economy. This also applies to planned economies, which, since the change-over to an intensive development model of growth, have become more sensitive to world economic effects than they were in the period of extensive development. Under normal international political circumstances, it is possible to shift unfavourable effects to other spheres, although this involves several negative consequences. But it is impossible and unreasonable to try to 'isolate' the economy completely from the unfavourable world shocks.

The economic performance of the small European socialist countries between 1974 and 1978 indicated that they reacted relatively slowly to world economic events. This phenomenon was due to several factors:

1. Policy-makers at that time misinterpreted the character of the crisis and regarded the deterioration of the terms of trade as an unprecedentedly strong and extreme cyclical phenomenon. They did not expect either the spreading of the crisis to other spheres or its persistence. Hoping that the 'normal situation' would be restored within two to three years, they undertook 'minimising' steps, without preparing for permanent structural and political changes. The misjudgement of the situation was the less excusable since from the very beginning of the crisis Hungarian economists pointed out that the energy crisis was only the initial stage of a change in world economic history, which would last for decades and would require a new economic policy in all countries. (Bognár, 1976 and 1980).
2. Socialist countries, after the decades of cold and hot wars, of blockades and embargos, were inclined to an 'introvertive' attitude and were unable to establish flexible structures and mechanisms to promote quick adjustment.

It should not be surprising that an economic policy which made attempts to 'minimise' world market effects, brought forth indebtedness and imbalance. Many resources and energies were wasted which, if appropriately used, could have led to 'gaining time' and to the establishment of a reaction system capable of promoting adjustment.

Moreover, the incurring of debts took place in a period of severe crisis in the international credit market, which caused problems of liquidity.

Since 1979 planned economies have gradually started to follow an adjustment policy by trying to reduce the effects which impaired economic-social-political change. But in order to re-establish the balance, the following measures are necessary:

1. Profitable exports must be increased; this implies essential structural changes.
2. A reasonable import-substitution process must be promoted, since the surplus of the balance of payments cannot be guaranteed exclusively by increasing exports.

3. The proportion of national income spent on investment must be reduced; giving priority at the same time to export-orientated investments and promoting the flexible allocation of capital.
4. Increases in consumption by the population must be limited.
5. The budget deficit must be gradually eliminated.

This economic policy requires changes not only in the economic sphere, but also in economic management and its institutional system.

The limitation of negative effects will not hold off the effects of world market events, but will allow some time for the implementation of the necessary reforms.

Naturally, the introduction of the necessary economic and social reforms requires special attention to the preservation of the identity and fundamental characteristics of the system. In this respect, it is necessary to point out that public opinion – and often scientific opinion too – considered as socialist features not only certain achievements (e.g. full employment, institutional assistance of the handicapped, etc.) but also institutions and methods which in the past decades helped the implementation of these achievements. It is also necessary to point out that the forms and methods of the implementation of the achievements may change with the course of historical development. For example, full employment should still be considered a socialist achievement, but not in the sense that a considerable proportion of labour is engaged in backward sectors, while up-to-date sectors or services suffer from significant labour shortages. Supporting the low paid or the handicapped remains a duty of a socialist society, but this support must be realised by welfare policy and not by distorting the price system.

The reactions of different economies nevertheless involve a great number of similar features. Export orientation, import substitution, anti-inflationary actions and the reduction of budget deficits are essential elements of almost every policy programme.

But there are also differences concerning the most serious problems. Developed capitalist countries have to face the problem of increasing unemployment, while developing countries suffer from 'double instability', and planned economies have the problem of extracting themselves from inherited socio-economic structures. The military build-up that is still pursued for policital reasons, in spite of budget deficits, and which entails high rates of interest and the danger of inflation, constitutes a special problem for the majority of countries. Substantial military expenditure involves severe consequences both for single economies and for the world economy.

The question arises as to what sort of influence the policy measures suggested above would exert on the world economy, when account is taken of its complex interdependence and the old and outworn system of international relations. It is obvious that we cannot cherish the hope that an 'invisible hand' will establish overall harmony.

Can a world recovery be promoted when everybody is attempting to increase exports and decrease imports? Can developed economies, which suffer from imbalance, and other economies, which suffer from indebtedness, import more? Can the international monetary system, which has plunged into a severe crisis since the beginning of the 1970s, promote these changes? Can the present world economy overcome the consequences of international political tension and confrontation?

The question can also be reversed. What influence will the worsening world economic circumstances exert on national economic programmes aimed at recovery?

Given the present situation, positive answers cannot be given to these dramatic questions.

A contradiction has arisen between what appears as a reasonable policy of promoting economic independence and the international political organisation, which is characterised by lack of co-operation, in a situation of diverging interests among 180 national economies. It is obvious that there is no basis for expecting the disappearance of national states and economies. Therefore, international problems can be solved only through co-operation. Such co-operation consists not only in the co-ordination of national economies, but also in the transformation of a historically established institutional system of international economic relations. This transformation no doubt requires political will and consensus.

There is no recovery without co-operation, economic and policital co-ordination and the transformation of institutional systems.

REFERENCES

Bognár, J. (1976) *Világgazdasági korszakváltás (Change of Era in the World Economy)* (Budapest: Közgazdasági és Jogi Könyvkiadó – Gondolat).

Bognár, J. (1980) *A fejlódés és az együttmüködés századvégi fordulópontjai (Turning Points in Development and Co-Operation at the End of the Century)* (Budapest: Közgazdasági és Jogi Könyvkiadó).

29 The Impact of External Shocks on Centrally Planned Economies: Theoretical Considerations

Richard Portes[1]
BIRKBECK COLLEGE, LONDON, AND
CENTRE FOR ECONOMIC POLICY
RESEARCH, LONDON

1 INTRODUCTION

Interest in the foreign trade and finance of centrally planned economies (CPEs) is relatively recent. Until the late 1970s, even less attention was devoted to the impact of external shocks on CPEs, partly because it was thought that the planning system insulated the domestic economy from the effects of such shocks. The USSR, as the largest and most self-sufficient CPE, was thought particularly immune to influence from the foreign sector.

Wiles (1968) analysed balance-of-payments crises in CPEs and considered in detail the USSR 1929–32, Hungary 1954–5 and Czechoslovakia 1962–4. He gave only two sentences to Soviet payments problems in 1946 and 1963, however, which he characterised as 'purely agricultural' (p. 108). Hoeffding (1968) argued that the grain imports of 1963–5 'were only the climax of a significant shift in the commodity structure of Soviet foreign trade which . . . had turned the USSR into a net importer of food' (p. 313), and went on to say that 'the Soviet difficulty, measured in absolute terms, was but a turbulence in a teapot' (p.314). The literature of the late 1970s on the responses of CPEs to external shocks acknowledges only one other major earlier paper, that of Holzman (1968), which was a general treatment of balance-of-payments adjustment mechanisms under Soviet central planning.

In practice, the USSR began to run substantial current account deficits in convertible currency and to accumulate debt to the West only in the 1970s, and the numbers were not really worth noticing until 1975–6. Its six East European CPE partners in the Council for Mutual Economic Assistance (CMEA) had started borrowing fairly substantial amounts a few years earlier. There was some recognition in the mid-1970s of the East–West Financial interdependence arising out of these payments disequilibria and the associated debt (Portes, 1977), and scholars began to follow up the earlier theoretical work of Holzman and Wiles on the relations between the foreign sector and the domestic macroeconomy of CPEs (e.g. Wolf, 1980, and Portes, 1979). Despite such analyses and their application to the CPEs' current problems (Neuberger and Tyson, 1980, and Portes, 1980), it took the Polish crisis of 1980–1 to draw the attention of policy-makers and the public to the debt and convertible currency payments problems of all the CMEA countries and their responses to events in world markets.

This paper will consider the impact of external market fluctuations on the CPEs in the CMEA. I have already co-authored a survey on this topic (Neuberger, Portes and Tyson, 1981), so here I shall highlight those key theoretical themes of my own and others' writings which bear most directly on the current economic policy problems of both the CPEs and their Western trading partners. I discuss only the 'standard' CPE; there are, of course, considerable differences now among the economic systems in the CMEA countries (especially Hungary).

2 STATISTICAL PROBLEMS

Statistical expression of any CMEA country's balance-of-payments constraint is made somewhat complicated by its trade and payments patterns. Trade carried out with its CMEA partners is almost all denominated in 'transferable rubles' (a small proportion is accounted for in convertible currency at world market prices). A small part of trade with other countries proceeds under bilateral clearing agreements, but most is carried out in convertible currencies, which for convenience will be discussed in terms of US dollars. The USSR reports all trade in 'foreign-trade rubles', which is a purely statistical concept. An official (accounting) rate of unity is used to convert transferable into foreign-trade rubles. The accounting rate for convertible currency trade varies; for 1980, it was $1.5406/foreign-trade ruble (with other currencies converted to dollars at market rates). Other CMEA countries use analogous concepts (devisa zloties, valuta lei, etc.)

For over two decades, prices in intra-CMEA trade have been based on 'world market prices'. Since the mid-1970s, they have been set at the beginning of each year as a function of the average of world market prices over the previous five years (before that, they were fixed for each five-year-plan period). But if the commodities sold in intra-CMEA trade actually appeared on world markets, the 'world market price' might change significantly (e.g. the price of oil would probably be affected if the USSR sold the 80 million tons it sells annually to the CMEA Six on world markets instead, and the CMEA Six had to buy all their supplies on those markets). Moreover, there are no obvious world market prices for many non-standard goods; in particular, it is believed that the relative prices of machinery in intra-CMEA trade substantially exceed whatever world market levels would be, taking account of quality differentials and of likely low world elasticities of demand for much of this machinery. For all these reasons, foreign-trade ruble statistics for intra-CMEA trade are strictly incommensurate with those for convertible-currency trade.

Thus, an aggregate balance of trade converting all Soviet foreign-trade ruble data into dollars at the current accounting rate is meaningless; the same holds true for the trade statistics of other CMEA countries. Nevertheless, the United Nations (for example) does report such balances. One reason why these are often used is that the detailed and precise information necessary to permit a recalculation – using alternative exchange rates – that would command wide agreement simply is not available. Still, it is important to try to obtain a global picture. This has been attempted by Marrese and Vanous (1983a, 1983b) for the USSR, and their work shows how different overall Soviet foreign trade can look using alternative valuations. They price Soviet exports to centrally planned economies (CPEs) – mainly fuels and raw materials – higher than the official exchange rate indicates, whereas they value Soviet imports from these countries - mainly machinery – at a much lower rate. On their calculations, the overall 1980 Soviet trade surplus reported at just under $8 billion becomes a 'true' surplus of slightly over $27 billion!

The difference is a calculated or 'implicit' subsidy of $16.4 billion to the CMEA Six and $2.9 billion to other CPEs. This does not allow for the changes in world market prices that would occur if all trade of socialist countries were conducted freely on those markets. With that strong reservation, it is still interesting to observe how much the shares of Soviet foreign trade with different country groupings change with alternative valuations. This is particularly pronounced for imports, where the share coming from the CMEA Six drops from 43 per cent at official transaction prices to 34 per cent in the recalculation, and that from the developed West rises from 35 per cent to 43 per cent.

Such calculations may be helpful in providing better information about real resource flows. Nevertheless, it remains the case that almost all trade inside the CMEA does not involve convertible currency, whereas almost all the CPEs' trade outside the CMEA does. These and similar non-trade flows generate a balance of payments in convertible currencies that is statistically and economically well-defined, although many of the relevant data are only imperfectly known to us.

3 CONVERTIBLE–CURRENCY TRANSACTIONS

If a CMEA country's convertible-currency transactions and assets could be aggregated with its other transactions, its overall balance-of-payments constraint could be translated into real resource terms and analysed in standard ways. For example, the 'absorption approach' could be applied without modification, so as to focus on the balance between total output and total resource utilisation (absorption) of the economy. The CPE would then appear similar to any country with a non-reserve currency and direct controls on capital account transactions. The major different would be the 'price equalisation account', which separates domestic from foreign prices and acts in some respects like a floating exchange rate, isolating the domestic monetary system from the effects of foreign trade (Portes, 1983; Neuberger *et al.*, 1981). The absorption approach is particularly suitable to balance-of-payments analysis for the standard CPE because of the rigidity of its internal relative prices and the unimportance of price effects on resource allocation. It is unlikely that the balance of payments of a CPE could usefully be analysed as a 'monetary phenomenon', but a suitably modified absorption approach has been applied by Portes (1980) and Holzman (1981).

While there are two separate sets of CPE foreign transactions, reflected in separate data, it is often the convertible-currency balance-of-payments alone that is called the balance-of-payments constraint for a CMEA country. That simplation might be appropriate for the smaller CPEs with less diverse and extensive resource bases, which could not easily switch trade between markets. But most Soviet exports to inconvertible-currency markets could easily be sold for convertible currency. Thus for the USSR, it should not matter that some goods are available only on convertible-currency markets, and the separation of convertible currency from other flows seems more a statistical necessity due to divergent systems of relative prices than a reflection of real economic constraints on Soviet decisions-makers.

On the other hand, the dependence of the CMEA Six on the USSR as supplier and market imposes reciprocal constraints. An immense economic shock would result if the CMEA Six had to import their fuels and raw materials from, and export their machinery to, world markets. To the extent that the USSR's exports to the CMEA Six cannot be diverted, its marginal exports for convertible currency may be limited to manufactures, which are difficult to sell at acceptable prices in Western markets. This non-economic condition is one determinant of the extent to which the convertible-currency balance of payments is a separate, binding economic constraint on the USSR.

An alternative approach would assume a convertible-currency constraint on the CMEA Six, which translates into a constraint on the USSR because of its 'obligations' to them. This might best be described as an overall CMEA convertible-currency constraint. While it is not entirely unreasonable to ignore the bilateralism of intra-CMEA trade and to see the CMEA as a unit, in real resource terms, relative to the rest of the world, this does *not* mean that their convertible currency receipts, expenditures or debts can be aggregated in any simple way. In particular, the view that a Soviet 'umbrella' would be extended to protect other CMEA countries with debt service problems was always dubious (Portes, 1977).

Within the CMEA, there has long been a distinction between 'hard goods', that could be sold easily and profitably on convertible-currency markets and 'soft goods' that could not. Planners have sought to balance trade bilaterally for each of the two categories taken separately. Viewing the CMEA as a unit suggests asking what are its aggregate 'hard good' reserves and how liquid these reserves are, in the sense of cost and time required for extraction and export. Convertible currency is simply a generalised, highly liquid 'hard good'.

4 THE FOREIGN TRADE SYSTEM AND THE BALANCE OF PAYMENTS

The 'standard' centrally planned economy does function quite differently from market economies. It therefore cannot be fully integrated into the world trading and financial system and its economic institutions under the same rules which apply to market economies.

The CPE's foreign trade is part of an all-embracing, centralised system for the physical allocation of goods; detailed directives inform enterprises what to produce and how, and distribution plans control their suppliers and the destinations of their output. Since domestic prices play a minimal role in this system, they are fixed for long periods with little relation to demand and supply conditions. The planning system and efforts by enterprises to fulfil their plans exert severe macro- and micro- level pressure on the economy. This is 'taut planning' or 'over-full employment planning': a generalised excess demand in productive sectors.

CPE foreign trade enterprises buy imports and sell exports at foreign currency prices, which, for their internal accounts, are converted to units of domestic currency at an accounting exchange rate that bears no relation to the domestic price level. But they sell the imports to and buy exports from domestic users and producers, respectively, at the domestic prices. The accounting profit or loss on the aggregate of these transactions is appropriated by the state budget. Thus there is no functioning exchange rate, no link between domestic and foreign prices, and no link between trade and foreign-exchange reserve flows on the one hand and monetary assets of households and firms on the other (there are only minor exceptions to these generalisations – see Holzman, 1974; Hewett, 1982; Neuberger *et al.*, 1981; Portes, 1983).

Most of the endogenous feedback mechanisms in market-economy macroeconomics are broken in CPEs, and the planners can and normally do directly ensure full employment. Exports have no Keynesian 'demand multiplier' effects, but they do finance the imports essential to production. Thus there can be a 'supply (or bottleneck) multiplier' if a fall in exports forces cuts in imports, thus in production, thus in export supply.

Indeed, with prices fixed we have in the CPE a sort of 'super crowding out', due to repressed inflation. Starting in full employment equilibrium with no excess demand and holding wages constant, a shift in output away from consumption (e.g. to exports) causes excess demand for consumer goods, which discourages labour supply. As workers find they cannot spend as much as they would like, they will react at least partly by working less. The result will be a fall in output, hence in the amount available for consumption, hence perhaps a further fall in labour supply, until this 'supply multiplier' process converges.

These circumstances also create an interesting parallel between CPE macroeconomics and monetarist macroeconomics in regard to the impact of external shocks, such as an increase in import prices. It has been suggested (Purvis, 1980) that the 'acid test' for a monetarist is the policy recommendation following an increase in the oil price for an oil importer. The monetarist would argue that this will require a reduction in real income and the real value of money holdings, so that the nominal stock of money should certainly not be increased; a non-monetarist, on the other hand, would argue that the oil price rise will have the deflationary effect of an indirect tax increase, so that monetary policy should be expansionary. On this test, the macroeconomics of central planning must be monetarist: the tax effect does not operate and full employment is not threatened (except in so far as the real income loss may induce bottlenecks in production). The only alternative to reducing real incomes and demand is to run an import surplus, exporting the excess demand created by the deterioration of the terms of trade.

For a CMEA country, a trade surplus in either, convertible currency or transferable rubles or both could correspond to a trade deficit in domestic prices. Conversely, a deficit in domestic prices implies nothing whatsoever about having to borrow either in dollars or in transferable rubles to 'finance' it.

5 EFFECTS OF INCONVERTIBILITY

Convertibility between the domestic currency and foreign exchange is simply not possible in this system. The planners cannot allow residents, much less non-residents, to purchase domestic goods freely, for this would disrupt the plan; nor can foreigners be permitted to exploit the divergences between domestic and world relative prices, because the domestic prices do not reflect relative costs. The consequent restrictions on exports amount to 'commodity inconvertibility', which entails currency inconvertibility. Non-residents cannot exchange foreign currency for rubles to buy domestic goods or assets at their ruble prices (except in limited amounts for tourism). It would require an internal shift towards market relations – perhaps to an even further extent than Hungary – to modify this extreme form of inconvertibility.

Ruble (or zloty, lei, etc.) inconvertibility is much wider. Non-residents cannot sell goods or capital assets to domestic residents for rubles, to be converted into foreign exchange; they sell to the foreign-trade enterprises and are paid directly in foreign currency (or credited with transferable-ruble balances, in the CMEA). Residents cannot purchase foreign currency for rubles, for either capital-account or current-account transactions (again, except for tourism).

The essential point is that inconvertibility must be recognised as fundamental to the economic system; it is not merely a barrier to capital flight or a defence of an overvalued exchange rate. While the dollar/foreign-trade ruble rate does, in fact, 'overvalue' the ruble in terms of domestic prices (relative to purchasing power parity), this is irrelevant, since exports and imports are not sold and bought at domestic prices converted at this rate (except through tourism). (Note that although domestic prices of tradables do not respond flexibly to world market prices, the peculiarities of intra-CMEA pricing rules are such that the speed of adjustment of the dollar/transferable ruble rate to dollar price inflation does affect intra-CMEA relatives price – see Marer, 1982).

Even within the CMEA, the transferable ruble is not transferable, much less convertible. A surplus accumulated in one bilateral relation cannot be used to finance a deficit or commodity purchases in another. In recent years, however, limited 'above-plan' quantities of 'hard goods' have been exchanged at world market prices for convertible currency, and it is now believed that the resulting balances are freely usable outside the CMA as well as to settle convertible-currency accounts within it. To this limited extent, 'hard goods' have functioned as a specialised form of convertible currency. The levels of imports and exports under this mode of settlement are not known, except for Hungary. Whatever the balance, this innovation does make Soviet primary product reserves more liquid in convertible currency. It further erodes the distinction between the Soviet economy's overall balance-of-payments constraint and the convertible-currency constraint.

It is not clear whether ruble inconvertibility itself very much affects the Soviet balance-of-payments constraints or its consequences. The USSR has always used convertible currency as the medium for its trade with non-CMEA countries and as a reserve asset. While its traditional (political) preference is for long-run state-to-state trade and credit agreements, the Soviet Union's trade with the West is fully multilateral. For example, in 1974–80 the USSR accumulated a trade deficit of $9.6 billion with the United States and surpluses of $4.8 billion with the United Kingdom, $3.4 billion with Italy, and $2.3 billion with Sweden (Kravalis, 1982, Tables A-9 and A-12).

Doubtless, bilateralism does impede efficient trade within the CMEA. The convertible-currency constraint itself motivates inefficient trades, as countries feel themselves forced to buy within the CMEA items whose real resource (even just transport) costs might be much less outside, in terms of what would have to be exported to pay for them. It might be said that inconvertibility hinders economic integration in the CMEA, but the underlying cause of both phenomena is the physical allocation mechanism (and resulting price system) within these economies.

It is therefore not clear why Roosa *et al.* (1982) identify inconvertibility as the major cause of financial constraints on East-West trade:

> What the entire CMEA group needs for a sustained expansion of East-West trade ... is a more fluid monetary system ... [which would extend to] the Trilateral countries ... [without] some form of ruble convertible with Western currencies, finance will become an operational limit on any substantial expansion of trade. (p. 73; see also pp. 106–7).

Roosa *et al.* do make an exception for the USSR, perhaps because its credit status is much better, but, as argued earlier, the Soviet convertible-currency constraint may be interpreted as a bloc-wide constraint. I repeat: only systemic reforms going even further than the Hungarian system of 1982 would permit full commodity convertibility, and such reforms are *a fortiori* necessary for currency convertibility affecting trade.

6 RESOURCE TRANSFERS AND THE NEW MERCANTILISM

The economic strategy underlying CPE trade differs from that in the West. In an economy dominated by excess real demand (over-full employment), growth is import-fed rather than export-led. Western countries are typically neomercantilist, seeking to loosen the balance-of-payments constraint on domestic stabilisation policy. CPE planners are antimercantilist, viewing exports as a necessary evil to pay for required imports. Western economies export unemployment with export surpluses in foreign trade; CPEs export excess demand with import surpluses. Both perceive an increase of the West's net exports to the East (the CMEA as a whole) as beneficial, so long as the Eastern deficits can be financed so that the resource transfer will eventually be requited (Portes, 1977, 1980).

The new emphasis in some Western policies on reversing that resource transfer appears to contradict this analysis. On the contrary, however, the justification given for continuing grain exports to the USSR confirms that a mercantilist view underlies these policies. Grain imports are said to be bad for the Soviet Union because it must give up treasure (convertible currency) in exchange, whereas pipe and equipment imports are good for the USSR because they will enable it to export gas and thereby accumulate treasure. This version of mercantilism pre-dates Adam Smith.

This reasoning ignores the economic axiom that choices reveal preferences: the USSR freely chooses to import massive quantities of grain, regardless of the sacrifice of treasure. It also neglects Adam Smith's argument that the gains from trade arise from reducing the resource cost of what you want by getting it in exchange for exports of other things in whose production you have a comparative advantage. The gains themselves are the imports, less what must be given up to obtain them. The Soviet comparative advantage in gas-for-grain trade is immense, and the gains correspondingly large. But they are grain net of the gas it costs, not the other way round.

Adam Smith also stressed that national wealth is real capital assets, not specie. The USSR's foreign exchange holdings do yield it an interest-rate return, so the relevant comparison is with the rate of return on imports. Feed grain is in fact a capital good which is invested in the livestock herd. There is no doubt that the Soviet planners judge the rate of return to be very high.

The gas pipeline to Western Europe will permit the USSR to earn foreign exchange. Grain imports permit the allocation to investment, in foreign-exchange-earning activities, of resources which would otherwise have to be used in agriculture. So far, the two are the same. But the other argument of the new mercantilism is that whereas cash purchases in convertible currency (for grain) are bad for the USSR, buying on credit (pipe and equipment) is in itself good for the USSR. This must suppose that the credits are subsidised or will not be repaid, or at least that the Soviets discount the future more heavily than does the market. This contradicts conventional wisdom about Soviet planners.

7 RESPONSE TO EXTERNAL EVENTS

Normally in a CPE, the balance of payments does not constrain the level of employment. The planners maintain 'over-full' employment by creating excess real demand. This can create a balance-of-payments problem, as it did for the CMEA Six in the 1970s (Portes, 1980). But dealing with this potential problem does not necessarily require reducing output in order to cut expenditure and absorption; the planners can use direct controls to change the allocation of resources, shifting them from domestic absorption into net exports. Thus the deficit will affect employment only if adjustment to it reduces imports of intermediate goods so much as to hit capacity utilisation and output through the 'bottleneck multiplier', or reduces consumer goods imports so much as to discourage work and activate the 'supply multiplier'. The former process has been dominant in the Polish crisis (Portes, 1981b) and, since the late 1970s, it has appeared elsewhere in Eastern Europe in a milder form. In general, however, if the balance of payments does constrain policy, it acts to slow investment and long-run growth, rather than to create short-run unemployment; and balance-of-payments concerns may make the planners more sensitive to relative prices and opportunity costs in foreign trade, at least at the margin.

The use of 'direct controls' similarly dominated the response by Soviet planners to their terms-of-trade improvement in the 1970s. They spent the increased convertible currency revenues directly on imports, rather than using the balance-of-payments slack to raise the growth rate of output, thereby drawing in more imports (Drabek,

1981). This confirms that the balance of payments was not a constraint on output.

There is a substantial recent literature on the adjustment of CPEs to external shocks, much of which addresses how such an economy would respond to a balance-of-payments constraint. I stress here only that the exchange rate is not a policy instrument in these economies – simply because it has no economic function (Holzman, 1979) – but the planners can instead reduce export supply prices in foreign currency and raise import prices in domestic currency. (They would not voluntarily prescribe offering higher foreign-currency prices for imports, simply to discourage foreign-trade enterprises from buying, even if the incentive system for those enterprises operated accordingly, which in general it does not.) Neither measure works 'automatically' like a devaluation, however, and raising import prices of consumer goods is politically costly, while the prices of inputs (imported or domestic) have little effect on producing enterprises. As for exports, there is some evidence that even where its market share in the West is large enough to create market power, the USSR is generally a price follower rather than a leader (Wolf, 1982). If it can price-discriminate among its customers, however, it will not have to take as much terms-of-trade loss (and 'secondary transfer burden') as an across-the-board devaluation would require to achieve the same increase in export revenues (Holzman, 1981).

The 'absorption approach' suggests that any balance-of-payments problem can be analysed with two equivalent representations of the difference between national expenditure and output: the excess of domestic investment (including government expenditure) over savings (including taxes net of transfers), or the current account deficit. Both 'gaps' must be reduced, but measures which could close one may not suffice to close the other, so either can be the binding constraint. The burden of raising the economy's net savings as much as is needed to reduce the trade deficit and service foreign debt will depend on how these requirements relate to the national output. Any given 'debt service ratio' (annual payments of principal and interest as a percentage of export revenues) will represent a smaller burden if trade is small relative to output.

Soviet 'trade participation ratios', imports or exports or their sum divided by total output, are relatively low, as is normal for a large country (although this empirical judgement is now somewhat controversial; see below). Moreover, convertible-currency trade is only a part of the total, so the resource shifts necessary to eliminate convertible-currency payments imbalances are that much smaller relative to output.

On the other hand, closing the 'absorption gap' will only generate the desired increase in net exports if import substitution is easy, the production of exportables can be expanded, and the demand for exports is highly elastic. For the CMEA countries, only part of the convertible-currency imports they financed by incurring debt in the 1970s went into investment which created capacities to produce convertible-currency tradables; and some of the new capacities themselves have a high output-elasticity of demand for convertible currency tradables.

Conversely, where internal resource reallocation has to be implemented through foreign trade, it may be blocked by inelasticities of import supply or export demand. In an LDC, for example, if capacities which produce consumption goods cannot switch to producing investment goods, the constraint on converting increased savings into capital formation will be the foreign elasticity of demand for domestically produced consumption goods; at the point of unit elasticity, any further savings go to foreigners through a deterioration in the terms of trade. The USSR might find it impossible to effect the opposite switch, if it tried to buy more consumer goods imports (food) by cutting investment so as to offer for export more capital goods, for which demand is inelastic. The convertible-currency balance-of-payments constraint would then restrict the composition of domestic absorption (Desai, 1979). Import supply inelasticity (an embargo, say) might have the same consequence.

It has been argued that the USSR and other CMEA countries face a 'structural' balance-of-trade deficit in convertible currencies because their weaknesses in selling, quality and innovation give them a comparative disadvantage in manufactures, even where their production costs are low (Holzman, 1979). The resulting inelasticity of demand for their exports means that they cannot earn enough to finance their debt service and the minimum of convertible-currency imports that they need.

While this might be a reasonable interpretation for most of the CMEA Six, it is not obvious that manufactures, rather than primary products or arms, are the marginal Soviet exports for convertible currency. Their fondness for counter-trade and compensation agreements might suggest recognition of the weaknesses cited, but it might also be a Soviet counterpart of Western 'project lending' – a tool deployed by conservative Soviet bankers who wish to be assured that they will be able to service the debts incurred for the project. But lending to finance specific projects in a CPE and trying to segregate their proceeds for debt service is meaningless (Portes, 1977) and futile (cf. the 'copper loans' to Poland). Similarly, CPE bankers are economically irrational to permit investment in any project whose output would not be marketable without a compensation agreement, unless they are explicitly purchasing marketing services. Counter-trade which disguises dumping is similarly irrational for the CPE (unless it is successful predatory dumping), since there is no employment-creation argument to offset the resource loss.

8 TRADE PARTICIPATION AND DEPENDENCE

For the USSR, the imports from Western markets which matter most are in automobiles, fertilisers, chemicals, feed grains, food, and the oil and gas industries. Dohan (1979) finds that the main Soviet benefits come from importing technology, grain and the materials and intermediate goods needed to meet 'deficits' in the material balances. He maintains, however, that the growing role of imports (from all sources) in the Soviet economy 'has not significantly increased the dependence of the Soviet economy on imports in a short-term strategic sense' (p. 366).

A recent study has been interpreted to the contrary by its sponsor, the US Bureau of the Census, which found evidence of Soviet economic 'vulnerability' in the conclusion that the 'Soviet Union's participation in world trade relative to its national income is in fact two to three times higher than has been recognised . . . The importance of this conclusion cannot be overemphasised' (Kostinsky and Treml, 1982, p. 30). It has been. The authors calculate trade participation ratios (percentage shares in national income of imports, exports and their sum) in terms of domestic ruble prices and find these have risen dramatically in the past two decades: exports are up from 3.7 per cent of domestic net material product (NMP) in 1960 to 6.9 per cent in 1980, and imports from 8.3 per cent to a striking 20.1 per cent of NMP in 1980 (the 1980 figures are given by Treml in Wharton CPEs Current Analysis, 6 August 1982). As Kostinsky and Treml say themselves, however, to ascertain the 'true role' of foreign trade in the Soviet economy would require re-computing all Soviet economic aggregates in terms of measures approaching 'equilibrium prices' (p. 40).

Their scholarly work has been misrepresented. It is remarkable that many who would explain Soviet economic inefficiency by the irrational distortions and rigidity of Soviet prices are nevertheless willing to draw far-reaching conclusions from calculations based on those absurd and useless prices. One substitute for 'equilibrium prices' would be world market prices. Vanous has estimated at these prices that the export and import shares of GNP for 1980 are 6.0 per cent and 4.1 per cent, respectively. Allowing for various criticisms by Treml, he puts an upper limit to these figures at 8 per cent and 6 per cent, with the figure for imports from the developed West at only 2.6 per cent (Wharton CPE Current Analysis, 6 August 1982). Similar methods indicate total export and import shares of around 2 per cent each in 1960 (without any upward adjustment), so Soviet trade participation has certainly risen over time. But the current levels are still comparatively low.

Trade participation has been growing fairly rapidly in all industrialised countries. Much of this, however, is intra-industry trade in differentiated products. The Soviet economy has also experienced growing simultaneous imports and exports of very similar goods (Dohan, 1979). The rise in trade participation ratios resulting from this specialisation indicates very little about 'vulnerability' or 'dependence'. This would require a microeconomic study of input-output relations between imports and domestic production and the substitutability among inputs. Such a study of Poland in the late 1970s might have predicted how drastically its industrial production would fall in consequence of convertible-currency shortages. The USSR would clearly not suffer similarly from any external shock.

9 CONCLUSION

Nevertheless, the analysis of this paper suggests that while the central planning system can indeed 'insulate' the economy from the macro-monetary effects of external shocks, there are still many channels through which these shocks do impinge on the CPEs, especially the smaller CMEA economies. No economy can be insulated from changes in its terms of trade or other real external variables, and the smaller CPEs are much more open than the USSR to such influences. The trend towards increasing openess is likely to continue, but less rapidly than in the 1960s and 1970s, following the overall slowdown in world trade and finance. But East–West financial and economic interdependence is now firmly established.

NOTE

1. I gratefully acknowledge research support from the UK SSRC, the Twentieth Century Fund, the Ford Foundation through the Maison des Science de l'Homme, and the Commissariat Général du Plan through the EHESS. I have had very helpful discussions with John Hardt, Ed Hewett and Jan Vanous, as well as comments from Bill Branson, Phil Hanson, Michael Kaser, Robin Marris, Joan Pearce and Stan Rudcenko. I thank them all and fully absolve them from responsibility. Much of the material in this paper is taken from a background report prepared for a Twentieth Century Fund conference and resulting pamphlet, *Deficits and Détente: Report of an International Conference on the Balance of Trade in the Comecon Countries* (New York: Twentieth Century Fund, 1983), and permission to use this material is gratefully acknowledged.

REFERENCES

Brown, A. and Neuberger, E. (eds) (1968) *International Trade and Central Planning* (Berkeley: University of California Press).
Desai, P. (1979) 'The Rate of Return on Foreign Capital Inflow to the Soviety Economy' in Joint Economic Committee (1979).
Dohan, M. (1979) 'Export Specialization and Import Dependence in the Soviet Economy 1970–1977', in Joint Economic Committee (1979).
Drabek, Z. (1981) 'Exports of Primary Commodities and the Soviet Terms of Trade', mimeo.
Hewett, E. (1982) 'The Foreign Sector in the Soviet Economy', in Bergson, A. and Levine, H. (eds) (1982) *The Soviet Economy to the Year 2000* (London: Allen & Unwin).
Hoeffding, O. (1968) 'Recent Structural Changes and Balance-of-Payments Adjustments in Soviet Foreign Trade', in Brown and Neuberger (1968).
Holzman, F. (1968) 'Soviet Central Planning and Its Impact on Foreign Trade and Adjustment Mechanisms', in Brown and Neuberger (1968).
Holzman, F. (1974) *Foreign Trade under Central Planning* (Cambridge, Mass.: Harvard University Press).
Holzman, F. (1979) 'Some Theories of the Hard Currency Shortages of Centrally Planned Economies', in Joint Economic Committee (1979).
Holzman, F. (1981) 'Creditworthiness and Balance of Payments Adjustment Mechanisms of Centrally Planned Economies', in Rosefielde, S. (ed.) *Economic Welfare and the Economics of Soviet Socialism* (Cambridge: Cambridge University Press).
Joint Economic Committee, US Congress (1979) *The Soviet Economy in a Time of Change* (Washington DC).
Joint Economic Committee, US Congress (1981) *East European Economic Assessment* (Washington DC).
Joint Economic Committee, US Congress (1982) *East–West Trade: the Prospects to 1985* (Washington DC).

Joint Economic Committee, US Congress (1983) *The Soviet Economy in the 1980s* (Washington DC).

Kostinksy, B. and Treml, V. (1982) *The Domestic Value of Soviet Foreign Trade* (Washington DC: US Bureau of Census).

Kravalis, H. (1982) 'USSR: An Assessment of US and Western Trade Potential with the Soviet Union Through 1985', in Joint Economic Committee (1982).

Marer, P. (1982) 'The Council for Mutual Economic Assistance: Integration or Domination?'. mimeo.

Marer, P. and Montias, J. M. (eds) (1980) *East European Integration and East–West Trade* (Bloomington: Indiana University Press).

Marrese, M. and Vanous, J. (1983a) 'Soviet Options in Trade Relations with Eastern Europe', in Joint Economic Committee (1983).

Marrese, M. and Vanous, J. (1983b) *Implicit Subsidies and Non–Market Benefits in Soviet Trade with Eastern Europe* (Berkeley: Institute for International Studies, University of California).

Neuberger, E., Portes, R. and Tyson, L. (1981) 'The Impact of International Economic Disturbances on the Soviet Union and Eastern Europe', in Joint Economic Committee (1981).

Neuberger, E. and Tyson, L. (1980) *The Impact of International Economic Disturbances on the Soviet Union and Eastern Europe* (New York: Pergamon).

Portes, R. (1977) 'East Europe's Debt to the West', *Foreign Affairs*, 55, pp. 751–82.

Portes, R. (1979) 'Internal and External Balance in a Centrally Planned Economy', *Journal of Comparative Economics*, 3, pp. 325–45.

Portes, R. (1980) 'Effects of the World Economic Crisis on the East European Economies', *The World Economy*, 3, pp. 13–52.

Portes, R. (1981a) 'East, West and South: The Role of the Centrally Planned Economies in the International Economy', in Grassman, S. and Lundberg, E. (eds) *The World Economic Order: Past and Prospects* (London: Macmillan).

Portes, R. (1981b) *The Polish Crisis: Western Economic Policy Options* (London: Royal Institute of International Affairs).

Portes, R. (1983) 'Central Planning and Monetarism: Fellow Travellers?', in Desai, P. (ed.) *Marxism, Planning and the Soviet Economy* (Cambridge, Mass.: MIT Press).

Purvis, D. (1980) 'Monetarism: a Review', *Canadian Journal of Economics*, 13, pp. 96–122.

Roosa, R., Matsukawa, M. and Gutowski, A. (1982) *East–West Trade at a Crossroads* (New York: NYU Press for the Trilateral Commission).

Wiles, P. (1968) *Communist International Economics* (Oxford: Blackwell).

Wolf, T. (1980) 'On the Adjustment of Centrally Planned Economies to External Economic Disturbances', in Marer and Montias (1980).

Wolf, T. (1982) 'Soviet Market Power and Pricing Behaviour in Western Export Markets', *Soviet Studies*, 34, pp. 529–46.

30 World Markets and Socialist Economies

M. M. Maximova
INSTITUTE OF WORLD ECONOMY
AND INTERNATIONAL RELATIONS
ACADEMY OF SCIENCES, USSR

The growing importance for each national economy of international relations and world markets is universally recognised. The influence of international relations has become especially apparent during the last twenty-five years. In the middle of the 1950s about 9 per cent of the aggregate gross national product of the world was going through the channels of world trade. By the beginning of the 1980s this figure was already over 15 per cent. As a consequence, there was an intensification of interdependence and co-operation between different national economies. Governments and international organisations were increasingly faced with the necessity of considering the changes occurring in the international sphere.

All countries experience the influence of the external environment upon their internal economic development. The scale and extent of such influence depend, as is well-known, on the availability of natural resources in the country, the scope of its industrial, scientific and technological potential, the intensity of its participation in the international division of labour, etc.

The socio-economic specificity of countries, their social systems and their foreign economic policy are of particular importance. The presence of socialist, capitalist and also developing countries with different social orientations in the contemporary world naturally causes a specific impact of international conditions on these various groups of countries. The ability of different social systems to counteract negative events in the international sphere varies to quite a large extent.

Several approaches to the analysis of the influence of the world market upon the socialist economies, predominantly that of the Soviet Union, are discussed in this paper.

1 POINTS OF DEPARTURE

In the West there are different and sometimes opposite points of view concerning the role of external markets for socialist economies.

In particular, some economists believe that the market mechanism is incompatible with the very nature of planned economies and that, because of this, the trend 'towards self-isolation' is inevitable in the socialist countries. These economists maintain that foreign trade is used by socialist countries, not as the means of raising national economic efficiency, but as a temporary forced measure for 'loosening bottlenecks' and eliminating commodity shortages.[1] Other economists consider that socialist countries actually gain more from relations with the capitalist countries than their Western partners. Appeals to restrict and even to curtail Western economic relations with the socialist countries originate from this opinion.

As is well known, the leaders of the present American administration are trying hard to support this thesis.

Some economists believe that the socialist countries would be incapable of withstanding economic recessions in the West. Other economists, on the contrary, argue that economic crises in the capitalist countries are favourable to the socialist countries. According to Marxist ideology, such crises would shorten the length of time before the collapse of the capitalist system.

Let us turn our attention to the Soviet conception of the role of markets.

According to a profound conviction of Marxist economists, the contemporary economy of any country could not be developed efficiently without international economic relations. This statement applies to socialist countries as well. The growth of the international division of labour and the internationalisation of economies constitute an objective process, conditioned by the requirements of the progress of the world productive forces. Moreover, the growing role of science and technology in the life of contemporary societies, the necessity of solving global problems – energy, environment, etc. – considerably intensify the need for effective international economic co-operation, for the co-ordination of policies in all countries – socialist, capitalist and developing.

Nowadays, the significance of such co-operation is increased, while the international situation is worsening and the risk of war is growing. Economic relations between countries with different social systems would help to ease tension and therefore would improve the world political climate. This is vital for the peoples of different countries all over the world.

The Soviet Union and other socialist countries are following just such an approach. Their foreign economic activity is not based on short-term considerations, nor is it based on any isolationist attitude. Rather it is based on long-term goals dictated by the requirements of broad economic co-operation with all interested countries in order to promote peace and social progress.

The question has to be raised: is the world market and the market mechanism in general compatible with a planned-economy system? In relation to this question, it would be desirable to emphasise the following points.

Marxists have never denied the importance of markets for the socialist economy. Markets, commodities and financial relations represent fundamental elements in planned socialist economies. In principle, the main difference between a socialist market and a capitalist market is that the former is based upon state ownership of the means of production and is managed on the basis of planning methods; the latter is based on private ownership, and that determines its spontaneous character. Monopoly regulations only restrict, but do not eliminate, the spontaneous nature of the capitalist market.

Let us turn our attention to the world market. On the one hand, the world market is an outcome of the progress of productive forces, of the international specialisation and division of labour. On the other hand, it is a combination of two different types of international markets: capitalist and socialist. The common features lies in the fact that both capitalist and socialist markets constitute two spheres of the circulation of international commodities characterised by demand and supply, prices, credit, exchange rates, and so on. But there also are other distinctions.

Business organisations representing the socialist governments, which possess a monopoly over foreign economic relations, are the actual agents in the international socialist market. Private companies, both national and transnational, behaving according to the principles of competition, are the main agents in the international capitalist market. Commodities and money relations in the international socialist market are regulated by planning with the help of different methods, such as the co-ordination of mutual supplies of commodities by the CMEA member countries, and a floating basis for the conversion of the ruble. The rules of the international capitalist market are practically beyond any control. Its main regulator – the relationship of demand and supply – is settled basically as a spontaneous outcome of competition.

It is quite natural that the international socialist market is capable of satisfying the requirements of planned economies much better than that of capitalist economies, although its functioning is far from ideal and requires many improvements. According to law, the Soviet Union gave and still gives preference to the co-operation with the CMEA member countries and other socialist countries. Nowadays more than half of their foreign trade (57.2 per cent in 1980) is comprised of trade among themselves. This circumstance should be taken into consideration when analysing the scope and influence of world trade upon the socialist economies.

But there is another fact: experience has proved that countries with planned economic systems can, and do, co-operate with countries characterised by the so-called market (or capitalist) economy, in many different spheres of business. Naturally they co-operate on the sole possible basis for them, that is, on the basis of full equal rights and mutual benefits. This is one of the general principles for the peaceful co-existence of countries belonging to different systems.

To conclude, to trade or not to trade with countries characterised by different social systems is no problem for socialist countries.

But there are other questions: how does a socialist planned economy interact with the world capitalist market? And how does it react to world economic fluctuations?

2 MEANS OF CO-OPERATION

Socialist countries have co-operated with the world capitalist countries for many years. But it can be stated without exaggeration that the problem of neutralising the negative feedbacks from the world economic situation has never been so acute as in the late 1970s and early 1980s.

The scope of co-operation between socialist countries and Western countries has increased. It is quite enough to recall that the average annual rate of growth of trade between the CMEA member countries and Western countries was 5 per cent in 1951–60, 12 per cent in

1962–70, and 22 per cent in 1971–80. In the 1970s these percentages were greater than the rates of growth of world trade as a whole.[2] The aggregate exports of the CMEA member countries to the West European market is now comparable with American exports to this market.

But the main point lies elsewhere. First, the specific economic situation of the Western world in the last decade played a significant role. A synchronisation of cyclical development, in combination with a protracted economic crisis, sharp fluctuations in world prices, inflation and high interest rates, have aggravated the conditions of international trade for all countries including the socialist ones.

During the post-war years the socialist countries had to cope with 'sanctions' of various kinds and other restrictions in the sphere of trade, credit and payments, as a result of a discrimination policy pursued by the US administration.

When appraising the influence of these factors upon the socialist economies, it is necessary first of all to emphasise the following. The system of a planned economy, the state monopoly of foreign economic relations and opportunities inherent in the socialist economic systems allow the socialist countries sufficiently to countervail the negative consequences of international conditions. The evidence of many years confirms this conclusion quite convincingly.

It does not follow, of course, that the socialist economies do not experience difficulties related to the influence of international factors. Moreover, international factors play a different role in the various socialist countries depending on their different degrees of involvement with the international division of labour. For example, at the beginning of the 1980s, the share of exports in the national income was 8 per cent in the USSR, 27 per cent in Rumania, 29 per cent in Czechoslovakia, 30 per cent in the GDR, 31 per cent in Poland, 40 per cent in Bulgaria, and 54 per cent in Hungary.[3] Correspondingly, the import share in these countries also differs widely.

The structure of foreign trade is also very different and, in particular, the nature of the interactions of the internal economy and the foreign economic sphere varies from one CMEA country to another. Finally, it has to be remembered that the Soviet Union has considerably greater opportunities for countervailing any negative international influence, as it possesses an enormous stock of natural resources, including gold, and has a powerful scientific, technological and industrial potential.

Close co-operation between the countries of the socialist group and such a powerful economy as that of the Soviet Union makes the process of adaptation of these countries to changing international conditions considerably easier.

Although there are differences, there is also much in common in the kind of influence that international conditions have on the foreign economic relations of the socialist countries. This influence is exerted by changes in the state of world affairs and business fluctuations. Let us consider this problem in detail.

Changes in the state of world affairs influence in general the export of commodities from the socialist countries to the capitalist market. In the low phase of the cycle and especially during Western economic recessions (as, for example, in 1979–82) the socialist countries experienced serious difficulties in selling their commodities in Western markets. These difficulties were less problematic for the Soviet Union, owing to the predominance in its exports of fuel and energy commodities (oil, natural gas, coal), the demand for which remained high, although not as high as before. However, even the USSR ran into difficulties in selling some commodities (especially machinery and equipment, including those meeting world technical standards).

It is often maintained that the slowing of economic development in the CMEA member countries in the later 1970s and early 1980s has been exclusively a result of economic crisis in the world capitalist economy. The fact that the worsening of the world crisis was reflected to a certain extent in the economic situation of the CMEA member countries can hardly be denied. In general, as it was stressed at the 26th Congress of the Communist Party of the Soviet Union, it should be said that during the last few years our countries had to solve difficult problems under complicated conditions, and the downturn in the world economy, added to the sharp fluctuations in prices, played a certain role.[4] However, there is another major fact. Socialist countries have entered into a transition period, from an extensive to an intensive type of economic model, characterised by a profound restructuring of their economies, which naturally influenced the pace of their economic development.

The dynamics of world prices in the last decade, and especially the twofold explosion of oil prices, exerted an unequal influence on the socialist countries. Those countries with a high share of fuel and raw materials commodities in their imports proved to be the most vulnerable to prices changes. In 1980 these commodities accounted for 27 per cent of the imports to Hungary, 31 per cent in Poland, 32 per cent in Czechoslovakia, 37 per cent in the GDR, 43 per cent in Bulgaria, and 50 per cent in Rumania.[5] Such countries satisfy an overwhelming part of their needs for these commodities by imports from the Soviet Union and also by mutual trade. However, they also have to enter the capitalist market, where they purchase a certain amount of oil, natural gas and other raw materials.

Large increases in world prices of manufactured goods and particularly of special types of machines and equipment also exerted a negative influence on the economies of virtually all the CMEA member countries (including the Soviet Union, which imports such commodities from capitalist countries). Socialist countries suffered from the sharp fluctuations in world prices of grain and other kinds of food which constitute not a small part of their imports.

As a consequence, the CMEA member countries had to withdraw a certain proportion of their resources from internal utilisation and divert them to exports to pay for their imports. A number of CMEA member countries had either to raise the prices of several groups of commodities or to increase budget subsidies to some enterprises. Certain corrections had to be introduced into national economic plans.

Credit conditions and international payments, which were relatively favourable during the 1970s, have worsened considerably since the early 1980s. Interest rates and bank premiums increased in the Western financial market. The terms of newly granted loans became more severe. Banks set a tight rationing restriction on international credit operations. All these measures affected the interest payments of different borrowing countries, including the socialist group. As a result, according to EEC data, the interest payments of the European CMEA member countries increased 3.3 times from 1977 to 1981, while the whole of their liabilities grew less than 1.5 times.[6] An inadequately thought-out credit policy has also played a certain role, for example, in the growth of the foreign debts of Poland. The strict credit policy of the West towards the CMEA member countries caused extremely unfavourable consequences. For example, in 1981, Hungary, the GDR, the USSR and Rumania were included in the group of countries with a high degree of risk, so that the conditions for credit to them were tightened up. As a result, the value of middle- and long-term credits obtained by the CMEA member countries in the international market was reduced from 4.7 billion dollars in 1979 to 1.51 billion dollars in 1981 and less than 1 billion dollars in 1982.[7]

The harsher credit conditions exerted a negative influence upon the East–West trade; but both socialist and Western countries are losing in equal proportions because of this situation.

As for the CMEA member countries, they are correcting export and import flows in order to regulate external liabilities. As a result, the Soviet Union has had a surplus in its trade with Western countries during the last three years. The other CMEA member countries reduced their trade deficit considerably.

It should be emphasised that the negative consequences of world economic trade were aggravated by the discriminatory policy of several Western countries, chiefly the USA, in trade with the socialist countries. It is enough to recall actions of the American administration such as an embargo on the supply of grain to the USSR, which was in force during 1981; an 'economic boycott' of Poland; a veto on the sale of new technology to the CMEA member countries and more restricted COCOM lists; attempts to prevent the construction of the Siberia–Western Europe gas pipeline; and the preparation of new laws on export, virtually aimed at the curtailment of economic relations with the socialist countries.

It is hardly necessary to prove the inconsistency of such intentions. Under contemporary conditions any attempt to dictate to other countries is doomed to fail. It is quite significant that an overwhelming majority of Western countries – not to mention developing countries – did not support the American sanctions and restrictions on trade with the socialist countries. This kind of policy does not correspond either to the spirit of the times or the objective needs of the countries, including those of the people of the USA.

3 A CONSTRUCTIVE APPROACH

The Soviet Union and the other socialist countries took measures in order to consolidate their economic and technological security and to countervail the negative consequences of the trends in the world economy. Such measures are an integral part of the common course pursued by the CMEA member countries and are directed at the improvement of their economies, at growing efficiency and at a broad utilisation of opportunities.

In every CMEA member country measures were taken which were directed at a more rational utilisation of natural resources; at economising in fuel, raw materials and energy; at a reduction in imports of expensive resources from the capitalist countries; and at a higher degree of autonomy in providing previously scarce foods and other commodities. In particular, these goals are fixed in the Energy and Food Programmes adopted in the Soviet Union and in a number of other CMEA member countries which are intended to span two or more decades. Many long-term programmes of co-operation within the CMEA are subordinate to these goals.

A perfecting of the national economic structure, the intensification of technological progress, the modernisation of traditional industries and the development of new ones such as electronics, nuclear energy, robot construction and automatic systems, and biotechology, are paramount problems to be solved in the Soviet Union and other CMEA member countries. The solution of such problems will be the basis for a considerable improvement in the foreign trade structure of these countries.

In the CMEA member countries great attention is paid to perfecting the management system of the economy, including foreign economic relations. First of all, there are the questions of increasing the flexibility of the management of these relations, of accumulating the necessary export and currency reserves, and of improving the structure of internal prices, taking world trends into consideration.

Measures directed at improving the level and quality of economic relations among the CMEA member countries in order to achieve a closer co-ordination of their internal and external economic policies were also undertaken.

The CMEA member countries have also planned a number of measures for diversifying their sources of raw materials by means of a further intensification of their relations with developing countries.

A certain time is necessary for the realisation of plans and programmes. Therefore, side by side with long-term and large-scale actions, the socialist countries are introducing the necessary amendments into current national economic plans, taking into account the peculiarities of the moment and the reality of the international situation.

The experience of the last decade convincingly showed that the planned economic systems of the CMEA member countries are flexible enough to avoid importing the crisis of the world capitalist economy into the socialist economy, without breaking ties with the capitalist market. This is proved by the dynamic economic performance of the CMEA member countries. From 1971 to 1981 the annual rate of growth of their industrial production was 6.8 per cent as against 3.0 per cent in the capitalist countries.[8] Then, as a result of a purposeful economic policy, the CMEA member countries managed to keep internal prices under complete control, and avoided being affected by the high inflation which shocked the capitalist economy. They have been able to cope with the problem of indebtedness in spite of the strict credit conditions imposed by the Western banks. Finally, and this is the main point, the Soviet Union and other CMEA member countries continued to ensure the full employment of their labour force over the whole period. They did not decrease, but in fact increased social expenditures and allowances, thereby raising the welfare of broad masses of the population. All this testifies to the fact that the socialist planned economy enjoys great opportunities. It is necessary to note also that the economic relations of the socialist countries with the capitalist and developing countries serve as an important stabilising factor in international economic relations. This is proved by the inter-governmental long-term agreements and co-operation programmes; by the strict fulfilment of the international obligations of the Soviet Union and other CMEA member countries; by their large-scale orders, which ensure employment for hundreds of thousands of workers in Western countries; and by extended economic assistance to developing countries.

The group of socialist nations is an integral part of contemporary civilisation considered as a whole. It cannot, and does not, stand aloof from the anxieties disturbing the peoples on Earth. It is concerned, first of all, with the main problem perturbing mankind – the problem of preserving peace. It is also concerned with the progress of international economic relations. The Soviet Union and other socialist countries are ready to participate in a dialogue and in joint action in order to improve these relations on a fair and equitable basis.

NOTES

1. See Bernstein (1980), p. 309.
2. Calculated according to UN, *UN Yearbook of International Trade Statistics*, 1959, 1963 and *Monthly Bulletin of Statistics*, July 1981.
3. See Bogomolov (1980), p. 233.
4. See CPSU (1981), p. 9.

5. See CMEA (1981).
6. Calculated according to UNO, *Bulletin Economique pour l'Europe*, 1981.
7. See OECD, *Financial Market Trends*, March, 1983, p. 33.
8. See Tsentralnoye Statisticheskoye Upravlenie SSSR (1982), p. 62.

REFERENCES

Bernstein, M. (1980) 'Systemic Aspects of the Response of East European Economies to Disturbances in the International Economy', in Neuberger, E. and Tyson, L. (eds) *The Impact of International Economic Disturbances on the Soviet Union and Eastern Europe. Transmission and Response*, (New York: Pergamon Press).
Bogomolov, O. T. (1980) *Strany socialisma v mezhdunarodnom razdelenii truda* (Moscow: Nauka).
CPSU (Communist Party of the Soviet Union) (1981) *Materialy XXVI s'ezda CPSS* (Moscow: Polit'izdat).
OECD (1983) *Financial Market Trends*, March (Paris: OECD).
CMEA (Council for Mutual Economic Assistance), Secretariat (1981) *Statistichesky ezhegodnik stran–chlenov SEV, 1980* (Moscow: Finansy i Statistica).
Tsentralnoye Statisticheskoye Upravlenie SSSR (1982) *SSSR v tsifrakh v 1981 g* (Moscow: Finansy i Statistica).
UN (1959, 1963) *UN Yearbook of International Trade Statistics*, (New York: United Nations, Central Statistics Office)
UN (1981) *Monthly Bulletin of Statistics*, July (New York: United Nations).
UN (1981) *Bulletin Economique pour l'Europe* (Geneva: United Nations Central Statistics Office).

31 Adjustment to External Shocks in Socialist and Private Market Economies

B. Balassa and L. Tyson
INTERNATIONAL BANK FOR
RECONSTRUCTION AND
DEVELOPMENT, WASHINGTON, DC

1 ANALYSING ADJUSTMENT POLICIES TO EXTERNAL SHOCKS

1.1 Introduction

This paper will examine policy response to external shocks in socialist and in private market economies during the period 1973–8. The distinction between the two groups of countries has been made on the basis of the ownership of the means of production. Countries where the means of production are largely in state ownership have been classified as socialist, while those where the means of production are largely in private hands have been classified as private market economies.

Among socialist countries, the investigation covers Hungary and Yugoslavia. This choice has been dictated by the availability of the data necessary to implement the analytical scheme employed. As a consequence, the study is limited to socialist countries which have undertaken reforms aimed at decentralising the decision-making process and applying market principles, to the exclusion of countries which have continued to rely on centralised decision-making.

For purposes of comparison, private market economies that are at levels of economic development similar to those of Hungary and

Yugoslavia have been selected for the investigation. They are the so-called newly industrialising countries (NICs), defined as having per capita incomes of between $1100 and $3500 in 1978 and value added in manufacturing in excess of 20 per cent of the gross domestic product in 1977 (Balassa, 1981). The study covers all NICs other than Greece, Hong Kong and Spain.

The NICs have been divided into two groups, depending on whether they applied outward-oriented or inward-oriented development strategies during the period under consideration. Outward-orientation strategies are characterised by the provision of similar incentives to export promotion and import substitution. By contrast, inward-orientated strategies imply a bias in the system of incentives against exports and in favour of import substitution.

Three Far Eastern economies, Korea, Singapore and Taiwan, adopted an outward-oriented development strategy in the early 1960s. After 1973, they were joined by Chile and Uruguay, which had earlier applied an inward-oriented strategy but turned outward following the external shocks that originated in the quadrupling of oil prices in 1973–4 and the world recession of 1974–5. In turn, Argentina, Brazil, Israel, Mexico, Portugal and Turkey have been classified under the inward-oriented country group. While these countries had made certain efforts to reduce the extent of the bias in their incentive system against exports after the mid-19860s, they increasingly turned inward in response to the 1973–5 external shocks.

The paper will present estimates of the balance-of-payments effects of external shocks resulting from the deterioration of the terms of trade and the slowdown of foreign demand for exports in the 1974–8 period, for Hungary, Yugoslavia and the inward-oriented and outward-oriented newly industrialising country groups. Estimates will further be provided of the balance-of-payments effects of policy responses to these shocks, including reliance on additional net external financing, output-increasing policies of export promotion and import substitution and restrictive macroeconomic policies.

Following a brief description of the methodology applied, Section 2 presents estimates of the balance-of-payments effects of external shocks and of policy responses to these shocks for Hungary and Yugoslavia in their trade with private market and with socialist economies. In Section 3, the estimates for Hungary and Yugoslavia trade will be compared with similar estimates for the outward-oriented and inward-oriented newly industrialising country groups.[1]

Finally, Section 4 will evaluate the policies applied in the individual countries and country groups.

1.2 Measuring the Balance-of-Payments Effects of External Shocks and of Policy Responses to the Shocks

The balance-of-payments effects of external shocks, in the form of the deterioration of the terms of trade and the slowdown of foreign demand, have been estimated by postulating a situation that would have existed in the absence of external shocks. Terms-of-trade effects have been derived as the difference between the current price values of exports and imports and their constant price values, estimated in the prices of the 1971–3 (1972) base period. They have further been decomposed into a 'pure terms-of-trade effect', calculated on the assumption that the balance of trade expressed in terms of '1972' prices was in equilibrium, and an 'unbalanced trade effect', indicating the impact of the rise of import prices on the deficit (surplus) in the balance of trade, expressed in '1972' prices.[2]

The effects of the slowdown of foreign demand on the exports of the countries studied, the so-called export volume effects, have been calculated as the difference between the trend value of exports and hypothetical exports. The trend value of exports has been derived on the assumptions that the growth rate of foreign demand for individual products and product groups remained the same as in the 1963–73 period and that the particular country maintained its '1972' market share in these exports. In turn, hypothetical exports have been estimated on the assumption that the country maintained its '1972' market share in the actual exports of individual products and product groups during the period under consideration.[3]

The balance-of-payments effects of policy responses have also been estimated by hypothesising a situation that would have occurred in the absence of external shocks. Additional net external financing has been derived as the difference between the actual merchandise trade balance and the trade balance that would have been obtained if trends in imports and exports observed in the 1963–73 period continued and the prices of exports and imports remained at their '1972' level. The effects of export promotion have been calculated as the difference between actual exports and hypothetical exports and reflect changes in exports resulting from changes in the country's '1972' export market shares. Import substitution has been defined as

Table 31.1 Balance-of-payments effects of external shocks and of policy responses to these shocks, 1974–8 (US $ millions)

	1974	1975	1976	1977	1978	Average 1974–78	1974	1975	1976	1977	1978	Average 1974–78	1974	1975	1976	1977	1978	Average 1974–78
			Private Market						Socialist						Total			
Hungary																		
I External shocks																		
Terms-of-trade effects	458	570	334	419	641	485	−17	104	155	231	399	175	441	674	489	650	1040	660
Export volume effects	21	165	77	228	283	155	9	100	159	177	314	152	30	265	236	405	597	307
Together	479	735	411	647	924	639	−7	204	314	407	713	326	472	939	725	1054	1637	965
II Policy responses																		
Additional Nwt external financing	618	678	525	766	1271	772	−5	201	78	−54	364	117	613	879	603	712	1635	889
Increase in export market shares	−149	−132	−285	−221	−316	−220	−24	26	176	349	207	147	−173	−106	−109	128	−109	−73
Import substitution	20	206	140	105	−63	82	38	9	40	140	134	72	58	215	180	245	71	154
Effects of lower GNP growth rate	−11	−16	31	−3	32	7	−17	−32	21	−28	−10	−10	−28	−48	52	−31	40	−3
Together	479	735	411	647	924	639	−7	204	314	407	713	326	472	939	725	1054	1637	965
Yugoslavia																		
I External shocks																		
Terms-of-trade effects	1,554	1,815	1,265	1,945	2,093	1735	159	59	111	376	304	202	1,713	1,874	1,376	2,231	2,397	1,937
Export Volume effects	28	261	110	320	392	222	−9	47	86	91	150	73	19	308	196	411	542	295
Together	1,582	2,076	1,375	2,265	2,485	1957	150	106	197	467	454	275	1,732	2,182	1,572	2,732	2,939	2,232
II Policy responses																		
Additional net external financing	2,039	1,892	430	1,383	1,460	1,441	80	−104	53	554	468	210	2,119	1,788	483	1,937	1,928	1,651
Increase in export market shares	−437	−302	−372	−626	−862	−520	59	135	103	−190	−134	−5	−378	−167	−269	−816	−996	−525
Import substitution	225	422	1,173	1,491	2,017	1,066	75	59	5	102	158	80	300	481	1,178	1,593	2,175	1,146
Effects of lower GNP growth rate	245	64	144	17	−130	−30	−64	16	36	1	−38	−10	−309	80	180	18	−168	−40
Together	1,582	2,076	1,375	2,265	2,485	1,957	150	106	197	467	454	275	1,732	2,182	1,572	2,372	2,939	2,232
		Outward-oriented newly industrialising countries						Inward-oriented newly industrialising countries						Newly industrialising countries				
I External shocks																		
Terms-of-trade effects	3,611	4,421	2,530	1,970	3,011	3,108	8,311	11,018	8,589	7,800	8,084	8,760	11,922	15,439	11,118	9,770	11,094	11,869
Export volume effects	14	1,490	738	1,993	2,533	1,354	451	1,951	1,409	2,834	3,540	2,037	465	3,441	2,147	4,827	6,074	3,391
Together	3,625	5,911	3,267	3,963	5,544	4,462	8,762	12,970	9,998	10,634	11,624	10,797	12,387	18,879	13,265	14,597	17,168	15,259
II Policy responses																		
Additional net external financing	2,609	1,686	−2,901	−4,441	−4,592	−1,528	12,444	12,498	6,013	3,648	1,686	7,258	15,053	14,184	3,112	−793	−2907	5,730
Increase in export market shares	463	890	2,357	3,094	4,360	2,233	−1,230	−980	−1,757	−1,257	−956	−1,236	−767	−90	600	−1,838	3,404	997
Import substitution	−237	1,325	2,088	3,872	5,090	2,428	−2,180	81	3,571	4,995	6,309	2,555	−2,417	1,406	5,659	8,867	11,399	4,983
Effects of lower GNP growth rate	790	2,010	1,723	1,438	686	1,329	−273	1,371	2,171	3,247	4,586	2,220	517	3,381	3,894	4,685	5,271	3,550
Together	3,625	5,911	3,267	3,963	5,544	4,462	8,762	12,970	9,998	10,633	11,624	10,797	12,387	18,880	13,265	14,597	17,168	15,259

Source: World Bank economic and social data bank and text.

savings in imports associated with a decrease in the income elasticity of import demand compared with the 1963–73 period, with separate estimates made for fuel and non-fuel imports. Finally, the effects on imports of changes in GNP growth rates in response to restrictive macroeconomic policies have been calculated on the assumption that the income elasticities of import demand remained at its 1963–73 level.[4]

2 EXTERNAL SHOCKS AND POLICY RESPONSES TO THESE SHOCKS IN TRADE WITH PRIVATE MARKET AND SOCIALIST ECONOMIES: HUNGARY AND YUGOSLAVIA

2.1 The Balance-of-Payments Effects of External Shocks

Table 31.1 provides estimates of the balance-of-payments effects of external shocks, in the form of terms-of-trade effects and export volume effects, for Hungary and Yugoslavia in their trade with private market and socialist economies. In turn, Table 31.2 relates terms-of-trade effects to the average value of exports and imports (average trade) and to the gross national product, and export volume effects to the value of exports and to the gross national product (gross domestic product in the case of Hungary), all expressed in '1972' prices. The estimates pertain to the years 1974–8, taken individually, as well as to averages for these years.

In interpreting the estimates, it should be noted that during the 1974–8 period private market economies accounted for 39 per cent of Hungary's exports and for 48 per cent of its imports, whereas the corresponding ratios were 57 per cent and 73 per cent in Yugoslavia.[5] There were also differences in the *modus operandi* of trade with socialist economies in the two countries. Hungary is a member of the Council for Mutual Economic Assistance (CMEA) and carries out the bulk of its trade with the other CMEA countries in the framework of long-term bilateral trade agreements. These agreements regulate the quantities traded as well as prices, which generally follow world market prices with a lag. In turn, Yugoslavia is not a member of the CMEA, and only its trade with the Soviet Union is carried out in the framework of bilateral agreements. Yugoslavia's trade with the Soviet Union, too, was largely paid at current world market prices, although the bulk of its trade with socialist countries involved bilateral clearing.[6]

Table 31.2 Balance-of-payments effects of external shocks and policy responses to these shocks 1974–8 (per cent)

	1974	1975	1976	1977	1978	Average 1974–78	1974	1975	1976	1977	1978	Average 1974–78	1974	1975	1976	1977	1978	Average 1974–78
	Private market						Socialist						Total					
Hungary																		
I External shocks																		
Terms-of-trade effects/average trade	34.7	44.1	23.7	26.9	37.2	33.2	−1.1	6.2	8.5	11.3	19.3	9.6	15.5	22.7	15.1	18.1	27.4	20.1
Terms-of-trade effects/GNP	5.6	6.5	3.7	4.3	6.3	5.3	−0.2	1.2	1.7	2.4	3.9	1.9	5.4	7.7	5.4	6.7	10.2	7.2
Export Volume effects/exports	1.7	13.5	5.8	16.1	19.1	11.6	0.6	6.0	8.3	7.9	14.5	7.5	1.1	9.2	7.3	11.0	16.4	9.5
Export Volume effects/GNP	0.3	1.9	0.8	2.3	2.8	1.7	0.1	1.1	1.8	1.8	3.1	1.6	0.4	3.0	2.6	4.2	5.9	3.3
External shocks/GNP	5.8	8.4	4.5	6.7	9.1	7.0	−0.1	2.3	3.5	4.2	7.0	3.6	5.7	10.8	8.0	10.8	16.1	10.5
II Policy responses																		
Additional net external financing/average trade	46.8	52.4	37.2	49.2	73.7	52.8	−0.3	12.0	4.3	−2.6	17.6	6.4	21.5	29.7	18.6	19.8	36.0	27.0
Additional net external financing/GNP	7.5	7.8	5.8	7.9	12.5	8.4	−0.1	2.3	0.9	−0.6	3.6	1.3	7.5	10.1	6.7	7.3	16.1	9.7
Increase in export market shares/exports	−12.3	−10.8	−21.6	−15.6	−21.3	−16.6	−1.5	1.6	9.2	15.5	9.6	6.9	−6.2	−3.7	−3.4	3.5	−3.0	−2.3
Import substitution/imports	1.4	15.1	9.3	6.2	−3.2	5.1	2.5	0.5	2.3	7.7	6.8	4.1	2.0	7.1	5.6	6.9	1.8	4.6
Effects of lower GDP growth rate/imports	−0.7	−1.2	2.0	−0.2	1.6	0.4	−1.1	−1.9	1.2	−1.5	0.4	−0.6	−1.0	−1.6	1.6	−0.9	1.0	−0.1
Yugoslavia																		
I External shocks																		
Terms-of-trade effects/average trade	64.3	75.9	54.4	82.9	87.6	73.1	14.8	5.1	9.1	32.6	24.1	17.2	49.1	53.0	38.8	66.3	65.6	54.6
Terms-of-trade effects/GNP	5.3	6.2	4.1	5.8	5.7	5.4	0.5	0.2	0.4	1.1	0.8	0.6	5.9	6.4	4.4	6.9	6.6	6.1
Export volume effects/exports	2.0	17.7	6.2	20.1	24.6	14.2	−0.9	4.0	7.1	8.9	13.0	6.5	0.7	11.6	6.6	15.7	19.8	11.0
Export volume effects/GNP	0.1	0.9	0.4	1.0	1.1	0.7	0.0	0.2	0.3	0.3	0.4	0.2	0.1	1.0	0.6	1.2	1.5	0.9
External shocks/GNP	5.4	7.1	4.4	6.7	6.8	6.1	0.5	0.4	0.6	1.4	1.2	0.9	5.9	7.4	5.1	8.1	8.1	7.0
II Policy responses																		
Additional net external financing/average trade	84.4	79.1	18.5	59.0	61.1	60.7	7.4	−9.1	4.4	48.1	37.0	18.0	60.7	50.6	13.6	55.4	52.8	46.5
Additional net external financing/GNP	7.0	6.4	1.4	4.1	4.0	4.5	0.3	−0.4	0.2	1.6	1.3	0.7	7.2	6.1	1.6	5.8	5.3	5.2
Increase in export market shares/exports	−32.0	−20.4	−20.8	−39.3	−54.1	−33.2	5.5	11.4	8.5	−16.5	−11.6	−0.5	−15.5	−6.3	−8.9	−31.2	−36.3	−19.5
Import substitution/imports	6.5	12.8	41.0	48.1	63.3	33.5	6.9	5.3	0.4	8.0	11.4	6.5	6.6	10.9	28.8	36.4	47.6	26.0
Effects of lower GDP growth rate/imports	−7.1	1.9	5.0	0.6	−4.1	−0.9	−6.0	1.5	2.9	0.1	−2.7	−0.8	−6.8	1.8	4.4	0.4	−3.7	−0.9

	Outward-oriented newly industrialising countries						Inward-oriented newly industrialising countries						Newly industrialising countries					
I External shocks																		
Terms-of-trade effects/average trade	28.8	35.7	16.5	11.8	15.4	20.3	40.0	54.7	42.8	37.5	36.8	42.2	35.8	47.5	31.5	26.1	26.7	32.9
Terms-of-trade effects/GNP	7.4	8.9	4.6	3.3	4.5	5.6	3.0	3.9	2.9	2.5	2.5	2.9	3.7	4.6	3.1	2.6	2.8	3.3
Export volume effects/exports	0.1	2.9	4.8	12.2	13.3	9.2	3.0	12.7	8.4	15.9	18.2	12.0	1.8	12.6	6.7	14.1	15.8	10.7
Export volume effects/GNP	0.0	3.0	1.4	3.3	3.8	2.4	0.2	0.7	0.5	0.9	1.1	0.7	0.1	1.0	0.6	1.3	1.5	1.0
External shocks/GNP	7.5	12.0	6.0	6.6	8.3	8.0	3.2	4.5	3.4	3.4	3.6	3.6	3.8	5.6	3.8	3.9	4.4	4.3
II Policy responses																		
Additional net external financing/ average trade	20.8	13.6	−19.0	−26.7	−23.5	−10.0	59.8	62.0	30.0	17.6	7.7	35.0	45.2	43.6	8.8	−2.1	−7.0	15.9
Additional net external financing/GNP	5.4	3.4	−5.3	−7.4	−6.9	−2.7	4.5	4.4	2.0	1.2	0.5	2.4	4.6	4.2	0.9	−0.2	−0.7	1.6
Increase in export market shares/exports	4.1	7.7	15.5	18.9	23.0	15.2	−8.1	−6.4	−10.4	−7.1	−4.9	−7.3	2.9	−0.3	1.9	5.4	8.8	3.2
Import substitution/imports	−1.7	10.1	13.6	22.8	25.2	15.3	−8.2	0.3	15.3	21.0	25.8	10.4	6.0	3.7	14.6	21.8	25.5	12.3
Effects of lower GNP growth rate/imports	5.8	15.3	11.2	8.5	3.4	8.4	−1.0	5.5	9.3	13.7	18.8	9.0	1.3	8.9	10.1	11.5	11.8	8.8

Source: Table 31.1 and text.

In Hungary, the adverse terms-of-trade effects, expressed as a ratio of the average value of exports and imports, were larger in trade with private market economies (an average of 33 per cent in the 1974–8 period) than in trade with socialist countries (an average of 10 per cent during the same period). The large terms-of-trade loss in trade with private market economies reflected in part relatively small increases in the prices of foodstuffs exported by Hungary and in part the rapid rise in the prices of manufactured goods, in which Hungary had a large trade deficit *vis-à-vis* private market economies. While the overwhelming share of Hungary's oil imports came from socialist countries, terms-of-trade effects were smaller in trade with these countries as Soviet export prices of oil in intra-CMEA trade lagged considerably behind world market prices. The lagged adjustment of oil prices also explains the gradual increase in terms-of-trade effects from −1 per cent of the average value of trade with socialist countries in 1975 to 19 per cent by 1978.

In Yugoslavia, as in Hungary, the adverse terms-of-trade effects were larger in trade with private market economies than in trade with socialist countries: 73 per cent of average trade in the first case and 17 per cent in the second. At the same time, Yugoslavia suffered substantially greater terms-of-trade losses than Hungary in trade with private market economies, which provide much of its oil imports. As Yugoslavia pays world market prices for oil imported from socialist countries, its adverse terms-of-trade effects in trade with these countries were also larger than those of Hungary.

Adverse export volume effects in the two countries, too, were greater in trade with private market economies than in trade with socialist countries during the 1974–8 period. The effects averaged 12 per cent of total exports in trade with the first group of countries and 8 per cent in trade with the second in Hungary; the comparable figures were 14 per cent and 7 per cent for Yugoslavia. Apart from a decline between 1975 and 1976 in the export shortfall experienced in trade with private market economies, the adverse export volume effects increased over time.

The larger export shortfall for Hungary and Yugoslavia in trade with private market economies reflected the fact that the slowdown in the growth of imports was more pronounced in these economies than in socialist countries. The differences are largely explained by the greater deceleration of economic growth in private market economies than in socialist countries after 1973, with little variation shown in the income elasticities of import demand.

With terms-of-trade effects as well as export volume effects being larger in trade with private market economies than in trade with socialist countries, Yugoslavia's relatively high share of trade with the former group placed it at a disadvantage *vis-à-vis* Hungary. Expressed as a proportion of their overall trade, the adverse terms-of-trade effects averaged 55 per cent in Yugoslavia and 20 per cent in Hungary between 1974 and 1978. In the same period, the adverse export volume effects averaged 11 per cent of the volume of exports in Yugoslavia and 10 per cent in Hungary.

2.2 Policy Responses to External Shocks

The balance-of-payments effects of the policies applied in the two countries are shown in Table 31.1 while Table 31.2 relates the results to the value of exports, imports, average trade, and the gross national product, as the case may be, all expressed in '1972' prices. In turn, Table 31.3 provides information on debt service and external debt ratios.

In trade with private market economies, Hungary's principal policy response to external shocks was to step up borrowing abroad. This reflects Hungary's failure to reduce the rate of growth of aggregate expenditure, matched by the willingness of foreign banks to meet its borrowing requirements. With continued foreign borrowing, additional net external financing exceeded the balance-of-payments effects of external shocks in trade with private market economies by about one-fifth during the period under consideration.

In turn, Hungary's export shares in private market economies declined more or less continuously, thus augmenting the adverse balance-of-payment effects of external shocks by about one-third, on average. Losses in export market shares were concentrated in manufactured goods as Hungary managed to maintain its average market share in primary commodities, notwithstanding the losses it suffered as a result of the imposition of quotas on its livestock and meat exports by the European Common Market.

Hungary's losses of market shares in manufactured exports were largely the result of domestic policies. The authorities attempted to minimise the effects of changes in world market prices on domestic prices by revaluing the forint and increasing the use of firm-specific taxes and subsidies. The consequences of these policies were a decline in the competitiveness of Hungarian exports and a growing

Table 31.3 Net debt service and net external debt ratios in convertible currencies ($US million)

	1973	1974	1975	1976	1977	1978	1973	1974	1975	1976	1977	1978
	Hungary						Yugoslavia					
Debt service	900	1,500	2,000	2,800	3,400	4,600	1,168	1,359	1,962	1,424	1,733	2,249
Merchandise exports	8,501	9,557	10,950	12,690	14,174	16,573	1,911	2,113	2,154	2,837	2,934	3,168
Debt service ratio	10.6	15.7	18.3	22.1	24.0	27.8	61.1	64.3	91.1	50.2	59.1	71.0
External debt							2,972	3,944	5,134	5,486	7,095	8,887
Gross national product							26,794	33,370	36,710	40,622	4,6695	54,341
External debt ratio							11.1	11.8	14.0	13.5	15.2	16.4
	Outward-oriented newly industrialising countries						Inward-oriented newly industrialising countries					
Debt service	1,425	1,890	2,167	3,036	3,566	4,652	5,792	6,288	8,911	11,666	14,919	21,924
Merchandise exports	12,771	18,619	17,686	25,065	30,375	38,528	19,234	24,183	23,836	28,450	33,942	39,575
Debt service ratio	11.2	10.2	12.3	12.1	11.7	12.1	30.1	26.0	37.4	41.0	44.0	55.4
External debt	5,130	7,909	10,123	10,180	10,797	13,798	18,725	32,621	48,584	58,382	71,480	86,825
Gross national product	48,861	56,300	62,842	72,994	85,261	101,719	269,760	318,907	359,948	395,536	438,755	490,314
External debt ratio	10.5	14.0	16.1	13.9	12.6	13.6	6.9	10.2	13.5	14.8	16.3	17.1

Sources:
Hungary: Net external debt – Marer (1981), p.180; Gross domestic product – World Bank economic and social data base.
Other countries: Exports, interest payments, and amortization – International Monetary Fund, *Balance of Payments Statistics*; Net external debt – World Bank economic and social data base; Gross domestic product – World Bank economic and social data base.

wedge between world market and domestic prices which reduced incentives for exporting by domestic firms.

While some import substitution occurred in Hungary's trade with private market economies, the resulting import savings were quantitatively small and disappeared by 1978. At the same time, the Hungarian authorities failed to reduce domestic demand pressures in response to external shocks, both because of their inability to control investment demand and their unwillingness to cut consumption demand, so that there were no import savings on this count.

In turn, in Hungary's trade with socialist economies, additional net external financing offset, on average, 35 per cent of the adverse balance-of-payments effects of external shocks during the 1974–8 period. The Soviet Union supplied the additional financing by allowing Hungary, like the other members of the CMEA, to run up a ruble trade deficit so as to ease the impact of rising fuel prices.

Hungary further responded to the adverse balance-of-payments effects of external shocks by increasing its export market shares in socialist countries, thereby offsetting 45 per cent of the balance-of-payments effects of external shocks between 1974 and 1978, on average. Gains in market shares in part reflected the diversion of some of Hungary's exports from Western to Eastern markets which was particularly attractive for so-called 'hard' goods, like livestock and meat products, which encountered marketing difficulties in the EEC countries and could be sold for convertible currencies to socialist countries.[1] Another contributory factor was demand on the part of the other socialist countries, motivated by shortages in the domestic availability of certain commodities. Finally, while some import substitution occurred, the lack of restrictive macroeconomic policies was also apparent in Hungary's trade with socialist countries.

To get an overall picture of Hungary's policy responses to the balance-of-payments effects of external shocks, it is necessary to add Hungary's trade with private market economies and with socialist economies. This procedure may be criticised on the grounds that Hungary cannot utilise its earnings of non-convertible rubles from exports to socialist economies to finance imports in convertible currencies from private market economies. However, Hungarian trade flows with the two groups of countries are interrelated both because of substitution in sales between the two markets and because inputs imported from one group may be used in the production of exports to the other. Furthermore, as already noted, part of Hungary's trade with the socialist economies was carried out on a convertible currency basis during the period under consideration.[8]

In the aggregate, additional net external financing was the principal policy response to external shocks in Hungary, nearly equalling the balance-of-payments effects of these shocks. While some import substitution occurred, the resulting import savings were relatively small. At the same time, losses in export market shares in trade with private market economies were offset only to some extent by gains made in trade with socialist countries. Finally, Hungary's failure to impose restrictive macroeconomic policies to reduce imports is reflected in the aggregate calculations as in the country group calculations.

In Yugoslavia, the two most important policy responses to external shocks in trade with private market economies were additional net external financing and import substitution. During the 1974–8 period, additional net external financing offset three-quarters of the balance-of-payments effects of external shocks in this trade. Reliance on external financing reflected the failure of Yugoslavia, like Hungary, to reduce the rate of economic growth in response to adverse external shocks, and it was accommodated by the willingness of foreign banks to meet Yugoslavia's borrowing requirements. Like the Hungarian authorities, the Yugoslav government was both unwilling to sacrifice domestic growth objectives and unable to control domestic demand pressures, especially those associated with investments.

Yugoslavia also experienced large losses in export market shares in its trade with private market economies. Lossess occurred in all commodity groups, especially manufactured goods and copper; they averaged 33 per cent of export value during the 1974–8 period compared with 17 per cent for Hungary. The large losses in the Yugoslav case are mainly attributable to the appreciation of the dinar in real terms and to the growing bias in the system of incentives against exports that resulted from the increasing use of quantitative import restrictions.

Increased protection of the domestic market and the concentration of investment efforts on import replacement projects in conjunction with the 1976–80 plan contributed to import substitution in Yugoslavia's trade with private market economies.[9] The resulting import savings averaged one-third of the value of imports during the 1974–8 period. The calculations further indicate that in Yugoslavia losses in export market shares and import savings due to import substitution increased during the 1974–8 period as incentives increasingly shifted against exports.

As far as its trade with socialist economies is concerned, Yugoslavia's predominant policy response was additional net external financing, equalling on average three-quarters of the balance-of-payments effects of external shocks in this trade between 1974 and 1978. In turn, losses in export market shares in trade with socialist countries were negligible, reflecting some shift of exports from private markets to socialist economies. Finally, there was some import substitution in trade with socialist economies during the 1974–8 period while macroeconomic policies did not lead to import savings.

Thus in the aggregate, Yugoslavia's principal policy response to external shocks was additional net external financing, followed by import substitution, while macroeconomic policies did not give rise to import savings. Losses in export market shares aggravated the adverse effects of external shocks.

3 EXTERNAL SHOCKS AND POLICY RESPONSES TO THESE SHOCKS: SOCIALIST AND PRIVATE MARKET ECONOMIES COMPARED

3.1 The Balance-of-Payments Effects of External Shocks

In the 1974–8 period, on average, adverse terms-of-trade effects equalled 55 per cent of the average value of exports and imports in Yugoslavia and 42 per cent in the inward-oriented NICs. The ratio was 20 per cent in Hungary, which benefited from relatively slow price increases on imports from socialist countries, accounting for over one half of its total imports, and in outward-oriented NICs, which benifited from the higher than average increases in the prices of manufactured goods, accounting for two-thirds of their exports.

A different picture emerges if comparisons are made with the gross national product. In Hungary and in the outward-oriented NICs, both of which have trade shares much above the average, the terms-of-trade loss equalled 7.2 per cent and 5.6 per cent of GNP respectively. The loss was only 2.9 per cent of GNP in the inward-oriented NICs which have a trade share much below the average; it was 6.1 per cent in Yugoslavia, which occupies an intermediate position in regard to the share of trade in the gross national product.

Pure terms-of-trade effects accounted for seven-eighths of the deterioration of the terms of trade in the outward-oriented NICs and for four-fifths in Hungary. In turn, they represented one-third of the terms-of-trade deterioration in the inward-oriented NICs and one-fifth in Yugoslavia, indicating the existence of a large trade deficit in these countries in terms of '1972' prices.

The export shortfall associated with the deceleration of the growth of foreign demand varied from 9.2 per cent of export value in the outward-oriented NICs and 9.5 per cent in Hungary to 11.0 per cent in Yugoslavia and 12.0 per cent in the inward-oriented NICs. Again, Hungary benefited from its larger trade with socialist countries, where import demand slowed to a lesser extent than in private market economies, while outward-oriented NICs benefited from their share of manufactured exports, for which demand increased more rapidly than the average.

As in the case of terms-of-trade effects, however, the results are reversed if comparisons are made with GNP rather than with export value. The resulting estimates show export volume effects to have been the largest in Hungary (3.3 per cent), followed by the outward-oriented NICs (2.4 per cent), Yugoslavia (0.9 per cent), and the inward-oriented NICs (0.7 per cent).

All in all, the adverse balance-of-payments effects of external shocks, expressed as a proportion of GNP, were the largest in Hungary (10.5 per cent), followed by the outward-oriented NICs (8.0 per cent), Yugoslavia (7.0 per cent), and the inward-oriented NICs (3.6 per cent). The differences in the results are in large part explained by the relative degree of openness of the national economies, as represented by the share of exports and imports in their gross national product.

The time pattern of external shocks was similar in the outward-oriented and the inward-oriented NICs. The balance-of-payments effects of external shocks peaked in 1975, when the real price of oil was the highest and the world recession was at its deepest. A considerable improvement occurred in 1976, followed by a deterioration in subsequent years. Despite this deterioration, the balance-of-payments effects of external shocks did not again regain their 1975 level.

By contrast, in Yugoslavia, and to an even greater extent in Hungary, the 1975 balance-of-payments effects of external shocks were surpassed in 1978. This is largely because the adverse balance-of-payment effects increased over time in trade with socialist countries as the Soviet Union raised its oil price and the deceleration of economic growth continued.

3.2 Policy Responses to External Shocks

In 1974, the outward-oriented NICs offset 72 per cent of the balance-of-payments effects of external shocks through additional net external financing, while import savings associated with restrictive macroeconomic policies accounted for a further 22 per cent. Additional net external financing turned negative after 1976, averaging −34 per cent of the effects of external shocks during the 1974–8 period as a whole. Also, with the acceleration of economic growth, import savings due to restrictive macroeconomic policies declined over time, amounting to only 12 per cent of the balance-of-payments effects of external shocks by 1978.

The results indicate the extent of reliance placed on domestic adjustment through higher exports and import replacement in the outward-oriented NICs. In these countries, export promotion and import substitution, taken separately, nearly matched the adverse balance-of-payment effects of external shocks in 1978. For the entire 1974–8 period, additional exports stemming from export promotion equalled 50 per cent, and import savings stemming from import substitution 54 per cent, of the adverse balance-of-payments effects of external shocks.

In the inward-oriented NICs, additional net external financing exceeded the balance-of-payments effects of external shocks in 1974 and, despite decreases in subsequent years, averaged 67 per cent of these effects in the 1974–8 period. The countries in question stepped up their economic growth in 1974, leading to higher imports, while subsequent declines in growth rates resulted in import savings averaging 21 per cent of the balance-of-payments effects of external shocks in the period taken as a whole.

Import substitution also turned from negative to positive in the inward-oriented NICs, but offset only 24 per cent of the balance-of-payments effects of external shocks in the 1974–8 period, on average. In turn, these countries continued to lose export market shares, with the resulting losses averaging 11 per cent of the balance-of-payments effects of external shocks for the entire period. Taken together, additional exports from export promotion and import savings from import substitution equalled only 12 per cent of these effects during the 1974–8 period, compared with 104 per cent for the outward-oriented NICs.

Differences in the policies applied are reflected in changes in net debt services ratios (the net payments of interests and dividends, expressed as a proportion of merchandise exports) and net external debt ratios (the ratio of net external debt to the gross national product) in the two groups of NICs. While these ratios underwent little change in the outward-oriented NICs, net debt service ratios increased from 30.1 per cent to 55.4 per cent, and net external debt ratios from 6.9 to 17.7 per cent in the inward-oriented NICs.

As noted earlier, Hungary failed to take macroeconomic adjustment measures in response to the external shocks it suffered in 1974 and 1975. Rather, the growth of domestic expenditures (in particular, investment demand) accelerated, and reliance was placed on additional net external financing. Some restrictive measures were introduced in 1976, followed by accelerated expansion in 1977 and another slowdown in 1978.

On the whole, import savings associated with macroeconomic policies were nil in Hungary. At the same time, gains made in exporting to socialist countries did not fully offset losses in export market shares in trade with private market economies and import substitution remained small overall. Correspondingly, additional net external financing nearly equalled the balance-of-payments effects of external shocks. Hungary borrowed largely in convertible currencies, and its net indebtedness in these currencies rose from 10.6 per cent of GNP in 1973 to 27.8 per cent in 1978.

In Yugoslavia, additional net external financing exceeded the balance-of-payments effects of external shocks by a substantial margin in 1974, with borrowing taking place largely in convertible currencies. As a result, Yugoslavia's net debt service ratio in convertible currencies increased further from the already high 1973 level, reaching 91 per cent in 1975.[10] Its high debt service ratio made it necessary for Yugoslavia to cut back foreign borrowing, requiring the application of strong restrictive measures. The resulting slowdown, however, gave place to an acceleration of economic growth in 1977 and 1978 as expansionary policies were again applied.

The 1973–8 experience is characteristic of Yugoslavia's stop-go cycles of macroeconomic policy and economic growth. Years of excessive expansion that spill over into balance-of-payments difficulties are followed by short-lived periods of deceleration in response to restrictive policies that are relaxed as soon as the external payments position improves, and thus the cycle continues.

Additional net external financing largely followed the course of these stop-go cycles in Yugoslavia. After reaching high levels in 1974 and 1975, it fell to a considerable extent in 1976 but increased again to 5.8 per cent of GNP in 1977, declining only to 5.3 per cent in 1978. As a result, the ratio of net external debt to GNP reached 16.4 per cent in 1978, compared with 11.1 per cent in 1973. However, despite increased borrowing, Yugoslavia's debt service ratio did not again attain the lofty heights of 1975 and was 71 per cent in 1978.

4 THE ADJUSTMENT EXPERIENCE OF PRIVATE MARKET AND SOCIALIST ECONOMIES

4.1 Adjustment Policies and Economic Growth

For the sake of limiting the growth of their foreign debt, the outward-oriented NICs accepted a temporary decline in the rate of economic growth following the quadrupling of oil prices. At the same time, they increasingly relied on output-increasing adjustment policies that involved increased in exports and import substitution in approximately equal measure.

Output-increasing policies, in turn, led to the acceleration of economic growth in the outward-oriented NICs. While the average rate of growth of GNP declined from 7.4 per cent in 1963–73 to 5.9 per cent in 1973–6 in response to restrictive macroeconomic policies, it increased again to 9.7 per cent in 1976–9 in response to output-increasing adjustment policies. Over the entire 1973–9 period, the growth rate averaged 8.4 per cent, exceeding the 1963–73 growth rate despite adverse external circumstances (Table 31.4).

In the outward-oriented NICs, exports and import substitution were encouraged by the adoption of realistic exchange rates and the provision of similar incentives to sales in domestic and foreign markets. The experience of these countries indicates that outward-orientation can promote efficient import substitution *pari passu* with exports by encouraging the exploitation of economies of scale and by avoiding discrimination against primary activities and the capital goods sector, which are generally disadvantaged under inward-orientation (Balassa, 1981).

Table 31.4 Expenditure shares, incremental capital-output ratios and growth rates

	1963-73	1970-3	1973-6	1976-9	1973-9	1963-73	1970-3	1973-6	1976-9	1973-9
		Hungary					Yugoslavia			
Domestic expenditure shares (as % of GDP)										
Private consumption	na	57.2	58.5	57.8	58.1	55.0	57.8	57.1	53.2	55.2
Public consumption	na	9.9	10.3	10.3	10.3	17.2	16.5	17.7	17.5	17.6
Total consumption	na	67.1	68.6	68.1	68.4	72.2	74.3	74.8	70.7	72.8
Gross domestic investment	na	33.0	36.6	37.6	37.1	30.4	29.8	31.9	35.3	33.6
Net foreign investment	na	−0.1	−5.4	−5.7	−5.5	−2.6	−4.1	−6.7	−6.0	−6.4
Incremental capital-output ratios	na	5.3	6.4	7.7	7.1	5.7	6.2	4.6	4.5	4.6
growth rates (constant prices)										
Gross national product	5.7	6.4	5.2	4.9	5.1	5.6	5.2	6.6	6.9	6.8
Population	0.3	0.3	0.5	0.4	0.4	1.0	0.9	0.9	0.9	0.9
Per capita GNP	5.4	6.1	4.7	4.5	4.6	4.6	4.2	5.7	5.9	5.8
	Outward-oriented newly industrialising countries					*Inward-oriented newly industrialising countries*				
Domestic expenditure shares (as % of GDP)										
Private consumption	70.5	67.5	65.9	61.2	63.5	68.3	68.4	68.0	65.1	66.6
Public consumption	12.6	13.5	12.9	13.0	13.0	11.4	11.6	11.9	13.7	12.8
Total consumption	83.1	81.0	78.8	74.2	76.5	79.7	80.0	79.9	78.7	79.3
Gross domestic investment	20.1	21.6	25.8	27.3	26.5	21.7	22.2	24.8	24.5	24.7
Net foreign investment	−3.2	−2.6	−4.6	−1.5	−3.0	−1.5	−2.2	−4.7	−3.2	−4.0
Incremental capital-output ratios	3.0	3.3	4.9	2.7	3.4	3.1	2.8	4.4	4.9	4.6
Growth rates (constant prices)										
Gross national product	7.4	7.9	5.9	9.7	8.4	6.9	8.5	5.0	5.0	4.9
Population	2.1	1.9	1.8	1.7	1.8	2.5	2.6	2.6	2.6	2.6
Per capita GNP	5.3	6.0	4.1	8.0	6.6	4.4	5.9	2.4	2.4	2.3

Sources: Hungary: *Statisztika Évkönyv* (Statistical Yearbook), various issues.
Other countries: World Bank economic and social data base.

The inward-oriented NICs relied largely on external financing in response to 1973–5 external shocks. Foreign borrowing provided only a temporary remedy, however, and losses in export market shares and negative import substitution adversely affected economic growth in the years 1974–5. Import substitution turned positive in subsequent years but, with continued losses in export market shares, foreign borrowing continued, albeit at reduced rates, and earlier rates of economic growth were not re-established.

GNP growth rates in the inward-oriented NICs averaged 5.0 per cent in 1973–6 as well as in 1976–9, compared with 6.9 per cent in 1963–73. Thus while the outward-oriented NICs were able to surpass earlier rates of economic growth, notwithstanding the large external shocks they experienced, the inward-oriented NICs experienced a decline in growth rates even though the adverse effects of external shocks were smaller relative to their GNP than in the case of the outward-oriented NICs.

The relatively poor economic performance of the inward-oriented NICs was largely the consequence of the policies applied by these countries. Exports were discouraged as a result of the appreciation of the real exchange rate and increased import protection. Although the protective measures more than offset the adverse effects of exchange rate appreciation as far as incentives for import substitution are concerned, there was less import substitution in the inward-oriented than in the outward-oriented NICs. Furthermore, buffeted by the 1979–80 oil price increase and the subsequent world recession, as well as by higher interest rates on their large foreign debt, the inward-oriented NICs eventually had to apply strongly restrictive macro-economic policies.

Hungary, like the inward-oriented NICs, lost export market shares in private market economies, while import substitution remained limited throughout the period under consideration. As in the inward-oriented NICs, these results may be explained by reference to the policies followed. After 1973 the forint appreciated in real terms *vis-à-vis* the US dollar, and export incentives were reduced. Also, continued rapid growth of aggregate expenditure exerted pressure on producers to service domestic markets and created a spillover into imports that were also encouraged by firm-level incentives (Balassa, 1983).

With limited efforts made at domestic adjustment, Hungary continued to rely on external financing. The rapid accumulation of foreign debt could not continue indefinitely, however. The situation was aggravated by the external shocks of 1979–80 – the increase in oil prices by two-and-a-half times, the ensuing world recession, and the rise in real interest rates – necessitating the application of restrictive policies.

The policies applied involved substantial reductions in investment activity and some slowdown in the rise of consumption, leading to a decline in the rate of economic growth to 2.7 per cent in 1979, with practically no further increase in 1980. Rates of economic growth averaged 5.7 per cent in 1963–73, 5.2 per cent in 1973–6, and 4.9 per cent in 1976–9.

In Yugoslavia, GNP growth rates increased from 5.6 per cent in 1963–73 to 6.6 per cent in 1973–6. Growth accelerated again in subsequent years, averaging 6.9 per cent in 1976–9. Yugoslavia experienced considerable losses in export market shares, but this was more than offset by import substitution. Exports were adversely affected by the appreciation of the real exchange rate as well as by an increased bias in favour of import substitution through the application of quantitative restrictions. While the 1976–80 plan called for import substitution in raw materials, the restrictions pertained largely to the importation of finished goods (Tyson, 1981).

Yugoslavia's increased foreign indebtedness and the external shocks of 1979–80 necessitated the application of restrictive measures, involving a tight monetary policy and direct controls on investment after 1978. As a result, economic growth slowed down, with increases of 3.7 per cent in 1979 and 1.8 per cent in 1980.

4.2 Factors Affecting Growth Performance

Economic growth is influenced by the efficiency of investment, the rate of domestic savings, and the availability of foreign savings. An often used, although highly imperfect, measure of investment efficiency is the incremental capital-output ratio (ICOR). With all the customary caveats, this will be utilised in the following discussion.

As shown in table 31.4, among the countries and country groups under consideration, incremental capital-output ratios were traditionally by far the lowest in the outward-oriented NICs. After an increase in 1973–6, when deflationary policies were followed, the average ICOR in these countries decreased below the 1963–73 level during the 1976–9 period. the apparently high level of investment efficiency in the outward-oriented NICs may be explained by the policy choices.

To begin with, the lack of a bias against exports contributed to the efficient allocation of resources between exports and import substitution. The same result was obtained in resource allocation between industry and agriculture, since the countries in question generally provided similar incentives to the two sectors. The lack of bias against exports also permitted the exploitation of economies of scale and encouraged technological improvements through external competition. At the same time, in the absence of serious distortions in the price mechanism, limited intervention by public authorities in investment decisions, and positive interest rates on loans to the private sector contributed to the efficient allocation of investment funds.

Allocative efficiency was compromised through the bias of the incentive system against exports and against agriculture in the inward-oriented NICs. Also, the government played an important role in allocating investment funds in these countries, often invoking non-economic considerations or using inadequate project evaluation procedures, while negative real interest rates necessitated credit rationing in the private sector. Correspondingly, incremental capital-output ratios increased to a considerable extent, from an average of 3.1 in the 1963–73 period to 4.6 in the 1973–9 period. By 1976–9, the average ICOR for the inward-oriented NICs exceeded that of the outward-oriented NICs by four-fifths.

Notwithstanding some decline after 1973, the average ICOR in Yugoslavia remained at a level comparable to that in the inward-oriented NICs during the entire 1973–9 period, and it began to rise once again at the end of the 1970s. The relatively high incremental capital-output ratio in Yugoslavia may be explained by several features of the policy environment, including the bias in incentives against exports and agriculture; the relatively slow profitability of a number of priority investment projects; and the adverse effects of recurrent stop-go investment cycles, which led to inefficient investments in boom periods, the rejection of desirable projects when investment funds were cut back, and a gradual lengthening of the period of project completion (Tyson, 1983).

These considerations also apply to Hungary, where the investment cycle and their adverse effects were especially pronounced. Investment efficiency in Hungary was further reduced as a result of the gradual recentralisation of a substantial part of investment decisions that began in the early 1970s. Moreover, as part of the movement towards recentralisation, domestic producer prices and world market prices increasingly diverged and central intervention in firm decision-making increased.

As a result of these influences, the incremental capital-output ratio increased to a considerable extent in 1973–6 in Hungary. Some improvement occurred in subsequent years, however, as domestic producer prices were again brought nearer to world market price and a fund for export finance was established, reducing the bias against export activities.

Differences in GNP growth rates as between the outward-oriented and the inward-oriented NICs were increased further as a result of higher domestic savings ratios in the former that were offset only in part by a larger inflow of foreign capital in the latter. Apart from interest rate policy, differences in domestic savings ratios may be explained by differences in public savings that tended to be greater in the outward-oriented than in the inward-oriented NICs.

Measured domestic savings ratios were far higher in Hungary and Yugoslavia than in private market economies. While the difference was partly due to price distortions associated with consumer subsidies, adjusted savings ratios were still considerably higher in the two socialist countries than in the newly industrialising country groups.[11] High savings ratios in the socialist countries reflect public decisions regarding the amount to be consumed and the use of public revenues for investment. At the same time, part of domestic investment was financed by foreign borrowing, which averaged 6.4 per cent of the gross domestic product in Yugoslavia and 5.5 per cent in Hungary in 1973–9; the corresponding figures were 4.0 per cent in the inward-oriented NICs and 3.0 per cent in the outward-oriented NICs.

5 CONCLUSIONS

The results reported in this paper permit one to derive some general conclusions about adjustment policies and their relative effects under outward- and inward-oriented development strategies. It appears that, differences in their social system notwithstanding, the policies applied by Hungary and Yugoslavia in response to the external shocks of the 1973–8 period and the effects of these policies had much in common with the inward-oriented NICs and contrasted with the experiences of the outward-oriented NICs.[12]

Hungary, Yugoslavia and the inward-oriented NICs wished to maintain earlier rates of economic growth in the face of external shocks. This objective was pursued by increased foreign borrowing, while the countries in question lost export market shares, and the net effects of output-increasing policies through export promotion and import substitution were small or even negative. By contrast, the outward-oriented NICs placed little reliance on foreign borrowing, gained export market shares, and engaged in import substitution, so that output-increasing policies more than offset the balance-of-payments effects of external shocks.

Differences in the experiences of the outward-oriented NICS on the one hand and Hungary, Yugoslavia and the inward-oriented NICs on the other may be explained by differences in the policies applied. The two socialist countries and the inward-oriented NICs let their exchange rates appreciate in real terms and increased the bias of the incentive system against exports. At the same time, while protection favoured import substitution, the extent of import replacement in manufactured goods was limited by the size of national markets which were not large enough to permit exploiting economies of scale in many industries without an expansion of exports. The protection of the industrial sector also entailed discrimination against primary activities, discouraging not only exports but also import substitution in the primary sector.

Moreover, import substitution in the highly protected industrial sector became increasingly costly as it proceeded into areas where domestic market limitations were more constraining. This fact, together with the lack of sufficient consideration of economic profitability in the public sector and distorted price signals in the private sector, constributed to the low level of investment efficiency observed in Hungary, Yugoslavia and the inward-oriented NICs.

The relatively small output effects and low investment efficiency point to the fact that the countries in question did not make good use of borrowed funds. At the same time, as their external indebtedness increased, they came to encounter limitations for further borrowing. The decline of the borrowing capabilities of the two socialist countries and the inward-oriented NICs was made worse by the general deterioration of the international financial climate, and they were constrained to apply strongly restrictive macroeconomic policy measures. Thus, while the relative ease in obtaining foreign loans following the external shocks of 1973–5 allowed these countries to continue with expansionary policies, the subsequent decline in the availability of loans reinforced the need for the application of restrictive measures following the external shocks of 1979–81.

In order to increase their creditworthiness and to re-establish economic growth on a sound basis, the countries in question would further need to reform their system of incentives. This conclusion is buttressed by the experience of the outward-oriented NICs during the 1973–9 period. In providing similar incentives to sales in domestic and foreign markets and to manufacturing and primary activities, these countries encouraged exports as well as import substitution and attained relatively high levels of investment efficiency.

The policies applied led to the acceleration of economic growth despite relatively large external shocks. At the same time, by limiting reliance in foreign capital and investing the proceeds in high-yielding activities, the outward-oriented NICs were able to avoid excessive indebtedness. Correspondingly, they were better prepared for the external shocks of the years 1979–81 and did not have to apply strongly restrictive policies.

It may be concluded that outward orientation, which is often regarded as a 'fair weather' strategy suitable to buoyant world economic conditions, is also superior to inward orientation as an adjustment policy in response to external shocks. From the evidence provided in this paper, it would further appear that this conclusion applies irrespective of the system of social and economic organisation. In fact, it is the advantages of outward orientation that have motivated the recent policy changes in Hungary.

NOTES

1. Because of the smallness of the trade of the NICs with socialist countries, accounting for about 3 per cent of their total trade, separate estimates for this trade have not been made.
2. This procedure reflects the assumption that price increases after 1971–3 were due to external shocks, in particular the direct and indirect effects of the quadrupling of oil prices.
3. In trade with private market economies, trend and hypothetical values of exports have been calculated with respect to the world exports of each country's traditional export products, defined as primary products that accounted for at least 1.5 per cent of their total exports in '1972', and with respect to the developing countries' exports of fuels, non-traditional primary products other than fuels, and manufactured goods. The view underlying the calculations is that each country competes against all suppliers in the world market for its traditional exports, while its non-traditional exports compete against those of the developing countries.

   In turn, in Hungary's and Yugoslavia's trade with socialist countries, trend and hypothetical values of exports have been calculated with respect to the imports of socialist countries from CMEA member

countries. The view underlying the calculation is that in their export trade with socialist economies Hungary and Yugoslavia compete with CMEA suppliers.
4. For more detail on the procedures for calculating the balance-of-payments effects of external shocks and of policy responses to these shocks, see Balassa (1981), pp. 145–51.
5. These ratios should be interpreted as rough approximations, particularly for Hungary, because the prices used in calculating trade flows with socialist countries are not directly comparable with the prices used in calculating trade flows with private market economies.
6. Data on trade with private market economies and on Yugoslavia's trade with socialist countries originate in the GATT trade tapes. In turn, unit value indices published by the Food and Agriculture Organisation have been used for each country's traditional primary exports taken individually, while unit value indices published by the United States have been utilised for the exports of non-traditional primary products, fuels, and manufactured goods. Finally, the country's own import price indices have been employed for total imports and the UN index for fuel imports.

Hungary's trade with the socialist countries is expressed in terms of rubles, and the estimates made in rubles have been converted into US dollars by utilising the forint/ruble exchange rate derived as a ratio of Hungary's balance of trade published in terms of forints and in terms of rubles in the *Külkereskedelmi Evkönyv* (Foreign Trade Yearbook), 1980. We are indebted to Jan Vanous of Wharton Econometric Forecasting Associates, who supplied the estimates of Hungary's trade with socialist countries and of CMEA exports and imports, all expressed in terms of rubles, as well as the unit value indices for this trade.
7. During the 1974–8 period, Hungary maintained a surplus in its convertible currency trade with socialist countries, which equalled about one-third of its convertible currency deficit with private market economies (Marer, 1981).
8. For example, in 1978, 18 per cent of Hungary's exports to and 13 per cent of Hungary's imports from socialist countries were on a convertible currency basis.
9. It should be noted that while in Yugoslavia increased inward-orientation was the result of deliberate actions, in Hungary this was a concomitant of policies aimed at reducing the effects of fluctuations abroad on the national economy.
10. In interpreting this ratio, it should be noted that the export data do not include services and private transfers, which are of considerable importance in Yugoslavia (tourism and workers' remittances) but not in Hungary or in the NICs.
11. For Hungary, the relevant estimates are shown in Kravis, Heston and Summers (1982), pp. 170, 186.
12. For a similar conclusion regarding the policies followed in the post-war period up to the mid-1960s, see Balassa (1970).

REFERENCES

Balassa, B. (1970) 'Growth Strategies in Semi-Industrial Countries', *Quarterly Journal of Economics*, vol. 84, no. 1, pp. 24–47.

Balassa, B. (1981) 'The Newly-Industrializing Developing Countries After the Oil Crisis', *Weltwirtschaftliches Archiv*, vol. 117, no. 1, pp. 142–94.

Balassa, B. (1983) 'The Hungarian Economic Reform, 1968–82', *Banca Nazionale del Lavoro, Quarterly Review*, no. 144, pp. 163–84.

Kravis, I. B., Heston, A. and Summers, R. (1982) *World Product and Income: International Comparisons of Real Gross Product* (Baltimore: Johns Hopkins University Press).

Marer, P. (1981) 'The Mechanism and Performance of Hungary's Foreign Trade, 1968–79', Hare, P., Radice, H. and Swain, H. (eds) *Hungary: a Decade of Economic Reform* (London: Allen & Unwin).

Tyson, L. (1981) *The Yugoslav Economic System and Its Performance in the 1970s* (Berkeley: University of California, Institute for International Studies).

Tyson, L. (1983) 'Investment Allocation: Comparison of Reform Experiences of Hungary and Yugoslavia', *Journal of Comparative Economics*, vol. 7, no. 3, pp. 288–305.

32 Impact of External Market Fluctuations on Centrally Planned and Market Economies: A Systematic Comparative Approach

W. Trzeciakowski
INSTITUTE OF ECONOMICS, POLISH ACADEMY OF SCIENCES

1 CHANNELS OF IMPACT AND CHARACTERISTICS OF INTERDEPENDENCE

The growth of current and capital transactions between centrally planned economies (CPEs) and market economies (MEs) has increased the vulnerability of CPEs to external market fluctuations. Those market fluctuations were transmitted through the following main channels:
1. changes in the general level of world prices (inflation);
2. changes in exchange rates;
3. changes in particular prices leading to terms-of-trade changes;
4. changes in demand for exports and import supplies;
5. changes in interest rates and credit availability.

The shares of foreign trade in the national income of CPEs are shown in Table 32.A1 at the end of this paper. Table 32.A2 illustrates annual rates of growth and income elasticities of imports and exports in the period 1960–80. Both tables characterise the economic dependence of CPEs, especially the smaller six Eastern European countries, upon foreign trade.

The increase in dependence on foreign trade with the West, resulting from the acceptance of an outward-oriented strategy, came just at the time when the West became unstable. This strategy was permitted by the willingness of Western financial institutions to lend (see Table 32.A3).

Changes in the terms and availability of foreign credits were the major sources of disturbances in CPEs. Each CPE attempted to fulfil the planned rates of growth of investment and consumption in spite of adverse trends in Western markets. This resulted in a drastic expansion of borrowing in the Western banking system. The changes in indicators of creditworthiness resulted in sharp fluctuations in the level of interest rates and in the volume of available credits. These developments resulted in harmful adjustment processes, and in some countries endangered the continuity of debt servicing, resulting in new refinancing of credit arrangements, moratorium procedures and conversion of debts.

No country can insulate its internal economy from fluctuations of foreign demand, changes of terms of trade or terms of credits. However, CPEs can shape the structure of final demand so as to restrict the dependence on foreign countries and, within given limits, adopt inward-oriented or outward-oriented development policies. Adjustment policies can be executed by central directives and/or may be induced indirectly by management. Which policy is effective depends to a large extent on the size of the country, its raw material base and the commodity structure of its exports. Evidently there are trade-offs between the maintenance of overall stability and rational adjustment processes at the level of enterprises. The choice of adjustment policy determines the type of control system (direct-centralised or indirect-centralised).

2 THE ADJUSTMENT SYSTEM IN CPEs

2.1 Direct Central Adjustment in a Traditional CPE

In a traditional CPE there is a built-in preference for a macro-stability, hence for an inward-oriented development, minimising the dependence on countries abroad. Imports are usually treated as indispensable supplies, unavoidable for the elimination of internal shortages or for acquiring new technology. Exports are treated as a means of covering the expenses of indispensable imports. There is a general tendency to insulate the domestic system of prices and costs, investment plans, the structure of production and consumption and the maintenance of full employment from the direct impact of external fluctuations on foreign markets. Long-term goals and medium-term targets are implemented within the framework of a centralised directive planning system and a system of central price control. Planned targets are expressed in physical units of domestic prices, independent of foreign prices.

This system eliminates the direct impact of external fluctuations on the behaviour of enterprises. Hence macro-stability is maintained at the expense of micro-efficiency, as adjustment processes take place exclusively through changes in the central plan, and the use of indirect measures is non-existent. The centralised decision-making system operates effectively in the sphere of raw material exports, but cannot ensure efficiency in industrial exports. The centralised system is oriented towards the preservation of stability of directive plans, full employment and income distribution and is feasible in a large economy, characterised by a rather limited share of foreign trade in the national income, and by a large share of raw materials in overall exports to the west. This is the case of the USSR.

However, this traditional centralised directive system creates huge problems in small open economies, whose exports are composed of highly processed commodities.

2.2 Direct and Indirect Decentralised Adjustment in Reformed CPEs

In reformed CPEs the system deviates from the principles of a traditional CPE. It is a mixed system within which central directives coexist with indirect methods of management and with the operation of market forces. Some spheres of decision-making are centralised as in the traditional system; some are based on decentralised indirect management rules of profit maximisation, relying on prices fixed by the centre; and finally some sectors operate in accordance with market forces, where prices are determined by the market mechanism. Structural investments are determined centrally. Short-term decision-making is decentralised and enterprises fix autonomously the allocation of resources. Foreign market prices determine decision-making in imports and exports. Price control is more flexible, partly determined by enterprises. Domestic prices are in part closely linked to foreign prices by foreign trade exchange rates. Hence in sectors in which these rules apply, external changes in foreign prices, supply and demand directly affect the domestic economy. Equally the changes in foreign exchange rates, though with a certain time-lag, affect the level of domestic exchange rates. To the extent that enterprises subordinate their allocation decisions to the profit maximisation criterion, adjustment processes to external fluctuations are similar to the adjustment processes undertaken by enterprises in market economies. Therefore the indirect decentralised mechanism of adjustment ensures, within the limits of its operation, an efficient allocation of resources at a micro level.

The closest practical approximation of the idealised model of mixed direct and indirect adjustment is the Hungarian system and, to a lesser extent, the Polish system. Both countries are small open economies, relying heavily on foreign trade. However, the adjustment to external fluctuations within the reformed system proved to be unsuccessful in practice, as it resulted in the accumulation of huge debts and permanent problems with the expansion of exports to market economies.[1]

The failure to adjust to external disturbances is caused by the lack of internal consistency of the reformed system:

1. The planned character of the system (the maintenance of stability) is often incompatible with the acceptance of adjustment processes. The temptation of the central planner to reserve the right to choose freely whether to adjust or to insulate leads to inconsistencies in the operation of the system. Whatever the motivations (whether the protection of jobs in inefficient enterprises, or simply the preservation of power in the hands of central administrative organs), inefficiencies are tolerated.

2. In order to preserve this freedom of manoeuvre, instead of using marginal rates of exchange, non-marginal rates are applied; this necessitates the use of corrective taxes and subsidies leading to bargaining procedures.
3. Inefficiencies lead to the low competitiveness of exports; among imports from Western countries raw materials and productive imports, for which there exist no substitutes, predominate. When recessionary conditions hit Western markets there was a sharp drop in CPEs' exports to these market economies; the possible policy responses were painful cuts in import plans, or costly additional credits.
4. Rational and uniformly determined adjustment regimes were incompatible with the ruling egalitarian principles. The need for 'social justice' was usually stronger than efficiency requirements.
5. Where cost-plus forming rules are applied in monopolistic conditions, non-parametric and hence 'manipulable' prices prevail. In these conditions financial authorities are forced to constrain increases in wages by highly progressive taxation rules. This destroys the motivational dynamism of the system, which proves to be especially harmful for export expansion.

Hence successful adjustment to external market fluctuations necessitates an improvement in the reformed system in order to make it more strongly 'efficiency-oriented'. This seems to be especially important in the export sector.

3 COMPARATIVE ANALYSIS OF ADJUSTMENT PROCESSES

Different adjustment rules characterising CPEs and MEs can be explained by the fundamentally different preferences ruling in both systems; namely the preference for stability in a CPE, and the preference for constant adjustment in an ME.

At the one extreme, consecutive five-year plans and yearly plans are supposed to conform to binding long-term directives (development goals, the distribution of income, full employment, etc.) Plans covering longer time-spans have then to include all the necessary specifications for building up the shorter-term plans, and, at the same time, their context should be relatively independent of short-term changes in the economy (see Figure 32.1).

At the other extreme, longer-term programmes are looked upon as subsidiary instruments for analysis and forecast, and planning consists of the constant adaptation of decisions to changing conditions (see Figure 32.2).

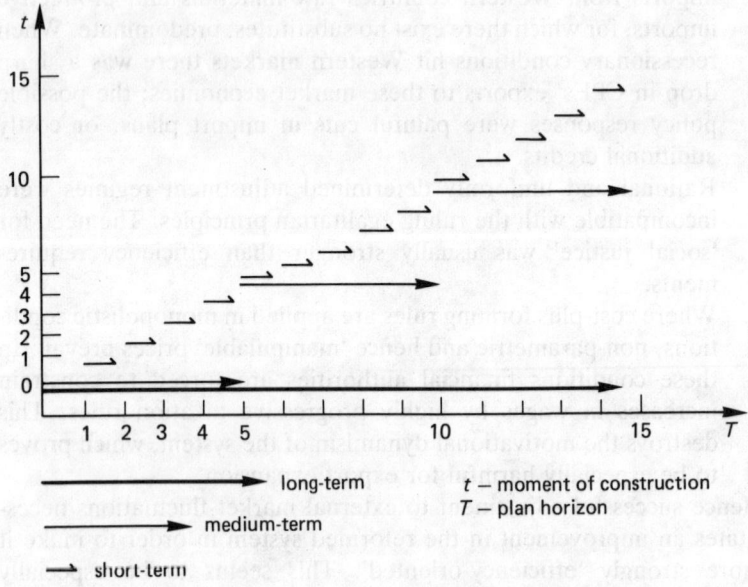

Figure 32.1 CPE: preference for stability

It is obvious that the basic preference for stability in a CPE restricts adjustment processes to external market fluctuations, whereas the preference for constant adaptation in an ME facilitate the adjustment to external disturbances.

In the traditional CPE the fixed accounting exchange rate, operating with a system of variable taxes and subsidies, is aimed at insulating stable domestic prices from changing foreign prices.

In an ME the managed flexible exchange rate system operating with constant taxes and subsidies is aimed at linking domestic prices with foreign prices.

The reformed CPE applies mixed adjustment processes, partly insulating and partly transmitting the external fluctuations into the domestic economy.

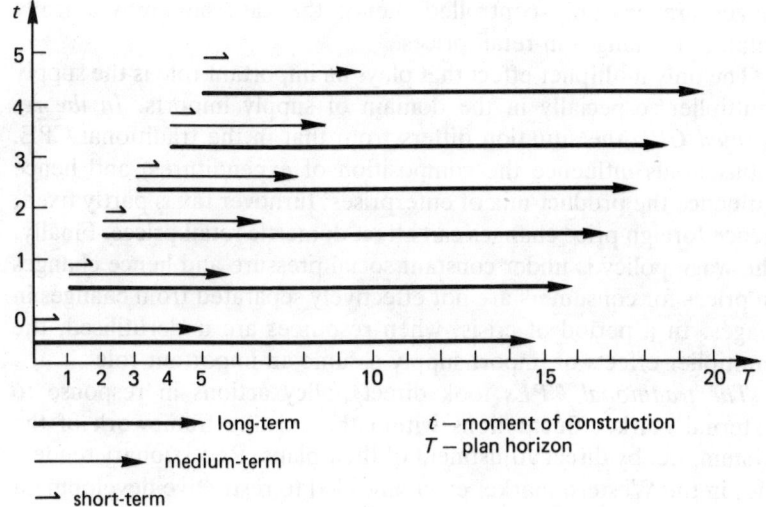

Figure 32.2 ME: constant decision-adaptation to changing conditions

In the traditional CPE producers are separated from foreign trade transactions and there is complete central control over all foreign trade decisions. Equally, there is complete central control over foreign capital market decisions.

In MEs foreign trade decisions are decentralised and profits from domestic activities are integrated with profits from foreign trade activities. In principle, foreign capital market decisions are equally decentralised.

In reformed CPEs, as already mentioned, the exchange rate regime connected with the tax subsidy system permits foreign price changes to be transmitted, but not for all commodities.

In the traditional CPE – contrary to an ME – there occur neither demand-multiplier effects, nor real-balance effects. The first are excluded, as the central plan directly adjusts aggregate demand and production in order to ensure the full employment of resources. The second do not occur, as the changes in foreign reserves do not determine the supply of money. Equally, price-wage substitution effects do not occur, as retail prices are insulated from wholesale prices by variable subsidies and turnover taxes. On the other hand, wages are centrally controlled, hence they are not automatically related to changes in retail prices.

The only multiplier effect that plays an important role is the supply multiplier, especially in the domain of supply imports. *In the reformed CPE* the situation differs from that in the traditional CPE. Households influence the composition of expenditures, and hence influence the product-mix of enterprises; turnover tax is partly fixed, hence foreign price changes can affect domestic retail prices. Finally, the wage policy is under constant social pressure and hence changes in prices for consumers are not effectively separated from changes in wages. In a period of crisis, when resources are underutilised, the multiplier effects of import supply assume an important role.

The traditional CPEs took direct policy actions in response to external market fluctuations within the existing framework of the system, i.e. by direct adjustment of their plans. Recessionary tendencies in the Western market economies led to restrictive development policies aimed at reducing investment and consumption. There were attempts to re-orient foreign trade policies so as to alter the geographic composition of trade by increasing the share of intra-CMEA trade. Policy measures were taken aimed at reducing the dependence upon imports from free currency markets by various measures (by increasing import substitution by undertaking common CMEA investments). In order to reduce the strong terms-of-trade effects in intra-CMEA trade (due to the increased raw material prices of USSR exports), special long-term credits were granted to the worst affected importers of those raw materials.

In MEs instead of the direct quantitative adaption of plans, policy responses took the form of changes in monetary and fiscal policies, floating exchange rates, price and wage controls, trade controls and capital market controls.

In CPEs as well as MEs there are similarities in the case of protective policies aimed at insulating domestic prices from foreign prices: the variable tax-subsidy regime applied in the European Economic Common Market in agricultural commodities is similar to the insulation schemes used in the traditional CPEs.

4 CONCLUSIONS

1. No economy can insulate itself against external market fluctuations: changes in the terms of trade, shifts in demand and

supply, and variation in interest rates and credit availability.
2. Policy responses to these external market fluctuations rely in CPEs usually on direct plan adjustment and in MEs on indirect measures.
3. Reformed CPEs use direct and indirect adjustment measures.
4. Direct adjustment applied in CPEs is aimed at maintaining the stability of plans and at controlling consciously the transmission of an external disturbance in the domestic economy in order to regulate its distributional effects. The weakness of direct adjustment processes lies in the lack of ability to ensure micro-efficiency at the enterprise level.
5. In a very large economy with a relatively low share of foreign trade and with a raw material structure of exports, the use of central directives in adjustment processes seems to be a workable solution. The advantages of ensuring domestic stability are probably more valuable to the decision-makers than the losses in micro-efficiency.
6. Small CPEs cannot switch to inward-oriented development without endangering further growth prospects. In order to adjust to external fluctuations they must decentralise and rationalise their system of decision-making, especially in the foreign trade sector.
7. The reformed CPE system as it actually works seems to be insufficiently internally consistent to ensure adequate expansion of efficient exports. Hence systemic solutions must be further improved so as to eliminate the weaknesses discussed earlier and ensure the competitiveness of exports both to the West and to the East. This seems to be the best solution.
8. This best solution is feasible on the assumption that the Western banking system will have to renegotiate new terms of credits (conversion of debts accumulated in the last decade on acceptable terms) in order to avoid massive defaults of debtor countries.
9. If this solution proves to be unrealistic, the lack of adequate adjustment to external market fluctuations may lead to a long-run re-orientation of economic relations from the West to the East. However, this would require new, more effective changes in the system, dynamising CMEA integration processes, which up till now have been rather ineffective. This seems to be the second-best scenario.
10. If the opening up of small CPEs proves not to be feasible (neither

to the Western nor the Eastern point of view) it is highly probable that their rates of growth will decrease in the foreseable future.

NOTE

1. It should be stressed that the economic results of Hungary are much better than those of Poland. Hungary kept internal prices under control with a consumer's market in equilibrium, whereas Poland ran into troubles and deep crisis, caused by an irresponsible development strategy. Both countries maintained full employment.

REFERENCES

Csaba, L. (1980) 'World Economic Changes and the CMEA' *Acta Oeconomica*, Budapest, vol. 25, no. 1–2.

Drabeck, Z. (1982) *Changes in Relative World Prices and their Transmission into Economies Protected by Foreign Trade Monopoly* (Geneva: UNCTAD).

Neuberger, E. and Tyson, L. (eds) (1980) *The Impact of International Economic Disturbances on the Soviet Union and Eastern Europe* (New York: Pergamon Press).

Trzeciakowski, W. (1978) *Indirect Management in a CPE* (Amsterdam: North-Holland).

Wojciechowski, B. (1982) 'Economic Measures Bearing Upon Trade of the Socialist Countries' (Geneva: UNCTAD), unpublished paper.

Wolf, T. A. (1980) 'On the Adjustment of CPEs to External Economic Disturbances', in: Marer, P. and Montias, J. (eds) *East European Integration and East–West Trade* (Bloomington: Indiana University Press).

Table 32.A1 Percentage of imports and exports of national income (in current domestic prices)

Years	Bulgaria		Czechoslovakia		GDR		Hungary		Poland		Rumania		USSR*	
	Imports	Exports	Imports	Exports	Imports	Exports	Imports	Exports	Imports	Exports	Imports	Exports	Imports	Exports
1970	20.0	21.9	8.6	8.8	18.6	17.5			24.5	22.9	5.7	5.4	3.7	4.0
1971	24.0	25.0	8.9	9.8					24.0	21.9			3.7	4.1
1972	25.0	25.0	9.0	9.5					26.1	23.1			4.2	4.1
1973	26.4	26.4	10.0	9.9					31.1	24.3			4.6	4.7
1974	32.1	28.2	11.4	10.7					36.5	27.7			5.3	5.8
1975	36.4	31.5	12.5	11.6	27.6	24.6	52.9	47.1	38.9	30.5	7.3	7.4	7.3	6.6
1976	35.8	34.4	13.6	12.6	31.1	26.8	55.8	49.8	36.7	27.8	7.6	7.7	7.4	7.3
1977	39.4	38.7	15.4	14.2	32.2	26.9	58.0	46.4	35.5	28.4	8.1	8.1	7.4	8.2
1978	41.7	40.5	15.8	14.7	31.5	28.7	55.7	50.9	34.0	28.4	8.8	8.0	8.2	8.4
1979	41.2	43.5	16.6	15.4	33.8	31.4	51.6	48.4	35.6	31.4	10.0	8.9	8.6	9.6
1980	40.5	43.4	16.8	16.5	33.7	30.5			37.2	31.6	9.9	10.7	9.6	10.8
1981	45.2	45.2	18.4	18.7					30.1	24.9			10.9	11.8

*Imports and exports based on current prices, expressed in transferable rubles.
Sources: UN foreign trade statistics, domestic statistical yearbooks and own estimates.

Table 32.A2 Growth rates and income estimates by type of country 1960–80

Areas/Countries	Gross national product			Annual rates of growth in %						Income elasticities					
				Imports*			Exports*			Imports			Exports		
	1960–70	1970–80	1960–80	1960–70	1970–80	1960–80	1960–70	1970–80	1960–80	1960–70	1970–80	1960–80	1960–70	1970–80	1960–80
World total††	5.3	4.0	4.6	8.0	5.5	6.7	7.8	4.8	6.3	1.50	1.38	1.45	1.45	1.20	1.37
Market type economies	5.4	3.7	4.4	8.0	5.3	6.6	7.8	4.7	6.2	1.57	1.43	1.50	1.53	1.27	1.41
Developed market economies	5.1	3.3	4.2	8.9	4.8	6.9	8.4	6.5	7.4	1.75	1.45	1.64	1.65	1.97	1.76
Developing countries	5.3	5.7	5.5	5.2	7.1	6.2	7.0	1.5	4.2	0.98	1.25	1.13	1.32	0.26	0.76
Petroleum-exporting countries	6.6	6.3	6.5	4.8	13.5	9.0	8.7	1.0	3.8	0.58	2.14	1.38	1.32	0.16	0.58
Other	4.9	5.4	5.1	5.3	4.0	4.6	4.8	6.8	5.8	1.08	0.74	0.90	0.98	1.26	1.14
Socialist countries (east'n europe)	6.7	5.3	6.0	8.1	7.4	7.8	9.3	7.0	8.1	1.21	1.33	1.30	1.39	1.32	1.35
USSR	7.2	5.0	6.1	6.2	8.0	7.1	9.3	4.9	7.1	0.86	1.62	1.16	1.29	0.98	1.16
Other (6 countries)	6.4	5.5	5.9	10.1	7.4	8.8	9.2	8.4	8.8	1.58	31.35	1.49	1.44	1.53	1.49
Bulgaria	8.2	7.1	7.6	11.6	8.7	10.2	13.9	11.6	12.7	1.41	1.23	1.34	1.69	1.63	1.67
Czechoslovakia	4.2	4.7	4.4	7.4	4.7	6.0	6.7	6.3	6.5	1.76	1.00	1.36	1.60	1.34	1.48
GDR	4.5	4.8	4.6	8.8	6.2	7.5	8.1	7.4	7.7	1.96	1.29	1.63	1.80	1.54	1.67
Hungary	5.4	5.4	5.4	10.4	5.6	8.0	10.3	8.2	9.2	1.92	1.04	1.48	1.91	1.52	1.70
Poland	6.2	6.0	6.1	9.4	8.3	8.9	10.3	7.3	8.8	1.52	1.38	1.46	1.66	1.22	1.44
Rumania	8.6	9.9	9.2	9.9	...	11.8	11.1	...	11.3	1.15	...	1.28	1.29	...	1.22

* Volumes: GNP – 1970 prices; imports and exports – 1978 prices.
** For socialist countries, material product.
† Without socialist countries of Asia
†† Rough estimate by author because of lack of official figures for years 1974–80.

Sources: *Handbook of International Trade and Development Statistics*, 1981 Supplement, Tables 2.1., 2.2., 6.2.; *Year-Book of International Trade Statistics 1980*, vol. I; *Economic Survey of Europe in 1981*, pp. 287, 291; *Facts on Czechoslovak Foreign Trade 1981*; *Statistisches Jahrbuch der DDR 1981*; *Statistisches Jahrbuch für die BRD 1982*; *Rocznik Statystyczny Handlu Zagranioznego Polski 1981*. Compiled by Wojciechowski (1982).

Table 32.A3 Indebtedness of CMEA countries 1975–82

Year	Indebtedness, CMEA 7		Indebtedness, CMEA 6		Indebtedness
	in $bn	rate of growth in %, previous year = 100	in $bn	rate of growth in %, previous year = 100	USRR in $bn
1975	32.9	53	22.3	43	10.6
1976	42.4	29	28.8	29	13.6
1977	49.8	17	34.5	20	15.3
1978	55.1	11	41.2	19	13.9
1979	64.7	17	50.7	23	14.0
1980	69.5	7	56.5	11	13.0
1981	80.7	16	61.3	8	19.4
1982	76.8	−5	60.9	−1	15.9

Net indebtedness of individual CMEA countries, 1980–2, 1985

Year	Total	Bulgaria	Czechosl.	GDR	Poland	Rumania	Hungary	USRR
1980	69.5	4.0	3.8	10.3	22.1	7.9	8.4	13.0
1981	80.7	2.6	3.5	13.0	24.3	10.2	7.7	19.4
1982	76.8	2.3	3.4	12.2	25.0*	10.3	7.7	15.9
1985	83–100	2–3	4–5	14–16	30–32	10–12	6–7	17–25

*Including arrears in interests.
Sources: 'L'endettement des pays de l'Est vis-à-vis de l'Occident', Problèmes Economiques, no. 1327, 1983.
'Der harte Dollar als Wohltat für den Comecon', Neue Züricher Zeitung, 25 March 1983.
GUS/Central Statistical Office (1983) Report on the Economic Situation of Poland, Warszawa.
Zelechowska J; 1982 'Sytuacja platnicza RWPG', Rynki Zagraniczne, no. 109, and estimates by J.J. Sztaudynger, Lodz University Institute of Econometrics.

33 Impact of External Market Fluctuations on Centrally Planned and Market Economies: Discussion and Conclusions

J. Bognár
INSTITUTE FOR WORLD ECONOMICS
OF THE HUNGARIAN ACADEMY OF
SCIENCES

The papers collected here discuss on a comparative basis the impact of external market fluctuations on planned and market economies. I would like to start with some brief remarks.

In my opinion the expression 'external market fluctuations' is insufficient to describe the processes and impacts that are taking place in the world economy. Many experts talk of a world economic crisis, while others, including myself (Bognár, 1976 and 1980) talk of the beginning of a new era. In any case, both expressions indicate wider, more complex and longer lasting phenomena than the concept of 'external market fluctuations'.

The high-standard lectures that have been delivered have dealt with the impact of external circumstances on national economies, but failed to discuss the opposite effects.

It is obvious, however, that the sensitivity of the world economy has increased, precisely because of the crisis. Consequently, some other phenomena, which would not have caused any distortion under more favourable circumstances, can also worsen the situation. I am referring not only to the fact that neither theory nor practice of a global issues management have as yet been developed, but also to another problem. Nowadays a powerful country, acting in the spirit of 'enlightened self-interest', may contribute to a deterioration of the world economic situation to an extent which will not only negatively affect other countries, but also eventually strike back at the 'enlightened' powerful country. I shall return to this issue later on.

In the course of the debate a consensus has been achieved on the fact that at present each national economy has the problem of adjusting to external impacts, since an increasing proportion of national production and consumption is affected by the international economic process. Such a change is taking place both in the developed and in the developing world, which have to be complementary to each other in one way or another. In other words, interdependence has reached such a high level that a *qualitative* change has occurred.

These considerations, as was stressed by lecturers and contributors, hold good for both planned and market economies.

Of course, considering the character and pace of response, economies belonging to various socio-political systems show fundamental differences. By thorough comparative research, Béla Balassa has come to the conclusion that the newly industrialising countries (NICs) are quicker and more resolute in responding to the world economic 'challenges' than the Hungarian or Yugoslav economies. I agree with the judgement, which has been strongly supported by data, that export-oriented economies have achieved better results in import substitution than the other countries.

Lecturers and participants from planned-economy countries, including Witold Trzeckiakowski and Maria Maximova, gave strong evidence of factors that weakened the adaptability of some socialist countries, including, among other things, the initial uncertainty in judging the world economic crisis, a certain weakness in management organisation, and above all the fact that the European socialist countries had to face an unfriendly, even 'hostile' international economic environment (blockades, cold war and embargoes). Such processes and tendencies can still be felt today. It is, of course, easier and more reasonable to 'adjust' to a 'friendly' international economic environment than to an 'unfriendly' one. Finally, as far as the Soviet Union is concerned, the first phase of the world economic crisis (up to 1979) was accompanied by several advantages for its economy (the rise in the price of primary energy and some raw materials). Consequently, for the Soviet Union, the re-arrangement of certain economic and political factors to maintain balance was not mandatory in that phase.

The contributors mainly discussed the situation as it has developed until 1979, but the crisis has spread since then, and economies have to face not only inflation, unemployment and imbalance, but also the stagnation of international trade, which has been evident for years, and the increasing danger of a monetary and liquidity crisis.

Under these circumstances, the reaction of national economies has resulted in no more than a certain re-arrangement of economic power relations between states. This kind of reaction reminds me of the zero sum game, in which one of the players wins the other player's money without any change in the total sum. Besides the stagnation of international trade, the monetary and liquidity crisis represents a serious problem, which includes the breaking up of the Bretton Woods system and a stock of debts of about 1,000 billion dollars. The high level of interest rates is also a matter for concern, especially in the case of short-term debts, for the indebted countries.

Under these circumstances, the stagnation of international trade is caused not only by restrictive domestic economic policies but also by the lack of financial resources in debtor countries.

Although imports are of fundamental importance in ensuring economic development, indebted countries are unable to import. On the other hand, developed countries are unable to increase exports; but recovery in an export-oriented country is impossible when export stagnates or declines. (It is well-known that 35 to 40 per cent of the exports of developed countries go to developing countries, i.e. to the countries that are most in debt.)

The danger of a deepening economic crisis is intensified by a persistent political and security crisis. This crisis itself brings about growing political tensions, with an increase in the number of conflicts and an intensification of the arms race. Unfortunately, the conventional way of thinking of the economic profession still starts from the view that economic developments are determined only by economic factors. Although this supposition may be considered necessary at a first stage of analysis, at a later stage – especially when working out interdependent economic policies – it can lead to a dangerous illusion.

It is obvious, however, that mutual mistrust revealed by an increasing political tension over armaments constitutes a very difficult obstacle to the achievement of the co-operation required by interdependence.

Of course, the adjustment of national economies involves certain policy elements which can be accomplished even in difficult and unstable world economic conditions, such as, among other things, energy and raw material austerity, the reduction of public expenditure, and the rationalisation of investments. Governments, however, find themselves in a delicate situation if – due to external economic circumstances – they have to implement unpopular programmes in stagnating economic conditions. It also must be taken into consideration that certain social groups (old people, young people, women, coloured people, minorities) will get into a particularly difficult situation as a consequence of the persistence of the crisis.

A lively debate has developed on whether we can or cannot overcome the crisis and on whether a certain recovery can or cannot be expected in the near future.

According to several contributors, the current recovery of the US economy will also carry other economies with it. Nevertheless, the supporters of this view were not optimistic about the possibility of a sustained expansion in Western Europe, while they thought that Canada, Australia, Japan and South-East Asia could follow the US recovery.

According to a less optimistic opinion, the most dynamic group of countries in a stagnating world economy could only increase their exports at the expense of other groups. As the success of the former group involves a reduction in the purchasing power of the latter groups, a boom will be followed by a slump, especially if other crisis elements (including large budget deficits, high military expenditure, persistent unemployment and high interest rates) are not eliminated. The advocates of the less optimistic opinion also pointed out that the fundamental elements of the world economic crisis remained unchanged (namely, the basic contradiction between the population explosion and lack of purchasing capacity; the food crisis; the increasingly ambivalent nature of science and technology; the problems of structural and technological change; the dangers of nuclear techniques; the arms race based on the balance of reciprocal deterrence; the limitation of the natural sources of energy, etc.), which leads to the world becoming less and less 'controllable'.

The most essential problem nowadays is whether or not mankind is able to break out from this 'vicious circle'.

We are of the opinion that a way out of the crisis can be found if three conditions are fulfilled:
1. A stop to the arms race and the establishment of a mutually acceptable security system.
2. The establishment of a co-operative atmosphere among nations.
3. The introduction of institutional reforms, based on a consensus, which could fill the gap between the goals of mankind and national economic interests.

The 'less optimistic' assessment of the world economic crisis indicates that policy programmes have to be worked out that are suitable for the management of global economic problems. In other words, the understanding and the management of the new world economic situation requires a brand new approach.

The understanding of this new interaction of economic, political and security factors is a fundamental element of the new approach. Therefore the consideration of external non-economic factors appears relevant for any economic analysis.

The current political structure of the world (which includes 180 national economies) cannot be radically transformed in the near future. Therefore research has to find the ways and means to replace unfriendly economic relations with co-operation.

International economics can be useful to mankind if it is able to show the way to possible solutions of these, at present apparently insoluble, problems.

REFERENCES

Bognár, J. (1976) *Világgazdasági korszakváltás* (Change of Era in the World Economy) (Budapest: Közgazdasági és Jogi Könyv-kiadó).

Bognár, J. (1980) *A fejlődés és az együttműködés század-végi fordulópontjai* (Turning Points of Development and Co-operation at the End of the Century) Budapest: Közgazdasági és Jogi Könyv-kiadó).

Part VII

Economic Aspects of Alternative Energy Sources

34 Economic Aspects of Alternative Energy Sources: An Introduction

P. Maillet
UNIVERSITÉ DE LILLE I

1 LESSONS FROM THE PAST

The economic experience of the last decade has taught us two important lessons about energy economics and energy policy. First, the era of focusing world-wide on one main source of energy has come to an end; after the dominance of wood in the past centuries (but still nowadays in many developing countries), then of coal for many decades, especially at the time of industrial take-off in the now developed countries, and finally of oil after the Second World War, we are entering a period in which we will use many sources of energy at the same time, some not renewable, other renewable or very slowly exhaustable. The issue of delineating the best mix of these alternative sources of energy comes to the forefront when defining an energy policy. Though this problem is set up in different ways in different countries, according, of course, to geographical endowments, but also to the standard of the equipment industry, it has to be solved in all of them, whether they are rich or poor in sources of energy.

Secondly, the impact of energy on the working of the national economy has become of vital importance. Certainly, we have known for a long time that a sufficient supply of energy is a must for the satisfactory working of the economy, due to the ubiquitous role of this product. This is illustrated by (a) the role of the coal mines in the development of industrial activities in certain countries in the nineteenth century (the UK, Germany, the USA, France and Belgium) and the backwardness of some others which were lacking in energy; (b) the possibility on the contrary of expanding industry in many Western countries (like Italy or the Netherlands) after the Second World War, thanks to the possibility of using cheap oil or natural gas; (c) the help given to the fast economic growth of the Western world between 1955 and 1973 by the low price of oil. All these facts are well known, and the same type of impact will be observed in the future for the developing countries. But we have more recently realised that the conditions of the supply of energy are also decisive for the smooth functioning of the economy, through its impact on the balance of payments, on national investment and finally on employment, with the consequence that a good energy policy cannot be defined without taking account very carefully of the interrelations between the energy sphere and the economic sphere as a whole.

2 ENERGY AND THE THEMES OF THIS CONFERENCE

As a consequence, energy is at the very junction of the three themes of this Congress:
1. The appearance of new sources of energy is the result of an intensive striving through research and development. The possibilities of domestically and economically new sources of energy, and also of technically transforming some primary sources to various end-products (benzine from coal is only one example) are being extensively studied in private or public laboratories. But this energy evolution is also at the root of substantial structural changes: changes in the different industrial technologies, but also changes in the world specialisation of various activities, due to the fact that the comparative costs of energy-intensive activities have changed a lot among countries in the last decade.
2. The most important sources of energy are fairly unevenly distributed over the world; energy has long been, but is more and more, a source of interdependence among nations. This interdependence is sometimes the source of political conflicts, and is of ever-increasing importance in economic life.
3. Economic development may be helped or hampered by the economic conditions of energy supply and by the more or less efficient energy policy adopted by each country.

Two steps are decisive in the energy field: the preliminary step of preparing the best decisions, which mainly involves comparison between alternative energy sources, giving due weight to the whole set of criteria which have to be considered; and the final step of implementation, by means of measures which will orientate the energy balance of the nation (or of a set of nations) in the right direction. The methodological aspects of economic studies in the fields of energy and the practical problems of delineating and implementing an energy policy have been the main topics of the papers and discussions in this specialised session.

35 Main Economic Aspects of Energy Choices and Policies

P. Maillet
UNIVERSITÉ DE LILLE I

For a long time, national energy policies have concentrated on one major option, i.e. determining the optimal distribution of energy supply as between the available sources, both domestic and imported. More recently, the problem of energy-saving has also become of prominent importance.

With the increasing number of energy sources and the economic and political necessity, for most countries, of diversifying their energy supply, the problem of comparing alternative energy sources and options must receive increasing attention; at the same time, the problem of implementing the chosen option is becoming more difficult. Both these aspects – of preliminary studies and of implementation – will be touched on in turn.

1 COMPARING ENERGY ALTERNATIVES

The basic methodological instrument used to approach the problem has for long been, and still remains in a number of cases, of a micro economic order: that is, accepting general economic parameters, such as current price and cost levels, as a fundamental reference frame, a comparison of costs to the end-user is then made and the alternatives are expressed in rank order.

There is now increasing awareness of the inadequacies of this approach, which can be listed under three main headings:

1. Energy consumption is not an end in itself, but a means to achieving an end-service which can often be attained by other means.
2. The spectrum of criteria of comparison (and the order in which they are placed) is not the same for all the economic agents concerned (the multitude of end-users, the small number of producers, the political authorities).
3. Major energy options are not just insignificant ones such as would leave untouched the other factors ruling the economy as a whole: they are not micro, but meso-decisions.

This means that we must compare not only specific sources of energy, but whole energy supply systems, applying a wide range of criteria, and then explicitly relate those comparisons to the overall view of the economy and its complex machinery.[1] Let us insist on the meso-economic nature of high-level energy policy decisions.

The separate decisions of individual end-users are virtually without effect on the general economy of a country, but the situation is quite different for decisions taken by the government or by major energy producers. This contrast is highlighted if we consider the two questions of capital investment and the balance of payments.

The energy sector accounts for roughly 12 per cent of total capital investment (excluding housing) in industrial countries. At the same time, the ratio of investment to effective energy output varies considerably as between one energy mode, or supply-line, and another. Even if individual producers tend to assume that there are unlimited financial resources at going rates, people in government must take a different view: knowing that the overall national investment capacity is not very elastic, they must bear in mind that an energy strategy requiring heavy investment will reduce the possibilities of developing other capital-intensive sectors of the economy or of combating unemployment by adequate investment in labour-intensive sectors.

As concerns imported products, industrial operators reckon their costs on the basis of current and foreseeable future exchange rates, which are for them a standard parameter, whereas the national executive must adopt a more flexible attitude. Increased imports are offset by increased exports in very different proportions according to the country with which the trade flow is proceeding: if it has a state-controlled economy, the trade relationship works rather like a one-for-one barter system, but if it has a free market economy, then a triangular system of payments obtains. Hence it is clear that the geographical origin of energy imports can weigh heavily on the balance of payments as a whole. Furthermore, when a country's balance of payments is unfavourable, this can be a serious obstacle to a general policy of economic growth. Thus, depending on whether an energy option tends to improve or worsen the payments position, it will influence, for better or worse, the overall economic trend in that country.

More generally, prices and observed levels of other economic parameters can be unsatisfactory indicators in relation to energy policy options (whereas these same options can have significant indirect repercussions on the national economy as a whole). Consequently, it is essential for a proper evaluation of energy options to make a careful prior evaluation of connections at the interface between energy and the rest of the economy. This may be illustrated by four main points.

1.1 Social Costs and Benefits

Here we are concerned with economic components (both costs and benefits) which are directly linked to the development of a given energy technology or production system, but which for various reasons do not enter into the economic calculations of the producer or the end-user, because they are not directly charged for the costs and derive no direct advantage from the benefits.

There are two examples which come prominently to mind. Some social costs are represented by the pollution and other dangers associated with operating plant: the discharge of effluents into the atmosphere or rivers, industrial accidents, and risks to the surrounding population. Conversely, social benefits can derive from the research and development work accompanying an energy product or supply-line which give an economic fall-out in other directions by stimulating improvements in intermediate products or technical processes.

Assessment of the financial impact of these costs and benefits generally depends on political judgements and on the local economic structure, so that it is highly likely that this will vary from one country to another.

1.2 Effects on the Balance of Payments

Under the standard micro economic approach, the decisive factor affecting these comparisons is the foreign exchange rate, assumed to depend on the overall economic position and to be unrelated to the energy option itself.

A meso-economic analysis of the energy economy must on the contrary take full account both of the economic dissimilarities between potential outside suppliers of energy and of the wider economic implications of maintaining the balance of payments. In the last decade, due to the increase in the cost of primary energy, the question has become of vital importance.

If additional energy imports are not to upset the trade and payments balances, they must be offset by additional exports of equivalent value. How can these imports generate the exports required?

In the most frequent case (with due exception paid to the state-trading countries) the energy supplier engages in indiscriminate international trading on a multilateral basis and its receipts from energy sales can be spent anywhere in the world.

Some of these receipts find their way back to the energy-importing country. This gives a direct feedback ratio obtained by dividing the value of energy imports by that of exports to the energy seller country. Another part of these receipts returns indirectly to the energy-importing country via triangular transactions involving one or more third countries. This gives us an indirect feedback ratio.

The value of the direct feedback ratio depends on the degree of complementarity between the products or services required by the energy seller country and those which can be supplied by the energy-importing country on competitive terms. That of the indirect feedback ratio depends on the balance-of-payments techniques of the third country or countries involved.

The overall feedback ratio is, of course, obtained by aggregating the direct and indirect components. It may equal one or be below. This leads us to the conclusion that the incidence on the balance of payments of a given increase in energy imports varies according to country of origin and often, therefore, to the energy form considered. For instance, in terms of the balance of payments, the incidence of importing energy to a value of 1 billion dollars is not the same, for a European country, if the energy is in the form of American, Australian or Polish coal, Russian or Algerian gas, or Saudi Arabian, Mexican or Nigerian oil.

In some economic situations, the need to maintain the balance of payments in equilibrium is liable to hinder economic growth and the even balance might be achieved to the detriment of the home employment situation (unemployment external equilibrium): the transfer to another level of equilibrium, corresponding to a greater volume of imports, would stimulate activity at home and thus greatly benefit the economy as a whole.

This is the case when there is a fairly rigid link between GNP and import volume, when the level of the trade deficit is limited by the necessity of finding other means of closing the overall payments gap and finally when the net value of exports cannot be increased by currency devaluation, because the aggregate elasticity is less than one (theorem of critical elasticies or Lerner conditions).

Here, to a given import volume M is tied a given domestic production level Y, which may imply underemployment. Consequently, any increase that can be achieved in M contributes to relieving the pressure on Y from external sources, and thus to increasing the general level of economic activity. In other words, the currency exchange rate, in so far as it reflects a balance-of-payments position in which the volume of foreign trade corresponds to unemployment, might be a very unreliable indicator of the true economic value of the foreign currency considered.

This being so, one can formulate an activity multiplier in relation to the improvement of the balance-of-payments position.

1.3 Dependence on Foreign Energy Supplies

Foreign energy supplies are obviously vulnerable to uncontrolled events: price fluctuations (resulting from a monopoly situation or other examples of a seller's market), a supply embargo or restriction. Such events may exert a bad impact on the working of the economy, and this impact may differ according to which energy product falls short.

When making comparisons between alternative sources of energy, therefore, it is necessary not only to consider the element of risk involved by each, but also to have a perfectly clear idea of what measures are practically available to counter that risk – for example, what underground storage capacity will be available to accompany imports of natural gas[2].

1.4 Energy Options in Relation to Employment

In a situation of full employment, with no shortage of skilled manpower, the additional labour cost can properly be represented by the remuneration (including wages and related social contributions) awarded to the additional workers engaged; the microeconomic approach is quite adequate for determining that cost. But things are very different when there is a labour surplus or shortage.

The importance of present unemployment leads to the macroeconomic question: is it possible to gear national energy policy for the purpose of economic expansion at home? The ideas put forward refer to two macroeconomic notions: the Keynesian multiplier, and the loosening of external constraints.

The creation of domestic employment by increasing domestic energy production, and also activities tending to decrease energy consumption, set off a cumulative process which applies both to the additional investment expenditure and additional current expenditure (provided they are directed to the domestic market). Examples are the making and fitting of solar appliances (a typical energy-producing investment), work on energy-saving systems (insulation, heat-pumps, and so on), or to raising the current level of output from coal-mines. This is accompanied by a loosening of the external constraint: increased domestic production of energy and the reduction of energy imports, through introducing energy-saving devices and by reducing the marginal reliance on imports, enable domestic economic activity to expand at a higher rate.

The above argument is limited, however, by the very mechanism of the multiplier effect itself. In the first phase, activity is created due to an injection of new expenditure; when this expenditure is called off, the activity it created disappears as well. This is avoided only if the spurt of expenditure has encouraged capital investment which in turn creates new jobs of a more permanent kind. But this is an effect produced by investment, and no longer by increased expenditure.

Furthermore, the multiplier effect exists only if it involves monetary creation. If this in fact takes place, the stimulation of the economy is due not to the energy policy as such, but to monetary growth – which would have approximately the same effect whatever its purpose.

The true economic relationship between a domestic energy programme and the domestic employment situation is thus a most ambiguous one: expenditure on an energy drive will undoubtedly produce an increase in the demand for labour, although this can be said of any kind of expenditure; and there will probably be some kind of multiplier effect, although this can be said of any expenditure which involves monetary creation. Consequently, the job-creation potential of a domestic energy drive, whether resulting directly from the added expenditure or from the multiplier effect, is to some extent illusory: it is not the energy factor which counts, but the effect of additional expenditure *per se* ('additional' in the sense of not reducing the expenditure under other headings). Before embarking on such energy expenditures, one must test very carefully that they are more efficient in the energy sphere than somewhere else in the economy.

1.5 Limitations of Existing Comprehensive Models

Interrelations between energy choices and economic development appear to be numerous: beside the old goal of having a sufficient (and low-cost) energy supply there are new worries about balance of payments and employment, which make the comparison between energy options more complex. To make proper allowance for these interrelations it is necessary to spell out the economic, technological and political implications affecting each energy choice. In other words, we must think in terms of comprehensive scenarios.

Certain costs and benefits of any scenario have links between them, and the only way of dealing with these interrelationships is to use a mathematical model. But the available macroeconomic models are not suitable because energy is treated as a whole (and sometimes included in industry). Hence it might be necessary to develop specific models[3].

2 IMPLEMENTING CHOICES

So much for preliminary studies; let us turn now to the specific problem of policy.

One of the most fundamental questions for the implementation of energy goals deals with the role of the government. Political and social uncertainties, the international and political dimension of the energy market, technological risk and the risk of underprovision of fuels at some future date are the main reasons for having an element of planning in even the most market-oriented of economic systems.

The element of externalities might be a further reason for such public intervention. But, in practice, the main option is to define the optimal allocation of the burden of choices between planners in central government and planners in individual enterprises (and households), and on this point a wide range of opinions can be expressed.

It can be stressed very strongly that the identification of market failure is only a necessary prerequisite for government interference but not a sufficient requirement. It has been said that 'The real world choices are between imperfect markets and imperfect governments'. The degree of imperfection may vary from market to market and from government to government, and the evaluation of this degree of imperfection is also a subjective one, differing from observer to observer.

These problems are in fact common to all attempts to implement at ground level the decisions taken following cost-benefit analysis at the highest level, to the extent that the individuals affected do not see things in quite the same way as the decision-makers in charge of defending the general interest.

Many energy end-users – especially when energy costs are only a minor item of overall expenditure where they are concerned – tend to base their judgement on the energy price current at the time. They have to make a decision, and to assume this price to be constant even though they are increasingly aware that other factors such as labour costs or borrowing rates must be viewed in a evolutionary context. There is thus a tendency to invest excessively in forms of energy whose cost in real terms is likely to increase, and insufficiently in those forms where it is likely to decrease.

Some components of the problem are not taken into account by individual actors. This is first of all the case – although to a lesser extent in the recent term – with environmental damage (air pollution, water pollution, thermal discharges, etc). As a natural consequence, indiscriminate use is made of energy forms which pollute the environment, without sufficient attention being paid to alleviating their effects (which involves a cost factor). But this is also the case with macroeconomic consequences.

A specific item left out of individual assessments is the implied cost of lost national independence, even when the individual concerned is intellectually aware of the risks involved in relying on foreign sources of supply, because he feels that his personal contribution to combating those risks would not be significant.

The same applies to the indirect effects on the economy of individual energy options. Consequently, the 'civic' reaction of saving energy and thereby assisting the national balance of payments is by no means the general rule.

In order to reduce the disturbing effects of these differences, some corrective actions are needed from government authorities which will use the standard instruments of economic policy.

1. Information designed to make energy users more aware of the main trends in the energy economy and encourage them to consider a whole range of factors when making decisions.
2. Regulations designed to internalise some of the indirect effects of those decisions.
3. Financial incentives, particularly to encourage research and investment which, although justified in the overall view, would be neglected if left to purely individual initiative.
4. Manipulation of energy prices to consumers.

As will be seen from Figure 35.1, these energy prices are the central feature of the interface between the energy economy and the general economy. Pricing policy is thus the corner-stone of energy policy as a whole.

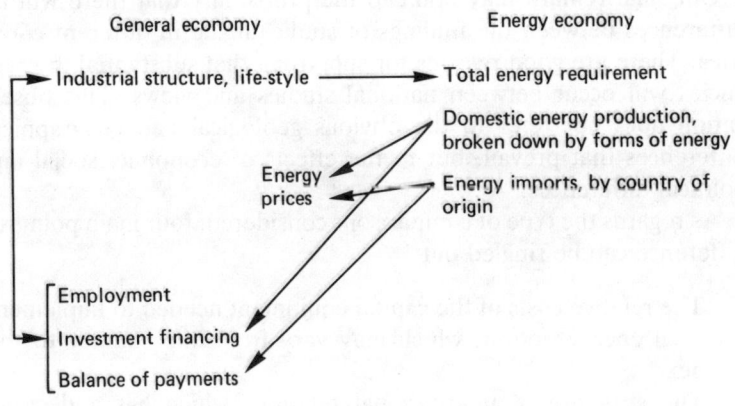

Figure 35.1 Relation between the energy economy and the general economy

The basic idea is that energy prices are influencing users' decisions, regarding either the amount of energy or the kind of energy that is used. A social optimal decision will be reached if the user tries to minimise his own cost, in face of prices which correctly reflect the social cost of energy products (and also other products, mainly equipment goods). But both conditions must be fulfilled at the same time: the rule of expected marginal cost is valid only if prices anticipate correctly the evolution of costs *and* if users react fully and rapidly to price modifications. If, for various reasons these conditions are not fulfilled, (e.g. sellers use today's costs and users express some inertia)[4], the decisions taken might be wrong and government might act along two lines. First, it can try voluntarily to disconnect prices from expected costs (for instance by increasing prices for stimulating energy saving). Such behaviour is dangerous for when prices are manipulated too often, the price pattern starts to lose any real meaning after a certain time, and this can be damaging for the economy as a whole. Hence it might be better to use specific actions – usually temporary subsidies – to accelerate among users changes in the pattern of their behaviour which spontaneously would be too small or too slow.

In any case, it is important that such prices (whether they are administered or not) should be consistent with the national energy options. This concern over consistency might seem self-evident, but it would be quite illusory to assume that it is always fulfilled.

Our final remark may point to the probability that there will be differences between the findings of studies made in different countries. There are good reasons for supposing that substantial discrepancies will occur between national studies and views. This observation does not refer to the obvious geological and geographical differences that prevail, but to the effects of economic, social and political differences.

As regards the type of comparisons considered, four main points of difference can be singled out:

1. The relative costs of the capital equipment needed to implement each energy option, which may vary from one country to the next.
2. The structure of international relations which has a decisive influence on balance-of-payments mechanisms, with special reference to what was earlier called the 'feedback ratio'.
3. The evaluation of political terms of socialised factors, such

evaluations not being made generally in the context of the market-place.
4. The values placed on the main economic indicators, such as consumption levels and import/export ratios. These are so closely linked to local, social and economic conditions that they are likely to be assessed very differently from one country to another, especially as between countries of contrasting levels of development.

As concerns the implementation of an energy policy, the fundamental choice of policy instruments must be made by reference to the foreseeable response of energy and end-users: in particular, the extent of price-demand elasticity determines whether pricing mechanisms can be a decisive element of policy, or whether they must be used in conjunction with other and more direct types of incentives and disincentives.

This all adds up to saying that we must expect to be faced with differences in the energy policies of different countries, both as concerns the main choices and the means adopted to implement those policies.

NOTES

1. For further details, see our report to the Tokyo Conference (Maillet, 1982).
2. For an estimation of this goal of energy supply and independence see the report by Gouni at the Tokyo Conference (Gouni, 1982).
3. Such as the French mini-DMS energy model.
4. Many surveys show such an inertia.

REFERENCES

Gouni, L. (1982) 'Reflections on Energy Planning in France', in Maillet, P., Hague, D. and Rowland, C. (eds) *The Economics of Choice Between Energy Sources*, proceedings of a Conference held by the International Economic Association in Tokyo, Japan (London: Macmillan).

Maillet, P. (1982) 'Energy Options: Interface Connections between the Energy Sphere and the Rest of the Economy', in Maillet, P., Hague, D. and Rowland, C. (eds), *The Economics of Choice between Energy Sources* (London: Macmillan).

36 The Special Source of Alternative Energy: Comparing Energy Conservation Performance of the East and West

Istvan Dobozi
INSTITUTE FOR WORLD ECONOMY,
BUDAPEST

This paper attempts to provide a comparative perspective on the energy conservation performance of the advanced market-economy countries and the European socialist countries. An attempt is made to identify the common and different characteristics of the demand response of the two systems both to the first and the second oil price explosions. The first part of the paper is devoted to the analysis of the advanced market economies' experience. The second part discusses the policy responses of the socialist countries. The paper concludes with a comparison of the conservation performance.

1 THE ADVANCED MARKET ECONOMY COUNTRIES

1.1 A Shift from Supply-oriented Energy Policy Towards Demand Management

The acceleration of economic growth and, in connection with this, the heightening of international market competitiveness became the foremost objective of government economic policy in the Western countries after the Second World War. Macro policy directed towards the promotion of growth and world market competitiveness imposed considerable demands on energy supply. The goal of energy policy was to ensure the guaranteed and unhindered meeting of the demand for energy at the lowest possible cost and allowing consumers a free choice. The growth rate and structure of demand were treated as the givens, not as objects of policy. Policy and planning were thus equated with developing the 'necessary supply'. Governmental resource policy became reduced to a supply policy. The regulation of demand with proper governmental policies (e.g. conservation, industrial development, urban planning, transportation) was, to a large extent, neglected (Lindberg, 1977).

The transformation of the traditional international energy supply system and the higher prices in the 1970s have fundamentally altered the conditions of national energy management in almost all countries. The operation of the international energy supply system has become more conflict-prone and less predictable. As a result, policy-making is carried out under conditions of increasing uncertainty. Policy-making has shifted in the direction of increased instability and uncertainty within individual countries, too.

In the new situation following the energy crisis, Western governments are devoting considerably more attention than previously to influencing the demand side in order to moderate its growth. Each country uses a number of policy instruments to regulate demand, but administrative methods have also been used in some countries. Besides, a powerful campaign for popularisation has unfolded to encourage the so-called 'conservation ethic'.

The West European governments have been expecting a substantial moderation in the growth of energy demand from the measures adopted in the interest of energy conservation, from the rise in the price of energy and from the anticipated long-term slackening in economic growth.

1.2 Macro-micro Conflicts in the Adjustment Process

As shown above, policies designed to moderate demand growth are one of the most salient features of post-crisis Western energy policies. Empirical studies consistently show that a very significant conservation potential exists in the individual sectors of the Western economies.

Since 1973 there has been a continuous decrease in the energy per unit of GDP, even though energy/GDP was reasonably constant or increasing over the 1960s for most OECD countries. For the OECD countries the ratio of total energy use per US $1,000 of GDP has fallen by about 2 per cent a year between 1973 and 1980. This has meant a saving of about 15 per cent, or 500 million tons of oil equivalent in 1980 (World Bank, 1981, p. 36). Table 36.1 shows the reduction of energy use/GDP for the seven leading OECD countries: between 1973 and 1981 energy intensity decreased by 14 per cent. The drop in oil intensity was twice as much. Not all of this, however, is real savings because industrial output has not recovered to the same extent as GDP. The energy-intensive basic industries, namely metals, minerals and chemicals, are still producing at or below 1973 levels, whereas reflationary measures have kept private consumer expenditure artificially high. For example, in 1980 the output of the basic metals sector (ISIC 37) was 6 per cent below the 1973 level, whereas the GDP increased by 20.6 per cent (OECD, 1979 and 1981a; United Nations, 1981). A part of this structural offset is probably temporary, and hence part of the apparent savings should be discounted. Even allowing for this factor, conservation is apparently largely responsible for the reduction in energy per unit of GDP (Shell Petroleum, 1979).

Table 36.1 Energy and oil intensity in the seven leading OECD countries, 1973–1981 (percentage changes)

	Oil intensity**			Energy intensity*		
	1973–76	1978–81*	1973 81*	1973 76	1978–81*	1973–81*
United States	− 2.7	− 8.8	−14.0	2.7	−25.2	−23.8
Japan	− 0.3	−13.5	−19.1	− 9.7	−25.6	−36.4
Germany, Federal Republic	− 4.4	−16.3	−14.1		−28.0	−37.5
France	−10.3	− 1.7	−11.0	− 7.8	−14.8	−31.5
United Kingdom	− 9.7	− 3.9	−15.1	−14.9	−21.1	−37.5
Italy	− 3.4	− 4.3	−11.0	−19.3	− 7.8	−21.7
Canada	− 5.1	− 3.6	− 9.3	−10.5	−12.1	−20.9
				− 6.6		
Total of above countries	− 3.7	− 7.9	−14.0	−13.2	−23.4	−27.6

*Index of primary energy demand divided by index of real GDP.
**Index of primary oil demand divided by index of real GDP.
*Estimate.

Source: OECD Economic Outlook 30 (Paris: OECD) December, 1981, p. 50.

Empirical evidence suggests that some measure of conservation has indeed been realised in the OECD countries since 1973, but the results are less than expected. The expectation that a decrease in demand could be achieved was largely based on the assumption that energy demand would be highly responsive to price increases. Long-run price elasticities of demand for energy estimated for the United States and West European economies were surprisingly high: 0.8 (*The Economist*, 1978, p. 84). Another estimate put the medium-term elasticity of demand for crude oil at 0.8 (Sweeney, 1977, p. 122). The elasticity calculations have proved to be both erroneous and misleading. For example, between 1972 and 1980 in the EEC countries a 10 per cent increase in the import prices of oil was associated with a 0.16 per cent decline in overall demand. The actual response of import demand for oil to the drastic price increases has proved to be *inelastic*. Why has energy consumption not reacted more sharply to the world market oil price rise of the past decade? The most probable reasons are as follows:

1. Final product prices have changed very little relative to the rise in the import price of crude oil.
2. Each nation's capital stock is replaced only gradually, particularly at a time of economic recession and falling or stagnating real incomes.
3. Energy conservation has not had a larger impact because of the short pay-back time that most private consumers expect from a cost-saving measure.

Each of these will be examined in turn

Final Product Price

As Ray notes, the real price of crude oil may be of importance at the macroeconomic level, but in fact nobody, apart from refineries, consumes crude oil. If the high relative price of energy is to have any impact on consumption, the relevant prices are those of the oil products, as well as other forms of energy (Ray, 1980, p. 197). Compared to the severalfold increase in the real price of crude oil, until 1978 the real energy price for consumers in the OECD countries increased only moderately. Between 1973 and 1978 the real energy prices to final users in the major industrial market economies increased by only 44 per cent, whereas the real world price of crude oil tripled (World Bank, 1981, p. 37). Table 36.2 shows that in the years immediately following the first oil shock real energy prices in some countries increased only marginally. In order to keep down final energy prices, governments have used price controls, allowed their energy tax rates to fall and raised subsidies.

Most of the Western governments started to implement more serious domestic energy price increases in real terms only after the second oil shock. In 1979 and 1980, in the major industrial market economies real energy prices for final users increased by 35.4 per cent. That is about the same increase as occurred in the preceding five years.

Table 36.2 Real energy prices to final users

	Percentage changes in real energy prices*		
	1973–76	1978–81†	1973–81†
United States	27.2	35.7	76.7
Japan	79.6	76.7	176.1
Germany, Federal Republic	17.1	34.7	52.0
France	23.2	20.2	53.2
United Kingdom	16.0	19.3	32.0
Italy	77.4	34.5	134.9
Canada	13.2	27.7	55.9
Total of above countries	32.7	37.7	82.4

*Energy component of consumer and wholesale price indices divided by total indices excluding energy. Relative energy prices at the wholesale level have been weighted by the share of industry in total final energy demand.
†Estimate
Source: CECD Economic Outlook 30, (Paris: OECD) December 1981, p. 52

Capital Stock is Replaced only Gradually

Both consumers and producers are 'locked in' their appliances, the dwellings they live in, the productive processess they operate, the products they produce and the technologies they apply (Ray, 1980, p. 206). The existing 'energy-consuming infrastructure' will not vanish overnight. Thus, although some retro-fitting is economically attractive and hence justifiable, the bulk of improved energy efficiency must be expected from new, more energy-efficient equipment. Because it is generally uneconomic to scrap existing equipment for the sake of energy conservation, the rate of growth and hence turnover of equipment has a very profound influence on the amount of improvement in energy efficiency that can be realised (ECE, 1978, p. 15). The economic recession is only one factor. The relatively small increase in real consumer prices has also contributed to the slow replacement of existing 'energy-consuming infrastructure'.

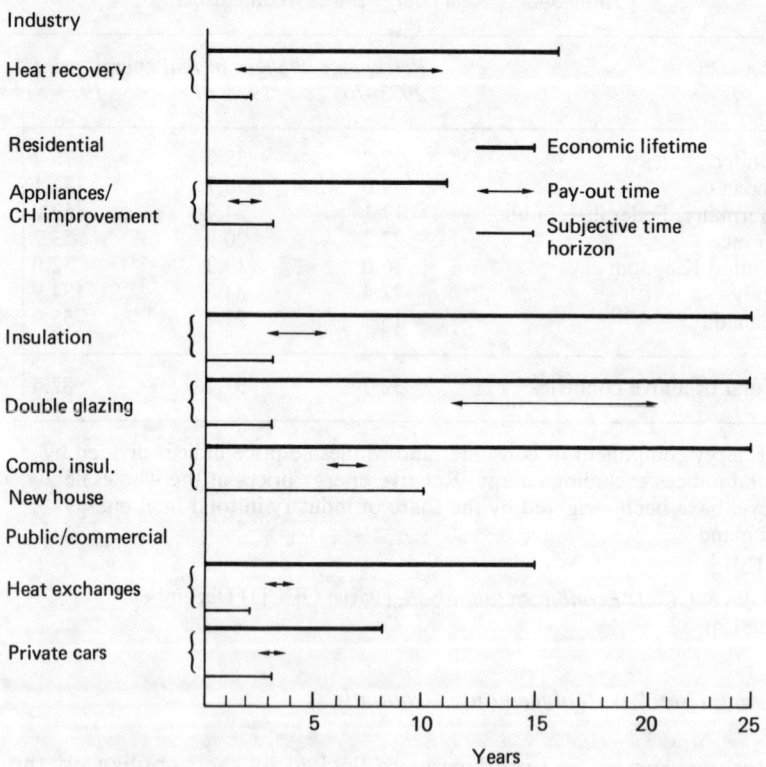

Figure 36.1 Comparison of economic lifetime, actual payout time and typical consumer's subjective payout requirement

Source: Shell Petroleum (1979).

Energy Conservation

The actual pay-back time of various energy conservation measures is shorter than the economic lifetime, but the pay-back time demanded by the consumer is even shorter (Figure 36.1). In the West European industrial sector the maximum pay-back time allowed for cost-saving measures currently seems to be about two years. In the household sector two to four years is the maximum period most homeowners will allow for the pay-back time of an investment. As a Shell Petroleum study has put it:

> Many options that are economically attractive when properly evaluated face the very real psychological barrier inherent in the need to spread a capital investment over a long period of time (divided by an invisible commodity – the energy saved). Thus, many options may fall very short of their potential impact, and attain only a low rate of penetration. Owing to a lack of awareness, to a lack of knowledge or to competition for available capital, many consumers will probably leave significant energy-saving opportunities untapped, that could otherwise have worked in their own long-term advantage. It is the prospect of lengthening the consumer's time horizon that provides an opportunity to develop to a much greater extent the 'invisible' source of energy conservation. (Shell Petroleum, 1979, p. 5).

Between 1973 and 1981 the energy conservation efforts did not significantly affect the general investment process; the conservation efforts, being less investment-oriented, have not provided new impetus to the generally sluggish investment process. Although conservation considerations alone have not been used to justify a massive replacement of capital stock, potential energy savings are taken into account during the replacement induced by non-conservation factors. Thus, effective conservation possibilities are connected to the general growth process and especially to the dynamics of investment activity.

In the 1970s and early 1980s, the declining share of gross fixed capital formation as a percentage of GDP in most OECD countries has resulted in an *increase in physically and technologically obsolete capital stock*. The age of the capital stock has increased in most of the advanced market economy countries. Table 36.3 shows the average annual increase or decrease in the age of the US capital stock by industry. The results reinforce the view that the net capital stock is ageing. If the assumption is made that newer plant and equipment is more energy efficient, because it embodies greater technological advances in conservation, then it may be concluded that the relatively

Table 36.3 Changes in the age of capital stock in the United States

Industry (SIC)*	Percentage change 1971–6	Average age of net capital stock, 1971 (years)
Food (20)	+1.2	8.0
Tobacco (21)	−6.6	9.0
Textiles (22)	+6.6	6.0
Apparel (23)	+2.6	6.3
Lumber (24)	+0.0	9.0
Furniture (25)	+3.0	6.5
Paper and products (26)	+5.2	7.3
Printing/publishing (27)	+8.4	6.7
Chemicals (28)	+6.2	6.5
Petroleum/coal products (29)	−2.8	10.0
Rubber (30)	+6.6	4.7
Leather products (31)	+2.8	7.0
Stone/clay/glass (32)	0.0	9.8
Primary metals (33)	+1.6	9.6
Fabricated metals (34)	+2.6	7.5
Non-electrical machinery (35)	+4.2	6.6
Electrical machinery (36)	+6.8	6.2
Transportation (37)	+6.2	7.3
Instruments (38)	+7.2	5.6
Miscellaneous (39)	0.0	7.0

*Standard Industrial Classification.
Source Leipziger, D.M. (1980) 'Productivity in the United States and its International Implications', *The World Economy*, June, p.123.

inadequate conservation performance by the United States is in part due to an impoverishment of its capital base.

The above-mentioned factors are largely responsible for the 'micro-macro' contrast that has developed in the area of energy conservation in most of the advanced market economy countries. The individual or corporate reaction is insufficient in view of the national problems created in the area of balance of payments, public budget disequilibrium, security of supply, etc., as a result of the world market oil price increases. For example, an increase of US $1 in the price of a barrel of crude oil can be very serious in balance-of-payments terms, yet the price of petrol at the pump, if the crude price increase were spread evenly over petroleum products, would not go up by more than about two cents per gallon. (DuMoulin and Eyre, 1979, p. 79).

The conservation approach is of great importance from the 'macro' point of view. Although the 'national' benefits of energy conservation, such as slower domestic resource depletion, reduced environmental impact of energy use, increased employment opportunities and reduced burden on the balance of payments and public budget can rightly be expounded as strong arguments in favour of active conservation, these arguments weigh little with the prime actor and decision-maker: the decentralised consumer. Given the fact that the share of energy costs in total industrial costs and household expenditure did not rise to such a level that a change in equipment or habits occurred rapidly, and due to the various technical and behavioural inelasticities existing in the demand sector, the insufficient consumer response to the higher world energy prices, as compared with the macro problems which the latter created, is understandable and logical.

Thus an important aspect of the 'macro-micro' contrast in the adjustment to higher world energy prices has to do with the frequent difference between the micro- and macro- level efficiency of demand reduction. There is persuasive empirical evidence that capital used to conserve energy brings more social and economic benefits than capital used to produce more energy. We have seen, however, that on the micro level energy conservation is slow to take hold. Thus an important internal contradiction in the area of energy conservation is reflected by the fact that conservation still appears to be more of a governmental concern than a microeconomic one.

As pointed out above and illustrated by Table 36.1, over the short and medium term the domestic demand for energy is quite insensitive to price changes. Between 1973 and 1981 a 1 per cent real price increase to final users – along with other non-price-motivated conservation measures – resulted in only a 0.1 per cent drop in the energy intensity of GDP. Table 36.1 demonstrates that in 1978–81, as compared with the period 1973–6, the speed with which energy use has been cut in the production process has doubled and the speed with which oil has been replaced by other fuels has risen dramatically. This achievement is partly due to favourable weather, but the most important factors are:

(i) a larger rise in real energy prices to final users combined with lagged responses to the 1974 price rise;

(ii) the cumulative response to non-price measures introduced since 1974 (and subsequently strengthened) to promote energy demand restraint, especially in the case of oil;
(iii) the altered state of expectations, with energy and oil prices expected to stay high for some time.

Some indication of the importance of the lagged demand responses and the altered state of expectations is provided by a comparison of 'price effectiveness' for both adjustment periods: in 1973–6, a 1 per cent rise in real energy prices to final users supported by non-price measures was apparently associated with a decline in energy intensity

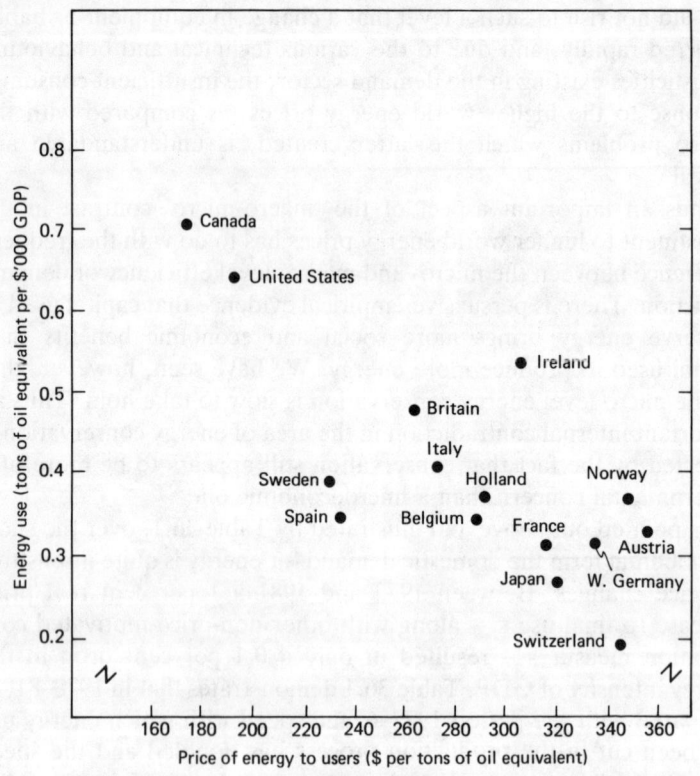

Figure 36.2 The relationship between inter-country differences in energy prices and energy intensity, 1978

Source: International Monetary Fund, quoted by *The Economist*, 26 December 1981, p.66.

of production of 0.1 per cent. In 1978–81, the corresponding ratio was twice as high (OECD, 1981b, p. 50).

As Figure 36.2 shows, there is a relationship between the differences in real energy price levels of various countries and the inter-country differences in energy intensity. The 1978 data reflect cumulatively not only the price effects of the energy crisis, but also the price differences in the pre-energy crisis period. It is a fact that even before 1973–4 domestic real energy prices were signficantly higher in Western Europe than in North America. Figure 36.2 reinforces the view that inter-country differences in relative energy prices influence to a considerable extent the inter-country differences in energy intensity. This fact underlines the importance of price policy in any long-term energy-demand management strategy.

2 THE EAST EUROPEAN CMEA COUNTRIES

2.1 The Main Features of Energy Policy before 1973–4

Even before the price explosion of 1973–4, problems related to energy had a special importance for the European CMEA countries. For a number of reasons the growth of energy supply-side was unable to keep pace with expansion of demand.

The situation described above can, generally speaking, be attributed to the combined effect of limited national energy resources, the 'extensive' type of industrial development, and the relatively inadequate level of development of international energy co-operation within the CMEA. The structural causes of energy shortage that have developed in the European CMEA countries must be sought on both the demand and supply sides. In reviewing the causes, one finds an energy policy which is typically supply-oriented one in which the demand-side figures are an externally given condition and not the main object of policy. The macro-level management of demand is much more 'interventionist' in nature than the supply policy. From this point of view the East European socialist countries were in a more favourable situation than the West European countries, but they did not make adequate use of this 'institutional' advantage. Indeed, macro policy exerted an influence in the opposite direction, towards the excessive growth of energy demand. Within the system of economic management then established, sufficiently effective management of demand was not carried out at the level of industrial enterprises. Instead, in some cases, the incentive system with its emphasis on *gross* production value or *gross* sales as success indicators created a counter-incentive which acted towards over-consumption and permanent excess demand. Other properties of the dominant Eastern European growth pattern have acted in a similar direction, such as the persistent expansion drive and investment hunger, as well as the 'soft' budget constraint (Kornai, 1981).

2.2 Energy Policy after 1973–4

The higher oil imports prices and the growing difficulties in obtaining incremental supplies both from CMEA and non-CMEA sources have resulted in important policy shifts. The maximum exploitation of national energy sources became the policy of most of the CMEA countries. The development of coal-mining has been especially emphasised. Unfortunately, geological conditions are generally poor, and it is quite likely that investments in national energy will result in rapidly diminishing returns. Because of these diminishing returns, the decision to increase domestic energy supplies is likely to require an ever-increasing rise in the level and share of investments devoted to energy. The rapidly increasing share of energy-related investment to total industrial investment, which in some countries has already reached 40–45 per cent, or will do so in a few years, may 'crowd out' investments in other sectors, which will, with a lag, reduce the growth rate of the non-energy-producing capital stock. That, in turn, will cause a shrinkage in the expansion of non-energy production, including the production of all final goods and services. Assuming imports cannot rise due to a debt ceiling, that will mean a slowdown in the expansion of consumption and investment (Hewett, 1981, p. 13).

As in the case of the advanced market economies, the desirability of a policy shift towards demand management is substantiated by studies which show that in the East European context, too, energy-saving investments are an attractive economic proposition and, in general, the rate of return on capital to save energy is greater than on expansion of supply. For instance, in the case of the Soviet Union it has been estimated that with sharply rising production and transport costs for additional output, per energy unit, conservation costs little more than half as much as new supplies (Nekrasov, 1979). Another Soviet estimate gives an even more significant cost advantage for energy savings (Shelest, 1982).

The substantial rise in the import price of energy and the fact that procurement within the CMEA has become more difficult have obliged all the CMEA countries in recent years to give up their one-sided supply-expanding approach and to devote considerably greater attention to the demand side of energy management. In theory, the CMEA countries should react more strongly to the price increase in the area of demand management policy than did the West European countries. The reason is that the CMEA countries use substantially more energy to produce a unit of national income than the advanced Western countries, and a price rise of the same magnitude affects their international cost competitiveness more strongly.

2.3 Energy Demand Growth: Some Unexpected Empirical Facts

Table 36.4 shows the trends in energy demand for the CMEA as a whole and the individual European member countries before and after the 1973. The striking fact is that in four countries, Czechoslovakia, the GDR, Poland and Hungary, the rate of growth of demand for primary energy increased between 1974 and 1980. The energy/national income growth elasticity shows an increase during this same period for these four countries and for the USSR. These data indicate that the OPEC and CMEA price rises basically left energy use patterns in most of the CMEA countries unaffected.

Some of the reasons for the grossly inadequate response to higher world energy prices are similar to those we have seen in the case of advanced market economy countries. They include the following:

1. Real energy product prices have changed very little relative to the increase in the world market price of crude oil. The CMEA countries have relied in their domestic energy pricing to an even smaller extent on world market prices than the advanced market econony countries.

2. The technical and behavioural inelasticities existing in the demand sector, resulting from consumers 'locked-in' by their energy-consuming 'infrastructure', short pay-back time demanded, lack of information, and resistance to change, etc.

Table 36.4 Trends in primary energy consumption in CMEA countries before and after 1974 (average annual rate of growth, per cent)

	1965–73			1974–80		
	Total consumption	Per capita consumption	Energy elasticity*	Total consumption	Per capita consumption	Energy elasticity*
Bulgaria	7.2	6.6	0.88	5.3	4.8	0.79
Czechoslovakia	1.8	1.4	0.28	2.7	1.8	0.60
GDR	1.5	1.5	0.28	2.2	2.5	0.50
Hungary	1.1	0.7	0.17	3.8	3.4	0.86
Poland	3.7	2.9	0.50	4.1	3.1	1.14
Rumania	8.2	7.0	0.90	5.6	4.6	0.67
Soviet Union	4.6	3.5	0.64	3.5	2.6	0.79
European CMEA	4.2	3.2	–	3.7	2.7	–

*Ratio of the annual percentage change in energy consumption to the annual percentage change in national income (net material product).

Source: Based on *World Energy Supplies 1950–1974* (New York: United Nations, 1976); *1980 Yearbook of World Energy Statistics* (New York: United Nations, 1981); and *Statisticheskii Ezhegodnik Stran-chlenov Soveta Ekonomicheskoi Vzaimopomoshchi* (Moscow: Statistika, various issues).

There are also *system-specific reasons* for the slow CMEA response:

1. In the typical centrally planned economy enterprises are not given enough incentives to minimise cost, and the input-price system does not ration scarcity. Therefore input-price increases do not necessarily result in reduced input use.
2. Because of CMEA trade pricing rules, until the early 1980s the net energy-importing countries have enjoyed substantial 'subsidies' on their imports from socialist sources *vis-à-vis* their imports from non-socialist sources. Therefore, the average import price for the socialist countries has been significantly lower than for the Western countries.
3. The credits provided by the advanced market economy countries and the USSR to the Eastern European countries helped, to a considerable extent, to improve the balance-of-payments situation despite steadily deteriorating terms of trade. This policy of 'borrowing rather than adjusting' to higher energy prices reduced the necessity for quick demand adjustment.
4. The 1975–80 national plans of the Eastern European countries were based on bilateral oil supply agreements with the USSR, which allowed them greatly to increase the oil imported. In most of these countries the central development programmes, many of them energy-intensive, were based on these supply agreements. The most oil-intensive technologies and equipment were introduced exactly at the time when the Western countries were shifting away from oil and energy-intensive technologies. Only after the completion of the development programmes and the second oil shock was it discovered that the programmes were based on an incorrect analysis of anticipated economic and technological trends.

As a result of the insufficient demand response to higher world energy prices, there exists today in the CMEA countries an even sharper 'micro-macro' contrast in the area of energy policy than is the case with the Western countries. It has been predominantly the governments of the socialist countries that have absorbed the impact of higher energy import prices by accepting a deterioration of their balance of payments, increased budgetary deficits, etc. The enterprise and household reaction has proved strikingly inadequate to the gravity of macro problems that higher import prices and changing world market conditions have created.

The second oil price explosion of 1979, along with the resulting economic problems, the increasing difficulties of borrowing due to the high indebtedness of most of the East European countries and the growing realisation that oil imports from CMEA sources cannot be increased in the foreseeable future have finally forced the majority of CMEA countries to introduce comprehensive energy conservation measures.

These measures have been compatible with the organisational and institutional framework of the East European countries, and administrative measures ('conservation by decree') have assumed a central role in energy conservation. Since 1980 in the GDR enterprises are provided with energy quotas. Czechoslovakia instituted reduced energy deliveries for the major users. In Rumania the useable amount of energy is fixed for every enterprise, and the allocated quantity cannot be surpassed. In the more decentralised Hungarian economy it has been recognised that the price system plays a meaningful role in influencing economic decisions and that it should reflect scarcity values. It was recognised that domestic energy price should reflect marginal cost. As a result of the new pricing mechanism, the real domestic price of energy has increased significantly.

As a result of the combined impact of comprehensive conservation measures and a slowdown in economic activity in 1980 and subsequently, the rate of growth of primary energy consumption showed a decreasing trend in every CMEA country.

However, the decrease in the rate of growth of energy consumption or its absolute drop in certain cases is only in part the result of the more significant domestic price increases and conservation measures. An important factor has been the decrease in output of several energy-intensive sectors. In Hungary, for example, the output of the metallurgical sector decreased by 7.2 per cent in 1980 and by 4.3 per cent in 1981. The output of the mining sector declined 5.2 per cent in 1980 and 3.2 per cent in 1981. Production in the chemical industry in 1981 was 3.9 per cent lower than in 1979. These energy-intensive sectors in 1980 accounted for 60 per cent of the total direct industrial energy consumption and about one-fourth of the national energy consumption (Központi Statisztikai Hivatal, 1981 and 1982). By taking into account these impacts of the structural modifications which is due to a slowdown in activity, the 'real' saving becomes significantly smaller than the recorded saving. Some of the recorded saving will probably disappear with an upswing in these sectors.

3 SOME COMPARATIVE CONCLUSIONS

Before the energy crisis, in both groups of countries the goal of government energy policy was to ensure the guaranteed and unhindered meeting of energy demand. Policy and planning were equated with developing the 'necessary supply'. The regulation of demand through proper governmental policies was to a large extent neglected.

The world energy picture has changed dramatically since 1973. In this new situation moderation of the growth of energy demand has become a major policy objective of both groups of countries.

Between 1973 and 1981 the advanced market economies have shown a significantly better conservation performance than the CMEA countries. While growth of energy demand slowed down in the advanced market economy countries, it accelerated in the majority of CMEA countries. Some measure of conservation has been going on in the OECD countries since 1973, whereas in the case of CMEA countries meaningful conservation efforts were instituted only after 1979.

The majority of governments in both the advanced market economies and the CMEA countries only after the second oil shock have instituted stronger and more comprehensive conservation measures. In the West, the most significant change has taken place in the domestic energy price policy, which has allowed a quicker and more flexible adjustment of domestic prices to world market prices. Characteristically enough, in most CMEA countries administrative measures have received strong emphasis.

As a result of more radical and more comprehensive conservation measures since 1979, in both groups of countries the decrease of energy intensity of GDP has accelerated over recent years. However, the total drop in energy intensity cannot be considered strictly as savings, because in both groups of countries the significant structural shifts of a partly temporary nature in the economy have also played a considerable role in the drop in energy intensity. The 'real' saving is thus significantly smaller than the 'apparent' one.

There is substantial empirical evidence to show for both groups of countries that conservation investments are an attractive economic proposition and that, in general, the rate of return on capital to conserve energy is greater than on expansion of supply. Thus it is in the interests of governments in both groups of countries to make greater conservation an attractive business opportunity for the household and corporate consumers. This is possibly the best way (if not the only one) to reduce or eliminate the gap between the private (or microeconomic) and social rate of return on conservation measures, and, in the final analysis, to eliminate the present 'micro-macro' adjustment conflict in the area of energy conservation in both groups of countries. The analysis suggests that a major source of energy conservation which the so far under-performing European CMEA countries can tap is economic reform towards decentralisation and a more rational price system.

REFERENCES

DuMoulin, H. and Eyre, P. (1979) 'Energy Scenarios: A Learning Process', *Energy Economics*, April.
Economic Commission for Europe (1978) *New Issues Affecting the Energy Economy of the ECE Region in the Medium and Long Term* (Geneva: EC), ECE/2, 18 January.
The Economist (1978) 'Europe's Energy', *The Economist*, 25 March.
Hewett, E. A. (1981) 'An Essay on Energy Activity in Eastern Europe', prepared for the 13th National AAASS Conference, Monterey, CA., September 20–23, mimeo.
Kornai, J. (1981) 'Some Properties of the Eastern European Growth Pattern', *World Development*, nos. 9–10.
Központi Statisztikai Hivatal (1981) *Statisztikai Évkönyv 1980* (Budapest: Központi Statisztikai Hivatal).
Központi Statisztikai Hivatal (1982) *Statisztikai Havi Közlemények* (Budapest: Központi Statisztikai Hivatal), various issues.
Lindberg, L. N. (ed.) (1977) *The Energy Syndrome: Comparing National Responses to the Energy Crisis* (Lexington and Toronto: Lexington Books).
Nekrasov, A. M. (1979) *Materialno-tekhicheskoye Snabzsehiye*, No. 3.
OECD (1979) and (1981a) *Main Economic Indicators* (Paris: OECD), May 1979 and December 1981.
OECD (1981b) *OECD Economic Outlook 30* (Paris: OECD), November.
Ray, G. (1980) 'The Influence of Relative Prices on Energy Consumption', in Saunders, C. T. (ed) *East and West in the Energy Squeeze* (Vienna: Vienna Institute for Comparative Studies).
Shelest, V. A. (1982) 'Alternative Sources of Energy in the National Economy of the Soviet Union', International Economic Association Conference on Economics of Alternative Sources of Energy, Tokyo, 27 September – 1 October, 1982, mimeo.

Shell Petroleum (1979) *Energy Conservation: The Prospects for Improved Energy Efficiency* (London: Shell International Petroleum Company).

Sweeney, R. (1977) 'Alternative Tariff and Quota Mechanism in the Face of Monopolistic Exporter of a Non-renewable Resource', *Weltwirtschaftliches Archiv*, No. 1.

United Nations (1981) *Monthly Bulletin of Statistics* (New York: United Nations), November.

World Bank (1981) *World Development Report 1981* (New York: Oxford University Press for World Bank).

37 Governments in Energy Markets

M. V. Posner
PEMBROKE COLLEGE, CAMBRIDGE

1 INTRODUCTION

This paper discusses the role of governments in energy markets – how that role should be chosen, how it should be exercised, and the difficulties that have to be overcome.[1]

It is possible to specify a highly abstract, closed-market economy in which the authorities have no more reason to adopt 'an energy policy' than a policy for strawberries or bath plugs. Admittedly, fuel is a basic commodity and the production and transformation of fuels require very long gestation periods, but flexibility at the margin can significantly lessen the importance of these two constraints.

In formal terms, Leontief interdependence does not imply fixed coefficients, and, in the energy case, inter-fuel substitution is a potent escape mechanism from shortages or 'errors' in the provision of any particular fuel. Moreover, 'energy shortage' as a catchword arouser of environmental worries can be somewhat neutralised when we remember that 'energy' is more a physicist's concept than an economist's.

Choices which may seem ineluctable for the world as a whole may be genuinely avoidable by one particular country. For instance, it is possible that the world as a whole will really 'need' nuclear energy on a fairly large scale in the next century, but the United Kingdom or any other country in an n-country system could in principle refuse to undertake nuclear investment, and instead hope to be able to purchase its necessary alternative fuel input on the world market.

All this must lead an economist to view with some suspicion facile popular assumptions about the absolute necessity for energy policies. Nevertheless, it is the theme of this paper that a general case for some active form of energy policy does remain and, therefore, that the problems of formulating, pursuing and achieving the eventual policy targets are worthy of analysis.

2 THE FRAMEWORK OF CHOICE

It follows from my introductory remarks that simple 'energy balance' approaches to policy-making are inappropriate. It is not possible or sensible to proceed by predicting total demand twenty-five years ahead and establishing likely supply trends of the various fuels. Prices and costs have to be introduced as explicit arguments of the planning process, and this leads naturally to the 'cost minimisation' approach to energy planning: to find that mix of fuels which will satisfy a forecast energy demand at some future date at minimum social cost. But the level of demand is not only subject to all sorts of external variables and shocks; it contains an endogenous element – the future demand for energy depends in part on the future expected cost of energy. So *the process of planning becomes an iterative process*, with supply and demand interrelated by cost and price terms. Some of the feedback loops in the economic system which is being modelled can be quite complex: for instance, experience of the last decade has taught us that variations in energy prices can have not just a resource cost effect, but also, through changes in the international distribution of purchasing power, very powerful effects on both the level and pattern of final demand in the world economy as a whole. The modelling process needs, in principle, to take all such effects into account.

Finally, the model must take account of risk and uncertainty in all its forms, in relation to all of the exogenous assumptions and most of the endogenous relationships. The forecasting of technological change is a hazardous business, and is now apparent that we need to forecast not only technological possibilities – whether a fast breeder reactor would work within certain technical parameters – but also the political and social acceptability of certain technologies. The rate at which North Americans will switch to small cars, or the environmental lobby accept strip mining in the Rocky Mountains, or domestic households accept the discipline of district heating techniques, are as important as the rate of change of political attitudes to nuclear energy.

These political and social uncertainties are one main reason for preserving an element of planning in even the most market-oriented of economic systems.

A second reason is the international and political dimension to the energy market: to what extent can individual decision-makers within one country be permitted by their national authorities to assume a perfectly elastic supply of fuels in the international market at some future date? During the 1950s and 1960s, United Kingdom policy was content to make such an assumption, with the result that almost all the growth in energy demand was satisfied by imported oil, and to a greater or lesser extent this was also the experience of most Western countries. Once bitten, several times shy, and it is not conceivable that such a happy-go-lucky attitude will be taken in the future: the question of national self-sufficiency, once raised, will not go away.

Finally, technological risk and the risk of underprovision of fuels at some future date must both be of concern to governments. In principle, no doubt, the market could provide insurance systems and associated forward contracts to deal with both types of risk, but in no economic system have such arrangements been developed to anything like the necessary extent. Recent experience lends emphasis to this point.

Governments (or, generally, planning authorities) therefore have the following task. They have to estimate in a satisfactorily iterative or simultaneous way demand and supply trends both in their domestic market and in the international economy. They have to take a view on the likely pattern of technological developments and of changes in social and political attitudes both at home and, to some extent, abroad. They have to develop a preference pattern for the treatment of risk and uncertainty, and in particular about the extent to which it is wise to carry 'over-capacity' in energy production at home. And they have to equip themselves with the necessary instruments by which policies can be implemented and targets reached. All this is consistent with a wide range of philosophies, from *laissez-faire* to interventionism. The decisions can be left to the market, but governments will need at least to equip themselves to judge whether the market solutions are at least politically defensible at the next election.

This leaves a reasonable freedom of choice, and it is no surprise that different national authorities have taken different approaches, both in the degree of planning intervention which they have chosen and in the emphasis they have decided to put on different policy targets or instruments. The first reaction to the events of 1973 was a general search for an increase in the degree of national self-sufficiency. Where the market had gone wrong, in the eyes of the consumers now faced with sharply higher prices, the market should be avoided in the future.

But the validity of this approach depends on the validity of the belief that the price increases of the 1970s were a response to market rigging, or to non-market forces. If one believes instead that the price trajectory actually followed was a belated response to changing market appreciation of the future balance between supply and demand forces for the rest of the century, then the correct national policy might be to encourage a smooth but rapid adaptation of domestic fuel use to the new higher prices, with attention given to conservation. Whereas a belief that the market had collapsed, or had been taken over by political cartels, would have justified widespread investment in high-cost alternative sources of fuel in all domestic ecnomies, a belief that market forces were merely reflecting real technological facts encouraged instead a degree of indifference about domestic energy production – shortfalls in domestic supplies in the future would, it could be argued, always be offset, at a price, by purchases on the international market.

Perhaps the change in American attitudes over the last five years can best be understood as the rebound of a faith in market forces, and therefore a diminution in insistence on national self-sufficiency in the future.

But this is only part of the story. Most observers would agree that the increase in energy prices during the 1970s has played some substantial part in the continuing deep Western recession. By accommodating themselves to high energy prices, large OPEC surpluses and general inflation, by policies which lowered the rate of growth of real demand, the OECD countries have implicitly at any rate colluded in a form of international energy policy which works exclusively on the demand side: energy demand has been depressed as a direct result of a depression in the general level of demand and output. If ever there was a case of the 'invisible hand of the market working by strangulation', this is it. Moreover, any one country, or any one company, which has stepped out of line and made investments which implicitly depended upon high energy demand and, therefore, prices much higher than those of today, has had its expectations falsified, and has lost money as a result. This episode provides a clear reminder that, among the exogenous forces which a planner must take into account is the reaction of other economic agents.

It is not only the possibly perverse reactions of 'foreign' decision-makers which have to be taken into account, but also those of one's own citizens. British policies for our indigenous coal industry are a good case in point. Throughout the 1950s, and at an increasing pace in the 1960s, deliberate steps were taken to contract the size of the coal industry, with the intention of simultaneously switching from coal to oil or nuclear energy, and at the same time concentrating coal production in the relatively low-cost collieries. Both intentions were thwarted by political considerations; nevertheless, by 1973 coal output had been halved from its post-war peak, and the number of collieries was radically reduced. The oil price increases of the 1970s convinced most observers that this process of contraction should be halted if not reversed, and (since many of the remaining collieries were approaching geological exhaustion) a large programme of investment in new coalfields was envisaged. Environmental considerations, which we will discuss below, provided some constraint on this programme, but the main brake on investment came from the increasing fear of the authorities that real wage costs per unit of output would rise in tune with energy prices elsewhere. During the miners' strike of 1974, and in subsequent episodes of confrontation with successive governments, calculations were freely made in public purporting to show the amount of 'headroom' for miners' wages to rise. Given the world price of alternative fuels and the productivity at home of British coal-miners, the maximum wage per man-year which would leave British coal 'competitive with alternative fuels' could be read off. This upwards pull of world energy prices, combined with the short-term control over the supply of primary fuel input into electricity generation, and with an unwillingness of the miners to see even high-cost collieries close, made investment in coal seem a far less favourable instrument of energy policy than the planners had suggested in the early 1970s.

This episode can be seen as merely one example of the general tendency for all costs and prices to rise to the level determined by the market leader in an oligopolistic situation. Some observers, however, would see it also as a good example of the foolishness of any one small country attempting to insulate itself from the world market. From an economist's point of view, it remains an intellectual puzzle whether a rise in miners' wages of this sort – which after all is merely a transfer payment in terms of social accounting or welfare economics – can properly be regarded as a rise in the real resource costs of home-produced fuel. If it cannot be so regarded, is it appropriate for planners to ignore it in making investment decisions about the future pattern of energy use? Whatever technical answer we give to that conundrum, there is no doubt that, politically, increases in miners' wages are a strong argument against investment in coal, and this is a consideration which planners ignore at their peril.

A final example of the complexities that face planners is the growth in expected generating costs of nuclear electric power. Environmental or safety hazard, for any engineer, is a challenge which can be designed away, at non-zero cost. Safety in highly sophisticated equipment is never an absolute; more can always be purchased. The concept, much developed by the tradition of governmental safety inspectors in many fields in the United Kingdom for many decades, of 'best available practice' is sufficient evidence that standards of safety and acceptable environmental hazard are raised through time as knowledge and wealth both increase. As technology in fuel production and conversion changes, it appears that many of the production hazards which were formerly internalised to those who earn their living in the industry, become external, perceived and to some extent objectively incurred by the community as a whole. Moreover, not only are the risks and environmental unpleasantness externalised, but engineers develop a fairly explicit notion of 'head-room for further safety provisions' in very much the same way as British coal-miners developed notions of the scope for increases in their own pay. Economic rent can take various forms, and higher standards of safety or environmental protection is one of them.

In making their choices, therefore, energy planners find the measuring rods they need to use can expand, contract, and even change their shape as the planning process continues. This does not mean that their job is useless or impossible; it does mean, however, that the apparent simplicities of the naive forecasting or planning model can conceal more than it reveals.

3 COSTS AS A DEPENDENT VARIABLE

The two examples given above of costs in some sense tending to rise in real terms through time are not the only nor the most important examples. Every economist working in this field is familiar with the puzzling tendency for successive estimates of the cost of a new technology to be higher, relative both to earlier estimates about the characteristics of the same technology and relative to other fuels. In part, this is no doubt merely the result of engineering optimism in the early days of new developments. In part, there is a well-known tendency for those concentrating on the characteristics of a specific technology to assume that progress on all competing, old technologies will cease. But in the case of energy technologies in the last decade, there is a more fundamental economic process at work. There is no doubt that, for instance, at least half of North Sea oil production would not be economically viable if the real price of oil had stayed at its early 1973 levels, although much of the exploration and some of the original investment in extraction was committed before the 1973 price rise took place. A new technology, a new oil province, or a new coal-mining region might be economically viable on a small, carefully controlled scale, in carefully chosen sites; but if competitive conditions are favourable – 'if sufficient headroom exists' (in the terminology of the preceding section) – then developments will take place at both the intensive and extensive margin so as to bring the marginal cost of the new technology up to the prices set by the exploitation of the old technologies.

To say this is not to suggest that there is a universal, rapid and complete tendency to 'thermal equivalent pricing' for all competing fuels. Even when allowance has been made for spatial differentiation, and differences in the convenience or acceptability of the fuel (gas against coal for domestic space heating for instance), thermal equivalent prices must be expected to diverge for a run of years for market reasons. An energy industry that is striving to increase its market share will often need to persist with a price advantage over its nearest competitors for several years, and differences in the structure of costs between two fuels may rationally encourage differences in the structure of prices charged even in steady-state equilibrium.

The price mechanism will encourage a large degree of matching or marriage between suppliers with specific cost structures and customers whose structure of demand can be more compatible with one set of supply characteristics than another.

The aspect of risk on which we concentrate here is concerned with costing the price of world traded energy – typically the world oil price – towards the end of the century. In a world of complete certainty, with OPEC oil available in virtually unlimited quantities at a known future price, most traditional reasons for energy planning become invalid. As uncertainty is introduced, there are three possibilities to examine: first, that the planning authorities 'know differently' than individual economic agents; secondly, that the planners can control risk and uncertainty, or at least the impact of that risk on domestic markets; and thirdly, that the attitude, rationally, of the planning authorities to risk and uncertainty may be different from the expected approach of the aggregate of individual economic agents.

'Knowing better' is not a claim that can easily be made by planning authorities, in the light of thirty years' experience of commodity stabilisation schemes, of mistaken official forecasts of the relative terms of trade of manufactured goods and primary products, and of the rise and fall of the 'Club of Rome' environmentalists.[2]

Moreover, most large energy users themselves have access to the same type of energy forecasting as governments or planning authorities, and it would be an unusual as well as a brave government official who asserted otherwise.

If governments cannot claim to 'know better', they do have a clear record for 'knowing worse' in a number of key cases. Centralised decision-making might well lead to a set of decisions which, on average, will be worse than a decentralised system.

It remains possible, however, that the willingness to bear risk and uncertainty, and choice of behaviour in the face of ignorance, will differ systematically between planning authorities and individual economic agents. From the point of view of a potential domestic investor in a form of energy alternative to world traded oil, the risk which has to be hedged is that the world oil price will fall short of the minimum level required to validate his proposed investment. If the planning authority believes this to be a risk worth incurring for the country as a whole, then it can rationally insure the investor against the risk which he fears.

For instance, it has been suggested that over the last few years key western countries have been operators in an unconscious stabilising mechanism to keep oil prices low. On this argument, there is a maximum value (say zero) for the continuing surplus of oil-producing countries on current account; any rise in the oil price above its equilibrium level would increase this surplus, because the short-run elasticity of response between oil revenues and expenditure out of those revenues is small, and therefore an oil price increase must be modelled as a rise in the required current account deficit of all net oil importers. Because the target current account deficit is a fixed and inflexible component in the preference pattern of public authorities, they react to a rise in their actual deficit by implementing policies which are restrictive of output, employment, and therefore demand for energy. The net result of such policies is to reduce the spot demand for oil, reduce its price, and thereby return the world to the oil price from which it started. Similarly, an initial drop in the oil price (perhaps caused by new oil discoveries, or successful innovation in low-cost alternative fuels) would set up an expansionary process, which would lead to the oil price rising again to the level from which it started.

To the extent that such a mechanism at present prevails, there would be a net advantage if the public authorities instead encouraged investment in alternative forms of energy at home, even if the costs of such energy supplies were to exceed the level which most observers believe to be the sustainable world traded price of energy. This is because the existence of such alternative sources would allow each national authority, and therefore all national authorities collectively, to escape the continuing underemployment equilibrium which would need to prevail to keep oil producers' surpluses from rising.

Considerations such as these, and perhaps a systematic concern with somewhat longer time horizons than might preoccupy individual agents, lead the public authorities to place greater stress on the potential risks of underprovision of alternative energy supplies than the reverse – a greater stress on the upside risk of high world traded prices for oil than on the possibility of low prices.

In formal terms, such insurance can be offered in a number of alternative ways: the planning authority can promise that the domestic price will follow a certain trajectory, whatever the world circumstances suggest; it can guarantee a market for the output of a given investment, at whatever price is necessary to cover production costs; or it can provide something closer to a conventional insurance policy against the risk that the world price will drop. Simple theoretical reasoning suggests that the insurance route is the best, but most of the relevant considerations appear regardless of which policy instrument the planning authority uses.

A possible formula might be developed as follows. Against a background of general forward projections, estimates are prepared of the range within which market-clearing prices for energy might be established on a 'high employment assumption' for the OECD countries as a whole. In concrete terms the centre of that band might correspond to a rate of growth of OECD industrial production for something like three-quarters of the growth rate achieved over the last two decades. Investment projects which seem to offer reasonable prospects of thermal equivalent prices at or below the centre of that range would be eligible for insurance cover. The expenditures to be insured would be those committed to the project over the coming five years, and cover once given will not be withdrawn. But each year, for the life of the project, the commitment will be extended by one further year into the future, so that there will always be five years of insured time ahead until the project came to fruition. New information about the development cost and prospects of the project would become available as time rolled forward, and new assessments of the world energy scene would also become available to all interested parties. Either insurer or underwriter could withdraw from further contractual obligation at any point. Withdrawal by the project sponsor, unilaterally, would relieve the underwriter of any responsibility: the 'policy' would be surrendered (there might be some provision for the return of premium). Withdrawal by the underwriter – the planning authority – could not abrogate his responsibilities for that proportion of the total life-time cost of the project which he had already undertaken to insure. If the underwriter did withdraw, it would be up to the project sponsor to decide whether to cancel further expenditure, to carry on in the hope that the underwriter would return at some future stage, or to bear all the future risk of the project himself.

One possible arithmetical measure of the risk to be insured would be the difference between the centre of the range of foreseen outcomes for the world traded price of energy and its lower limit – the underwriter could insure that element of the risk. But, more persuasively, it could be argued that it is the risk of the *unknown* – true uncertainty – that concerns any manager of long-lived projects, and on that approach the investor himself would bear all the risk within the perceived band of possible outcome, and the public authority would underwrite any shortfall below the recognised range of possible outcomes.

4 SOME ENVIRONMENTAL ISSUES

Environmental issues in energy planning have several different interpretations. First, they can emphasise potential shortages, as one or other source of raw materials or fuel becomes exhausted – spaceship earth must conserve its resources or perish. Secondly, those concerned with the environment can stress specific ecological constraints on technical progress, radiation hazards, the effects of CO_2 or SO_2 on the earth's atmosphere as coal is burned, or disturbance of the balance of nature as power station sites are exhausted in crowded islands like Japan or the United Kingdom. Thirdly, and most generally, those who stress environmental factors seek to remind us of considerations which while they may be external to a particular productive process are internal to society as a whole. It is this generalised interpretation of environmental considerations that concerns us here.

There is no doubt that externalities loom larger in the energy business than in most others. Chemical engineering in general runs us a good second, but any economist who has been involved in the discussion of the choice of technique, the choice of site or the choice of scale of electricity generation cannot believe that similar problems occur elsewhere. No doubt some of this interference with decision-making is irrational – Californians instal air-conditioning in all their dwellings, but don't want any more electric power stations. Some environmental pressures are merely of the parish pump variety: 'yes we need power stations, but not in my back garden'. And some is of the 'enforced holiness type': 'I like wearing wool next to the skin, you should too'. A country which has an effective system for making decisions will ride fairly brutally over this sort of 'environmentalism', rightly in my view.

But there is more to environmentalism than that. There *are* considerations to be borne in mind which are not just those of private profit. In the study of *Coal and the Environment* carried out by the UK Commission on Energy and the Environment and published in 1981, there was a detailed study of all the likely consequences of obtaining, transporting and using coal with available and likely-to-be-available techniques. The Commission developed clear views on what types of coal use were environmentally desirable (burning in large and efficient modern boilers, and conversion in adequately controlled synthetic fuel plants); on the way coal should be transported (mainly by rail); and on the types of controls that were necessary before new collieries or strip mining permissions were granted. Overriding the whole of the discussion was the concept of best practicable means: 'best practicable means does not necessarily mean all technically possible means. In some cases such a requirement would involve unsupportable costs. Existing equipment must be allowed a reasonable economic life unless it is grossly ineffective (section 1.37 of the report). The essence of this approach is that each form of energy extraction or transformation should, where newly installed, be at the frontier of environmental acceptability, judged by the standards of the reasonable person and 'reasonable costs'.

Some of this argumentation frankly has the flavour of comforting the qualms of an anguished but poorly informed community – examining their fears one by one and showing them to have little foundation. This is more social or political therapy than economic policy-making. But there is more to the environmental lobby than that. There is no doubt that pressures for safety, for the avoidance of pollution and for aesthetic quality in energy conversion plants have sharply increased the cost of energy production in most countries, and have substantially swayed much argument against both hydrocarbons and nuclear energy in favour of the so-called renewable energy sources. In every way save their effects on the atmosphere and chemical pollution, these renewable energy sources are as full of problems as their traditional equivalents. The vast number of windmills required to replace one modern power station makes it implausible that the public will ever prefer wind power to coal power. The size of much investment in tidal barrages or wave power gadgetry in order to produce adequate amounts of electricity involve environmental change on a large scale. And yet these techniques prove attractive to the general public because their perceived hazards are less incomprehensible, apparently more familiar, more easily contained by normal engineering practice.

It is, I believe, the wish of our fellow citizens to understand and control what is happening around them that is the key to the planning process in environmental matters. Perhaps it is unsophisticated to fear the unknown, or to object to changes which seem inevitable to the technicians, or, most of all, to refuse to accept the natural consequences in energy *production* of one's own decisions about energy *consumption*. But a planning authority which refuses the mechanism for talking these issues through with its own citizens is asking for trouble.

5 CONCLUSIONS

In this paper I have tried to describe some of the practical problems of energy planning. None of them are easy to handle, and all of them (with the possible exception of the environmental issues) can be to some extent avoided by governments who are determined to rely on the market. But that is just to shunt the problem of choice sideways from the planners in central government to the planners in individual enterprises. The issues cannot be finally evaded.

NOTES

1. The paper builds on and develops the theme I spoke on at the Tokyo Conference in 1982 (Posner, 1982).
2. In the years immediately after the first OPEC oil price rise a certain amount of public education about energy prices was necessary, but recent investigations in the United Kingdom at any rate show no lack of recognition of the possibility that energy prices will remain at or above their present level in real relative terms.

REFERENCES

Posner, M. (1982) 'Problems Concerning the Implementation of Energy Policies', in Maillet, P., Hague, D. and Rowland, C. (eds) *The Economics of Choice between Energy Sources*, proceedings of a Conference held by the International Economic Association in Tokyo Japan (London: Macmillan, 1987).

38 Economic Development in Third World Countries: The Role of Existing Sources of Energy and Alternative Choices

V. S. Mahajan
PUNJAB UNIVERSITY, CHANDIGARH

1 ENERGY AND MARKET STRUCTURE IN DEVELOPING ECONOMIES

While developing countries are legitimately anxious to achieve high growth rates, they in fact find it very difficult to do so mainly due to underdeveloped resources and domestic markets. Most of the developing economies, moreover, do not have enough natural resources, especially minerals, and those that do, have only partially exploited these. For example, the fact that a number of developing countries have an abundant supply of hydro resources does not help them unless such hydro potential is harnessed for energy generation. Similarly, the existence of coal in areas remote from the centre of industrial activity is of little help unless either the centre of industrial activity is brought close to the coal-mining areas, which would facilitate the optimal operation of thermal plants, or there exists an efficient transport system for the quick transportation of coal to feed power plants which are located at a distance.

Those developing countries which do not possess minerals would have either to import these or the final product. For example, if they are not endowed with energy resources, they would either be importing energy inputs like coal, oil, etc., or energy itself, if there is excess generation in a neighbouring country. Such arrangements, however, generally do not work smoothly for technical and/or political reasons, with the result that most of these small developing countries are left with no alternative other than to develop their own energy resources irrespective of cost.

Not only are the basic inputs (like coal and oil) not easily available, but the escalation in their prices (particularly of oil which is at present an essential import item for all non-oil-producing developing economies) makes a large hole in their already difficult balance-of-payments position. On top of all this, there is a serious dearth of skills in these countries for the successful installation, maintenance and operation of plants. Further, instability in the political sphere, a common feature in most developing economies, discourages the adoption of a long-term industrial and energy policy.

Thus there exists a vicious circle: while economic compulsions demand the creation of an interdependent framework of economic development, at the same time the lack of resources, political instability, regional factionalism (every region trying to outwit the other in grabbing the scarce resource irrespective of needs) and serious market distortions, do not help to achieve it. Rather, the continuation of such an atmosphere further worsens the balance-of-payments situation in these countries, when fast rising imports, both developmental and non-developmental, are not matched by exports. The situation is made even more complicated by the worsening terms of trade of these developing economies.

It is a recognised axiom that for the realisation of maximum benefits from, say, a power plant, the contribution made by the domestic markets is unique. If markets are viable, these would be in a position to sustain a high level of energy consumption for industrial activity. Thus expanding markets would automatically encourage a chain of economic activities.

Unfortunately, such a market situation does not exist in developing countries. While almost all of them are committed to planned development, hardly any effective planning exists for forging appropriate links between the basic facilities on the one hand and the user industries on the other. Often one meets the situation where facilities exist but user industries are absent, or vice versa.

Western economists often emphasise that developing economies should use labour-intensive techniques in production, which are capital-saving (as capital is a scarce factor in these economies) and labour-using (as labour is an abundant factor). However, it is not adequately appreciated that even the labour-intensive technology is power-using for, without power, productivity per unit of input cannot be raised and ultimately it is productivity which is the key factor in economic development. For instance, in agriculture, which is the major economic activity in developing economies, supporting between 60 and 90 per cent of the population, it is the growth of productivity that would help to raise total farm output as well as incomes of farmers. Similarly, in the development of small industries which provide large opportunities outside the highly crowded farm sector, it is again the availability of power and the appropriate technology that would help these industries become economically viable. India's experience shows that, despite all-out attention being devoted to the growth of tiny and small industrial units over the past three decades, as well as providing them with liberal financial and fiscal support, these units have neither become viable nor helped to expand employment opportunities. The main reason for this is poor productivity and also the lack of appropriate avenues for marketing their output.[1]

2 RURAL ENERGY: A LOW PRIORITY SECTOR

Thus it is abundantly clear that rising productivity through energy and better technology (especially in the rural sector) and favourable markets would play a key role in the development of newly emerging economies.

Unfortunately, experience shows that so far the development of the energy sector in these countries has had a heavy urban bias, and very little attention has been paid to the development of rural energy sources. Due to the long colonial status of a majority of countries in the southern hemisphere comprising South and South East Asia, the Middle East, most of Africa and Latin America, what little development that occurred in the energy sector before their independence was almost exclusively to serve the needs of the small urban population; here again energy was utilised mainly for street-lighting and meeting household needs, as these countries had very little industrialisation.

Such a lop-sided energy development, which these countries inherited at the time of their independence, was not helpful for their economic development. Therefore, after independence almost all these countries accorded a high priority to the development of the energy sector in their plans. However, in their anxiety to achieve rapid development, which was generally associated with the setting up of large manufacturing plants in new industries, mainly using capital-intensive technology, energy development during the early phases of plans virtually followed the pre-colonial pattern, i.e. heavy investment was made in creating urban sources of energy, mainly thermal plants.

Even in those countries that were rich in hydro resources, for example, the development of hydro energy has not been matched by the growth of industry, with the result that vast areas which this energy network traverses provide a rich scope for its pilferage and leakage. This state of affairs has only encouraged further dependence on thermal energy. The existence of thermal plants in the crowded urban centres leads to a serious pollution hazard and has also given rise to difficulties in the transportation as well as stocking of coal (which is the main input for these plants). Further, if coal is to be brought from distant areas, which is the case for a majority of thermal plants in a country like India, then the availability of an appropriate number of railway wagons has to be planned in advance. Usually this proves to be a difficult exercise in a growing economy, where there are simultaneous pressures on these wagons from alternative commodities (particularly agricultural and industrial products). Even when wagons are available, these might not move according to schedule because of congestion on the railways. The situation becomes even more difficult if these power plants are imported which they usually are in the developing countries, since these countries are then dependent on foreign countries for spares and technical maintenance.

Because there is a high urban bias in energy development in India, which is also true for most developing countries, there has been a high concentration of industry in a few cities, and this has given rise to the widening gaps in regional development. All this has happened despite the fact that the licensing policy in India, for instance, specifically emphasises that there should be balanced regional industrial development.[2]

2.1 Central Grid Electricity

Lately, most of the developing countries have begun to realise that a rural electrification programme is essential for the rapid development of the rural sector. Thus in the recent energy plans of these countries emphasis has been laid on rural electrification.[3] The options available for rural electrification are, however, limited. One of these, which has already gained popularity in some developing countries,[4] is to extend the supply of energy from the existing large power plants – usually urban-based – to the rural areas. However, this option has its disadvantages. The foremost is that because the transmission equipment is laid across sparsely inhabited areas, there is a probability of leakage as well as the pilferage of power. Besides this, the maintenance cost of new equipment is likely to be high. Both these factors would raise the cost of distributing power to the rural areas. Thus unless power is subsidised, rural households would be reluctant to make use of this facility, which they mainly need for farm operation since very little power is used for domestic needs in villages.

Thus justification for the supply of power through the central grid system is questionable when 'the social and economic benefits of subsidising residential consumer electrical prices [might] outweigh the economic penalties upon the finances of electrical utilities.' (Johnson, 1983) p. 268) As a result of extending power facilities to rural areas through the central grid system in India, the losses suffered by the State Electricity Boards in just one year – 1976–7 –were Rs 1570 million.[5]

2.2 Mini Hydro Projects

While mini-hydro projects offer encouraging potential for supplying power to rural areas, these are commercially viable only in those developing countries which are better off, have a high population density and an adequate water supply all the year round. These schemes are particularly suitable for mountainous areas. Thus, while most of the developing countries have a high hydro potential, only a few would qualify for these mini-hydro plants. With this limitation, it is not clear how China would be able to generate 12 MKW of power through mini hydro schemes during the next decade (Guanglin, 1982). Sadli, on the other hand, in discussing the hydro potential of Indonesia, does not commit himself to any figure but merely adds that there exists a high potential for tapping energy through mini hydro plants which could over time make a significant contribution to rural development (Sadli, 1982). At the same time, he says that where the hydro potential exists, but the population is thin and development poor, then these factors are not helpful for exploiting hydro potential. Similarly, while the Philippines holds out good prospects for the development of mini hydro schemes – and for this purpose 4,539 potential sites have already been identified and the 1980 Five Year Plan has envisaged the construction of 3.9 MW of mini-hydro capacity (Johnson, 1983, p. 275), it is difficult to visualise what shape this programme will finally take and what difficulties will be faced. But this experience will certainly help other developing economies which are potential applicants for these mini plants.

2.3 Biogas

Energy based on tapping rural waste matter (biomass) has already gained popularity in those developing countries which have a high population density and a large cattle population. In China, for instance, a large number of biogas digesters are serving the needs of the rural population, both directly and indirectly: directly in cooking, general heating and lighting, and indirectly by making available a vast quantity of manure (which is a by-product from these plants) for helping agriculture.

India, on the other hand, despite over a decade and a half's research in biogas technology, has not made any significant advance in this direction. Two major difficulties are being found. First, technology is yet to emerge which is within the range of an average rural household. Secondly, there is the problem of the collection and distribution of inputs (like dung and farm wastes) which are essential for the operation of these plants. While it is hoped that the efforts of the Indian government through the Khadi and Village Industries Commission, which as a fully fledged directorate of biogas, will result in the development of technology which meets with the needs of rural households, the problem of an adequate supply of inputs for the working of the plants is indeed going to be difficult. An average rural household does not have enough cattle or farmland to ensure a regular supply of inputs. Therefore, a planned programme which ensures a regular supply of inputs for these biogas plants is an essential precondition of the large-scale acceptance by households.[7]

Furthermore, the biogas plants according to the existing technology, would meet only the limited domestic needs of the rural population (e.g. cooking, heating, lighting, etc.), and would not be able to meet the needs of agricultural operations and rural industrial development for which some new source of energy (other than the central grid system) has to be found.

One way, of course, is to extend the biogas technology through appropriate research to meet this need. This might be possible after intensive research on the part of individual governments of developing countries.[8] However, because of the basic constraint in the availability of inputs for the operation of commercial-sized biogas plants, rural areas will have to tap alternative sources, mainly for powering the pumpsets used for irrigation which are at present operated either by diesel or electricity.

2.4 Wind Power

Wind power, which is a renewable source of energy, could be developed for irrigation. As one writer[9] puts it:

> It is possible to design cheaper and smaller windmills which irrigate a one-hectare wheat or rice field in a region with wind velocities averaging 10 km. per hour for about 10 hours a day. In any case, the fact that windmills are powered by a free and renewable resource whereas electric and diesel pumping sets consume rapidly vanishing fossil fuels is too important a consideration to be lightly brushed aside by a mere superficial comparison of the comparative costs of the two types of pumping sets. Even if the windmill . . . costs more initially, it is fully justified because of the high cost of electrification via a central grid.

Thus, in view of the high initial cost of windmills, a subsidy would have to be provided to farmers to enable them to change to this source of energy. But then this subsidy would be justified for conserving both oil and electricity, which could be put to better alternative use.

3 BETTER USE OF OIL

While we have laid emphasis on the predominant role of the rural sector in developing countries and stressed that there is a need for developing energy sources which are relevant to these countries, it is at the same time to be recognised that petroleum and related products are essential items in these economies, especially in the transport sector. This is clearly brought out in Table 38.1, where we show that the share of oil use in developing countries as a percentage of total primary energy consumption in their domestic market has been rising recently, and a major share of this consumption is by the commercial sector.

Thus the steep increase in oil prices over the past decade has adversely affected the balance-of-payments position of these countries (excepting, of course, oil-producing economies).[10] It is further found that the value of oil imports in developing countries varies between one-fifth to four-fifths of total imports, which certainly puts them in a difficult corner.

Table 38.1 Proportion of oil use in total primary energy consumption in selected countries

	1970		1980	
	Total	Commercial	Total	Commercial
Brazil	0.38	0.63	0.40	0.56
Mexico	0.49	0.60	0.61	0.71
India	0.15	0.31	0.17	0.33
Republic of Korea	0.46	0.58	0.58	0.62
Philippines	n.a.	n.a.	0.63	0.91
Indonesia	0.35	0.83	0.44	0.81
Thailand	0.64	0.84	0.71	0.82
Pakistan	0.16	0.33	0.20	0.36
Malaysia	0.83	0.92	0.93	0.96
Bangladesh	0.27	0.79	0.27	0.46
Kenya	0.26	0.88	0.28	0.85
Jamaica	0.84	0.98	0.88	0.98
Panama	0.69	0.92	0.61	0.78
Ethiopia	0.03	0.87	0.04	0.80
Mauritius	n.a.	1.00	0.64	1.00

Source: Johnson (1983).

3.1 Alternative Options

One could think of two alternatives to reduce dependence on imported oil: (a) intensify the domestic hunt for oil, and (b) reduce consumption of oil through encouraging alternative sources of energy and also by economising its use. As far as the former alternative is concerned, the prospects for the majority of developing countries are not encouraging. Even though a developing country like India might be able to tap extra oil through offshore drilling, the prospects of obtaining any significant quantity of oil in this way do not appear to be bright. The costs of exploration and exploitation of future possible oil resources, especially in sparsely populated developing economies (for example, in most of Africa and Latin America) would also stand in the way of developing new oil sources. Thus the overall situation, at least over the next couple of decades, is that there is not much possibility of developing countries tapping additional oil.

3.2 Energy Policy

Before we deal with possible alternative sources, let us look at the present policies adopted by developing countries towards the energy sector *vis-à-vis* other sectors. This has been summed up by Johnson as follows:

> For industrialists and governments investment in productive plant is likely to attract greater support than that in, say a coal-importing distribution infrastructure system, even if the latter can show a rather better economic return on investment. Before 1974, the emphasis, both within governments of developing countries and in external lending and aid agencies, was on optimising use of capital to achieve maximum overall benefit for development of the economy. Quite reasonably such emphasis persists. However, capital projects designed to reduce operating costs in the form of energy expenditure are not always perceived to be potentially of as much long-term value to the economy as a direct increase in industrial or agricultural output, even when the former leads to a vital reduction in the foreign exchange burden. (Johnson, 1983, pp. 250–1).

The last line of the above quote is important, and shows that the developing countries are far less interested in investing in those projects which are designed to reduce energy costs than in projects which would help to raise industrial and agricultural output. This is by and large true.

Johnson goes on to point out that (deceptive) social welfare receives higher priority than economic rationale in the energy policies of developing countries:

> Policies designed to encourage efficient energy use and promote oil substitution can, in developing countries, sometimes conflict with other economic and social and economic priorities. For example, cheap oil fuel may be seen as important in fostering industrial growth, relieving the fuel cost burden of the poor, and minimising inflationary pressure. As a matter of policy, oil fuel prices may be controlled so that they are less than the true costs of supply, or, as is often the case, less than world oil prices. In contrast to the situation in industrialised countries, excise tax is not often imposed on oil fuels. (Johnson, 1983, p. 251).

Sadli (1982) also confirms the above view in his study of Indonesia. He adds that kerosene prices in Indonesia are much below their world market prices. He also does not find much support for arguments advanced in support of such action, which claim that it would discourage inflation, improve income distribution and discourage cutting down of forests for fuels. Similarly in India, it is found that, notwithstanding the increase in the price of kerosene and diesel, these products are still cheaper in the local market compared with world market prices. Again, social welfare arguments were behind this move, such as that it would benefit low-income consumers who would shift to kerosene in place of wood and thus save forests. Further low prices of diesel would benefit small farmers and transporters. However, it is doubtful whether subsidised prices of diesel and kerosene have actually benefited small consumers. It appears more likely that much of this benefit has actually accrued to more affluent sections of the community.

4 ALTERNATIVE ENERGY OPTIONS

Let us next review the feasibility of developing countries adopting alternative energy fuels.

As far as the industrial sector is concerned, the substitution of oil by solid fuels (coal, etc.) faces certain limitations. Only those developing countries which have a high initial advantage in industrialisation would find such a switchover economically justified. For others, such a switchover is going to be rather difficult. This is because it is only in

> energy-intensive industries where sufficient economies of scale exist and for which energy costs are more than 10 per cent of the output value, which are likely candidates for oil substitution. Principal among these would be the steel, metal, smelting, petrochemicals (which can use coal, gas or gas condensates), cement and brick, and cement industries; to a lesser extent food and textiles industries might be included. (Johnson, 1983, p. 261)

Obviously such types of industrial structure would be found only in a few developing countries.

It is in the transport sector, which is also a major consumer of oil and products, that the possibility exists for developing alternative fuels. This is particularly so for countries which have developed sources of natural gas or have a favourable population-to-land ratio. For example, a country like Brazil, with a favourable population-to-land ratio, has already successfully developed alternative fuel, alcohol (or gasohol), from sugarcane, for which there is a considerable market in running automobiles (Johnson, 1983, p. 263).[11] But here it is the high cost of production of such fuel which is the major constraint in its replacing oil. Although a country like India is favourably situated in so far as the production of sugarcane is concerned, its high density of population makes it impossible to switchover to alcohol production on a commercial scale.

Similarly, while technically there also exists the possibility of substituting diesel oil with vegetable oil 'as a blend, as there are indications that engine lubrication problems occur with 100% vegetable oil' (Johnson, 1983, p. 263), on economic grounds such substitution depends on the market price of vegetable oil *vis-à-vis* that of diesel. Here only a few countries have found such substitution feasible. For example:

> Surplus coconut oil in the Philippines has resulted in the government recommending the blending of 5% of this oil into diesel from September 1982. Other developing countries showing interest in this form of substitution include Brazil, with its 'pro-oleo' program-

me based on soya and palm oil, and Zimbabwe (sunflower oil). (Johnson, 1983, p. 264)

Still another possibility of substituting diesel in commercial vehicles is through the use of wood/charcoal gasifiers, which were used during the Second World War. Brazil and the Philippines have introduced these on a commercial scale. Here these gasifiers have been adapted to commercial vehicles, stationary engines (e.g. pumps) and small boats. Notwithstanding the fact that such developments are also taking place in a number of other developing countries, it is as yet in its teething stage.

Thus the final picture that emerges after analysing different substitutes for oil is that the development of these substitutes would very much depend on the development of appropriate technology, the availability of surplus land, and also the existence of active government support and favourable market conditions in individual developing countries. All this will take time; in the meantime oil and products will continue to play a significant role in the energy market economy of developing countries. As such it would be appropriate to adopt measures which would help oil conservation and its better use. Here developing economies could benefit from the experience of developed countries, e.g. in the adoption of measures like better care and maintenance of the existing transport media, as well as of roads, and a shift to the use of alternative fuel in industries where oil is used at present. All this, however, would need substantial investment and certain major changes in the energy-using sectors.[12]

5 OVERVIEW AND POLICY IMPLICATIONS

For years to come the developing countries will have to depend on existing sources of energy such as coal, hydro and oil. Over time, there might be a possibility of developing alternative sources of energy such as wind, solar and tidal power. But unless these and other likely sources become commercially viable, they will not be able to replace existing sources.

However, as the major existing fossil resources, coal and oil, are limited in supply, it is imperative that great care is exercised in using these energy sources. This is all the more true of oil, which has already become an expensive commodity. Both oil and non-oil developing economies will have to devote their resources to ensuring conservation of this basic fuel, which still plays a major role in agriculture, transport and households in developing countries. Here, besides developing equipment which could economise the use of oil, there is an equally important need to follow an appropriate pricing policy which is at least based on a cost plus basis.

In so far as nuclear energy is concerned, with the present state of development and the rural-based economic structure of developing countries, it would not be feasible either on economic or technical grounds to set up nuclear plants. Apart from their high initial cost and the advanced skills needed for their operation and maintenance, there is also the major problem of obtaining inputs for feeding these plants.

The rural character of these developing countries, therefore, calls for special attention to be paid to developing simple energy sources which could effectively serve the various needs of the rural population. Here the developing countries are likely to benefit through mutual co-operation.

As in the long run non-replenishable sources of energy such as like oil and coal are going to be exhausted, it is essential that both developing and developed countries join hands in tapping alternative energy sources such as the wind, the sun and the waves, which are replenishable and are also available in abundance, particularly in developing countries.

NOTES

1. This is particularly true of units in the smallest sector which constitutes a significant share of the rural industrial economy. For example, the Ambar Charkha (an improved yarn spinning wheel) programme, which occupies a significant place in the Indian rural economy is, according to Sen, 'inflationary and is also likely to affect capital accumulation adversely. Far from creating any flow of surplus, it produces a flow of output value less than even its recurring costs' (Sen, 1972, p. 110).
2. This policy is enshrined in the Industrial (Development and Regulation)Act of 1951. But due to pressure from politicians and big businesses, the provisions of the Act are grossly violated when licenses are issued.
3. In India it was only during the late 1960s and 1970s, after the country had been through the first three five-year plans, that attention began to be focused on rural electrification.

4. For example, in India there has been heavy reliance on the central grid system for the supply of energy to the rural sector.
5. See Ramesh, S., 'Pricing Policy for Power', in Madan *et al.* (1983), p. 357.
6. According to Zheng Guanglin (1982) of the Institute of Scientific and Technical Information in China: 'By the end of 1981, within the whole country, there were more than 6 million biogas plants'. He adds that by the end of this century biogas family plants would number 100 million. In other words, in less than 20 years these plants will increase by more than six times.
7. In China, Zheng Guanglin (1982) adds that the problem of supply of inputs to feed biogas plants has been solved through encouraging the cultivation of energy plants and firewood forests. However, the growing of plants on a sufficiently large scale to meet the targeted biogas production would need an enormous amount of land which could be exclusively devoted to the cultivation of this input. Can China afford to spare so much land? Would it not affect its food balance? This question has not been dealt with in the paper.
8. India has already made some advance in this direction. For instance, the development of larger community biogas plants are expected to help farm operations (e.g. by supplying power for running pumpsets for irrigation). These plants would also help small and medium industrial units to set up in rural areas. India's Sixth Plan has laid down a target of installing 100 such community plants. This, however, is a modest target for a country the size of India, and it shows that the Planning Commission is adopting a cautious approach. Ultimately, the effectiveness of these plants will very much depend on the co-operation of rural households in the supply of inputs. Experience so far in this direction has not been encouraging.
9. See Jagjit Singh, 'Our Energy Choices Now', in Madan *et al.* (1983), p. 314.
10. For instance, in the case of India the deficit in the balance of payments, mainly on account of the increase in the price of oil, has risen from Rs 3.6 billion in 1978–9 to Rs 31.5 billion in 1981–2. That the worsening of balance-of-payments situation in India is by and large due to oil imports is also confirmed by the fact that while such imports were 12 per cent of the aggregate value of imports in 1970–1, their share had gone up to around 50 per cent a decade later.
11. See also Barros de Castro (1982).
12. See also Prasad and Ramesh (1982). While appreciating the role of various measures to save energy, the authors suggest that it would be a temporary expedient, as the long-term solution is only possible by developing existing or alternative sources of energy.

REFERENCES

Barros de Castro, A. (1982) 'Brazilian Energy Policy at a Crossroad', in Maillet, P., Hague, D. and Rowland, C. (eds) *The Economies of Choice between Energy Sources*, proceedings of a Conference held by the International Economics Association in Tokyo, Japan (London: Macmillan).

Guanglin, Z., (1982) 'The Rural Energy Situation in China Today and Its Development in Future', in Maillet, P., Hague, D. and Rowland, C. (eds) *The Economics of Choice between Energy Sources* (London: Macmillan).

Madan, K. D. *et al.* (eds) (1983) *Policy Making in Government* (New Delhi: Publication Division, Government of India).

Johnson, R. (ed.) (1983) *Oil Substitution World Outlook to 2020*, report by the Oil Substitution Task Force (New Delhi: Oxford University Press).

Prasad, K. and Ramesh, S. (1982) 'Energy Development Choices for India', in Maillet, P., Hague, D. and Rowland, C. (eds) *The Economics of Choice between Energy Sources* (London: Macmillan).

Sadli, M. (1982) 'Alternative Energy Options in Indonesia', in Maillet, P., Hague, D. and Rowland, C. (eds) *The Economics of Choice between Energy Sources* (London:Macmillan, 1987).

Sen, A. K. (1972) *Choice of Techniques* (New Delhi: Oxford University Press).

39 Economic Aspects of Alternative Energy Sources: Discussion and Conclusions

P. Maillet
UNIVERSITÉ DE LILLE I

The papers presented in this part of the book were discussed at the Congress together with the following papers, which are not published here:

> Heinrichs, Wolfgang (Berlin, GDR) 'Evaluation of Macroeconomic Consequences of Intensified Extraction and Utilisation of Domestic Brown Coal'.
> Banks, (Uppsala, Sweden) 'The Political Economy of European Natural Gas'.
> Paraskevospoulos, Christos (York University, Toronto, Canada), 'Energy Demand Modelling for Oil-based Economies'.
> Street, James H. (Rutgers University, New Jersey, USA) 'Latin American Science and Technology Policy in the Era of Energy Substitution'.

From the discussion, six conclusions may be drawn which might be of interest both to scholars and to decision-makers.

1. A quite general consensus emerged on *the necessity for tapping simultaneously all sources of energy*. This diversification appears necessary, either for economic, geographical or political reasons. One result in the future will be that, on the world market, all energy prices will interact much more than in the past. The main reasons for this

increasing interdependence are the increasing importance of international trade and the increasing technical possibility of transforming one energy product into another. This lesson has been learnt, and most of the prospective studies of the balance between supply and demand of energy for the next decade make this process of diversification quite clear on the supply side.

2. Although each country is confronted with a very different situation, the general approach to energy problems is *not fundamentally different among countries*. The methodological dialogue does not seem difficult between developed and developing countries, between market-oriented and centrally planned economies, even if practical solutions could diverge vastly. Quite interestingly, no objection was raised to the idea that *some governmental intervention in the field of energy is necessary*, but also that these interventions have to be backed by very serious economic studies.

Even if one could think theoretically of a closed-market economy where there would be no reason to adopt an energy policy, because of the degree of flexibility that reliance on markets may offer, a general case for some active form of energy policy would remain (owing to rigidities, risk and uncertainties).

The political and social uncertainties, the international and political dimension of the energy market, technological risk and the risk of underprovision of fuels at some future date are the main reasons for an element of planning even in the most market-oriented of the economic systems. The elements of externalities might be a further reason for such public intervention.

Such energy planning should naturally use the 'cost minimisation' approach, but it should also have regard to cost functions, rather than costs for particular output levels, and should adopt prices as the instruments of the planning process. Expressed in such a general way, the necessity of some kind of energy policy is recognised by everyone. In practice, the main problem is to define the optimal allocation of the burden of choices between planners in central government and planners in individual enterprises (and households), and on this point, a wide range of opinions has been expressed.

It has been stressed very strongly that the identification of market failure is only a necessary prerequisite for government interference but not a sufficient requirement. 'The real world choices are between imperfect markets and imperfect governments', and this is not specific to energy issues. The degree of imperfection may vary from market to market and from government to government, and the evaluation of this degree of imperfection is also a subjective one, differing from observer to observer. It is not surprising that the discussion on this point showed fairly different opinions.

One important reason for planning the energy sector in the national economy is the attitude of the decision-makers towards risk and uncertainty. The idea was expressed that national planning authorities should ensure investors against risk. The insurance could be offered in a number of alternative ways, for example by promising that the domestic price will follow a certain trajectory, whatever the world circumstances, or by guaranteeing a market for the output of investment, or by providing an insurance against the risk that the world price will drop. When relying on such an insurance, however, one must be cautious not to reduce the efficiency of the economic system.

Finally, the role of central government may vary extremely from case to case: for instance introducing new sources of energy cannot be the same in small rural villages which hardly know how to use money and in urban regions where comparative prices play a decisive role for consumers' choices among alternative commercial sources of energy.

More particularly, in the less developed countries (like India or China, but also many African countries), the agricultural sector is still a dominant one, and the need for increased food production is absolutely urgent. Although rural energy should be a high priority sector, it is in fact a low priority sector. The high urban bias in energy development in India is given as an example of this mis-orientation of efforts. Another frequent error in energy policies lies in the discrepancy between prices and the economic costs of energy products: for various alleged reasons, prices are fixed much below costs, leading to waste and misallocation of scarce national resources.

3. Energy is an area in which all decisions should be taken in a long-term *framework*, even if the distant future is very uncertain. *A good evaluation of expected cost* is a decisive factor for a good choice. Too many decisions are taken on subjective impressions of relative costs, or on external values which are not valid in the country, and thus prove completely wrong some years later.

4. The *conservation of energy* plays an increasing role in the evolution of energy consumption. From the social point of view, it

might be that the rate of return on capital to conserve and save energy is greater than on expansion of supply in most countries. However, a micro-macro conflict in the area of energy conservation appears in many countries, in particular in those where energy prices are relatively low. The individual and corporate consumer reaction is insufficient in view of the national problems concerning the balance of payments and the security of supply. The best policy for making energy conservation attractive to consumers' agents is probably to rely both on market incentives and governmental interventions.

A look at the *comparative performance* of the advanced market economy countries and the European socialist countries is extremely illuminating. In both groups of countries, the emphasis was put on the supply side up to 1973; the main issue was to supply the economy with as much energy as it needed, without taking care of the way these 'needs' were met. On the contrary, after the first oil shock, all these countries did engage in a process of striving to reduce energy intensity, but with contrasting results: between 1973 and 1981, the advanced market economies showed a significantly better conservation performance than the CMEA countries. Despite the fact that in the first group there is some opposition between micro and macro attitudes, and that final energy product prices have changed little relative to the rise in the import price of crude oil, energy intensity has decreased, while, over the same period, it has continued to increase in socialist countries, the main reason for this being the lack of strong incentives in these countries to minimise costs.

5. *A good correspondence between energy planning and the overall expected economic scenario is a vital condition of an efficient choice.* The interrelationships between energy and and the economy are so numerous and so strong that by missing or under-evaluating some of them one introduces a definite bias in the planning.

In the past, most of the economic studies dealing with energy relied on microeconomic analysis. The recent global economic situation has made economists more conscious of the necessity of widening the range of criteria and looking at the interrelationships between energy choices and some broad economic variables such as employment, investment and the balance of payments. This necessity follows from the fact that the main energy choices are not of a micro type, where it is possible to suppose constant economic variables. One should pay special attention to the importance of the geographical origin of imported energy (which is an aspect of the diversification of supply):

imports of energy have to be paid for by exports, and the opportunities for exporting goods and services are not equal amongst countries; export capabilities have to be fitted to the needs of the energy-producing country; certain privileged economic links exist between countries (for historical, geographical or political reasons); all these factors help to explain the differences. As for employment, the validity of the argument frequently used in these times of unemployment, according to which one should systematically choose a labour-intensive process for producing energy, should also be carefully scrutinised. As a whole, three important points should be emphasised:

(a) All elements of choices are intricately related, and only by using a model of interdependence can one prepare the main choices.
(b) The different criteria are not evaluated with the same weights by all economic agents concerned, hence there is a specific role for public authorities when framing and implementing energy policy.
(c) Real energy and economic situations, cost evaluations, the hierarchy of criteria are so different among countries that it is to be expected that optimal choices and optimal policies should also be fairly different.

6. Finally there is no apparent reason why the various national energy policies, having been formulated separately, should be consistent with each other. The optimum energy balance for each country will not necessarily be the same, according to whether it is drawn up from a strictly national standpoint or forms part of a wide framework such as one of the existing continental economic communities or is even on a planetary scale. There is still ample opportunity to attempt to *reconcile these geographical partial approaches.*

Index

Absorption approach, balance of payments analysis 412–13, 420–1
Adelsheim, P. D. 335, 351
Adjustment
 centrally planned economies 406–7, 467–9, 480–1
 external shocks 439–43, 455–60
 industrially advanced countries 2
 investment costs 14
 market economies 109–20
 new industries 94–7, 99
Administered markets 345–6
Administered price thesis 337
Affluence 276
AFL–CIO 118
Agricultural prices 388, 398
Agriculture
 developing countries 305, 539, 555
 India 307, 309–10, 314, 316, 321
 protection 116, 208 n2
Ahmad, S. 33
Alcohol, automotive fuel 260 n19, 547
Allocation, resources 14
Allocative efficiency *see* assignative efficiency
Alternative energy sources 489, 534
 developing countries 537–50
 economic aspects 4, 487–9, 553–7
 investment 531
 see also energy
Ambar Charkha 549 n1
Amendola, 104
Anderson, K. 209 n6
Annerstadt, J. 43 n2
Argentina 440
Arrow, K. 57
ASEAN 198, 208 n5
Asia 189
Assignative efficiency 52–3, 58–9, 60, 61–2
Atomistic competition model, price behaviour 338
Auction markets 345–6
Australia 3, 482
 imports from LDCs 189–201
 protection 189–90, 208 n2, 265
Australia. Industries Assistance Commission 193, 209 n6

Automation, electronics industry 228
Automobile industry, structural change 18–20
Automobile prices 116

BACHGUROO model 157 n1
Balance of payments
 Brazil 264
 CMEA countries 377–9, 379–80, 409–10, 412–13, 419–20
 effects of energy imports 494–5
 effects of energy prices 517
 effects of external shocks 440, 441–3, 443–7, 451–3
 India 550 n10
 Singapore 213–14
 Soviet Union 417
Balassa, B. 2, 4, 123, 128, 135, 139, 143, 144, 147 n12, 183, 439, 455, 457, 463 n4, 463 n11, 480
Banks, 553
Barros de Castro, A. 550 n11
Becher, J. 75
Becher principle 75–7
Bergsman, J. 258 n2
Bernstein, M. 436 n1
BEST 223, 231 n9
Bhagwati, J. 117
Bilateral trade agreements 443, 517
Binswanger, H. P. 43 n5
Biogas 548–9, 550 n6, 550 n7, 550 n8
Birch, D. 162, 164, 165
Birnberg, T. B. 208 n4
Black economy 114, 290
Blanchard, O. J. 347
Blinder, A. 341
Blue collar employment 206, 210 n19
Bognar, J. 4, 405, 406, 479
Bogomolov, O. T. 275, 436 n3
Boisguillebert, 76
Boot, J. C. 392 n2
Borpujari, J. G. 2, 75, 76, 103, 104
Boyer, R. 161
Brandt Report 265
Brazil 3, 284, 440, 547, 548
 economic modelling 234–44
 growth pattern 247–51
 inflation 381–92, 398–9

558

investment requirements 251–4
structural change 233–4, 264
Bretton Woods system 481
Britain *see* United Kingdom
British Steel 116
Brocard, R. 169
Brody, A. 24
Bruno, M. 258 n3, 259 n6, 259 n11, 346, 352
Buckley, P. 56
Budget deficit 325
  centrally planned economies 407
  developing countries 306
  India 312–13, 315, 322, 324
  United States 288
Bulgaria 363, 370, 377, 431, 433
Bureau of Labor Statistics, US 85
Bureaucratic organisations 59, 67
Burns, A. F. 92, 100, 100 n3, 101 n9
Business cycles, equilibrium models 342

Cable, B. 118
Cagan, P. 335, 350
Campos, R. de O. 391 n1
Camus, A. 75
Canada 124, 140, 143, 208 n2, 482
  trade with developing countries 126, 127, 129, 131, 133, 134
Capacity
  expansion 16–17
  growth rate 97–8
  utilisation 77
Capital, public sector 311
Capital accumulation 94
Capital Assistance Scheme 224
Capital deepening 294, 298
Capital flows, free 283
Capital formation 324
Capital goods, as indirect labour 34–5
Capital goods capacity, LDCs 37
Capital goods sectors, Brazil 243
Capital inflows, USA 288
Capital requirements, products 29
Capital stock
  energy equipment 507–8
  obsolescence 509–10
Capital-intensive production 183
Capital-intensive technologies 31, 32
Capital-labour ratios 280
  industrialised countries 142–3
Capital–land ratio, agriculture 309
Capitalist markets 429–30
Capitalists 149

Carlton, D. 332, 334
Carter, A. P. 2, 13, 21, 103, 104
Casson, M. 56
Census of Manufacturing, US 138
Central banks, intervention 289
Central directives, planning 467–8
Central grid electricity, developing countries 541
Central Provident Fund 22, 231 n7
Centrally planned economies 4, 25, 359–80, 409–24, 465–77, 479–83
  adjustment 406–7, 467–72, 480–1
  adjustment processes 467–72
  balance of payments 377–9
  energy conservation 513–18, 556
  external market fluctuations 465–77
  external shocks 405–6, 409–10
  foreign debt 433–4
  foreign trade 360–1, 414–15
  inconvertibility 415–17
  resource transfers 418–19
  response to external events 419–22
  retail prices 375–7
  terms of trade 361–7
  trade participation 422–3
  trade statistics 410–12
  wholesale prices 368–75
  world markets and 427–36
  see also socialist countries
CEPME 168, 170, 174
Cheap-labour countries, imports 189
Chemicals, international trade 135, 137, 138
Chenery, H. B. 259 n6
Chia Siow-Yue 3, 213, 264
Chile 440
China 42, 198, 209 n14, 323, 542, 550 n6, 556 n7
Civil Construction Cost Index, Brazil 392 n9
Clark, P. B. 258 n1, 259 n6
Clearing arrangements, CMEA trade 410
Cline, W. R. 208 n2, 208 n4, 209 n12
Clothing
  consumer spending 79–81
  international trade 135, 137, 138
  protection 198
Clothing industry, Singapore 219, 225–8
CMEA 359, 410, 437 n5, 473, 477
CMEA countries 430
  economic performance 434–6
  energy conservation 513–19, 556

Hungarian trade with 443
  slowdown in economic
    development 432–3
  Western trade 430–1
Coal 546–7
  developing countries 540
Coal industry, UK 527, 533
Coal mines 487–8
  developing countries 537
Cobb-Douglas production
  functions 277, 280
COCOM agreement 434
Coen, R. M. 293, 294, 295, 297, 298, 299
Coleman, J. S. 100 n1
Commission on Energy and the
  Environment, UK 533
Committee on Australia's Relations
  with the Third World 208 n3
Commodities
  Australian imports 199–201
  demand 77–8, 104–5
Commodity composition
  consumer demand 88
  international trade 123, 135–8
Commodity prices 432
  effects on inflation 351–2
  rises 397
Commodity structure, CMEA
  trade 363–4
Common Agricultural Policy 118
Communist Party of the Soviet
  Union 436 n4
Companies
  creation and destruction 172–3
  see also small companies
Compensation agreements 421
Compensatory accounts, stable price
  maintenance 369, 371
Competition
  allocation of resources and 14
  effects on pricing behaviour 351
  market-orientated economies 2
  restriction 58
Competitive price behaviour 337–8
Complementarity, public
  investment 319–20
Complete contracts 56
Computer industry 116, 228
  Conselho de Desenvolvimento
  Industrial 259 n15
Consulting teams, technology
  transfer 57

Consumer demand 77–9, 88, 244
Consumer electronics, Singapore 228
Consumer goods 281–3
  import prices 420
  international trade 135, 137, 138
  production 399
Consumer preferences, learning
  process 94–5
Consumer prices, India 314
Consumer spending
  energy 505
  essentials 79–81
Consumer tastes, North–South
  differences 40
Consumers
  energy conservation pay-back
    times 508–9
  response to energy prices 511
Consumer goods, CMEA prices 375, 376
Consumption 75–7
  limiting 407
  oil 545
Consumption patterns 2, 75–89
Continuing education programme,
  Singapore 223, 231 n9
Contract-theoretic framework,
  heterogenous markets 345
Contracts
  price flexibility 332–5
  price inflexibility 344
Convertible currency 410–11, 412–14,
  420–1, 449, 450, 463 n7
Cooper, R. J. 152–6, 157 n3
Cost effectiveness, new
  technology 17–18
Cost minimisation, incentives 517
Cost of Living Index of Rio de Janeiro
  City 388, 389, 392 n9
Costs
  energy systems 528–32
  price changes 336
  pricing response to 346
  technical change 23–4
  technological progress 13–14
Counter-trade agreements 421
Cournot equilibrium framework,
  prices 341
Coutts, K. 331
Creative destruction 24, 25, 103, 105
Credit conditions, CMEA
  countries 433–4
Crop yields 325
Crowding out, public
  investment 319–20

Index

Crude oil, import prices 506–7, 510
Current account deficit
  CMEA countries 420
  Soviet Union 410
  Czechoslovakia 363, 371, 409, 431, 433, 515, 518

Dadli, M. 546
Data, for process modelling 67–71
Data Resources Inc, 24
Davidson, P. 344, 392 n1
Davies, S. 101 n10
De Groof, 265
Debt
  international 481
  renegotiation 473, 477
Debt service ratios 420, 454
Debt servicing, centrally planned economies 422, 466
Decentralisation, reformed centrally planned economies 467–9
Decision-making
  centrally planned economies 467, 468
  energy supply 492
  foreign trade 471
  investment 16–17
Deindustrialisation 2, 177–8, 183
Delattre, M. 164, 165, 169
Demand
  commodities 77–8, 104–5
  effects on prices 331–2, 336
  energy 504
  growth 8, 94–5, 97–8
  pricing response to 346
Demand elasticities, imports 208 n4
Demand management, energy 514–15
Demographic imbalances, world 273
Department of Statistics, Singapore 217, 230 n1, 231 n8
Depression 24, 160, 165
Desai, P. 421
Developing countries 3, 124, 323
  effects on industrialised countries' employment 138–42
  energy 537–50
  export-orientated strategy 135
  foreign debt 276, 288–9
  imports 183
  inflation 398
  inflation-generating impulses 305–7
  instability 407
  internal problems 276, 290–1
  non-OPEC 129–30, 133–4

  structural change 287
  trade by commodities 135–8
  trade with industrialised countries 123–35
Development, rural energy sources 539–41
Development aid 291
Development economics 89 n5
Development strategies 440, 460
Didier, M. 2, 159, 161, 163, 165, 185
Diesel oil, substitution 546, 547
Diewert, 61, 62, 64
Diffusion, innovation 95, 101, n10, 103–4
Direct controls, resource allocation 419–20
Direct discrimination, trading policy 190
Direct foreign investment, Singapore 216, 218, 220
Direct labour, costs 35–6
Directly unproductive activites 117, 120
Disclosure, information 57
Distribution, wealth 276–7
Distributive effects, new technology 41–2
Dixon, P. B. 2, 149, 157 n2, 184, 193
Dobb, M. 43 n1
Dobozi, I. 4, 503
Dohan, M. 422, 423
Domestic borrowing, India 312, 313
Domestic investment, excess 420
Domestic market
  energy consumption 538
  Singapore 230 n4
Domestic prices
  CMEA countries 414
  energy 531–2
Domestic producers, protection 25–6
Domestic savings, India, 308
Domestic savings ratios 460
Donati, 104
Dornbusch, R. 392 n2
Downs, A. 117
Drabek, Z. 419
Dubois, P. 162
DuMoulin, H. 510
DUP activities 117, 120

East Germany 363, 371, 377, 431, 433, 515, 518
Eastern Europe 3
Eckstein, O. 331

Ecological equilibrium 278–9
Economic activity
  effects of import prices 316–17
  technical change and 32–4
Economic aspects, alternative energy sources 487–9, 553–7
Economic co-operation, international 428–34
Economic Commission for Europe 367, 508
Economic Commission of the United Nations 178, 179, 180, 181
Economic crisis, world 432, 479–83
Economic equilibrium 77, 86–7
Economic growth 3, 269, 275, 303
  adjustment policies and 455–8
  constraints 9
  external shocks and 460
  factors affecting 458–60
  government policy 503–4
  modelling 104
  prospects 323–4
  Singapore 264
  structural change and 275–6, 287
  United States 24, 293–300
Economic models
  Brazil 234–44
  India 306–7, 308–15
  world 272, 301, 302
Economic performance, CMEA countries 434–6
Economic policy
  balance of payments effects 440, 441–3
  Brazil 233–4
  effects of entrepreneurs 114–16
  response to external shocks 439–43, 477–51
  world 272
Economies
  consumption patterns 81–2
  impact of energy 487–8
  typical Southern 28
Economies of scale, international trade 143–4
Economist 506
Education, Singapore 223, 231 n9
Efficiency 47–72
  investment 458–60
  measurement 61–5, 71
  MNCs 58–9
  technical progress and 49–56
Effluent discharge 493
EFTA 124, 140, 143

trade with developing countries 126, 127, 130, 131, 133, 134
Elasticity of demand, imports 194, 209 n12
Electricity, prices 541
Electrification, developing countries 541
Electronics industry, Singapore 216, 219, 225–8
Emmanuel, A. 44 n11
Employers, solvency 111–12
Employment 269–74, 275–91
  centrally planned economies 419
  effects of energy systems 496–7
  effects of import quotas 208 n4
  effects of international trade 144
  effects of new technology 38–9
  effects of reduced protection 204–6
  electronics industry 227–8
  Europe 177–8
  India 314
  industrialised countries 138–42
  public sector 311
  redistribution 2
  sectoral 180–1
  Singapore 213
  structural change and 162–5
  structural dynamics 11
Employment policy, Keynesian 275, 284–6
Employment relation, stability 110–11
End-users, energy 492, 498–500
Energy
  comparing alternatives 491–7
  decrease in use 505–6
  developing countries 537–50
  impact on national economy 487–8
  imports 492–3, 494–5, 517, 556–7, 538
  national self-sufficiency 525
  new sources 488
  terms of trade 324
  see also alternative energy sources
Energy conservation 4, 518–19, 539–40
  CMEA countries 513–18
  market economies 503–13
  pay-back times 508–9
Energy consumption
  CMEA countries 518
  domestic markets 538
Energy demand
  CMEA countries 513–14
  depression 526
  prediction 524

Index

restraint 511–12
Energy equipment, capital stock 507–8
Energy forecasting 530
Energy planning
 environmental issues 532–4
 uncertainty 529–30
Energy policy 488
 CMEA countries 513–15
 developing countries 545–3
 government 492, 523–35, 554–5
 implementation 497–501
Energy prices 294–5, 498, 499–500, 526, 529–32
 consumer response 511
 interaction 553–4
 public awareness 535 n2
 real 506–7, 511–13
 stabilisation 531–2
Energy producers 492
Energy quotas 518
Energy sector, rural 539–43
Energy supply
 decision-making 492
 dependence on foreign 495
Energy systems
 costs 528–32
 effects on employment 496–7
 externalities 533
 less developed countries 539
 modelling 497
 planning 524–6, 554–5
 social costs and benefits 493
Engel curves 287
Engel, E. 40, 76
Engel's Law 8, 77, 78, 94, 99, 105
Engineering process models 69–71
Engineering products, international trade 135, 137, 138, 143
Engineering technology 48–9
Engleman, F. 104
entrepôt, Singapore as 214, 216
Entrepreneurs
 incentives 184
 market for 109, 113–16, 120
 pursuit of innovations 33
 role 120 n3
 Singapore 229
Environmental damage, energy systems 498
Environmental hazards, nuclear power 528
Environmental issues, energy planning 532–4
Environmental protection 274

Environmental requirements, growth 278–80
Equilibrium models, business cycles 342
Equipment demand, Brazil 243
Essentials, consumer spending 79–81
Europe, market economies 109–20
European Community 116, 118, 119, 124, 140, 190, 447
 employment gains 140
 protectionism 208 n2, 472
 trade with developing countries 124, 126, 127, 130, 131, 133, 134
European Economic Commission 178, 179, 180, 181
Exchange rates 276, 280, 289, 325, 461
 centrally planned economies 372, 468, 469, 470, 471
 energy imports and 495
 fluctuations 361, 364–5, 465
 inward orientated NICs 457
Expansion, capacity 16–17
Expectations, lags in formation 346
Expenditure, energy systems 496–7
Experimental data, for process modelling 67–71
Export demand, inelasticity 421
Export expansion 233, 235, 245–7, 249, 253, 255, 258, 258 n4, 264
Export flows, changes 124–7
Export manufacturing, Singapore 230 n4
Export performance, productivity patterns and 85–6
Export prices, centrally planned economies 420
Export promotion 3, 133, 440, 441, 461
Export share
 gains 89 n4
 Hungary 447, 449, 454, 457
 Yugoslavia 450, 451
Export structures
 changing 181–2
 Singapore 241–19
Export volume effects, foreign demand 441, 452
Export-orientated investment 407
Exports
 Brazil 237
 centrally planned economies 360–1, 414–15, 431, 467
 incentives against 440, 450
 increase 406

Japan 85
outward-orientated NICs 453, 455
Singapore 216, 218, 228
small companies 165–6
Soviet Union 411
External financing, policy response to external shocks 447, 450, 451, 453, 454, 455, 457–8
Externalities
  cost of 14
  energy systems 493, 498, 533
  structural change 22–3
Eymard-Duvernay, F. 171
Eyre, P. 510

Factor costs, industry price changes 336
Factors of production 8, 10, 113, 277
Farrell, M. 48, 49, 50, 61, 72 n3
Federal Republic of Germany *see* Germany
Feedback ratios, energy imports 494
Fetter, F. A. 76
Fibreglass, automobile bodies 18–20
Firms
  large 115–16
  regulations 289
Fiscal expansion 272
Fiscal incentives, industrial restructuring 223–4
Fiscal policy 305, 402
  inflation and 382, 388, 391, 398–9
Fischer, S. 341, 349, 392 n2
Fisher, F. 338
Flexible exchange rates 280, 289, 364–5, 470
Florence, F. S. 161
Food, consumer spending 79–81
Food and Agriculture Organisation 463 n6
Food prices, India 307, 309, 310
Food production, LDCs 555
Foodgrains, output 309
Forecasting
  energy 530
  technological change 524
Foreign capital, inflows 3
Foreign competition 25–6
  effects on pricing behaviour 351
Foreign currency, CMEA restrictions 416
Foreign debt
  Brazil 264

centrally planned economies 377–9, 410, 422, 433–4, 466, 468, 473, 477
developing countries 133–4, 135, 276, 288–9
Hungary 447, 457–8
inward-orientated NICs 457
Yugoslavia 458
Foreign demand, slowdown 441, 452
Foreign exchange reserves,
  India 307–8, 313
Foreign investment, Singapore 216, 218, 220, 227 228, 229, 231 n13, 264
Foreign prices, effects on CMEA wholesale prices 368–75
Foreign trade
  benefits 280–4
  centrally planned economies 360–1, 414–15, 428, 466, 475
  decision-making 471
  intra-CMEA 430, 472
  Soviet Union 411–12, 422–3
Foreign trade rubles, USSR trade 411
Foreign workers, Singapore 222–3
Fossil fuels 548–9
Fothergill, S. 163
France 161, 163–4, 166, 168, 169–70, 172, 185
Free trade 25–6
  advantages 280–4
Freeman, C. 100 n2
Fromm, G. 331
Frontier production functions, efficiency 50–5, 61, 65, 66–71, 72 n8
Frydman, R. 338, 346, 351
Fuel exports, Soviet Union 432
Fuel imports
  CMEA countries 432–3
  developing countries 306
  India 308
Fuel prices
  developing countries 546
  India 316–17
Fuels, thermal equivalent prices 529
Full employment 9, 77, 86–8, 113, 407, 414, 496
Fundação Getulio Vargas 259 n7

Gaffard, 104
Galbraith, J. K. 160
Galenson, S. 43 n1
Gandois, J. M. 169

Index

Garnaut, R. 209 n6
Gas pipeline, Siberia–Western Europe 418, 419, 434
Gasifiers, wood/charcoal 548
Gasohol 260 n19, 547
GATT 125, 128, 136, 141, 146 n6, 365, 463 n6
Gaudin, J. 174
GDP
  Brazil 237
  India 307, 311
  industrialised countries 127–30
General equilibrium models 149–57
  Australian economy 193–201, 207, 208 n1
  structural change 2, 149–57, 263
General Price Index, Brazil 388, 389, 392 n9
German Democratic Republic see East Germany
Germany 115–16, 161, 271, 323
Gibbons, M. 91, 103
Gionnaros, D. 396
Global efficiency 50–2, 53
Global frontiers, production 666–7, 68, 72 n8
GNP
  inward-orientated NICs 457
  outward-orientated NICs 455
  Singapore 213, 230 n3
  terms of trade loss 451–2
  United States 293, 296, 298
  Yugoslavia 458
Godley, W. 331
Gonzalez, N. 395
Gordon, R. J. 329, 330, 342, 343, 345, 346, 353
Gouni, L. 501 n2
Government, energy policy 523–35
Government assistance, market for 109, 116–19, 120
Government consumption, Brazil 243–4
Government credits, Reserve Bank 307, 308
Government expenditure 420
  Brazil 388–9
  India 312–13
Government intervention 25–6
  energy policy 554–5
  industrial restructuring 219–20
  industry 160
Government policies, effects on entrepreneurs 114–16

Government policy, economic growth 503–4
Government role, energy policy 497–8
Governments, energy policy 492
Grain embargo, Soviet Union 434
Grain imports, Soviet Union 295, 409, 418, 419
Green Revolution 307
Gross fixed capital formation, OECD 509
Growth rate, Brazil 247–51
Grubb, D. 331, 352
Gudgin, G. 163
Gupta, V. 331, 343
GUS/Central Statistical Office, Poland 477

Hall, R. E. 110
Hard goods, CMEA trade 413–14, 416, 449
Harries Committee 208 n3
Harris, D. J. 79
Harrod-neutral technical progress 277, 279, 280
Hawkins–Simon condition 101 n15
Hay, G. 331
Heinrichs, W. 553
Henwood, 167
Hernes, G. 101 n10
Heston, A. 84, 463 n11
Hewett, E. A. 414, 514
Hickman, B. G. 3, 293, 294, 295, 297, 298, 299, 323, 324, 325
Hickman–Coen model 294, 295, 298, 299
Hicks, J. 92, 100 n3
High technology production 183
High-powered money 307, 313, 314
Historical data, for process modelling 67–71
Historical validation, model of Indian economy 316
Hoeffding, O. 409
Hoffman, W. G. 94, 95
Holanda Barbosa, F. de 3, 381, 392 n1, 396, 398
Holzman, F. 409, 410, 413, 414, 420, 421
Hong Kong 226, 229, 230 n3, 231 n13, 291
Hughes, H. 231 n11
Human capital, effects of structural change 22–3
Human capital–labour ratios 142–3

Hungary   359, 416, 417, 431, 433, 456, 474 n1
  balance of payments   409, 433–7, 451–3
  energy demand   515
  ICOR   459–60
  industrial output   518
  open economy   468
  policy response to external shocks   439–43, 447–50, 454, 457–8, 460–1, 480
  retail prices   370, 371, 375, 376, 377
  terms of trade   363, 365–6
Hydro energy   537, 540, 541–2
Hymer, S.   58
Hyperinflation   353–4

ICOR   458–60
Immigrant workers, Singapore   222–3
IMPACT project   150, 152
Implicit deflator, wholesale prices   373–4
Implicit Output Deflator, Brazil   388
Import flows, changes   124–7
Import prices
  centrally planned economies   420
  effects of commodity prices   351–2
  energy   517
  India   314, 316–17
  raw materials   388
Import quotas, effects on employment   208 n4
Import restrictions, Yugoslavia   450
Import structures, changing   181–2
Import substitution   3, 133, 135, 233, 235, 245–7, 249, 253, 254, 255, 258, 258 n4, 264, 406, 440, 441, 443, 461
  centrally planned economies   472
  Hungary   449
  outward-orientated NICs   455
  policy response to external shocks   453–4
  Yugoslavia   450, 451, 458
Import supply, inelasticity   421
Imports
  Brazil   237
  centrally planned economies   360–1, 414–15, 467
  cheap-labour countries   189
  effects on pricing behaviour   351
  elasticity of demand   127–30, 146 n7, 194, 208 n4, 209 n12
  energy   492–3, 494–5
  from LDCs   189–201

  LDCs   133, 183, 201–6, 265
  Poland   374
  Soviet Union   411
Income elasticities, import demand   127–30, 146 n7
Income levels, per capita consumption   82–4
Incomplete contracts   56
Inconvertibility, centrally planned economies   415–17
Incremental capital–output ratio   456, 458–60
India   3, 42, 198, 209 n14, 305–22, 323, 545, 551, 553, 555 n1, 555 n3, 556 n10
  biogas   542–3, 550 n8
  central grid system   541, 550 n6
  economic models   306–7, 308–15
  energy development   540–1
  features of economy   307–8
  fuel prices   546
  hydro energy   542
  model simulation experiments   315–22
Indices of discrimination   194–9, 209 n13, 209 n14, 209 n15
Indirect discrimination, trading policy   190, 192
Indirect labour
  as capital goods   34–5
  costs   35–6
Indonesia   546
Industrial accidents   493
Industrial concentration   160–1
Industrial consumers, energy conservation pay-back times   508–9
Industrial consumption, energy   505
Industrial (Development and Regulation) Act 1951, India   549 n2
Industrial electronics, Singapore   228
Industrial employment, United Kingdom   163
Industrial growth, dynamics   98
Industrial policy   274, 325
Industrial prices, India   310, 311
Industrial production, CMEA countries   436
Industrial productivity   160–1
Industrial relations, Singapore   223
Industrial restructuring, Singapore   219–25
Industrial sector
  effects on inflation   318

Index

oil substitution 546–7
Industrialisation 290–1
  Singapore 214, 219–20, 230 n4
Industrialised countries 3, 124, 159–75
  capital–labour ratios 142–3
  employment 138–42
  GDP 127–30
  internal problems 276, 289–90
  manufactured exports 130–3
  structural adjustment 177–85, 287
  technical change 27–31
  trade by commodities 135–8
  trade with developing
    countries 123–35
  unemployment 407
Industries Assistance Commission,
  Australia 193, 209 n6
Industry
  declining 12
  differing price flexibility 332–5
  government intervention 160
  India 310–11, 321
  job losses 163
  new 92–101
  Singapore 221
  skill-intensive 220
  subsidies 116
Industry concentration, pricing
  behaviour 336, 337–41
Inflation 3–4, 11, 269–74, 275–91,
  293–300, 302, 323–4, 325
  Brazil 381–92, 398–9
  centrally planned economies 399
  developing countries 305–7, 398
  effects of commodity prices 351–2
  effects of import prices 316–17
  effects of relative price changes 341
  effects on savings 312
  India 307, 315, 317, 318, 321, 322
  industrialised countries 368, 378
  international causes 397–400
  money supply growth 318
  price variability 349
  structural model 382–8
  United States 270–1, 293–300
  world 395
Information
  disclosure 57
  price setting 338
Information value paradox 57, 58
Infrastructure, costs 14, 23
Innovation 85
  diffusion 95, 101 n10
  relationship with company

  size 166–8
  sequential process 104
  South 33
  see also technical change
Innovation possibility curves 33
Innovations
  clusters of basic 100 n2
  cost-reducing 33
  time-lag 92
Insurance, energy price rises 531–2,
  539
Interest groups 118–19
Interest payments, CMEA
  countries 377–9, 433
Interest rates 286, 325, 457, 458, 481
  reduction 272, 288–9
  United States 276, 288
International competition, pricing
  behaviour 350–3
International Monetary Fund 364, 368,
  448, 456
International monetary system 289
International trade 275
  commodity composition 123, 135–8
  manufactured goods 2, 123
  specialisation 181–2
  stagnation 481
  trends in 123–47
Inventory, decisions 341–2
Investment
  Brazil 242–3, 244, 251–4, 256–7, 259
    n4
  decision-making 16–17
  developing countries 306
  efficiency 458–60
  energy 492, 518–19, 527, 531, 545–6
  export-orientated 407
  India 308
  new technology 15–16
  OECD 509–10
  pay-back times 508–9
  promotion 220
  rate of profit 95–6
  reallocation 254–5
  resistance to 289
  savings 88
  Singapore 214, 224–5
  socialist countries 104
Investment allowances 224
Investment controls, Yugoslavia 458
Investment costs, adjustment 14
Investment efficiency 461
Investment goods 282
  prices 311

Inward-orientated NICs 440
 balance of payments 451–3
 GNP growth 460
 ICOR 459
 policy response to external
  shocks 451, 453–4, 460–1
 see also newly industrialising countries
Inward orientation, development
 strategy 460–2, 463 n9, 467
Iron and steel, international trade 135,
 137, 138
Irrigation 309, 543
Italy 114, 116, 417

Jackman, R. 331
Jaeger, A. 59
Jagjit Singh 556 n9
James, J. 43 n9, 44 n10
Japan 3, 85, 86, 124, 208 n2, 227, 284,
 323, 325, 482, 533
 trade with developing countries 126,
  127, 130, 131, 133, 134
Japan Productivity Center 85
Job creation, USA 162–3
Job stability 113
Johansen, L. 259 n8, 259 n10, 259 n11
Johnson, R. 541, 542, 544, 545, 546,
 547
Jonson, P. D. 152
Jungenfelt, K. 2, 177

Kahn, A. E. 43 n1
Kalecki, M. 76, 77
Kampuchea 42
Kattermann, D. 104
Kawasaki, S. 331, 333, 341
Kerosene 552
Keynes, J. M. 76, 285
Keynesian multiplier 496
Khadi and Village Industries
 Commission, India 542
Kindahl, J. K. 331
Kirkpatrick, C. H. 392 n1
Klein, L. R. 3, 269
Knowledge, production and
 implementation 56–7
Kolluri, B. 396
Kopp, R. J. 61, 62, 64, 72 n3
Korff, 116
Kornai, J. 380 n2, 514
Kostinsky, B. 422
Kozponti Statisztikai Hivatal 518
Kravalis, H. 417
Kravis, I. B. 84, 463 n11

Krelle, W. 3, 275, 323, 325
Krishnamurty, K. 3, 305, 323, 324, 325
Krueger, A. O. 117, 208 n4
Kuran, T. 349
Kuznets, S. 81, 91, 100, 100 n3

Labour costs 85
Labour force 273, 279
 Singapore 220, 231 n6, 264–5
Labour input coefficients 138, 140, 147
 n14
Labour market 119
 adjustment 109, 110–13
 Singapore 221–3
Labour productivity 285
Labour requirements, products 29
Labour shortage, Singapore 220, 227,
 228–9
Labour skills, effects of structural
 change 22–3
Labour supply 277
Labour-intensive manufacturing 31,
 220–1, 226, 539
Lall, S. 27
Lancaster, K. 39
Land, productivity 309
Landes, D. S. 100 n1
Lauderdale, 76
Lavigne, M. 380 n1
Layard, R. 331
Learning capacity, firms 346
Learning curves, new
 technology 17–18
Learning process, consumer
 preferences 94–5
Legislation, minimum wage 111
Leibenstein, H. 43 n1, 48, 49, 50, 60
Leipziger, D. M. 510
Lekvall, P. 101 n10
Leon, P. 92, 100 n3
Leontief interdependence 523
Leontief, W. 21
Lerner conditions 495
Less developed countries 3
 definition 208 n5
 energy systems 555
 exports to Australia 189–206
 imports 265
Lindberg, L. N. 504
Link, 43 n3
Liquidity crisis 481
Literacy 231 n9
Livestock exports, Hungary 447, 449
Living standards 276

Lloyd, P. J. 192, 207 n1, 209 n10, 263
Lobbying, government assistance 117
Lombardini, 104
Long period niches, new
 industries 92–4
Lopes, F. L. P. 258 n3
Low-income LDCs 198
Lucas, R. E. 342
Lustig, N. C. 76
Lydall, H. F. 168

Maccini, L. 346
McLaren, K. R. 152–6, 157 n3
McMillan, J. 331, 333, 341
MACRO model 152–6
Macro price models, price
 inflexibility 330–2
Macroeconomic adjustment, new
 forms 170–4
Macroeconomic conditions, affecting
 structural change 21
Macroeconomic equilibirum,
 post-war 160
Macroeconomic models 152–6
Magee, 116
Mahajan, V. S. 4, 537
Maillet, P. 4, 487, 491, 501 n1, 553
Malaysia 230 n4
Malinvaud, E. 161
Man-made fibres, reduced
 protection 200
Management structures 67
Managerial technology 48–9
Manne, A. S. 258 n2, 258 n3, 259 n6
Manpower, regulation 161–2
Manpower costs, small
 companies 169–70
Manpower managements, new
 forms 171–2
Mansfield, 43 n7
Manufactured exports
 developing countries 130–3
 industrialised countries 130–3
Manufactured goods
 definition 146 n5
 international trade 2, 123–47
 prices 397
 relative importance of trade
  in 130–3
Manufactured imports, developing
 countries 129
Manufacturing
 effects of reduced protection 201–4
 industrialised countries 138

labour-intensive 220–1
 protection 189–90
 Singapore 219–25, 230 n3
Marcuse, H. 89 n2
Marer, P. 448, 456, 463 n7
Marginal tax rates 112, 115
Market clearing prices, energy 531
Market economies 4
 ability to adjust to economic
  shocks 109–20
 adjustment processes 469–72
 effects of external market
  fluctuations 465–77
 energy conservation 503–13, 556
Market forces
 in centrally planned economies 468
 labour 111
Market share, small companies 165–6
Market share equilibrium 348–9
Market transactions, price flexibility
 and 332–5
Markets
 heterogeneity 345–8
 small companies 170–1
Marrese, M. 411
Marsden, J. R. 2, 47, 103
Mass production 161
Material costs 398
Maximova, M. M. 427, 480
Means, G. C. 337, 338
Measurement, efficiency 61–5, 71
Meat exports, Hungary 447, 449
Medical care, consumer spending
 81
Mercantilism, new 418–19
Metcalfe, J. S. 91, 101 n10, 103
Mexico 42, 284, 440
Meyers, K. 123
Microeconomic management, structural
 change 165–70
Military expenditure 270, 407
Miners, wages 527
Minimum wage legislation 111
Ministry of Science and Technology,
 Singapore 231 n12
Ministry of Trade and Industry,
 Singapore 215, 218, 225
Mistral, J. 161
Modelling
 Brazilian economy 234–44
 energy systems 497, 524
 Indian economy 308–15
 macroeconomic 152–6
 world economy 277–80

Momentum effect, price
    movements 346
Monetarism 395, 415
    Latin America 382, 391 n1
Monetary crisis 481
Monetary policy 272, 305, 402
    inflation and 382, 388, 391, 398–9
    US 295, 298–9
    Yugoslavia 458
Monetary system, international 275, 289
Money supply
    expansion 285–7, 305, 306, 324, 325, 383
    India 307, 313, 317–19, 321, 322
    US 295, 296, 298
Monopoly capitalism 159
Motor vehicles 198, 200, 203–4, 210 n18
Multifibre Arrangement 116, 137, 226
Multinational corporations 67, 68, 264
    Singapore 227
    technology transfer 57–9
Multiplier effect, energy expenditure 496–7
Multiplier effects 471–2
Murakami, Y. 24

Nadiri, M. I. 3, 329, 331, 338, 343, 351, 396, 398
Nardozzi, 105
Narodniks 76
National independence, effects of foreign energy sources 498
National Insititute of Research Advancement 302
National Monetary Council, Brazil 389
National self-sufficiency, energy 525
National Wages Council, Singapore 222
Natural employment rate, price stability 119
Natural gas 266, 488
Natural resources
    depletion 277, 278
    Soviet Union 431
Nekrasov, A. M. 514
Nelson, R. R. 33
Neoclassical analysis, factors of production 113
Neoclassical model, technical change 31–2
Neoclassical production functions 277
Net investment, Brazil 242–3

Netherlands 265–6
Neuberger, E. 410, 412, 414
Neue Zürcher Zeitung 477
New technologies 100 n2
    displacing old 38–9
    distorting effects on South 28–9
    distributive effects 41–2
    growth 92
    sales to CMEA countries 434
    see also technology
Newly industrialising countries 3, 165, 208 n5, 221, 229
    development strategies 440
    response to external shocks 480
    see also inward-orientated NICs, outward-orientated NICs
Newly industrialising country, Singapore as 213
Nishimizu, M. 50, 55, 63, 64
Nixson, F. I. 392 n1
Nominal wages 10–11, 298–9, 310, 311, 373
Non-convertible currency 449
Non-food prices, agricultural 310
Non-tariff barriers 116, 208 n2
Nordhaus, W. 331, 345, 346, 351
Norman, C. 28
North, technical change 27–43
North sea oil 529
Nuclear energy 523, 528, 549

Obsolescence 30
OECD 3, 147 n15, 208 n4, 209 n12, 266, 269, 270, 302, 437 n7, 505, 506, 507, 513, 526, 531
Oil 488 conservation 548–9
    domestic sources 545
    real price 529
    substitution 546–8
Oil imports 146 n6
    bilateral agreements 517
    CMEA countries 365, 366
    developing countries 538
    Hungary 446
    India 550 n10
    OPEC 124, 126
    prices 506, 514
    reducing dependence on 544–8
    Yugoslavia 446
Oil prices 133, 295, 298, 301, 306, 325, 362, 364, 368, 391, 432, 440, 452, 453, 455, 457, 458, 462 n2, 488, 518, 530–1
Oil product, prices 506–7

Okolski, 104
Okun, A. M. 345
Oligopolies, pricing behaviour 337–8, 340–1, 351
Olivera, J. H. G. 391 n1
Olson, M. 118, 119
OPEC 124, 126, 129, 133, 295, 298, 301, 382, 391, 515, 526, 529
ORANI model 150–6, 193–201, 207, 208 n1, 210 n19
Ouchi, W. G. 67, 72 n7
Output
 effects of demand 331
 effects of public investment 319–20
 effects of reduced protection 201–4
 maximisation 38
 structural dynamics 9–11
 United States 293, 294–5
Outward-orientated NICs 440
 adjustment policies 455
 balance of payments 451–3
 GNP growth 460
 ICOR 458–9
 policy response to external shocks 453–4, 455, 460, 461, 462
 see also newly industrialising countries
Outward-orientation, development strategy 460–2
Ow, C. H. 231 n10
Ozga, S. A. 101 n10

Page, T. 50, 55, 63, 64
Panel data, for process modelling 67–71
Paraskevospoulos, C. 553
Parmenter, B. R. 157 n2
Pasinetti, L. 7, 9, 34, 35, 43 n6, 77, 89 n4, 92, 100 n1, 100 n3, 101 n8, 101 n11, 103
per capita consumption, by income levels 82–4
per capita GNP, Singapore 213, 230 n3
per capita incomes
 consumption patterns and 81
 rising 78
 South 28
Petrochemical complex, Singapore 230 n5
Petroleum products, prices 510–11
Petroleum refining, Singapore 216, 218, 230 n2

Phelps, E. S. 338, 342
Philippines 542, 547, 548
Phillips curve 110, 113, 271
Phlips, L. 339, 340
Physical capital–labour ratios 142–3
Physical output, growth 9–10
Planning
 centrally planned economies 467, 469–70, 473
 energy systems 497–8, 524–6, 554–5
Poland 104, 266, 359, 373, 419, 423, 474 n1, 515
 economic performance 474 n1
 energy demand 515
 foreign debt 422
 foreign trade 361, 431, 433
 open economy 468
 retail prices 371, 375, 376, 377
 terms of trade 363, 366–7
 wholesale prices 373–4
Political crisis 481–2
Political lobbying 117
Political structures, developing countries 287
Pollution 493, 498
Pommerol, 171
Popkin, J. D. 347
Population growth
 as source of structural change 8
 Singapore 230 n6
Portes, R. 4, 409, 410, 412, 413, 414, 418, 419, 422
Portugal 440
Posner, M. V. 4, 523, 535 n1
Powell, A. A. 152–6, 157 n2, 157 n3
Power stations, siting 533
Prasad, K. 550 n12
Prebisch, R. 391 n1
Price adjustment 342–3
Price behaviour 398
 atomistic competition model 338
 industry concentration 336, 337–41
 international competition 350–3
 response to demand and costs 346
Price changes, CMEA terms of trade 361–7
Price control, centrally planned economies 468
Price elasticity of demand 348, 349, 350
 energy 506
Price equalisation account 412
Price flexibility 400
Price inertia 329–55

Price inflexibility 329–30
  extent of 330–6
  recession 348
  theoretical rationale 337–48
Price levels 285, 286
  asymmetric 348–50
Price movements, international 3–4, 359–80, 396
Price ratios 280–1
Price reforms, CMEA countries 371–2, 376–7, 380 n1
Prices rises 271
Price rules, firms 339–40
Price setting, information 338
Price stability 345
  unemployment and 119, 353
Price stickiness 341–2
Price strategies, oligopoly 340–1
Price studies, disaggregated 335–6
Price variability, inflation 349
Prices 9–11
  agricultural 309–10
  CMEA countries 362, 363–4
  collusive agreement 338, 339
  effects of public investment 320
  effects of stage of production process 347–8
  electricity 541
  energy 498, 499–500, 529–32
  fixed 285
  India 313–14
  inertia 347
  insensitivity to demand 329
  intra-CMEA trade 362, 411
  investment goods 311
  new commodities 96–7
  stable 344
  state regulation 400–1
  sturctural change and 16, 17, 18, 20, 21–2
  world 432–3
Primary commodities
  CMEA imports 365, 366
  prices 362, 364, 368, 370, 399
Private consumers, energy conservation pay-back times 508–9
Private disposal income, India 312
Private investment
  agriculture 309
  crowding out 319–20
  industry 310–11, 321
Private market economies
  Hungarian trade with 447, 449
  policy response to external shocks 451–60
  Yugoslav trade with 450–1
Private real investment, agriculture 309
Problèmes Economiques 477
Process models, production frontiers 65, 66–71
Process technology 92, 93
  technical change 31–9
Product Development Assistance Scheme 224
Product innovation, research and development 43 n3
Product technologies 92, 93
Production
  patterns of 2
  structural change 179–81
Production costs, state enterprises 373
Production efficiency 49
Production frontiers, process models 65, 66–71
Production functions, neoclassical 277
Production structure, Singapore 214–19
Productive capacity
  growth 95–6
  utilisation 9
Productive structures
  Brazil 247–51
  theoretical aspects of change 103–6
Productivity
  best practice 63, 64
  export performance and 85–6
  growth 78
  Japan 86
  land 309
  sectoral 180–1
  textile industry 226
  United States 293, 294–5, 298, 324
  world 324
Productivity gains 87
  overtime 54–5, 63
  technical change 105
Productivity patterns 75–89
Products, technical change 39–41
Professional associations 118
Profit rates 35, 95–6
Profit structures, small companies 168–9
Profits, entrepreneurs 114–15
Project lending 421–2
Project LINK 272
Projects, costs and benefits 43 n6

Index

Protection 3, 149, 221, 226, 231 n11, 287, 472
agriculture 116
Australia 189–201, 265
domestic producers 25–6
manufacturing sector 189–90
nominal rates 208 n2, 209 n7, 209 n9
structural effects of reduced 201–6
Public employment 184
Public investment, India 308, 309, 310–11, 314, 319–22, 324
Public irrigation works, India 309
Public policy, full employment 86–7
Public procurement 116
Public sector
growth 183–4
India 311, 312–13, 314, 321
Public sector borrowing, India 312
Public sector savings, India 308
Public spending 272
Purchasing power, currencies 289
Purvis, D. 415

Quadrio Curzio, A. 396
Qualifications, Singapore 231 n9
Quotas
meat and livestock 447
textile exports 231 n13

Raczkowski, S. 3, 359, 396, 399
Rainfall, effects on agriculture 309, 316
Ramesh, S. 550 n5, 550 n12
Rate of profit, uniform 104
Raw material prices, Brazil 388
Raw materials
CMEA imports 432–3
international trade 351
Ray, G. 506, 507
Reagan Administration 119
Real costs, structural change 21
Real demand, centrally planned economies 419
Real energy prices 506–7, 511–13, 515
Real GDP, India 307, 311
Real GNP, United States 293, 296, 298
Real output, Europe 177–8
Real per capital incomes, growth 8
Real price, oil 529
Real wages 265, 310, 352
USA 298–9
Rebelo, I. 118

Recession 270, 271–2, 335, 348, 432, 440, 457, 458, 526
Redundancy benefits 111
Regional changes, costs 23
Regulation
firms 289
manpower 161–2
Relative prices, effects on inflation 341
Relocation costs 14, 23
Rent seeking 117
Replacement, capacity 16–17
Replacement investment, Brazil 242, 243
Rerat, F. 172
Research and development
frontier technologies 303
product innovation 43 n3
promotion 325
Singapore 224, 231 n12
technical change 29
Research and Development Assistance Scheme 224
Research ratios 277, 278, 283
Reserve Bank, India 307, 308, 312, 313, 314, 315
Resource allocation 14
direct controls 419–20
Resource constraints, developing countries 306
Resource gap, public sector 308, 312–13, 315, 320
Resource transfers, centrally planned economies 418–19
Retail prices, CMEA countries 375–7, 379
Revaluation, Hungary 447
Revoil, J. P. 172
Risk
elimination 160
energy planning 539
Robinson, J. 76
Rocznik Statystyczny 360, 363, 367, 374
Roncin, A. 166
Roosa, R. 417
Rosenberg, N. 100 n2
Ross, S. A. 340
Rostow, W. 100 n1, 100 n2
Rotemberg, J. J. 342, 343
Rothwell, R. 161, 166, 167
Roughgardan, J. 101 n14
Ruble inconvertibility 416
Ruble trade deficit, Hungary 449
Rudra, A. 259 n6

Rumania 363, 377, 431, 433, 518
Rural economy, India 549 n1
Rural electrification, developing countries 541, 549 n3
Rural energy, developing countries 539–43

Saarstahl 116
Sachs, J. 346, 352
Sadli, M. 542
Safety, nuclear power 528
Sahal, D. 43 n3, 43 n7
Salaries 10
Salas-Fumas, V. 2, 47, 103
Salter, W. E. G. 32
Sanctions, trade 431
Savings 79
  India 308, 312
  investment 88
  Singapore 214
Savings ratios 277, 278, 280, 283
Savings School 75–7, 79
Scarf, H. 120 n2
Schumacher, E. F. 44 n11, 173
Schumpeter, J. A. 24, 25, 75, 92, 100 n3, 103, 113
Schumpeterian development 94, 99, 100, 103
Scientific advances 91–2
Scientific research, as source of structural change 8
Secretaria de Planejamento da Presidencia da Republica 259 n15
Security, workers 111–12
Security crisis 481–2
Seers, D. 391 n1
Selection, technology 42
Semi-manufactures, international trade 135, 137, 138
Sen, A. K. 43 n1, 549 n1
Service sector 163, 171, 183
  Singapore 215, 217, 221
Shelest, V. A. 514
Shell Petroleum 505, 509
Shishido, S. 3, 301, 302, 323, 325
Shoven, J. 351
Singapore 3, 213–14, 291, 440
  industrial restructuring 219–25
  production and export structures 214–19
  sectoral developments 225–8
  structural changes 264–5
Singapore, Department of Statistics 217, 230 n1, 231 n8

Singapore, Ministry of Science and Technology 231 n12
Singapore, Ministry of Trade and Industry 215, 218, 225
Singapore, National Wages Council 222
Sismondi, J. C. 76
Skill shortages 24
Skill-intensive industries 220
Skilled labour 344
Skills Development Fund 222, 223, 231 n7
Slobodkin, L. B. 101 n14
Small companies 159, 163, 173–4, 185
  complementarity with large 170–1
  job creation 163–5
  manpower costs 169–70
  market share 165–6
  profit structures 168–9
  subcontractors 168
  wages 171–2
Small Industries Scheme 224
Smith, Adam 418
Social insurance payments 290
Social programmes, financing 271
Social security contributions 296
Social structures, developing countries 287
Social welfare, fuel prices and 546
Socialist countries 3, 427–37, 439–63
  Hungarian trade with 449–50
  policy response to external shocks 451–60
  trade and investment policies 104
  Yugoslav trade with 451
  see also centrally planned economies
Soft goods, CMEA trade 413–14
Solid fuel 546–7
Solow, R. 31
Solvency, employers 111–12
South
  effects of technical change 27–43
  innovation 33
  technical change 27–31
  technical choice 34–9
South Korea 210 n18, 220, 229, 291, 440
South-East Asia 482
Soviet Union 288, 295, 361, 481, 517
  balance of payments 409
  centralised decision-making 467
  convertible currency constraint 417
  credit conditions 433
  current account deficit 410

Index

energy demand 515
  foreign trade 411–12, 431
  foreign trade rubles 411
  intra-CMEA trade 413
  oil prices 453
  prices 369–70, 371, 375, 376, 377, 472
  response to external events 419, 420–2
  terms of trade 363, 365, 367, 379
  trade participation 422–3
  world markets and 428–9
  Yugoslav trade with 443
Specialisation, international trade 143–4, 181–2
Spence, M. 76, 348
SPRU 167
Srinivasan, T. N. 259 n5
Stability, centrally planned economies preference for 467, 469–70, 473
Stable prices, CMEA countries 368–72
Stagflation 271, 301, 324, 325, 352, 395–6
  United States 293–6
Stagnation, European economies 177–8
Standards of living 276
State energy policies 4
State enterprises, production costs 373
State intervention, labour market 111–12
State investment, Brazil 244
State regulation, price 400–1
Statisztikai Evkonyzv 366
Steel, automobile bodies 18–20
Steel negotiations, US–EC 119
Steel policy
  EC 119
  rationalisation 115–16
Steel prices 116
Stewart, F. 2, 27, 30, 43 n8, 43 n9, 44 n10, 103
Stigler, G. J. 331, 338, 339, 340
Stock flow conversion factors, investment 243, 259 n6
Stop-go cycles, Yugoslavia 454–5
Storey, D. J. 163, 173
Street, J. H. 553
Streeten, P. 43 n8
Structural adjustment, industrialised countries 177–85
Structural change
  Brazil 233–4
  economic growth and 7–12, 275–6, 287
  employment and 162–5
  externalities 22–3
  general equilibrium models 2, 149–57
  microeconomic management 165–70
  multisectoral 18–20
  national economies 263–6
  pro-change bias 23–6
  production 179–81
  relationship with technical change 91–101, 103
  simultaneous 21–2
  Singapore 214–19
  single-sector 15–18
  sources of 7–9
  theoretical aspects 2
Structural dynamics, output and prices 9–11
Structural effects, reduced protection 201–6
Structural policies 273–4
Structuralism, Latin America 382, 391 n1
Subcontractors 170
  small companies 168
Subsidies 184
  firms 287
  industry 115, 116
Summers, R. 84, 463 n11
Sutton, J. 157 n2
Sweden 116, 417
Sweeney, R. 506

Taiwan 42, 220, 226, 229, 231 n13, 291, 440
Tan, A. H. H. 231 n10
Tandon, R. 396
Tariff barriers 116
Tariff equivalent, forms of protection 209 n7, 209 n9
Tastes, consumers 40
Tâtonnement 110, 120 n1, 120 n2
Tax holidays 220, 223
Tax rates, marginal 112, 115
Taxation 184, 290
  industrial restructuring 223–4
  USA 296, 298–9
Taylor, L. 259 n6
Technical change 12, 300
  advanced countries 27–31
  as sequential process 104
  costs 13–14, 23–4
  deceleration 294, 295

diffusion 2, 103–4
economic activity and 32–4
efficiency and 49–56
forecasting 524
Harrod-neutral 277, 279, 280
indigenous 42
in the North 27–43
process technology 31–9
products 39–41
relationship with structural
  change 8, 91–101
research and development 29
speed of 2
see also innovation
Technical choice 34–9
Technical efficiency 49, 50–2, 53–4, 60, 61–2, 63
Technological unemployment 87
Technology 13–26, 91–101
  choice of 2
  investment in new 15–16
  rejection 42
  selection 42
  speed of change 13–26
  see also new technologies
Technology transfer 2, 43 n7, 47–73, 104, 229–30
  process models 66–71
  transaction costs approach 56–65
Temporary workers 172
Terms of trade 89 n3
  centrally planned economies 361–7, 379, 406
  changes 465
  effects of external shocks 441, 451–2
  energy 271, 324
  Hungary 446
  Soviet Union 419
  Yugoslavia 446
Tertiary sector 163, 164
  India 311, 321
Textile and Garment Industry Training Board 227
Textile industry, Singapore 219, 225–8
Textiles
  international trade 135, 137, 138, 142
  protection 198, 231 n13
Theil, H. 392 n2
Theorem of critical elasticities 495
Thermal equivalent prices, fuels 529
Third World, energy 4
Tholon, 171
Thomas, 167
Time-lag, innovations 92
Total factor productivity ˙ 63–4
Townsend, 167
Trade
  CMEA–West 430–1
  intra-CMEA 430, 472
Trade balance
  India 308
  industrialised countries 124–7
  OPEC 133
  Soviet Union 411–12, 417
Trade barriers 26
  reduction 145–6
Trade Development Board 227
Trade liberalisation 272
Trade participation, centrally planned economies 422–3
Trade participation ratios, Soviet Union 420
Trade policies, socialist countries 104
Trade preferences, Australia 190, 192
Trade sanctions, centrally planned economies 431
Trade unions 149, 204, 223, 290, 344
Trades, job creation 163
Training, Singapore 223
Transaction costs approach, technology transfer 56–65
Transaction prices 331–2, 333
Transfer payments 289–90
Transferable rubles 410, 416
Transmission equipment, electricity 541
Transport equipment industry, Singapore 218–19
Transport sector, oil substitution 547–8
Treciokowski, W. 480
Treml, V. 422, 423
Trevor, R. G. 152
Trzeciakowski, W. 4, 465
Tsentralnoye Statisticheskoe Upravlenie 437 n8
Tsukuba-FAIS world model 302
Tsukui, J. 24
Tumlir, J. 119
Turkey 440
Tunrpike paths 24
Type Z organisations 59, 67
Tyson, L. 4, 410, 412, 414, 439, 458, 459

Uncertainty
  energy planning 529–30, 555

Index

price flexibility and   343–4
Underemployment   29
UNEDIC   163–4
Unemployment   78, 112, 184, 269, 271, 273, 284–7, 290, 331, 496
  costs of   23
  industrialised countries   407
  natural rate   119
  price stability and   353
  technological   87
  United States   24, 293–300
Unemployment insurance   111–12
United Kingdom   4, 116, 190, 271, 417, 533, 535 n2
  energy policy   525, 527, 533
  industrial employment   163
  new companies   172–3
  small companies   185
United Kingdom. Commission on Energy and the Environment   533
United Nations   146 n8, 146 n9, 288, 367, 411, 436 n1, 437 n6, 463, 475, 505, 516
United States   3, 116, 119, 124, 161, 227, 271, 293–300, 323, 417, 463 n6
  age of capital stock   509–10
  budget deficit   288
  economic growth   24
  economic recovery   482
  employment   140, 162–3
  import quotas   208 n4
  inflation   270–1
  interest rates   276, 288
  market share   85
  productivity   293, 294–5, 298, 324
  prospects   296–9
  protection   208 n2
  sanctions   431
  Soviet grain embargo   434
  stagflation   293–6
  steel negotiations   119
  trade with developing countries   126, 127, 129, 131, 133, 134
University of Sussex   166
Urban bias, energy development   540
Urbanisation   290
Uruguay   440
US Bureau of Labor Statistics   85
US Bureau of the Census   422
US Census of Manufacturing   138
US–Canadian Automotive Agreement   146 n10
Usher, D.   118
USSR *see* Soviet Union

Van Gemert,   265
Vanous, J.   411, 423, 463 n6
Variable prices, CMEA countries   369–70, 372
Vassille, L.   168, 171
Vegetable oil, fuel   547–8
Verdoorn Law   85
Villa,   104
Vincent, D. P.   157 n2
Vocational and Industry Training Board, Singapore   223

Wachtel, H. M.   335, 351
Wachter, M. L.   340, 344
Waelbroeck, J.   2, 109, 184
Wage earners, numbers   164
Wage rates   34–5, 285
  Brazil   392 n5
  fixed   285
Wages   10, 110–11
  inflexibility   344
  miners   527
  public sector   311
  Singapore   221–2
  small companies   169–70, 171–2
  textile industry   226
Wahlbin, C.   101 n10
Walrasian auctioneer   338
Warr, P. G.   189, 192, 207 n1, 209 n8, 263, 265
Wealth, distribution   276–7
Weather, effects on agriculture   305, 314, 316, 322, 325
Weiss, L. W.   311, 340
Welfare effects, new products   29, 39–40
Welfare policy   407
Welfare programmes   23
Welfare states   109
Werneck, R. L. F.   3, 233, 258 n3, 259 n12, 260 n24, 260 n25, 263, 264
West Germany *see* Germany
Western Europe   227
Wharton Econometric Forecasting Associates   269, 378, 463 n6
Whinston, A.   2, 47, 103
Wholesale Price Index, Brazil   388, 389, 392 n9
Wholesale prices
  centrally planned economies   368–75
  CMEA countries   379
  India   313, 317
Wilczynski, W.   396
Wiles, P.   409, 410

Williamson, O. E.   56, 57, 72 n6
Wind power, developing countries   543
Winiecki,   104
Winter, S. G.   338, 342
Winters, S.   33
Wojciechowski, B.   476
Wolf, M.   119
Wolf, T.   410, 420
Wood/charcoal gasifiers   548
Worker remittances, India   324
Workers
  market forces and   111
  safeguarded earnings   115
World Bank   128, 146 n8, 208 n5, 230 n3, 276, 442, 448, 456, 505, 506
World economy
  long term problems   276–84
  modelling   277–80, 301, 302
World market prices   423, 432–3, 447, 465
  CMEA trade   361–7, 411
World markets
  centrally planned economies
    and   427–36
  role   428–9
Wu, S. T.   344
Wyss, P.   331

X-efficiency   49, 50, 60

Youth unemployment   273
Yugoslavia   456
  balance of payments   443–7, 451–3
  debt service ratios   456
  domestic savings ratios   460
  ICOR   459
  policy response to external
    shocks   439–43, 450–1, 458, 460–1, 480

Z-form organisations   59, 67
Zegveld, W.   161, 166, 167
Zelechowska, J.   477
Zheng Guanglin   550 n6, 550 n7
Zimmerman, K. F.   331, 333, 341